JUVENILE DELINQUENCY

A Book of Readings

Also by Rose Giallombardo

SOCIETY OF WOMEN: A STUDY OF A WOMEN'S PRISON

JUVENILE DELINQUENCY
A Book of Readings

ROSE GIALLOMBARDO

NATIONAL OPINION RESEARCH CENTER
UNIVERSITY OF CHICAGO

JOHN WILEY AND SONS, INC.   *New York · London · Sydney*

PREFACE

This volume is designed to introduce the student of juvenile delinquency to some of the most important contemporary literature in the field. The distribution of the selections is such that this book of readings is easily adaptable to the framework of single-semester undergraduate and graduate courses in delinquency. It may be used along with supporting lectures and materials as the basic text, or it may be used to supplement the various basic textbooks in the field.

For some time there has been a need to bring together selections from the recent literature on juvenile delinquency which have been published in journals, books, and monographs. It is my contention that a knowledge of primary sources broadens the student's understanding of the subject matter by confrontation with the original expression of the scholars in the field. The intellectual excitement that is generated by reading the primary sources cannot be duplicated by study of the brief and skeletal summaries of source materials which are of necessity the expositions used in textbooks. The limited resources of many college libraries and ever-increasing class enrollments, however, pose problems which the instructor finds difficult and often impossible to resolve. In an effort to help remove this difficulty, the articles in this volume have been reprinted in their entirety.

The literature dealing with delinquency is prodigious, and the task of selecting articles requires the willingness to compromise in making choices. In a book of this kind, questions about why a particular selection was included and another excluded are inevitable. All subjects and all the excellent papers and pertinent material in the field of delinquency could not be included in a volume of this size. The selections reprinted here are for the most part articles from the professional journals in social science or lengthy selections from important books. They have been included because they deal with the sociological aspects of delinquency; and they either are important research contributions or provide valuable theoretical analyses and description. Nevertheless, even use of these restricting criteria in selecting materials did not make it possible to include all the worthy sociological studies. Psychological and biological studies have been omitted because, without sacrificing important sociological papers, their inclusion would have resulted in a book of unwieldy length. Historical treatments have been excluded for the same reason.

In order not to interfere with the work of the instructor who uses this volume, the brief introductory comments preceding each section do not impose a particular point of view on the student. They are intended solely to suggest connections and to bridge gaps between the individual selections. The book has been planned and designed with the hope that it will engage the imagination and critical thinking of discerning students.

My thanks are gratefully extended to the authors and their publishers who have generously permitted their works to be reprinted. I also wish to express my appreciation to Nancy T. Unger, Mrs. Carol Silverstein, and Mrs. Betty Ierrolino whose considerable help with editorial tasks made completion of this book possible.

Rose Giallombardo

Chicago, Illinois
August, 1966

Contents

Section I THE DATA OF DELINQUENCY: PROBLEMS OF DEFINITION AND MEASUREMENT

The difficulties and confusion involved in determining the causes of delinquency originate in the extremely ambiguous use of the concept itself. Without a clear awareness of precisely what is meant by delinquency, no delineation of cause is possible. As the term is used at present, it may encompass almost any type of youthful behavior. This problem stems largely, Tappan would maintain, from the contrasting views of those who deal with delinquents. Moreover, the problem of measurement is complicated by the distinction made between "adjudicated delinquents," those who have been processed through the courts, and "unofficial delinquents," those who are handled unofficially by the courts, police, and other agencies. Hence the statistics of juvenile delinquency are unreliable indices of the amount of juvenile misconduct or of variations in it from one time period to another. Official records are unreliable as a basis for determining the extent or the nature of delinquent behavior.

In the first selection the nature of delinquency, defining the conduct itself, and the legal status involved are cogently probed by Tappan. In order that the distinctions between delinquency, unofficial delinquency, and behavior problems may be understood, he contrasts the differing approaches of social work and of law to the youthful offender. In addition, the compromises that are present in the sociojudicial procedures of the children's court are discussed in relation to the general problem of definition and measurement. Throughout, Tappan stresses the importance of legal and social norms. The selection by Rubin, "The Legal Character of Juvenile Delinquency," further explores the legal conception of delinquency and analyzes the problems involved in the variation that exists from one state to another with respect to behavioral acts defined as delinquencies.

The literature suggests that the increase in delinquency rates during the past two decades does not represent a genuine index of delinquent behavior, but, rather, that the rates are linked to official policy. More specifically, the rates are related to the variable structures of family and community life, a description of the volume of cases through selected children's courts, and the variable nature of the court's function. In assessing the basic difficulties of computing the extent of delinquency, Teeters and Matza suggest that rates of one period may be "very high" only when they are compared with a period when rates were very low.

As pointed out previously, the data on the extent and distribution of delinquency are neither complete nor known, and this causes a good deal of misunderstanding and controversy. Using three Western and Midwestern small cities, with populations of 10,000 to 30,000, Short and Nye studied high school students to ascertain the extent of admitted offenses. The matter of "hidden delinquency" is also taken up by Murphy, Shirley, and Witmer in the assessment of the delinquency rate. They present data to show that court statistics are inadequate as a measure of the amount of youthful illegal behavior in the community. So frequent are the misdeeds of youths that even a moderate increase in the societal reaction to such misconduct by law enforcement authorities could create a so-called delinquency wave without a corresponding change in adolescent behavior.

1. The Nature of Juvenile Delinquency

PAUL TAPPAN

Annetta found some whisky at home and got drunk at the age of seven. Arnold stole some extract from a neighbor. His mother said, "Send him to the training school." Sarge whips his sisters. Cap stays out till midnight. J—— E—— and J—— B—— fight one another. Alvin stole his mother's stove and sold it. Melvin stole a pig from his father, who prevailed upon the juvenile court to commit him to the training school at the age of fifteen. An alcoholic parent complains that his daughter is "sassy." A boy strikes his alcoholic grandfather with a rock. Another is abusive to his mother and sister. Still another hacks up a package that his mother aims to send to another son. At the filling station that he was keeping during his father's absence Ritchey found a pint of whisky belonging to his father. Upon his father's return they got into a row. The father complained. Two months after a youth's father died, the boy wagered 40 cents against a bottle of wine in a game of dice. His mother said that she would send him to the training school next time. One mother complained that her boy was very troublesome and "just like his dad." Another parent heard that Jane left church one night and went to the school grounds with some boys. Gaylord is in when his mother is out and out when his mother is in. She works. Another mother had her fifteen-year-old son taken to jail from home because he was drunk. Jerry had a tantrum, during which he jerked the telephone off the wall. Speck's grandmother had him committed to the training school because he tried to leave town, and Mark's mother committed him after he stole a gallon of gasoline.[1]

What, then, is delinquency? Certainly there is no more central question in this study and probably none more difficult to answer. Yet it is important to see the nature of delinquency as clearly as possible and to understand the problems that have impeded efforts at definition. It is important, because on the interpretation of the term depend all those vital differences which set off the juvenile delinquent from the adult criminal at the one extreme and from the nonoffender at the other. In theory at least and, to a large degree, in fact, the delinquent child is dealt with differently from the criminal: in the conduct

[1] Austin L. Porterfield, *Youth in Trouble*, p. 17, 1946.

SOURCE. Paul Tappan, *Juvenile Delinquency*, New York: McGraw-Hill Book Company, 1949, pp. 3–13 and 15–30. Copyright 1949, McGraw-Hill Book Company. Reprinted with permission.

involved; the court and its methods employed; the treatment philosophy, purposes, and methods applied; and in the individual's status, reputation, and civil rights in the community after adjudication.

No less significant but far more difficult is the distinction between the delinquent and the individual who has no conflict with the law. Official delinquency usually implies involvement with the police, detention, court handling, damaging associations, semipunitive correctional treatment, and a role and stigma that are ineradicably injurious—notwithstanding all the idyllic euphemisms to the contrary that embellish the literature on "rehabilitative therapy." One must decide to whom these measures need to be applied and also who, in the name of justice, should be exempt from them. Incidentally, the student of the problem would like to know what phenomenon it is that he studies, its frequency, what is being done about it, and what should be done about it. It is a major thesis of the present work that, to a considerable extent, ineffective dealing with young deviants arises from the failure to determine and classify their problems and then to apply treatment that is appropriate to such careful classification.

The Legal View

The problem of definition flows in part from the contrasting views of those who deal with the delinquent. Broadly considered, two chief general types of approach may be observed: the judicial, or legal, view and the administrative, or case work, view. Conceptions of delinquency have been derived largely from these views, and they in turn tend to reflect the two main phases of juvenile court work: the adjudication of cases and their probation supervision. In the legal approach to misconduct, it is customary to describe offenses and penalties in specific terms in order to protect the citizen from arbitrary or unjust acts of police and judicial authority and, at the same time, to secure the community against those whose conduct has been shown in court to be dangerous. Lawyer and judge are inclined to stress as a precondition of treatment through criminal courts the following requirements: (1) that a specific charge be alleged against the defendant, (2) that it be defined in definite terms by law, (3) that the offense be proved rather conclusively, (4) that protection be given to the accused during trial against conviction by false, misleading, prejudicial, irrelevant, or immaterial evidence. The liberal political philosophy of Anglo-American democracy has evolved and refined these principles in reaction against the arbitrary, tyrannical excesses of political and administrative authoritarianism; they have become firmly embedded in the common law, constitutions, statutes, and institutional practices.

In relation to the young delinquent, as will be shown more fully below, this tradition of juristic liberalism has made for a partly "legalistic" handling of the offender, an attempt to distinguish as clearly as possible between delinquent and nondelinquent and to treat only the former with the sanctions of the state. The offender may be looked upon by the state as one functioning with greater or less freedom of will who has chosen to violate the law and who must be dealt with correctively to discourage him and others from further infractions. The full rigors of the criminal law are mitigated by reason of the offender's youth, but the judicial view would preserve in the hearings of children's courts a real test of the individual's status as a delinquent before applying to him the modern and individualized methods of treatment. The child is not a delinquent unless the court has found him so.

The Case Work Approach

In contrast with the procedural and normative formalism of the legal approach, case work brings to behavior problems a distinctly different set of methods and values. Its aims, generally, are therapeutic: to aid in the resolution of the individual's maladjustment by seeking out the social roots of his difficulties and attempting to mitigate the conflicts that have caused disturbance. Case work, then, essays to deal with a wide assortment of personal and group problems that represent failures in man's personal and social adjustments. Largely these are maladaptations in behavior: dependence, domestic conflict, desertion, drunkenness, unemployment, avoidance of responsibility, delinquency, the whole province of child-welfare work, and many others. Treating presumed causes and symptoms with methods devised to meet the particular needs of the individual situation is the essential function of case work.

The practitioner in applied sociology and case work ideally is nonmoralistic and nonpunitive in approach. His approach is nonmoralistic, because he either denies the freedom of the will or recognizes the profound significance of external forces in impelling conduct over which the individual has little or no control; he observes, moreover, that an understanding, sympathetic, nonmoralistic reaction encourages a more confident cooperation from the client, which facilitates treatment. His approach is nonpunitive, because the attribution of blame and the application of retributive measures are inconsistent with the recognition of causes of conduct extraneous to the individual "will" and, moreover, because experience shows the failure of retaliatory measures to produce the personal reconstruction which is sought. The social worker's approach is less formal than that of the legal mind, since categories and qual-ities of problem conduct are not so precisely established in the content of case work theory, nor are methods of treatment so definitively organized and equated, in general, to the problems of the case. In social work it is recognized that a given type of conduct may in different cases reflect quite different causes and that the treatment required to deal with the given behavior should depend on the factors that underlie the particular case rather than the behavior itself. It follows from this that there must be a far wider province of administrative discretion in the practice of case work than is employed by the judge in attempting to allocate responsibility for deviant behavior and to prescribe treatment suited to the subject. Moreover, interpretation and technique may differ considerably from one social agency to another or even, within an agency, from one case worker to another. To some extent the worker must operate empirically through trial and error to resolve the problems that confront him.

In contrast to the law's preoccupation with miscreants who have violated specific and official legal norms, then, social work is concerned with a multitude of problems of behavior that deviate from psychological, social, economic, and—sometimes—legal normality. Insofar as the case worker may deal with the law violator, he does so with the same nonmoralistic, nonpunitive assumptions that are applied to other deviants. The young antisocial child may be referred to any one of a variety of social agencies rather than to a court. In the agency his statutory infractions, if any, are not viewed separately from the remainder of his conduct but merely as incidents of the total problem to be dealt with for the purpose of improving adjustment. The focus of attention is upon the whole child. His illegalities are commonly interpreted as merely symptoms of the underlying maladjustments from which he suffers. In a proper case, where official authority appears to be needed, law-enforcement agencies may be called into operation, but much of the problem conduct that is handled by the case worker in the agency is identical with the illegal behavior that confronts the court. The agency, in the fulfillment of its purposes, makes no attempt at a specific definition of the type or degree of law violation or at a carefully controlled determination of the individual's innocence or guilt of the prohibited conduct. Rather, operating within the limitations of its means and purposes, the agency accepts as true the findings and interpretations of social investigation, and proceeds to over-all treatment of the case as inferred from the relatively loose methods (compared with the exacting requirements of legal evidence) of social inquiry. It should be noted, in addition, that the treatment techniques of the unofficial social agency lack the stigma of community disapproval that is inherent in the law's penalties. The very term "delinquent" is shunned because of its moralistic and legalistic implications. The child is called "unadjusted."

Judicial-Administrative Blending in the Children's Court

In the modern juvenile court there is a compromising of the legal and casework approaches: an effort at sociolegal handling of the child. Legal influences are inevitable and necessary in a court; they may be seen in the age limitations for delinquency, in the statutory specification of particular conduct deemed to be delinquent, in the preservation of some measure of procedural regularity and of due process rights, and in the very effort itself to provide children with special protec-

tion. Children were not only given a protected position, as early as the thirteenth century, at common law, before the ordinary courts, but also were considered in later chancery—along with other incompetents (females and imbeciles!)—to be wards of the state, shielded by the king's chancellor from injury or exploitation. The origin in chancery jurisdiction of many of the child's protections established an early informal and administration tradition in the legal handling of children's cases; thus, his contracts, property interests, and his rights and status might be ensured by administrative as well as strictly judicial measures. Much later, when juvenile courts were established, some followed this tradition as equity courts with wider powers and more informal methods than those of the common-law courts. However, equity, like the legal approach in general, has been characterized by rather definite rules of law governing conduct and regular procedures; its function has been chiefly the protection of those who lacked other adequate legal remedies.

In the nature of the juvenile court, case work practices are associated with probation treatment *after* the determination of delinquency. But in the emergence of specialized children's courts, the administrative approach was greatly extended beyond the limits that had been fixed in earlier law and equity. The developing ideology of social work was brought in to an increasing extent, particularly through the channels of a probation system that had already been set up in criminal courts before separate tribunals for juveniles were invented. After the birth of the juvenile court movement, the administrative approach received a great impetus from leaders in the field of juvenile probation who conceived the function of the court largely in terms of administrative social-work supervision, aimed at prevention and rehabilitation of problem cases.[2] Hence, important new influences developed to modify the traditional judicial process as it applied to the young offender. There is an expanded administrative emphasis today on the need to find the underlying social and psychological maladjustments of the child in the court, to see the total problem, and to resolve his difficulties by probation treatment. The specific delinquent act is considered to be relatively unimportant except as a symptom of the real problems. The model juvenile court statute of the National Probation Association neither defines the term "delinquent" nor applies it to court cases.[3]

The trend noted here has been fostered by the general terms in the provisions of children's court acts, which permit wide discretionary latitude in adjudication and treatment on the basis of vague standards of the conduct and the attitude of the child.[4] Thus a child whose behavior shows no specific and serious violation of the law may nevertheless be treated "preventively" if he is found to suffer from problems of social or psychological unadjustment. The growth of administrative process is seen in the effort of juvenile courts today to prevent misconduct through supervision by probation officers and to deal with children's problems in their early stages before more serious recalcitrance may develop. The large and growing amount of informal work performed by probation departments in cases that are not officially adjudicated is a part of this trend. This work reveals the effort of probation to function as an ordinary case work agency: "The juvenile court in its investigations and case work becomes an administrative social-work agency and must follow the example of the best private agencies in the fullest cooperation with others, taking advantage of the resources they offer in helping to work out the complicated and difficult problems often presented."[5] The significant point may be mentioned here, to be developed later, that in most jurisdictions neither

[2] Alice Scott Nutt, in "The Future of the Juvenile Court," *Nat. Prob. Assn. Yearb.*, 1939, p. 159, said: ". . . once certain services were begun as part of the court work they were continued as a matter of course and gathered strength through precedent, although the original reason for their initiation, namely, the absence in the community of other agencies performing these services, often no longer existed. The court frequently came to consider itself and to be considered a social agency rather than a socialized court, although strangely enough it often held itself apart from the social agencies of the community, and its probation officers spoke of themselves as a group separate and distinct from other social workers." (Reprinted by permission.)

[3] *A Standard Juvenile Court Act*, pp. 8–11, National Probation Association, New York, 1943.

[4] See Gilbert Cosulich, *Juvenile Court Laws of the United States*, pp. 34–47, National Probation Association, New York, 1939.

[5] It is not implied that professional case workers in private and public agencies share this view. To the contrary, see Alice Scott Nutt, *op. cit.*, pp. 163–164, where she says, "Because it is a court, the juvenile court has certain functions entirely apart from case work functions and a structure quite different from that of a nonjudicial agency. The court may use a socialized procedure, but because it is the offspring of the legal system this procedure is nevertheless a judicial one operating along legalistic lines. The handling of each official case in the juvenile court follows more or less a fixed routine. . . . The probation or case work is done under the direction of and within the framework of the law. . . . Several persons well known to this group have voiced their recognition of the limitations upon the development of the juvenile court as a case work agency and also their belief that instead of continuing to broaden its function it should concentrate on a definite and fairly limited field. They have argued that the court should limit its intake to children in whose cases a real issue arises; that the judicial and case work functions of the court should be separated; that the expansion of treatment services within the court administration should be opposed, and their development, specialization, and coordination in the educational and public welfare system should be encouraged."

probation staff nor judges are trained for a preventive case work function.

The administrative approach is revealed further by the quite successful resistance that comes frequently from probation officers, sometimes even from the judges themselves, to the legal requirements of proving an offense, excluding hearsay and prejudicial testimony, allowing counsel to the defendant, and permitting appeal. The argument runs that the court exists for the care, protection, and benefit of the child; it is therefore unnecessary to set up safeguards and frustrating limitations on the agency that would help him. There is a marked tendency among many leaders of the juvenile court movement today, in considering the child to be merely "unfortunate" or "unadjusted," to avoid reference to delinquency itself. They sometimes favor the burying of institutional statistics on the juvenile delinquent in some all-inclusive and innocuous category. This whole view appears to overlook the significant point that whatever he may be called, he is in fact treated as an offender through court control, and is himself often buried deeper in the correctional system than his statistics can be. A short quotation from each of two cases famous in the jurisprudence of the children's court will serve to illustrate this central problem of requiring proof of delinquency. How a particular jurisdiction resolves the issue determines to a great extent who may be considered a delinquent there.

The constitutional objections turn upon whether the act [the children's court act of Connecticut] is one for the punishment of crime and therefore subject . . . to the guaranties . . . in the Bill of Rights, or whether it is concerned with the care and protection which every state as *parens patriae* in some measure affords to all . . . who . . . are in some degree abnormal, and hence . . . *entirely of a civil nature* . . . if such courts are not of a criminal nature, then they are not unconstitutional because of the nature of their procedure depriving persons brought before them of certain constitutional guaranties in favor of persons accused of crime. This principle has been recognized in many states where juvenile courts exist; in only one [Texas] has such an act been held entirely void, while in Missouri the validity of the act was based upon the statute in relation to constitutional provisions regarding courts.[6]

The proceeding here is under a widely different statute. . . . The concept of crime and punishment disappears. To the child, delinquent through the commission of an act criminal in nature, the state extends the same aid, care, and training which it had long given to the child who was merely incorrigible, neglected, abandoned, destitute, or physically handicapped. . . .

When it is said that even in cases of law-breaking delinquency, constitutional safeguards and the technical procedure of the criminal law may be disregarded, *there is no implication that a purely socialized trial of specific issue may properly or legally be had. The contrary is true. There must be a reasonably definite charge. The customary rules of evidence shown by long experience as essential to getting at the truth with reasonable certainty in civil trials must be adhered to.* The finding of fact must rest on the preponderance of evidence adduced under those rules. Hearsay, opinion, gossip, bias, prejudice, trends of hostile neighborhood feeling, the hopes and fears of social workers are all sources of error and have no more place in children's courts than in any other court.[7]

It should be noted in the above that, holding the children's court and its procedure to be noncriminal, these appellate decisions nevertheless affirm that juvenile cases come under the procedure of the civil law *and its due*

[6] *Cinque v. Boyd*, 121 Atl. 678 (June 1, 1923). (Italics not in the original.)

[7] *In the Matter of Arthur Lewis*, 260 N.Y. 171. (Italics not in the original.) See also Paul W. Tappan, *Juvenile Delinquency*, New York: McGraw-Hill Book Company, 1949, Appendix A, pp. 551–553.

process protections of fair trial of a real issue. Nevertheless, again and again in the literature on probation and juvenile courts and, moreover, in the practices of many of these courts, there is an assumption that, since they are "remedial instead of punitive," such safeguards as "appeals, rules of evidence, appearance of counsel, etc., [are] details of jurisprudence from which the juvenile court has been relieved."

This wedding of judicial and administrative process has not produced a wholly compatible marriage. Each strains to dominate the union—with results that are not always beneficial to the child who is subjected to its influence. The special danger is that in an "overlegalistic" court the experience of trial will be severe and traumatic. The child will less frequently be adjudicated a delinquent, but if he is, the treatment imposed may be based upon a moralistic and punitive ideology. In an "oversocialized" tribunal, on the other hand, there is danger that individuals will be exposed to court machinery and treatment who do not require state sanctions and who may, indeed, be injured by the crude tools to which courts are limited in their treatment efforts.

Modern probation tends to reflect the preventive views and administrative methods of professional case work, meritorious values within the framework of nonofficial case work agencies. But it should be remembered, ideal standards to the contrary, that the probation officer is generally not a case worker by professional training but rather an untrained, overworked, and undersupervised individual whose ability to carry out effective treatment is limited in addition by the coercive authority that the court setting implies. Also, he exercises far more power over the liberty of the child than does any professionally trained private case

worker. The sociolegal compromise of the juvenile court fails when probation attempts to displace law and the courts by becoming an administrative social agency.[8] The compromise fails, too, when the judge attempts to operate a junior criminal court. Among the more than a thousand juvenile jurisdictions in the United States, both of those perversions of a liberalized justice are prevalent, but the former is becoming an especially common error. Later, consideration will be given to a better division of legal and social functions in the children's courts. Here concern has been only with the two conflicting spheres of ideology that have had so much to do with the determination of the official delinquent through the actual operation of the juvenile courts. The inclination of the court to assume a judicial attitude, on the one hand, or the administrative approach, on the other, determines to an important extent the probabilities of a child's being found delinquent and may influence as well the type of treatment he receives.

THE OFFICIAL DELINQUENT

The blending of conflicting concepts of delinquency is fully revealed in the definitions of juvenile delinquency that appear in children's court statutes. The disparity may be seen in the provisions for the courts possessing jurisdiction in these cases, in the age level of offenders covered by them, and in the types of conduct (substantive norms) established by law as delinquent.

Court Jurisdiction

The first juvenile court in the United States was one of equity jurisdiction, exemplifying the protective and noncriminal nature of the proceedings. Yet a majority of children's courts were originally set up as part of the criminal

[8] *Ibid.,* Chapter IX.

court system and, despite subsequent enactments, a large proportion of them still remains so. Thus juvenile cases are handled to a great extent today by some term of an ordinary court of original criminal jurisdiction or of general jurisdiction covering both criminal and civil cases; some are trial courts; others are courts of summary jurisdiction; a minority are distinct juvenile courts of separate jurisdiction; a few are probate or common pleas courts. Where special terms of court are established for children's cases, they are generally handled, nevertheless, by the nonspecialized judges, magistrates, and referees who try a variety of other cases. Usually the probation officers, too, are a part of the general system of probation that deals with adult criminal cases. In most juvenile courts there is a preservation of criminal court personnel, ideology, and, to a less marked extent, trial procedure and treatment methods. But the current trend is toward separate children's courts and separate probation departments to handle juveniles. There is a large and increasing admixture of informal, administrative, and case work methods filtering into these courts with considerable current dispute as to the role of legal and social methods in dealing with the child.

Age Levels of Delinquency

At common law the infant was held to be nonresponsible for crime up to the age of seven, lacking mental capacity to entertain the intent that is required for criminal behavior. From seven to fourteen the infant was presumed to be incapable of crime intellectually because of his immaturity, but this presumption might be rebutted by a showing that he had sufficient capacity to distinguish between right and wrong. From fourteen to twenty-one there was a rebuttable presumption

that the individual possessed criminal capacity and after twenty-one the presumption became conclusive insofar as age might affect capacity.[9] Distinctions in responsibility were based upon the notion of variations according to age among individuals deemed to possess free will in their power to distinguish right from wrong and thus to form the *mens rea* or culpable intent required in crime. This use of chronological maturity as a basis of discriminating between criminal and noncriminal has evolved into modern statutory law, with the underlying ideology preserved to a great extent.[10] A major change has been a pushing upward of the minimum age. Also, the presumption of juvenile nonresponsibility has been made absolute.

This use of chronological age as a criterion of delinquency may seem oddly arbitrary and out of place in an era of individualization. It is unfortunate, certainly, to hold a dull or emotionally unstable first offender criminally responsible if he is a young adult and to treat more leniently or with greater care an habitual, sophisticated, intelligent, and tough recalcitrant of fifteen (in some states sixteen, eighteen, or even twenty-one). From a psychiatric or case work point of view the individual's diagnosis and treatment should depend not on his years per se but on numerous more individuated

[9] See Blackstone, *Commentaries*, Book IV, Chap. II, quoted in Tappan, *op. cit.*, Chap. VIII, pp. 167–169.
[10] In *The Penal Law of the State of New York*, Sec. 817, appears the persisting survival of the common-law rule: "A child of the age of seven years and under the age of twelve years is presumed to be incapable of crime, but the presumption may be removed by proof that he had sufficient capacity to understand the act or neglect charged against him and to know its wrongfulness." This section is obsolete, except in regard to cases punishable by death or life imprisonment, but it survives in the statutes of this and other states.

factors, such as emotion, temperament, experiences, and physical condition. Despite the apparent excessive arbitrariness in the criterion of age, particularly in borderline cases where the child is just under or over the age set by statute, it should be recognized that the law must rely upon systems of rather definite classification to cover large numbers of cases. Arbitrariness is implicit in any system of classification; yet science as well as law is based upon classificatory devices. For the most part, legal categories have evolved as experience has shown their value for the purpose at hand.

Chronological age is a relevant criterion for distinguishing between antisocial groups, for it is a factor subject to easy verification and one which is highly correlated with specific items of maturity, balance, and physical condition with which the correctional system is properly concerned. Moreover, though it is impossible to individualize completely a system of justice, it is possible and usual today, within the framework of these age categories, to separate and subclassify treatment methods to meet particular groups of cases. The establishment of somewhat rough and variable age divisions, however lacking in nicety of discrimination the device may appear, does nevertheless promote a greater evenness of justice than would be possible under a legal system attempting to operate with a wide-open discretion for the judges and treatment experts. The requirements of justice are often enough disserved in the discretionary latitude now permitted where gross variations among authorities and their ideologies result in treating similar cases in radically dissimilar ways. A fair measure of just uniformity is ensured by classification norms such as age.

Under the statutes of a majority of states today, a child may be adjudi-cated delinquent if he is over the age of seven and under eighteen; thirty-two states confer either complete or partial jurisdiction over juvenile delinquency up to that age. Seven states extend jurisdiction to the age of twenty-one, but in each of these the criminal court has concurrent power to try serious cases, such as homicide, robbery, burglary, and rape. In eleven states, jurisdiction over the juvenile is terminated wholly or in part by the age of sixteen.

Delinquency as a Status

In addition to the shifting of the age factor, another significant change has developed in the establishment of delinquency as a status distinct from crime, dependent in part on age and in part on conduct. According to modern statutes a criminal charge against an infant must be dismissed on the ground of nonage: he is irresponsible by reason of immaturity. Nevertheless, such a person may be held as a juvenile delinquent and treated for his protection as a ward of the state. The status concept of delinquency has evolved from an appreciation of the danger that the young offender may easily become an adult criminal if no deterrent or rehabilitative influences play upon him. Hence, the contemporary effort to curb antisocial traits in their incipience. Adjudication to the status of delinquency does not establish a criminal record against the individual. Reports and records of the juvenile court may not be used against the child later in criminal trials. He loses no rights of citizenship, to hold public office, or to secure employment.

Nonetheless, these laws are generally a part of the criminal code; they are evolved from earlier criminal statutes governing incorrigible and wayward behavior. A considerable proportion of the child-defendants comes to the court (often, as indicated above, a part of the criminal court system) as serious offenders. It is natural that some of the contumely that devolves upon the adult criminal is attached to the young delinquent as well; the young offender is often considered and not infrequently treated as an intractable junior criminal. The curse of court adjudication and of institutional commitment or probation supervision is upon him. The stigma is just as real if not as horrendous as that of the convict.

Delinquency: Substantive Norms in the Law

Juvenile delinquency implies a special age range, a more or less distinct court jurisdiction, and a concept of status. These are all rather definite and specifically ascertainable. There is the further, most significant, and more difficult problem of the behavior denoted by that term. Here is real confusion in the purpose, philosophy, and content of the law—and a bewilderment to match in the practices of the courts.

A great part of the difficulty may be traced to the contrast drawn above between the legal and administrative approaches to the subject. The former characteristically specifies particular acts as offenses, operating under the theory that the blunt weapons of the law should be called into operation only after violations that appear clearly deleterious to social welfare. Exceptionally, as in the law of criminal attempt and of conspiracy, the effort is made to operate preventively by permitting prosecution where the conduct proscribed is not itself intrinsically harmful but, unless forestalled before the consummation of the intended acts, may seriously threaten harm to the group. Law of this sort has frequently been criticized for the ease with which evidence can be framed against innocent persons: usually the meaning of the statute is too imprecise and the

probabilities of social harm too obscure. By and large, the formulation of statutory rules of conduct has tended to rest upon the standards that Professors Michael and Wechsler have stated. These standards have a special importance for delinquency legislation: "(1) What sorts of conduct is it both desirable and possible to deter; (2) what sorts indicate that persons who behave in those ways are dangerously likely to engage in socially undesirable behavior in the future; (3) will the attempt to prevent particular kinds of undesirable behavior by the criminal law do less good, as measured by the success of such efforts, than harm, as measured by their other and harmful results."[11] An evolving jurisprudence of delinquency has been less sure of its ground in this issue of conduct to be made taboo, perhaps, than has any other branch of the law.

Under the statutes of the various states, juvenile delinquency has come to include in part conduct that is specifically defined and clearly injurious. In considerable part, however, it is composed of vague and imprecise standards that look to preventive efforts and to the amelioration of social and psychological problems. Of the first type is the characteristic provision that a juvenile delinquent is any child "who violates any law of this state or of the United States or any municipal ordinance or who commits any act which if committed by an adult would be a crime. . . ."[12] This substantive provision is as definite as are the statutes defining adult criminal acts (though the courts are often in fact much less rigorous in their requirements of proof).

The omnibus provisions of these statutes, probably more vague as to

[11] Jerome Michael and Herbert Wechsler, *Criminal Law and Its Administration,* p. 11, 1940.
[12] *The Penal Law of the State of New York,* Sec. 486, Subsec. (a).

the class of individuals intended than any other part of the criminal code, are best illustrated by the common definition that the delinquent is one "who so deports himself as willfully to injure or endanger the morals or health of himself or others." Other recurring phrases of similar indefiniteness include the individual "who is incorrigible, ungovernable, or habitually disobedient and beyond the control of his parents, guardian, or other lawful authority" or "who, without just cause and without the consent of his parent, guardian, or other custodian, deserts his home or place of abode."[13] Obviously adjudication under such substantive provisions as these imposes upon the judge an onerous task of determining what conduct is reprehensible and dangerous, with very little assistance from the statute. This extends the administrative powers of the court to implement the statutory objectives, but the law may neglect to establish even general conduct norms to guide the tribunal's decision—which is customarily done for an ordinary administrative agency. The adjudicator may be an arbitrary despot in the application of his peculiar preferences. He may be enlightened, objective, and nonmoralistic, or ignorant and prejudiced. Under the elastic course-of-conduct clauses of these acts, the risk of adjudication as a delinquent depends considerably on the point of view of the judge and the probation officer who influences him.

In two jurisdictions, California and the District of Columbia, there is not even a statutory definition of delinquency. This follows the practice recommended under the standard juvenile court act of the National Probation Association which, in line with the case work theory of avoiding the very concept of delinquency itself, simply establishes the jurisdiction of the chil-

dren's court over those "(b) Whose occupation, behavior, environment, or associations are injurious to his welfare. (c) Who deserts his home or who is habitually disobedient or beyond the control of his parent or other custodian. (d) Who, being required by law to attend school, willfully violates rules thereof or absents himself therefrom. (e) Who violates any state law or municipal ordinance."[14] Query: How much difference does this approach make in the repute of the officially adjudicated child?

Legal Exceptions to the Delinquency Status

The statutory definitions of delinquency appear to reflect a dual purposing: there are clauses of a judicial slant to discourage specific acts of illegality and others bent toward administrative control over courses of conduct, which are designed to prevent the development of crime. This mixture of legal motives is not irreconcilable in logic, whatever difficulties it may involve in practice. Conceivably the court might, in turn, be reformative to the serious offender and preventive to the potential offender. But a more obvious confusion of purposes does appear in exceptions established to the jurisdiction of the children's courts in a number of states, e.g., the limitation that a child otherwise of delinquent age may be tried as a criminal where he is accused of committing a capital crime or certain other crimes.[15] The provision in various states for concurrent juris-

---

[13] *Ibid.*, Subsecs. (b) and (d).

[14] *A Standard Juvenile Court Act*, p. 10, 1943.

[15] California, Delaware, Louisiana, Vermont, and West Virginia except capital crimes. Colorado, Iowa, Massachusetts, Montana, New York, South Carolina, Tennessee, and United States courts except crimes punishable by death or life imprisonment. Florida, Maryland, North Carolina, Pennsylvania, and Rhode Island except certain other specific offenses.

diction of the criminal court and children's courts similarly displays an anomaly in the purposes of delinquency statutes. They first assert that the child is too immature to be responsible for crime or to suffer punishment therefor, and then except those crimes which are most retributively penalized in the law. These two cases from recent news releases reveal very well the anomalous contradictions of policy in dealing with the youngster:

JURY REFUSES TO INDICT

Youth, 13, in Fatal Shooting Still to Face Children's Court

Thirteen-year-old Nicholas I—, of . . . , the Bronx, who last Friday shot and fatally wounded Rita P—, 8, . . . as she stood in front of 854 East 999 Street, will be arraigned today as a juvenile delinquent before Justice M— in Bronx Children's Court. Yesterday the Bronx Grand Jury refused to return an indictment against the youth after Chief Assistant District Attorney O— said he found no evidence of premeditation or intent to kill. Mr. O— said later that the Grand Jury could not return an indictment for manslaughter against a child under 16 years.[16]

BOY, 16, SENTENCED TO 25 YEARS TO LIFE

Nicholas T—, 16 years old, who had a record of juvenile delinquency for several years, was sentenced yesterday to serve twenty-five years to life for murder by Judge G— in Kings County Court. Only 15 at the time he was charged with the lead-pipe slaying . . . of Mrs. Pauline G—, 53, in her store . . . , the youth was found guilty May 7 of second-degree murder by an all-male blue-ribbon jury. Reviewing the boy's record of seven arrests since he was 8, Judge G— said he still had faith in the "fundamental goodness" of the youth of the country and absolved society from responsibility in the failure of the defendant to rehabilitate himself.

As the court concluded, the youth insisted that he was innocent of the crime. "What I did in the past, I admit, may have been bad," he said, "but of this charge I am not guilty. The jury was wrong."[17]

Observe the quaint spectacle of a child thirteen years old accused of murder. Such a child is ordinarily detained in jail without right to bail and goes before a police magistrate or justice of the peace for questioning in open court. There he may be bound over for action of the grand jury. In jail again, eventually he may be indicted by that body and held for trial before a jury "of his peers" whose duty it is to determine whether the child did commit a willful, deliberate, and premeditated homicide. (For any other offense it is conclusively presumed that he lacks the power of will and intent to commit crime.) But here it becomes the duty of the jury to decide whether this thirteen-year-old did "intend" to take the victim's life, whether he "planned" it—for even a moment—in advance. For the latter he may be punished by death or life imprisonment. For the former he may spend the entire productive period of his life in prison. Yet if, as in the case of Nicholas I——, the jury finds that the child acted without premeditation or intent, it can find him guilty of no crime at all. He may then be brought before the juvenile court as a delinquent to receive its relatively modest penalties or its therapy, as the case may be.

This is no mere relic of medieval justice or indeed even of nineteenth-century practice. It happens today as one may see all too often in the headlines of the daily papers. It is true that the child is no longer punished capitally for a long list of offenses. Nor, as in colonial days, for a short series (which included disobedience, smiting one's parents, and other "horrible"

---

[16] *The New York Times,* Sept. 6, 1946.

[17] *Ibid.,* May 28, 1946.

crimes).[18] But a child's age is not yet a bar to the death penalty or to a lifetime of retributive justice if he has deliberately taken the life of another.

BOY, 14, IS FREED IN GIRL'S DEATH[19]

TERM FOR BOY IN SHOOTING

Lad Who Fired "to See Someone Die" Gets 10 to 14 Years[20]

BOY, 15, GETS LIFE TERM

He Pleads Guilty to Slaying of Philadelphia Policeman[21]

BOY SLAYER GETS 30 YEARS

Codarre, 13, Is Sentenced for Attack on Girl of 10[22]

YOUTH, 15, ARRAIGNED IN MURDER OF BOY, 11[23]

BOY, 16, SEIZED AS SLAYER

Admits He Killed Youngster, 13, on Bronx Roof, Police Say[24]

4 CHILDREN SLAIN: BOY, 16, IS ACCUSED[25]

TEEN AGERS DESCRIBE KILLING POLICEMAN[26]

20 YEARS TO LIFE FOR ALBANY BOY, 15[27]

The Neglected or Dependent Child

Technically separate from juvenile delinquency, but included in the jurisdiction of the juvenile court, is the power to determine cases of neglected and dependent children. This protective function adds some further confusion to the effort to limit and define the delinquency concept, especially in

that these children are often detained in and sometimes committed to the same institutions where delinquents are held. Frequently, too, their conduct problems overlap with those of delinquents to such an extent that any realistic behavioral discrimination is impossible. Whether a child be held delinquent, neglected, or dependent may depend chiefly on the petitioner and his motive rather than either the child's conduct or his more basic problems of unadjustment. Clearly many juvenile offenses are bred in parental neglect. This suggests the larger problem confronting children's courts as to the behavioral or situational elements that should be taken to constitute delinquency, an issue that will be considered in the next section.

There are provisions in some states establishing, in the courts that handle delinquents and neglected children, jurisdiction over other related problems, e.g., the dependent child, adoption, custody, the physically handicapped child, the mentally defective or disordered child, illegitimacy, or marriage of girls under sixteen.[28] In some states the children's court has jurisdiction to try as a misdemeanant the parent, guardian, or other custodian whose negligence in his duties has caused or contributed to the delinquency of the child.[29] The common

---

18 For statute in Illinois, see Tappan, *op. cit.*, Appendix B, p. 554.

19 *The New York Times*, May 8, 1946, and Aug. 7, 1946.

20 *Ibid.*, May 28, 1947.

21 *Ibid.*, Mar. 20, 1947.

22 *Ibid.*, Dec. 7, 1943.

23 *Ibid.*, Oct. 29, 1946.

24 *Ibid.*, Oct. 24, 1946.

25 *Ibid.*, May 28, 1947.

26 *Ibid.*, May 29, 1947.

27 *PM*, July 8, 1947.

28 All but four states confer jurisdiction upon the children's court over neglect and dependency (Massachusetts, New York, New Mexico, and Texas). See Gilbert Cosulich, *op. cit.*, pp. 42–47, for a summary of the numerous states that provide for children's court control over the mentally defective or disordered child, issues of guardianship, adoption, custody, and legitimacy and for less common jurisdictional powers.

29 Thirty-one states are listed by Cosulich as possessing jurisdiction to try adults charged with contributing to the delinquency, neglect, or dependency of a child; in the remainder some other court has this jurisdiction. See Cosulich, *op. cit.*, pp. 69–70.

informality of procedures employed in children's courts, particularly the allowance of hearsay testimony and hearings on imprecise issues, has been extended to threaten unjudicious criminal adjudication of adults under conditions that do not guard against injustice as do procedures of the ordinary criminal courts.

JUVENILE DELINQUENCY: ITS BEHAVIORAL CONTENT

In the discussion above of the substantive norms defining delinquency and the conflicting ideas of legal and case work personnel, the problem of attempting to delimit the behavioral content of delinquency has appeared in its general aspects. It was suggested that the judicial approach would require the statement and proof of fairly definite offenses. The administrative view, to the contrary, is that, since delinquents and their courts are not criminal in character, the latter being designed to aid children who are unadjusted, the courts should not seek to define and segregate delinquency but to discover and treat the maladjustments of children who appear before them. Out of these opposed ideologies have come varied statutory specifications. It is clear that these do not resolve the central issue of who should be brought before the court and adjudicated. Is the precocious and adventurous child who has run away from home once, or several times, a delinquent? Is the one who reacts rebelliously in a home pervaded by an atmosphere of incessant hostility a delinquent? Is a daughter in "bobby sox" who stays out later than her mother used to do, who seems "a little wild," and causes her fearful family much anxiety, a delinquent? Is the boy who expresses a desire, thoroughly normal in a healthy maturing preadolescent, to emancipate himself emotionally and

socially from his family and who behaves in a very independent fashion a delinquent? Is the youth who refuses to turn over his entire wage to his family? Is the girl who has become pregnant through ignorance, seduction, or curiosity? What are the effects on the child, his family, and the community when a fraction of the children who behave in these ways are adjudicated?

How, then, may one distinguish the problem child, the predelinquent, and the delinquent? Who among them belongs in court? A series of categories of deviation are set up below in order to consider the level at which a children's court should take control:

1. Deviant situational factors, where the child is exposed to deleterious home and community influences:
    (a) Broken home
    (b) Variable, inadequate, or excessive discipline
    (c) Vice in the home
    (d) Economic insecurity
    (e) Unsupervised and unhealthy recreation
    (f) Slum neighborhood
    (g) Agencies of moral risk: cheap bars, theaters, poolrooms, etc.

2. Behavior problems that represent some measure of personal unadjustment to the environment:
    (a) Thumb-sucking
    (b) Nail-biting
    (c) Temper tantrums
    (d) Enuresis
    (e) Masturbation

3. Antisocial attitudes wherein the child reveals subjective reactions antagonistic to authority, but without serious overt aggressions:
    (a) Hostility
    (b) Isolation
    (c) Anxieties
    (d) Guilt feelings

4. "Waywardness" or "incorrigibility," the violation of relatively nonserious community conduct standards:

(a) Idleness
(b) Truancy
(c) Running away from home
(d) Fighting
(e) Disobedience

5. Serious illegalities, the violation of criminal conduct norms:

(a) Theft
(b) Burglary
(c) Robbery
(d) Assault
(e) Rape
(f) Homicide

To most students of the problem it is clear that there is some child behavior which requires court attention due to the seriousness of its influence upon the community and the danger of continued criminalism. It is easy enough to justify a court's assuming control in the parent's stead under category 5 above in order to apply therapeutic, corrective, or deterrent treatment. It is also apparent, perhaps, that certain types of situational factors, attitudes, and deviant conduct may better be dealt with by nonjudicial social agencies, public or private, whenever possible. Many would agree that categories 1, 2, and 3, above, should be handled outside of court by noncourt personnel. This, however, leaves exceedingly difficult issues to resolve. If the community lacks appropriate agency facilities, such as case work organizations, mentalhygiene clinics, psychiatric resources, etc., should the court then take over in these cases to do as well as it can, with a view to preventing later more serious maladjustment? Or, though the community may provide these other facilities, if the child comes first to the court, should it attempt to deal with the problems discovered as an "administrative social agency" striving to provide the fullest possible service? However these questions may be answered, there is still the problem of what should be done with the "wayward" child, with that large range of behavior, attitude, and situation that lies between the extremes of criminalism on the one hand and mere slight deviation on the other. The cases under category 4 may be dealt with today either by court or social agency; they lie within the province of the courts by ancient legal tradition, and yet the majority of such cases are handled by the home or by any of a variety of social agencies. In this area there is much overlapping of effort, sometimes competition of agency resources, and frequently needs are met very inadequately or not at all because of the failure to work out a systematic philosophy and program for treatment.

The court may essay to deal with these situations "preventively" because of the alleged dangers of later delinquency or because it conceives its function broadly. A case work or group work agency may handle similar situations regularly, though with different tools, specific objectives, and consequences.

Neva Deardorff, assistant executive director of the Welfare Council, New York City, has pointed up this problem of defining delinquency in instances of so-called "incorrigible" behavior:

Not all disobedience, for instance, carries a connotation of moral turpitude. As everyone knows there are family situations from which any sensitive child would inevitably wish to run away, and some would have the courage to do so even though in the process they become "runaways." It would have to be decided whether rebels of this kind should go on the register of delinquents and, if so, under what diagnosis. Everyone who gives any thought to the matter knows that when a parent claims that a child is ungovernable it is well to see the kind of government that the parent

Table 1

COURT AND AGENCY DELINQUENCY:* CHILDREN REGISTERED FOR SPECIFIED REASONS FOR REFERENCE BY ALL AGENCIES AND BY THE JUVENILE COURT†

(1) Reason for reference	(2) Children registered by all agencies for reason specified in (1)	(3) Children registered by the juvenile court for reason specified in (1)	(4) Per cent of all children registered for specified reason who were registered by the juvenile court for that reason
Traffic violations	591	585	99
Stealing	1,870	1,487	80
Assault, injury to person	187	148	79
Acts of carelessness or mischief	951	733	77
Being ungovernable	456	244	54
Sex offense	258	61	24
Truancy	3,488	177	5
Running away	819	16	2

* Edward E. Schwartz, Community Experiment in Delinquency Measurement, *Natl. Prob. Assn. Yearb.*, 1945, p. 173.

† Inasmuch as some children were referred to agencies for more than one reason, neither (2) nor (3) may be totaled without obtaining figures which include duplicate counts.

is imposing before jumping to the conclusion that the problem inheres in the child.[30]

Very convincing evidence of the difficulties inherent in the effort to define delinquency in terms of conduct appears in the results of two research studies on the incidence of court-adjudicated behavior and of similar behavior in other noncourt samples. The first of these studies came out of an effort, which was proposed by the U.S. Children's Bureau, to measure the total volume of delinquency in a single community, as recorded in court and by all the public agencies of the District of Columbia which have responsibility for dealing with delinquent children. The types of conduct that most frequently bring children into court are shown in

[30] Neva Deardorff, Central Registration of Delinquents, *Prob.*, vol. 13, p. 143, June, 1945. (Reprinted by permission.)

Table 1, together with data on the total number of children engaging in such behavior, the number brought before the juvenile court, and the proportion of all cases of the several types of conduct that appeared in court. It is apparent upon inspection that, save for the more serious types of law violation, juvenile court statistics include only a limited, and in some categories very small, proportion of cases of the kind with which criminal courts customarily deal. Moreover, these figures do not reveal the volume of similar cases handled by the private agencies of the community or by parents and others without resort to social agencies. Clearly whether or not one is officially delinquent depends not on his conduct alone but, to a great extent, on referral practices that obtain in the community (see Table 1).

The other study is even more suggestive of the anomaly implicit in juvenile court practices when conduct of the same order that may result in adjudication is regularly tolerated in vast numbers of other instances. Moreover, if a purpose of these courts is to prevent the development of serious misconduct, it is an error of function to manipulate many of these cases in court, since the result is so commonly recidivism and increasing recalcitrance. Professor Porterfield studied 2,049 cases of alleged delinquents in the Fort Worth area and broke down their conduct into fifty-five specific offenses ranging from "shooting spitwads at a wrestling match" to murder. He compared this sample with the admitted conduct of 337 students from three colleges of northern Texas. The summary table borrowed from his study reveals the frequency of these offenses in the histories of those who went to college rather than to court (see Table 2). It is of special interest to note in his detailed breakdown of the offenses and their frequency how often the college students had indulged in the "delinquent" or "predelinquent" peccadillos that send their less fortunate counterparts to court and frequently to the reformatory (see Table 3).

No clearer evidence is required to show the essentially sumptuary character of official definitions of delinquency as they operate from day to day in the court. It appears that the minor waywardness or incorrigibility of the college student's history is not only tolerated but proves to be of little detriment in his subsequent conformity to law and to the norms of society at large. What foundation is there to believe that the child of lower socioeconomic status with a similar conduct record will become seriously delinquent if he is not brought to court? It is known from disillusioning experience that many of them become progressively deviant *after* they have been exposed to court and training school. It is known, too, that similar cases dealt with simply by their parents or by nonstigmatic and unofficial social agencies do not become criminal. Does this not indicate that, in relation to "wayward" and other course-of-conduct provisions at any rate, control is better left whenever possible to noncourt facilities, the trenchant judicial authority being reserved for more serious cases that clearly require it? How frequently does society in effect manufacture, aggravate, and extend delinquency by preventive efforts on the predelinquent? Where is the administrative approach in the liberal and "socialized" but quasi-criminal court taking us?

Children's Court or Parents' Court?

A further and related problem affecting the behavioral content of delinquency remains to be stated: Whose

Table 2

PERCENTAGE OF STUDENTS REPORTING THE COMMISSION OF ONE OR MORE OF THE FIFTY-FIVE OFFENSES CHARGED AGAINST CHILDREN IN THE COURT AND AVERAGE NUMBER OF OFFENSES REPORTED BY EACH[*]

Offending group	Number in group	Percentage reporting one or more of the offenses	Average number of offenses reported
Precollege men	200	100.0	17.6
College men	100	100.0	11.2
Precollege women	137	100.0	4.7

[*] Porterfield, *Youth in Trouble*, p. 38.

Table 3

OFFENSES OF COLLEGE STUDENTS AND JUVENILE DELINQUENTS*

	Percentage of students						Percentage of juvenile court cases charged with the offense	
	Reporting the offense			Charged with the offense				
	Precollege		Col-lege men	Precollege		Col-lege men		
Offenses by types	Men	Women	men	Men	Women	men	Boys	Girls
Vagabondage:								
Suspicious character	0.0	0.0	0.0	0.0	0.0	0.0	9.0	4.9
Vagrancy	4.0	0.0	4.0	0.0	0.0	0.0	0.3	0.0
Begging	5.5	0.0	3.0	0.0	0.0	0.0	0.5	0.0
Peddling, no license	5.5	0.0	5.0	0.0	0.0	0.0	0.2	0.0
Runaway, wandering	14.5	4.3	2.0	0.0	0.0	0.0	42.0	31.5
Stranded transiency	14.5	0.0	12.0	0.0	0.0	0.0	†	†
Truancy	42.5	34.3	28.0	0.0	0.0	0.0	1.0	1.1
Loafing in a pool hall	48.0	0.0	46.0	0.0	0.0	0.0	0.3	0.0
Percentage charged in court: total				0.0	0.0	0.0	53.3	37.5
Liquor violations:								
Illegal manufacture	8.0	0.0	0.0	0.0	0.0	0.0	0.2	0.0
Illegal possession	35.5	2.9	47.0	0.0	0.0	0.0	0.1	0.0
Buying as a minor	38.0	2.2	53.0	0.0	0.0	0.0	0.1	0.0
Drunkenness	39.0	2.9	43.0	0.5	0.0	0.0	0.8	1.1
Percentage charged in court: total				0.5	0.0	0.0	1.2	1.1
Theft:								
Automobile theft	0.5	0.0	0.0	0.0	0.0	0.0	0.9	0.5‡
Bicycle theft	0.5	0.0	0.0	0.0	0.0	0.0	2.5	0.0
Theft of tools, money	5.5	0.0	1.0	0.0	0.0	0.0	3.8	0.0
Burglary	7.5	0.0	4.0	0.0	0.0	0.0	7.0	0.0
Shoplifting	10.0	1.5	5.0	0.0	0.0	0.0	10.0	11.4
Miscellaneous, petty	23.0	8.8	11.0	0.0	0.0	0.0	2.7	4.1
Stealing melons, fruit	69.0	16.0	15.0	0.0	0.0	0.0	0.3	0.0
Percentage charged in court: total				0.0	0.0	0.0	27.2	16.0
Dishonesty (other than stealing):								
Forgery	2.5	5.1	1.0	0.0	0.0	0.0	0.2	1.6
False collection	8.0	2.2	10.0	0.0	0.0	0.0	0.2	0.0
Possessing stolen goods	20.0	3.6	14.0	0.0	0.0	0.0	1.4	0.0
Passing slugs, bad coins	24.0	0.0	14.0	0.0	0.0	0.0	0.1	0.0
Gambling	58.5	17.4	60.0	0.0	0.0	0.0	0.7	0.0
Percentage charged in court: total				0.0	0.0	0.0	2.6	1.6
Sex offenses:								
Attempt to rape	5.5	0.0	3.0	0.0	0.0	0.0	0.1	0.0
Indecent exposure	24.5	2.2	23.0	0.0	0.0	0.0	0.1	0.0
Extramarital coitus	58.5	0.7	59.0	0.0	0.0	0.0	0.5	11.4
Percentage charged in court: total				0.0	0.0	0.0	0.7	11.4

Table 3 (continued)

Offenses by types	Percentage of students						Percentage of juvenile court cases charged with the offense	
	Reporting the offense			Charged with the offense				
	Precollege		College men	Precollege		College men		
	Men	Women		Men	Women		Boys	Girls
Other cases:								
Carrying concealed weapons	14.0	0.0	0.0	0.0	0.0	0.0	0.2	0.0
Homicide, murder	0.5	0.0	0.0	0.0	0.0	0.0	0.2	0.5§
Homicide, negligent	0.5	0.0	0.0	0.5	0.0	0.0	0.1	0.0
Incorrigible	0.0	0.0	0.0	0.0	0.0	0.0	1.4	10.3
Neglected, abused, etc.	0.0	0.0	0.0	0.0	0.0	0.0	0.1	12.0
Miscellaneous appearance in court				2.0	0.0	4.0	0.0	2.1
Percentage charged in court: total				2.5	0.0	4.0	2.0	24.9

* Porterfield, *Youth in Trouble*, p. 41.
† See "Runaway."
‡ As accomplice.
§ Self-defense.

interests does the juvenile court propose to protect? Is it the child, the parent, or some other petitioner who persuades the court to action? In legal theory the court acts in a role of protector to serve its wards who have suffered from insufficiency in the aid and guidance of their natural parents. As stated in *Commonwealth v. Fisher*,[31]

. . . it is not for the punishment of offenders, but for the salvation of children, and points out the way by which the state undertakes to save, not particular children of a special class, but all children under a certain age, whose salvation may become the duty of the state in the absence of proper parental care or disregard of it by wayward children. No child under the age of sixteen years is excluded from its beneficent provisions. Its protecting arm is for all who have not attained that age and who may need its protection.

At the same time that statute and cases observe the objective to save the

[31] *Commonwealth v. Fisher*, 213 Pa. 48 (1905). See Tappan, *op. cit.*, Appendix A for a more complete quotation of this case.

child, the courts often appear in practice to shrink from any real subrogation to the parental role, tending simply to support parental authority by the added prestige and power of the state. It is anomalous when the parents have been, as they often are, an important contributing factor to the unadjustment of their offspring or have failed in efforts to guide and control them for the court to take jurisdiction and accede to the demands of those parents on adjudication and treatment. Courts and judges vary considerably in their inclination either to stand behind the parents or to blame and condemn them. The custom of the courts has been largely to assist parents in the latter's program of controlling the child, however, rather than to make an independent plan for his care based upon the total situation. Definitions of delinquency are based in part upon violation of parental standards and the courts are often deemed to be acting in the role of the parents. An equally unfortunate but contrasting practice that has become popular recently in some jurisdictions is to punish the parents for their children's delinquencies, usually treating the children too as offenders.[32] The provisions in many statutes for penalties against those responsible for or contributing to delinquency have permitted this opposite approach, popular in California, New York, and elsewhere.

This whole issue of parent-court relationship is important here in that the risk of a child's adjudication depends to so considerable an extent on whether the court conceives its primary function as protection of the child or support to the parent. In the former instance adjudication may often be avoided entirely whereas in the latter it is facilitated, whatever may be the consequent injury to the child. It appears that whether the child is a delinquent depends too much on whether the parent says he is, rather than on his actual conduct.

[32] A recent instance of this, which stirred considerable interest, was the case of a mother sentenced to a year in prison for contributing to the delinquency of her fourteen-year-old son. Upon appeal to the Appellate Division, the decision was reversed on the grounds of the improper hearsay testimony which the judge had allowed at the trial in children's court. The defendant was subsequently found to be insane and not, therefore, responsible for her own behavior, let alone that of her son. As Edwin Lukas, director of the Society for the Prevention of Crime, which appealed this case, pointed out, this mother was as much the victim of circumstances as was her son: "Mrs. R— was sent to this country like a piece of baggage at the age of 8 by parents who had too large a family to worry about her. She lived with childless relatives here. When she was 16, they tried to marry her off to a man twice her age. At 19 she married an older man and had two children by the time she was 20. Her husband abandoned her and she tried to find work to support her children, boarded out over the years. The woman deteriorated—she had no strength left. She tried to support her children, but she couldn't. Parents have contributed a great deal to the delinquency of their children. But just as children are seen as the products and victims of their environment, so are parents products and victims too." See *The New York Times*, Mar. 18, 1947.

What Conduct Results in Adjudication?

Of those children who are adjudicated in children's courts, the relative frequency of various offenses may be inferred from the petitions issued. In most jurisdictions theft, including automobile theft, burglary, and robbery, is the primary type of delinquency with mischievous behavior fairly close. Endangering the morals of oneself or others and running away from home follow with high rates and other assorted offenses trail behind with but a small proportion of each, such as truancy, property damage, unlawful entry, possession of a dangerous weapon, homicide, etc. Among girls the most common offenses are sex violations, incorrigibility, and running away. The accompanying table shows the ground of petition as reported to the U.S. Children's Bureau for 1945 (see Table 4).

Obviously, adjudications or petitions offer no accurate picture of the actual rates of delinquent conduct, or even of the order of their frequency. Truancy, running away, and unlawful entry, for example, occur much more frequently than court statistics indicate; their relative rates of adjudication vary greatly in different cities. The charges of incorrigibility and endangering the morals or health of a child, in the very nature of the allegations, are such that any estimate of their real frequency is futile: adjudication depends on the interpretation of the court.

DELINQUENCY DEFINED

It is suggested that the general terms of juvenile delinquency statutes permit courts to take hold under broad and imprecise circumstances of conduct, attitude, or social situation; that to a large and increasing extent these courts do in fact exercise this discretion to deal with cases deemed either presently delinquent or in danger of becoming so; that the same types of behavior and situation are handled by unofficial social agencies without stigma to the client; and that, in consequence of all this, "delinquency" has little specific behavioral content either in law or in fact, other than the provision that acts which would otherwise be crimes, in a juvenile are delinquency.

Hence, one emerges from a consideration of the elements entering into delinquency with an indefinite and unsatisfying conclusion. *The juvenile delinquent is a person who has been adjudicated as such by a court of proper jurisdiction* though he may be no dif-ferent, up until the time of court contact and adjudication at any rate, from masses of children who are not delinquent. *Delinquency is any act, course of conduct, or situation which might be brought before a court and adjudicated* whether in fact it comes to be treated there or by some other resource or indeed remains untreated. It will be noted that under these definitions adjudicatable conduct may be defined as delinquent in the abstract, but it cannot be measured as delinquency until a court has found the facts of delinquency to exist.

Table 4

JUVENILE DELINQUENCY CASES, 1945: REASONS FOR REFERENCE TO COURT, IN BOYS' AND IN GIRLS' CASES DISPOSED OF BY 374 COURTS[*]

	Juvenile-delinquency cases					
	Number			Per cent		
Reason for reference to court	Total	Boys	Girls	Total	Boys	Girls
Total cases	122,851	101,240	21,611			
Reason for reference reported	111,939	92,671	19,268	100	100	100
Stealing	40,879	38,610	2,269	37	42	12
Act of carelessness or mischief	19,241	17,779	1,462	17	19	8
Traffic violation	9,852	9,659	193	9	10	1
Truancy	8,681	6,164	2,517	8	7	13
Running away	9,307	5,652	3,655	8	6	19
Being ungovernable	9,840	5,542	4,298	9	6	22
Sex offense	5,990	2,579	3,411	5	3	18
Injury to person	3,224	2,828	396	3	3	2
Other reason	4,925	3,858	1,067	4	4	5
Reason for reference not reported	10,912	8,569	2,343			

[*] *Social Statistics*, p. 11, U.S. Children's Bureau, 1945.

2. The Legal Character of Juvenile Delinquency

SOL RUBIN

The underlying purposes of the juvenile court movement are twofold—one, to remove child offenders from the ordinary criminal courts to courts specially adapted for dealing with children on a social treatment rather than a penal basis; and two, to have this specialized court render protection and treatment to other children needing them. The law is at the service of these admirable purposes.

With regard to the first purpose, it is considered that, for children in any event, the ordinary procedure obtaining in a criminal court is objectionable as being based on the personal responsibility of the offender. Contention between defendants and the state has produced an intricate, highly formalized procedure, the specific purpose of which is to determine the responsibility of the individual defendant for his act.

But in the development of juvenile courts there has been established a new type of proceeding for a group of offenders formerly dealt with in the criminal courts. For juveniles a procedure has been established in all states, although not applicable to all juveniles, which is informal, which does not limit itself to a particular act as does the criminal court, and whose function of social treatment of the offender is very widely asserted, becoming indeed the guiding principle of the court.

With regard to the second purpose of the juvenile court—to render special assistance to children needing protection —we may note that juvenile courts generally include in their jurisdiction children who are dependent and neglected, as well as children who are delinquent. It may have other jurisdiction as well. For these children the court renders judicial decree or order according to the needs of the child.

The creation of juvenile courts has been recognized everywhere as a first-rank development in the treatment of children. It is true, however, that the courts have had varying degrees of success. They have not reached their full expectations, for reasons which are well known and not denied. Two decades ago in *The Annals* they were summarized in an attack on the court entitled "The Juvenile Court at the Bar," by J. Prentice Murphy, then executive secretary of the Children's Bureau in Philadelphia. In brief, the inadequacies of the court were and are generally considered to be related primarily to

SOURCE. Sol Rubin, "The Legal Character of Juvenile Delinquency," from *The Annals of the American Academy of Political and Social Science,* Volume 261, January 1949, pp. 1–8. Reprinted with the permission of the American Academy of Political and Social Science and the author.

personnel standards—the caliber of the judge, the training and education of the probation staff, and their sufficiency in numbers.

It is agreed that the philosophy of the court is sound. However, the fact that the juvenile courts have been upheld as a constitutional device and as an important development in socialized justice does not obviate the need of examining them with a critical eye unrelated to constitutional requirements but focused rather on the social effectiveness of the court and its legal provisions.

WHAT IS JUVENILE DELINQUENCY?

First of all, *juvenile delinquency is what the law says it is.* It is a legal and sociological concept, not psychological. When psychologists and psychiatrists use the term, they use it in the legal sense, or more loosely as a sociological concept.[1]

As indicated, a chief purpose of the juvenile court is to take child offenders out of the criminal court and protect them from criminal procedure and its effects. We therefore find in the juvenile-court acts that every definition of delinquency includes violations of laws and ordinances by children. The definition of delinquency does not, however, stop there, but *starts* there. The list of other acts or conditions which may bring a child within the jurisdiction of the juvenile courts as a delinquent is painstakingly long. The following is a list of abbreviated definitions of acts or conditions included under the heading of delinquency in the juvenile court laws of the United States:

Violates any law or ordinance

[1] Fritz Schmidl comments, "We hear psychiatrists make a distinction between 'neurotic' and 'delinquent' behavior. [But] we have searched in vain for a definition of the term 'delinquent' in the psychiatric literature." "The Rorschach Test in Juvenile Delinquency Research," *American Journal of Orthopsychiatry*, Jan. 1947.

Immoral or indecent conduct

Immoral conduct around school

Engages in illegal occupation

(Knowingly) associates with vicious or immoral persons

Grows up in idleness or crime

(Knowingly) enters, visits house of ill repute

Patronizes, visits policy shop or gaming place

Patronizes saloon or dram house where intoxicating liquor is sold

Patronizes public poolroom or bucket shops

Wanders in streets at night, not on lawful business (curfew)

(Habitually) wanders about railroad yards or tracks

Jumps train or enters car or engine without authority

Habitually truant from school

Incorrigible

(Habitually) uses vile, obscene, or vulgar language (in public place)

Absents self from home without consent

Loiters, sleeps in alleys

Refuses to obey parent, guardian

Uses intoxicating liquors

Is found in place for permitting which adult may be punished

Deports self so as to injure self or others

Smokes cigarettes (around public place)

In occupation or situation dangerous to self or others

Begs or receives alms (or in street for purpose of)

Of course not every state, or any state, has all these items in its definition of delinquency. However, the laws average eight or nine items in addition to violations of law. *No* juvenile court law confines its definition of delinquency to violations of laws and ordinances.

Nor are these jurisdictional possibilities neglected. The latest national statistics of juvenile delinquency, the United States Children's Bureau juvenile court statistics for 1944 and 1945, inform us that "ungovernable" was the reason for reference to 380 juvenile courts in 9,853 cases, and running away in 9,688 cases—18 per cent of the total delinquency cases. Some of these possibly could have been represented as some violation of law. But undoubtedly many of these cases represented no violation of a penal law. Twenty per cent of the cases were referred for "acts of carelessness or mischief." Very likely many of these were not violations of penal law. Some would be torts rather than crimes if committed by adults.

As we have already said, the juvenile court laws go far beyond the purpose of taking child offenders out of the criminal courts. The juvenile courts have a proper function beyond delinquency jurisdiction. This question is present, however: Does inclusion in the delinquency definition of children who are not offenders but may be in need of protection complicate the concepts of the juvenile court? Does it confuse them?

There is no serious question that the juvenile court in its handling of child offenders is better—less harmful—than the criminal court. When the court goes beyond violators of the penal code, and takes in children who are not subject to the jurisdiction of a criminal court, the test becomes more exacting. It must then be established that the juvenile court, by initiating treatment of a group of children designated as delinquents who could not be criminals under the penal laws of the state, is making a positive contribution to the well-being of the community. Does the juvenile court by means of this widely inclusive delinquency definition lessen delinquency, or does it contribute to the solution of other problems of children and the community?

We must face the question of quality in the administration and practice of juvenile courts. It being recognized that probation staffs are inadequate in many courts, and that judges are inadequate in many courts, is it wise to augment the definition of delinquency as broadly as is done? Where the staff is not adequate, such augmentation may not only fail to help children who do not violate laws, but may impede the proper handling of children who are offenders against the penal law.

Furthermore, the extravagant expansion of the definition of delinquency may have a retrograde effect on jurisdiction over child offenders. At present the jurisdiction of some juvenile courts is severely limited as to child offenders. Although the age jurisdiction goes as high as eighteen in a majority of the states, in a substantial number of states it stops at sixteen. In a number of states the juvenile court is not given exclusive jurisdiction, and many child offenders are tried in the criminal courts. In some states certain offenses are *exclusively* the province of the *criminal court*.

The result is that although the juvenile courts everywhere go beyond the concept of a court only for child offenders, in many states they have not been given complete jurisdiction to fulfill their function of taking child offenders out of the criminal courts, and in some states the court has lost jurisdiction originally given to it.

It is perhaps in keeping with the present state of development of juvenile courts that jurisdiction be made most complete over child offenders before shaping delinquency definitions that include standards of conduct which go far beyond the prohibitions of the penal code.

STANDARDS OF CONDUCT FOR CHILDREN

Aside from the argument that as a matter of proper development of the juvenile court the delinquency definition ought not to be greatly expanded until well-nigh all child offenders have been taken out of the criminal courts, the problem of how comprehensive the definition of delinquency ought to be requires a sociopsychological examination. Do these parts of the delinquency definitions establish standards of conduct for children which are preferred rather than required? If there is justification for including in the delinquency definitions behavior which would *not* be criminal under the penal code, the justification would be most cogent as to behavior which is clearly predelinquent and likely to lead to delinquent or criminal behavior. If the behavior is dangerous to the community, or is intolerable behavior, delinquency is indicated. If, however, the *child*, and *not* the community, is in danger, the child needs protection, but delinquency is not indicated.

It is relevant to look to the penal codes not as standards of child behavior, but as guides to what the community considers dangerous and intolerable. A child who associates with immoral persons is doing nothing which in an adult would be considered criminal. Of course such a child requires community attention; but we are talking here of *delinquency* definitions. A child who absents himself from home without consent is doing nothing which in an adult would be deemed criminal.

Children and adolescents coming within the age jurisdiction of the juvenile courts are in process of continuous growth, experimentation, and development. Stringent rules of conduct are not realistic. Yet the adult is not so closely bound by the penal code as the child is by the delinquency definitions.

Perhaps we do not like children to smoke or drink. But there is no proof that children who smoke or drink are likely to become criminal offenders. Indeed, smoking and drinking are now important adult graces. Using vile or obscene language is not nice. Nor is it nor should it be criminal or delinquent. Highly questionable in a delinquency definition are such provisions as patronizing poolrooms or bucket shops. If these places are sufficiently awful, they should be wiped out.

An "ungovernable" child may require attention. Is categorizing such a child as "delinquent" the kind of attention required? Perhaps the parents need help. Perhaps the child would be "governable" if community facilities were available for greater assistance to parents and child.

BREADTH OF DELINQUENCY DEFINITIONS

It is clear from a reading of the various items that go into delinquency definitions that standards of conduct are applied to children which are not applied to adults, at least so far as the penal laws are concerned. Since we are greatly concerned with the wide incidence of delinquency, since the very finding of delinquency is popularly, sometimes officially, considered to be only a lesser evil than a conviction for crime, since, furthermore, the consequences of an adjudication of delinquency are sometimes evil,[2] the broad delinquency definitions should be carefully examined to give these adverse factors full weight. It is a matter to which far less attention has been given than the problem deserves.

The Standard Juvenile Court Act, published by the National Probation and Parole Association and most recently endorsed as a model for all the states at the National Conference on Juvenile Delinquency held in 1946, avoids most of these delinquency classes. The

[2] Our training schools for delinquents have been called junior prisons and schools of crime; delinquency is sometimes a quasi-criminal finding in effect.

Standard Act includes in its provisions corresponding to the usual delinquency definition only two items in addition to violation of law or ordinance. These items are: a child "who deserts his home or who is habitually disobedient or is beyond the control of his parent or other custodian; who, being required by law to attend school, willfully violates rules thereof or absents himself therefrom."

It is universally recognized that truancy is a mere symptom of more basic maladjustment. Modern school authorities wish to rely as little as possible on juvenile court proceedings in handling truancy. The Standard Act does not categorize truancy as delinquency, since it does not use the categories. Most juvenile courts do categorize truancy as delinquency.

With regard to the only other item contained in the Standard Act and usually found in the delinquency definition, I should like to see the psychologists and sociologists engage in a discussion of it. A child "who deserts his home or who is habitually disobedient or beyond the control of his parent . . ."— to what extent is this a family problem only, involving no inherent socially destructive element other than family disharmony? Should this be included in the delinquency definition? Would "neglect" be a sounder category? The Standard Act does not categorize disobedience as either delinquency or neglect. In many juvenile court laws such behavior is included in the definition of delinquency. This seems to have been accepted more or less routinely, without sufficient consideration.

With the present broad definitions of delinquency, a vast population of children, particularly children in slum areas, could be adjudicated delinquent. It would be hard to justify such a concept, just as it is hard to explain away the experience in California where a judge closed a juvenile institution because he was disgusted with the absence of sound treatment. The children had been neglected and abused in the institution. Most were simply sent home by the judge, some were placed in foster homes. The police predicted a crime wave; it never came. Six months later, out of 140 children taken out of the institution, only ten were in trouble again.

AVOIDING THE DELINQUENCY TAG

We have referred to the delinquency categories in the Standard Juvenile Court Act. The Standard Act, however, does not define delinquency, but merely describes situations and classifications of children over which the court has jurisdiction. Thus in the Standard Act a disobedient child is not called a delinquent. About half a dozen juvenile court acts similarly avoid the delinquency tag.

What is the purpose of avoiding the delinquency tag? It is to support the underlying philosophy that in a juvenile court a child is being protected and helped and not being categorized as antisocial. Avoiding the delinquency tag thus implements the common legislative declaration of policy that a juvenile court proceeding is noncriminal. It requires, in turn, administrative and community implementation. However, it is clearly an advantage, although the same result should obtain where the delinquency tag *is* used, since the effect of an adjudication of delinquency is likewise noncriminal. It is also true that the distinction between delinquency and neglect is not always clear; the concepts cannot always be separated.

Does avoiding the delinquency tag have any other advantage? None is apparent.

An incidental advantage in the *use* of the categories is facility in statistical reporting (although more is required than mere existence of the categories before statistics of delinquency can attain reliability). There are more important advantages in the use of the categories.

Where the categories of children within the jurisdiction of the juvenile court are separated into delinquent, dependent, and neglected, it is frequently provided that only the delinquent children may be committed to the training school or other institution for delinquent children. Where the delinquency tag is not used, a danger exists in the legal possibility that *any* child within the jurisdiction of the court, including dependent and neglected children, may be committed to the institution for delinquents. Possibly there are rare cases where a child not adjudicated delinquent would benefit from commitment to the training school. The question of training school commitments is apart from this discussion. It would seem, however, that the lost opportunity of placing in the training school children who are not delinquent is more than compensated for by lessening the danger of improper commitments of this kind.

There is also the danger, where the categories are not used, that the thinking of a court may become too vague for the proper protection of the child. A court without categories may engage in deciding that a child before it might benefit from the court facilities, without concerning itself with a clear legal test of jurisdiction and proof. With the categories, the court has to decide that the child is either dependent, neglected, or delinquent, and not merely that the court finds the child to be within its very generally described jurisdictional sections. If the distinction between delinquency and neglect is not always clear, the difficulty is not overcome by avoiding the terms. Avoiding the use of the terms "delinquency" and "neglect" does not avoid the use of categories, but merely avoids naming them.

AGE FLOOR FOR DELINQUENCY

Again, bearing in mind the inadequacies of many courts and juvenile institutions and the need for the most careful selection in institutional commitments, means of controlling commitments should be welcomed. Where the delinquency tag is used, it is possible to place an age floor on delinquency, therefore on children committable to the training schools.

The common law rule and the most common statutory rule is that a child under seven is conclusively presumed to be incapable of committing crime. A child between seven and fourteen is presumed incapable of committing crime. In a criminal proceeding the state must prove affirmatively that such a child has sufficient capacity to entertain a criminal intent (*doli capax*). In a juvenile court, these presumptions against responsibility of children do not exist. Some writers have accepted without discussion the proposition that in some way the rule carries over to the juvenile court. However, the presumptions are not in fact retained in the juvenile court laws as to delinquency. In several of the states the penal law provides that a child under a particular age—twelve years, or ten—may not be convicted of *crime*. In these states, however, a child under the specified age *may* be found delinquent for an act prohibited by the penal law. Children under seven years of age are adjudicated delinquents.

Is not the reason of the rule exempting children from criminal responsibilities applicable to delinquency? Accordingly, in some juvenile court acts the provision appears that a child under a stated age cannot be a delinquent, therefore cannot be committed as a delinquent. In Mississippi and Texas, for example, a child under ten cannot be adjudicated a delinquent. New York has an age floor of seven. By far most juvenile court laws have no floor; the definition applies to "children under 18" or whatever the upper age limit may be.

Retaining the delinquency tag permits a definition of delinquency to be applicable to a specifically limited age group, thus keeping the younger children out of the training schools. The same effect might be obtained in the noncategorized laws by providing that any one of the defined situations shall apply to children of a particular age. This is not done. It would require a corresponding particularity in the disposition section. Or it might be done by suitable provisions in the statute governing the institutions.

EUROPEAN AGE LIMITS

To a European juvenile court representative, the suggestion that an age floor be fixed in the delinquency definition would appear as a laggard proposition. It would be a matter of approaching what has long been established in a number of countries. Reviewing the delinquency jurisdiction of juvenile courts in Europe, M. Grünhut writes:

At present, the lower limit is 8 in England (though the law presumes that a child under 14 is *doli incapax* unless the prosecution rebuts the presumption by proving that the child understood the criminal nature of his act); 13 in France and Poland; 14 in Austria, Czechoslovakia, Germany, Norway; 15 in Denmark and Sweden. In Sweden the police have suggested a raising of the age limit to 16. The higher age limit is 17 in England and Poland and 18 in Austria, Czechoslovakia and Germany. Belgium, which followed the French *Code Pénal* in that it substituted the require-

ment of *discernement* for a statutory lower age limit, has the higher age limit of 16, and Holland likewise of 18. . . .[3]

For those cases of children whose delinquency consists of a criminal act as defined in the penal code, the term "criminal responsibility" is frankly used in the European juvenile court laws, as distinguished from the jurisdiction of the juvenile court over neglected and wayward children.

Can the delinquency age floor be safely lifted? Grünhut says:

To a certain extent, such age limits depend on ethnological factors which vary in different countries. Another factor is even more important. The more a thorough social and educational service by a Court, a Youth Welfare Authority, or the co-operation of both, has been developed and is working satisfactorily with regard to the treatment of wayward children, the more can the lower age limit of a Juvenile Court for offenders be raised. The Scandinavian countries with their well-established Child Welfare Councils have the highest lower age limit for juvenile offenders eligible for trial.

In a court with excellent personnel, facilities (including institutions), and practices, these factors supporting the use of the delinquency tag would have little relevancy. The court's discretion would be sufficient protection. This is perhaps applicable to model legislation also. In many courts, however, at the present state of their development, the categories, including delinquency, may still serve an important, desirable function.

[3] In an article entitled "The Juvenile Court: Its Competence and Constitution," in *Lawless Youth, A Challenge to the New Europe*, a Policy for the Juvenile Courts prepared by the International Committee of the Howard League for Penal Reform, 1942–1945, by Margery Fry, M. Grünhut, Hermann Mannheim, Wanda Grabinska, D. C. Reckham, London: George Allen and Unwin, Ltd., 1947.

A CHOICE OF JUVENILE COURT
CONCEPTS

Juvenile courts, like other social institutions, are in a continuous state of change. Some of our juvenile courts do not go far beyond the function of taking child offenders out of the criminal courts, and by having a comprehensive and exclusive jurisdiction they fulfill this function. Other juvenile courts perform this function rather poorly, leaving a wide jurisdiction over child offenders in the criminal courts. Many juvenile courts operate under laws which are concerned with standards of conduct on the part of children, standards which are not established as related to crime prevention.

Despite the fifty years' growth of the juvenile courts, they are still beset with difficulties on all sides. It might be the part of wisdom for the juvenile courts to go slow, to achieve important although limited purposes before embarking upon projects of doubtful urgency. If the juvenile court is to go beyond the problems of child offenders, if the juvenile court law is to set up special standards of conduct for children, it ought to do so cautiously and slowly, on the basis of generally accepted concepts on which child behavior experts are agreed. It may be that that is the course of speediest and most successful development for juvenile courts in the future.

If some of the foregoing concepts are controversial, the discussion is warranted. It will be beneficial if it is entered into by others, with tight hold of the single precept—what is best for the child. Jealousy of jurisdiction, or devotion to precedent for its own sake, ought to have no place in the development of the best means for protecting children. Not controversial, however, is the proposition that the delinquency definition is relatively unimportant when compared with the need for adequate court personnel and services, as well as other welfare and institutional services for children. It is the inadequacy of these services that often results in a court referral or institutionalization rather than a welfare service solution. Where social services are inadequate, it helps neither child nor court to increase the scope of the delinquency definition.

3. The Extent of Delinquency in the United States

NEGLEY K. TEETERS AND DAVID MATZA

During this year when preparations are being made for the Sixth White House Conference on Children and Youth, it is not out of place, in assaying the extent of delinquency, to quote from the third conference held in 1930: "There exists no accurate statement as to the amount of delinquency in this country, nor whether it is increasing or decreasing." And again: "There is no accurate conception as to what actually constitutes delinquency."[1] These same words might well be stated at the White House Conference in 1960.

The term "juvenile delinquency" does not appear in the literature until 1823 when a New York philanthropic society changed its name from the *Society for the Prevention of Pauperism* to the *Society for the Reformation of Juvenile Delinquents*. But there can be little doubt that there have always been juvenile delinquents. But as to "how many" we cannot know. They were referred to through the years as "wayward," "depraved," "unfortunate," "wild," "headstrong," "willful," or "handicapped." The first special insti-

[1] *The Delinquent Child*, New York: Century, 1932, p. 23.

tutions for delinquents in this country were the early Houses of Refuge established in New York in 1824, in Boston in 1826, and in Philadelphia in 1823. The first institution in the world for the treatment of delinquent youth was the *Hospice of San Michael* in Rome in 1704.

It has always been difficult—even impossible—to compute the extent of delinquency. It has always been popular for each generation to believe its children were the worst, the most lawless, and the most unruly. Sir Walter Scott, writing in 1812, deplored the insecurity of Edinburgh, where groups of boys between 12 and 20 scoured the streets at night and knocked down and robbed all who came in their way. In an article in the *Atlantic Monthly* for December, 1926 bearing the intriguing title "The Habit of Going to the Devil," Archer Butler Hulbert presents an array of diatribes against youth, as culled from the press during the early part of the nineteenth century. He found that in 1827 "a glance at our country and its moral conditions fills the mind with alarming apprehension; the moral desolation and flood tides of wickedness

SOURCE. Negley K. Teeters and David Matza, "The Extent of Delinquency in the United States," from *The Journal of Negro Education*, Volume 28 (Summer 1959 Yearbook), pp. 200–213. Reprinted with the permission of *The Journal of Negro Education* and the authors.

threaten to sweep away not only the blessings of religion, but the boasted freedom of our republican institutions as well." In 1828 he found: "No virtuous public sentiment frowns down upon the criminal to shame him into secrecy," and a year later, "And what of our youth? The lamentable extent of dishonesty, fraud, and other wickedness among our boys and girls shocks the nation." He found that in 1831, "Half the number of persons actually convicted of crime are youths who have not yet reached the age of discretion (how familiar that sounds in 1959)." He further finds that in 1830 "The army of youthful criminals from the slums are augmented by children abandoned by the shiftless of the working classes, by families wrecked by living beyond their means, and by wayward unfortunates from reputable families. Large numbers of these youngsters belong to organized gangs of thieves and cut-throats. . . . Of 256 convicts in the Massachusetts State Prison, forty-five were thieves at 16, and 127 had at that age become habitual drinkers."[2]

A century later, in 1930, we find the oft-quoted statement of the Wickersham Commission of the prison population of that year—54.8 per cent had been less than 21 years of age when convicted. In 1938 Harrison and Grant, in their startling study of young offenders in New York City, stated that of those persons arrested for lesser offenses, minors were responsible for only 4.5 per cent of the total, whereas of the more serious crimes, the arrest rates of those under 21 were many times higher.[3]

It was the startling data presented in this work that galvanized into motion

the American Law Institute to draw up the Youth Correction Authority Model Act of 1940 which subsequently was adopted in modified form in California and a few other states. Almost twenty years ago we found the following sober analysis of youthful delinquency and crime to substantiate the findings of Harrison and Grant; it could well have been written in 1959:

Youthful offenders are an especially serious factor in the crime problem. Young people between 15 and 21 constitute only 13 per cent of the population above 15, but their share in the total amount of serious crime committed far exceeds their proportionate representation. They are responsible for approximately 26 per cent of the robberies and thefts; they constitute some 40 per cent of our apprehended burglars and nearly half of our automobile thieves. Boys from 17 to 21 are arrested for major crimes in greater numbers than persons of any other four year group. They come into court, not for petty offenses but for serious crimes, twice as often as adults of 35 and 39; three times as often as those of 45 and 49; five times as often as men of 50 to 59. Nineteen year olds offend more frequently than persons of any other age, with 18 year olds next. Moreover, the proportion of youths less than 21 in the whole number arrested, has increased 15 per cent during the past three years; 108,857 not yet old enough to vote were arrested and fingerprinted last year.[4]

Such was the situation as reported in 1940.

Before analyzing the extent of delinquency, let us set down some data from the Uniform Crime Reports for 1957. Taking the serious categories of crime we find that arrests for all crimes reported (by the police in 1,473 cities

---

[2] *Atlantic Monthly*, 138: 804–806, December 1926.

[3] Leonard V. Harrison and Pryor M. Grant, *Youth in the Toils*. New York: Macmillan, 1939, pp. 44–45.

[4] Digested in the *Prison Journal*, April-July, 1940, pp. 57–58, from a pamphlet *The American Law Institute*. See also Thorsten Sellin, "The Criminality of Youth," Philadelphia: *The American Law Institute*, October 1940.

of over 2,500 representing a population of 40,176,369 based on the 1950 census) 19.3 per cent were of persons under 21 years of age. Of the arrests for the serious categories, 14.5 per cent of all for homicides were of those under 21; 44.7 per cent of the robberies; 16.9 per cent for all aggravated assaults; 44.1 per cent for the rapes; 68.0 per cent of all the burglaries; 62.4 per cent of all larcenies; and 80.6 per cent of all auto thefts.

At first glance and without interpretation this is indeed an alarming picture. But like all statistics, they do need considerable interpretation. We quote in this connection the former F.B.I. affiliate and presently operating Director of the Chicago Crime Commission, Mr. Virgil Peterson:

A few years ago the Attorney General of the United States . . . informed the people: "I have been asked to bring you the facts and the figures, the tragic evidence of juvenile crime. . . . Here are some . . . of the figures chargeable to some of our youth . . . 51 per cent of all burglaries, over half of them; 36 per cent of all robberies. . . ." Naturally, these figures given by the highest law enforcement official of the land were widely quoted in the press, over the radio, from speakers' platforms, and by crime prevention groups. Actually, the figures were based only on the available fingerprint cards of persons arrested and charged with burglary and robbery—a small sample from a huge army of burglars and robbers.[5]

Mr. Peterson points out that of all burglaries reported, only 31.3 per cent were cleared by arrest; and that of each ten burglaries reported no one knows who committed seven of them; and of the vast number arrested, the majority were youth. He continues:

Their youthful recklessness and inexperience in crime make it relatively easy to apprehend them. The professional crim-

[5] *Atlantic Monthly,* "Crime Does Pay." pp. 38–42, February 1953.

inal is more difficult to detect and apprehend. And it is reasonable to assume that he is responsible for a large percentage of our unsolved crimes. At any rate, the Attorney General's flat statement that over half of the burglaries were attributable to youth was little more than an opinion— an opinion that may be far from the truth.

Further along in his article Mr. Peterson adds this startling remark: "During the five year period from 1947 through 1951 over a million burglaries were reported to the police in about 2,200 cities. . . . No one knows who committed over 800,000 of them." But the bulk of those arrested were youth under 21 years of age. The same can be stated of practically all categories. The monetary value of articles stolen by youth is generally quite small. Lumped into these "burglaries" are thefts of hub caps or tire gauges from filling stations, or other objects of trifling value. It is important to note that the Federal Bureau of Investigation's definitions of robbery and burglary include "attempts" as well as the actual commission of these acts. The arrest rate also includes many instances of mistaken identity at the scene of the crime.

In order to present a picture of national delinquency trends between 1940 and 1957 it is necessary to use a number of different sources of information. The reason for this is that it is not possible to convert Uniform Crime Report data prior to 1952 into rates since there is no base population reported. Therefore, we shall infer the trends between 1940 and 1952 from the Juvenile Court Statistics. While this may be questioned, there seems to be good reason to believe there is considerable similarity between the direction or changes indicated by both collecting systems. As I. Richard Perlman of the Children's Bureau, states:

We find that despite the fact that neither of these series (Juvenile Court Cases and Police Arrest data from the Uniform Crime Reports between 1938 and 1947) represents a completely accurate measurement of juvenile delinquency and despite the differences in the unit of count, the extent of coverage and geographical representation, nevertheless there is remarkable similarity between the direction of changes indicated by the two lines. Both increased sharply from 1942 to 1943, both decreased between 1943 and 1944, both increased again in 1945 to the ten year peak and both showed sharp decreases in 1946 and 1947.[6]

If Perlman is right we are able to increase greatly the length of time subsumed by our descriptive series. Table 1 shows the increase in juvenile delinquency rates between 1940 and 1952 as indicated by the Juvenile Court Statistics. Table 2 shows the increase in

Table 1

JUVENILE DELINQUENCY CASES (AGES 10-17) 1940–1952. JUVENILE COURT STATISTICS [*]

Year	Per cent (1940 as 100)	Child population of United States, per cent (1940 as 100)
1940	100	100
1941	112	99
1942	125	98
1943	172	97
1944	165	96
1945	172	95
1946	148	94
1947	131	93
1948	128	93
1949	135	92
1950	141	91
1951	149	93
1952	165	95

[*] Herbert A. Block and Frank T. Flynn, *Delinquency, The Juvenile Offender in America Today*. New York: Random House, 1956, p. 27.

[6] "The Meaning of Juvenile Delinquency Statistics," *Federal Probation*, pp. 63–67.

Table 2

INCREASE IN DELINQUENCY RATES BETWEEN 1952 AND 1956 [*]

Year	Per cent (1952 as 100)
1952	100.0
1953	107.7
1954	111.6
1955	121.3
1956	147.9

[*] Rates computed from Uniform Crime Report data using estimated number of children (0-18) in reporting areas as base population.

juvenile delinquency rates between 1952 and 1956 as supplied by the Uniform Crime Reports.

We may infer from Tables 1 and 2 the following tendencies: A gradual increase between 1940 and 1942, a marked increase in delinquency beginning in 1943 and lasting through 1945 with a slight dip in 1944, a gradual decrease beginning in 1946 and continuing through 1948, a gradual increase from 1949 to 1951, a more marked increase between 1951 and 1952, a continuing gradual increase from 1952 to 1954, and finally another marked increase beginning in 1955 and lasting at least until 1957. Except for the period 1946 to 1948 and except for a slight dip in a high plateau in 1944, the picture revealed by official national statistics is one of continuous increase, sometimes gradual, sometimes rather rapid.

For the years between 1952 and 1957, we have computed delinquency rates by specific offense categories in order to obtain a more concise understanding of trends during this period. In Table 3 we present the delinquency rates per 100,000 persons using the number of persons in the populations represented in the Uniform Crime Reports as the base population. In Table 4 we present the delinquency rates

Table 3

DELINQUENCY RATES PER 100,000: USING THE UNIFORM CRIME REPORTS ESTIMATES OF REPRESENTED POPULATION AS THE BASE POPULATION: 1952-1957*

Offense	1952	1953	1954	1955	1956	1957	Per cent of 56-52	Per cent of 57-52
Criminal Homicide	.37	.36	.35	.39	.52	.52	141	141
(a) Murder and Nonnegligent Manslaughter	.22	.24	.20	.23	.34	.33	155	150
(b) Manslaughter by Negligence	.15	.12	.15	.16	.18	.19	120	127
Robbery	5.45	5.68	5.91	6.56	6.53	7.78	120	143
Aggravated Assault	2.75	3.43	3.37	4.14	4.78	5.20	174	189
Other Assault	6.91	9.63	10.48	12.02	13.49	15.06	195	218
Burglary (B&E)	46.56	48.77	50.61	56.02	60.72	70.14	130	151
Larceny-Theft	62.95	73.46	83.09	92.72	112.76	130.80	179	208
Auto-Theft	27.05	29.36	30.22	34.99	45.18	48.99	167	181
Embezzlement and Fraud	.83	1.16	.78	.72	.75	1.13	90	136
Stolen Property: buying, receiving, etc.	1.41	1.83	2.10	2.13	6.10	3.11	433	221
Forgery and Counterfeiting	1.04	1.27	1.18	1.20	1.41	1.64	136	158
Rape	1.27	1.75	1.51	1.99	2.04	2.32	161	183
Prostitution and Commercialized Vice	.63	.63	.48	.53	.37	.30	59	48
Other Sex Offenses	5.22	6.16	7.56	6.64	7.37	8.50	141	163
Narcotic Drug Laws	.41	.63	.41	.60	.71	.55	173	134
Weapons: carrying, possessing, etc.	3.07	4.15	4.60	5.74	6.82	7.46	222	243
Offenses Against Family and Children	2.95	3.30	4.10	2.40	.62	.72	21	24
Liquor Laws	4.62	7.71	9.45	10.06	13.90	17.73	301	384
Driving While Intoxicated	.92	1.04	.93	1.21	1.53	1.66	166	180
Disorderly Conduct	43.26	42.93	42.67	47.57	61.73	64.79	143	150
Drunkenness	11.71	12.33	12.00	13.33	15.69	16.87	134	144
Vagrancy	7.25	8.32	6.99	6.56	8.97	11.71	124	162
Gambling	1.12	1.22	.92	.96	1.25	1.53	112	137
Suspicion	24.41	31.08	23.60	27.78	38.47	39.75	158	163
All Other Offenses	106.78	105.91	120.26	131.79	157.15	173.49	147	163
Total	368.95	402.10	423.54	468.09	568.85	631.76	154	171

* These rates have been computed from data appearing in the Uniform Crime Reports, 1952-1957.

Table 4

DELINQUENCY RATES PER 100,000: USING THE ESTIMATED POPULATION OF CHILDREN (0–18) IN THE POPULATION REPRESENTED IN THE UNIFORM CRIME REPORTS: 1952–1956

Offense	1952	1953	1954	1955	1956	Per cent of 56–52
Criminal Homicide	1.11	1.08	1.01	1.10	1.48	133
(a) Murder and Nonnegligent Manslaughter	.66	.71	.58	.64	.97	147
(b) Manslaughter by Negligence	.45	.37	.43	.46	.51	113
Robbery	16.26	16.77	17.16	18.74	18.71	115
Aggravated Assault	8.20	10.12	9.78	11.81	13.70	167
Other Assaults	20.63	28.42	30.42	34.32	38.64	187
Burglary	139.02	144.01	146.93	159.96	173.95	125
Larceny-Theft	187.96	216.91	241.25	264.77	323.01	172
Auto-Theft	80.76	86.69	87.74	99.90	129.42	160
Embezzlement and Fraud	2.48	3.42	2.27	2.04	2.16	87
Stolen Property: buying, receiving, etc.	4.21	5.40	6.09	6.09	17.46	415
Forgery and Counterfeiting	3.11	3.75	3.43	3.44	4.04	130
Rape	3.80	5.17	4.39	5.68	5.84	154
Prostitution and Commercialized Vice	1.89	1.86	1.41	1.52	1.05	56
Other Sex Offenses	15.59	18.20	21.95	18.95	21.11	135
Narcotic Drug Laws	1.23	1.86	1.20	1.70	2.03	165
Weapons: carrying, possessing, etc.	9.17	12.25	13.34	16.40	19.55	213
Offenses Against Family and Children	8.81	9.74	11.92	6.85	1.79	20
Liquor Laws	13.80	22.76	24.73	28.72	39.81	288
Driving While Intoxicated	2.75	3.08	2.69	3.46	4.39	160
Disorderly Conduct	129.18	126.77	123.85	135.83	176.83	137
Drunkenness	34.97	36.42	34.85	38.06	44.96	129
Vagrancy	21.66	24.56	20.29	18.72	25.69	119
Gambling	3.34	3.59	2.66	2.75	3.58	107
Suspicion	72.88	91.76	68.51	79.53	110.19	151
All Other Offenses	318.84	312.74	349.16	376.33	450.17	141
Total	1101.66	1187.33	1229.72	1336.67	1629.55	148

per 100,000 children (0-18) using the estimated number of children in the populations represented in the Uniform Crime Reports as a base population.[7] We see in Tables 3 and 4 that there is considerable variation by offense in the shifting delinquency rates experienced during this period. In a few offenses, Embezzlement and Fraud, Prostitution and Offenses Against the Family, we observe decreasing rates of delinquency. These, however, are the exceptions. In all

[7] The base population in Table 3 is the number of persons residing in the cities included in the Uniform Crime Reports as of the 1950 Census. The base populations for Table 4 were computed by first correcting the total populations for increases that had taken place since 1950, and then applying the proportion of children for each year to the corrected total population. We are indebted to the Population Reference Bureau for the estimates of total population (1950–1958) and the estimates of youthful population (1950–1956).

other offense categories we see varying degrees of increase in the delinquency rates. In Table 5, we have classified the offenses according to the magnitude of the increase.

This series of tables represents the basis upon which we shall continue in this paper. The problem is obviously one of interpretation. What do the figures tell us?

Table 5

CLASSIFICATION OF OFFENSES BY AMOUNT OF INCREASE: 1952–1956 (ESTIMATED YOUTHFUL POPULATION USED AS BASE POPULATION). RATIO OF 1956 RATES TO 1952 RATES

High-Increase Offenses	
	(160 and above)
Receiving Stolen Property	415
Liquor Laws	288
Weapons	213
Other Assaults	187
Larceny	172
Aggravated Assault	167
Narcotics	165
Medium-Increase Offenses	
	(Between 136 and 160)
Auto-Theft	160
Driving While Intoxicated	160
Rape	154
Suspicion	151
Murder and Manslaughter	147
All Other Offenses	141
Disorderly Conduct	137
Low-Increase Offenses	
	(Between 100 and 139)
Other Sex Offenses	135
Forgery and Counterfeiting	130
Drunkenness	129
Burglary	125
Vagrancy	119
Robbery	115
Murder by Negligence	113
Gambling	107
Decrease Offenses	
	(Below 100)
Embezzlement and Fraud	87
Prostitution and Vice	56
Offenses Against Family	20

The fundamental question is whether this increase in delinquency is apparent or real. There are three positions that may be taken in attempting to come to any conclusion: First, that the data accurately reflect a real increase; second, that the increases are due to artifacts of data-collecting methods; and finally that the official statistics overrate the increase but that there has been some real increase.

The official description of delinquency trends is not readily accepted by the academician. The point of departure for the theoretical criminologists has been the insistence that the official increase represents, not a reflection of real increases, but rather a number of diverse artifacts inherent in the subtle processes involved in the collection of the data.

The academicians—who may be referred to here as skeptics—possess an antipathy to "alarmist" tendencies in the interpretation of delinquency statistics; furthermore, they are concerned with distortions and error usually inherent in any system of collecting information.

The strength of the "alarmist" point of view exists, for the most part, outside the university. It is found most frequently among spokesmen of mass media, law-enforcement officials, serious citizens, and practitioners who are face to face with the delinquent, especially juvenile court jurists. The public has aligned itself with this "alarmist" point of view, especially since its "common-sense" impression of the problem supports it. Thus, it is not surprising that many informed and most uninformed Americans are disturbed by the "rising tide" of juvenile delinquency during the past twenty years.

The academic intellectual finds it impossible to accept the obviousness of the "common-sense" approach. His skepticism sometimes manifests itself in a rather charming—even if irritating— "hide-bound conservatism." Yet, the reluctance to accept new ideas is simply a form of skepticism that is necessary in any scientific endeavor. Scholars or academicians are, by definition, endowed, rightly or wrongly, with a near-monopoly of expertness. Thus they are in the intellectually impossible situation of being the judges and the judged. Therefore, we must bend over backward to be certain that we consider carefully the "alarmist" point of view, precisely because our first impulse is to dismiss it. More important, we must sometimes supply the opposition point of view with the sophistication that it, unfortunately, so often lacks. In reality, the "alarmists" are not the best spokesmen for their own position. They often lack the technical skills necessary to support their position and thus become vulnerable to those trained in the arts of logic, argumentation, and scientific methodology.

There are a number of methods used by the "skeptics" in minimizing the apparent increases in delinquency. One is the thesis of the "expanding denominator" which contends that the growth of child population offsets the increase in delinquency rates. Empirically this argument has some validity but not too much. Thus, if we compare Table 3 with Table 4, we see that the delinquency rate of 1956 was 54 per cent higher than that of 1952 if we *do not* take into consideration the expanding youthful population for that period; but if we *do* take the growth into consideration we find the increase in delinquency about 48 per cent. Thus, while we may contend that the "expanding denominator" may reduce the cause for alarm, it by no means completely disarms the vocal proponents of common sense.

The second argument of the skeptics is more sophisticated. It may well be asserted that the legal definition of delinquency throughout the nation has become less precise, more confused and vague. Stated another way, there is more delinquency because more and more overt acts—as well as covert— are being defined or considered delinquent. In addition, more and more minors are being counted for the same act, e.g., "57 youths charged with homicide" with one murder tabulated; "20 youths charged with carrying firearms" when only one of the group possessed a pistol. The skeptics contend that it is official policy in administering justice that has changed rather than the actual content and substance of juvenile behavior. We should also add that quite frequently it is the same child who is arrested over and over again and thus increases the delinquency rate.

This argument is often coupled with the assertion that norms in urban communities become increasingly formalized. This results in certain types of youthful behavior being officially dealt with rather than being handled through unofficial or informal forces of control such as parents, storekeepers, and neighbors. In many cities, the agents of formal control usually have a penchant for "recording" and "bookkeeping" and "referring" which usually results in an almost insatiable hoarding of a wide variety of records and statistics. The norms of bureaucratic management therefore impel the recording of many trivial deviant acts rather than of disposing of such cases on a personal and informal level. Thus, in many of our large cities, we find records of cases labeled with the vague nomenclature, "adjusted" or "unofficially handled."

What empirical evidence is there that the changes in methods of law-enforcement are responsible for the alleged increase in delinquency? The available evidence leads us to believe that some, but by no means all, can be explained by these changes. For instance, if we examine the data between 1952 and 1956, there is little evidence that the bulk of the increase can be attributed to vague and diffuse definitions. This is admittedly a short period of time, but it is a period within which the data seem roughly comparable and it is, furthermore, a period during which a significant increase in delinquency rates took place (Table 6).

In Table 5 we divided the various offense categories into (*a*) High Increase Offenses; (*b*) Medium Increase Offenses; (*c*) Low Increase Offenses, and (*d*) Decrease Offenses. The four best examples of vaguely defined offenses which appear in the Uniform Crime Reports are "Suspicion," "Disorderly Conduct," "Vagrancy" and "All Other Offenses." Three of these are "Medium Increase" offenses. This means that the rates of increase for these offense categories was about the same as that for total delinquency. The fourth, "Vagrancy," was a "Low Increase" offense. The vaguely defined offenses, therefore, contributed *slightly less* than their share to the increases that had taken place in delinquency within this five-year period.

Another factor involves wider definitions of delinquency related to technological innovations. Traffic violations and the casual sale and use of guns are examples of anti-social behavior which parents and grandparents of modern youth could not have easily committed. Therefore, in some states—Utah, for example—traffic offenses comprise more than half of all delinquencies. In the period between 1954 and 1956, traffic violations in Utah constituted 58.4 per cent of all delinquencies. In that state traffic violations rose from 1 per 1,000 of school age children in 1935 to 40 per 1,000 in 1955. It must be pointed out, however, that in Utah, conventional delinquency followed the national pat-

Table 6

PERCENTAGE INCREASE IN DELINQUENCY RATES BETWEEN 1952 AND 1956. TOTAL DELINQUENCY VS. DIFFUSELY DEFINED OFFENSE CATEGORIES

Total Delinquency	48%
Suspicion	51%
All Other Offenses	41%
Disorderly Conduct	37%
Vagrancy	19%

tern. For example, out of each 1,000 school age children, there were 12 delinquents in 1935, 18 in 1940, 41 in 1943, 27 in 1945, 16 in 1950, and 30 in 1955.[8]

A final argument used by the skeptics pertains to the improvements in techniques of apprehending and recording delinquents. We have more delinquents simply because we are better able to capture and count them. Such improvements have taken place, but it is doubtful that a significant proportion of increased rates can be attributed to these improvements.

In discussing improved methods of collecting statistics, it must be remembered that every additional reporting area brings with it not only an additional number of recorded delinquents (the numerator) but also an increase in the base population (the denominator). With each increase in the numerator, there is an increase in the denominator. The question is whether the increase in the denominator is proportionate or disproportionate to increases in the numerator.

Let us assume that City X reports for the first time in 1954. If its rate of delinquency has been higher through the years than the average of cities reporting prior to 1954, then all previous rates were underestimated because City

[8] Biennial Report of the Director, Bureau of Services for Children, State Department of Public Welfare, Utah, Juvenile Courts, January 1, 1954 to June 30, 1956.

X, a high delinquency city, was not included in previous compilations. On the other hand, if City X has traditionally been a low delinquency area then all previous rates have been overestimated because it was not included in previous compilations. The answer to our question, therefore, depends on whether or not the cities that have only recently begun to report are relatively high or low delinquency areas. One may suggest that generally the larger cities tend to report first and smaller communities later. If delinquency is more concentrated in the large cities, as sociologists have traditionally held, then it may well be that we have *overestimated* the national rates of delinquency in the past and therefore *underrated* the differences between the rates of from 1940 to 1956.

While all of the above is quite conjectural, it can be stated that a major innovation in reporting that took place in 1953 was coupled with an increase that was rather "average" in all respects. We see in Table 7 that the Uniform Crime Reports in 1952 were based on data compiled from 232 cities with population over 25,000. Starting in 1953, there are a great many cities reporting, ranging from 1,174 in 1953 to a maximum of 1,551 in 1956 (all over 2,500). The increase in delinquency rates between 1952 and 1953, the year of the major innovation in the number and type of cities included in the compilation, was 7.7 per cent. Between 1953 and 1954 the increase was 3.9 per cent. Between 1954 and 1955 there was a 9.7 per cent increase. Between 1955 and 1956 there was a 26.6 per cent increase. Thus it would seem that there is no striking relationship between major changes in the system of data-gathering and the official increases in delinquency.

There remains the question of improved methods of apprehension. Once again our belief is that we cannot attribute much of the increase to this, important though it may be. If we did make this contention, we would be obliged to answer some knotty questions as, for example, how account for the decreased rates between 1946 and 1948? Was there a decrease in police effectiveness during those years? If there are any years during which a realistic decrease in police effectiveness might be assumed, it would be the wartime period 1942 through 1945 when there was a critical manpower shortage; yet in this period we find an extremely high rate of delinquency. The inescapable fact is that delinquency rates are highly fluctuating in character, whereas there is every reason to assume that methods of apprehension and police efficiency have constantly improved. We do not intend to dismiss completely the role played by increasing police effectiveness in artificially raising the official rates. We merely wish to point out that its importance can, like all other phases of the problem, be overemphasized.

Thus far our position has been somewhere between that of the "alarmist" and the "skeptic." For the years between 1940 and 1957 our belief is that although the official statistics perhaps overrate the increase in the delinquency rates, there has, nevertheless, been some real increase. However, we do not believe that one may assume lower and lower rates for years previous to 1940.

Table 7

POPULATION REPRESENTED IN UNIFORM CRIME REPORTS 1952–1957

1952	23,344,305	(232 cities over 25,000)
1953	37,255,808	(1174 cities over 2,500)
1954	38,642,183	(1389 cities over 2,500)
1955	41,792,800	(1477 cities over 2,500)
1956	41,219,052	(1551 cities over 2,500)
1957	40,176,369	(1473 cities over 2,500)

As we stated above, delinquency rates are highly fluctuating. They are not stable, nor theoretically should we expect them to be. Juveniles by their nature should be expected to respond quickly to abrupt changes in the social structure. Delinquency rates should be diagnostic of various forms of social disorganization and social reconstruction. This means that unless we adhere to the fashionable but superficial view that modern times are decadent and that some unspecified era in past history is the repository of all things good, there is reason to suppose that delinquency rates were high in other periods —perhaps as high as those currently experienced. The early years of nineteenth century England immediately come to mind.

We argued earlier that there is nothing drastically new about the content or substance of delinquency. It has always been a feature of human existence—a part of the "backwash" of our culture. But one may ask, is it not true that there is a great deal more delinquency among modern youth? The answer depends a good deal on how far back one wishes to go for comparisons. It is often assumed that if the present rates are really higher than those of, let us say, 1935, then they are *ipso facto* higher than the rates experienced in all years prior to 1935. There takes place, unconsciously to be sure, that curious reversal of the "evolutionary" mentality, the mentality of the "golden age." Just as the gloomy demographers of the thirties erred in extrapolating short-run tendencies into the future, so a disgruntled and neo-traditionalist public errs in simply extrapolating short-run tendencies back into the dark and unknown recesses of history.

There is one obvious reason why both predictions of the future and assessments of the past can be treated in so cavalier a fashion. We know little

that is measurable about either. It is highly probable that the rates of delinquency of the late fifties seem dramatically high only because we have been forced by the data to choose a slice of history that *accidentally* begins with relatively low rates and culminates in relatively high rates. The fact that we happen to be "cheek to jowl" with them gives us no little concern. Put another way, the delinquency rates of the late fifties may be "very high" only when we compare them to the "very low" rates of the late thirties.

We may see some scant evidence for this point if we turn to scattered local statistics that go back beyond the middle thirties. Table 8 shows the number of delinquency complaints and the rates for Cuyahoga County, Ohio for the years between 1918 and 1957. The city of Cleveland is located within Cuyahoga County.[9]

We may make two inferences from this table. First, the pattern of fluctuation between 1932 and 1957 is roughly similar to that experienced by the nation as a whole. Second, and more important, we note that the rates in Cleveland and the rest of the county were twice as high in the period during and after World War I than the rates experienced during the early and late fifties. The delinquency rate was 65.9 per 1,000 children (12-17) in 1918, 63.2 in 1919, and 52.0 in 1920. In 1925 the rate was 41.5; in 1932 it was 35.8; in 1939 it was 21; in 1943 it was 31.7; in 1945 it was 34.7; in 1950 it was 25.2; and in 1957 it was 33.5.

What was the rate before World War I? We do not know. We can say,

[9] We are indebted to Mr. John J. Alden, Chief of Probation Services for the Juvenile Court of Cuyahoga County, Cleveland, Ohio, for these very interesting statistics. Population based on resident births (uncorrected for deaths, in-migration, out-migration). Source: A Sheet-a-Week, prepared by Howard Whipple Green, March 5, 1953.

Table 8

NUMBER OF DELINQUENCY COMPLAINTS AND DELINQUENCY RATES FOR THE YEARS 1918–1957

Year	Population —ages 12 through 17	Official delinquency cases	Unofficial delinquency cases	Grand total delinquency cases	Number cases excluding unofficial traffic violations	Delin- quency rate per thousand children
1918	89,138	3434	2505	5939	5877	65.9
1919	98,387	3502	2433	5935	5901	63.2
1920	96,108	3108	1911	5019	5000	52.0
1921	100,160	2495	1298	3793	3785	37.8
1922	104,117	2433	1018	3451	3436	33.0
1923	108,410	2546	1434	3980	3963	36.6
1924	110,051	2379	1804	4183	4163	37.8
1925	110,943	2519	2129	4648	4602	41.5
1926	113,119	2622	2144	4766	4736	41.9
1927	115,795	2675	1883	4558	4548	39.3
1928	117,940	2142	1770	3912	3858	32.7
1929	122,462	2564	2124	4688	4683	38.2
1930	128,396	2562	3078	5640	5637	43.9
1931	134,653	2560	3259	5819	5816	43.2
1932	138,134	2232	2708	4940	4939	35.8
1933	140,580	2082	2566	4648	4648	33.1
1934	143,129	2204	2479	4683	4676	32.7
1935	141,605	2113	2060	4173	4169	29.4
1936	140,292	1910	1939	3849	3847	27.4
1937	139,541	2101	1763	3864	3864	27.7
1938	140,269	1713	1466	3179	3179	22.7
1939	139,228	1595	1324	2919	2919	21.0
1940	137,183	1674	1388	3062	3059	22.3
1941	135,411	1790	1376	3166	3138	23.2
1942	131,559	1814	1428	3242	3123	23.7
1943	127,695	2244	2032	4276	4047	31.7
1944	122,926	2036	1685	3721	3546	28.9
1945	117,543	2323	1945	4268	4077	34.7
1946	111,250	1740	2053	3793	3166	28.5
1947	106,565	1534	2125	3659	2804	26.3
1948	102,674	1470	2140	3610	2761	26.9
1949	98,833	1321	2370	3691	2579	26.1
1950	97,604	1256	2275	3531	2458	25.2
1951	98,644	1671	2979	4650	2852	28.9
1952	100,437	1609	3753	5362	3213	32.0
1953	103,420	1687	4027	5714	3395	32.8
1954	109,326	1645	3867	5512	3305	30.2
1955	118,257	1807	4324	6131	3511	29.7
1956	126,493	2275	5089	7364	4090	32.3
1957	130,705	2467	5968	8435	4385	33.5

however, that despite the better reporting, despite the better detection, the delinquency rates of at least one large metropolitan area were twice as high in World War I than in World War II. Of course, this does not prove too much, if anything. We have no idea how typical the experience of this one large urban county is. We cite it in order to suggest the intriguing possibility that the extent of delinquency, as well as its character, was just as serious, if not more so, in the dark and unknown recesses of history.

4. Extent of Unrecorded Delinquency, Tentative Conclusions

JAMES F. SHORT, JR. AND F. IVAN NYE

The frequency and nature of delinquent behavior committed by adolescents never arrested or committed to institutions has been regarded by criminologists as an important but unknown dimension of delinquent behavior. The informed layman also is aware that only a portion of delinquent behavior is followed by arrest and conviction; further, that conviction and committal to a "training school" is much more likely to follow delinquent behavior if the adolescent is from the "wrong side of the tracks." The picture of delinquent behavior obtained from official records only, and particularly the punitive action of the courts, is known to be incomplete and seriously biased.

That concern with unrecorded delinquency is high is indicated by the great interest shown in the pioneer studies of Robinson,[1] Schwartz,[2] Porterfield,[3] and the Cambridge-Somerville Youth Study,[4] in texts and in recent papers by the writers.[5] Cohen has called for an extension of such studies,[6] and a number of other investigators are pursuing research projects dealing with unrecorded delinquency.[7]

* From two larger studies of adolescent delinquency and adjustment supported in part by grants from the Social Science Research Council and the College Committee on Research of the State College of Washington.

[1] Sophia Robison, *Can Delinquency Be Measured?* (New York: Columbia University Press, 1936).

[2] Edward E. Schwartz, "A Community Experiment in the Measurement of Juvenile Delinquency," reprinted from *Nat. Prob. Assoc. Yearbook,* 1945 (Washington: U.S.G.P.O., 1947).

[3] Austin L. Porterfield, *Youth in Trouble* (Fort Worth: Leo Potishman Foundation, 1946), Chapter 2.

[4] Fred J. Murphy, Mary M. Shirley, and Helen L. Witmer, "The Incidence of Hidden Delinquency," *Am. Jour. of Orthopsychiatry,* 16 (October, 1946), 686–696.

[5] Albert K. Cohen, *Delinquent Boys: The Culture of the Gang* (Glencoe, Illinois: The Free Press, 1955), 37–41; for the authors' statement as to the importance of such data, see James F. Short, Jr. and F. Ivan Nye, "Reported Behavior as a Criterion of Deviant Behavior," *Soc. Problems* (Winter, 1957–1958).

[6] Albert K. Cohen, *Sociological Research in Juvenile Delinquency,* paper read before American Orthopsychiatric Association, March, 1956.

[7] The authors are aware of studies under way in Chicago, Kansas City, Indiana,

SOURCE. James F. Short, Jr. and F. Ivan Nye, "Extent of Unrecorded Delinquency, Tentative Conclusions," from *Journal of Criminal Law, Criminology and Police Science,* Volume 49, November-December 1958, pp. 296–302. Copyright © 1958, The Williams and Wilkins Company, Baltimore, Maryland.

Table 1

REPORTED DELINQUENT BEHAVIOR AMONG BOYS IN THREE SAMPLES

Type of offense	Percent admitting commission of offense			Percent admitting commission of offense more than once or twice		
	M.W.	West	Tr.S.	M.W.	West	Tr.S.
Driven a car without a driver's license or permit	81.1	75.3	91.1	61.2	49.0	73.4
Skipped school	54.4	53.0	95.3	24.4	23.8	85.9
Had fist fight with one person	86.7	80.7	95.3	32.6	31.9	75.0
"Run away" from home	12.9	13.0	68.1	2.8	2.4	37.7
School probation or expulsion	15.3	11.3	67.8	2.1	2.9	31.3
Defied parents' authority	22.2	33.1	52.4	1.4	6.3	23.6
Driven too fast or recklessly	49.7	46.0	76.3	22.7	19.1	51.6
Taken little things (worth less than $2) that did not belong to you	62.7	60.6	91.8	18.5	12.9	65.1
Taken things of medium value ($2–$50)	17.1	15.8	91.0	3.8	3.8	61.4
Taken things of large value ($50)	3.5	5.0	90.8	1.1	2.1	47.7
Used force (strong-arm methods) to get money from another person	6.3	—	67.7	2.4	—	35.5
Taken part in "gang fights"	24.3	22.5	67.4	6.7	5.2	47.4
Taken a car for a ride without the owner's knowledge	11.2	14.8	75.2	4.5	4.0	53.4
Bought or drank beer, wine, or liquor (include drinking at home)	67.7	57.2	89.7	35.8	29.5	79.4
Bought or drank beer, wine, or liquor (outside your home)	43.0	—	87.0	21.1	—	75.0
Drank beer, wine, or liquor in your own home	57.0	—	62.8	24.1	—	31.9
Deliberate property damage	60.7	44.8	84.3	17.5	8.2	49.7
Used or sold narcotic drugs	1.4	2.2	23.1	0.7	1.6	12.6
Had sex relations with another person of the same sex (not masturbation)	12.0	8.8	10.9	3.9	2.9	3.1
Had sex relations with a person of the opposite sex	38.8	40.4	87.5	20.3	19.9	73.4
Gone hunting or fishing without a license (or violated other game laws)	74.0	62.7	66.7	39.6	23.5	44.8
Taken things you didn't want	15.7	22.5	56.8	1.4	3.1	26.8
"Beat up" on kids who hadn't done anything to you	15.7	13.9	48.7	3.1	2.8	26.2
Hurt someone to see them squirm	22.7	15.8	33.4	2.8	3.2	17.5

The methodology of the investigations which form the basis for this paper have been described elsewhere and will not be repeated here.[8] The

present paper deals with (1) types and frequency of delinquent behavior as indicated by 23 specific delinquent acts ranging from driving without a license to grand larceny and drug use, and by the use of delinquency scales derived from these items; (2) comparison of

Tennessee, Columbus, Ohio, New York City, and in the State of Washington.

[8] F. Ivan Nye and James F. Short, Jr., "Scaling Delinquent Behavior," *Amer. Sociol. Rev.*, 22 (June, 1957); F. Ivan Nye, *Family Relationships and Delinquent Behavior* (New York: John Wiley and Sons, 1958) Chapter 1; James F. Short, Jr., *The Study of Juvenile Delinquency by*

Reported Behavior—An Experiment in Method and Preliminary Findings, paper read at the annual meetings of the American Sociological Society, Washington, D. C., 1955 (dittoed).

delinquent behavior in western and mid-western high school students; and (3) comparison of unrecorded delinquency with official records of delinquency.

The data were gathered by anonymous questionnaire in the classroom under the supervision of the writers. A 75 percent sample was taken from the three western high schools (cities of 10,000 to 30,000 population) and a 100 percent sample in three smaller mid-western communities. Approximately 99 percent of the questionnaires were usable.[9] In addition to being considered generally suitable for present research purposes, these particular communities possessed the positive advantage that active and informed lay people were ready to sponsor the project and interpret it to the community.

The measures of delinquent behavior used in this paper are based upon a list of behavior items commonly referred to in the laws relating to delinquent and criminal behavior. Delinquency has been defined in descriptive terms rather than in terms of legalistic categories. For example, we refer to stealing things of a certain value, rather than to descriptions of property offenses, e.g., robbery, burglary, larceny, etc.

HIGH SCHOOL POPULATIONS

Because they seem likely to be more representative of the general population than are college or training school populations, we have concentrated our research on high school populations. Table 1 presents the percentage of boys in our two high school samples, western and mid-western, and in the western

training school group, who report committing each of 21 delinquency items, and the percentage who admit committing these offenses more than once or twice. Table 2 presents these data for the high school and training school girls.

From these tables it is apparent that the types of delinquent behavior studied are extensive and variable in the populations studies. We have compared students in the western and mid-western samples in order to secure an estimate of the stability of responses in two non-institutionalized populations. Populations in these two regional samples differ in such respects as city size and population mobility. The mid-western sample is comprised of three small communities: a suburb of a large city, a rural town, and a consolidated rural school district. The western sample comprises three small contiguous cities. The population of the mid-western communities has been fairly stable since 1940, in contrast to the rapid population growth experienced by the western cities. These samples are alike in important respects, however. Ethnic composition is similar, both populations being overwhelmingly native caucasian, and age and sex are controlled. Perhaps of greater importance, both populations are non-institutionalized.

Few statistically significant differences between our two non-institutionalized groups are found in Tables 1 and 2.[10] This may be taken as an indication

[9] Questionnaires were administered by one or both writers, assisted by other staff members or graduate students of the Department of Sociology of the State College of Washington. For further methodological details, see references cited in footnote 8.

[10] Samples from both finite and hypothetical universes are treated. The western state samples represent 25 per cent regular-interval samples of the high school population. Mid-western and training school samples represent 100 per cent samples of the individuals in those selected grades in the mid-western high schools and 100 per cent samples of the training schools.

Nine of 21 possible comparisons of the percentage of western and mid-western boys who admit committing these offenses are significant at least at the .05 level. Eight of these 9 offenses are committed

Table 2

REPORTED DELINQUENT BEHAVIOR AMONG GIRLS IN THREE SAMPLES

Type of offense	Percent admitting commission of offense			Percent admitting commission of offense more than once or twice		
	M.W.	West	Tr.S.	M.W.	West	Tr.S.
Driven a car without a driver's license or permit	60.1	58.2	68.3	33.6	29.9	54.4
Skipped school	40.3	41.0	94.0	10.1	12.2	66.3
Had fist fight with one person	32.7	28.2	72.3	7.4	5.7	44.6
"Run away" from home	9.8	11.3	85.5	1.0	1.0	51.8
School probation or expulsion	2.7	3.7	63.4	0.3	0.2	29.3
Defied parents' authority	33.0	30.6	68.3	3.7	5.0	39.0
Driven too fast or recklessly	20.9	16.3	47.5	5.7	5.4	35.0
Taken little things (worth less than $2) that did not belong to you	36.0	30.0	77.8	5.7	3.5	48.1
Taken things of medium value ($2–$50)	3.4	3.9	58.0	1.0	0.6	29.6
Taken things of large value ($50)	2.0	1.3	30.4	1.7	0.9	10.1
Used force (strong-arm methods) to get money from another person	1.3	—	36.7	0.3	—	21.5
Taken part in "gang fights"	9.7	6.5	59.0	1.7	1.1	27.7
Taken a car for a ride without the owner's knowledge	5.4	4.5	36.6	1.0	0.6	20.7
Bought or drank beer, wine, or liquor (include drinking at home)	62.7	44.5	90.2	23.1	17.6	80.5
Bought or drank beer, wine, or liquor (outside your home)	28.7	—	83.9	10.8	—	75.3
Drank beer, wine, or liquor in your own home	54.2	—	71.1	16.4	—	42.2
Deliberate property damage	21.7	13.6	65.4	5.7	1.6	32.1
Used or sold narcotic drugs	1.3	0.5	36.9	0.3	0.3	23.8
Had sex relations with another person of the same sex (not masturbation)	5.4	3.6	25.0	1.7	0.5	12.5
Had sex relations with a person of the opposite sex	12.5	14.1	95.1	4.1	4.8	81.5
Gone hunting or fishing without a license (or violated other game laws)	20.6	20.3	27.5	5.7	3.9	21.3
Taken things you didn't want	6.4	3.6	43.0	0.7	0.6	13.9
"Beat up" on kids who hadn't done anything to you	5.7	3.1	37.8	1.0	0.9	18.3
Hurt someone to see them squirm	10.4	9.3	35.4	1.0	1.1	20.7

by a higher percentage of mid-western boys. When percentage of boys admitting commission of these offenses more than once or twice is compared, only 6 significant differences (at .05 level) are found, 5 of these being higher for the mid-western boys. When mid-western and western girls are compared as to commission of these offenses, 5 significant differences are found, all being committed by a higher percentage of mid-western girls. Only 1 significant difference between these groups of non-institutionalized girls is found when percentages admitting commission of the 21 offenses more than once or twice is compared.

of stability and reliability of the responses obtained from the two samples. Comparison of 16 and 17 year old high school boys on a seven-item delinquency scale, based upon these same data, indicates agreement between the two groups of boys in 90.7 percent of the scale responses.[11] We note that such

[11] These data are described and graphically presented in F. Ivan Nye and James F. Short, Jr., "Scaling Delinquent Behavior," *op. cit.*

differences as are found in Tables 1 and 2 indicate that delinquent behavior is somewhat more widespread in the smaller, older, more structured midwestern sample than in the larger, newer, growing western communities.

The most common offenses reported "more than once or twice" by high school boys and girls in Tables 1 and 2 are traffic offenses, truancy, and drinking. Boys also report considerable fighting, stealing (of small things), heterosexual relations, and game violations.

Comparisons of western institutionalized and non-institutionalized boys and girls on the delinquency items in Tables 1 and 2 indicate that significantly higher proportions of the "official" delinquents commit virtually all of the offenses, and commit them more often, than do the high school students.[12] Exceptions to this pattern are found only in the case of homosexual relations among the boys, driving a car without a license among girls, and game violations among both boys and girls. In spite of the statistical significance of these comparisons, however, it is apparent that there is a good deal of "overlapping" between institutionalized and non-institutionalized boys and girls in the frequency of commission of our delinquency items.

In order to specify more precisely the amount of such overlapping, indexes of delinquent behavior in the form of Guttman-type scales have been constructed. Scales for 16 and 17 year old boys, consisting of seven and eleven delinquency items, have been described elsewhere.[13] These scales proved to

be nearly equal in their ability to differentiate between institutionalized and non-institutionalized boys. On the seven-item scale, a cutting point is found which maximizes the difference in delinquency involvement between the two groups of boys at 71 percent (see Table 3). At this cutting point, 86 percent of the non-institutionalized boys had been accounted for, as compared with only 14 percent of the training school boys. This difference on the eleven-item scale was maximized at 67 percent.[14] The amount of overlapping between institutionalized and non-institutionalized boys is here specified more closely than has been done in previous research. We have cited only the maximum differences between the two groups. Thus, if we were to study "delinquent" and "non-delinquent" boys by comparing our institutionalized and

things (worth less than $2) that did not belong to you, buying or drinking beer, wine, or liquor (include drinking at home), skipping school without a legitimate excuse, purposely damaging or destroying public or private property, sex relations with a person of the opposite sex, and defying parents' authority to their faces. Offenses added for the eleven-item scale were: taking things of medium value, taking things of large value, running away from home, and narcotics violations. These data were rescored following the Israel "Gamma" technique in order to remove "idiosyncratic" elements, prior to scaling. For the procedure, and an exposition of its rationale, see M. W. Riley, J. W. Riley, and Jackson Toby, *Scale Analysis* (New Brunswick: Rutgers University Press, 1954), Chapter 18.

14 It is interesting to compare these findings with results of the delinquency scale of the California Psychological Inventory, as obtained by Gough. Comparing a broad cross section of delinquents (as indicated by their being institutionalized or classed as "high school disciplinary problems") and non-delinquents on this scale, he found a cutting point above which 70 percent of his male delinquents fell, as compared to 20 percent of his male non-delinquents. See Harrison Gough, *Systematic Validation of a Test for Delinquency*, paper delivered at the annual meeting of the American Psychological Association, 1954 (mimeographed).

12 This conclusion is based upon statistical comparison of figures presented in Tables 1 and 2, for our institutionalized and non-institutionalized western state boys and girls.

13 F. Ivan Nye and James F. Short, Jr., *op. cit.* The seven-item scale included the following delinquency items: driving a car without a license or permit, taking little

Table 3

DELINQUENT BEHAVIOR SCORES OF HIGH SCHOOL AND TRAINING SCHOOL BOYS AGED 16 AND 17°

Scale type	Delinquent behavior score	High school		Training school	
		Frequency	Cumulative percent	Frequency	Cumulative percent
1	00	0	0	0	0
2	01	128	22	0	0
3	02	40	29	0	0
4	03	60	40	0	0
5	04	105	58	3	2
6	05	28	63	2	4
7	06	26	68	3	6
8	07	25	72	2	8
9	08	80	86	7	14
10	09	31	92	24	32
11	10	27	96	8	39
12	11	6	97	11	48
13	12	6	98	15	60
14	13	5	99	16	72
15	14	3	100	34	100
		570		125	

° No scores were obtained for one training school and eight high school boys.

non-institutionalized groups, on the basis of the seven-item scale we would in fact be studying a group of delinquent boys, 14 percent of whom are less delinquent than are 14 percent of the "non-delinquent" boys. Comparisons can, of course, be obtained at any point along the scale.

A nine-item scale for the 16 and 17 year old western high school and training school girls differentiates somewhat more clearly between the two groups.[15] On this scale a maximum difference of 80 percent is found at scale type 09 (see Table 4). At this point on the scale 90.4 percent of the high school girls and only 10.4 percent of the training school girls are accounted for. That is, only about 10 percent of the high school girls are more delinquent than is indicated by scale type 08, while nearly 90 percent of the training school girls fall into this more delinquent category.

SEX DIFFERENCES

Comparison of boys and girls within the high school sample indicates a higher proportion of boys committing nearly all offenses. With few exceptions such differences are statistically significant (at .01 level). This finding is similar to that revealed by official data, though the 5 to 1 ratio of boys to girls reported by the Children's Bureau[16] is not found in many cases, suggesting a bias in under-reporting female delinquency on the part of official data. Offenses for which significant differences between the sexes are not found are generally those offenses for which girls are most often apprehended, e.g. running away from home, defying

[15] The girls' scale consisted of the offenses included in the eleven-item boys' scale, with the exception of taking things of large value and narcotics violations.

[16] U. S. Department of Health, Education and Welfare, Social Security Administration, Children's Bureau, *Juvenile Court Statistics*, 1955, Children's Bureau Statistical Series, *Number 37*.

Table 4

DELINQUENT BEHAVIOR SCORES OF HIGH SCHOOL AND TRAINING SCHOOL GIRLS AGED 16 AND 17[*]

Scale type	Delinquent behavior score	High school		Training school	
		Frequency	Cumulative percent	Frequency	Cumulative percent
1	00	135	26	1	2
2	01	72	40	0	2
3	02	21	44	1	4
4	03	74	59	1	6
5	04	61	71	0	6
6	05	52	81	0	6
7	06	15	84	1	8
8	07	11	86	1	10
9	08	22	90	0	10
10	09	10	92	1	12
11	10	23	97	6	25
12	11	9	99	4	33
13	12	2	99	7	48
14	13	5	100	25	100
		512		48	

[*] No scores were obtained for two training school and one high school girls.

parents' authority (incorrigibility), and drinking. The fact that significantly higher proportions of boys in both samples report engaging in heterosexual relations and the fact that girls are most often referred to court for such activities presumably reflects society's greater concern for the unsupervised activities of girls.

Fewer statistically significant differences are found between training school boys and girls than was the case in our samples of high school students. Significantly greater percentages of the boys report committing 11 of the 24 offenses studied, and 13 of these offenses "more than once or twice." For nine of these offenses the recorded differences are not significant. Four of the offenses are reported by larger percentages of training school girls. These include running away from home, defying parents' authority, narcotics violations, and homosexual relations. A higher percentage of girls also report heterosexual relations, though this difference is not statistically significant. With the exception of nar-

cotics violations, these are offenses for which girls are most often apprehended. The offenses reported by the highest percentage of training school boys, with the exception of fighting, which is a part of "growing up," are also those for which boys are most often apprehended, viz., stealing and traffic offenses.

ARREST RATES

Arrest rates for the high school and training school samples described above are not available. Data from the first phase of our research program, comparing college and training school students, indicate that non-institutionalized (college) students experience arrest in a far smaller proportion of offenses which they report committing than do training school students.[17] This is es-

[17] James F. Short, Jr., "A Report on the Incidence of Criminal Behavior, Arrests, and Convictions in Selected Groups," *Proc. of the Pacific Sociol. Soc.*, 1954, published as Vol. 22, No. 2 of *Research Studies of the State College of Washington* (June 1954), 110–118, see Table 3, p. 117.

pecially true of girls, for college girls report arrests only for traffic offenses. These arrest data bear a close relationship to officially available data. For both training school boys and girls arrest rates are highest for offenses against the person exclusive of sex offenses. Arrest rates for property offenses are more than twice as high among boys as among girls in the training school populations, while the reverse is true of sex offenses among these groups. Arrests among college men are reported in only a small percentage of property offenses (.3 percent as compared to 13.7 percent for training school boys), behavior problem offenses (2.3 percent compared to 15.1 percent for training school boys), and "casual" offenses (1.9 percent compared to 5.2 percent).

SOCIO-ECONOMIC DISTRIBUTION

Finally, the socio-economic characteristics associated with delinquent behavior among our high school and training school populations have been studied.[18] For this purpose analysis of delinquent behavior by individual behavior items and by scale type was made, holding constant sex categories and two age groups in the western and midwestern states. Similar analysis was made for adolescents 16 and older in the "training schools" of the western state. Few significant differences were found between socio-economic strata. Such differences as were found indicated greater delinquent involvement within the highest socio-economic category as often as in the lowest.

CONCLUSIONS

While recognizing the limitations of our definition of delinquent behavior,

in terms of the behavior categories studied, and the limitations of the samples employed, it appears that the following tentative conclusions regarding the extent of juvenile delinquency in the non-institutionalized population are warranted:

1. Delinquent conduct in the non-institutionalized population is extensive and variable.

2. Delinquent conduct as we have measured it is similar in extent and nature among non-institutionalized high school students in widely separated sections of the country.

3. Delinquent conduct *reported* by institutionalized and non-institutionalized students is similar to delinquency and crime as treated officially in the following respects:

(*a*) Non-institutionalized boys admit committing virtually all delinquencies more frequently than do non-institutionalized girls, "once or twice" and "more than once or twice"; fewer differences exist, and these differences are smaller, between institutionalized boys and girls.

(*b*) The offenses for which boys are most often arrested are generally those which they most often admit committing, e.g., property offenses, traffic violations, truancy, destruction of property, drinking; a few offenses are reported by large proportions of boys which are not often recorded in official statistics, e.g., game violations and fist fights.

(*c*) The offenses for which girls are most often arrested are, with the exception of sex offenses among high school girls, generally the offenses which girls most often admit committing, e.g., sex offenses, incorrigibility, running away. A few offenses are reported by high proportions of girls which do not find their way into official statistics.

(*d*) Significantly greater proportions of training school boys and girls admit

18 F. Ivan Nye, James F. Short, Jr., and V. J. Olson, "Socio-Economic Status and Delinquent Behavior," *Amer. Jour. of Sociol.*, 63 (January, 1958).

committing virtually all delinquencies, and admit committing them more frequently, than do high school boys and girls.

(*e*) When training school students are compared with high school students on a composite scale of delinquency activities, there is considerable overlapping between groups of both boys and girls, but training school students as a group rank significantly higher, in terms of seriousness of involvement in delinquent behavior, than do high school students.

(*f*) Differences on the delinquency scales, and in the commission of individual delinquencies, are greater between high school and training school girls than between high school and training school boys.

(*g*) Variation in the proportion of reported delinquencies which result in arrest are similar to variations in the "cleared by arrest" figures collected by the Federal Bureau of Investigation.

4. Delinquent conduct reported by non-institutionalized students differs from official data in the following ways:

(*a*) Arrests—comparison of college and training school students indicates that training school students are arrested in higher proportions of all classes of delinquencies which they admit committing than college students.

(*b*) Socio-economic status—delinquency within the non-institutionalized populations studied is distributed more evenly throughout the socio-economic structure of society than are official cases, which are found disproportionately in the lower socio-economic strata.

Further research of this nature may be expected to provide additional clues as to the extent and nature of delinquent behavior in various segments of the population. By such means the structural correlates of delinquency, together with other important etiological considerations, may be better understood. Reported delinquent behavior as a method warrants and requires further investigation.[19] The present status of research by reported behavior is regarded as still in a pioneer stage. It provides an alternative to the use of institutionalized populations and court records, with new opportunities for research in delinquent behavior and comprehension of it.

[19] For a discussion of advantages, as well as methodological problems of this approach, see James F. Short, Jr., and F. Ivan Nye, "Reported Behavior as a Criterion of Deviant Behavior," *op. cit.*

5. *The Incidence of Hidden Delinquency*

FRED J. MURPHY, MARY M. SHIRLEY, AND HELEN L. WITMER

Mental hygienists have always been concerned, on the one hand, that many a youthful violator of the law goes unprosecuted and even undetected until a delinquent pattern becomes deeply ingrained; and on the other, that many a lad receives a juvenile court record for a relatively innocent misdemeanor. Students of juvenile delinquency have long suspected that juvenile court statistics do not reflect adequately the extent of youthful misconduct and that a considerable number of violations and violators never find their way into official court records. Hitherto, research workers have been baffled as to how to get at this pool of hidden delinquency. The Cambridge-Sommerville Youth Study, which has maintained an intimate contact with a large group of boys throughout their adolescent years, has afforded a unique opportunity to arrive at some measure of the amount of juvenile law-breaking that is hidden from public view. From our case records, it is possible to make a minimum estimate of how frequently the group of boys under study committed acts that *could* have brought them into court if someone in the community had wanted to register a court complaint.

This program of character building and delinquency prevention sponsored by the late Dr. Richard Cabot directed its efforts chiefly toward underprivileged boys who lived amidst the congestion and squalor of high delinquency areas. The plan of treatment involved close contact with the subjects and their parents by case workers who became trusted friends and were consequently afforded the boys' confidences. In the course of work the case workers acquired a great deal of information concerning misdeeds that had never become a matter of official court complaint.

Before extracting the pertinent data from the case histories, certain terms had to be understood and procedures developed and explained. The General Laws of Massachusetts define a delinquent as "A child between seven and seventeen years who violates any city ordinance or town by-law or commits an offense not punishable by death or by imprisonment for life." Our classification as to an unofficial or official delinquent depended upon whether or not a court complaint had been granted for an offense. The distinction was arbitrarily established at this point because

SOURCE. Fred J. Murphy, Mary M. Shirley, and Helen L. Witmer, "The Incidence of Hidden Delinquency," from *The American Journal of Orthopsychiatry*, Volume 16, No. 4, October 1946, pp. 686–696. Copyright, The American Orthopsychiatric Association, Inc. Reprinted with the permission of the authors.

Juvenile Court statistics are computed upon the basis of the number of court complaints issued. This step was decided upon in collaboration with an official of the Boston Juvenile Court, now Justice John J. Connelly, a recognized authority on delinquency.

Because the length of a period of probation or the term of institutional commitment for juvenile offenses do not serve as an adequate measure of the seriousness of an act, three groupings by nature of offenses were formulated with the assistance of the aforementioned authority. The three categories as developed in the order of seriousness were:

1. *Violations of city ordinances,* such as shining shoes or vending without a license, street ball playing, hopping street cars, swimming and/or fishing in forbidden places, and curfew laws.

2. *Minor offenses,* of the nature of truancy, petty stealing (5 and 10¢ stores), trespassing, running away, stubborn child, sneaking into movies.

3. *More serious offenses,* involving such acts as breaking and entering, larceny, assault, drunkenness, sex offenses.

The comprehensive list of approximately 50 offenses was drawn up on individual work sheets which provided space for identifying material on the boy and columns for tabulating his law violations.

A group consultation with the case workers, later to be interviewed individually, was held. This was done to avoid confusion and to assure consistency in the workers understanding the procedure. The project was thoroughly explained and their advice sought particularly in reference to the tabulation of the frequency of unofficial acts wherein it did not always make for accurate enumeration. Case workers often knew that a boy had repeatedly committed a certain infraction during a given period, but they would have been at a loss to enumerate the individual occurrences. Hence, it was decided to use—*rarely, occasionally,* and *frequently*—giving to each a range of numerical value which would represent the number of violations in a given year of a boy's life. *Rarely* denoted a frequency span of from one to three offenses per year; *occasionally,* from four to nine, and *frequently,* ten and over. By this method it was obvious that we would have to be satisfied in most instances with a numerical approximation of a youth's unofficial offenses. This was termed a "score" of law infractions.

In the process of tabulating a boy's offenses, the case worker and I (F.J.M.) jointly reviewed each page of the case record. Any uncertainty as to whether an offense had been committed, either because the record was vague or because it seemed possible that the boy was entertaining his case worker with a story of fantasied misdeeds, always resulted in his being given the benefit of the doubt, and no tally was recorded. Likewise, in totaling the number of misdemeanors of a boy in a given year, we conservatively employed the lowest weighting; i.e., *rarely* was given a weight of 1, *occasionally,* 4, and *frequently,* 10. When an incident might have two possible interpretations, the less serious was utilized. For example, one little culprit disturbed a theater manager no end by dropping a lighted match into his pocket. This situation never reached the court, but if it had, we speculated that one of two complaints could have been made—a charge of malicious mischief, or a more serious one of assault and battery. In this instance we used the former label. As the result of these precautions, our estimate of the number of violations and of their seriousness is a very conservative one.

Table 1

COMPARISON OF VIOLATIONS FOR UNOFFICIAL AND OFFICIAL DELINQUENTS
(Based on records of 114 boys, ages 11–15)*

Violation	Unofficial delinquents	Official delinquents	Both
	N 61	N 40	N 101
City ordinance	739	655	1394
Minor offenses	1913	2493	4406
Serious offenses	174	442	616
Total	2826	3590	6416

* Of 114 boys, 13 had no violations to the case workers' knowledge.

In order to obtain uniformity in the delinquency scores, it was necessary to select an age span that could be consistent for all cases. From a survey of the entire case load, it was found that the majority had received service throughout the age span from 11 to 16 years. A total of 114 boys had been given service throughout this five-year period, and the present study is based upon their analyses.

To the workers' knowledge, only 13 of the boys had never committed an offense for which a complaint might have been made in court. The rest had all been more or less serious juvenile offenders; 40 designated as official delinquents because complaints were registered in court, and 61 as unofficial delinquents because they "got by" without court complaint.

The numerical scores hereafter re-represent the minimum number of law ferred to as "number of violations" infractions committed by these boys between their eleventh and sixteenth years. At our conservative estimate, these boys had committed a minimum of 6,416 infractions of the law during the five-year period; while only 95 of their violations had become a matter of official complaint. In other words, authorities took official action in less than 1½ per cent of the infractions. Approximately 1,400 of these infractions were violations of city ordinances, none of which became a matter of court complaint. Of 4,400 minor offenses, only 27 (.60%) were prosecuted. Of 616 serious offenses, 68 (11%) were prosecuted.

Lest the small proportion of infractions resulting in court complaints should lead to the inference that law enforcement was lax in these communities, it must be explained that during the period covered by this study there was a policy of handling a large proportion of juvenile offenders informally. Hence, many of our boys were apprehended and warned by police but no complaint was registered in court. Furthermore, lest it be thought that CSYS case workers were protecting the boys from court involvement, it must be mentioned that in many instances the boys revealed their delinquencies months or even years after they had occurred. In reminiscing on their activities, they often owned up to earlier law violations hitherto unsuspected.

Analysis of the type of infractions for which court complaints were registered indicated that larceny and breaking and entering were the charges of highest frequency. Truancy and school offenses were a matter of official court complaint only rarely in comparison to the frequency with which these were committed. This suggests that school authorities manifest a considerable degree of tolerance of such juvenile of-

Table 2

NUMBER AND PROPORTION OF VIOLATIONS RESULTING IN COURT COMPLAINTS

Type of violation	Number court complaints	Official delinquents	Both groups
City ordinance	0	0.00%	0.00
Minor offenses	27	1.08	.61
Serious offenses	68	15.39	11.04
Total	95	2.72	1.47

fenses and tend to handle them by their own methods rather than to call upon the help of the court.

In the main, the transgressions of the official offenders were more frequent and more serious than those of the unofficial group. The total scores of violations for the officials ranged from 5 to 323 with a median of 79; whereas the unofficials ranged from 0 to 266 with a median of 30. Furthermore, the median official delinquent over the five-year period scored 10 city ordinance infractions, 53 minor acts, and 6 more serious offenses; whereas the median unofficial delinquent had scored 0 on city ordinance violations, only 20 on minor offenses, and 0 on serious offenses. There were, however, a number of exceptions because 5 boys having official records had total scores less than 30, the median of the unofficials; and 13 unofficials equaled or exceeded in minor and more serious offenses the median score of the official delinquents. In computing the percentiles for the scores of delinquent acts for the two respective groups, it was found that for the most part from year to year, 11 through 16, the pattern of asocial behavior was fairly even and consistent. The amount of delinquency exhibited in the eleventh year remained surprisingly constant in the ensuing four years.

Relevant to the bearing that intelligence might have as a differentiating factor between the two groups, we at first speculated that perhaps higher mental endowments enabled the un-

official delinquents to remain out of court. However, upon compiling the figures, it was found that there was no appreciable difference. The official offenders had IQ's on the revised Stanford-Binet ranging from a low of 59 to a high of 117 with a median of 93.25, as compared to a median of 93.70 for the unofficials who ranged from 65 to 149. Thus, our study seems to substantiate the present more or less accepted contention that law violators, known officially by the courts and authorities, do not differ markedly from the general population.

We were interested further in ascertaining what the case records revealed concerning the personalities of these boys, especially insofar as these enabled us to judge whether the delinquencies seemed to spring from a neurotic basis or whether they resulted largely from the boys' acquiescence to the prevailing juvenile pattern of their communities. It was also hoped that the records might throw light on why some relatively law-abiding boys had court records and why some of the chronic offenders escaped court action. We therefore studied the case records of the five official delinquents who had low scores and the 13 unofficial delinquents with high scores. It appeared that three of the five official delinquents were dull, passive boys, who had considerable security within their own families and were not particularly troublesome in the community. For these three, court involvement seemed to be a piece of ill luck. Two

Table 3

PERCENTILE SCORES FOR UNOFFICIAL AND OFFICIAL DELINQUENTS

Percentile	Unofficial delinquents[*]				Official delinquents[*]			
	CO	MO	SO	All	CO	MO	SO	All
First	0	0	0	0	0	0	0	5
Tenth	0	1	0	2	0	12	0	27
Twenty-fifth	0	8	0	10	0	30	1	39
Fiftieth	0	20	0	30	10	53	6	79
Seventy-fifth	14	48	0	71	24	70	16	102
Ninetieth	50	84	5	107	40	118	32	194
Hundredth	88	134	44	266	90	187	46	323

[*] Type of offense
CO = City Ordinance
MO = Minor Offenses
SO = Serious Offenses

were perhaps the victims of police vigilance directed toward their entire families.

Ned, one of the boys, had always been a quiet stay-at-home, but regularly throughout Ned's childhood the father had been arrested for drunkenness and assault, and the older brother had been sent to a correctional school on a charge of larceny. Hence, when Ned was discovered with a "borrowed" bicycle, the police, being aware of the hazards surrounding children in this family, brought him into court and he was placed on probation. The other two, with a small number of violations, gave the impression of being greatly disturbed, with neurotic trends springing largely from difficult home relationships. Henry's father regarded his wife as his inferior; he constantly belittled his son, and remarked openly that the boy took after his mother's family and would sooner or later end up in a penal institution. The mother was ambivalent toward the boy, occasionally indulging him but more often railing at him. As he grew into adolescence, Henry's toleration of this treatment lessened, and the case worker believed that his removal from the home would be the only way of safeguarding him from an aggressive attack upon his parents or

from some serious delinquency outside. The parents were eager to have him placed out, but were not willing to have the placement go through court. The placement agency was reluctant to accept the boy without a court order. While placement negotiations were under way, Henry was summoned to a police station to give testimony concerning a sex pervert of whom he had been a victim, but he was led to believe that he would not be implicated. Upon learning of this private hearing, the placement worker, in an effort to obtain court custody, started a rumor that Henry was being protected in his delinquencies. When this rumor, much enlarged, reached the ears of the officer he was disturbed, had Henry reappear and prosecuted him on a charge of lewdness. Embittered by what he considered as "being framed," Henry walked out of court muttering "I'll show that officer what I can do"; whereupon he entered a haberdashery, stole a pair of braces from the counter, was apprehended by the store detective and again handed over to the police.

Percy, the last of these five boys, seems to have had a delinquency score that was spuriously low, due to the fact that he was in foster homes in rural villages during much of his eleventh to sixteenth years. Prior to CSYS contact he and his brothers had been sent out by their mother to steal. Her desertion led to breaking up of the home and to placement of the children in areas that either presented fewer temptations or were more tolerant of youthful misdemeanors. On the other hand, the foster mothers may have been less willing to recount to the case worker, at his infrequent visits, all of Percy's bad deeds lest their own status as worthy foster mothers be questioned. Percy was in and out of foster homes and correctional schools throughout the entire period, and his inability to settle down and accept the advantages of a good placement, when such was provided, was indicative of his general instability.

Of greater interest are the personalities of the 13 who avoided court records in spite of having committed a larger number of minor or serious infractions than the median official delinquent. These likewise could be grouped in a general way into two categories—gregarious, fairly well-adjusted boys whose delinquencies seemed free from a neurotic component; and emotionally disturbed boys whose asocial behavior seemed primarily the outgrowth of tension or friction within the home. There were five boys in the first group; eight in the second.

The four most frequent and most serious of these offenders gave no evidence of being poorly adjusted, in that their behavior reflected the mores of their particular group. Marcus, whose minor infractions totaled 134 and whose 44 serious offenses included larceny from parked cars, assault, picking the pockets of a service man, and breaking and entering, was a confirmed gang member from early childhood. Although his mother was psychotic and was hospitalized a good part of the period under consideration, her illness and ab-

sence from the home seemed to have little effect on the boy's pleasant, outgoing personality and his popularity with the gang with whom he roved the neighborhood. His infractions increased from begging on the streets at age 11 and peddling Christmas wreaths stolen from front doors, to the mysterious possession of a seaman's wallet containing more than $200 at the age of 14. In this last escapade, his accomplice was a boy on probation through whom the incident became known to the probation officer. The boys declared they had found the wallet on the floor of a theater. Since no loss was reported they got by with their story. Marcus's father, having first salted the money away in war bonds, hired an attorney to discuss his rights with a probation officer. On some of their other larcenies the gang's activities were known and Marcus was warned by the police. Often he tended to drop out when he believed serious mischief was in the wind. While he has never manifested particular strengths, he has maintained good standing with his friends throughout and now seems to be making an adequate adjustment in the Merchant Marine.

Denny, with a score of 84 minor offenses and 25 serious ones, manifested considerable strength and independence in the management of his own life when his home was broken up by the accidental death of his besotted stepmother. Reviewing this period of his life later with his case worker, he told how his gang had taken a bike here and there until they had so many of them they didn't know what to do. He told that he had often stolen food, and when he was ill-shod in winter he and a pal had snatched a purse containing $40. "Every now and then I see that woman on the street and it makes me feel pretty mean," he added. While some of these early larcenies seemed prompted by a desire for excitement, many seemed to the case worker to have been directed toward survival. Though only 14 when his home dissolved, Denny took things into his own hands, obtaining working papers and making his way back and forth to the home of a friendly Vermont farmer each summer. Winters, he lived either with his aunt or with his employer, an ash hauler. Denny demonstrated his ability to fend for himself at an early age, and he kept himself out of trouble with the law by being very street-wise.

Al, with a score of 96 minor infractions, seemed an independent, self-sufficient boy, with inner strengths that fortified him against the more contaminating influences of a highly delinquent neighborhood. On the whole, his family life was one of harmony and integration. During the early years, he had the companionship of his grandfather which seemed to have represented a character-building force in his life. His case worker observed that his gang membership seemed in a peripheral capacity so far as group activities went, but that he had a close enough association with each of the members to obtain a companion in a dual project—one for swimming and another for bicycle trips. Thus, the gang did not have sway over his activities, for he knew what he wanted and always had command of the situation. His most frequent offenses were street fighting, sneaking into movies, swimming in forbidden places, and shining shoes without a license. Only occasionally did he engage in petty stealing, and never in more serious larceny.

Jerry, with a score of 108 minor offenses, was a passive, lackadaisical boy who tended to go along with the gang in their less serious infractions and to avoid becoming involved in more serious episodes. This seemed a sign of weakness and cowardice, and was all of a pattern with his tendency to give up school at the slightest difficulty and to postpone until tomorrow or next week or until he was 16 appointments for job interviews arranged for him. He was, in fact, a quitter, and his avoidance of serious law infractions was not a matter of ego strength. In spite of these signs of weakness, Jerry showed no symptoms of deep, underlying anxieties. He lived on the surface, and made as little effort as possible, following perhaps the pattern of his two ne'er-do-well brothers rather than that of his steady, hard-working father.

John, the last of these five reasonably well-adjusted boys, had a score of 61 minor infractions, and was once warned by the police for trespassing during a realistic game of commandos. Temper outbursts during his early school years were perhaps suggestive of some emotional disturbance, but these had been overcome by the time he was 11. He was a favorite with his teachers and had friends among the boys in the neighborhood. John's father was given to drunken sprees, during which his mother seemed to lean on John as the eldest of her three boys. He accepted this responsibility in a rather mature way. Throughout the years, the case workers tried to draw him out on the subject of family relationships, thinking he well might feel considerable hostility toward his father. They were never able to elicit anything except matter-of-fact comments and occasional genuine admiration of his father's athletic prowess, and concluded that he felt no resentment and really took the father's drunkenness and periodic upsets in the home in his stride.

In contrast to these five, the other eight unofficial delinquents all seemed to be suffering to some degree from neurotic difficulties springing largely from discord within the home.

Between Mrs. B. and her eldest son,

Herbert, a cordial hatred existed, stemming perhaps from the paternal grandparents' belief that their son had married beneath him. They compensated for their dislike of the mother by indulging Herbert, encouraging him to seek haven in their home when he and his mother came to blows, which sometimes occurred. Herbert's 104 minor offenses consisted largely of aggression and profanity directed toward the mother. His eight serious offenses were composed of occasional physical assaults on his mother and some sex play with one of his sisters. Since his infractions were for the most part confined to aggression within the home, it is understandable that they did not come to the attention of the police.

Edwin, whom the police had warned because his mother complained that he was stubborn and sometimes assaulted her, had adequate provocation for attacks on his mother. This childish widow never stopped lamenting that her only child had not been a girl, and never ceased to nag for every little fault, from failure to brush his hair to ripping a button from his shirt at play. She constantly harped on her own imaginary ailments and upon her many sacrifices for her son. She tried her best to train him into girlish behavior, and to some extent succeeded, so that he was considered a sissy by his contemporaries. Small wonder that his response to all these frustrations developed from childish pinching and pommeling of his mother to adolescent attacks with a chair, and finally to bitter cursing and turning away. His mother often expressed to the case worker her wonderment that she, being such a good woman, could have such a bad boy. She often threatened to have him sent to a correctional school, but it was apparent that she could not part with him, nor could he emancipate himself from her.

Dan, a colored boy whose father had deserted during Dan's infancy, had close physical contact with his mother, even sleeping with her until late childhood. Many of his aggressions seemed to have a sexual basis, his most serious offense being that of assaulting white girls. In the opinion of the case worker, they were only girls who were sexually promiscuous with colored boys. The worker summarized Dan's record by saying "Certain antisocial problems exist not because of any conflict between Dan and his environment, but because Dan is so akin to his environment."

The most neurotic boy of all this group early exhibited traits suggestive of Levy's "affect hunger" cases. Andy's mother had died in his infancy. The father placed him and his much older brother in various boarding homes where they suffered a good deal of neglect and abuse. When Andy was three, the father married a rather young woman who later claimed that her love of children and the knowledge that she would never have any of her own had entered into her decision to marry Mr. T. and bring up his motherless boys. At the beginning of the study, Andy was a disturbing element in the primary grades, being unable to concentrate on his lessons and annoying the teachers and other children. His parents also found him a problem at home, and the father controlled him with very strict discipline. The stepmother worked, thus leaving the elder brother to enforce the stringent rules laid down by the father.

Andy's attitude toward his case worker was that of teasing and begging for little gifts and for trips and excursions. The worker recognized him as a very disturbed child and sought the help of a child guidance clinic. There Andy and his mother received treatment for several months, with little improvement in his behavior. Eventually, he was removed from his home, which shortly after placement was dissolved, leaving the boy entirely without anchorage. He was resentful at being sent to a boarding school for difficult children and ran away twice. Andy's delinquencies consisted mainly of truancy, school offenses, and stubborn, unruly behavior. He engaged in petty stealing only twice, and in breaking and entering once. The depth of his emotional disturbance was indicated by his failure to use the help of either his CSYS case workers or of the psychiatrist in a constructive way. He has developed into a youth who borders on the psychopathic personality.

The chief contribution of this study is that we have been able to arrive at a minimal estimate of the amount of unofficial delinquency that takes place among a sizable group of underprivileged boys. Both official and unofficial delinquents commit numerous infractions of juvenile laws which do not become a matter of official record. Although both groups differ somewhat in the frequency and seriousness of offenses, there is much overlapping between the two.

While it has not been within the scope of this paper to make a comprehensive analysis of factors which may perhaps differentiate the official and unofficial delinquents, some marked similarities between the two groups have been found. Both have a wide range in intelligence as measured by standard tests and show no difference in this respect. Both groups contain boys who are socially well adjusted to the pattern of life within their particular subcultures and whose asocial acts could not be considered as springing from emotional conflict or turmoil within themselves. These boys seem to commit most of the violations of property rights, such as larceny, breaking and entering, and destruction of property. Both groups also contain boys whose offenses seem to arise out of deep neurotic disturbance within themselves. These boys, with a neurotic component in their delinquencies, tend to commit aggressions directed toward the home or school in greater frequency than they commit violations against property rights. This observation is consistent with the findings of other students of delinquency and is what one would be led to expect from psychological theory. It is hoped that further analysis of the material will reveal factors that differentiate between the groups of official and unofficial delinquents.

Section II   DEVELOPMENT OF
DELINQUENT BEHAVIOR

Many theories have been advanced to account for the development of delinquent behavior, and explanations offered for delinquent behavior vary with time and place. Sociology has expanded the analysis of delinquency and crime well beyond the narrow individual-centered theories that once prevailed. Attempts by sociologists to relate delinquency to the social structure have helped us to understand delinquent and criminal acts as though they were integral elements of social life rather than aberrations.

The student will appreciate how knowledge of the legal definition of delinquency is important in understanding the statutory norms which stipulate that certain forms of behavior are consigned delinquent status. This status is part of the long process that leads to delinquent careers. In outlining the development of the delinquent career, Tannenbaum shows how being processed by various agencies, labeled as a delinquent, and stigmatized ascribe to the individual a social role, change his public image and self-conception, and generate a set of appropriate responses. These responses often involve exclusion from avenues of legitimate opportunity and hence may function to make attractive illegitimate events.

Sutherland's "Theory of Differential Association" is essentially a culture transmission view. He hypothesizes that criminal behavior is learned in a pattern of communication. Persons acquire patterns of criminal behavior by the same learning process with which they acquire patterns of lawful behavior. The delinquent career, then, is integrally related to an excess of definitions favorable to violation of law over definitions unfavorable to violation of law. According to Sutherland, when a person becomes criminal, he does so because of isolation from anticriminal patterns. An empirical test of Sutherland's hypothesis that differential associations may vary in several important ways is described in the selection by Short. He attempts to measure the frequency, duration, priority, and intensity of interaction with delinquent peers, the degree of exposure to delinquency in the community, as well as knowledge of and association with adult criminals.

According to the anomie theory of Merton, deviant behavior at least in part involves "selective adherence to accepted social norms and occurs in areas of specific structural strains in a social system." Merton suggests that anomie develops because of a breakdown in the relationship between goals which place great stress on success and to which all groups in our society are indoctrinated, without equivalent emphasis on institutional or legitimate channels of access to such goals. In the areas where the discrepancy between goals and means is greatest, a condition of anomie prevails, and individuals resort to illegitimate means to achieve the goals.

A modification of Merton's theory appears in Cohen's theory of delinquent subcultures. This concept is also rooted in the discrepancy between culture goals and institutionalized means. However, according to Cohen's formulation, the delinquent subculture is a reaction formation to socially induced stresses that our social-class system inflicts on working-class boys. He attempts to explain the formation of what he describes as the "non-utilitarian, malicious, and negativistic" behavior of working-class gang boys. Critiques of Cohen's position have been made on several grounds. Kitsuse and Dietrich contend that the postulation of a sharp break between the value systems of the middle and working classes is dubious, and that support for the theory is inadequate. Sykes and Matza question whether a gang boy actually rejects middle-class values, and they suggest that he rationalizes his deviant behavior by five techniques of neutralization or rationalization. Another response to Cohen's thesis is the portrayal of lower-class gang delinquency by Miller, who suggests that lower-class boys are virtually unaffected by middle-class traditions. He contends that much of lower-class delinquency may be seen as a reflection of certain "focal concerns" which are characteristic of the urban lower-class way of life.

The selection by Kobrin clarifies our understanding of delinquency areas by suggesting that they differ in the degree to which deviant and conventional value systems are integrated with each other. Kobrin postulates the simultaneous existence of two conflicting value systems in the delinquency areas, one favoring law-abiding behavior and the other favoring delinquency.

Cloward and Ohlin distinguish varieties of delinquent subcultures and try to account for them in terms of socially structured anomie based on interclass conflict and the availability of legitimate and illegitimate opportunity structures differentially organized on an ethnic and neighborhood basis. This theory has had a great impact on our approach to delinquency and its prevention in several action programs throughout the country.

The selection by Nye, Short, and Olson questions the differential status distribution of delinquent behavior which was so forcefully propounded in earlier selections. Data obtained from noninstitutionalized and institutionalized high school students revealed no significant difference in the amount of delinquent behavior of boys and girls in different socioeconomic strata. Clark and Wenninger question the conclusions drawn by Nye, Short, and Olson. They suggest that illegal acts within small communities or "status areas" of a large metropolitan center are related to community-wide norms to which juveniles adhere regardless of their social-class origins. Finally, the problem is further explored by Reiss and Rhodes, who examine the relationship between life style and delinquent behavior.

There is wide belief that the chief source of delinquent behavior lies in family disorganization. The practice followed by a few judges, of punishing the parents of delinquents, is a reflection of this belief, although the nature of the family influences that might be related to delinquent behavior are seldom specified apart from vague references to, for example, "lack of proper supervision." Although it is extremely difficult to indicate exactly what influence the family may have on delinquency, a number of studies suggest that the broken home and socialization to delinquent norms within the family may be related to delinquency. The selection by Monahan stresses the deleterious influence of a broken home on the child's development, whether through death, desertion, long separation, or divorce, and the consequences for delinquent behavior.

This section concludes with an attempt by Reckless to explain why all children living in a delinquency area do not engage in deviant behavior.

6. Point of View

FRANK TANNENBAUM

The criminal is a social human being; he is adjusted; he is not necessarily any of the things that have been imputed to him. Instead of being unadjusted he may be quite adjusted to his group, and instead of being "unsocial" he may show all of the characteristics we identify as social in members of other groups. The New York Crime Commission says, "He is adjusted to his own social group and violently objects to any social therapy that would make him maladjusted to it."[1]

Crime is a maladjustment that arises out of the conflict between a group and the community at large. The issue involved is not whether an individual is maladjusted to society, but the fact that his adjustment to a special group makes him maladjusted to the large society because the group he fits into is at war with society.

The difficulty with the older theory [of deviant behavior] is that it assumed that crime was largely an individual matter and could be dealt with when the individual was dealt with. Instead, most delinquencies are committed in groups; most criminals live in, operate

with, and are supported by groups. We must face the question of how that group grew up into a conflict group and of how the individual became adjusted to that group rather than to some other group in society. The study of the individual in terms of his special physical or psychical idiosyncrasies would have as much bearing on the question why he became a member of a criminal group as it would on the question why he joined the Ku Klux Klan, was a member of a lynching bee, joined the I. W. W., became a member of the Communist or Socialist party, joined the Seventh Day Adventists or the Catholic Church, took to vegetarianism, or became a loyal Republican. The point is that a person's peculiar physical or psychic characteristics may have little bearing on the group with which he is in adjustment.

The question is not how a criminal is distinguished in his nature from a non-criminal, but how he happened to be drawn into a criminal group and why that criminal group developed that peculiar position of conflict with the rest of society. The important facts, therefore, are to be sought in his behavior history.

Criminal behavior originates as part

[1] State of New York. Report of the Crime Commission, 1930. Legislative Document (1930) No. 98, p. 243.

SOURCE. Frank Tannenbaum, "Point of View," *Crime and the Community*, Boston: Ginn and Company, 1938, pp. 8–22. Copyright 1938, Columbia University Press.

of the random movement of children in a world of adults, a world with attitudes and organized institutions that stamp and define the activities of the little children. The career of the criminal is a selective process of growth within that environment, and the adult criminal is the product and summation of a series of continued activities and experience. The adult criminal is usually the delinquent child grown up.

The delinquent child is all too frequently "the truant of yesterday."[2] The truant is the school child who found extra-curricular activities more appealing and less burdensome than curricular ones. The step from the child who is a behavior problem in school to the truant is a natural one; so, too, is the step from truancy to delinquency, and that from delinquency to crime. In the growth of his career is to be found the important agency of the gang. But "the majority of gangs develop from the spontaneous play-group."[3]

The play group becomes a gang through coming into conflict with some element in the environment. A single illustration will indicate the process.

The beginning of the gang came when the group developed an enmity toward two Greeks who owned a fruit store on the opposite corner. The boys began to steal fruit on a small scale. Finally they attempted to carry off a large quantity of oranges and bananas which were displayed on the sidewalks, but the Greeks gave chase. This was the signal for a general attack, and the fruit was used as ammunition. The gang had a good start from this episode.[4]

But even after the gang has been formed, in its early stages its activities are not necessarily delinquent, and de-

linquent and non-delinquent activities may have the same meaning for the children. "We would gather wood together, go swimming, or rob the Jews on Twelfth Street."[5] The conflict may arise from play.

We did all kinds of dirty tricks for fun. We'd see a sign "Please keep the street clean," but we'd tear it down and say, "We don't feel like keeping it clean." One day we put a can of glue in the engine of a man's car. We would always tear things down. That would make us laugh and feel good, to have so many jokes.[6]

Or the jokes may be other ways of annoying people. "Their greatest fun consists in playing tag on porches and having people chase them."[7] Or it may be more serious annoyance: "such as throwing stones at windows of homes and ridiculing persons in the street who are known as 'odd characters.'"[8] Even a murder may arise out of the ordinary by-play of two gangs of young boys in rivalry.

Dey picked on us for two years, but even den we wouldn't a shot if "Stinky" —the big guy and the leader of the El-stons—hadn't jumped out of his dugout in a coal pile Saturday and waved a long bayonet wid a red flag on one end of it and an American flag upside down on de udder and dared us to come over de tracks.[9]

Once the gang has been developed, it becomes a serious competitor with other institutions as a controlling factor in the boy's life. The importance of the gang lies in its being the only social world of the boy's own age and, in a sense, of his own creation. All other agencies belong to elders; the gang belongs to the boy. Whether he is a

---

[2] State of New York. Report of the Crime Commission, 1927. Legislative Document (1927) No. 94, p. 285.
[3] Frederic M. Thrasher, *The Gang*, p. 29. Chicago, 1927.
[4] Thrasher, *op. cit.*, p. 29.

[5] *Ibid.*, p. 36.
[6] *Ibid.*, pp. 94–95.
[7] New York Crime Commission, 1927 Report, p. 371.
[8] *Ibid.*, p. 370.
[9] Thrasher, *op. cit.*, p. 180.

leader or just one of the pack, whether his assigned rank has been won by force or ingenuity or represents a lack of superior force or ingenuity, once that rank is established the child accepts it and abides by the rules for changing it.

Children are peculiarly sensitive to suggestion.

It is known that young people and people in general have little resistance to suggestion, that fashions of thought and fashions of dress spread rapidly through conversation and imitation, and that any form of behavior may be normalized through conversation and participation of numbers.[10]

In the boy's gang, conversation, gossip, approval, participation, and repetition will make any kind of behavior whatsoever normal.

The gang is important because the reaction of others is the source of the greater part of the individual's conduct. Conduct is learned in the sense that it is a response to a situation made by other people. The smile, the frown, approval and disapproval, praise and condemnation, companionship, affection, dislike, instruments, opportunities, denial of opportunities, are all elements at hand for the individual and are the source of his behavior. It is not essential that the whole world approve; it is essential that the limited world to which the individual is attached approve. What other people think is the more important because what they think will express itself in what they do and in what they say; and in what they do or say, in the way they look, in the sound of their voices, in the physical posture that they assume, the individual finds the stimuli that call out those particular attitudes that will bring the needed and desired approval from his immediate face-to-face companionship.

10 William I. Thomas and Dorothy S. Thomas, *The Child in America*, p. 164. New York, 1928.

It is here that we must look for the origin of criminal behavior. It is here, largely, that the roots of conduct difficulties are to be found. What one learns to do, one does if it is approved by the world in which one lives. That world is the very limited world which approves of the conduct one has learned to seek approval for. The group, once it becomes conscious of itself as an entity, tends to feed and fortify itself in terms of its own values. The contrast with the rest of the world merely strengthens the group, and war merely enhances its resistance.

THE GROUP AND THE COMMUNITY

Once the differentiation of the gang has taken place, it becomes a competitor for the child's allegiance, and wins in a certain number of cases.

The growing child in a modern large city is exposed to a variety of conflicting stimuli, interests, and patterns. Not only are there differences between the family, the school, the church, and the street gang, but the family itself may be representative of a series of differences between parents and children, between father and mother, between older and younger children. The pattern is uneven, the demands are contradictory. What is approved in one place is derided and condemned in another.

Behavior is a matter of choice as to whose approval you want. And whose approval you want may be determined by such invisible and subtle influences as whom you like, who has given you pleasure, who has commended you. Conflicting demands for the growing child's loyalty are the source of much of the difficulty.

The fact that the gang wins in many instances does not reflect upon the children. It reflects upon the other agencies that are competing for the child's adherence. Of a dozen children who have come into conflict with the other groups in the community and have given their loyalty to the gang instead, the victory of the gang may have had a different cause in each case.

The family by its internal weakness may have been a contributory factor. The father or mother or an older brother may have been delinquent, or there may have been sharp conflict of opinions and attitudes in the family, or constant bickering and incompatibility between the parents. The father may have been dead and the mother forced away from home so that the children were left unsupervised, or an ignorant and poverty-stricken mother may have encouraged the child to bring in food or money whether earned or stolen, or the father may have been a drunkard and given to seriously mistreating the child and breaking down the loyalty and unity which are essential to the slow maturation of systematic habit formation. In these and innumerable other examples that might be cited of family inadequacy we have a source for the acceptance by the child of his playmates and gang affiliates *as a substitute for the home.* Gang membership under these circumstances may be a perfectly natural reaction and a seeking for fun, contentment, and status. That the fun may take on delinquent forms is another matter and depends on the opportunities for such uses of leisure within the environment as make delinquency an alternative, or by-product, of gang activity.

If the family itself is a unit and well co-ordinated, it still may contribute to delinquency by forcing upon the child an incompatible pattern. The dislike of the pattern, again, may arise from many different reasons, none of which are in themselves evidence of moral turpitude or psychical deficiency on the part of the child.

The objections to going to school may arise from lack of good hearing, from poor eyesight, from undernourishment, from being left-handed, from dislike for the teacher because of favoritism, from being taken away from playmates because the family moves, from lack of interest in intellectual pursuits, from being either too big or too small for the grade, from undue competition with other children within the family, from a desire for excitement which the school does not provide, from having poor clothes and being ashamed to go to school, from a too rapid maturing, from a too slow development, from losing a grade because of illness, or from any number of other causes. That is, even in a "good" family, where moral standards are rigid, habits regular, ambitions high, there may still be adequate cause for the child to fall out of the pattern of the family interest because there are insufficient insight and sympathy for his needs, with the consequent conversion of the difficulty into conflict.

Truancy may in some degree have its roots in physical defect.

Thus, only 2.9 per cent of normal school children were suffering from malnutrition, whereas 26.2 per cent of truants were undernourished. Seven and three-tenths per cent of normal school children had defective vision, whereas 20.1 per cent of truants were so handicapped. Forty-nine and four-tenths per cent of normal children had defective teeth, whereas 91.2 per cent of truants had bad teeth.[11]

The physical defect may not be a direct cause of truancy, but it may contribute to that disgust with the school which may be directly responsible for truancy. "These are children in whom a definite attitude of dislike or even of disgust toward school has been built up."[12]

[11] New York Crime Commission, 1927 Report, p. 287.
[12] *Ibid.,* p. 285.

If the deviation could be compensated by having its need met, then the conflict might never arise and the competition of the gang would not be serious. But ordinarily it is not met.

Under our system of compulsory education we force into schools many, many children who would otherwise have been kept, or at least allowed to stay, at home —the "delicate" child, the excessively shy child, the child with some obvious defect, the child who does not care especially for books or activities that appeal only to the intellect. Now we make all of these children attend school, but we have not yet adapted our educational system to their needs.[13]

The difficulties of the child who is forced out of step in the school system, either through poor health or through lack of aptitude for scholastic endeavor, are met by the school authorities in terms of conflict, discipline, and tradition.

This group has been regarded by school teachers and administrators as more or less of an enigma, because these children stand out so decidedly from their playmates as being free from the domination of school discipline. Threats, punishment, hearings at the Bureau of Attendance, pleas of parents, frequently even commitments to the truant school do not seem to be successful in breaking up this attitude of unyielding resistance to compulsory schooling. It is because the truant is usually such an enigma to the average school administrator that he arouses so much ire. The response of the school administrator to the problem of truancy takes very little cognizance of the specific factors which have entered into the individual case of truancy. His response is in terms of an established tradition.[14]

Another source of failure of the other agencies within the community to fulfill the demands made upon them for winning the loyalty and cooperation of the child who ultimately becomes delinquent may have no direct relation to the family or to the school, but be the result of the environment. The family may live in such crowded quarters as to force the child into the street to such an extent that street life takes the place of family life. The family may be living in a neighborhood where houses of prostitution are located; where gangsters gather; where there is a great deal of perversion of one sort or another; where street pilfering is a local custom; where there is hostility to the police; where there is race friction and warfare; where the children, without the knowledge of their parents, may find means of employment in illicit ways such as acting as procurers for prostitutes or as messengers and go-betweens for criminals; where they can observe the possession of guns, the taking of dope; where they can hear all sorts of tales and observe practices or be invited to participate in practices, or become conscious of habits, attitudes, morals, which are entirely in conflict with the teaching, habits, and points of view of the family in which they live. And because the family under these conditions may be an inadequate instrument for the purpose of supervising and co-ordinating all the child's activities, the family may lose the battle for the imposition of its own standards just because there was a lack of time, energy, space, for the doing of the things that needed to be done or for the provision of the room that the children required for the development of their normal play life.

The activities which are taken as a substitute for those provided by the community may be innocent enough in themselves. The New York Crime Commission found that the activities of truants, as a rule, were not delinquent

[13] White-Williams Foundation: Five Years' Review for the Period Ending December 31, 1921, p. 8.
[14] New York Crime Commission, 1927 Report, p. 285.

activities: the children flew pigeons, went fishing, rode in the subway and the "L," went to the movies, went to a park, shot craps, collected junk, went to work, peddled fruit, went auto riding with older boys, hitched on the backs of wagons, delivered wet wash, and stole lead pipe for sale. These activities, we see, were for the children an adequate substitute for the school which they did not particularly enjoy; instead of doing required things which were not particularly attractive to them— they almost all liked mechanical shop work but were generally indifferent to purely intellectual endeavor—these children turned to the endless opportunities for adventure in the city streets. Here they are free of physical restraint, can avoid any authority they do not wish to acknowledge, may use their wits and legs and voices for objectives they themselves set.

But these and other activities carried on during truancy or in spare time are carried on in a group. The gang tends to dominate the children's activities as soon as conflict arises. And conflict arises frequently over issues much less conspicuous than stealing. In the congested neighborhoods where most of the young delinquent gangs arise, the elements of conflict between the old and the young are natural and difficult to avoid. The old want peace, security, quiet, routine, protection of property. The young want just the opposite: chiefly room, noise, running about, unorganized mischief, fighting, shouting, yelling.

The crowded homes provide no place for the children, and therefore force them into the streets for play. Not only the homes are congested, but the streets are, too. In densely populated sections children engaged in even the mildest activities seem in the way. The absence of open spaces on the one hand and the conflict of interests on the other provide many occasions for opposition, dispute, and difference.

Gang KK. This group of 12 boys, ranging in age from 12 to 15 years, were all American-born. They were fond of athletics and had made a habit of playing hand-ball against the rear wall of a moving picture theatre. Their yells disturbed the patrons of the theatre, and the management frequently ordered them away from the premises. They left, but returned. Finally, in anger, the movie proprietor called a patrol wagon and had them loaded into it. They were arraigned in the Children's Court, but discharged. None of these boys had previous court records. They consisted partly of boys who lived in the immediate neighborhood, and partly of former residents, who still kept up their intimacy with the group.[15]

Here is an illustration of the difficulty in its simplest form. It is no crime to play handball against a wall. Nor is it a crime to yell and shout while the playing proceeds. In fact, the shouting, yelling, rough-housing, are an integral part of the game. It would be no game at all if this loud verbalization could not go on. The patrons are watching a picture and the noise disturbs them. The owner wants to keep his customers. A natural conflict has arisen, and no compromise is possible: the children cannot promise not to play or shout, the patrons cannot help being annoyed. The alternative is a different place to play. But a different place may not exist; there may be only one available wall and ground in the neighborhood. The children are arrested. A definition of evil has been created, a court record has been set up. The beginning of a career may have been marked. A differentiation has now been created which would never have arisen if the interests of the children were as highly considered as those of

[15] State of New York. Report of the Crime Commission, 1928, p. 620. Legislative Document (1928) No. 23.

the patrons of the theater or of the owner. The children needed space and a wall; these should have been provided in some form that would not involve the children with the court, the police, the patrol wagon, with which they had had no previous contact.

The process of gang formation may be stimulated also by the natural efforts of parents to maintain their own social standards in a continual process of classification, of separation of the "good" and the "bad," the right and the wrong. Parents carry their attitudes over to their children by talk, gossip, approval, condemnation, punishment, and reward. A system of values, judgments, differentiations, and classifications makes itself felt very early in the children's lives, and may have any number of grounds: religious, racial, economic, social, professional, and occupational. The more differentiation in the community, the greater the heterogeneity of the population, the less internal unity and sympathy, the greater the ease with which gangs are formed. In a sense, therefore, the gangs derive from the natural conflict that exists within the community itself.

Gangs are not merely spatial relationships—blocks, neighborhoods—but they are social relationships. The Irish gangs, the Jewish gangs, the Italian gangs, the Polish gangs, the gangs of English-speaking and non-English-speaking members of the community, are all evidence of the range of conflict within which the individual finds an outlet, recognition, and companionship.

A MATTER OF DEFINITION

In the conflict between the young delinquent and the community there develop two opposing definitions of the situation. In the beginning the definition of the situation by the young delinquent may be in the form of play, adventure, excitement, interest, mis-

chief, fun. Breaking windows, annoying people, running around porches, climbing over roofs, stealing from pushcarts, playing truant—all are items of play, adventure, excitement. To the community, however, these activities may and often do take on the form of a nuisance, evil, delinquency, with the demand for control, admonition, chastisement, punishment, police court, truant school. This conflict over the situation is one that arises out of a divergence of values. As the problem develops, the situation gradually becomes redefined. The attitude of the community hardens definitely into a demand for suppression. There is a gradual shift from the definition of the specific acts as evil to a definition of the individual as evil, so that all his acts come to be looked upon with suspicion. In the process of identification his companions, hang-outs, play, speech, income, all his conduct, the personality itself, become subject to scrutiny and question. From the community's point of view, the individual who used to do bad and mischievous things has now become a bad and unredeemable human being. From the individual's point of view there has taken place a similar change. He has gone slowly from a sense of grievance and injustice, of being unduly mistreated and punished, to a recognition that the definition of him as a human being is different from that of other boys in his neighborhood, his school, street, community. This recognition on his part becomes a process of self-identification and integration with the group which shares his activities. It becomes, in part, a process of rationalization; in part, a simple response to a specialized type of stimulus. The young delinquent becomes bad because he is defined as bad and because he is not believed if he is good. There is a persistent demand for consistency in character. The community cannot deal with people whom it cannot define. Reputation is this sort of public definition. Once it is established, then unconsciously all agencies combine to maintain this definition even when they apparently and consciously attempt to deny their own implicit judgment.

Early in his career, then, the incipient professional criminal develops an attitude of antagonism to the regulated orderly life that he is required to lead. This attitude is hardened and crystallized by opposition. The conflict becomes a clash of wills. And experience too often has proved that threats, punishments, beatings, commitments to institutions, abuse and defamation of one sort or another, are of no avail. Punishment breaks down against the child's stubbornness. What has happened is that the child has been defined as an "incorrigible" both by his contacts and by himself, and an attempt at a direct breaking down of will generally fails.

The child meets the situation in the only way he can, by defiance and escape—physical escape if possible, or emotional escape by derision, anger, contempt, hatred, disgust, tantrums, destructiveness, and physical violence. The response of the child is just as intelligent and intelligible as that of the schools, of the authorities. They have taken a simple problem, the lack of fitness of an institution to a particular child's needs, and have made a moral issue out of it with values outside the child's ken. It takes on the form of war between two wills, and the longer the war lasts, the more certainly does the child become incorrigible. The child will not yield because he cannot yield —his nature requires other channels for pleasant growth; the school system or society will not yield because it does not see the issues involved as between the incompatibility of an institution and a child's needs, sometimes physical needs, and will instead attempt to twist the child's nature to the institution with that consequent distortion of the child which makes an unsocial career inevitable. The verbalization of the conflict in terms of evil, delinquency, incorrigibility, badness, arrest, force, punishment, stupidity, lack of intelligence, truancy, criminality, gives the innocent divergence of the child from the straight road a meaning that it did not have in the beginning and makes its continuance in these same terms by so much the more inevitable.

The only important fact, when the issue arises of the boy's inability to acquire the specific habits which organized institutions attempt to impose upon him, is that this conflict becomes the occasion for him to acquire another series of habits, interests, and attitudes as a substitute. These habits become as effective in motivating and guiding conduct as would have been those which the orderly routine social institutions attempted to impose had they been acquired.

This conflict gives the gang its hold, because the gang provides escape, security, pleasure, and peace. The gang also gives room for the motor activity which plays a large role in a child's life. The attempt to break up the gang by force merely strengthens it. The arrest of the children has consequences undreamed of, for several reasons.

First, only some of the children are caught though all may be equally guilty. There is a great deal more delinquency practiced and committed by the young groups than comes to the attention of the police. The boy arrested, therefore, is singled out in specialized treatment. This boy, no more guilty than the other members of his group, discovers a world of which he knew little. His arrest suddenly precipitates a series of institutions, attitudes, and experiences which the other children do not share. For this boy there suddenly appear the police, the patrol wagon, the police station, the other delinquents and criminals found in the police lock-ups, the court with all its agencies such as bailiffs, clerks, bonds-men, lawyers, probation officers. There are bars, cells, handcuffs, criminals. He is questioned, examined, tested, investi-gated. His history is gone into, his fam-ily is brought into court. Witnesses make their appearance. The boy, no different from the rest of his gang, sud-denly becomes the center of a major drama in which all sorts of unexpected characters play important roles. And what is it all about? About the accus-tomed things his gang has done and has been doing for a long time. In this en-tirely new world he is made conscious of himself as a different human being than he was before his arrest. He be-comes classified as a thief, perhaps, and the entire world about him has sud-denly become a different place for him and will remain different for the rest of his life.

THE DRAMATIZATION OF EVIL

The first dramatization of the "evil" which separates the child out of his group for specialized treatment plays a greater role in making the criminal than perhaps any other experience. It can-not be too often emphasized that for the child the whole situation has be-come different. He now lives in a differ-ent world. He has been tagged. A new and hitherto non-existent environment has been precipitated out for him.

The process of making the criminal, therefore, is a process of tagging, de-fining, identifying, segregating, describ-ing, emphasizing, making conscious and self-conscious; it becomes a way of stimulating, suggesting, emphasizing, and evoking the very traits that are complained of. If the theory of relation of response to stimulus has any mean-ing, the entire process of dealing with

the young delinquent is mischievous insofar as it identifies him to himself or to the environment as a delinquent person.

The person becomes the thing he is described as being. Nor does it seem to matter whether the valuation is made by those who would punish or by those who would reform. In either case the emphasis is upon the conduct that is disapproved of. The parents or the policeman, the older brother or the court, the probation officer or the juve-nile institution, insofar as they rest upon the thing complained of, rest upon a false ground. Their very enthu-siasm defeats their aim. The harder they work to reform the evil, the greater the evil grows under their hands. The persistent suggestion, with whatever good intentions, works mischief, be-cause it leads to bringing out the bad behavior that it would suppress. The way out is through a refusal to dram-atize the evil. The less said about it the better. The more said about some-thing else, still better.

The hard-drinker who keeps thinking of not drinking is doing what he can to initi-ate the acts which lead to drinking. He is starting with the stimulus to his habit. To succeed he must find some positive interest or line of action which will inhibit the drinking series and which by instituting another course of action will bring him to his desired end.[16]

The dramatization of the evil there-fore tends to precipitate the conflict situation which was first created through some innocent maladjustment. The child's isolation forces him into companionship with other children sim-ilarly defined, and the gang becomes his means of escape, his security. The life of the gang gives it special mores, and the attack by the community upon

[16] John Dewey, *Human Nature and Conduct*, p. 35. New York, 1922.

these mores merely overemphasizes the conflict already in existence, and makes it the source of a new series of experiences that lead directly to a criminal career.

In dealing with the delinquent, the criminal, therefore, the important thing to remember is that we are dealing with a human being who is responding normally to the demands, stimuli, approval, expectancy, of the group with whom he is associated. We are dealing not with an individual but with a group.

In a study of 6,000 instances of stealing, with reference to the number of boys involved, it was found that in 90.4 per cent of the cases two or more boys were known to have been involved in the act and were consequently brought to court. Only 9.6 per cent of all the cases were acts of single individuals. Since this study was based upon the number of boys brought to court, and since in many cases not all of the boys involved were caught and brought to court, it is certain that the percentage of group stealing is therefore even greater than 90.4 per cent. It cannot be doubted that delinquency, particularly stealing, almost invariably involves two or more persons.[17]

That group may be a small gang, a gang of children just growing up, a gang of young "toughs" of nineteen or twenty, or a gang of older criminals of thirty. If we are not dealing with a gang we may be dealing with a family. And if we are not dealing with either of these especially we may be dealing with a community. In practice all these factors—the family, the gang, and the community—may be important in the development and the maintenance of that attitude towards the world which makes a criminal career a normal, accepted and approved way of life.

Direct attack upon the individual in these circumstances is a dubious under-

[17] Clifford R. Shaw and Earl D. Myers, "The Juvenile Delinquent," The Illinois Crime Survey, pp. 662-663. Chicago, 1929.

taking. By the time the individual has become a criminal his habits have been so shaped that we have a fairly integrated character whose whole career is in tune with the peculiar bit of the environment for which he has developed the behavior and habits that cause him to be apprehended. In theory isolation from that group ought to provide occasion for change in the individual's habit structure. It might, if the individual were transplanted to a group whose values and activities had the approval of the wider community, and in which the newcomer might hope to gain full acceptance eventually. But until now isolation has meant the grouping in close confinement of persons whose strongest common bond has been their socially disapproved delinquent conduct. Thus the attack cannot be made without reference to group life.

The attack must be on the whole group; for only by changing its attitudes and ideals, interests and habits, can the stimuli which it exerts upon the individual be changed. Punishment as retribution has failed to reform, that is, to change character. If the individual can be made aware of a different set of values for which he may receive approval, then we may be on the road to a change in his character. But such a change of values involves a change in stimuli, which means that the criminal's social world must be changed before he can be changed.

THE SCAPEGOAT IS A SNARE AND A DELUSION

The point of view here developed rejects all assumptions that would impute crime to the individual in the sense that a personal shortcoming of the offender is the cause of the unsocial behavior. The assumption that crime is caused by any sort of inferiority, physiological or psychological, is here completely and unequivocally repudiated.

This of course does not mean that morphological or psychological techniques do not have value in dealing with the individual. It merely means that they have no greater value in the study of criminology than they would have in the study of any profession. If a poor IQ is a bad beginning for a career in medicine, it is also a poor beginning for a career in crime. If the psychiatrist can testify that a psychopath will make an irritable doctor, he can prove the same for the criminal. But he can prove no more. The criminal differs from the rest of his fellows only in the sense that he has learned to respond to the stimuli of a very small and specialized group; but that group must exist or the criminal could not exist. In that he is like the mass of men, living a certain kind of life with the kind of companions that make that life possible.

This explanation of criminal behavior is meant to apply to those who more or less consistently pursue the criminal career. It does not necessarily presume to describe the accidental criminal or the man who commits a crime of pas-sion. Here perhaps the theories that would seek the cause of crime in the individual may have greater application than in attempting to deal with those who follow a life of crime. But even in the accidental criminal there is a strong presumption that the accident is the outcome of a habit situation. Any habit tends to have a background of social conditioning.

A man with the habit of giving way to anger may show his habit by a murderous attack upon some one who has offended. His act is nonetheless due to habit because it occurs only once in his life. The essence of habit is an acquired predisposition to *ways* or modes of response, not to particular acts except as, under special conditions, these express a way of behaving. Habit means special sensitiveness or accessibility to certain classes of stimuli, standing predilections and aversions, rather than bare recurrence of specific acts. It means will.[18]

In other words, perhaps the accidental criminal also is to be explained in terms such as we used in discussing the professional criminal.

[18] Dewey, *op. cit.,* p. 42.

7. The Theory of Differential Association

EDWIN H. SUTHERLAND

The following paragraphs state a genetic theory of criminal behavior on the assumption that a criminal act occurs when a situation appropriate for it, as defined by the person, is present. The theory should be regarded as tentative, and it should be tested by the factual information and theories which are applicable.

GENETIC EXPLANATION OF CRIMINAL BEHAVIOR

The following statement refers to the process by which a particular person comes to engage in criminal behavior.

1. *Criminal behavior is learned.* Negatively, this means that criminal behavior is not inherited, as such; also, the person who is not already trained in crime does not invent criminal behavior, just as a person does not make mechanical inventions unless he has had training in mechanics.

2. *Criminal behavior is learned in interaction with other persons in a process of communication.* This communication is verbal in many respects but includes also "the communication of gestures."

3. *The principal part of the learning of criminal behavior occurs within intimate personal groups.* Negatively, this means that the impersonal agencies of communication, such as movies and newspapers, play a relatively unimportant part in the genesis of criminal behavior.

4. *When criminal behavior is learned, the learning includes (a) techniques of committing the crime, which are sometimes very complicated, sometimes very simple; (b) the specific direction of motives, drives, rationalizations, and attitudes.*

5. *The specific direction of motives and drives is learned from definitions of the legal codes as favorable or unfavorable.* In some societies an individual is surrounded by persons who invariably define the legal codes as rules to be observed, while in others he is surrounded by persons whose definitions are favorable to the violation of the legal codes. In our American society these definitions are almost always mixed, with the consequence that we have culture conflict in relation to the legal codes.

6. *A person becomes delinquent because of an excess of definitions favorable to violation of law over definitions*

SOURCE. Edwin H. Sutherland, *Principles of Criminology,* fifth edition, revised by Donald R. Cressey, Philadelphia: J. B. Lippincott Company, 1955, pp. 77–80. Reprinted with the permission of J. B. Lippincott Company.

unfavorable to violation of law. This is the principle of differential association. It refers to both criminal and anti-criminal associations and has to do with counteracting forces. When persons become criminal, they do so because of contacts with criminal patterns and also because of isolation from anti-criminal patterns. Any person inevitably assimilates the surrounding culture unless other patterns are in conflict; a Southerner does not pronounce "r" because other Southerners do not pronounce "r." Negatively, this proposition of differential association means that associations which are neutral so far as crime is concerned have little or no effect on the genesis of criminal behavior. Much of the experience of a person is neutral in this sense, e.g., learning to brush one's teeth. This behavior has no negative or positive effect on criminal behavior except as it may be related to associations which are concerned with the legal codes. This neutral behavior is important especially as an occupier of the time of a child so that he is not in contact with criminal behavior during the time he is so engaged in the neutral behavior.

7. *Differential associations may vary in frequency, duration, priority, and intensity*. This means that associations with criminal behavior and also associations with anti-criminal behavior vary in those respects. "Frequency" and "duration" as modalities of associations are obvious and need no explanation. "Priority" is assumed to be important in the sense that lawful behavior developed in early childhood may persist throughout life, and also that delinquent behavior developed in early childhood may persist throughout life. This tendency, however, has not been adequately demonstrated, and priority seems to be important principally through its selective influence. "Intensity" is not precisely defined but it has

to do with such things as the prestige of the source of a criminal or anti-criminal pattern and with emotional reactions related to the associations. In a precise description of the criminal behavior of a person these modalities would be stated in quantitative form and a mathematical ratio be reached. A formula in this sense has not been developed, and the development of such a formula would be extremely difficult.

8. *The process of learning criminal behavior by association with criminal and anti-criminal patterns involves all of the mechanisms that are involved in any other learning*. Negatively, this means that the learning of criminal behavior is not restricted to the process of imitation. A person who is seduced, for instance, learns criminal behavior by association, but this process would not ordinarily be described as imitation.

9. *While criminal behavior is an expression of general needs and values, it is not explained by those general needs and values since non-criminal behavior is an expression of the same needs and values*. Thieves generally steal in order to secure money, but likewise honest laborers work in order to secure money. The attempts by many scholars to explain criminal behavior by general drives and values, such as the happiness principle, striving for social status, the money motive, or frustration, have been and must continue to be futile since they explain lawful behavior as completely as they explain criminal behavior. They are similar to respiration, which is necessary for any behavior but which does not differentiate criminal from non-criminal behavior.

It is not necessary, at this level of explanation, to explain why a person has the associations which he has; this certainly involves a complex of many things. In an area where the delinquency rate is high, a boy who is sociable, gregarious, active, and athletic is very likely to come in contact with the other boys in the neighborhood, learn delinquent behavior from them, and become a gangster; in the same neighborhood the psychopathic boy who is isolated, introverted, and inert may remain at home, not become acquainted with the other boys in the neighborhood, and not become delinquent. In another situation, the sociable, athletic, aggressive boy may become a member of a scout troop and not become involved in delinquent behavior. The person's associations are determined in a general context of social organization. A child is ordinarily reared in a family; the place of residence of the family is determined largely by family income; and the delinquency rate is in many respects related to the rental value of the houses. Many other aspects of social organization affect the kinds of associations a person has.

The preceding explanation of criminal behavior purports to explain the criminal and non-criminal behavior of individual persons. As indicated earlier, it is possible to state sociological theories of criminal behavior which explain the criminality of a community, nation, or other group. The problem, when thus stated, is to account for variations in crime rates and involves a comparison of the crime rates of various groups or the crime rates of a particular group at different times. The explanation of a crime rate must be consistent with the explanation of the criminal behavior of the person, since the crime rate is a summary statement of the number of persons in the group who commit crimes and the frequency with which they commit crimes. One of the best explanations of crime rates from this point of view is that a high crime rate is due to social disorganization. The term "social disorganization" is not entirely satisfactory, and it seems preferable to substitute for it the term "differential social organization." The postulate on which this theory is based, regardless of the name, is that crime is rooted in the social organization and is an expression of that social organization. A group may be organized for criminal behavior or organized against criminal behavior. Most communities are organized both for criminal and anti-criminal behavior, and in that sense the crime rate is an expression of the differential group organization. Differential group organization as an explanation of variations in crime rates is consistent with the differential association theory of the processes by which persons become criminals.

8. Differential Association and Delinquency

JAMES F. SHORT, JR.

An important task of research in the field of juvenile delinquency, and indeed in sociology and science generally, is the testing of theories set forth in the literature but not previously subjected to empirical inquiry. The social sciences contain many such theories, based on case studies, historical examples, or the synthesis of other theoretical and empirical work. Some of these become virtually sacrosanct through continued usage, particularly in textbook form, though they remain untested in any systematic way.

° Paper delivered at the annual meeting of the American Sociological Society in Detroit, September 7, 1956. The project of which this paper is a partial report is made possible by a Faculty Research Fellowship grant from the Social Science Research Council and a grant from the College Committee of Research, State College of Washington. I am indebted to these groups for their encouragement in this area of study. Thanks are due also to F. Ivan Nye, director of the Sociological Laboratory of the State College of Washington, for assistance in developing the questionnaire utilized in this study; to Mrs. Frances Romeo and Mr. James McCorkhill for statistical aid, and to Mr. McCorkhill for help in administering the questionnaire as well; and to various members of the Department of Sociology, State College of Washington, for critical appraisal of this paper.

The researcher who would test such theories must do so with trepidation and not a little humility. The latter state is a healthy one in any research and is particularly appropriate when the theory to be tested has been propounded out of the considered experience and thought of pioneers in the field. The former is occasioned by the fact that, to test such theories, it is often necessary to reformulate them in testable form (9). This inevitably involves the loss of some of the "flavor" imparted to concepts by their formulators and exposes one to scorn from detractors and/or proponents of the theory being investigated, as well as from those who deplore the "crass empiricism" which dominates contemporary sociology.

Still, theories demand testing, and the process may yield additional precision and even insight to earlier formulations. The subject of this paper is the most truly sociological of all theories which have been advanced to explain criminal and delinquent behavior, Edwin H. Sutherland's "differential association" hypothesis (13, pp. 74 ff.). This theory has been attacked many times and for many reasons, yet

SOURCE. James F. Short, Jr., "Differential Association and Delinquency," from *Social Problems*, Volume 4, No. 3, January 1957, pp. 233-239. Reprinted with the permission of the Society for the Study of Social Problems and the author.

it is still widely used as a description of basic processes involved in such behavior. Stated in Sutherland's terms, this principle, as he calls it, holds that "a person becomes delinquent because of an excess of definitions favorable to violation of law over definitions unfavorable to violation of law" (13, p. 78).

In such terms, the theory is not testable. The equation involving definitions "favorable to" and "unfavorable to" violation of law cannot be specified in any meaningful quantitative terms. It is, perhaps, for this reason that the theory has not been systematically investigated. For although the data of many studies support the theory, whether or not their compilers recognize the fact (1, 6, 8), systematic study of the theory itself is almost non-existent. Cressey's empirical investigation of the violation of financial trust, in which the theory was found wanting in some respects, and his theoretical article treating applicability of the differential association theory to cases of "compulsive crimes" stand alone as attempts to orient specifically towards verification of the differential association theory (2, 4; see also 3).

Sutherland's use of the concept, and the usage which has become common, is not so restrictive of empirical investigation. For, in effect, differential association has come to imply differential access to delinquent and conventional values through interaction with other people and with various aspects of the larger society. Sutherland's statement that "differential associations may vary in frequency, duration, priority, and intensity" suggests the main dimensions of differential association which this paper investigates. Specifically, we attempt to measure the frequency, duration, priority, and intensity of interaction with delinquent peers, the degree of presumed exposure to crime and delinquency in the community, and

knowledge of and association with adult criminals.

SAMPLE AND INSTRUMENTS

The subjects under study in this paper were students in the state training schools for boys and girls in a western state during the month of February, 1955. Because of age in relation to delinquent behavior, we have restricted this analysis to sixteen- and seventeen-year-old boys and girls. A total of 126 boys and 50 girls were administered a questionnaire developed by the writer in consultation with the Sociological Laboratory of the State College of Washington. Respondents answered the questionnaire anonymously. No direct refusals were encountered, though approximately 10 per cent of the boys' questionnaires and 4 per cent of the girls' could not be used either because responses were obviously frivolous or because there was excessive non-response. Some of the latter was due to school retardation.

The delinquency scales employed in the study consisted of selected delinquency items from the questionnaire which were re-scored according to the Israel Gamma technique (7) and scaled by the Cornell technique (12). The scale for the boys developed in an earlier study (11), originally comprised 11 items and 18 scale types. A group of 570 public-school boys from the same state was combined with the training-school boys in the construction of the scale. The boys' scale utilized in this paper consists of a reassignment of the original scale types to the training-school boys in the present study. This was necessary because these boys were not represented in all the original scale types. The present scale, consisting of 11 scale types, appears in Table 1. The delinquency scale for girls likewise was first developed by combining sixteen- and seventeen-year-old girls from the

Table 1

DELINQUENCY SCALE TYPES FOR BOYS°

Scale type	Offense†											No. in scale type
	1	2	3	4	5	6	7	8	9	10	11	
00	1	1	1	1	0	0	0	0	0	0	0	3
01	2	1	1	1	0	0	0	0	0	0	0	2
02	2	1	1	1	1	1	0	0	0	0	0	3
03	2	2	1	1	1	1	0	0	0	0	0	20
04	2	2	2	1	1	1	1	0	0	0	0	20
05	2	2	2	2	1	1	1	1	1	0	0	3
06	2	2	2	2	1	1	2	1	1	0	0	1
07	2	2	2	2	2	1	2	1	1	0	0	8
08	2	2	2	2	2	2	2	1	1	0	0	26
09	2	2	2	2	2	2	2	1	1	1	1	5
10	2	2	2	2	2	2	2	2	1	1	1	34
Total												125

° The coefficient of reproducibility of the original scale was .975.

† Numbers refer to the following delinquents acts:

1. Driving a car without a driver's license or permit.
2. Buying or drinking beer, wine, or liquor (including drinking at home).
3. Skipping school without a legitimate excuse.
4. Taking little things (worth less than $2) that did not belong to you.
5. Purposely damaging or destroying public or private property.
6. Sex relations with a person of the opposite sex.
7. Taking things of medium value (worth $2 to $50).
8. "Running away" from home.
9. Taking things of large value (worth more than $50).
10. Defying parents' authority to their faces.
11. Narcotics violations.

An "0" centered in the table indicates that the offense has not been committed by subjects in the scale type. In the case of all items except heterosexual relations, "1" indicates commission of the offense once or twice and a "2" indicates commission of the offense three times or more. A "1" for heterosexual relations indicates commission of the offense from one to four times, while a "2" indicates commission more than four times.

training school and girls in this age group from the same public schools as were included in the construction of the boys scales, a total of 512 girls. Again, reassignment of scale types was necessary because the training-school girls were not always represented in the original scale types. Table 2 presents the girls' delinquency scale employed in this paper.

Measures of differential association were obtained from the answers to the following questions:

1. Think of the friends you have been associated with *most often*. Were

(or are) any of them juvenile delinquents?

2. Think of the friends you have known *for the longest time*. Were (or are) any of them juvenile delinquents?

3. Think back to the *first* friends you can remember. Were any of them juvenile delinquents at the time you first knew them?

4. Have any of your *best* friends been juvenile delinquents while they were your best friends?

5. Was there much crime or delinquency committed by young people (in their teens or below) in the community in which you grew up?

Table 2

DELINQUENCY SCALE TYPES FOR GIRLS*

Scale type	Offense†									No. in scale type
	1	2	3	4	5	6	7	8	9	
00	0	0	0	0	0	0	0	0	0	0
01	1	1	0	0	0	0	0	0	0	1
02	1	1	1	0	0	0	0	0	0	1
03	2	1	2	1	0	0	0	0	0	1
04	2	1	2	1	1	0	0	0	0	1
05	2	2	2	1	1	1	0	0	0	1
06	2	2	2	1	1	1	1	0	0	6
07	2	2	2	1	1	2	1	0	0	4
08	2	2	2	1	1	2	1	1	0	7
09	2	2	2	1	1	2	1	1	1	25
Total										48

* The coefficient of reproducibility of the original scale was .979.
† Numbers refer to the following delinquent acts:
1. Driving a car without a driver's license or permit.
2. Skipping school without a legitimate excuse.
3. Buying or drinking beer, wine, or liquor (including drinking at home).
4. Defying parents' authority to their faces.
5. Taking little things (worth less than $2) that did not belong to you.
6. Sex relations with a person of the opposite sex.
7. "Running away" from home.
8. Purposely damaging or destroying public or private property.
9. Taking things of medium value (worth $2 to $50).

Numbers entered in the table have the same significance as those in Table 1, except that heterosexual relations are scored in the same way as other items.

6. Have any of your friends been "juvenile delinquents"?

7. Are any of your present friends juvenile delinquents?

8. Do you know any adult criminals?

9. How well have you known criminals?

Each question was followed by an appropriate set of four or five responses, such as "most were," "several were," "very few were," and "none were"; or "very well," "fairly well," "not very well," "only knew their names," and "didn't even know their names." The responses were numbered consecutively, the highest number representing minimum association in each case.

A "specific differential association score," designed to reflect the cumulative effect of frequency, duration, priority, and intensity of interaction with delinquent friends, was obtained for each subject by adding together the numbers of his answers to the first four of these questions. This permitted scores ranging from 4 to 16, the smaller sum indicating higher differential association. "General differential association scores" were obtained by adding the numbers symbolizing the answers to the last five questions. A "total differential association score" was then computed by adding the specific and general scores of each individual. The range of total scores was from 9, representing the highest degree of differential association, to 38, representing minimum answers to all the questions.

In the course of administering the questionnaires, we attempted to emphasize the subject's *own feelings*. If a respondent asked about the meaning of the questions, we explained that we were not interested in official records or in reputations. What the respondent himself felt was the important thing. This was done for reasons consistent with social-psychological theory, but it does raise certain hazards, and it may not have gotten across to all our respondents. We were interested in reality *as perceived by our respondents,* whether or not this perceived situation was in fact real. The disadvantages of this approach were felt to be considerably outweighed by the advantages. Tentative analysis of data from interviews carried out in conjunction with the questionnaires suggests that the desired interpretation was understood by the great majority of our respondents.

FINDINGS

Tables 3, 4, and 5 present the coefficients of correlation between the dif-

Table 3

SPECIFIC DIFFERENTIAL ASSOCIATIONS AND DELINQUENCY

Components of differential association	For boys	For girls
Frequency	.580°°	.552°°
Duration	.423°°	.347°°
Priority	.288°°	.379°
Intensity	.580°°	.473°°
Total specific score	.581°°	.606°°

° Significant at the 5 per cent level.
°° Significant at the 1 per cent level.

Table 5

TOTAL DIFFERENTIAL ASSOCIATION AND DELINQUENCY

	Excluding adult criminal questions	Including adult criminal questions
Boys	.620°°	.672°°
Girls	.667°°	.506°°

°° Significant at the 1 per cent level.

ferential association and delinquency measures, separately for each sex. To determine the efficiency of the measures of differential association as predictors of delinquency, the coefficient of correlation for proportions (rp), developed by Davies,° has been used.

° I am indebted to Dr. Davies for the following description of r: In arranging a contingency table for prediction purposes, the values for each trait are combined, if necessary, so that for each resulting category of x there is a single predictive category for the y trait, the consequence being that both traits are set up with the same number of categories. The raw frequencies in the cells of the table are next translated into proportions of each category of x as subdivided according to the categories of y. Then c prediction cells are selected, conforming to a prediction rule that best fits the data, where $c =$ the number of categories for each trait. If $p' =$ the proportion shown in any prediction cell, a correlation coefficient conforming to the prediction rule used can be shown to be:

$$\frac{r}{p} = \frac{\Sigma p' - 1}{c - 1}$$

The standard error of this coefficient,

Table 4

GENERAL DIFFERENTIAL ASSOCIATION AND DELINQUENCY

Components of differential association	For boys	For girls
Delinquency committed by young people in the community in which you grew up	.404°°	.279°
Have any of your friends ever been juvenile delinquents?	.613°°	.400°°
Are any of your present friends juvenile delinquents?	.447°°	.501°°
Do you know any adult criminals?	.446°°	.286°
How well have you known criminals?	.352°°	.164
Total general score	.679°°	.393°°

° Significant at the 5 per cent level.
°° Significant at the 1 per cent level.

Before computing the coefficients, the data were grouped into four-fold tables, because the delinquency scale types lacked the stability necessary for more detailed analysis of their relation to the measures of differential association. This form of analysis is admittedly crude, but it is probably as refined as the instruments and data warrant.

The most notable finding from these tables is the consistently positive relationship between delinquent behavior and delinquent association. In no case is a negative relationship between these variables found. This coefficients are, furthermore, of such magnitude as to give confidence in the theory.

Technically, the findings must be regarded as parameter values, i.e., characteristic only of the populations studied. To regard these populations as samples from which generalizations may be made, even to other training-school groups, would be unwarranted in view of the assumptions which would have to be made regarding randomness, constancy of population, etc. Statisticians point out, however, that any sample may be assumed to be a random sample of some universe, and the variables studied here may be quite independent of any known bias which is present in any given sample. Since our interest transcends the particular cases we are studying, it seems useful to apply tests of statistical significance to our findings. In any case, such tests involve controls over the manipulation of data which aid us in interpreting our findings. This is especially helpful when

for samples where the sub-totals for the x trait are constant, can be shown to be:

$$s = \sqrt{\frac{\dfrac{\Sigma p'q'}{n}}{c-1}}$$

The restriction that the sub-totals be constant is the same as that required for the chi-square test of independence.

measures are applied to samples of different sizes, as is the present case. We recognize that the assumptions governing tests of significance are not met by our research design. Generalization beyond these groups must, therefore, be recognized as speculation, but as the sort of healthy speculation calculated to assess more inclusive theoretical significance. More generalized demonstration requires study of other populations under carefully controlled sampling conditions.

It is important to the differential association theory that the summary measures of delinquent association have generally higher correlations with delinquent behavior, as measured by our scale, than do their component parts. Such a cumulative trend suggests that the addition of other aspects of differential association to those included in our study would account for virtually all the delinquent behavior, and the lack of it, among the respondents. It should also be noted that the individual components of differential association in most cases bear a closer relationship to delinquent behavior among the boys than among the girls.

The correlation of the general differential association scores with the delinquency scales calls for additional comment. A general score was first obtained by adding together the answers to questions 5, 6, and 7 only, thus eliminating consideration of the adult criminal questions. When this is done, the correlation of the general score with the boys' delinquency scale types is lowered to .572 (as compared to .679 in Table 4), while this correlation for the girls is .412, slightly larger than that which appears in Table 4. The correlations for total differential association scores are similarly affected when the adult criminal questions are not included, as can be seen in Table 5. Association with adult criminals is clearly more closely related to delinquent behavior among our boys than it is for our girls.

CONCLUSION

Space does not permit detailed treatment of the relation of our measures of differential association to particular delinquencies or to different patterns of delinquent behavior. Suffice it to say that correlations have been computed between our summary measures of differential association and each of the 26 delinquencies included in the larger list from which the delinquencies comprising our scales were chosen. For the training-school boys, these correlations are all significantly larger than zero at the 1 per cent level, with the exception of the correlations with homosexual behavior (and these are significant at the 5 per cent level). More of the correlations with the delinquencies of girls fail to reach statistical significance. No significant correlations are found for the girls between our summary measures of differential association and the five delinquencies of skipping school, strong-arm robbery, homosexual behavior, "taking things you really didn't want," and hurting or inflicting pain on someone just to see them squirm. For the remaining 21 delinquencies, significant correlations at the 5 per cent level or higher are found with at least one of our summary measures of differential association, and usually for two or all three of them.

The fact that our study was conducted on an institutionalized delinquent group, and therefore a more seriously delinquent group, must be taken as a restriction on the generalizability of this study. It may be that the close relationships demonstrated here between differential association and delinquency are limited to such seriously delinquent groups. We have collected data on three midwestern public-school groups which will aid us in resolving this question. Further, our study of differential association is "negative," in the sense that no measures of anti-delinquent peer relationships and other associations are studied.

Finally, it may be objected that this approach is "factorial" and not within the spirit and intention of Sutherland's theory. To this we can say only that our attempt has been merely to explore the relationship of various aspects of differential association to the delinquent conduct specified. Within these limitations, strong support has been found for the differential association theory. Further investigation may reveal types of delinquency, or patterns of delinquency, which are more closely related to particular types of differential association, or to the very process itself, than are others. Again, it may be possible to find patterns of behavior which are not so closely related to differential association, of the types we have measured in any case, as they are to patterns of emotional adjustment or maladjustment.[*] Lastly, the concept of differential association includes differential social organization and other aspects of social integration not touched upon in this paper—e.g., differential identification or reference, parental associations, etc. (5).

[*] A previous study found that, among the training-school girls, five of the 26 delinquencies had statistically significant correlations with a psychosomatic complaint scale (10).

References

1. Burgess, E. W., "Can Potential Delinquents Be Identified Scientifically?," *Twenty-Fourth Annual Governor's Conference on Youth and Community Service* (Springfield, Ill.: Illinois Youth Commission, 1955), 33-39.
2. Cressey, Donald R., "Application and Verification of the Differential Association Theory," *Journal of Criminal Law, Criminology, and Police Science*, 43 (May-June, 1952), 43-52.
3. Cressey, Donald R., "Changing Criminals: The Application of the Theory of Differential Association," *American Journal of Sociology*, 61 (September, 1955), 116-120.
4. Cressey, Donald R., "The Differential Association Theory and Compulsive Crimes," *Journal of Criminal Law, Criminology, and Police Science*, 45 (May-June, 1954), 29-40.
5. Glaser, Daniel, "Criminality Theories and Behavioral Images," *American Journal of Sociology*, 61 (March, 1956), 433-444.
6. Reiss, Albert J., Jr., "Unraveling Juvenile Delinquency. II. An Appraisal of the Research Methods," *American Journal of Sociology*, 57 (September, 1951), 115-120.
7. Riley, Matilda White, John W. Riley, Jr., and Jackson Toby, *Sociological Studies in Scale Analysis* (New Brunswick, N. J.: University Press, 1954), chap. 18.
8. Rubin, Sol, "Unraveling Juvenile Delinquency. I. Illusions in a Research Project Using Matched Pairs," *American Journal of Sociology*, 57 (September, 1951), 107-114.
9. Sewell, William H., "Some Observations on Theory Testing," presidential address to the Rural Sociological Society, 1955.
10. Short, James F., Jr., "Psychosomatic Complaints, Institutionalization, and Delinquency," *Research Studies of the State College of Washington*, 24 (June, 1956), 150-159.
11. Short, James F., Jr., "The Study of Juvenile Delinquency by Reported Behavior: An Experiment in Method and Preliminary Findings," paper delivered at the annual meeting of the American Sociological Society, September, 1955.
12. Stouffer, Samuel A., et al., *Measurement and Prediction*, vol. 4 of *Studies in Social Psychology in World War II* (Princeton, N. J.: Princeton University Press, 1950).
13. Sutherland, Edwin H., *Principles of Criminology* (5th ed., rev. by Donald R. Cressey; Philadelphia: Lippincott, 1955).

9. Social Structure and Anomie

ROBERT K. MERTON

There persists a notable tendency in sociological theory to attribute the malfunctioning of social structure primarily to those of man's imperious biological drives which are not adequately restrained by social control. In this view, the social order is solely a device for "impulse management" and the "social processing" of tensions. These impulses which break through social control, be it noted, are held to be biologically derived. Nonconformity is assumed to be rooted in original nature.[1] Conformity is by implication the result of an utilitarian calculus or unreasoned conditioning. This point of view, whatever its other deficiencies, clearly begs one question. It provides no basis for determining the nonbiological conditions which induce deviations from prescribed patterns of conduct. In this paper, it will be suggested that certain phases of social structure generate the circumstances in which infringement of social codes constitutes a "normal" response.[2]

The conceptual scheme to be outlined is designed to provide a coherent, systematic approach to the study of socio-cultural sources of deviate behavior. Our primary aim lies in discovering how some social structures *exert a definite pressure* upon certain persons in the society to engage in nonconformist rather than conformist conduct. The many ramifications of the scheme cannot all be discussed; the problems mentioned outnumber those explicitly treated.

Among the elements of social and cultural structure, two are important for our purposes. These are analytically separable although they merge imperceptibly in concrete situations. The first consists of culturally defined goals, purposes, and interests. It comprises a frame of aspirational reference. These goals are more or less integrated and

[1] E.g., Ernest Jones, *Social Aspects of Psychoanalysis*, 28, London, 1924. If the Freudian notion is a variety of the "original sin" dogma, then the interpretation advanced in this paper may be called the doctrine of "socially derived sin."

[2] "Normal" in the sense of a culturally

oriented, if not approved, response. This statement does not deny the relevance of biological and personality differences which may be significantly involved in the *incidence* of deviate conduct. Our focus of interest is the social and cultural matrix; hence we abstract from other factors. It is in this sense, I take it, that James S. Plant speaks of the "normal reaction of normal people to abnormal conditions." See his *Personality and the Cultural Pattern*, 248, New York, 1937.

SOURCE. Robert K. Merton, "Social Structure and Anomie," from *American Sociological Review*, Volume 3, October 1938, pp. 672-682. Reprinted with the permission of the American Sociological Association and the author.

involve varying degrees of prestige and sentiment. They constitute a basic, but not the exclusive, component of what Linton aptly has called "designs for group living." Some of these cultural aspirations are related to the original drives of man, but they are not determined by them. The second phase of the social structure defines, regulates, and controls the acceptable modes of achieving these goals. Every social group invariably couples its scale of desired ends with moral or institutional regulation of permissible and required procedures for attaining these ends. These regulatory norms and moral imperatives do not necessarily coincide with technical or efficiency norms. Many procedures which form the standpoint of *particular individuals* would be most efficient in securing desired values, e.g., illicit oil-stock schemes, theft, fraud, are ruled out of the institutional area of permitted conduct. The choice of expedients is limited by the institutional norms.

To say that these two elements, culture goals and institutional norms, operate jointly is not to say that the ranges of alternative behaviors and aims bear some constant relation to one another. The emphasis upon certain goals may vary independently of the degree of emphasis upon institutional means. There may develop a disproportionate, at times, a virtually exclusive, stress upon the value of specific goals, involving relatively slight concern with the institutionally appropriate modes of attaining these goals. The limiting case in this direction is reached when the range of alternative procedures is limited only by technical rather than institutional considerations. Any and all devices which promise attainment of the all important goal would be permitted in this hypothetical polar case.[3]

[3] Contemporary American culture has been said to tend in this direction. See

This constitutes one type of cultural malintegration. A second polar type is found in groups where activities originally conceived as instrumental are transmuted into ends in themselves. The original purposes are forgotten, and ritualistic adherence to institutionally prescribed conduct becomes virtually obsessive.[4] Stability is largely ensured while change is flouted. The range of alternative behaviors is severely limited. There develops a tradition-bound, sacred society characterized by neophobia. The occupational psychosis of the bureaucrat may be cited as a case in point. Finally, there are the intermediate types of groups where a balance between culture goals and institutional means is maintained. These are the significantly integrated and relatively stable, though changing, groups.

André Siegfried, *America Comes of Age,* 26–37, New York, 1927. The alleged extreme(?) emphasis on the goals of monetary success and material prosperity leads to dominant concern with technological and social instruments designed to produce the desired result, inasmuch as institutional controls become of secondary importance. In such a situation, innovation flourishes as the *range of means* employed is broadened. In a sense, then, there occurs the paradoxical emergence of "materialists" from an "idealistic" orientation. Cf. Durkheim's analysis of the cultural conditions which predispose toward crime and innovation, both of which are aimed toward efficiency, not moral norms. Durkheim was one of the first to see that "contrairement aux idées courantes le criminel n'apparait plus comme un être radicalement insociable, comme une sorte d'élément parasitaire, de corps étranger et inassimilable, introduit au sein de la société; c'est un agent régulier de la vie sociale." See *Les Règles de la Méthode Sociologique,* 86–89, Paris, 1927.

[4] Such ritualism may be associated with a mythology which rationalizes these actions so that they appear to retain their status as means, but the dominant pressure is in the direction of strict ritualistic conformity, irrespective of such rationalizations. In this sense, ritual has proceeded farthest when such rationalizations are not even called forth.

An effective equilibrium between the two phases of the social structure is maintained as long as satisfactions accrue to individuals who conform to both constraints, viz., satisfactions from the achievement of the goals and satisfactions emerging directly from the institutionally canalized modes of striving to attain these ends. Success, in such equilibrated cases, is twofold. Success is reckoned in terms of the product and in terms of the process, in terms of the outcome and in terms of activities. Continuing satisfactions must derive from sheer *participation* in a competitive order as well as from eclipsing one's competitors if the order itself is to be sustained. The occasional sacrifices involved in institutionalized conduct must be compensated by socialized rewards. The distribution of statuses and roles through competition must be so organized that positive incentives for conformity to roles and adherence to status obligations are provided *for every position* within the distributive order. Aberrant conduct, therefore, may be viewed as a symptom of dissociation between culturally defined aspirations and socially structured means.

Of the types of groups which result from the independent variation of the two phases of the social structure, we shall be primarily concerned with the first, namely, that involving a disproportionate accent on goals. This statement must be recast in a proper perspective. In no group is there an absence of regulatory codes governing conduct, yet groups do vary in the degree to which these folkways, mores, and institutional controls are effectively integrated with the more diffuse goals which are part of the culture matrix. Emotional convictions may cluster about the complex of socially acclaimed ends, meanwhile shifting their support from the culturally defined implementation of these ends. As we shall see, certain aspects of the social structure may generate countermores and antisocial behavior precisely because of differential emphases on goals and regulations. In the extreme case, the latter may be so vitiated by the goal-emphasis that the range of behavior is limited only by considerations of technical expediency. The sole significant question then becomes, which available means is most efficient in netting the socially approved value?[5] The technically most feasible procedure, whether legitimate or not, is preferred to the institutionally prescribed conduct. As this process continues, the integration of the society becomes tenuous and anomie ensues.

Thus, in competitive athletics, when the aim of victory is shorn of its institutional trappings and success in contests becomes construed as "winning the game" rather than "winning through circumscribed modes of activity," a premium is implicitly set upon the use of illegitimate but technically efficient means. The star of the opposing football team is surreptitiously slugged; the wrestler furtively incapacitates his opponent through ingenious but illicit techniques; university alumni covertly subsidize "students" whose talents are largely confined to the athletic field. The emphasis on the goal has so attenuated the satisfactions deriving from sheer participation in the competitive activity that these satisfactions are vir-

---

[5] In this connection, one may see the relevance of Elton Mayo's paraphrase of the title of Tawney's well-known book. "Actually the problem *is not that of the sickness of an acquisitive society; it is that of the acquisitiveness of a sick society.*" *Human Problems of an Industrial Civilization*, 153, New York, 1933. Mayo deals with the process through which wealth comes to be a symbol of social achievement. He sees this as arising from a state of anomie. We are considering the unintegrated monetary-success goal as an element in producing anomie. A complete analysis would involve both phases of this system of interdependent variables.

tually confined to a successful outcome. Through the same process, tension generated by the desire to win in a poker game is relieved by successfully dealing oneself four aces, or, when the cult of success has become completely dominant, by sagaciously shuffling the cards in a game of solitaire. The faint twinge of uneasiness in the last instance and the surreptitious nature of public delicts indicate clearly that the institutional rules of the game *are known* to those who evade them, but that the emotional supports of these rules are largely vitiated by cultural exaggeration of the success-goal.[6] They are microcosmic images of the social macrocosm.

Of course, this process is not restricted to the realm of sport. The process whereby exaltation of the end generates a *literal demoralization,* i.e., a deinstitutionalization, of the means is one which characterizes many[7] groups in which the two phases of the social structure are not highly integrated. The extreme emphasis upon the accumulation of wealth as a symbol of success[8] in our own society militates against the completely effective control of institutionally regulated modes of acquiring a fortune.[9] Fraud, corruption, vice, crime, in short, the entire catalogue of proscribed behavior, becomes increasingly common when the emphasis on the *culturally induced* success-goal becomes divorced from a coordinated institutional emphasis. This observation is of crucial theoretical importance in examining the doctrine that antisocial behavior most frequently derives from biological drives breaking through the restraints imposed by society. The difference is one between a strictly utilitarian interpretation which conceives man's ends as random and an analysis which finds these ends deriving from the basic values of the culture.[10]

Our analysis can scarcely stop at this juncture. We must turn to other aspects of the social structure if we are to deal with the social genesis of the varying rates and types of deviate behavior characteristic of different societies. Thus far, we have sketched three ideal types of social orders constituted by distinctive patterns of relations between culture ends and means. Turning from

[6] It is unlikely that interiorized norms are completely eliminated. Whatever residuum persists will induce personality tensions and conflict. The process involves a certain degree of ambivalence. A manifest rejection of the institutional norms is coupled with some latent retention of their emotional correlates. "Guilt feelings," "sense of sin," "pangs of conscience" are obvious manifestations of this unrelieved tension; symbolic adherence to the nominally repudiated values or rationalizations constitute a more subtle variety of tensional release.

[7] "Many," and not all, unintegrated groups, for the reason already mentioned. In groups where the primary emphasis shifts to institutional means, i.e., when the range of alternatives is very limited, the outcome is a type of ritualism rather than anomie.

[8] Money has several peculiarities which render it particularly apt to become a symbol of prestige divorced from institutional controls. As Simmel emphasized, money is highly abstract and impersonal.

However acquired, through fraud or institutionally, it can be used to purchase the same goods and services. The anonymity of metropolitan culture, in conjunction with this peculiarity of money, permits wealth, the sources of which may be unknown to the community in which the plutocrat lives, to serve as a symbol of status.

[9] The emphasis upon wealth as a success-symbol is possibly reflected in the use of the term "fortune" to refer to a stock of accumulated wealth. This meaning becomes common in the late sixteenth century (Spenser and Shakespeare). A similar usage of the Latin *fortuna* comes into prominence during the first century B.C. Both these periods were marked by the rise to prestige and power of the "bourgeoisie."

[10] See Kingsley Davis, "Mental Hygiene and the Class Structure," *Psychiatry,* 1928, 1: esp. 62–63; Talcott Parsons, *The Structure of Social Action,* 59–60, New York, 1937.

these types of *culture patterning*, we find five logically possible, alternative modes of adjustment or adaptation *by individuals* within the culture-bearing society or group.[11] These are schematically presented in the following table, where (+) signifies "acceptance," (−) signifies "elimination," and (±) signifies "rejection and substitution of new goals and standards."

	Culture goals	Institu- tionalized means
I. Conformity	+	+
II. Innovation	+	−
III. Ritualism	−	+
IV. Retreatism	−	−
V. Rebellion[12]	±	±

Our discussion of the relation between these alternative responses and other phases of the social structure must be prefaced by the observation that persons may shift from one alternative to another as they engage in different social activities. These categories refer to role adjustments in specific situations, not to personality *in toto*. To treat the development of this process in various spheres of conduct would introduce a complexity unmanageable within the confines of this paper. For this reason, we shall be concerned primarily with economic activity in the broad sense, "the production, exchange, distribution, and consumption of goods

and services" in our competitive society, wherein wealth has taken on a highly symbolic cast. Our task is to search out some of the factors which exert pressure upon individuals to engage in certain of these logically possible alternative responses. This choice, as we shall see, is far from random.

In every society, Adaptation I (conformity to both culture goals and means) is the most common and widely diffused. Were this not so, the stability and continuity of the society could not be maintained. The mesh of expectancies which constitutes every social order is sustained by the modal behavior of its members falling within the first category. Conventional role behavior oriented toward the basic values of the group is the rule rather than the exception. It is this fact alone which permits us to speak of a human aggregate as comprising a group or society.

Conversely, Adaptation IV (rejection of goals and means) is the least common. Persons who "adjust" (or maladjust) in this fashion are, strictly speaking, *in* the society but not *of* it. Sociologically, these constitute the true "aliens." Not sharing the common frame of orientation, they can be included within the societal population merely in a fictional sense. In this category are *some* of the activities of psychotics, psychoneurotics, chronic autists, pariahs, outcasts, vagrants, vagabonds, tramps, chronic drunkards, and drug addicts.[13] These have relinquished, in certain spheres of activity, the culturally

11 This is a level intermediate between the two planes distinguished by Edward Sapir; namely, culture patterns and personal habit systems. See his "Contribution of Psychiatry to an Understanding of Behavior in Society," *Amer. J. Sociol.*, 1937, 42:862-870.

12 This fifth alternative is on a plane clearly different from that of the others. It represents a *transitional* response which seeks to *institutionalize* new procedures oriented toward revamped cultural goals shared by the members of the society. It thus involves efforts to *change* the existing structure rather than to perform accommodative actions *within* this structure, and introduces additional problems with which we are not at the moment concerned.

13 Obviously, this is an elliptical statement. These individuals may maintain some orientation to the values of their particular differentiated groupings within the larger society or, in part, of the conventional society itself. Insofar as they do so, their conduct cannot be classified in the "passive rejection" category (IV). Nels Anderson's description of the behavior and attitudes of the bum, for example, can readily be recast in terms of our analytical scheme. See *The Hobo*, 93-98, *et passim*, Chicago, 1923.

defined goals, involving complete aim-inhibition in the polar case, and their adjustments are not in accord with institutional norms. This is not to say that in some cases the source of their behavioral adjustments is not in part the very social structure which they have in effect repudiated nor that their very existence within a social area does not constitute a problem for the socialized population.

This mode of "adjustment" occurs, as far as structural sources are concerned, when both the culture goals and institutionalized procedures have been assimilated thoroughly by the individual and imbued with affect and high positive value, but where those institutionalized procedures which promise a measure of successful attainment of the goals are not available to the individual. In such instances, there results a twofold mental conflict insofar as the moral obligation for adopting institutional means conflicts with the pressure to resort to illegitimate means (which may attain the goal) and inasmuch as the individual is shut off from means which are both legitimate *and* effective. The competitive order is maintained, but the frustrated and handicapped individual who cannot cope with this order drops out. Defeatism, quietism, and resignation are manifested in escape mechanisms which ultimately lead the individual to "escape" from the requirements of the society. It is an expedient which arises from continued failure to attain the goal by legitimate measures and from an inability to adopt the illegitimate route because of internalized prohibitions and institutionalized compulsives, *during which process the supreme value of the success-goal has as yet not been renounced.* The conflict is resolved by eliminating *both* precipitating elements, the goals and means. The escape is complete, the conflict is eliminated, and the individual is associalized.

Be it noted that where frustration derives from the inaccessibility of effective institutional means for attaining economic or any other type of highly valued "success," that Adaptations II, III, and V (innovation, ritualism, and rebellion) are also possible. The result will be determined by the particular personality, and thus, the *particular* cultural background, involved. Inadequate socialization will result in the innovation response whereby the conflict and frustration are eliminated by relinquishing the institutional means and retaining the success-aspiration; an extreme assimilation of institutional demands will lead to ritualism wherein the goal is dropped as beyond one's reach but conformity to the mores persists; and rebellion occurs when emancipation from the reigning standards, due to frustration or to marginalist perspectives, leads to the attempt to introduce a "new social order."

Our major concern is with the illegitimacy adjustment. This involves the use of conventionally proscribed but frequently effective means of attaining at least the simulacrum of culturally defined success,—wealth, power, and the like. As we have seen, this adjustment occurs when the individual has assimilated the cultural emphasis on success without equally internalizing the morally prescribed norms governing means for its attainment. The question arises, Which phases of our social structure predispose toward this mode of adjustment? We may examine a concrete instance, effectively analyzed by Lohman,[14] which provides a clue to the answer. Lohman has shown that specialized areas of vice in the near north side of Chicago constitute a "normal" response to a situation where the cultural emphasis upon pecuniary success has

[14] Joseph D. Lohman, "The Participant Observer in Community Studies," *Amer. Sociol. Rev.*, 1937, 2:890–898.

been absorbed, but where there is little access to conventional and legitimate means for attaining such success. The conventional occupational opportunities of persons in this area are almost completely limited to manual labor. Given our cultural stigmatization of manual labor, and its correlate, the prestige of white collar work, it is clear that the result is a strain toward innovational practices. The limitation of opportunity to unskilled labor and the resultant low income cannot compete *in terms of conventional standards of achievement* with the high income from organized vice.

For our purposes, this situation involves two important features. First, such antisocial behavior is in a sense "called forth" by certain conventional values of the culture *and* by the class structure involving differential access to the approved opportunities for legitimate, prestige-bearing pursuit of the culture goals. The lack of high integration between the means-and-end elements of the cultural pattern and the particular class structure combine to favor a heightened frequency of antisocial conduct in such groups. The second consideration is of equal significance. Recourse to the first of the alternative responses, legitimate effort, is limited by the fact that actual advance toward desired success-symbols through conventional channels is, despite our persisting open-class ideology,[15] relatively rare and difficult for those handicapped by little formal education and few economic resources. The dominant pressure of group standards of success is, therefore, on the gradual attenuation of legitimate, but by and large ineffective, strivings and the increasing use of illegitimate, but more or less effective, expedients of vice and crime. The cultural demands made on persons in this situation are incompatible. On the one hand, they are asked to orient their conduct toward the prospect of accumulating wealth and on the other, they are largely denied effective opportunities to do so institutionally. The consequences of such structural inconsistency are psychopathological personality, and/or antisocial conduct, and/or revolutionary activities. The equilibrium between culturally designated means and ends becomes highly unstable with the progressive emphasis on attaining the prestige-laden ends by any means whatsoever. Within this context, Capone represents the triumph of amoral intelligence over morally prescribed "failure," when the channels of vertical mobility are closed or narrowed[16] *in a*

15 The shifting historical role of this ideology is a profitable subject for exploration. The "office-boy-to-president" stereotype was once in approximate accord with the facts. Such vertical mobility was probably more common then than now, when the class structure is more rigid. (See the following note.) The ideology largely persists, however, possibly because it still performs a useful function for maintaining the *status quo*. For insofar as it is accepted by the "masses," it constitutes a useful sop for those who might rebel against the entire structure, were this consoling hope removed. This ideology now serves to lessen the probability of Adaptation V. In short, the role of this notion has changed from that of an approximately valid empirical theorem to that of an ideology, in Mannheim's sense.

16 There is a growing body of evidence, though none of it is clearly conclusive, to the effect that our class structure is becoming rigidified and that vertical mobility is declining. Taussig and Joslyn found that American business leaders are being *increasingly* recruited from the upper ranks of our society. The Lynds have also found a "diminished chance to get ahead" for the working classes in Middletown. Manifestly, these objective changes are not alone significant; the individual's subjective evaluation of the situation is a major determinant of the response. The extent to which this change in opportunity for social mobility has been recognized by the least advantaged classes is still conjectural, although the Lynds present some suggestive materials. The writer suggests that a case in point is the increasing frequency of cartoons which observe in a tragi-comic vein that "my old man says everybody can't be President. He says if ya can get three days a week steady on W.P.A. work ya ain't

society which places a high premium on economic affluence and social ascent for all its members.[17]

This last qualification is of primary importance. It suggests that other phases of the social structure besides the extreme emphasis on pecuniary success must be considered if we are to understand the social sources of antisocial behavior. A high frequency of deviate behavior is not generated simply by "lack of opportunity" or by this exaggerated pecuniary emphasis. A comparatively rigidified class structure, a feudalistic or caste order, may limit such opportunities far beyond the point which obtains in our society today. It is only when a system of cultural values extols, virtually above all else, certain *common* symbols of success *for the population at large* while its social structure rigorously restricts or completely eliminates access to approved modes of acquiring these symbols *for a considerable part of the same population* that antisocial behavior ensues on a considerable scale. In other words, our egalitarian ideology denies by implication the existence of noncompeting groups and individuals in the pursuit of pecuniary success. The same body of success-symbols is held to be desirable for all.

These goals are held to *transcend class lines,* not to be bounded by them, yet the actual social organization is such that there exist class differentials in the accessibility of these *common* success-symbols. Frustration and thwarted aspiration lead to the search for avenues of escape from a culturally induced intolerable situation; or unrelieved ambition may eventuate in illicit attempts to acquire the dominant values.[18] The American stress on pecuniary success and ambitiousness for all thus invites exaggerated anxieties, hostilities, neuroses, and antisocial behavior.

This theoretical analysis may go far toward explaining the varying correlations between crime and poverty.[19] Poverty is not an isolated variable. It is one in a complex of interdependent social and cultural variables. When viewed in such a context, it represents quite different states of affairs. Poverty as such, and consequent limitation of opportunity, are not sufficient to induce a conspicuously high rate of criminal

---

doin' so bad either." See F. W. Taussig and C. S. Joslyn, *American Business Leaders,* New York, 1932; R. S. and H. M. Lynd, *Middletown in Transition,* 67 ff., chap. 12, New York, 1937.

[17] The role of the Negro in this respect is of considerable theoretical interest. Certain elements of the Negro population have assimilated the dominant caste's values of pecuniary success and social advancement, but they also recognize that social ascent is at present restricted to their own caste almost exclusively. The pressures upon the Negro which would otherwise derive from the structural inconsistencies we have noticed are hence not identical with those upon lower class whites. See Kingsley Davis, *op. cit.,* 63; John Dollard, *Caste and Class in a Southern Town,* 66 ff., New Haven, 1936; Donald Young, *American Minority Peoples,* 581, New York, 1932.

[18] The psychical coordinates of these processes have been partly established by the experimental evidence concerning *Anspruchsniveaus* and levels of performance. See Kurt Lewin, *Vorsatz, Willie und Bedurfnis,* Berlin, 1926; N. F. Hoppe, "Erfolg und Misserfolg," *Psychol. Forschung,* 1930, 14:1–63; Jerome D. Frank, "Individual Differences in Certain Aspects of the Level of Aspiration," *Amer. J. Psychol.,* 1935, 47:119–128.

[19] Standard criminology texts summarize the data in this field. Our scheme of analysis may serve to resolve some of the theoretical contradictions which P. A. Sorokin indicates. For example, "not everywhere nor always do the poor show a greater proportion of crime . . . many poorer countries have had less crime than the richer countries . . . . The [economic] improvement in the second half of the nineteenth century, and the beginning of the twentieth, has not been followed by a decrease of crime." See his *Contemporary Sociological Theories,* 560–561, New York, 1928. The crucial point is, however, that poverty has varying social significance in different social structures, as we shall see. Hence, one would not expect a linear correlation between crime and poverty.

behavior. Even the often mentioned "poverty in the midst of plenty" will not necessarily lead to this result. Only insofar as poverty and associated disadvantages in competition for the culture values approved for *all* members of the society are linked with the assimilation of a cultural emphasis on monetary accumulation as a symbol of success is antisocial conduct a "normal" outcome. Thus, poverty is less highly correlated with crime in southeastern Europe than in the United States. The possibilities of vertical mobility in these European areas would seem to be fewer than in this country, so that neither poverty *per se* nor its association with limited opportunity is sufficient to account for the varying correlations. It is only when the full configuration is considered, poverty, limited opportunity, and a commonly shared system of success symbols, that we can explain the higher association between poverty and crime in our society than in others where rigidified class structure is coupled with *differential class symbols of achievement.*

In societies such as our own, then, the pressure of prestige-bearing success tends to eliminate the effective social constraint over means employed to this end. "The-end-justifies-the-means" doctrine becomes a guiding tenet for action when the cultural structure unduly exalts the end and the social organization unduly limits possible recourse to approved means. Otherwise put, this notion and associated behavior reflect a lack of cultural coordination. In international relations, the effects of this lack of integration are notoriously apparent. An emphasis upon national power is not readily coordinated with an inept organization of legitimate, i.e., internationally defined and accepted, means for attaining this goal. The result is a tendency toward the abrogation of international law, treaties become scraps of paper, "undeclared warfare" serves as a technical evasion, the bombing of civilian populations is rationalized,[20] just as the same societal situation induces the same sway of illegitimacy among individuals.

The social order we have described necessarily produces this "strain toward dissolution." The pressure of such an order is upon outdoing one's competitors. The choice of means within the ambit of institutional control will persist as long as the sentiments supporting a competitive system, i.e., deriving from the possibility of outranking competitors and hence enjoying the favorable response of others, are distributed throughout the entire system of activities and are not confined merely to the final result. A stable social structure demands a balanced distribution of affect among its various segments. When there occurs a shift of emphasis from the satisfactions deriving from competition itself to almost exclusive concern with successful competition, the resultant stress leads to the breakdown of the regulatory structure.[21] With the resulting attenuation of the institutional imperatives, there occurs an approximation of the situation erroneously held by utilitarians to be typical of society generally wherein calculations of advantage and fear of punishment are the sole regulating agencies. In such situations, as Hobbes observed, force and fraud come to constitute the sole virtues in view of their relative efficiency in attaining goals—which were for him, of course, not culturally derived.

It should be apparent that the fore-

[20] See M. W. Royse, *Aerial Bombardment and the International Regulation of War,* New York, 1928.

[21] Since our primary concern is with the socio-cultural aspects of this problem, the psychological correlates have been only implicitly considered. See Karen Horney, *The Neurotic Personality of Our Time,* New York, 1937, for a psychological discussion of this process.

going discussion is not pitched on a moralistic plane. Whatever the sentiments of the writer or reader concerning the ethical desirability of coordinating the means-and-goals phases of the social structure, one must agree that lack of such coordination leads to anomie. Insofar as one of the most general functions of social organization is to provide a basis for calculability and regularity of behavior, it is increasingly limited in effectiveness as these elements of the structure become dissociated. At the extreme, predictability virtually disappears and what may be properly termed cultural chaos or anomie intervenes.

This statement, being brief, is also incomplete. It has not included an exhaustive treatment of the various structural elements which predispose toward one rather than another of the alternative responses open to individuals; it has neglected, but not denied the relevance of, the factors determining the specific incidence of these responses; it has not enumerated the various concrete responses which are constituted by combinations of specific values of the analytical variables; it has omitted, or included only by implication, any consideration of the social functions performed by illicit responses; it has not tested the full explanatory power of the analytical scheme by examining a large number of group variations in the frequency of deviate and conformist behavior; it has not adequately dealt with rebellious conduct which seeks to refashion the social framework radically; it has not examined the relevance of cultural conflict for an analysis of culture-goal and institutional-means malintegration. It is suggested that these and related problems may be profitably analyzed by this scheme.

10. The Delinquency Subculture

ALBERT K. COHEN

In the following pages we present a portrait of the delinquent subculture. In presenting a thumbnail description of any widely distributed subculture it is impossible to do full justice to the facts, for no brief account can deal with all the varieties and nuances which actually exist. The subcultures of the medical profession, the professional gambler or the jitterbug have many local versions, as does the delinquent subculture. Nonetheless, it is possible, for each of these subcultures, to draw a picture which represents certain themes or traits which run through all the variants. This "ideal-typical" or "full-blown" picture will be fully realized in some of the variants and only approximated, in various degrees, in others. This much, however, may be said for our description of the delinquent subculture. It is a real picture, drawn from life. It is the picture most familiar to students of juvenile delinquency, especially those who, like the group worker, encounter the delinquent gang in its natural habitat, the streets and alleys of our cities. It is the picture that stands out most prominently in the literature of juvenile delinquency. Compare it to a generalized picture of a pear, in which the distinctively pear-like features are accentuated. Many pears will look very like our picture; others will only approximate it. However, if our picture is truly drawn, it will give us a good idea of the shape which distinguishes pears in general from other fruits. This is the kind of validity which we claim for our portrait of the delinquent subculture.

THE CONTENT OF THE DELINQUENT SUBCULTURE

The common expression, "juvenile crime," has unfortunate and misleading connotations. It suggests that we have two kinds of criminals, young and old, but only one kind of crime. It suggests that crime has its meanings and its motives which are much the same for young and old; that the young differ from the old as the apprentice and the master differ at the same trade; that we distinguish the young from the old only because the young are less "set in their ways," less "confirmed" in the same criminal habits, more amenable to treatment and more deserving, because of their tender age, of special consideration.

The problem of the relationship be-

SOURCE. Albert K. Cohen, *Delinquent Boys: The Culture of the Gang,* Glencoe, Illinois: The Free Press, 1958, pp. 23–36, 121–137, 183–184, 185–186, 192, and 193. Copyright © 1955, The Free Press, a Corporation. Reprinted with the permission of The Macmillan Company.

tween juvenile delinquency and adult crime has many facets. To what extent are the offenses of children and adults distributed among the same legal categories, "burglary," "larceny," "vehicle-taking," and so forth? To what extent, even when the offenses are legally identical, do these acts have the same meaning for children and adults? To what extent are the careers of adult criminals continuations of careers of juvenile delinquency? We cannot solve these problems here, but we want to emphasize the danger of making facile and unproven assumptions. If we assume that "crime is crime," that child and adult criminals are practitioners of the same trade, and if our assumptions are false, then the road to error is wide and clear. Easily and unconsciously, we may impute a whole host of notions concerning the nature of crime and its causes, derived from our knowledge and fancies about adult crime, to a large realm of behavior to which these notions are irrelevant. It is better to make no such assumptions; it is better to look at juvenile delinquency with a fresh eye and try to explain what we see.

What we see when we look at the delinquent subculture (and we must not even assume that this describes *all* *juvenile* crime) is that it is *non-utilitarian, malicious* and *negativistic.*

We usually assume that when people steal things, they steal because they want them. They may want them because they can eat them, wear them or otherwise use them; or because they can sell them; or even—if we are given to a psychoanalytic turn of mind—because on some deep symbolic level they substitute or stand for something unconsciously desired but forbidden. All of these explanations have this in common, that they assume that the stealing is a means to an end, namely, the possession of some object of value, and that it is, in this sense, rational and

"utilitarian." However, the fact cannot be blinked—and this fact is of crucial importance in defining our problem—that much gang stealing has no such motivation at all. Even where the value of the object stolen is itself a motivating consideration, the stolen sweets are often sweeter than those acquired by more legitimate and prosaic means. In homelier language, stealing "for the hell of it" and apart from considerations of gain and profit is a valued activity to which attaches glory, prowess and profound satisfaction. There is no accounting in rational and utilitarian terms for the effort expended and the danger run in stealing things which are often discarded, destroyed or casually given away. A group of boys enters a store where each takes a hat, a ball or a light bulb. They then move on to another store where these things are covertly exchanged for like articles. Then they move on to other stores to continue the game indefinitely. They steal a basket of peaches, desultorily munch on a few of them and leave the rest to spoil. They steal clothes they cannot wear and toys they will not use. Unquestionably, most delinquents are from the more "needy" and "underprivileged" classes, and unquestionably many things are stolen because they are intrinsically valued. However, a humane and compassionate regard for their economic disabilities should not blind us to the fact that stealing is not merely an alternative means to the acquisition of objects otherwise difficult of attainment.[1]

[1] See H. M. Tiebout and M. E. Kirkpatrick, "Psychiatric Factors in Stealing," *American Journal of Orthopsychiatry,* 2 (April, 1932), 114–123, which discusses, in an exceptionally lucid manner, the distinction between motivating factors which center around the acquisition of the object and those which center around the commission of the act itself.

The non-utilitarian nature of juvenile delinquency has been noted by many stu-

Can we then account for this stealing by simply describing it as another form of recreation, play or sport? Surely it is that, but why is this form of play so attractive to some and so unappealing to others? Mountain climbing, chess, pinball, number pools and bingo are also different kinds of recreation. Each of us, child or adult, can choose from a host of alternative means for satisfying our common "need" for recreation. But every choice expresses a preference, and every preference reflects something about the chooser or his circumstances that endows the object of his choice with some special quality or virtue. The choice is not self-explanatory nor is it arbitrary or random. Each form of recreation is distributed in a characteristic way among the age, sex and social class sectors of our population. The ex-

planation of these distributions and of the way they change is often puzzling, sometimes fascinating and rarely platitudinous.

By the same logic, it is an imperfect answer to our problem to say: "Stealing is but another way of satisfying the universal desire for status." Nothing is more obvious from numberless case histories of subcultural delinquents that they steal to achieve recognition and to avoid isolation or opprobrium. This is an important insight and part of the foundation on which we shall build. But the question still haunts us: "Why is stealing a claim to status in one group and a degrading blot in another?"

If stealing itself is not motivated by rational, utilitarian considerations, still less are the manifold other activities which constitute the delinquent's repertoire. Throughout there is a kind of *malice* apparent, an enjoyment in the discomfiture of others, a delight in the defiance of taboos itself. Thrasher quotes one gang delinquent:

We did all kinds of dirty tricks for fun. We'd see a sign, "Please keep the streets clean," but we'd tear it down and say: "We don't feel like keeping it clean." One day we put a can of glue in the engine of a man's car. We would always tear things down. That would make us laugh and feel good, to have so many jokes.°

The gang exhibits this gratuitous hostility toward non-gang peers as well as adults. Apart from its more dramatic manifestations in the form of gang wars, there is keen delight in terrorizing "good" children, in driving them from playgrounds and gyms for which the gang itself may have little use, and in general in making themselves obnoxious to the virtuous. The same spirit is evident in playing hookey and in misbehavior in school. The teacher and her

---

dents. ". . . while older offenders may have definitely crystallized beliefs about profitable returns from anti-social conduct, it is very clear that in childhood and in earlier youth delinquency is certainly not entered into as a paying proposition in any ordinary sense." William Healy and Augusta F. Bronner, *New Light on Delinquency and Its Treatment* (New Haven, Conn.: Yale University Press, 1936), p. 22. "The juvenile property offender's thefts, at least at the start are usually 'for fun' and not for gain." Paul Tappan, *Juvenile Delinquency* (New York: McGraw-Hill Book Company, 1949), p. 143. "Stealing, the leading predatory activity of the adolescent gang, is as much a result of the sport motive as of a desire for revenue." Frederic M. Thrasher. *The Gang* (Chicago: University of Chicago Press, 1936), p. 143. "In its early stages, delinquency is clearly a form of play." Henry D. McKay, "The Neighborhood and Child Conduct," *Annals of the American Academy of Political and Social Science*, 261 (January, 1949), 37. See also Barbara Bellow et al., "Prejudice in Seaside," *Human Relations*, 1 (1947), 15–16 and Sophia M. Robison et al., "An Unsolved Problem in Group Relations," *Journal of Educational Psychology*, 20 (November, 1946), 154–162. The last cited paper is an excellent description of the non-utilitarian, malicious and negativistic quality of the delinquent subculture and is the clearest statement in the literature that a satisfactory theory of delinquency must make sense of these facts.

° Frederic M. Thrasher, *The Gang* (Chicago: University of Chicago Press, 1936), pp. 94–95.

rules are not merely something onerous to be evaded. They are to be *flouted*. There is an element of active spite and malice, contempt and ridicule, challenge and defiance, exquisitely symbolized, in an incident, described to the writer by Mr. Henry D. McKay, of defecating on the teacher's desk.[2]

All this suggests also the intention of our term "negativistic." The delinquent subculture is not only a set of rules, a design for living which is different from or indifferent to or even in conflict with the norms of the "respectable" adult society. It would appear at least plausible that it is defined by its "negative polarity" to those norms. That is, the delinquent subculture takes its norms from the larger culture but turns them upside down. The delinquent's conduct is right, by the standards of his subculture, precisely *because* it is wrong by the norms of the larger culture.[3]

"Malicious" and "negativistic" are foreign to the delinquent's vocabulary, but he will often assure us, sometimes ruefully, sometimes with a touch of glee or even pride, that he is "just plain mean."

In describing what might be called the "spirit" of the delinquent culture, we have suggested also its *versatility*. Of the "antisocial" activities of the delinquent gangs, stealing, of course, looms largest. Stealing itself can be, and for the gang usually is, a diversified occupation. It may steal milk bottles, candy, fruit, pencils, sports equipment and cars; it may steal from drunks, homes, stores, schools and filling stations. No gang runs the whole gamut but neither is it likely to "specialize" as do many adult criminal gangs and "solitary" delinquents. More to our point, however, is the fact that stealing tends to go hand-in-hand with "other property offenses," "malicious mischief," "vandalism," "trespass" and "truancy." This quality of versatility and the fusion of versatility and malice are manifest in the following quotation:

> We would get some milk bottles in front of the grocery store and break them in somebody's hallway. Then we would break windows or get some garbage cans and throw them down someone's front stairs. After doing all this dirty work and running through alleys and yards, we'd go over to a grocery store. There, some of the boys would hide in a hallway while I would get a basket of grapes. When the man came after me, why the boys would jump out of their places and each grab a basket of grapes.[°]

Dozens of young offenders, after relating to the writer this delinquent episode and that, have summarized: "I guess

conduct which result in personal degradation and dishonor in a conventional group, serve to enhance and elevate the personal prestige and status of a member of the delinquent group."

[°] Clifford R. Shaw and Henry D. McKay, *Social Factors in Juvenile Delinquency, op. cit.,* p. 18.

---

[2] To justify the characterization of the delinquent subculture as "malicious" by multiplying citations from authorities would be empty pedantry. The malice is evident in any detailed description of juvenile gang life. We commend in particular, however, the cited works of Thrasher, Shaw and McKay and Robison et al. One aspect of this "gratuitous hostility" deserves special mention, however, for the benefit of those who see in the provision of facilities for "wholesome recreation" some magical therapeutic virtue. "On entering a playground or a gym the first activity of gang members is to disrupt and interrupt whatever activities are going on. Nongang members flee, and when the coast is clear the gang plays desultorily on the apparatus or carries on horseplay." Sophia Robison et al., *op. cit.,* p. 159. See, to the same effect, the excellent little book by Kenneth H. Rogers, *Street Gangs in Toronto* (Toronto: The Ryerson Press, 1945), pp. 18–19.

[3] Clifford R. Shaw and Henry D. McKay, in their *Social Factors in Juvenile Delinquency,* Vol. 2 of National Commission on Law Observance and Enforcement, *Report on the Causes of Crime* (Washington: U. S. Government Printing Office, 1931), p. 241, come very close to making this point quite explicitly: "In fact the standards of these groups may represent a complete reversal of the standards and norms of conventional society. Types of

we was just ornery." A generalized, diversified, protean "orneriness," not this or that specialized delinquent pursuit, seems best to describe the vocation of the delinquent gang.[4]

Another characteristic of the subculture of the delinquent gang is *short-run hedonism*. There is little interest in long-run goals, in planning activities and budgeting time, or in activities involving knowledge and skills to be acquired only through practice, deliberation and study. The members of the gang typically congregate, with no specific activity in mind, at some street corner, candy store or other regular rendezvous. They "hang around," "rough-housing," "chewing the fat" and "waiting for something to turn up." They may respond impulsively to somebody's suggestion to play ball, go swimming, engage in some sort of mischief or do something else that offers excitement. They do not take kindly to organized and supervised recreation, which subjects them to a regime of schedules and impersonal rules. They are impatient, impetuous and out for "fun," with little heed to the remoter gains and costs. It is to be noted that this short-run hedonism is not inherently delinquent, and indeed it would be a serious error to think of the delinquent gang as dedicated solely to the cultivation of juvenile crime. Even in the most seriously delinquent gang only a small fraction of the "fun" is specifically and intrinsically delinquent. Furthermore, short-run hedonism is not characteristic of delinquent groups alone. On the contrary, it is common throughout the social class from which delinquents characteristically come. However, in the delinquent gang it reaches its finest flower. It is the fabric, as it were, of which delinquency is the most brilliant and spectacular thread.[5]

Another characteristic not peculiar to the delinquent gang but a conspicuous ingredient of its culture is an emphasis on *group autonomy*, or intolerance of restraint except from the informal pressures within the group itself. Relations with gang members tend to be intensely solidary and imperious. Relations with other groups tend to be indifferent, hostile or rebellious. Gang members are unusually resistant to the efforts of home, school and other agencies to regulate, not only their delinquent activities, but any activities carried on within the group, and to efforts to compete with the gang for the time and other resources of its members. It may be argued that the resistance of gang members to the authority of the home may not be a result of their membership in gangs but that membership in gangs, on the contrary, is a result of ineffective family supervision, the breakdown of parental authority and the hostility of the child toward the parents; in short, that the delinquent gang recruits members who have already achieved autonomy. Certainly a previous breakdown in family controls facilitates recruitment into delinquent

[4] *Federal Probation*, 18 (March, 1954), 3–16 contains an extremely valuable symposium on vandalism, which highlights all of the characteristics we have imputed to the delinquent subculture. . . .

[5] See the splendid report on "Working with a Street Gang" in Sylvan S. Furman (ed.), *Reaching the Unreached* (New York: New York City Youth Board, 1952), pp. 112–121. On this quality of short-run hedonism we quote, p. 13:
One boy once told me, "Now, for example, you take an average day. What happens? We come down to the restaurant and we sit in the restaurant, and sit and sit. All right, say, er . . . after a couple of hours in the restaurant, maybe we'll go to a poolroom, shoot a little pool, that's if somebody's got the money. O. K., a little pool, come back. By this time the restaurant is closed. We go in the candy store, sit around the candy store for a while, and that's it, that's all we do, man."
See also Barbara Bellow et al., *op. cit.*, pp. 4–15, and Ruth Topping, "Treatment of the Pseudo-Social Boy," *American Journal of Orthopsychiatry*, Vol. 13 (April, 1943), pp. 353–360.

gangs. But we are not speaking of the autonomy, the emancipation of *individuals*. It is not the individual delinquent but the gang that is autonomous. For many of our subcultural delinquents the claims of the home are very real and very compelling. The point is that the gang is a separate, distinct and often irresistible focus of attraction, loyalty and solidarity. The claims of the home versus the claims of the gang may present a real dilemma, and in such cases the breakdown of family controls is as much a casualty as a cause of gang membership.[6]

SOME ATTEMPTS AT EXPLANATION

The literature on juvenile delinquency has seldom come to grips with the problem of accounting for the content and spirit of the delinquent subculture. To say that this content is "traditional" in certain areas and is "handed down" from generation to generation is but to state the problem rather than to offer a solution. Neither does the "social disorganization" theory[7] come to grips with the facts. This theory holds that the delinquent culture flourishes in the "interstitial areas" of our great cities. These are formerly "good" residential areas which have been invaded by industry and commerce, are no longer residentially attractive, and are inhabited by a heterogeneous, economically depressed and highly mobile population with no permanent stake in the community. These people lack the solidarity, the community spirit, the motivation and the residential stability necessary for organization, on a neighborhood basis,

for the effective control of delinquency. To this argument we may make two answers. First, recent research has revealed that many, if not most, such "interstitial" and "slum" areas are by no means lacking in social organization. To the observer who has lived in them, many such areas are anything but the picture of chaos and heterogeneity which we find drawn in the older literature. We find, on the contrary, a vast and ramifying network of informal associations among like-minded people, not a horde of anonymous families and individuals, strangers to one another, rudely jostling one another in the struggle for existence. The social organization of the slum may lack the spirit and the objectives of organization in the "better" neighborhoods, but the slum is not necessarily a jungle. In the "delinquency area" as elsewhere, there is an awareness of community, an involvement of the individual in the lives and doings of the neighborhood, a concern about his reputation among his neighbors. The organization which exists may indeed not be adequate for the effective control of delinquency and for the solution of other social problems, but the qualities and defects of organization are not to be confused with the absence of organization.[8] However, granting the absence of community pressures and concerted action for the repression of delinquency, we are confronted by a second deficiency in this argument. It is wholly negative. It accounts for the presence of delinquency by the absence of effective constraints. If one is disposed to be delinquent, the absence of constraint will facilitate the expression of these impulses. It will not, however, account for the presence of these impulses. The social disorganization argument leaves

---

[6] The solidarity of the gang and the dependence of its members upon one another are especially well described in Barbara Bellow et al., *op. cit.*, p. 16 and Sophia Robison et al., *op. cit.*, p. 158.

[7] See Clifford R. Shaw and Henry D. McKay, *Social Factors in Juvenile Delinquency, op. cit.*, p. 111.

[8] See William Foote Whyte, "Social Organization in the Slums," *American Sociological Review*, 8 (February, 1943), 34–39.

open the question of the origin of the impulse, of the peculiar content and spirit of the delinquent subculture.

Another theory which has enjoyed some vogue is the "culture conflict" theory.[9] According to this view, these areas of high mobility and motley composition are lacking in cultural unity. The diverse ethnic and racial stocks have diverse and incongruent standards and codes, and these standards and codes are in turn inconsistent with those of the schools and other official representatives of the larger society. In this welter of conflicting cultures, the young person is confused and bedeviled. The adult world presents him with no clear-cut and authoritative models. Subject to a multitude of conflicting patterns, he respects none and assimilates none. He develops no respect for the legal order because it represents a culture which finds no support in his social world. He becomes delinquent.

From the recognition that there exists a certain measure of cultural diversity, it is a large step to the conclusion that the boy is confronted by such a hodge-podge of definitions that he can form no clear conception of what is "right" and "wrong." It is true that some ethnic groups look more tolerantly on certain kinds of delinquency than others do; that some even encourage certain minor forms of delinquency such as picking up coal off railroad tracks; that respect for the courts and the police are less well established among some groups and that other cultural differences exist. Nonetheless, it is questionable that there is any ethnic or racial group which positively encourages or even condones stealing, vandalism, habitual truancy and the general negativism which characterizes the delinquent subculture. The existence of culture conflict must not be allowed to obscure the important measure of consensus which exists on the essential "wrongness" of these activities, except under special circumstances which are considered mitigating by this or that ethnic subculture. Furthermore, if we should grant that conflicting definitions leave important sectors of conduct morally undefined for the boy in the delinquency area, we must still explain why he fills the gap in the particular way he does. Like the social disorganization theory, the culture conflict theory is at best incomplete. The delinquent subculture is not a fund of blind, amoral, "natural" impulses which inevitably well up in the absence of a code of socially acquired inhibitions. It is itself a positive code with a definite if unconventional moral flavor, and it demands a positive explanation in its own right.

Another view which currently commands a good deal of respect we may call the "illicit means" theory.[10] According to this view our American culture, with its strongly democratic and equalitarian emphasis, indoctrinates all social classes impartially with a desire for high social status and a sense of ignominy attaching to low social status. The symbols of high status are to an extraordinary degree the possession and the conspicuous display of economic goods. There is therefore an unusually intense desire for economic goods diffused throughout our population to a degree unprecedented in other societies. However, the means and the opportunities for the legitimate achieve-

<hr>

[9] See Clifford R. Shaw and Henry D. McKay, *Social Factors in Juvenile Delinquency, op. cit.*, p. 115.

[10] See Clifford R. Shaw and Henry D. McKay, *Juvenile Delinquency and Urban Areas: A Study of Rates of Delinquents in Relation to Differential Characteristics of Local Communities in American Cities* (Chicago: University of Chicago Press, 1942), pp. 180–181. Henry D. McKay, *op. cit.*, p. 35, and Robert K. Merton, "Social Structure and Anomie," *American Sociological Review*, 3 (October, 1938) 672–682.

ment of these goals are distributed most unequally among the various segments of the population. Among those segments which have the least access to the legitimate channels of "upward mobility" there develop strong feelings of deprivation and frustration and strong incentives to find other means to the achievement of status and its symbols. Unable to attain their goals by lawful means, these disadvantaged segments of the population are under strong pressure to resort to crime, the only means available to them.

This argument is sociologically sophisticated and highly plausible as an explanation for adult professional crime and for the property delinquency of some older and semi-professional juvenile thieves. Unfortunately, it fails to account for the non-utilitarian quality of the subculture which we have described. Were the participant in the delinquent subculture merely employing illicit means to the end of acquiring economic goods, he would show more respect for the goods he has thus acquired. Furthermore, the destructiveness, the versatility, the zest and the wholesale negativism which characterizes the delinquent subculture are beyond the purview of this theory. None of the theories we have considered comes to grips with the data: the distinctive content of the delinquent subculture. . . .

WHAT THE DELINQUENT SUBCULTURE HAS TO OFFER

The delinquent subculture, we suggest, is a way of dealing with the problems of adjustment we have described. These problems are chiefly status problems: certain children are denied status in the respectable society because they cannot meet the criteria of the respectable status system. The delinquent subculture deals with these problems by providing criteria of status which these children *can* meet.

This statement is highly elliptical and is based upon a number of assumptions whose truth is by no means self-evident. It is not, for example, self-evident that people whose status positions are low must necessarily feel deprived, injured or ego-involved in that low status. Whether they will or not depends upon several considerations.

Our ego-involvement in a given comparison with others depends upon our "status universe." "Whom do we measure ourselves against?" is the crucial question. In some other societies virtue may consist in willing acceptance of the role of peasant, low-born commoner or member of an inferior caste and in conformity to the expectations of that role. If others are richer, more nobly born or more able than oneself, it is by the will of an inscrutable Providence and not to be imputed to one's own moral defect. The sting of status inferiority is thereby removed or mitigated; one measures himself only against those of like social position. We have suggested, however, that an important feature of American "democracy," perhaps of the Western European tradition in general, is the tendency to measure oneself against "all comers." This means that, for children as for adults, one's sense of personal worth is at stake in status comparisons with all other persons, at least of one's own age and sex, whatever their family background or material circumstances. It means that, in the lower levels of our status hierarchies, whether adult or juvenile, there is a chronic fund of motivation, conscious or repressed, to elevate one's status position, either by striving to climb within the established status system or by redefining the criteria of status so that one's present attributes become status-giving assets. It has been suggested, for example, that such typically working-class forms of Protestantism as the Holiness sects owe their appeal to the fact that they reverse the respectable status system; it is the humble, the simple and the dispossessed who sit at the right hand of God, whereas worldly goods, power and knowledge are as nothing in His eyes. In like manner, we offer the view that the delinquent subculture is one solution to a kindred problem on the juvenile level.

Another consideration affecting the degree of privation experienced in a given status position is the "status source." A person's status, after all, is how he stands in somebody's eyes. Status, then, is not a fixed property of the person but varies with the point of view of whoever is doing the judging. I may be revered by some and despised by others. A crucial question then becomes: "Whose respect or admiration do I value?" That *you* think well or ill of me may or may not *matter* to me.

It may be argued that the working-class boy does not *care* what middle-class people think of him, that he is ego-involved only in the opinions of his family, his friends, his working-class neighbors. A definitive answer to this argument can come only from research designed to get at the facts. This research, in our opinion, is yet to be done. There is, however, reason to believe that most children are sensitive *to some degree* about the attitudes of *any persons* with whom they are thrown into more than the most superficial kind of contact. The contempt or indifference of others, particularly of those like schoolmates and teachers, with whom we are constrained to associate for long hours every day, is difficult, we suggest, to shrug off. It poses a problem with which a person may conceivably attempt to cope in a variety of ways. He

may make an active effort to change himself in conformity with the expectations of others; he may attempt to justify or explain away his inferiority in terms which will exculpate him; he may tell himself that he really doesn't care what these people think; he may react with anger and aggression. But the least probable response is simple, uncomplicated, honest indifference. If we grant the probable truth of the claim that most American working-class children are most sensitive to status sources on their own level, it does not follow that they take lightly rejection, disparagement and censure from other status sources.

Even on their "own" social level, the situation is far from simple. The "working-class," we have repeatedly emphasized, is not culturally homogeneous. Not only is there much diversity in the cultural standards applied by one's own working-class neighbors and kin, so that it is difficult to find a "working-class" milieu in which "middle-class" standards are not important. In addition, the "working-class" culture we have described is, after all, an ideal type; most working-class *people* are culturally ambivalent. Due to lack of capacity, of the requisite "character structure" or of "luck," they may be working class in terms of job and income; they may have accepted this status with resignation and rationalized it to their satisfaction; and by example, by class-linked techniques of child training and by failure to support the middle-class agencies of socialization they may have produced children deficient in the attributes that make for status in middle-class terms. Nevertheless, all their lives, through all the major media of mass indoctrination—the schools, the movies, the radio, the newspapers and the magazines—the middle-class powers-that-be that manipulate these media have been trying to "sell" them on middle-class values and the middle-class standard of living. Then there is the "propaganda of the deed," the fact that they have seen with their own eyes working-class contemporaries "get ahead" and "make the grade" in a middle-class world. In consequence of all this, we suspect that few working-class parents unequivocally repudiate as intrinsically worthless middle-class objectives. There is good reason to believe that the modesty of working-class aspirations is partly a matter of trimming one's sails to the available opportunities and resources and partly a matter of unwillingness to accept the discipline which upward striving entails.

However complete and successful a person's accommodation to an humble status, the vitality of middle-class goals, of the "American dream," is nonetheless likely to manifest itself in his aspirations for his children. His expectations may not be grandiose, but he will want his children to be "better off" than he. Whatever his own work history and social reputation may be, he will want his children to be "steady" and "respectable." He may exert few positive pressures to "succeed," and the experiences he provides his children may even incapacitate them for success; he may be puzzled at the way they "turn out." But whatever the measure of his own responsibility in accounting for the product, he is not likely to judge that product by unadulterated "corner-boy" standards. Even "corner-boy" parents, although they may value in their children such corner-boy virtues as generosity to friends, personal loyalty and physical prowess, are likely also to be gratified by recognition by middle-class representatives and by the kinds of achievement for which the college-boy way of life is a prerequisite. Even in

the working-class milieu from which he acquired his incapacity for middle-class achievement, the working-class corner-boy may find himself at a status disadvantage as against his more upwardly mobile peers.

Lastly, of course, is that most ubiquitous and inescapable of status sources, oneself. Technically, we do not call the person's attitudes towards himself "status" but rather "self-esteem," or, when the quality of the self-attitude is specifically moral, "conscience" or "superego." The important question for us is this: To what extent, if at all, do boys who are typically "working-class" and "corner-boy" in their overt behavior evaluate themselves by "middle-class," "college-boy" standards? For our overt behavior, however closely it conforms to one set of norms, need not argue against the existence or effectiveness of alternative and conflicting norms. The failure of our own behavior to conform to our own expectations is an elementary and commonplace fact which gives rise to the tremendously important consequences of guilt, self-recrimination, anxiety and self-hatred. The reasons for the failure of self-expectations and overt conduct to agree are complex. One reason is that we often internalize more than one set of norms, each of which would dictate a different course of action in a given life-situation; since we can only *do* one thing at a time, however, we are forced to choose between them or somehow to compromise. In either case, we fall short of the full realization of our own expectations and must somehow cope with the residual discrepancy between those expectations and our overt behavior.

We have suggested that corner-boy children (like their working-class parents) internalize middle-class standards to a sufficient degree to create a fundamental ambivalence towards their own corner-boy behavior. Again, we are on somewhat speculative ground where fundamental research remains to be done. The coexistence within the same personality of a corner-boy and a college-boy morality may appear more plausible, however, if we recognize that they are not simple antitheses of one another and that parents and others may in all sincerity attempt to indoctrinate both. For example, the goals upon which the college-boy places such great value, such as intellectual and occupational achievement, and the college-boy virtues of ambitiousness and pride in self-sufficiency are not as such disparaged by the corner-boy culture. The meritoriousness of standing by one's friends and the desire to have a good time here and now do not by definition preclude the desire to help oneself and to provide for the future. It is no doubt the rule, rather than the exception, that most children, college-boy and corner-boy alike, would like to enjoy the best of both worlds. *In practice,* however, the substance that is consumed in the pursuit of one set of values is not available for the pursuit of the other. The sharpness of the dilemma and the degree of the residual discontent depend upon a number of things, notably, the intensity with which both sets of norms have been internalized, the extent to which the life-situations which one encounters compel a choice between them, and the abundance and appropriateness of the skills and resources at one's disposal. The child of superior intelligence, for example, may find it easier than his less gifted peers to meet the demands of the college-boy standards without failing his obligations to his corner-boy associates.

It is a plausible assumption, then, that the working-class boy whose status is low in middle-class terms *cares* about that status, that this status confronts him with a genuine problem of adjustment. To this problem of adjustment there are a variety of conceivable responses, of which participation in the creation and the maintenance of the delinquent subculture is one. Each mode of response entails costs and yields gratifications of its own. The circumstances which tip the balance in favor of the one or the other are obscure. One mode of response is to desert the corner-boy for the college-boy way of life. To the reader of Whyte's *Street Corner Society* the costs are manifest. It is hard, at best, to be a college-boy and to run with the corner-boys. It entails great effort and sacrifice to the degree that one has been indoctrinated in what we have described as the working-class socialization process; its rewards are frequently long-deferred; and for many working-class boys it makes demands which they are, in consequence of their inferior linguistic, academic and "social" skills, not likely ever to meet. Nevertheless, a certain proportion of working-class boys accept the challenge of the middle-class status system and play the status game by the middle-class rules.

Another response, perhaps the most common, is what we may call the "stable corner-boy response." It represents an acceptance of the corner-boy way of life and an effort to make the best of a situation. If our reasoning is correct, it does not resolve the dilemmas we have described as inherent in the corner-boy position in a largely middle-class world, although these dilemmas may be mitigated by an effort to disengage oneself from dependence upon middle-class status-sources and by withdrawing, as far as possible, into a sheltering community of like-minded working-class children. Unlike the delinquent response, it avoids the radical rupture of good relations with even working-class adults and does not represent as irretrievable a renunciation of upward mobility. It does not incur the active hostility of middle-class persons and therefore leaves the way open to the pursuit of some values, such as jobs, which these people control. It represents a preference for the familiar, with its known satisfactions and its known imperfections, over the risks and uncertainties as well as the moral costs of the college-boy response, on the one hand, and the delinquent response on the other.

What does the delinquent response have to offer? Let us be clear, first, about what this response is and how it differs from the stable corner-boy response. The hallmark of the delinquent subculture is the explicit and wholesale repudiation of middle-class standards and the adoption of their very antithesis. *The corner-boy culture is not specifically delinquent.* Where it leads to behavior which may be defined as delinquent, e.g., truancy, it does so not because nonconformity to middle-class norms *defines* conformity to corner-boy norms but because conformity to middle-class norms *interferes with* conformity to corner-boy norms. The corner-boy plays truant because he does not like school, because he wishes to escape from a dull and unrewarding and perhaps humiliating situation. But truancy is not defined as intrinsically valuable and status-giving. The member of the delinquent subculture plays truant because "good" middle-class (and working-class) children do not play truant. Corner-boy resistance to being herded and marshalled by middle-class figures is not the same as the delinquent's flouting and jeering of those middle-class figures and active ridicule of those who submit. The corner-boy's ethic of reciprocity, his quasi-communal attitude toward the property of in-group members, is shared by the delinquent.

But this ethic of reciprocity does not sanction the deliberate and "malicious" violation of the property rights of persons outside the in-group. We have observed that the differences between the corner-boy and the college-boy or middle-class culture are profound but that in many ways they are profound differences in emphasis. We have remarked that the corner-boy culture does not so much repudiate the value of many middle-class achievements as it emphasizes certain other values which make such achievements improbable. In short, the corner-boy culture temporizes with middle-class morality; the full-fledged delinquent subculture does not.

It is precisely here, we suggest, in the refusal to temporize, that the appeal of the delinquent subculture lies. Let us recall that it is characteristically American, not specifically working-class or middle-class, to measure oneself against the widest possible status universe, to seek status against "all comers," to be "as good as" or "better than" anybody—anybody, that is, within one's own age and sex category. As long as the working-class corner-boy clings to a version, however attenuated and adulterated, of the middle-class culture, he must recognize his inferiority to working-class and middle-class college-boys. The delinquent subculture, on the other hand, permits no ambiguity of the status of the delinquent relative to that of anybody else. In terms of the norms of the delinquent subculture, defined by its negative polarity to the respectable status system, the delinquent's very nonconformity to middle-class standards sets him above the most exemplary college boy.

Another important function of the delinquent subculture is the legitimation of aggression. We surmise that a certain amount of hostility is generated among working-class children against middle-class persons, with their airs of superiority, disdain or condescension and against middle-class norms, which are, in a sense, the cause of their status-frustration. To infer inclinations to aggression from the existence of frustration is hazardous; we know that aggression is not an inevitable and not the only consequence of frustration. So here too we must feel our way with caution. Ideally, we should like to see systematic research, probably employing "depth interview" and "projective" techniques, to get at the relationship between status position and aggressive dispositions toward the rules which determine status and toward persons variously distributed in the status hierarchy. Nevertheless, despite our imperfect knowledge of these things, we would be blind if we failed to recognize that bitterness, hostility and jealousy and all sorts of retributive fantasies are among the most common and typically human responses to public humiliation. However, for the child who temporizes with middle-class morality, overt aggression and even the conscious recognition of his own hostile impulses are inhibited, for he acknowledges the *legitimacy* of the rules in terms of which he is stigmatized. For the child who breaks clean with middle-class morality, on the other hand, there are no moral inhibitions on the free expression of aggression against the sources of his frustration. Moreover, the connection we suggest between status-frustration and the aggressiveness of the delinquent subculture seems to us more plausible than many frustration-aggression hypotheses because it involves no assumptions about obscure and dubious "displacement" of aggression against "substitute" targets. The target in this case is the manifest cause of the status problem.

It seems to us that the mechanism of "reaction-formation" should also play a part here. We have made much of the corner-boy's basic ambivalence, his uneasy acknowledgement, while he lives by the standards of his corner-boy culture, of the legitimacy of college-boy standards. May we assume that when the delinquent seeks to obtain unequivocal status by repudiating, once and for all, the norms of the college-boy culture, these norms really undergo total extinction? Or do they, perhaps, linger on, underground, as it were, repressed, unacknowledged but an ever-present threat to the adjustment which has been achieved at no small cost? There is much evidence from clinical psychology that moral norms, once effectively internalized, are not lightly thrust aside or extinguished. If a new moral order is evolved which offers a more satisfactory solution to one's life problems, the old order usually continues to press for recognition, but if this recognition is granted, the applecart is upset. The symptom of this obscurely felt, ever-present threat is clinically known as "anxiety," and the literature of psychiatry is rich with devices for combatting this anxiety, this threat to a hard-won victory. One such device is reaction-formation. Its hallmark is an "exaggerated," "disproportionate," "abnormal" intensity of response, "inappropriate" to the stimulus which seems to elicit it. The unintelligibility of the response, the "over-reaction," becomes intelligible when we see that it has the function of reassuring the actor against an *inner* threat to his defenses as well as the function of meeting an external situation on its own terms. Thus we have the mother who "compulsively" showers "inordinate" affection upon a child to reassure herself against her latent hostility and we have the male adolescent whose awkward and immoderate masculinity reflects a basic insecurity about his own sex-role. In like manner, we would expect the delinquent boy who, after all, has been socialized in a society dominated by a middle-class morality and who can never quite escape the blandishments of middle-class society, to seek to maintain his safeguards against seduction. Reaction-formation, in his case, should take the form of an "irrational," "malicious," "unaccountable" hostility to the enemy within the gates as well as without: the norms of the respectable middle-class society.[11]

[11] No single strand of our argument concerning the motivation of the delinquent subculture is entirely original. All have been at least adumbrated and some quite trenchantly formulated by others.

The idea that aggressive behavior, including crime and delinquency, are often reactions to difficulties in achieving status in legitimate status systems has been remarked by many, although the systematic linkage between the particular status problems we have described and social class position has not been well developed in the literature. Caroline B. Zachry, for example, in *Emotion and Conduct in Adolescence* (New York: D. Appleton-Century Company, 1940), pp. 187, 200–209, 245–246, has a thoughtful discussion of the ego-damage resulting from inability to compete effectively in school and of the function of aggressive behavior in maintaining self-esteem. Arthur L. Wood, in Social Disorganization and Crime," *Encyclopedia of Criminology* (New York: Philosophical Library, 1949), pp. 466–471, states that the highest crime rates tend to occur in those minority culture groups "which have become acculturated to the majority-group patterns of behavior, but due to hostility toward them they have failed to succeed in competition for social status." Robert B. Zajonc, in "Aggressive Attitudes of the 'Stranger' as a Function of Conformity Pressures," *Human Relations*, 5 (1952), 205–216, has experimentally tested the general hypothesis, although not in connection with delinquency or crime, that a "need to conform" with a pattern of behavior coupled with inability to conform successfully generates hostile attitudes towards that pattern.

The general notion of negativism as an ego-salving type of reaction-formation, which plays such an important part in the theory we have outlined, is common in the psychoanalytical literature. It has been brilliantly developed with specific reference to criminality in a paper by George Devereux, "Social Negativism and Criminal Psychopathology," *Journal of Criminal Psychopathology*, 1 (April, 1940), 322–338 and applied to other behavior problems in

If our reasoning is correct, it should throw some light upon the peculiar quality of "property delinquency" in the delinquent subculture. We have already seen how the rewardingness of a college-boy and middle-class way of life depends, to a great extent, upon general respect for property rights. In an urban society, in particular, the possession and display of property are the most ready and public badges of reputable social-class status and are, for that reason, extraordinarily ego-involved. That property actually is a reward for middle-class morality is in part only a plausible fiction, but in general there is certainly a relationship between the practice of that morality and the possession of property. The middle-classes have, then, a strong interest in scrupulous regard for property rights, not only because property is "intrinsically" valuable but because the full enjoyment of their status requires that that status be readily recognizable and therefore that property adhere to those who earn it. The cavalier misappropriation or destruction of property, therefore, is not only a diversion or diminution of wealth; it is an attack on the middle-class where their egos are most vulnerable. Group stealing, institutionalized in the delinquent subculture, is not just a way of *getting* something. It is a means that is the antithesis of sober and diligent "labour in a calling." It expresses contempt for a way of life by making its opposite a criterion of status. Money and other valuables are not, as such, despised by the delinquent. For the delinquent and the non-delinquent alike, money is a most glamorous and efficient means to a variety of ends and one cannot have too much of it. But, in the delinquent subculture, the stolen

George Devereux and Malcolm E. Moos, "The Social Structure of Prisons, and the Organic Tensions," *Journal of Criminal Psychopathology*, 4 (October, 1942), 306–324.

dollar has an odor of sanctity that does not attach to the dollar saved or the dollar earned.

This delinquent system of values and way of life does its job of problem-solving most effectively when it is adopted as a group solution. The efficacy of a given change in values as a solution and therefore the motivation to such a change depends heavily upon the availability of "reference groups" within which the "deviant values" are already institutionalized, or whose members would stand to profit from such a system of deviant values if each were assured of the support and concurrence of the others. So it is with delinquency. We do not suggest that joining in the creation or perpetuation of a delinquent subculture is the only road to delinquency. We do believe, however, that for most delinquents delinquency would not be available as a response were it not socially legitimized and given a kind of respectability, albeit by a restricted community of fellow-adventurers. In this respect, the adoption of delinquency is like the adoption of the practice of appearing at the office in open-collar and shirt sleeves. Is it much more comfortable, is it more sensible than the full regalia? Is it neat? Is it dignified? The arguments in the affirmative will appear much more forceful if the practice is already established in one's milieu or if one senses that others are prepared to go along if someone makes the first tentative gestures. Indeed, to many of those who sweat and chafe in ties and jackets, the possibility of an alternative may not even occur until they discover that it has been adopted by their colleagues.

This way of looking at delinquency suggests an answer to a certain paradox. Countless mothers have protested that their "Johnny" was a good boy until he fell in with a certain bunch. But the mothers of Johnny's compan-

ions hold the same view with respect to their own offspring. It is conceivable and even probable that some of these mothers are naive, that one or more of these youngsters are "rotten apples" who infected the others. We suggest, however, that all of the mothers may be right, that there is a certain chemistry in the group situation itself which engenders that which was not there before, that group interaction is a sort of catalyst which releases potentialities not otherwise visible. This is especially true when we are dealing with a problem of status-frustration. Status, by definition, is a grant of respect from others. A new system of norms, which measures status by criteria which one can meet, is of no value unless others are prepared to apply those criteria, and others are not likely to do so unless one is prepared to reciprocate.[12]

We have referred to a lingering ambivalence in the delinquent's own value system, an ambivalence which threatens the adjustment he has achieved and which is met through the mechanism of reaction-formation. The delin-

[12] The distinguished criminologist, Sutherland, apparently had this in mind when he wrote: "It is not necessary that there be bad boys inducing good boys to commit offenses. It is generally a mutual stimulation, as a result of which each of the boys commits delinquencies which he would not commit alone." Edwin H. Sutherland, *Principles of Criminology* (Philadelphia: J. B. Lippincott Company, 1947), p. 145. Having made the point, however, Sutherland failed to develop its implications, and in his general theory of criminal behavior the function of the group or the gang is not collectively to *contrive* delinquency but merely to *transmit* the delinquent tradition and to provide protection to the members of the group. Fritz Redl, on the other hand, in "The Psychology of Gang Formation and the Treatment of Juvenile Delinquents," *The Psychoanalytic Study of the Child*, Vol. 1 (New York: International Universities Press, 1945), pp. 367–377, has developed at considerable length the ways in which the group makes possible for its members behavior which would otherwise not be available to them.

quent may have to contend with another ambivalence, in the area of his status sources. The delinquent subculture offers him status *as against* other children of whatever social level, but it offers him this status *in the eyes of* his fellow delinquents only. To the extent that there remains a desire for recognition from groups whose respect has been forfeited by commitment to a new subculture, his satisfaction in his solution is imperfect and adulterated. He can perfect his solution only by rejecting as status sources those who reject him. This too may require a certain measure of reaction-formation, going beyond indifference to active hostility and contempt for all those who do not share his subculture. He becomes all the more dependent upon his delinquent gang. Outside that gang his status position is now weaker than ever. The gang itself tends toward a kind of sectarian solidarity, because the benefits of membership can only be realized in active face-to-face relationships with group members.

This interpretation of the delinquent subculture has important implications for the "sociology of social problems." People are prone to assume that those things which we define as evil and those which we define as good have their origins in separate and distinct features of our society. Evil flows from poisoned wells; good flows from pure and crystal fountains. The same source cannot feed both. Our view is different. It holds that those values which are at the core of "the American way of life," which help to motivate the behavior which we most esteem as "typically American," are among the major determinants of that which we stigmatize as "pathological." More specifically, it holds that the problems of adjustment to which the delinquent subculture is a response are determined, in part, by those very values which respectable society holds most sacred. The same value system, impinging upon children differently equipped to meet it, is instrumental in generating both delinquency and respectability.

11. Delinquent Boys: A Critique

JOHN I. KITSUSE AND DAVID C. DIETRICK

One of the most provocative theoretical formulations concerning juvenile delinquency is that contained in Albert K. Cohen's *Delinquent Boys: The Culture of the Gang.*[1] The reviews of Cohen's monograph are enthusiastic in their praise,[2] and one textbook has already incorporated the theory of the delinquent subculture as the major framework for the discussion of juvenile delinquency.[3] Sykes and Matza, Wilensky and Lebeaux, Merton, and Kobrin and Finestone[4] have questioned various propositions and implications of Cohen's thesis, but their discussions are limited to rather specific issues. In view of the impressive reception which has greeted Cohen's work, his theory of the delinquent subculture deserves a more detailed and systematic examination.

The primary concern of Cohen's inquiry is stated clearly and repeatedly throughout the study: the theoretical task is to explain the content and distribution of the delinquent subculture. Cohen offers his theory to fill a gap in the cultural transmission theories of delinquency which assert that individuals become delinquent because they learn the values, attitudes, and techniques of the delinquent group. The theory of the delinquent subculture attempts to account for the content of what the delinquent learns. Thus, Cohen does *not* purport to present a theory of delinquency.

° This paper has benefited from the criticism and suggestions from many sources. We wish especially to acknowledge the helpful comments of Aaron V. Cicourel, Scott Greer, and Donald R. Cressey.

[1] Glencoe, Ill.: Free Press, 1955.

[2] See reviews by Frank E. Hartung, *American Sociological Review,* 20 (December, 1955), pp. 751–752; Donnell M. Poppenfort, *American Journal of Sociology,* 62 (July, 1956), pp. 125–126; Hermann Mannheim, *British Journal of Sociology,* 7 (June, 1956), pp. 147–152; Max Benedict, *The British Journal of Delinquency,* 7 (October, 1956), pp. 323–324; Gilbert Shapiro, *Dissent,* 3 (Winter, 1956), pp. 89–92.

[3] Jessie Bernard, *Social Problems at Midcentury,* New York: Dryden, 1957, Chapter 18.

[4] See, respectively, Gresham M. Sykes and David Matza, "Techniques of Neutralization," *American Sociological Review,* 22 (December, 1957), pp. 664–670; Harold Wilensky and Charles Lebeaux, *Industrial Society and Social Welfare,* New York: Russell Sage Foundation, 1958, Chapter 9; Robert K. Merton, *Social Theory and Social Structure,* Glencoe, Ill.: Free Press, 1957, pp. 177–179; and Solomon Kobrin and Harold Finestone, "A Proposed Framework for the Analysis of Juvenile Delinquency," presented at the meeting of the American Sociological Society, August, 1958.

SOURCE. John I. Kitsuse and David C. Dietrick, "Delinquent Boys: A Critique," from *American Sociological Review,* Volume 24, April 1959, pp. 208–215. Reprinted with the permission of the American Sociological Association and the authors.

Although Cohen is explicit about the limited and specific nature of the problem he is addressing, his theory has been interpreted and discussed as a theory of juvenile delinquency.[5] Indeed, the psychological terms in which Cohen couches his discussion and the logic of his thesis invite such an interpretation. In this paper, therefore, Cohen's thesis is critically examined both as a theory of the delinquent subculture and as a theory of delinquency. We contend that (1) Cohen does not present adequate support, either in theory or in fact, for his explanation of the delinquent subculture, (2) the methodological basis of the theory renders it inherently untestable, (3) the theory is ambiguous concerning the relation between the *emergence* of the subculture and its *maintenance*, and (4) the theory should include an explanation of the persistence of the subculture if it is to meet an adequate test. In the following section, we remain close to Cohen's statements and analyze them for their internal consistency.

THE THEORY OF THE DELINQUENT SUBCULTURE

Cohen addresses himself to the task of constructing a theory which will explain two sets of "known facts": first, the content of what he calls the "delinquent subculture," which is characterized by maliciousness, non-utilitarianism, and negativism; and, second, the concentration of that subculture among the male, working-class segment of the population.[6]

[5] See, e.g., Bernard, *op. cit.*; Marshall B. Clinard, *Sociology of Deviant Behavior*, New York: Rinehart, 1957, pp. 182–183.

[6] Cohen, *op. cit.*, pp. 36–44. It should be noted that Cohen's assertion that the *delinquent subculture* is concentrated in the working-class is based on an inference from data, not specifically classified with respect to their subcultural character, which suggest the concentration of *delinquency* in that social stratum.

The propositions in Cohen's theory may be stated briefly as follows:

1. The working-class boy faces a characteristic problem of adjustment which is qualitatively different from that of the middle-class boy.

2. The working-class boy's problem is one of "status-frustration," the basis of which is systematically generated by his early exposure to the working-class pattern of socialization.

3. The working-class boy's socialization handicaps him for achievement in the middle-class status system.

4. Nevertheless, he is thrust into this competitive system where achievement is judged by middle-class standards of behavior and performance.

5. Ill-prepared and poorly motivated, the working-class boy is frustrated in his status aspirations by the agents of middle-class society.

6. The delinquent subculture represents a "solution" to the working-class boy's problem, for it enables him to "break clean" with the middle-class morality and legitimizes hostility and aggression "without moral inhibitions on the free expression of aggression against the sources of his frustration."[7]

7. Thus, the delinquent subculture is characterized by non-utilitarian, malicious, and negativistic values as "an attack on the middle-class where their egos are most vulnerable. . . . It expresses contempt for a way of life by making its opposite a criterion of status."[8]

The Working-Class Boy's Problem

What are the logic and the evidence presented in support of Cohen's theory? He begins by noting the class differentials in the socialization experience of the child which handicap the working-class boy in his competition for status in

[7] *Ibid.*, p. 132.
[8] *Ibid.*, p. 134.

the middle-class system. For example: the working-class boy's social and cultural environment does not systematically support the middle-class ethic of ambition to get ahead; he is not socialized in techniques of discipline and hard work; his behavior is oriented to immediate satisfactions rather than to future goals. Thus, the working-class boy is not socialized to middle-class norms. "To this extent he is less likely to identify with these norms, to 'make them his own,' and to be able to conform to them easily and 'naturally.' "⁹

What then is the basis for the working-class boy's fundamental ambivalence toward the middle-class system that seeks and finds a solution in the delinquent subculture? His ambivalence, according to Cohen, is due to the fact that, in American society, children are compared with "all comers" by a single standard of performance which embodies the norms of the middle class. Neither the working-class boy nor his parents can ignore or deny the dominance of middle-class norms, for they comprise the code of "the distinguished people who symbolize and represent the local and national communities with which the children identify."¹⁰ Confronted by the obvious dominance and prestige of middle-class values, the working-class boy is drawn to the "American Dream."

We note a persistent ambiguity in Cohen's statements. The working-class boy faces a problem of adjustment "to the degree to which he values the good opinion of middle-class persons or because he has to some degree internalized middle-class standards himself. . . ."¹¹ On the other hand, Cohen acknowledges, "it may be argued that the working-class boy does not *care* what middle-class people think of

him."¹² He suggests, and rightly so, that this is an empirical question. Nevertheless, Cohen proceeds to develop his thesis with the assertion that "there is, however, reason to believe that most children are sensitive *to some degree* about the attitudes of *any persons* with whom they are thrown into more than the most superficial kind of contact."¹³

Cohen's reasons for rejecting the argument that the working-class boy may not care what middle-class people think (which is crucial for his theory) are not convincing. Indeed, his statements about the working-class boy's socialization lend strong support to the contrary view.¹⁴ If there are in fact class differences in socialization, surely they may be expected to insulate the working-class boy from the responses of middle-class people. Furthermore, it would appear that the working-class boy's problem is a minor one if it depends on "the degree to which he values middle-class persons" or if it rests upon the argument that he is "sensitive *to some degree*" about the attitudes of others. On the strength of his statements, the rejected proposition seems equally plaus-

---

⁹ *Ibid.*, p. 97.
¹⁰ *Ibid.*, p. 87.
¹¹ *Ibid.*, p. 119.

¹² *Ibid.*, p. 123, Cohen's emphasis.
¹³ *Ibid.*, p. 123, Cohen's emphases.
¹⁴ Thus Cohen states, "In general, the working-class person appears to be more dependent upon and 'at home' in primary groups [presumably among his own social class] and to avoid secondary, segmental relationships more than the middle-class person" (*ibid.*, p. 97). Again, "The working-class child is more often thrown upon his own or the company of an autonomous group of peers" (p. 100). He suggests further that "At the same time, it seems likely, although this aspect of differential socialization has not been so well explored, that the working-class child is more dependent emotionally and for the satisfaction of many practical needs upon his relationships to his peer groups. . . . Satisfactory emotional relationships with his peers are likely to be more important, their claims to be more imperious, and the rewards they offer to compete more effectively with parental [and we might add, teacher] expectations" (p. 101).

ible, namely, that the working-class boy is *not* oriented to status in the middle-class system. As Cohen himself suggests, "satisfactory emotional relationships with his peers are likely to be more important" for the working-class boy than for his middle-class counterpart.

The Reaction-Formation Concept

Cohen's explanation of the distinctive content of the delinquent subculture and "what it has to offer" to the working-class boy is anchored in the concept of "reaction-formation." His use of this psychological concept deserves careful examination, for reaction-formation provides the key to his explication of the non-utilitarian, malicious, and negativistic character of the delinquent subculture.

A reaction-formation is a psychological mechanism which "attempts to deny or to repress some impulses, or to defend the person against some instinctual danger. . . . the original opposite attitudes still exist in the unconscious."[15] In the context of Cohen's argument, the "impulse" is the working-class boy's desire for middle-class status which, if expressed, would only be frustrated. Therefore, the reaction-formation is instituted against it.

Is the ambivalence described by Cohen sufficient warrant for the introduction of this psychological concept? Cohen states that the reaction-formation in the case of the working-class boy who responds to the delinquent subculture "should take the form of an 'irrational,' 'malicious,' and 'unaccountable' hostility to the enemy within the gates as well as without: the norms of the respectable middle-class society." He suggests: "the unintelligibility of the response, the 'overreaction,' becomes

intelligible when we see that it has the function of reassuring the actor against an *inner* threat to his defenses as well as the function of meeting an external situation on its own terms. . . . we would expect the delinquent boy, who, after all, has been socialized in a society dominated by a middle-class morality and who can never quite escape the blandishments of middle-class society, to seek to maintain his safeguards against seduction."[16]

Clearly, Cohen's use of reaction-formation assumes that the delinquent boy is *strongly and fundamentally ambivalent* about status in the middle-class system, and that he "cares" so intensely about improving his status within the system that he is faced with a genuine problem of adjustment. Cohen's theory stands on this assumption which is, by his own admission, on "somewhat speculative ground where fundamental research remains to be done."[17]

Cohen's description of the social and cultural conditions of the working-class boy is a tenuous base from which to posit the internalization of middle-class values. A more reasonable and obvious question is: How under such conditions are such values significantly communicated to the working-class boy at all? According to Cohen, in his daily encounters with the middle-class system, the working-class boy suffers humiliation, shame, embarrassment, rejection, derision, and the like as a consequence of his family background. Similarly, in the settlement houses, recreation centers, and other welfare agencies, the working-class boy is exposed to the "critical or at best condescending surveillance of people who are 'foreigners' to his community and who appraise him in terms of values *which he does not share*. . . . To win favor of the peo-

---

[15] Otto Fenichel, *Psychoanalytic Theory of Neurosis*, New York: Norton, 1945, p. 151.

[16] Cohen, *op. cit.*, p. 133, Cohen's emphasis.

[17] *Ibid.*, p. 127.

ple in charge he must change his habits, his values, his ambitions, his speech and his associates. Even were these things possible, the game might not be worth the candle. So, having sampled what they have to offer, he turns to the street or to his 'clubhouse' in a cellar where 'facilities' are meager but human relations more satisfying."[18] In this description of the working-class boy's perceptions of the middle-class system, the implication is clear that it is not that the working-class boy's status aspirations are frustrated (that is, he is motivated but is unable to achieve prestigeful status in the middle-class system), but rather that he does not want to strive for status in the system, and that he resents the intrusion of "foreigners" who seek to impose upon him an irrelevant way of life.

Cohen's image of the working-class boy, who admittedly is extremely dependent upon his gang, standing alone to face humiliation at the hands of middle-class agents is difficult to comprehend. To add to this picture of the pre-teen and teen-ager an intense desire to gain status in the middle-class system, which when frustrated provides sufficient basis for a reaction-formation response, is to overdraw him beyond recognition. Even in "Elmtown," to which Cohen refers, it is difficult to conceive of the working-class boy exposed to the middle-class environment unprotected by the support of his peer group. When we realize that Cohen's formulation applies, presumably, more directly to schools in urban areas which are predominantly working-class in composition, confusion is compounded.

Again, *why* does Cohen insist upon the working-class boy's ambivalence toward the middle-class system? His discussion of alternative subcultural responses among working-class boys to the problem of status-frustration may

provide a clue. He specifies three modes of response: that of the college boy, of the "stable corner-boy," and of the delinquent boy. The college boy deserts the corner-boy way of life and accepts the "challenge of the middle-class status system," conforming to its rules.[19] The stable corner-boy culture "does not so much repudiate the value of middle-class achievements as it emphasizes certain other values which make such achievements improbable. . . . the corner-boy culture temporizes the middle-class morality."[20] It is the delinquent response, legitimized by the subculture, that represents the reaction-formation of a whole-hearted repudiation of middle-class morality.

It would appear that, of the three categories of respondents, the working-class boys who find a solution in the delinquent subculture are those who are faced with the most serious problems of status-frustration and ambivalence. The logic of the reaction-formation thesis leads us to conclude that, of the three modes of adjustment, the delinquent boys' is an expression of the *most serious* problems of status-frustration and ambivalence. We must assume that the intensity of the hostility and aggression against the middle-class system is a measure of status-frustration and ambivalence.

Theoretically, the college boy is equally ambivalent about the middle-class system, yet Cohen does not invoke the concept of reaction-formation to account for *his* (the college boy's) rejection of (or reaction against) working-class values. If the price of the working-class boy's accommodation to the middle-class system is that he must "change his habits, his values, his ambitions, his speech and his associates," would not the college-boy response entail more than an acceptance of the

---

[18] *Ibid.*, p. 117, emphasis added.

[19] *Ibid.*, p. 128.
[20] *Ibid.*, p. 130.

challenge to compete within the system on its own terms?[21]

The Description of the Delinquent Subculture

Cohen's emphasis upon the "positive" aspect of the college-boy response contrasts with his stress upon the "negative" aspect of the delinquent response, which leads him, we suggest, to describe the delinquent subculture as an irrational, malicious attack on the middle-class system. This raises the more fundamental question about his *description* of the subculture, "the facts to be explained."

"Non-utilitarian," "malicious," and "negativistic" are, we suggest, interpretive categories of description which are not independent of Cohen's explanation of the delinquent subculture. For example, the imputation of intent, implicit in his description of malice, is open to serious doubt.[22] We do not deny that subculture delinquency is marked by such distinctive characteristics as the systematic extortion of money from younger, defenseless children. What is at issue here is the interpretation of this kind of delinquent behavior, an interpretation directed systematically at the middle-class as a consequence of the frustration of ambivalent status aspirations.

It is important that we keep apace the facts. Cohen's description of the delinquent subculture does not fit the behavior of contemporary delinquent gangs.[23] They are not engaged in replacing one stolen hat with another from store to store, or delighting in the terrorizing of "good" children by driving them from playgrounds and gyms. The delinquents whose activities are organized by a delinquent subculture are attending to more serious enterprises. There is no absence of rational, calculated, utilitarian behavior among delinquent gangs, as they exist today. To describe the activities of such gangs as non-utilitarian, malicious, and negativistic gives the misleading view that they somehow represent a child's angry outbursts against the injustices of a world he never made.

It is also important to guard against the tendency to apply different standards for interpreting the behavior of class-differentiated groups. There is ample evidence in the daily press that middle-class adolescents are engaged in the kinds of activities that Cohen cites to support his description of the working-class delinquent subculture. To be sure, such reports appear less frequently under banner headlines than do the exploits of working-class delinquents; and middle-class delinquency does not prompt, as does working-class delinquency, editorial clamor for a radical and thorough revision of programs of control. For example, acts of vandalism committed by college boys on the facilities rented for fraternity dances and other occasions occur with

---

[21] *Ibid.,* p. 127.

[22] Martha M. Eliot, Chief of the Children's Bureau, has observed, "We are too inclined to make vandalism a catch-all phrase which imputes to the vandal hostile antagonisms toward society, then to compound the catch-all by saying that vandals, by and large, are teen-agers. But if teen-agers are vandals, why are they any more so than children of any age?" What is Vandalism"? *Federal Probation,* 18 (March, 1954), p. 3.

[23] See, e.g., Sam Glane, "Juvenile Gangs in East Side Los Angeles," *Focus,* 29 (September, 1950), pp. 136–141; Dale Kramer and Madeline Karr, *Teen-Age Gangs,* New York: Henry Holt, 1953; Stacy V. Jones, "The Cougars—Life with a Brooklyn Gang," *Harper's Magazine,* 209 (November, 1954), pp. 35–43; Paul C. Crawford, Daniel I. Malamud, and James R. Dumpson, *Working with Teen-Age Gangs,* New York: New York Welfare Council, 1950; Harrison E. Salisbury, "The Shook-Up Generation," *New York Times,* March 24–30, 1958; Dan Wakefield, "The

annual regularity.[24] In view of the great probability that such instances of middle-class gang delinquency are substantially under-reported, it would be an arbitrary preconception to dismiss them as no more than scattered and rare occurrences.

THE TEST OF COHEN'S THEORY

In the preceding discussion we argue that, first, Cohen does not present adequate support for his formulation of "the working-class boy's problem," second, his description of the working-class boy's ambivalence toward the middle-class system does not warrant the use of the reaction-formation concept, and third, his description of the delinquent subculture, the "facts" to which his theory is addressed, is open to question. While these criticisms are presented as logical ambiguities and inconsistencies in Cohen's statements, it may be maintained nevertheless that empirical research demonstrates the validity of his major thesis. In turning to this question, we suspend the criticisms formulated above, and examine the methodology of Cohen's theory.

Gang That Went Good," *Harper's Magazine,* 216 (June, 1958), pp. 36–43.

[24] One Southern California college fraternity has depleted a long list of rental facilities where their patronage is no longer solicited. The last dance held by this fraternity was the scene of a minor riot which required a force of thirty regular and reserve police officers to control. Acts of vandalism included ripping fixtures from the walls, entering the ballroom dripping with water from the swimming pool, tearing radio antennae from police cars, etc. Lest this example be dismissed as institutionalized saturnalia, other instances may be cited which the community was less willing to view as mere pranks. In Los Angeles, a group of high school seniors of undisputedly middle-class families committed an "unprovoked" act of setting fire to a school building. In another case, several middle-class adolescents in Glendale, California were convicted for stomping on the hoods and roofs of automobiles in that city. And so on.

The Historical Method and Empirical Research

What, then, are the research directives of the theory of the delinquent subculture? When this problem is analyzed, Cohen's methodology presents numerous difficulties, for his theory is an historical construction addressed to the explanation of the *emergence* of an existing subculture and its *present* concentration among the working-class male population. Furthermore, the basic propositions of this explanation utilize concepts which require data about the psychological characteristics of past populations.

Cohen's use of the present indicative in the development of his theory is misleading, for the interpretation of the rise of the delinquent subculture requires historical data. It is not that the working-class boy *is* ambivalent about middle-class values; the theory requires only that at some unspecified time when the delinquent subculture emerged, the working-class boy *was* ambivalent about middle-class values.

Subculture Maintenance and Motivation

There is no objection per se to a plausible explanation that cannot be tested if the explanation is viewed as an heuristic device for the generating of hypotheses. If then a direct test of Cohen's theory through the measurement of deduced empirical regularities is not possible as a practical matter, is it feasible to approach the problem from a functional point of view? The question may be phrased: What are the necessary conditions for the maintenance of the delinquent subculture? On this question, Cohen's statements are quite explicit. Commenting on the fact that his theory is not concerned with the processes by which one boy becomes delinquent while another does not, Cohen writes:

We have tried to show that a subculture owes its existence to the fact that it provides a solution to certain problems of adjustment shared among a community of individuals. However, it does not follow that for every individual who participates these problems provide the sole or sufficient source of motivation. Indeed, there may be some participants to whose motivation these problems contribute very little. . . . Our delinquent subculture . . . is not a disembodied set of beliefs and practices but is "carried" and supported by groups with distinctive personnel. A position in this organization or affiliation with this or that particular member may offer other satisfactions which help to account for the participation of certain members but do not help to explain the content of the culture in which they participate.[25]

An implication of this statement is that the maintenance of the delinquent subculture is not wholly dependent upon the motivational structure which explains its emergence. Not *every* individual who participates in the delinquent subculture need be so motivated and, for some, such motivation may be peripheral if not irrelevant. Clearly an investigation of the motivations which lead individuals to participate in the delinquent subculture does not constitute even an indirect test of the theory. For the statement may be read to mean that once the subculture is established, it can be maintained by the behavior of individuals who bring a diverse range of motivations to the gangs which embody the delinquent subculture. Thus, functionally, the delinquent subculture requires another explanation.

The Double Dilemma: Theory and Method

The theoretical significance of Cohen's explanation of the emergence of

[25] Cohen, *op. cit.*, p. 148.

the delinquent subculture, however, lies precisely in its relevance for an explanation of the maintenance of that subculture. Were this not so, the theory could be dismissed as merely plausible and untestable or as incapable of generating hypotheses about regularities other than the pre-existing "facts" which it explains. We suggest that the statement quoted above presents a methodological dilemma by divorcing the dynamics of the etiology of the delinquent subculture from the dynamics of its maintenance. Cohen is correct of course in asserting that, theoretically, the former does not necessarily require the same motivational dynamics as the latter. However, the ambiguity of his statement lies in his implicit concession that *some* of the participants in the subculture must have the characteristic motivational structure posited in the theory.

The research dilemma posed by Cohen's theory is two-fold. Methodologically, the historical method relies upon data concerning the psychological dynamics of a population which are difficult if not impossible to obtain. Theoretically, the motivational dynamics posited as necessary for the *emergence* of the delinquent subculture is considered either (a) independent of the motivational dynamics necessary for the *maintenance* of the subculture, or (b) dependent upon it in some unspecified relationship.

In view of these difficulties, it may be fruitful to turn the problem around and ask: What are the consequences of participation in the delinquent subculture for the motivational structure of the participants? This question places the theory of the delinquent subculture in its proper relation to the value-transmission theories of delinquency and directs us to examine the heuristic value of Cohen's theory. Viewing his theory from this perspective, the following propositions about the maintenance of the delinquent subculture may be stated:

1. The individual learns the values of the delinquent subculture through his participation in gangs which embody that subculture.

2. The motivations of individuals for participating in such gangs are varied.

3. The malicious, non-utilitarian, and negativistic behavior which is learned through participation in the subculture is met by formal negative sanctions, rejection, and limitation of access to prestigeful status within the middle-class system.

4. Thus, participation in the delinquent subculture creates similar problems for all its participants.

5. The participants' response to the barriers raised to exclude them from status in the middle-class system (that is, the "problem") is a hostile rejection of the standards of "respectable" society and an emphasis upon status within the delinquent gang.

6. The hostile rejection response reinforces the malicious, non-utilitarian, and negativistic norms of the subculture.

The formulation suggested here relates Cohen's explanation of the emergence of the delinquent subculture with an explanation of its maintenance. It hypothesizes that the delinquent subculture persists because, once established, it creates for those who participate in it the very problems which were the bases for its emergence. It is possible to derive the further hypothesis that the motivational structure of the participants of the subculture displays characteristics similar to those described by Cohen.

CONCLUSIONS

In this paper, we have critically examined Cohen's monograph for its implications for theory and method. The problems raised in the first part of our critique cannot be resolved by logical argumentation. Indeed, we have suggested that insofar as they are consequences of the historical method, research to test the validity of Cohen's statements, as a practical matter, is impossible. If, however, the theory of the delinquent subculture is read for its heuristic value, its significance for theory and research is not limited to the field of juvenile delinquency, but extends to the more general problem of the dynamics of subcultural maintenance.

12. Techniques of Neutralization: A Theory of Delinquency

GRESHAM M. SYKES AND DAVID MATZA

In attempting to uncover the roots of juvenile delinquency, the social scientist has long since ceased to search for devils in the mind or stigma of the body. It is now largely agreed that delinquent behavior, like most social behavior, is learned and that it is learned in the process of social interaction.

The classic statement of this position is found in Sutherland's theory of differential association, which asserts that criminal or delinquent behavior involves the learning of (a) techniques of committing crimes and (b) motives, drives, rationalizations, and attitudes favorable to the violation of law.[1] Unfortunately, the specific content of what is learned —as opposed to the process by which it is learned—has received relatively little attention in either theory or research. Perhaps the single strongest school of thought on the nature of this content has centered on the idea of a delinquent sub-culture. The basic characteristic of the delinquent sub-culture,

it is argued, is a system of values that represents an inversion of the values held by respectable, law-abiding society. The world of the delinquent is the world of the law-abiding turned upside down, and its norms constitute a countervailing force directed against the conforming social order. Cohen[2] sees the process of developing a delinquent sub-culture as a matter of building, maintaining, and reinforcing a code for behavior which exists by opposition, which stands in point by point contradiction to dominant values, particularly those of the middle class. Cohen's portrayal of delinquency is executed with a good deal of sophistication, and he carefully avoids overly simple explanations such as those based on the principle of "follow the leader" or easy generalizations about "emotional disturbances." Furthermore, he does not accept the delinquent sub-culture as something given, but instead systematically examines the function of delinquent values as a viable solution to the lower-

[1] E. H. Sutherland, *Principles of Criminology*, revised by D. R. Cressey, Philadelphia: Lippincott, 1955, pp. 77–80.

[2] Albert K. Cohen, *Delinquent Boys*, Glencoe, Ill.: The Free Press, 1955.

SOURCE. Gresham M. Sykes and David Matza, "Techniques of Neutralization: A Theory of Delinquency," from *The American Journal of Sociology*, Volume 22, December 1957, pp. 664–670. Copyright © 1957, University of Chicago Press. Reprinted with the permission of the University of Chicago Press.

class, male child's problems in the area of social status. Yet in spite of its virtues, this image of juvenile delinquency as a form of behavior based on competing or countervailing values and norms appears to suffer from a number of serious defects. It is the nature of these defects and a possible alternative or modified explanation for a large portion of juvenile delinquency with which this paper is concerned.

The difficulties in viewing delinquent behavior as springing from a set of deviant values and norms—as arising, that is to say, from a situation in which the delinquent defines his delinquency as "right"—are both empirical and theoretical. In the first place, if there existed in fact a delinquent sub-culture such that the delinquent viewed his illegal behavior as morally correct, we could reasonably suppose that he would exhibit no feelings of guilt or shame at detection or confinement. Instead, the major reaction would tend in the direction of indignation or a sense of martyrdom.[3] It is true that some delinquents do react in the latter fashion, although the sense of martyrdom often seems to be based on the fact that others "get away with it," and indignation appears to be directed against the chance events or lack of skill that led to apprehension. More important, however, is the fact that there is a good deal of evidence suggesting that many delinquents *do* experience a sense of guilt or shame, and its outward expression is not to be dismissed as a purely manipulative gesture to appease those in authority. Much of this evidence is,

to be sure, of a clinical nature or in the form of impressionistic judgments of those who must deal first hand with the youthful offender. Assigning a weight to such evidence calls for caution, but it cannot be ignored if we are to avoid the gross stereotype of the juvenile delinquent as a hardened gangster in miniature.

In the second place, observers have noted that the juvenile delinquent frequently accords admiration and respect to law-abiding persons. The "really honest" person is often revered, and if the delinquent is sometimes overly keen to detect hyprocrisy in those who conform, unquestioned probity is likely to win his approval. A fierce attachment to a humble, pious mother or a forgiving, upright priest (the former, according to many observers, is often encountered in both juvenile delinquents and adult criminals) might be dismissed as rank sentimentality, but at least it is clear that the delinquent does not necessarily regard those who abide by the legal rules as immoral. In a similar vein, it can be noted that the juvenile delinquent may exhibit great resentment if illegal behavior is imputed to "significant others" in his immediate social environment or to heroes in the world of sport and entertainment. In other words, if the delinquent does hold to a set of values and norms that stand in complete opposition to those of respectable society, his norm-holding is of a peculiar sort. While supposedly thoroughly committed to the deviant system of the delinquent sub-culture, he would appear to recognize the moral validity of the dominant normative system in many instances.[4]

[3] This form of reaction among the adherents of a deviant sub-culture who fully believe in the "rightfulness" of their behavior and who are captured and punished by the agencies of the dominant social order can be illustrated, perhaps, by groups such as Jehovah's Witnesses, early Christian sects, nationalist movements in colonial areas, and conscientious objectors during World Wars I and II.

[4] As Weber has pointed out, a thief may recognize the legitimacy of legal rules without accepting their moral validity. Cf. Max Weber, *The Theory of Social and Economic Organization* (translated by A. M. Henderson and Talcott Parsons), New York: Oxford University Press, 1947, p.

In the third place, there is much evidence that juvenile delinquents often draw a sharp line between those who can be victimized and those who cannot. Certain social groups are not to be viewed as "fair game" in the performance of supposedly approved delinquent acts while others warrant a variety of attacks. In general, the potentiality for victimization would seem to be a function of the social distance between the juvenile delinquent and others, and thus we find implicit maxims in the world of the delinquent such as "don't steal from friends" or "don't commit vandalism against a church of your own faith."[5] This is all rather obvious, but the implications have not received sufficient attention. The fact that supposedly valued behavior tends to be directed against disvalued social groups hints that the "wrongfulness" of such delinquent behavior is more widely recognized by delinquents than the literature has indicated. When the pool of victims is limited by considerations of kinship, friendship, ethnic group, social class, age, sex, etc., we have reason to suspect that the virtue of delinquency is far from unquestioned.

In the fourth place, it is doubtful if many juvenile delinquents are totally immune from the demands for conformity made by the dominant social order. There is a strong likelihood that the family of the delinquent will agree with respectable society that delinquency is wrong, even though the family may be engaged in a variety of illegal activities. That is, the parental posture conductive to delinquency is

not apt to be a positive prodding. Whatever may be the influence of parental example, what might be called the "Fagin" pattern of socialization into delinquency is probably rare. Furthermore, as Redl has indicated, the idea that certain neighborhoods are completely delinquent, offering the child a model for delinquent behavior without reservations, is simply not supported by the data.[6]

The fact that a child is punished by parents, school officials, and agencies of the legal system for his delinquency may, as a number of observers have cynically noted, suggest to the child that he should be more careful not to get caught. There is an equal or greater probability, however, that the child will internalize the demands for conformity. This is not to say that demands for conformity cannot be counteracted. In fact, as we shall see shortly, an understanding of how internal and external demands for conformity are neutralized may be crucial for understanding delinquent behavior. But it is to say that a complete denial of the validity of demands for conformity and the substitution of a new normative system is improbable, in light of the child's or adolescent's dependency on adults and encirclement by adults inherent in his status in the social structure. No matter how deeply enmeshed in patterns of delinquency he may be and no matter how much this involvement may outweigh his associations with the law-abiding, he cannot escape the condemnation of his deviance. Somehow the demands for conformity must be met and answered; they cannot be ignored as part of an alien system of values and norms.

In short, the theoretical viewpoint

---

125. We are arguing here, however, that the juvenile delinquent frequently recognizes *both* the legitimacy of the dominant social order and its moral "rightness."

5 Thrasher's account of the "Itschkies"—a juvenile gang composed of Jewish boys —and the immunity from "rolling" enjoyed by Jewish drunkards is a good illustration. Cf. F. Thrasher, *The Gang,* Chicago: The University of Chicago Press, 1947, p. 315.

6 Cf. Solomon Kobrin, "The Conflict of Values in Delinquency Areas," *American Sociological Review,* 16 (October, 1951), pp. 653–661.

that sees juvenile delinquency as a form of behavior based on the values and norms of a deviant sub-culture in precisely the same way as law-abiding behavior is based on the values and norms of the larger society is open to serious doubt. The fact that the world of the delinquent is embedded in the larger world of those who conform cannot be overlooked, nor can the delinquent be equated with an adult thoroughly socialized into an alternative way of life. Instead, the juvenile delinquent would appear to be at least partially committed to the dominant social order in that he frequently exhibits guilt or shame when he violates its proscriptions, accords approval to certain conforming figures, and distinguishes between appropriate and inappropriate targets for his deviance. It is to an explanation for the apparently paradoxical fact of his delinquency that we now turn.

As Morris Cohen once said, one of the most fascinating problems about human behavior is why men violate the laws in which they believe. This is the problem that confronts us when we attempt to explain why delinquency occurs despite a greater or lesser commitment to the usages of conformity. A basic clue is offered by the fact that social rules or norms calling for valued behavior seldom if ever take the form of categorical imperatives. Rather, values or norms appear as *qualified* guides for action, limited in their applicability in terms of time, place, persons, and social circumstances. The moral injunction against killing, for example, does not apply to the enemy during combat in time of war, although a captured enemy comes once again under the prohibition. Similarly, the taking and distributing of scarce goods in a time of acute social need is felt by many to be right, although under other circumstances private property is held inviolable. The normative system of a society, then, is marked by what Williams has termed *flexibility;* it does not consist of a body of rules held to be binding under all conditions.[7]

This flexibility is, in fact, an integral part of the criminal law in that measures for "defenses to crimes" are provided in pleas such as nonage, necessity, insanity, drunkenness, compulsion, self-defense, and so on. The individual can avoid moral culpability for his criminal action—and thus avoid the negative sanctions of society—if he can prove that criminal intent was lacking. *It is our argument that much delinquency is based on what is essentially an unrecognized extension of defenses to crimes, in the form of justifications for deviance that are seen as valid by the delinquent but not by the legal system or society at large.*

These justifications are commonly described as rationalizations. They are viewed as following deviant behavior and as protecting the individual from self-blame and the blame of others after the act. But there is also reason to believe that they precede deviant behavior and make deviant behavior possible. It is this possibility that Sutherland mentioned only in passing and that other writers have failed to exploit from the viewpoint of sociological theory. Disapproval flowing from internalized norms and conforming others in the social environment is neutralized, turned back, or deflected in advance. Social controls that serve to check or inhibit deviant motivational patterns are rendered inoperative, and the individual is freed to engage in delinquency without serious damage to his self-image. In this sense, the delinquent both has his cake and eats it too, for he remains committed to the dominant normative system and yet so

[7] Cf. Robin Williams, Jr., *American Society*, New York: Knopf, 1951, p. 28.

qualifies its imperatives that violations are "acceptable" if not "right." Thus the delinquent represents not a radical opposition to law-abiding society but something more like an apologetic failure, often more sinned against than sinning in his own eyes. We call these justifications of deviant behavior techniques of neutralization; and we believe these techniques make up a crucial component of Sutherland's "definitions favorable to the violation of law." It is by learning these techniques that the juvenile becomes delinquent, rather than by learning moral imperatives, values, or attitudes standing in direct contradiction to those of the dominant society. In analyzing these techniques, we have found it convenient to divide them into five major types.

The Denial of Responsibility

Insofar as the delinquent can define himself as lacking responsibility for his deviant actions, the disapproval of self or others is sharply reduced in effectiveness as a restraining influence. As Justice Holmes has said, even a dog distinguishes between being stumbled over and being kicked, and modern society is no less careful to draw a line between injuries that are unintentional, i.e., where responsibility is lacking, and those that are intentional. As a technique of neutralization, however, the denial of responsibility extends much further than the claim that deviant acts are an "accident" or some similar negation of personal accountability. It may also be asserted that delinquent acts are due to forces outside of the individual and beyond his control such as unloving parents, bad companions, or a slum neighborhood. In effect, the delinquent approaches a "billiard ball" conception of himself in which he sees himself as helplessly propelled into new situations. From a psychodynamic viewpoint, this orientation toward one's own actions may represent a profound alienation from self, but it is important to stress the fact that interpretations of responsibility are cultural constructs and not merely idiosyncratic beliefs. The similarity between this mode of justifying illegal behavior assumed by the delinquent and the implications of a "sociological" frame of reference or a "humane" jurisprudence is readily apparent.[8] It is not the validity of this orientation that concerns us here, but its function of deflecting blame attached to violations of social norms and its relative independence of a particular personality structure.[9] By learning to view himself as more acted upon than acting, the delinquent prepares the way for deviance from the dominant normative system without the necessity of a frontal assault on the norms themselves.

The Denial of Injury

A second major technique of neutralization centers on the injury or harm involved in the delinquent act. The criminal law has long made a distinction between crimes which are *mala in se* and *mala prohibita*—that is between acts that are wrong in themselves and acts that are illegal but not immoral—and the delinquent can make the same kind of distinction in evaluating the wrongfulness of his behavior. For the delinquent, however, wrongfulness may turn on the question of whether or not anyone has clearly been hurt by his deviance, and this matter is open to a variety of interpretations. Vandalism, for example, may be defined by the

[8] A number of observers have wryly noted that many delinquents seem to show a surprising awareness of sociological and psychological explanations for their behavior and are quick to point out the causal role of their poor environment.

[9] It is possible, of course, that certain personality structures can accept some techniques of neutralization more readily than others, but this question remains largely unexplored.

delinquent simply as "mischief"—after all, it may be claimed, the persons whose property has been destroyed can well afford it. Similarly, auto theft may be viewed as "borrowing," and gang fighting may be seen as a private quarrel, an agreed upon duel between two willing parties, and thus of no concern to the community at large. We are not suggesting that this technique of neutralization, labeled the denial of injury, involves an explicit dialectic. Rather, we are arguing that the delinquent frequently, and in a hazy fashion, feels that his behavior does not really cause any great harm despite the fact that it runs counter to law. Just as the link between the individual and his acts may be broken by the denial of responsibility, so may the link between acts and their consequences be broken by the denial of injury. Since society sometimes agrees with the delinquent, e.g., in matters such as truancy, "pranks," and so on, it merely reaffirms the idea that the delinquent's neutralization of social controls by means of qualifying the norms is an extension of common practice rather than a gesture of complete opposition.

The Denial of the Victim

Even if the delinquent accepts the responsibility for his deviant actions and is willing to admit that his deviant actions involve an injury or hurt, the moral indignation of self and others may be neutralized by an insistence that the injury is not wrong in light of the circumstances. The injury, it may be claimed, is not really an injury; rather, it is a form of rightful retaliation or punishment. By a subtle alchemy the delinquent moves himself into the position of an avenger and the victim is transformed into a wrong-doer. Assaults on homosexuals or suspected homosexuals, attacks on members of minority groups who are said to have gotten "out of place," vandalism as revenge on an unfair teacher or school official, thefts from a "crooked" store owner—all may be hurts inflicted on a transgressor, in the eyes of the delinquent. As Orwell has pointed out, the type of criminal admired by the general public has probably changed over the course of years and Raffles no longer serves as a hero;[10] but Robin Hood, and his latter day derivatives such as the tough detective seeking justice outside the law, still capture the popular imagination, and the delinquent may view his acts as part of a similar role.

To deny the existence of the victim, then, by transforming him into a person deserving injury is an extreme form of a phenomenon we have mentioned before, namely, the delinquent's recognition of appropriate and inappropriate targets for his delinquent acts. In addition, however, the existence of the victim may be denied for the delinquent, in a somewhat different sense, by the circumstances of the delinquent act itself. Insofar as the victim is physically absent, unknown, or a vague abstraction (as is often the case in delinquent acts committed against property), the awareness of the victim's existence is weakened. Internalized norms and anticipations of the reactions of others must somehow be activated if they are to serve as guides for behavior; and it is possible that a diminished awareness of the victim plays an important part in determining whether or not this process is set in motion.

The Condemnation of the Condemners

A fourth technique of neutralization would appear to involve a condemnation of the condemners or, as McCorkle and Korn have phrased it, a rejection of the rejectors.[11] The delinquent shifts

[10] George Orwell, *Dickens, Dali, and Others,* New York: Reynal, 1946.
[11] Lloyd W. McCorkle and Richard

the focus of attention from his own deviant acts to the motives and behavior of those who disapprove of his violations. His condemners, he may claim, are hypocrites, deviants in disguise, or impelled by personal spite. This orientation toward the conforming world may be of particular importance when it hardens into a bitter cynicism directed against those assigned the task of enforcing or expressing the norms of the dominant society. Police, it may be said, are corrupt, stupid, and brutal. Teachers always show favoritism and parents always "take it out" on their children. By a slight extension, the rewards of conformity—such as material success—become a matter of pull or luck, thus decreasing still further the stature of those who stand on the side of the law-abiding. The validity of this jaundiced viewpoint is not so important as its function in turning back or deflecting the negative sanctions attached to violations of the norms. The delinquent, in effect, has changed the subject of the conversation in the dialogue between his own deviant impulses and the reactions of others; and by attacking others, the wrongfulness of his own behavior is more easily repressed or lost to view.

The Appeal to Higher Loyalties

Fifth, and last, internal and external social controls may be neutralized by sacrificing the demands of the larger society for the demands of the smaller social groups to which the delinquent belongs, such as the sibling pair, the gang, or the friendship clique. It is important to note that the delinquent does not necessarily repudiate the imperatives of the dominant normative system, despite his failure to follow them.

Rather, the delinquent may see himself as caught up in a dilemma that must be resolved, unfortunately, at the cost of violating the law. One aspect of this situation has been studied by Stouffer and Toby in their research on the conflict between particularistic and universalistic demands, between the claims of friendship and general social obligations, and their results suggest that "it is possible to classify people according to a predisposition to select one or the other horn of a dilemma in role conflict."[12] For our purposes, however, the most important point is that deviation from certain norms may occur not because the norms are rejected but because others norms, held to be more pressing or involving a higher loyalty, are accorded precedence. Indeed, it is the fact that both sets of norms are believed in that gives meaning to our concepts of dilemma and role conflict.

The conflict between the claims of friendship and the claims of law, or a similar dilemma, has of course long been recognized by the social scientist (and the novelist) as a common human problem. If the juvenile delinquent frequently resolves his dilemma by insisting that he must "always help a buddy" or "never squeal on a friend," even when it throws him into serious difficulties with the dominant social order, his choice remains familiar to the supposedly law-abiding. The delinquent is unusual, perhaps, in the extent to which he is able to see the fact that he acts in behalf of the smaller social groups to which he belongs as a justification for violations of society's norms, but it is a matter of degree rather than of kind.

"I didn't mean it." "I didn't really

Korn, "Resocialization Within Walls," *The Annals of the American Academy of Political and Social Science*, 293 (May, 1954), pp. 88–98.

[12] See Samuel A. Stouffer and Jackson Toby, "Role Conflict and Personality," in *Toward a General Theory of Action*, edited by Talcott Parsons and Edward A. Shils, Cambridge, Mass.: Harvard University Press, 1951, p. 494.

hurt anybody." "They had it coming to them." "Everybody's picking on me." "I didn't do it for myself." These slogans or their variants, we hypothesize, prepare the juvenile for delinquent acts. These "definitions of the situation" represent tangential or glancing blows at the dominant normative system rather than the creation of an opposing ideology; and they are extensions of patterns of thought prevalent in society rather than something created *de novo*.

Techniques of neutralization may not be powerful enough to fully shield the individual from the force of his own internalized values and the reactions of conforming others, for as we have pointed out, juvenile delinquents often appear to suffer from feelings of guilt and shame when called into account for their deviant behavior. And some delinquents may be so isolated from the world of conformity that techniques of neutralization need not be called into play. Nonetheless, we would argue that techniques of neutralization are critical in lessening the effectiveness of social controls and that they lie behind a large share of delinquent behavior. Empirical research in this area is scattered and fragmentary at the present time, but the work of Redl,[13] Cressey,[14] and others has supplied a body of significant data that has done much to clarify the theoretical issues and enlarge the fund of supporting evidence. Two

[13] See Fritz Redl and David Wineman, *Children Who Hate*, Glencoe, Ill.: The Free Press, 1956.

[14] See D. R. Cressey, *Other People's Money*, Glencoe, Ill.: The Free Press, 1953.

lines of investigation seem to be critical at this stage. First, there is need for more knowledge concerning the differential distribution of techniques of neutralization, as operative patterns of thought, by age, sex, social class, ethnic group, etc. On a priori grounds it might be assumed that these justifications for deviance will be more readily seized by segments of society for whom a discrepancy between common social ideals and social practice is most apparent. It is also possible, however, that the habit of "bending" the dominant normative system—if not "breaking" it—cuts across our cruder social categories and is to be traced primarily to patterns of social interaction within the familial circle. Second, there is need for a greater understanding of the internal structure of techniques of neutralization, as a system of beliefs and attitudes, and its relationship to various types of delinquent behavior. Certain techniques of neutralization would appear to be better adapted to particular deviant acts than to others, as we have suggested, for example, in the case of offenses against property and the denial of the victim. But the issue remains far from clear and stands in need of more information.

In any case, techniques of neutralization appear to offer a promising line of research in enlarging and systematizing the theoretical grasp of juvenile delinquency. As more information is uncovered concerning techniques of neutralization, their origins, and their consequences, both juvenile delinquency in particular and deviation from normative systems in general may be illuminated.

13.   Lower Class Culture as a Generating Milieu of Gang Delinquency

WALTER B. MILLER

The etiology of delinquency has long been a controversial issue and is particularly so at present. As new frames of reference for explaining human behavior have been added to traditional theories, some authors have adopted the practice of citing the major postulates of each school of thought as they pertain to delinquency, and of going on to state that causality must be conceived in terms of the dynamic interaction of a complex combination of variables on many levels. The major sets of etiological factors currently adduced to explain delinquency are, in simplified terms, the physiological (delinquency results from organic pathology), the psychodynamic (delinquency is a "behavioral disorder" resulting primarily from emotional disturbance generated by a defective mother-child relationship), and the environmental (delinquency is the product of disruptive forces, "disorganization," in the actor's physical or social environment).

This paper selects one particular kind of "delinquency"[1]—law-violating acts

[1] The complex issues involved in deriving a definition of "delinquency" cannot

committed by members of adolescent street corner groups in lower class communities—and attempts to show that the dominant component of motivation underlying these acts consists in a directed attempt by the actor to adhere to forms of behavior, and to achieve standards of value, as they are defined within that community. It takes as a premise that the motivation of behavior in this situation can be approached most productively by attempting to understand the nature of cultural forces impinging on the acting individual as they are perceived *by the actor himself* —although by no means only that segment of these forces of which the actor is consciously aware—rather than as they are perceived and evaluated from the reference position of another cul-

be discussed here. The term "delinquent" is used in this paper to characterize behavior or acts committed by individuals within specified age limits which if known to official authorities could result in legal action. The concept of a "delinquent" individual has little or no utility in the approach used here; rather, specified types of *acts* which may be committed rarely or frequently by few or many individuals are characterized as "delinquent."

SOURCE. Walter B. Miller, "Lower Class Culture as a Generating Milieu of Gang Delinquency," from *The Journal of Social Issues*, Volume 14, No. 3, 1958, pp. 5–19. Reprinted with the permission of *The Journal of Social Issues*.

tural system. In the case of "gang" delinquency, the cultural system which exerts the most direct influence on behavior is that of the lower class community itself—a long-established, distinctively patterned tradition with an integrity of its own—rather than a so-called "delinquent subculture" which has arisen through conflict with middle class culture and is oriented to the deliberate violation of middle class norms.

The bulk of the substantive data on which the following material is based was collected in connection with a service-research project in the control of gang delinquency. During the service aspect of the project, which lasted for three years, seven trained social workers maintained contact with twenty-one corner group units in a "slum" district of a large eastern city for periods of time ranging from ten to thirty months. Groups were Negro and white, male and female, and in early, middle, and late adolescence. Over eight thousand pages of direct observational data on behavior patterns of group members and other community residents were collected; almost daily contact was maintained for a total time period of about thirteen worker years. Data include workers' contact reports, participant observation reports by the writer —a cultural anthropologist—and direct tape recordings of group activities and discussions.[2]

2 A three-year research project is being financed under National Institutes of Health Grant M-1414 and administered through the Boston University School of Social Work. The primary research effort has subjected all collected material to a uniform data-coding process. All information bearing on some seventy areas of behavior (behavior in reference to school, police, theft, assault, sex, collective athletics, etc.) is extracted from the records, recorded on coded data cards, and filed under relevant categories. Analysis of these data aims to ascertain the actual nature of customary behavior in these areas and

FOCAL CONCERNS OF LOWER CLASS CULTURE

There is a substantial segment of present-day American society whose way of life, values, and characteristic patterns of behavior are the product of a distinctive cultural system which may be termed "lower class." Evidence indicates that this cultural system is becoming increasingly distinctive, and that the size of the group which shares this tradition is increasing.[3] The lower class way of life, in common with that of all distinctive cultural groups, is characterized by a set of focal concerns—areas or issues which command widespread and persistent attention and a high degree of emotional involvement. The specific concerns cited here, while by no means confined to the American lower classes, constitute a distinctive *patterning* of concerns which differs significantly, both in rank order and weighting, from that of American middle class culture. Chart 1 presents a highly schematic and simplified listing of six of the major concerns of lower class culture. Each is conceived as a "dimension" within which a fairly wide and varied range of alternative behav-

the extent to which the social work effort was able to effect behavioral changes.

3 Between 40 and 60 per cent of all Americans are directly influenced by lower class culture, with about 15 per cent, or twenty-five million, comprising the "hard core" lower class group—defined primarily by its use of the "female-based" household as the basic form of child-rearing unit and of the "serial monogamy" mating pattern as the primary form of marriage. The term "lower class culture" as used here refers most specifically to the way of life of the "hard core" group; systematic research in this area would probably reveal at least four to six major subtypes of lower class culture, for some of which the "concerns" presented here would be differently weighted, especially for those subtypes in which "law-abiding" behavior has a high overt valuation. It is impossible within the compass of this short paper to make the finer intracultural distinctions which a more accurate presentation would require.

Chart 1

FOCAL CONCERNS OF LOWER CLASS CULTURE

Area	Perceived alternatives (state, quality, condition)	
1. Trouble:	law-abiding behavior	law-violating behavior
2. Toughness:	physical prowess, skill; "masculinity"; fearlessness, bravery, daring	weakness, ineptitude; effeminacy; timidity, cowardice, caution
3. Smartness:	ability to outsmart, dupe, "con"; gaining money by "wits"; shrewdness, adroitness in repartee	gullibility, "con-ability"; gaining money by hard work; slowness, dull-wittedness, verbal maladroitness
4. Excitement:	thrill; risk, danger; change, activity	boredom; "deadness," safeness; sameness, passivity
5. Fate:	favored by fortune, being "lucky"	ill-omened, being "unlucky"
6. Autonomy:	freedom from external constraint; freedom from superordinate authority; independence	presence of external constraint; presence of strong authority; dependency, being "cared for"

ior patterns may be followed by different individuals under different situations. They are listed roughly in order of the degree of *explicit* attention accorded each and, in this sense, represent a weighted ranking of concerns. The "perceived alternatives" represent polar positions which define certain parameters within each dimension. As will be explained in more detail, it is necessary in relating the influence of these "concerns" to the motivation of delinquent behavior to specify *which* of its aspects is oriented to, whether orientation is *overt* or *covert, positive* (conforming to or seeking the aspect) or *negative* (rejecting or seeking to avoid the aspect).

The concept "focal concern" is used here in preference to the concept "value" for several interrelated reasons: (1) It is more readily derivable from direct field observation. (2) It is descriptively neutral—permitting independent consideration of positive and negative valences as varying under dif-

ferent conditions, whereas "value" carries a built-in positive valence. (3) It makes possible more refined analysis of subcultural differences, since it reflects actual behavior, whereas "value" tends to wash out intracultural differences since it is colored by notions of the "official" ideal.

Trouble

Concern over "trouble" is a dominant feature of lower class culture. The concept has various shades of meaning; "trouble" in one of its aspects represents a situation or a kind of behavior which results in unwelcome or complicating involvement with official authorities or agencies of middle class society. "Getting into trouble" and "staying out of trouble" represent major issues for male and female, adults and children. For men, "trouble" frequently involves fighting or sexual adventures while drinking; for women, sexual involvement with disadvantageous consequences. Expressed desire to avoid behavior which violates moral or legal norms is often based less on an explicit commitment to "official" moral or legal standards than on a desire to avoid "getting into trouble," e.g., the complicating consequences of the action.

The dominant concern over "trouble" involves a distinction of critical importance for the lower class community —that between "law-abiding" and "non-law-abiding" behavior. There is a high degree of sensitivity as to where each person stands in relation to these two classes of activity. Whereas in the middle class community a major dimension for evaluating a person's status is "achievement" and its external symbols, in the lower class personal status is very frequently gauged along the law-abiding–non-law-abiding dimension. A mother will evaluate the suitability of her daughter's boyfriend less on the basis of his achievement potential than on the basis of his innate "trouble" potential. This sensitive awareness of the opposition of "trouble-producing" and "non-trouble-producing" behavior represents both a major basis for deriving status distinctions and an internalized conflict potential for the individual.

As in the case of other focal concerns, which of two perceived alternatives—"law-abiding" or "non-law-abiding"—is valued varies according to the individual and the circumstances; in many instances there is an overt commitment to the "law-abiding" alternative, but a covert commitment to the "non-law-abiding." In certain situations, "getting into trouble" is overtly recognized as prestige-conferring; for example, membership in certain adult and adolescent primary groupings ("gangs") is contingent on having demonstrated an explicit commitment to the law-violating alternative. It is most important to note that the choice between "law-abiding" and "non-law-abiding" behavior is still a choice *within* lower class culture; the distinction between the policeman and the criminal, the outlaw and the sheriff, involves primarily this one dimension; in other respects they have a high community of interests. Not infrequently brothers raised in an identical cultural milieu will become police and criminals respectively.

For a substantial segment of the lower class population "getting into trouble" is not in itself overtly defined as prestige-conferring, but is implicitly recognized as a means to other valued ends, e.g., the covertly valued desire to be "cared for" and subject to external constraint, or the overtly valued state of excitement or risk. Very frequently "getting into trouble" is multi-functional and achieves several sets of valued ends.

Toughness

The concept of "toughness" in lower class culture represents a compound combination of qualities or states. Among its most important components are physical prowess, evidenced both by demonstrated possession of strength and endurance and by athletic skill; "masculinity," symbolized by a distinctive complex of acts and avoidances (bodily tatooing, absence of sentimentality, non-concern with "art," "literature," conceptualization of women as conquest objects, etc.); and bravery in the face of physical threat. The model for the "tough guy"—hard, fearless, undemonstrative, skilled in physical combat—is represented by the movie gangster of the thirties, the "private eye," and the movie cowboy.

The genesis of the intense concern over "toughness" in lower class culture is probably related to the fact that a significant proportion of lower class males are reared in a predominantly female household and lack a consistently present male figure with whom to identify and from whom to learn essential components of a "male" role. Since women serve as a primary object of identification during pre-adolescent years, the almost obsessive lower class concern with "masculinity" probably resembles a type of compulsive reaction-formation. A concern over homosexuality runs like a persistent thread through lower class culture. This is manifested by the institutionalized practice of baiting "queers," often accompanied by violent physical attacks, an expressed contempt for "softness" or frills, and the use of the local term for "homosexual" as a generalized pejorative epithet (e.g., higher class individuals or upwardly mobile peers are frequently characterized as "fags" or "queers"). The distinction between "overt" and "covert" orientation to aspects of an area of concern is especially important in regard to "toughness." A positive overt evaluation of behavior defined as "effeminate" would be out of the question for a lower class male; however, built into lower class culture is a range of devices which permit men to adopt behaviors and concerns which in other cultural milieux fall within the province of women, and at the same time to be defined as "tough" and manly. For example, lower class men can be professional short-order cooks in a diner and still be regarded as "tough." The highly intimate circumstances of the street corner gang involve the recurrent expression of strongly affectionate feelings towards other men. Such expressions, however, are disguised as their opposite, taking the form of ostensibly aggressive verbal and physical interaction (kidding, "ranking," roughhousing, etc.).

Smartness

"Smartness," as conceptualized in lower class culture, involves the capacity to outsmart, outfox, outwit, dupe, "take," "con" another or others and the concomitant capacity to avoid being outwitted, "taken," or duped oneself. In its essence, smartness involves the capacity to achieve a valued entity—material goods, personal status—through a maximum use of mental agility and a minimum use of physical effort. This capacity has an extremely long tradition in lower class culture and is highly valued. Lower class culture can be characterized as "non-intellectual" only if intellectualism is defined specifically in terms of control over a particular body of formally learned knowledge involving "culture" (art, literature, "good" music, etc.), a generalized perspective on the past and present conditions of our own and other societies, and other areas of knowledge imparted by formal educational institutions. This particular type of mental attainment is, in general, overtly disvalued and frequently associated with effeminacy; "smartness" in the lower class sense, however, is highly valued.

The lower class child learns and practices the use of this skill in the street corner situation. Individuals continually practice duping and outwitting one another through recurrent card games and other forms of gambling, mutual exchanges of insults, and "testing" for mutual "con-ability." Those who demonstrate competence in this skill are accorded considerable prestige. Leadership roles in the corner group are frequently allocated according to demonstrated capacity in the two areas of "smartness" and "toughness"; the ideal leader combines both, but the "smart" leader is often accorded more prestige than the "tough" one—reflecting a general lower class respect for "brains" in the "smartness" sense.[4]

[4] The "brains-brawn" set of capacities are often paired in lower class folk lore or accounts of lower class life, e.g., "Brer

The model of the "smart" person is represented in popular media by the card shark, the professional gambler, the "con" artist, the promoter. A conceptual distinction is made between two kinds of people: "suckers," easy marks, "lushes," dupes, who work for their money and are legitimate targets of exploitation; and sharp operators, the "brainy" ones, who live by their wits and "getting" from the suckers by mental adroitness.

Involved in the syndrome of capacities related to "smartness" is a dominant emphasis in lower class culture on ingenious aggressive repartee. This skill, learned and practiced in the context of the corner group, ranges in form from the widely prevalent semi-ritualized teasing, kidding, razzing, "ranking," so characteristic of male peer group interaction, to the highly ritualized type of mutual insult interchange known as "the dirty dozens," "the dozens," "playing house," and other terms. This highly patterned cultural form is practiced on its most advanced level in adult male Negro society, but less polished variants are found throughout lower class culture—practiced, for example, by white children, male and female, as young as four or five. In essence, "doin' the dozens" involves two antagonists who vie with each other in the exchange of increasingly inflammatory insults, with incestuous and perverted sexual relations with the mother a dominant theme. In this form of insult interchange, as well as on other less ritualized occasions for joking, semi-serious, and serious mutual invective, a very high premium is placed on ingenuity, hair-trigger responsiveness, inventiveness, and the acute exercise of mental faculties.

Fox" and "Brer Bear" in the Uncle Remus stories, or George and Lennie in "Of Mice and Men."

Excitement

For many lower class individuals the rhythm of life fluctuates between periods of relatively routine or repetitive activity and sought situations of great emotional stimulation. Many of the most characteristic features of lower class life are related to the search for excitement or "thrill." Involved here are the highly prevalent use of alcohol by both sexes and the widespread use of gambling of all kinds—playing the numbers, betting on horse races, dice, cards. The quest for excitement finds what is perhaps its most vivid expression in the highly patterned practice of the recurrent "night on the town." This practice, designated by various terms in different areas ("honky-tonkin' "; "goin' out on the town"; "bar hoppin' "), involves a patterned set of activities in which alcohol, music, and sexual adventuring are major components. A group or individual sets out to "make the rounds" of various bars or night clubs. Drinking continues progressively throughout the evening. Men seek to "pick up" women, and women play the risky game of entertaining sexual advances. Fights between men involving women, gambling, and claims of physical prowess, in various combinations, are frequent consequences of a night of making the rounds. The explosive potential of this type of adventuring with sex and aggression, frequently leading to "trouble," is semi-explicitly sought by the individual. Since there is always a good likelihood that being out on the town will eventuate in fights, etc., the practice involves elements of sought risk and desired danger.

Counterbalancing the "flirting with danger" aspect of the "excitement" concern is the prevalence in lower class culture of other well-established patterns of activity which involve long periods of relative inaction or passivity. The term "hanging out" in lower class culture refers to extended periods of standing around, often with peer mates, doing what is defined as "nothing," "shooting the breeze," etc. A definite periodicity exists in the pattern of activity relating to the two aspects of the "excitement" dimension. For many lower class individuals the venture into the high risk world of alcohol, sex, and fighting occurs regularly once a week, with interim periods devoted to accommodating to possible consequences of these periods, along with recurrent resolves not to become so involved again.

Fate

Related to the quest for excitement is the concern with fate, fortune, or luck. Here also a distinction is made between two states—being "lucky" or "in luck" and being unlucky or jinxed. Many lower class individuals feel that their lives are subject to a set of forces over which they have relatively little control. These are not directly equated with the supernatural forces of formally organized religion, but relate more to a concept of "destiny," or man as a pawn of magical powers. Not infrequently this often implicit world view is associated with a conception of the ultimate futility of directed effort towards a goal: if the cards are right, or the dice good to you, or if your lucky number comes up, things will go your way; if luck is against you, it's not worth trying. The concept of performing semi-magical rituals so that one's "luck will change" is prevalent; one hopes as a result to move from the state of being "unlucky" to that of being "lucky." The element of fantasy plays an important part in this area. Related to and complementing the notion that "only suckers work" (Smartness) is the idea that once things start going your way, relatively independent of your own effort, all good

things will come to you. Achieving great material rewards (big cars, big houses, a roll of cash to flash in a fancy night club), valued in lower class as well as in other parts of American culture, is a recurrent theme in lower class fantasy and folk lore; the cocaine dreams of Willie the Weeper or Minnie the Moocher present the components of this fantasy in vivid detail.

The prevalence in the lower class community of many forms of gambling, mentioned in connection with the "excitement" dimension, is also relevant here. Through cards and pool which involve skill, and thus both "toughness" and "smartness"; or through race horse betting, involving "smartness"; or through playing the numbers, involving predominantly "luck," one may make a big killing with a minimum of directed and persistent effort within conventional occupational channels. Gambling in its many forms illustrates the fact that many of the persistent features of lower class culture are multifunctional—serving a range of desired ends at the same time. Describing some of the incentives behind gambling has involved mention of all of the focal concerns cited so far—Toughness, Smartness, and Excitement, in addition to Fate.

Autonomy

The extent and nature of control over the behavior of the individual—an important concern in most cultures—has a special significance and is distinctively patterned in lower class culture. The discrepancy between what is overtly valued and what is covertly sought is particularly striking in this area. On the overt level there is a strong and frequently expressed resentment of the idea of external controls, restrictions on behavior, and unjust or coercive authority. "No one's gonna push *me* around," or "I'm gonna tell him he can take the job and shove it. . . ." are commonly expressed sentiments. Similar explicit attitudes are maintained to systems of behavior-restricting rules, insofar as these are perceived as representing the injunctions and bearing the sanctions of superordinate authority. In addition, in lower class culture a close conceptual connection is made between "authority" and "nurturance." To be restrictively or firmly controlled is to be cared for. Thus the overtly negative evaluation of superordinate authority frequently extends as well to nurturance, care, or protection. The desire for personal independence is often expressed in such terms as "I don't need *nobody* to take care of me. I can take care of myself!" Actual patterns of behavior, however, reveal a marked discrepancy between expressed sentiment and what is covertly valued. Many lower class people appear to seek out highly restrictive social environments wherein stringent external controls are maintained over their behavior. Such institutions as the armed forces, the mental hospital, the disciplinary school, the prison or correctional institution, provide environments which incorporate a strict and detailed set of rules, defining and limiting behavior and enforced by an authority system which controls and applies coercive sanctions for deviance from these rules. While under the jurisdiction of such systems, the lower class person generally expresses to his peers continual resentment of the coercive, unjust, and arbitrary exercise of authority. Having been released, or having escaped from these milieux, however, he will often act in such a way as to insure recommitment, or choose recommitment voluntarily after a temporary period of "freedom."

Lower class patients in mental hospitals will exercise considerable ingenuity to insure continued commitment while voicing the desire to get out; delinquent boys will frequently "run" from a correctional institution to activate efforts to return them; to be caught and returned means that one is cared for. Since "being controlled" is equated with "being cared for," attempts are frequently made to "test" the severity or strictness of superordinate authority to see if it remains firm. If intended or executed rebellion produces swift and firm punitive sanctions, the individual is reassured, at the same time that he is complaining bitterly at the injustice of being caught and punished. Some environmental milieux, having been tested in this fashion for the "firmness" of their coercive sanctions, are rejected, ostensibly for being too strict, actually for not being strict enough. This is frequently so in the case of "problematic" behavior by lower class youngsters in the public schools, which generally cannot command the coercive controls implicitly sought by the individual.

A similar discrepancy between what is overtly and covertly desired is found in the area of dependence-independence. The pose of tough rebellious independence often assumed by the lower class person frequently conceals powerful dependency cravings. These are manifested primarily by obliquely expressed resentment when "care" is not forthcoming rather than by expressed satisfaction when it is. The concern over autonomy-dependency is related both to "trouble" and "fate." Insofar as the lower class individual feels that his behavior is controlled by forces which often propel him into "trouble" in the face of an explicit determination to avoid it, there is an implied appeal to "save me from myself." A solution appears to lie in arranging things so that his behavior will be coercively restricted by an externally imposed set of controls strong enough to forcibly restrain his inexplicable inclination to get into trouble. The periodicity observed in connection with the "excitement" dimension is also relevant here; after involvement in trouble-producing behavior (assault, sexual adventure, a "drunk"), the individual will actively seek a locus of imposed control (his wife, prison, a restrictive job); after a given period of subjection to this control, resentment against it mounts, leading to a "break away" and a search for involvement in further "trouble."

FOCAL CONCERNS OF THE LOWER CLASS ADOLESCENT STREET CORNER GROUP

The one-sex peer group is a highly prevalent and significant structural form in the lower class community. There is a strong probability that the prevalence and stability of this type of unit is directly related to the prevalence of a stabilized type of lower class child-rearing unit—the "female-based" household. This is a nuclear kin unit in which a male parent is either absent from the household, present only sporadically, or, when present, only minimally or inconsistently involved in the support and rearing of children. This unit usually consists of one or more females of childbearing age and their offspring. The females are frequently related to one another by blood or marriage ties, and the unit often includes two or more generations of women, e.g., the mother and/or aunt of the principal childbearing female.

The nature of social groupings in the lower class community may be clarified if we make the assumption that it is the *one-sex peer unit* rather than the two-parent family unit which represents the most significant relational unit for both sexes in lower class communities. Lower class society may be pictured as comprising a set of age-graded one-sex groups which constitute the major psychic focus and reference group for

those over twelve or thirteen. Men and women of mating age leave these groups periodically to form temporary marital alliances, but these lack stability, and after varying periods of "trying out" the two-sex family arrangement, they gravitate back to the more "comfortable" one-sex grouping, whose members exert strong pressure on the individual *not* to disrupt the group by adopting a two-sex household pattern of life.[5] Membership in a stable and solidary peer unit is vital to the lower class individual precisely to the extent to which a range of essential functions —psychological, educational, and others—are not provided by the "family" unit.

The adolescent street corner group represents the adolescent variant of this lower class structural form. What has been called the "delinquent gang" is one subtype of this form, defined on the basis of frequency of participation in law-violating activity; this subtype should not be considered a legitimate unit of study per se, but rather as one particular variant of the adolescent street corner group. The "hanging" peer group is a unit of particular importance for the adolescent male. In many cases it is the most stable and solidary primary group he has ever belonged to; for boys reared in female-based households the corner group provides the first real opportunity to learn essential aspects of the male role in the context of peers facing similar problems of sex-role identification.

The form and functions of the adolescent corner group operate as a selective mechanism in recruiting members.

[5] Further data on the female-based household unit (estimated as comprising about 15 per cent of all American "families") and the role of one-sex groupings in lower class culture are contained in Walter B. Miller, Implications of Urban Lower Class Culture for Social Work. *Social Service Review*, 1959, 33, No. 3.

The activity patterns of the group require a high level of intragroup solidarity; individual members must possess a good capacity for subordinating individual desires to general group interests as well as the capacity for intimate and persisting interaction. Thus highly "disturbed" individuals, or those who cannot tolerate consistently imposed sanctions on "deviant" behavior cannot remain accepted members; the group itself will extrude those whose behavior exceeds limits defined as "normal." This selective process produces a type of group whose members possess to an unusually high degree both the *capacity* and *motivation* to conform to perceived cultural norms, so that the nature of the system of norms and values oriented to is a particularly influential component of motivation.

Focal concerns of the male adolescent corner group are those of the general cultural milieu in which it functions. As would be expected, the relative weighting and importance of these concerns pattern somewhat differently for adolescents than for adults. The nature of this patterning centers around two additional "concerns" of particular importance to this group—concern with "belonging," and with "status." These may be conceptualized as being on a higher level of abstraction than concerns previously cited, since "status" and "belonging" are achieved *via* cited concern areas of Toughness, etc.

Belonging

Since the corner group fulfills essential functions for the individual, being a member in good standing of the group is of vital importance for its members. A continuing concern over who is "in" and who is not involves the citation and detailed discussion of highly refined criteria for "in-group" membership. The phrase "he hangs with us" means "he is accepted as a member in good standing by current consensus"; conversely, "he don't hang with us" means he is not so accepted. One achieves "belonging" primarily by demonstrating knowledge of and determination to adhere to the system of standards and valued qualities defined by the group. One maintains membership by acting in conformity with valued aspects of Toughness, Smartness, Autonomy, etc. In those instances where conforming to norms of this reference group at the same time violates norms of other reference groups (e.g., middle class adults, institutional "officials"), immediate reference group norms are much more compelling since violation risks invoking the group's most powerful sanction: exclusion.

Status

In common with most adolescents in American society, the lower class corner group manifests a dominant concern with "status." What differentiates this type of group from others, however, is the particular set of criteria and weighting thereof by which "status" is defined. In general, status is achieved and maintained by demonstrated possession of the valued qualities of lower class culture—Toughness, Smartness, expressed resistance to authority, daring, etc. It is important to stress once more that the individual orients to these concerns *as they are defined within lower class society;* e.g., the status-conferring potential of "smartness" in the sense of scholastic achievement generally ranges from negligible to negative.

The concern with "status" is manifested in a variety of ways. Intragroup status is a continued concern and is derived and tested constantly by means of a set of status-ranking activities; the intragroup "pecking order" is constantly at issue. One gains status within the group by demonstrated superiority in

Toughness (physical prowess, bravery, skill in athletics and games such as pool and cards), Smartness (skill in repartee, capacity to "dupe" fellow group members), and the like. The term "ranking," used to refer to the pattern of intra-group aggressive repartee, indicates awareness of the fact that this is one device for establishing the intragroup status hierarchy.

The concern over status in the adolescent corner group involves in particular the component of "adultness," the intense desire to be seen as "grown up," and a corresponding aversion to "kid stuff." "Adult" status is defined less in terms of the assumption of "adult" responsibility than in terms of certain external symbols of adult status—a car, ready cash, and, in particular, a perceived "freedom" to drink, smoke, and gamble as one wishes and to come and go without external restrictions. The desire to be seen as "adult" is often a more significant component of much involvement in illegal drinking, gambling, and automobile driving than the explicit enjoyment of these acts as such.

The intensity of the corner group member's desire to be seen as "adult" is sufficiently great that he feels called upon to demonstrate qualities associated with adultness (Toughness, Smartness, Autonomy) to a much greater degree than a lower class adult. This means that he will seek out and utilize those avenues to these qualities which he perceives as available with greater intensity than an adult and less regard for their "legitimacy." In this sense the adolescent variant of lower class culture represents a maximization or an intensified manifestation of many of its most characteristic features.

Concern over status is also manifested in reference to other street corner groups. The term "rep" used in this regard is especially significant and has broad connotations. In its most frequent and explicit connotation, "rep" refers to the "toughness" of the corner group as a whole relative to that of other groups; a "pecking order" also exists among the several corner groups in a given interactional area, and there is a common perception that the safety or security of the group and all its members depends on maintaining a solid "rep" for toughness vis-a-vis other groups. This motive is most frequently advanced as a reason for involvement in gang fights: "We *can't* chicken out on this fight; our rep would be shot!"; this implies that the group would be relegated to the bottom of the status ladder and become a helpless and recurrent target of external attack.

On the other hand, there is implicit in the concept of "rep" the recognition that "rep" has or may have a dual basis —corresponding to the two aspects of the "trouble" dimension. It is recognized that group as well as individual status can be based on both "law-abiding" and "law-violating" behavior. The situational resolution of the persisting conflict between the "law-abiding" and "law-violating" bases of status comprises a vital set of dynamics in determining whether a "delinquent" mode of behavior will be adopted by a group, under what circumstances, and how persistently. The determinants of this choice are evidently highly complex and fluid, and rest on a range of factors including the presence and perceptual immediacy of different community reference-group loci (e.g., professional criminals, police, clergy, teachers, settlement house workers), the personality structures and "needs" of group members, the presence in the community of social work, recreation, or educational programs which can facilitate utilization of the "law-abiding" basis of status, and so on.

What remains constant is the critical importance of "status" both for the members of the group as individuals and for the group as a whole insofar as members perceive their individual destinies as linked to the destiny of the group, and the fact that action geared to attain status is much more acutely oriented to the fact of status itself than to the legality or illegality, morality or immorality of the means used to achieve it.

LOWER CLASS CULTURE AND THE MOTIVATION OF DELINQUENT BEHAVIOR

The customary set of activities of the adolescent street corner group includes activities which are in violation of laws and ordinances of the legal code. Most of these center around assault and theft of various types (the gang fight; auto theft; assault on an individual; petty pilfering and shoplifting; "mugging"; pocketbook theft). Members of street corner gangs are well aware of the law-violating nature of these acts; they are not psychopaths, or physically or mentally "defective"; in fact, since the corner group supports and enforces a rigorous set of standards which demand a high degree of fitness and personal competence, it tends to recruit from the most "able" members of the community.

Why, then, is the commission of crimes a customary feature of gang activity? The most general answer is that the commission of crimes by members of adolescent street corner groups is motivated primarily by the attempt to achieve ends, states, or conditions which are valued and to avoid those that are disvalued within their most meaningful cultural milieu, through those culturally available avenues which appear as the most feasible means of attaining those ends.

The operation of these influences is well illustrated by the gang fight—a prevalent and characteristic type of corner group delinquency. This type of activity comprises a highly stylized and culturally patterned set of sequences. Although details vary under different circumstances, the following events are generally included. A member or several members of group A "trespass" on the claimed territory of group B. While there they commit an act or acts which group B defines as a violation of their rightful privileges, an affront to their honor, or a challenge to their "rep." Frequently this act involves advances to a girl associated with group B; it may occur at a dance or party; sometimes the mere act of "trespass" is seen as deliberate provocation. Members of group B then assault members of group A, if they are caught while still in B's territory. Assaulted members of group A return to their "home" territory and recount to members of their group details of the incident, stressing the insufficient nature of the provocation ("I just *looked* at her! Hardly even said anything!"), and the unfair circumstances of the assault ("About *twenty* guys jumped just the *two* of us!"). The highly colored account is acutely inflammatory; group A, perceiving its honor violated and its "rep" threatened, feels obligated to retaliate in force. Sessions of detailed planning now occur; allies are recruited if the size of group A and its potential allies appears to necessitate larger numbers; strategy is plotted, and messengers dispatched. Since the prospect of a gang fight is frightening to even the "toughest" group members, a constant rehearsal of the provocative incident or incidents and declamations of the essentially evil nature of the opponents accompany the planning process to bolster possibly weakening motivation to fight. The excursion into "enemy" territory sometimes results in a full scale fight; more often group B cannot be found, or the police appear and stop the fight, "tipped off" by an anonymous informant. When this occurs, group members express disgust and disappointment; secretly there is much relief; their honor has been avenged without incurring injury; often the anonymous tipster is a member of one of the involved groups.

The basic elements of this type of delinquency are sufficiently stabilized and recurrent as to constitute an essentially ritualized pattern, resembling both in structure and expressed motives for action classic forms such as the European "duel," the American Indian tribal war, and the Celtic clan feud. Although the arousing and "acting out" of individual aggressive emotions are inevitably involved in the gang fight, neither its form nor motivational dynamics can be adequately handled within a predominantly personality-focused frame of reference.

It would be possible to develop in considerable detail the processes by which the commission of a range of illegal acts is either explicitly supported by, implicitly demanded by, or not materially inhibited by factors relating to the focal concerns of lower class culture. In place of such a development, the following three statements condense in general terms the operation of these processes:

1. Following cultural practices which comprise essential elements of the total life pattern of lower class culture automatically violates certain legal norms.

2. In instances where alternate avenues to similar objectives are available, the non-law-abiding avenue frequently provides a relatively greater and more immediate return for a relatively smaller investment of energy.

3. The "demanded" response to certain situations recurrently engendered within lower class culture involves the commission of illegal acts.

The primary thesis of this paper is that the dominant component of the motivation of "delinquent" behavior engaged in by members of lower class corner groups involves a positive effort to achieve states, conditions, or qualities valued within the actor's most significant cultural milieu. If "conformity to immediate reference group values" is the major component of motivation of "delinquent" behavior by gang members, why is such behavior frequently referred to as negativistic, malicious, or rebellious? Albert Cohen, for example, in *Delinquent Boys* (Glencoe, Ill.: Free Press, 1955) describes behavior which violates school rules as comprising elements of "active spite and malice, contempt and ridicule, challenge and defiance." He ascribes to the gang "keen delight in terrorizing 'good' children, and in general making themselves obnoxious to the virtuous." A recent national conference on social work with "hard-to-reach" groups characterized lower class corner groups as "youth groups in conflict with the culture of their (*sic*) communities." Such characterizations are obviously the result of taking the middle class community and its institutions as an implicit point of reference.

A large body of systematically interrelated attitudes, practices, behaviors, and values characteristic of lower class culture are designed to support and maintain the basic features of the lower class way of life. In areas where these differ from features of middle class culture, action oriented to the achievement and maintenance of the lower class system may violate norms of middle class culture and be perceived as deliberately non-conforming or malicious by an observer strongly cathected to middle class norms. This does not mean, however, that violation of the middle class norm is the dominant component of motivation; it is a by-product of action primarily oriented to the lower class system. The standards of lower class culture cannot be seen merely as a reverse function of middle class culture—as middle class standards "turned upside down"; lower class culture is a distinctive tradition many centuries old with an integrity of its own.

From the viewpoint of the acting individual, functioning within a field of well-structured cultural forces, the relative impact of "conforming" and "rejective" elements in the motivation of gang delinquency is weighted preponderantly on the conforming side. Rejective or rebellious elements are inevitably involved, but their influence during the actual commission of delinquent acts is relatively small compared to the influence of pressures to achieve what is valued by the actor's most immediate reference groups. Expressed awareness by the actor of the element of rebellion often represents only that aspect of motivation of which he is explicitly conscious; the deepest and most compelling components of motivation—adherence to highly meaningful group standards of Toughness, Smartness, Excitement, etc.—are often unconsciously patterned. No cultural pattern as well established as the practice of illegal acts by members of lower class corner groups could persist if buttressed primarily by negative, hostile, or rejective motives; its principal motivational support, as in the case of any persisting cultural tradition, derives from a positive effort to achieve what is valued within that tradition, and to conform to its explicit and implicit norms.

14.   The Conflict of Values in Delinquency Areas

SOLOMON KOBRIN

The circumstance that fewer than one-quarter of the boys in the urban areas of high rates of delinquents are brought into the juvenile court charged as delinquents appears to invalidate the hypothesis that in the disorganized city areas delinquency is primarily a product of cultural rather than of personality or psychological processes.[1] Some of the official statistics of delinquency seem to suggest that most children conform to the legal norms of the wider society even in those urban areas where the culture of the local community is relatively favorable to the transmission of delinquent conduct patterns.[2] These

statistics therefore leave the inference that even in this situation variables other than culture are of possibly greater importance in delinquency causation than the customary sociological explanations would concede.

While the literature of juvenile delinquency is replete with discussions of the inadequacy of delinquency statistics in general as a basis for measuring the extent of officially proscribed behavior in the larger administrative areas,[3] the present paper will attempt

---

* Paper read at the annual meeting of the American Sociological Society held in Denver, September 7-9, 1950.

[1] The ecological studies of Shaw and McKay in Chicago show that the proportion of juvenile court-age boys on whom delinquency petitions were filed in the highest rate square mile areas were: for the 1917–1923 series, 19.4 per cent; for the 1927–1933 series, 18.9 per cent; and for the 1934–1940 series, 21.8 per cent. C. R. Shaw and Henry D. McKay, *Juvenile Delinquency and Urban Areas*, Chicago: University of Chicago Press, 1942, pp. 53 and 59. The figure for the 1934–1940 series is based on unpublished material by the same authors.

[2] Tappan observes that these statistics indicate that "most people living in such associations and under such social and psy-

chological influences as those of the deteriorated slum do not violate the law." Paul W. Tappan, *Juvenile Delinquency,* New York: McGraw-Hill Book Co., 1949, p. 142. The ambivalence of many students in this field regarding the validity of delinquency statistics as a basis for judgments about the extent of proscribed behavior among children is revealed in the same author's assertion which appears earlier in the same work that "statistical data on the volume of delinquency give no valid picture of its actual extent." *Ibid.*, p. 37.

[3] Among recent evaluations of this problem are: Negley K. Teeters and John O. Reinemann, *The Challenge of Delinquency,* New York: Prentice-Hall, Inc., 1950, pp. 12–19; and Paul W. Tappan, *op. cit.,* pp. 31–52. Relevant discussion is also provided in Sophia M. Robison, "Wanted—An Index of Crime and Delinquency," *Proceedings,* American Prison Association, 1945, pp. 203–212; Edward E. Schwartz, "Statistics of Juvenile Delinquency in the

---

SOURCE. Solomon Kobrin, "The Conflict of Values in Delinquency Areas," from *American Sociological Review,* Volume 16, October 1951, pp. 653–661. Reprinted with the permission of the American Sociological Association and the author.

to provide a demonstration of the inadequacies of these statistics with respect to the extent of delinquent behavior in the urban slum areas. This is deemed necessary only because the high proportion of official non-delinquency in these areas is sometimes construed as vital evidence bearing on the nature of the problem of delinquency. In addition, an attempt will be made to formulate a hypothesis with reference to delinquency in the high rate urban areas consistent with the statistical evidence of its extent in such areas, and to subject this hypothesis to preliminary examination in terms of certain widely observed features both of slum delinquency and its enveloping social structure.

I

As is well known, enumerations of delinquents based on different measures of delinquency produce different impressions of its extent. With increasing degrees of inclusiveness these measures range from commitments to training schools and other custodial institutions, through official and unofficial juvenile court cases, to police complaint cases. On the grounds of either accuracy or completeness no conclusive arguments may be adduced for regarding any of these enumerations as preferable, since each may serve to measure accurately a defined level of deviational behavior, or official action, or both.[4]

United States," *The Annals*, 261 (1949), 9-20; I. Richard Perlman, "The Meaning of Juvenile Delinquency Statistics," *Federal Probation*, September 1949, 63–67; F. J. Murphy, M. M. Shirley, and H. L. Witmer, "The Incidence of Hidden Delinquency," *American Journal of Orthopsychiatry*, 16 (1946), 686–696; and W. S. Robinson, "Ecological Correlations and the Behavior of Individuals," *American Sociological Review*, 15 (June 1950), 351–357.

[4] Insofar as any of these measures may be assumed to bear a constant ratio to the total volume of proscribed behavior, they may be used as indexes of delinquency. These indexes, in turn, may be validly

Thus, the range of possible enumerations of delinquents in the high rate areas may be illustrated by the data from one representative jurisdiction. During the seven-year period 1927–1933 the rate of commitment per 100 boys of juvenile court age residing in Chicago in the ten square mile areas with highest rates was 6.1.[5] In the highest rate square mile area this rate was 9.2. During the same period the rate of official court delinquents in the ten square mile areas of highest rates was 14.6, with a rate of 18.9 in the top square mile area.

In contrast to both commitments and juvenile court appearances, police complaint cases, as may be anticipated, include in the delinquent classification a considerably larger proportion of boys residing in urban delinquency areas. Thus, the Chicago data show that the average rate of delinquents based on police complaints for the ten square mile areas of highest rates for the year 1926 was 20.6. In this police series the top area had a rate of 26.6.[6] However, these rates are not computed on the basis of the seven-year period of age eligibility, and therefore do not parallel rates of commitments or court appearances. To restore comparability between the rates of police complaints here presented and rates of commitments and court appearances, it is necessary to multiply by seven the annual rate given. Since the data for the police series do not eliminate duplications of individuals, the multiplication required would result in a rate which exceeds the total age-eligible boy population

used only to gain a picture of the relative volume of delinquency in subdivisions of the same juvenile court jurisdiction during a period of time when administrative practices remain unchanged.

[5] Clifford R. Shaw and Henry D. McKay, *op. cit.*, p. 70.

[6] From police data available in the Sociology Department, Illinois Institute for Juvenile Research.

ulation of these areas. Unfortunately, a count of unduplicated individuals who became police cases in the ten highest rate areas of Chicago is not available for 1926.

However, such a count is available for an area of moderate rates for the standard seven-year period of juvenile court eligibility. A count of the unduplicated juveniles dealt with by the police during the 1927–1933 period disclosed that the police complaint rate for this area was 28.8, as compared to an average annual rate of police cases of 9.2 for the area. This indicates that the proportion of unduplicated individuals who become police cases during their seven-year period of eligibility is approximately three times larger than the rate of police cases for a single given year. Since the rate of police cases for the ten highest rate areas in Chicago in the single year 1926 was 20.6, the suggested relative magnitudes of single and seven-year rates indicate that the rate of police cases for the top ten square mile areas in Chicago during the seven-year period centering on 1926 was 65.9.[7] This is the proportion of individuals who, as they moved from their first to their seventh year of age eligibility, engaged in misbehavior serious enough to warrant recorded police attention. And this is the rate which is more nearly comparable, in terms of the basis of computation, to the rates of commitment and court appearance of 6.1 and 14.6 respectively, cited above. Thus, it is evident that when the most inclusive measure based on official records is used, not one-fifth but almost two-thirds of the boys in delinquency areas may be regarded as official delinquents.

The validity of such official cases for the measurement of delinquency rests not only on its inclusiveness of all offi-

cial delinquents, but on its capacity to mark out as well a homogeneous segment of the juvenile population which is consistently delinquent in terms of behavior content. It is of course with reference to the latter function that the official statistics of delinquency are more severely limited. After making the distinctions between the types of measures discussed, and concluding that police complaints probably represent the most inclusive measure, we are still confronted with the question whether the group thus identified is a distinctively delinquent group in contrast to the balance of the juvenile population. In other words, does even this inclusive measure include all juveniles who engage in delinquent activity? The answer, of course, is that it does not since it is well known that many delinquent juveniles who are never apprehended are known to social agencies, neighbors, friends, and associates.

Even if a defensible division of boys between delinquent and non-delinquent could be made, the prognostic value of the concept "delinquent," in its official sense, would still be uncertain. This is indicated by the findings of a recent follow-up of the careers of 83 public school boys who in 1929 resided in one of Chicago's delinquency areas. The individuals in this group were ascertained to be without records of appearances before the juvenile court prior to 1929. In 1949 an examination of their records of law violations during their adult careers revealed that 51 per cent of this group had been arrested for offenses other than infraction of the traffic laws. While a sample of 69 boys with juvenile court records drawn from the same neighborhood during the same year exhibited an adult arrest rate of 75 per cent, illustrative of the tendency of juvenile courts to deal primarily with the more serious and persistent offenders, the fact remains that over half the

[7] *Ibid.*

boys in the group of putative non-delinquents became adult offenders.[8]

It is altogether unlikely that these individuals stoutly resisted influences in the direction of delinquency during their youth only to succumb as adults. It is more reasonable to assume that as children they, too, engaged in delinquent activity, but perhaps less persistently or with greater success in avoiding detection and treatment in the court. If the terms "delinquent" and "non-delinquent" had dependable descriptive value, the large proportion of boys who were non-delinquent officially would not have appeared as adult offenders.

Taken together, the data presented above indicate that enumerations of delinquents in urban areas of high rates of delinquents exhibit a wide range. It is clear that (a) assertions of the preponderance of non-delinquency in these areas are based on relatively uninclusive official records, and (b) the more inclusive official records indicate the proportion of delinquents to be approximately two-thirds of the age eligibles. Moreover, even so inclusive a category as police complaint cases cannot be regarded as including the total number of offenders, since the police neither know of all offenses committed nor apprehend all offenders.

II

These observations suggest that delinquency is widely diffused in the urban high rate areas and therefore represents normative behavior which, like all normative behavior, generates a systematic scheme of values and institutional forms for its expression. The statistics of delinquency also indicate that a significantly large number of boys in these areas are free of the kind

of involvement in delinquency practices which ordinarily results in the acquisition of a police record or in the development of adult criminality. With respect to the careers of these individuals it seems necessary to assume the ultimate dominance of the norms of conventional society. Thus, a duality of conduct norms in the high rate areas rather than the hegemony of either conventional or criminal value systems may be regarded as the fundamental sociological fact in the culture of these communities.[9] This conclusion is suggested largely by the statistics of delinquency. Its validity may be subjected to further examination by using it in an attempt to explain selected aspects of the problem of delinquency in the high rate urban areas.

The Variability of Behavior Status in the Delinquency Area

The facts indicate that in areas of high rates of delinquents there are not only many boys who engage in delinquent activity without becoming official delinquents, but that a substantial number of boys who do possess police and court records become conventional and law-abiding adults. Moreover, there is evidence that of those who are without juvenile records, many become adult offenders. These apparent reversals of career lines are incomprehensible except on the assumption that the

[8] Unpublished materials available in the Sociology Department, Illinois Institute for Juvenile Research.

[9] This view is related both to Sutherland's concept of "differential association" and to Sellin's emphasis on the primacy of culture conflict, in one form or another, in the etiology of crime. E. H. Sutherland, *Principles of Criminology*, Philadelphia: J. B. Lippincott Co., 1939; and T. Sellin, *Culture Conflict and Crime*, New York: Social Science Research Council, 1938. The present discussion may be regarded, in fact, as an effort to identify and describe with a modicum of detail some of the co-ordinates of culture conflict in the urban delinquency area, and to mark out one type of problem involved in "associating differentially."

individual participates simultaneously in both criminal and conventional value systems. Observation of the social experiences of young persons in the delinquency areas supports this assumption and indicates that the simultaneous participation occurs in two ways.[10]

First, groupings of boys based on play interests frequently include at any given moment of time three types of individuals with reference to delinquent conduct: those who at the time are occasionally delinquent; those who at the time are actively and persistently delinquent; and those who at the time refrain completely from delinquent activity. In terms of propinquity and opportunity for association, delinquents have many contacts with non-delinquents and vice versa. The play of influence with respect to the development of values and goals is simultaneously exerted in both directions, even though delinquents may be expected to have more frequent and more intimate contacts with other delinquents than with non-delinquents.

Second, taken from the standpoint of the developmental pattern of the

individual, marked variability is encountered, particularly in the younger age groups, with respect to the degree of delinquent activity in which the individual is involved from time to time. Thus, the same person, either within the same group or in a succession of groups, may interchangeably occupy the role of persistent delinquent, occasional delinquent, or non-delinquent. He is thus provided an opportunity to experience in a direct and personal manner the full meaning of the alternative value systems implicit in each mode of conduct.

Simultaneous participation in the conventional and criminal value systems in either of the ways indicated is not inconsistent with the fact that over a long period of time persons in delinquency areas who come to occupy either the conventional or the delinquent role will develop more intimate associations and relationships with persons of the same role traits. As a result, progressive alienation from either the criminal or the conventional value scheme ensues, and the person may come in time to live more completely in terms of one rather than in terms of the other value scheme.

These observations emphasize the inadequacy, for purposes of either description or analysis, of designating boys in delinquency areas as delinquent or non-delinquent. In a real sense they are neither and they are both. The world of meanings in which they must find theiy way is an amalgam compounded in widely varying proportions of two implicitly inharmonious codes of conduct. As an amalgam of this character the world of the delinquency area represents an experience for the growing child which is qualitatively different from either the conventional world of the middle class child or the world of the child reared in an outcast society. It is, in fact, a world in which, because

---

[10] Concern with the social and psychological processes resulting in delinquent careers has led to a relative neglect of those aspects of the life of the "submerged" urban areas which center on the conventional and traditional institutions of the wider community. However, the presence of an emphatic strain of conventionality in these areas is indicated in W. F. Whyte, *Street Corner Society*, Chicago: University of Chicago Press, 1943. Ample reflection of the impact of such institutions and agencies as schools, police, social settlements, and churches may be found in C. R. Shaw and H. D. McKay, "Social Factors in Juvenile Delinquency," *Report on the Causes of Crime*, Vol. 2, National Commission on Law Observance and Enforcement, Washington, D.C., 1931; and C. R. Shaw et al., *Brothers in Crime*, Chicago: University of Chicago Press, 1938. There exists, in addition, a large if popular biographical literature detailing the rise of children of poor immigrant families to positions of prominence, power, and wealth within conventional hierarchies.

of its two-scale value orientation, boys move readily between the delinquent and the non-delinquent classifications. Thus, when applied to the boy who resides in an urban area of high rate of delinquents, the term "non-delinquent" becomes ambiguous. This designation has stable meaning primarily in the social world of those who are conventional and law-abiding.

Varieties of Delinquency Areas

The culture of delinquency areas and specific group patterns of delinquency in these areas may be regarded as in large part determined by the character of the interaction between the conventional and the criminal value systems. This fact suggests the possibility of a typology of delinquency areas based on variations in the relationship between these two systems.

Delinquency areas exhibit important differences in the degree to which integration between the conventional and criminal value systems is achieved.[11] Areas range from those in which the integration is well advanced to those in which it is minimal. The two polar types on this continuum may be briefly described.

[11] Competing value systems tend to accommodate to one another by mutual incorporation of elements common to or compatible with each. The criminal culture shares with the conventional culture the goal of a large and assured money income, and like the conventional culture utilizes the flexible processes of politics to achieve this goal. The use of the political process by organized crime entails the development of relationships with functionaries of the established power structure which transcend the symbiotic precisely because both the goal and in general form the methods of achieving the goal are truly shared by representatives of both cultures. The term "integration" as used in this connection denotes a situation in which such relationships are firmly established. When these relationships are haphazard, occasional, or undependable, it appears logical to conceptualize such a situation as representing only partial integration.

In areas where the two systems are highly integrated adult violative activity tends to be systematic and organized. This tendency is revealed in the development in these areas of groups of adults engaged in the promotion and management of consistently profitable illegal enterprises. Leaders in these enterprises frequently maintain membership in such conventional institutions of their local communities as churches, fraternal and mutual benefit societies, and political parties. While participation in the political party organizations is usually required by the character of their occupational activity, participation in churches and the other social organizations of the community represents a spontaneous quest for status in the social structure within which they have become acculturated. Within this framework the influence of each of the two value systems is reciprocal, the leaders of illegal enterprise participating in the primary orientation of the conventional elements in the population, and the latter, through their participation in a local power structure sustained in large part by illicit activity, participating perforce in the alternate, criminal value system.

The stable position of illicit enterprise in the adult society of the community is reflected in the character of delinquent conduct on the part of children. While delinquency in all high rate areas is intrinsically disorderly in that it is unrelated to official programs for the education of the young, in the type of community under discussion boys may more or less realistically recognize the potentialities for personal progress in the local society through success in delinquency. In a general way, therefore, delinquent activity in these areas constitutes a training ground for the acquisition of skill in the use of violence, concealment of offense, evasion of detection and arrest, and the purchase of immunity from punishment. Those who come to excel in these respects are frequently noted and valued by adult leaders in the rackets who are confronted, as are the leaders of all income-producing enterprises, with problems of the recruitment of competent personnel.

As a consequence of this situation delinquency tends to occur within a partial framework of social controls, insofar as delinquent activity in these areas represents a tolerated means for the acquisition of an approved role and status. Thus, while delinquent activity here possesses the usual characteristics of violence and destructiveness, there tend to develop effective limits of permissible activity in this direction. Delinquency is, in other words, encompassed and contained within a local social structure, and is marginally but palpably related to that structure.

The contrasting polar type of delinquency area is characterized principally by the absence of systematic and organized adult activity in violation of law, despite the fact that many adults in these areas commit violations. The presence of violators as adult models in the community legitimizes activity in opposition to law from the point of view of delinquent juveniles. In this situation conventional and criminal systems of values are not merely not integrated, but are in extreme and open opposition to one another. As a consequence, the delinquency in areas of this type tends to be unrestrained by controls originating *at any point* in the adult social structure.

Areas of this type are frequently produced by drastic changes in the class, ethnic, or racial characteristics of its population. Such transitions, as is well known, tend to devitalize the older institutions of the area, and to introduce a period during which institutional and other controls are at a mini-

mum. During these interim periods the bearers of the conventional culture and its value system are without the customary institutional machinery, and therefore in effect partially demobilized with reference to the diffusion of their value system. In these conditions the alternative criminal value system is able to gain both ground and vigor, and to persist on the local scene without effective opposition.

Because adult crime in this type of area is itself unorganized, its value system remains implicit and hence incapable of generating norms which function effectively on a groupwise basis. As a result, juvenile violators readily escape not merely the controls of the conventional persons in the community, but those of adult violators as well. It should be noted that the emergence of group norms on the part of persistent and systematic violators in the contemporary urban milieu is usually accompanied by regularized and dependable accommodations with such representatives of the wider society as police and politicians. It is at this point that the implicit value system of criminality becomes explicit, moves toward integration with conventionality, and undergoes an enhancement of its capacity to exert control over the behavior of violators.

In areas where such integration is absent the delinquencies of juveniles tend to acquire a wild, untrammeled character. Delinquents in this kind of situation more frequently exhibit the personality traits of the social type sometimes referred to as the hoodlum. Both individually and in groups violent physical combat is engaged in for its own sake, almost as a form of recreation. Here groups of delinquents may be seen as excluded, isolated conflict groups dedicated to an unending battle against all forms of constraint. The escape from controls originating in any social structure, other than that provided by unstable groupings of the delinquents themselves, is here complete.

All delinquency areas fall somewhere between the polar types described. Moreover, changes in the character of a given delinquency area may be explained in terms of changes in the degree of integration existing from time to time between the criminal and the conventional value systems. It is, in fact, the specific form of the interaction between these opposing value systems which helps to explain the character of juvenile group activity in specific delinquency areas, as well as changes in these activities in either a criminal or a conventional direction.

Thus, duality of value orientation in the high rate urban areas may be regarded as a fundamental property of a wide variety of specific community situations. While delinquency areas may move toward or away from the integration of these opposing systems of values, the basic character of the social life of these communities appears to be determined in large part by the explicit presence of this duality.

Personality of the Delinquent and Conflicting Value Systems

Juvenile groupings based on common interest in the pursuit of delinquent activity develop a body of shared attitudes which may be regarded as making up a distinctive culture. In a thoughtful analysis of the origin of this culture, Albert K. Cohen[12] has suggested that it arises in a framework of lower socio-economic class status in which many persons are unable, in terms either of achievement or the disciplining of behavior necessary for achievement, to acquire the symbols of

success current in the conventional, respectable, and dominant middle-class culture of the wider society.[13] As a result, young persons are exposed to the invidious judgments of those who, within the range of social contacts of the lower-class child, represent and exemplify the norms of middle-class culture. Such persons, moreover, symbolize, by virtue both of their roles and their class position, the power and prestige of the wider society in which the lower-class area is set.[14] One of several adjustive responses available to young males in this situation is to reject the imputation of inferiority and degradation by emphasizing those activities and personal traits which distinguish them from striving, upward mobile persons. The common response inaugurates new norms of conduct out of which develop the distinctive criteria of status in the delinquent group. Thus, a coherent social milieu is created in which status is distributed according to success in attacking the symbols of middle-class respectability. Since property represents a central symbol of merit and virtue in the culture of this class, stealing and destructiveness become a principal though not the only form taken by the attack.

This analysis constitutes a framework within which personality process and culture process may be in part related for purposes of understanding the delinquent as a person. This analysis also throws light on a further aspect of the conflict of value systems which has

---

[12] Thesis statement submitted to Department of Human Relations, Harvard University, 1949.

[13] The relation of social structure to the delinquency of the high rate urban areas is lucidly analyzed in Robert K. Merton, "Social Structure and Anomie," in *Social Theory and Social Structure*, Glencoe, Ill.: The Free Press, 1949, pp. 134–140.

[14] The significance of the social class identification of teachers for their attitudes toward lower-class children is in part indicated in W. Lloyd Warner, *Democracy in Jonesville*, New York: Harper and Brothers, 1949, pp. 208–210.

been seen as an essential characteristic of delinquency areas.

The aggressively hostile response of the young male in the delinquency area to his devaluation by representatives of the conventional culture arises entirely from the fact that the criteria of status in the conventional culture have validity for him. This is indicated not in the hostile response as such, but in certain sentiments and emotions which accompany the hostility. These associated sentiments are reflected in the acts of defiance and contempt which frequently accompany ordinary depredations of property. Nowhere is this more apparent than in the not uncommon burglaries of schools in delinquency areas in which the delinquent escapade is sometimes crowned, as it were, by defecating upon the school principal's desk. This supreme gesture of defiance and contempt can be understood as an effort on the part of the delinquents to counteract their own impulses to accept and accede to the superior status of such representatives of the conventional order as school principals. In a sense, such an act is a dramatically exaggerated denial of a system of values which the delinquent has at least partially introjected, but which for the sake of preserving a tolerable self-image he must reject. In this interplay of attitudinal elements the vigor of the rejection of the value system is the measure of its hold upon the person. In other words, the mood of rebellion which characterizes these young males is created not alone by the negative judgments of the surrogates of middle-class culture, but by the negative self-judgment as well.

Such overtones of rebellion, on the other hand, do not characterize members of subculture groups who are totally excluded from participation in the dominant culture of the wider society. For example, those groups which live by systematic depredations upon property, like the criminal castes of India or the professional thieves of our own society, are relatively impervious to the negative judgments of conventional persons, and do not ordinarily resort to the kind of behavior described.[15] Their devaluation and rejection by conventional society is not transmuted into self-rejection, since their criteria of worthiness diverge sharply from those encountered in conventional society. In contrast, the young male who occupies the role of delinquent in the delinquency area resorts to purposive destructiveness and exaggerates the differences between himself and conventional persons precisely because he cannot exclude from his system of values the conventional criteria of personal worth. His delinquency may hence be seen as a defensive adaptation in which he creates an opposing system of values, since by virtue of his lower-class culture background he remains relatively unequipped to move toward the goals explicit in the middle-class culture of the wider society.

The general conclusions suggested by these observations are (a) that a delinquent subculture originates in a setting of cross-group hostility; (b) that this subculture is a groupwise elaboration of individual adaptations serving ego-defense needs; and (c) that the conflict of cultures generated in this situation is reflected on its social psychological side in the introjection by the delinquent of a dual value orientation as exhibited principally in the delinquent's aggressive destructiveness.[16]

[15] M. Kennedy, *Criminal Tribes of the Bombay Presidency*, Bombay, 1908; E. H. Sutherland, *The Professional Thief*, Chicago: University of Chicago Press, 1937.

[16] Discussions of this problem in the psychoanalytic literature, illuminating and

SUMMARY

Analysis of the problem of the causation of delinquency in urban areas of high rates of delinquents is frequently confused by allusions to statistical data which suggest that, while the proportion of delinquents in these areas is

---

suggestive as they are, do not deal explicitly with those variables related to delinquency which originate in intergroup relations. Thus Aichhorn covers the customary range of etiologies when he observes that the child may become delinquent when his psychic apparatus is defective, when he develops defects in the superego or conscience functions of personality as a result of distorting or shocking experiences in his family relationships, or when, as in the instance of the gang boy or child of delinquent parents, he acquires an ego-ideal which is socially unacceptable. August Aichhorn, *Wayward Youth,* New York: The Viking Press, 1935, pp. 222–225. The problem of etiology is further complicated when we consider the effect upon normal personality of constraints to identify with models defined by the subculture as hostile and inimical.

high, this class nonetheless represents a distinct minority of the age-eligible population. Examination of delinquency statistics indicates that no conclusive judgments regarding this matter may be made on the basis of these statistics.

On the other hand, the statistics do support the proposition that urban areas of high rates of delinquents are characterized by a duality of conduct norms rather than by the dominance of either a conventional or a criminal culture.

This hypothesis appears to be useful in explaining the variability of behavior status on the part of boys in delinquency areas; in constructing a typology of delinquency areas based on degrees of integration of opposing value schemes; and in accounting for certain psychological mechanisms involved in the origin and persistence of the subculture of the delinquent boys' gang.

15. Illegitimate Means, Differential Opportunity and Delinquent Subcultures

RICHARD CLOWARD AND LLOYD E. OHLIN

THE AVAILABILITY OF
ILLEGITIMATE MEANS

Social norms are two-sided. A prescription implies the existence of a prohibition, and vice versa. To advocate honesty is to demarcate and condemn a set of actions which are dishonest. In other words, norms that define legitimate practices also implicitly define illegitimate practices. One purpose of norms, in fact, is to delineate the boundary between legitimate and illegitimate practices. In setting this boundary, in segregating and classifying various types of behavior, they make us aware not only of behavior that is regarded as right and proper but also of behavior that is said to be wrong and improper. Thus the criminal who engages in theft or fraud does not invent a new way of life; the possibility of employing alternative means is acknowledged, tacitly at least, by the norms of the culture.

This tendency for proscribed alternatives to be implicit in every prescription, and vice versa, although widely recognized, is nevertheless a reef upon which many a theory of delinquency has foundered. Much of the criminological literature assumes, for example, that one may explain a criminal act simply by accounting for the individual's readiness to employ illegal alternatives of which his culture, through its norms, has already made him generally aware. Such explanations are quite unsatisfactory, however, for they ignore a host of questions regarding the *relative availability* of illegal alternatives to various potential criminals. The aspiration to be a physician is hardly enough to explain the fact of becoming a physician; there is much that transpires between the aspiration and the achievement. This is no less true of the person who wants to be a successful criminal. Having decided that he "can't make it legitimately," he cannot simply choose among an array of illegitimate means, all equally available to him. It is assumed in the theory of anomie that access to conventional means is differentially distributed, that some individuals, because of their social class, enjoy

SOURCE. Richard Cloward and Lloyd E. Ohlin, "Illegitimate Means, Differential Opportunity and Delinquent Subcultures," from *Delinquency and Opportunity*, Glencoe, Illinois: The Free Press, 1961, pp. 145–159. Copyright © 1960, The Free Press, a Corporation. Reprinted with the permission of The Macmillan Company.

certain advantages that are denied to those elsewhere in the class structure. For example, there are variations in the degree to which members of various classes are fully exposed to and thus acquire the values, knowledge, and skills that facilitate upward mobility. It should not be startling, therefore, to suggest that there are socially structured variations in the availability of illegitimate means as well. In connection with delinquent subcultures, we shall be concerned principally with differentials in access to illegitimate means within the lower class.

Many sociologists have alluded to differentials in access to illegitimate means without explicitly incorporating this variable into a theory of deviant behavior. This is particularly true of scholars in the "Chicago tradition" of criminology. Two closely related theoretical perspectives emerged from this school. The theory of "cultural transmission," advanced by Clifford R. Shaw and Henry D. McKay, focuses on the development in some urban neighborhoods of a criminal tradition that persists from one generation to another despite constant changes in population.[1] In the theory of "differential association," Edwin H. Sutherland described the processes by which criminal values are taken over by the individual.[2] He asserted that criminal behavior is learned, and that it is learned in interaction with others who have already incorporated criminal values. Thus the first theory stresses the value systems of different areas; the second, the systems of social relationships that facilitate or impede the acquisition of these values.

Scholars in the Chicago tradition, who emphasized the processes involved in learning to be criminal, were actually pointing to differentials in the availability of illegal means—although they did not explicitly recognize this variable in their analysis. This can perhaps best be seen by examining Sutherland's classic work, The Professional Thief. "An inclination to steal," according to Sutherland, "is not a sufficient explanation of the genesis of the professional thief."[3] The "self-made" thief, lacking knowledge of the ways of securing immunity from prosecution and similar techniques of defense, "would quickly land in prison . . . a person can be a professional thief only if he is recognized and received as such by other professional thieves." But recognition is not freely accorded: "Selection and tutelage are the two necessary elements in the process of acquiring recognition as a professional thief. . . . A person cannot acquire recognition as a professional thief until he has had tutelage in professional theft, *and tutelage is given only to a few persons selected from the total population.*" For one thing, "the person must be appreciated by the professional thieves. He must be appraised as having an adequate equipment of wits, front, talking-ability, honesty, reliability, nerve and determination." Furthermore, the aspirant is judged by high standards of performance, for only "a very small percentage of those who start on this process ever reach the stage of professional thief. . . ." Thus motivation and pressures toward deviance do not fully account for deviant

---

[1] See esp. C. R. Shaw, The Jack-Roller (Chicago: University of Chicago Press, 1930); Shaw, The Natural History of a Delinquent Career (Chicago: University of Chicago Press, 1931); Shaw et al., Delinquency Areas (Chicago: University of Chicago Press, 1940); and Shaw and H. D. McKay, Juvenile Delinquency and Urban Areas (Chicago: University of Chicago Press, 1942).

[2] E. H. Sutherland, ed., The Professional Thief (Chicago: University of Chicago Press, 1937); and Sutherland, Principles of Criminology, 4th Ed. (Philadelphia: Lippincott, 1947).

[3] All quotations in this paragraph are from The Professional Thief, op. cit., pp. 211–213. Emphasis added.

behavior any more than motivation and pressures toward conformity account for conforming behavior. The individual must have access to a learning environment and, once having been trained, must be allowed to perform his role. Roles, whether conforming or deviant in content, are not necessarily freely available; access to them depends upon a variety of factors, such as one's socioeconomic position, age, sex, ethnic affiliation, personality characteristics, and the like. The potential thief, like the potential physician, finds that access to his goal is governed by many criteria other than merit and motivation.

What we are asserting is that access to illegitimate roles is not freely available to all, as is commonly assumed. Only those neighborhoods in which crime flourishes as a stable, indigenous institution are fertile criminal learning environments for the young. Because these environments afford integration of different age-levels of offender, selected young people are exposed to "differential association" through which tutelage is provided and criminal values and skills are acquired. To be prepared for the role may not, however, ensure that the individual will ever discharge it. One important limitation is that more youngsters are recruited into these patterns of differential associations than the adult criminal structure can possibly absorb. Since there is a surplus of contenders for these elite positions, criteria and mechanisms of selection must be evolved. Hence a certain proportion of those who aspire may not be permitted to engage in the behavior for which they have prepared themselves.

Thus we conclude that access to illegitimate roles, no less than access to legitimate roles, is limited by both social and psychological factors. We shall here be concerned primarily with socially structured differentials in illegit-imate opportunities. Such differentials, we contend, have much to do with the type of delinquent subculture that develops.

LEARNING AND PERFORMANCE STRUCTURES

Our use of the term "opportunities," legitimate or illegitimate, implies access to both learning and performance structures. That is, the individual must have access to appropriate environments for the acquisition of the values and skills associated with the performance of a particular role, and he must be supported in the performance of the role once he has learned it.

Tannenbaum, several decades ago, vividly expressed the point that criminal role performance, no less than conventional role performance, presupposes a patterned set of relationships through which the requisite values and skills are transmitted by established practitioners to aspiring youth:

It takes a long time to make a good criminal, many years of specialized training and much preparation. But training is something that is given to people. People learn in a community where the materials and the knowledge are to be had. A craft needs an atmosphere saturated with purpose and promise. The community provides the attitudes, the point of view, the philosophy of life, the example, the motive, the contacts, the friendships, the incentives. No child brings those into the world. He finds them here and available for use and elaboration. The community gives the criminal his materials and habits, just as it gives the doctor, the lawyer, the teacher, and the candlestick-maker theirs.[4]

Sutherland systematized this general point of view, asserting that opportunity consists, at least in part, of learning structures. Thus "criminal behavior is

[4] Frank Tannenbaum, "The Professional Criminal," *The Century*, Vol. 110 (May-Oct. 1925), p. 577.

learned" and, furthermore, it is learned "in interaction with other persons in a process of communication." However, he conceded that the differential-association theory does not constitute a full explanation of criminal behavior. In a paper circulated in 1944, he noted that "criminal behavior is partially a function of opportunities to commit [i.e., to perform] specific classes of crime, such as embezzlement, bank burglary, or illicit heterosexual intercourse." Therefore, "while opportunity may be partially a function of association with criminal patterns and of the specialized techniques thus acquired, it is not determined entirely in that manner, and consequently differential association is not the sufficient cause of criminal behavior."[5]

To Sutherland, then, illegitimate opportunity included conditions favorable to the performance of a criminal role as well as conditions favorable to the learning of such a role (differential associations). These conditions, we suggest, depend upon certain features of the social structure of the community in which delinquency arises.

DIFFERENTIAL OPPORTUNITY: A HYPOTHESIS

We believe that each individual occupies a position in both legitimate and illegitimate opportunity structures. This is a new way of defining the situation. The theory of anomie views the individual primarily in terms of the legitimate opportunity structure. It poses questions regarding differentials in access to legitimate routes to success-goals; at the same time it assumes either that illegitimate avenues to success-goals are freely available or that differentials in their availability are of little signifi-

cance. This tendency may be seen in the following statement by Merton:

Several researches have shown that specialized areas of vice and crime constitute a "normal" response to a situation where the cultural emphasis upon pecuniary success has been absorbed, but where there is little access to conventional and legitimate means for becoming successful. The occupational opportunities of people in these areas are largely confined to manual labor and the lesser white-collar jobs. Given the American stigmatization of manual labor *which has been found to hold rather uniformly for all social classes,* and the absence of realistic opportunities for advancement beyond this level, the result is a marked tendency toward deviant behavior. The status of unskilled labor and the consequent low income cannot readily compete *in terms of established standards of worth* with the promises of power and high income from organized vice, rackets and crime. . . . [Such a situation] leads toward the gradual attenuation of legitimate, but by and large ineffectual, strivings and the increasing use of illegitimate, but more or less effective, expedients.[6]

The cultural-transmission and differential-association tradition, on the other hand, assumes that access to illegitimate means is variable, but it does not recognize the significance of comparable differentials in access to legitimate means. Sutherland's "ninth proposition" in the theory of differential association states:

Though criminal behavior is an expression of general needs and values, it is not explained by those general needs and values since non-criminal behavior is an expression of the same needs and values. Thieves generally steal in order to secure money, but likewise honest laborers work in order to secure money. The attempts by many scholars to explain criminal behavior by general drives and values, such as the happiness principle, striving for so-

---

[5] See A. K. Cohen, Alfred Lindesmith, and Karl Schuessler, eds., *The Sutherland Papers* (Bloomington, Ind.: Indiana University Press, 1956), pp. 31–35.

[6] R. K. Merton, *Social Theory and Social Structure,* Rev. and Enl. Ed. (Glencoe, Ill.: Free Press, 1957), pp. 145–146.

cial status, the money motive, or frustration, have been and must continue to be futile since they explain lawful behavior as completely as they explain criminal behavior.[7]

In this statement, Sutherland appears to assume that people have equal and free access to legitimate means regardless of their social position. At the very least, he does not treat access to legitimate means as variable. It is, of course, perfectly true that "striving for social status," "the money motive," and other socially approved drives do not fully account for either deviant or conforming behavior. But if goal-oriented behavior occurs under conditions in which there are socially structured obstacles to the satisfaction of these drives by legitimate means, the resulting pressures, we contend, might lead to deviance.

The concept of differential opportunity structures permits us to unite the theory of anomie, which recognizes the concept of differentials in access to legitimate means, and the "Chicago tradition," in which the concept of differentials in access to illegitimate means is implicit. We can now look at the individual, not simply in relation to one or the other system of means, but in relation to both legitimate and illegitimate systems. This approach permits us to ask, for example, how the relative availability of illegitimate opportunities affects the resolution of adjustment problems leading to deviant behavior. We believe that the way in which these problems are resolved may depend upon the kind of support for one or another type of illegitimate activity that is given at different points in the social structure. If, in a given social location, illegal or criminal means are not readily available, then we should not expect a

criminal subculture to develop among adolescents. By the same logic, we should expect the manipulation of violence to become a primary avenue to higher status only in areas where the means of violence are not denied to the young. To give a third example, drug addiction and participation in subcultures organized around the consumption of drugs presuppose that persons can secure access to drugs and knowledge about how to use them. In some parts of the social structure, this would be very difficult; in others, very easy. In short, there are marked differences from one part of the social structure to another in the types of illegitimate adaptation that are available to persons in search of solutions to problems of adjustment arising from the restricted availability of legitimate means.[8] In this sense, then, we can think of individuals as being located in two opportunity structures—one legitimate, the other illegitimate. Given limited access to success-goals by legitimate means, the nature of the delinquent response that may result will vary according to the availability of various illegitimate means.[9]

[8] For an example of restrictions on access to illegitimate roles, note the impact of racial definitions in the following case: "I was greeted by two prisoners who were to be my cell buddies. Ernest was a first offender, charged with being a 'hold-up' man. Bill, the other buddy, was an old offender, going through the machinery of becoming a habitual criminal, in and out of jail. . . . The first thing they asked me was, 'What are you in for?' I said, 'Jack-rolling.' The hardened one (Bill) looked at me with a superior air and said, 'A hoodlum, eh? An ordinary sneak thief. Not willing to leave jack-rolling to the niggers, eh? That's all they're good for. Kid, jack-rolling's not a white man's job.' I could see that he was disgusted with me, and I was too scared to say anything" (Shaw, *The Jack-Roller, op. cit.*, p. 101).

[9] For a discussion of the way in which the availability of illegitimate means influences the adaptations of inmates to prison life, see R. A. Cloward, "Social Con-

[7] *Principles of Criminology, op. cit.*, pp. 7–8.

ILLEGITIMATE OPPORTUNITIES AND THE SOCIAL STRUCTURE OF THE SLUM

When we say that the form of delinquency that is adopted is conditioned by the presence or absence of appropriate illegitimate means, we are actually referring to crucial differences in the social organization of various slum areas, for our hypothesis implies that the local milieu affects the delinquent's choice of a solution to his problems of adjustment. One of the principal ways in which slum areas vary is in the extent to which they provide the young with alternative (albeit illegitimate) routes to higher status. Many of the works in the cultural-transmission and differential-association tradition are focused directly on the relationship between deviant behavior and lower-class social structure. By reconceptualizing aspects of that tradition, we hope to make our central hypothesis more explicit.

Integration of Different Age-Levels of Offender

In their ecological studies of the urban environment, Shaw and McKay found that delinquency tended to be confined to limited areas and to persist in these areas despite demographic changes. Hence they spoke of "criminal traditions" and of the "cultural transmission" of criminal values.[10] As a result of their observations of slum life, they concluded that particular importance must be assigned to the relationships between immature and sophisticated offenders—which we call the integration of different age-levels of offender. They suggested that many

youngsters are recruited into criminal activities as a direct result of intimate associations with older and more experienced offenders:

Stealing in the neighborhood was a common practice among the children and approved of by the parents. Whenever the boys got together they talked about robbing and made more plans for stealing. I hardly knew any boys who did not go robbing. The little fellows went in for petty stealing, breaking into freight cars, and stealing junk. The older guys did big jobs like stick-ups, burglary, and stealing autos. The little fellows admired the "big shots" and longed for the day when they could get into the big racket. Fellows who had "done time" were the big shots and looked up to and gave the little fellows tips on how to get by and pull off big jobs.[11]

Thus the "big shots"—conspicuous successes in the criminal world—become role-models for youth, much more important as such than successful figures in the conventional world, who are usually socially and geographically remote from the slum area. Through intimate and stable associations with these older criminals, the young acquire the values and skills required for participation in the criminal culture. Further, structural connections between delinquents, semimature criminals, and the adult criminal world, where they exist, provide opportunities for upward mobility; where such integrative arrangements do not exist, the young are cut off from this alternative pathway to higher status.

Integration of Conventional and Deviant Values

Shaw and McKay were describing deviant learning structures—that is, alternative routes by which people seek access to the goals that society holds to be worthwhile. Their point was that

---

trol in the Prison," *Theoretical Studies of the Social Organization of the Prison*, Bulletin No. 15 (New York: Social Science Research Council, March 1960), pp. 20–48.

[10] See esp. *Delinquency Areas, op. cit.*, Chap. 16.

[11] Shaw, *The Jack-Roller, op. cit.*, p. 54.

access to criminal roles and advancement in the criminal hierarchy depend upon stable associations with older criminals from whom the necessary values and skills may be learned. Yet Shaw and McKay failed to give explicit recognition to the concept of illegitimate means and the socially structured conditions of access to them—probably because they tended to view slum areas as "disorganized." Although they consistently referred to illegitimate *activities* as "organized," they nevertheless tended to label high-rate delinquency *areas* "disorganized" because the values transmitted were criminal rather than conventional. Hence they sometimes made statements which we now perceive to be internally inconsistent, such as the following:

This community situation was not only disorganized and thus ineffective as a unit of control, but it was characterized by a high rate of juvenile delinquency and adult crime, not to mention the widespread political corruption which had long existed in the area. Various forms of stealing and many organized delinquent and criminal gangs were prevalent in the area. These groups exercised a powerful influence and tended to create a community spirit which not only tolerated but actually fostered delinquent and criminal practices.[12]

Sutherland was among the first to perceive that the concept of social disorganization tends to obscure the stable patterns of interaction which exist among carriers of criminal values: "the organization of the delinquent group, which is often very complex, is social disorganization only from an ethical or some other particularistic point of view."[13] Like Shaw and McKay, he had observed that criminal activities in lower-class areas were organized in

terms of a criminal value system, but he also observed that *this alternative value system was supported by a patterned system of social relations*. That is, he recognized the fact that crime, far from being a random, unorganized activity, is often an intricate and stable system of arrangements and relationships. He therefore rejected the "social disorganization" perspective: "At the suggestion of Albert K. Cohen, this concept has been changed to differential group organization, with organization for criminal activities on one side and organization against criminal activities on the other."[14]

William F. Whyte, in his classic study of an urban slum, carried the empirical description of the structure and organization of illegal means a step further. Like Sutherland, Whyte rejected the position of Shaw and McKay that the slum is *dis*organized simply because it is organized according to principles different from those in the conventional world:

It is customary for the sociologist to study the slum district in terms of "social disorganization" and to neglect to see that an area such as Cornerville has a complex and well-established organization of its own. . . . I found that in every group there was a hierarchical structure of social relations binding the individuals to one another and that the groups were also related hierarchically to one another. Where the group was formally organized into a political club, this was immediately apparent, but for informal groups it was no less true.[15]

But Whyte's view of the slum differed somewhat from Sutherland's in that Whyte's emphasis was not on "differential group organization"—the idea that the slum is composed of two discrete

[12] Shaw, *The Natural History of a Delinquent Career, op. cit.*, p. 229.

[13] Cohen, Lindesmith, and Schuessler, eds., *The Sutherland Papers, op. cit.*, p. 21.

[14] *Ibid.*

[15] W. F. Whyte, *Street Corner Society*, Enl. Ed. (Chicago: University of Chicago Press, 1955), p. viii.

systems, conventional and deviant. He stressed, rather, the way in which the occupants of various roles in these two systems become integrated in a single, stable structure which organizes and patterns the life of the community. Thus Whyte showed that individuals who participate in stable illicit enterprises do not constitute a separate or isolated segment of the community but are closely integrated with the occupants of conventional roles. He noted, for example, that "the rackets and political organizations extend from the bottom to the top of Cornerville society, mesh with one another, and integrate a large part of the life of the district. They provide a general framework for the understanding of the actions of both 'little guys' and 'big shots.' "[16]

In a recent article, Kobrin has clarified our understanding of slum areas by suggesting that they differ in the *degree* to which deviant and conventional value systems are integrated with each other. This difference, we argue, affects the relative accessibility of illegal means. Pointing the way to the development of a "typology of delinquent areas based on variations in the relationship between these two systems," Kobrin describes the "polar types" on such a continuum. The integrated area, he asserts, is characterized not only by structural integration between carriers of the two value systems but also by reciprocal participation by carriers of each in the value system of the other. Thus, he notes:

Leaders of [illegal] enterprises frequently maintain membership in such conventional institutions of their local communities as churches, fraternal and mutual benefit societies and political parties. . . . Within this framework the influence of each of the two value systems is reciprocal, the leaders of illegal enterprise participat-

ing in the primary orientation of the conventional elements in the population, and the latter, through their participation in a local power structure sustained in large part by illicit activity, participating perforce in the alternate, criminal value system.[17]

The second polar type consists of areas in which the relationships between carriers of deviant and conventional values break down because of disorganizing forces such as "drastic change in the class, ethnic, or racial characteristics of [the] population." Kobrin suggests that in such slums "the bearers of the conventional culture and its value system are without the customary institutional machinery and therefore in effect partially demobilized with reference to the diffusion of their value system." At the same time, areas of this type are "characterized principally by the absence of systematic and organized adult activity in violation of the law, despite the fact that many adults in these areas commit violations." Thus both value systems remain implicit, but the fact that neither is "systematic and organized" precludes the possibility of effective integration.

How does the accessibility of illegal means vary with the relative integration of conventional and criminal values in a given area? Although Kobrin does not take up this problem explicitly, he does note that the integrated area apparently constitutes a "training ground" for the acquisition of criminal values and skills. Of his first polar type he says:

The stable position of illicit enterprise in the adult society of the community is reflected in the character of delinquent conduct on the part of children. While delinquency in all high-rate areas is intrinsically disorderly in that it is unrelated

16 *Ibid.,* p. xii.

17 Solomon Kobrin, "The Conflict of Values in Delinquency Areas," *American Sociological Review,* Vol. 16 (Oct. 1951), pp. 657–658.

to official programs for the education of the young, in the [integrated community] boys may more or less realistically recognize the potentialities for personal progress in local society through access to delinquency. In a general way, therefore, delinquent activity in these areas constitutes a training ground for the acquisition of skill in the use of violence, concealment of offense, evasion of detection and arrest, and the purchase of immunity from punishment. Those who come to excel in these respects are frequently noted and valued by adult leaders in the rackets who are confronted, as are the leaders of all income-producing enterprises, with problems of the recruitment of competent personnel.[18]

Kobrin makes no mention of the extent to which learning structures and opportunities for criminal careers are available in the unintegrated area. Yet the fact that neither conventional nor criminal values are articulated in this type of area as he describes it suggests that the appropriate learning structures —principally integration of different age-levels of offenders—are not available. Furthermore, Kobrin's description of adult violative activity in such areas as "unorganized" suggests that illegal opportunities are severely limited. Even if youngsters were able to secure adequate preparation for criminal roles, the social structure of such neighborhoods would appear to provide few opportunities for stable criminal careers. Kobrin's analysis—as well as that of Whyte and others before him—supports our conclusion that *illegal opportunity structures tend to emerge only when there are stable patterns of accommodation between the adult carriers of conventional and of deviant values*. Where these two value systems are implicit, or where the carriers are in open conflict, opportunities for stable criminal-role performance are limited. Where stable accommodative relationships exist between the adult carriers of criminal and conventional values, institutionalized criminal careers are available. The alienated adolescent need not rely on the vagaries of private entrepreneurship in crime, with the attendant dangers of detection and prosecution, imprisonment, fluctuations in income, and the like. Instead, he may aspire to rise in the organized criminal structure and to occupy a permanent position in some flourishing racket. Secure in such a position, he will be relatively immune from prosecution and imprisonment, can expect a more or less stable income, and can look forward to acceptance by the local community—criminal and conventional.

Some urban neighborhoods, in short, provide relief from pressures arising from limitations on access to success-goals by legitimate means. Because alternative routes to higher status are made available to those who are ambitious, diligent, and meritorious, the frustrations of youth in these neighborhoods are drained off. Where such pathways do not exist, frustrations become all the greater.

[18] *Ibid.*

16.   Socioeconomic Status and Delinquent Behavior

F. IVAN NYE, JAMES F. SHORT, JR., AND VIRGIL J. OLSON

Delinquency is commonly described in the literature as primarily a phenomenon of the lower economic strata.[1]

Such studies, dealing with the relationship between juvenile delinquency and socioeconomic level, have used court records, police files, and other official records of delinquency. These bases are adequate, within certain limitations, for an examination of "official delinquency," but they are unreliable as an index of "delinquent behavior" in the general population.[2] Estimates of the extent of delinquent behavior in the general population indicate that such behavior may be more evenly distributed in the various socioeconomic strata than official records lead one to believe.

° From two studies of adolescent delinquent behavior supported in part by grants from the College Committee on Research of the State College of Washington and the Social Science Research Council.

[1] Ernest W. Burgess, "The Economic Factor in Juvenile Delinquency," *Journal of Criminal Law, Criminology and Police Science*, 48 (May-June, 1952), 29–42; Cletus Dirksen, *Economic Factors in Delinquency* (Milwaukee: Bruce Publishing Co., 1948); Bernard Lander, *Juvenile Delinquency* (New York: Columbia University Press, 1954); J. B. Maller, "Juvenile Delinquency in New York City," *Journal of Psychology*, 3 (January, 1937), 1–25; Earl R. Moses, "Differentials in Crime Rates between Negroes and Whites in Comparisons of Four Socioeconomically Equated Areas," *American Sociological Review*, 12 (August, 1947), 411–420; W. C. Reckless, *Vice in Chicago* (Chicago: University of Chicago Press, 1933); Clifford R. Shaw and H. D. McKay, *Juvenile Delinquency and Urban Areas* (Chicago: University of Chicago Press, 1942); T. Earl Sullenger, *Social Determinants in Juvenile Delinquency* (New York: John Wiley and Sons, 1936), 170–180; William W. Wattenberg and J. J. Balistrieri, "Gang Membership and Juvenile Delinquency," *American Sociological Review*, 15 (December, 1950), 744–752; Paul Wiers, *Economic Factors in Michigan Delinquency* (New York: Columbia University Press, 1944).

[2] Clement S. Mihanovitch, "Who Is the Juvenile Delinquent?" *Social Science*, 22 (1947), 45–50; Sophia M. Robison, *Can Delinquency Be Measured?* (New York: Columbia University Press, 1936); Edward Schwartz, "A Community Experiment in the Measurement of Juvenile Delinquency," *National Probation Association Yearbook*, 1945, pp. 157–182; Thorsten Sellin, "The Basis of a Crime Index," *Journal of Criminal Law and Criminology*, 22 (September, 1931), 335–356; Jeremiah Shalloo, "Youth and Crime," *Annals of the American Academy of Political and Social Science*, 194 (November, 1937), 79–86; Henry D. Sheldon, "Problems in Statistical Study of Juvenile Delinquency," quoted in Edwin H. Sutherland and Donald R. Cressey, *Principles of Criminology* (Philadelphia: J. B. Lippincott Co., 1955).

SOURCE. F. Ivan Nye, James F. Short, Jr., and Virgin J. Olson, "Socioeconomic Status and Delinquent Behavior," from *The American Journal of Sociology*, Volume 63, January 1958, pp. 381–389. Copyright © 1958, University of Chicago Press. Reprinted with the permission of the University of Chicago Press.

Porterfield, for instance, found that college students committed many more delinquent acts than is commonly known and that these delinquent acts were as serious as those which brought other young people, less fortunate economically, into court.[3] Research by Murphy, based on the case histories of adolescents, yielded similar results.[4] Wallerstein and Wyle found that, in a group of upper-income individuals, 99 per cent answered affirmatively to one or more offenses.[5] Short's research on criminal behavior in selected groups likewise bears testimony to the fact that delinquent and criminal behavior are by no means limited to the lower economic groups.[6]

Despite the abundance of criticism that has been leveled against the use of official records as an index of delinquent behavior in the various socioeconomic levels, recent studies continue either to confuse "official delinquency" with "delinquent behavior" or to equate the two phenomena. An example of the former is provided by Dirksen, who presents one of the more extreme positions in assessing the role of the economic variable in juvenile delinquency.[7] His study may indicate the class differential in alleged or official delinquency, but generalizations to delinquent behavior in the general population cannot be made from these results.

Other recent studies utilize such data as obtained from court files and other official records as an index of delinquency.[8]

Cohen, in one of the most recent treatments of juvenile delinquency, has said concerning the disparity between official delinquency rates and delinquent behavior rates in the general population: "If many delinquencies of upper-class children fail to find their way into the police and court records, the same is apparently true also of many delinquencies of working-class children, and conceivably even more true."[9] Although Cohen indicates that the best *available* evidence supports the traditional and popular conception of the distribution of juvenile delinquency in the class structure, he calls for research that will make known the extent of delinquent behavior in the population not judged "delinquent."[10]

The present analysis (Table 1) shows that, in one of the states from which a sample was drawn, the relationship between socioeconomic status and commitment to the state "training school" is similar to that shown by the studies quoted above. A disproportionate number of the official delinquents come from the lower socioeconomic categories.

After an examination of this literature, it is the opinion of the writers that the use of a measure of reported delinquent behavior rather than official records of delinquency will yield results somewhat different from those supporting the traditional conceptions of the

[3] Austin L. Porterfield, *Youth in Trouble* (Fort Worth: Leo Potishman Foundation, 1946).

[4] Fred J. Murphy, M. Shirley, and H. L. Witmer, "The Incidence of Hidden Delinquency," *American Journal of Orthopsychiatry*, 16 (October, 1946), 686–696.

[5] James S. Wallerstein and C. J. Wyle, "Our Law-abiding Law-breakers," *Probation*, 25 (April, 1947), 107–112.

[6] James F. Short, Jr., "A Report on the Incidence of Criminal Behavior, Arrests, and Convictions in Selected Groups," *Proceedings of the Pacific Sociological Society, 1954*, pp. 110–118 (published as Vol. 22, No. 2, of "Research Studies of the State College of Washington" [Pullman, Wash., 1954]).

[7] Cletus Dirksen, *Economic Factors in Delinquency* (Milwaukee: Bruce Publishing Co., 1948).

[8] E.g., Bernard Lander, *Juvenile Delinquency* (New York: Columbia University Press, 1954).

[9] Albert K. Cohen, *Delinquent Boys: The Culture of the Gang* (Glencoe, Ill.: Free Press, 1955), pp. 37–41.

[10] *Ibid.*, pp. 170–171.

Table 1

PERCENTAGE DISTRIBUTION OF BOYS IN WESTERN HIGH SCHOOLS AND STATE TRAINING
SCHOOL SAMPLES BY SOCIOECONOMIC LEVEL

	Western high schools		State training schools	
Socioeconomic level	No.	Per cent	No.	Per cent
(High) 4	114	13.6	6	4.1
3	282	33.5	19	13.0
2	333	39.6	48	32.9
(Low) 1	112	13.3	73	50.0
Total	841	100.0	146	100.0

$$\chi^2 = 117.01 \qquad P < .001 \qquad \bar{C} = .45$$

status distribution of delinquency. We are not here concerned with etiology but with this question: Does delinquent behavior occur differentially by socioeconomic status?

The present study tests the null hypothesis that there is no significant difference in delinquent behavior of boys and girls in different socioeconomic strata.

THE RESPONDENTS

The Sample

In this study there are two principal sources of data—selected high-school groups in western and midwestern communities. In the western sample, data were gathered by questionnaire from 2,350 boys and girls in Grades IX through XII in the high schools of three western cities. These cities ranged in size from 10,000 to 25,000. They are thus clearly urban but not metropolitan.

The three western communities sampled in this study differ from the state in which they are located in two significant characteristics. They experienced a much higher growth from 1940 to 1950, and the average income level was higher. (See Table 2.) Related to the higher growth rate is the lower average age and the smaller proportion of old people in these communities. From a state-wide sample drawn in another

Table 2

SELECTED POPULATION CHARACTERISTICS FOR WESTERN COMMUNITIES FROM WHICH
SAMPLE IS DRAWN, COMPARED WITH THOSE CHARACTERISTICS FOR WESTERN STATE
AND THE UNITED STATES[*]

Selected population characteristics	Communities from which sample is drawn	Western state	United States
Median years of school (25 years old or over):			
Male	11.1	11.3	10.0
Female	11.1	12.1	10.3
Median age	27.5	31.8	31.6
Per cent 65 and over	3.0	9.3	8.2
Per cent over 14 years of age in labor force:			
Male	89.1	77.9	79.3
Female	32.1	31.6	33.2
Median income—families	$4,515.00	$3,755.00	$3,431.00

[*] *United States Census* (1950). Urban statistics are used for western state and the United States. Comparable data are not available for midwestern communities.

study[11] it was found, as would be expected, that horizontal mobility was greater in the present sample than for the state and is presumably greater than that for the country as a whole.

The midwestern data were gathered by a questionnaire soliciting comparable data from 250 boys and 265 girls in Grades IX through XII in the high schools of three midwestern communities. One of the high schools is located in a suburban residential town with a population of less than 2,500. The second is a rural town of less than 2,500 population. The third is a consolidated high school in a rural township. The population of these three communities has remained fairly stable since 1940.

No samples from large cities or from large non-Caucasian groups are included, and generalizations to such populations must await further research.

MEASURE OF DELINQUENT BEHAVIOR

Delinquent behavior in the present study was measured by means of an anonymous delinquency check list administered to adolescents who are not adjudged delinquent[12] and by a delin-

quency scale constructed from it. The list is designed to include a broad sampling of juvenile misconduct, though it does not include several of the more serious types of delinquency (e.g., rape, breaking and entering, and armed robbery).

MEASURE OF SOCIOECONOMIC LEVEL

The occupation of the father was utilized as an index of socioeconomic level of the respondent. A combination of the North-Hatt and Mapheus Smith scales was employed. These scales were combined and applied to data gathered from a sample of Washington State high-school students by Empey in a study of occupational aspiration and anticipation.[13]

Research in social stratification lends support to the use of occupation as a measure of socioeconomic status.[14] It has the following advantages: (1) Occupation correlates highly with other criteria of class and status position, such as subjective class affiliation, income, educational level, subjective class ratings, and others. (2) Occupation is related not only to income but to values, attitudes, and goals; to a certain extent it determines the social relations among societal members. (3) The use of occupation as a criterion of socioeconomic status makes it possible to correlate a child's delinquent behavior with

---

[11] LaMar T. Empey, "Relationship of Social Class and Family Authority Patterns to Occupational Choice of Washington High School Students" (unpublished Doctoral dissertation, State College of Washington, 1955).

[12] The actual items in the delinquency check list are as follows: defied parents' authority, taken things you didn't want or need; "beat up" on kids that hadn't done anything to you; hurt or inflicted pain on someone just to see them squirm; purposely damaged property; taken things under $2.00 in value; taken things between $2.00 and $50.00; taken things $50.00 and over; driven recklessly in a car; bought or drank intoxicants; used or sold narcotics, homosexual relations; heterosexual relations; taken someone's car without asking; taken part in gang fights; run away from home; had a fist fight; and probation or expulsion from school.

[13] Empey, op. cit.; see also LaMar T. Empey, "Social Class and Occupational Aspiration: A Comparison of Absolute and Relative Measurement," American Sociological Review, 21 (December, 1956), 703–709.

[14] Raymond B. Cattell, "The Concept of Social Status," Journal of Social Psychology, 15 (May, 1942), 293–308; Joseph A. Kahl and J. A. Davis, "A Comparison of Indexes of Socio-economic Status," American Sociological Review, 15 (December, 1955), 317–325; National Opinion Research Center, "The Quarter's Polls–Occupations," Public Opinion Quarterly, 11 (1947–1948), 138–171.

the socioeconomic level of his immediate family rather than with the demographic area in which he lives. (4) In addition, data on the occupation of the father are generally obtained more accurately from adolescents than income, years of schooling of the parents, value of the home, rental, and other items with which the adolescent may not be familiar.

Comparison of the percentage distribution by major occupational groups for the western sample and the midwestern sample indicated that the differences between the proportions of each sample falling in the several socioeconomic levels were not significant. The two samples are not significantly different as to range or distribution of occupations. The combined occupational prestige scale contains ten categories of occupations, each representing a range of occupations within the total scale. In the present study these ten categories were combined into four status groupings which include the following types of occupations: (1) unskilled and semiskilled labor (e.g., migratory worker to restaurant cook); (2) skilled labor and craftsmen (e.g., housepainter to linotype operator); (3) white collar and small business (e.g., newspaper columnist to owner-operator of a mine); and (4) professional and large business (e.g., interior decorator to United States Supreme Court justice). No attempt was made to classify adolescents who live in families in which there was no adult male. Elimination of this small group (108 out of a total of approximately 2,350 cases) does not seriously influence the findings of the study. Separate analysis of this group indicates that its members tend to be more delinquent than all others; but, when status is held constant by two independent measures (education of mother and comparison of income with that of "others"), no significant

relationship between status and delinquency is found.

FINDINGS

The data were subjected to five tests in an attempt to locate significant differences in delinquent behavior by socioeconomic status. First, four-by-four tables were constructed in which social status was categorized as described above. Delinquent behavior on each item was divided into four categories. Typically these were: (1) did not commit the act; (2) committed the act once or twice; (3) committed the act several times; (4) committed the act very often. The distribution of each delinquent act by social status was tested separately by the chi-square test. Tests were computed separately for boys' and girls' samples, followed by tests in which the boys' and girls' samples were combined for 21 delinquency items. This was done separately for the western and midwestern samples. In all, 126 chi-square tests were made with the western and midwestern data.

In the western samples two significant differences were found. Since 63 chi-squares were computed from the western data, three differences significant above the 5 per cent level might be expected to occur by chance.[15] These two differences did not follow any consistent pattern. "Heterosexual relations" were committed most frequently by lower-class boys, but "purposely damaged or destroyed property" was committed most frequently by upper-class boys and girls. In the midwestern samples three significant differences were found. Since 63 chi-squares were computed from the midwestern

[15] This assumes independence of variables and of each of the tests. The assumption in this case is valid except where boys and girls are combined following tests performed on data for boys and girls separately. For a summary of significant differences see Table 3 and comment below.

data, three differences significant above the 5 per cent level might be expected to occur by chance. Furthermore, the three do not follow any consistent pattern. "Taking a car without permission" was committed most frequently by lower-class boys; "running away from home," most frequently by upper-class girls. It was concluded, therefore, on the basis of the chi-square test of the four-by-four tables, that there is no reason to reject the null hypothesis.

However, it was possible that the differences in delinquent behavior might be cumulative and that a simple dichotomy of "committed" or "did not commit" the act might reveal differences not apparent in the more detailed analysis.[16] Thus a second test was made in which all delinquent behavior items were dichotomized and in which the relationship of delinquent behavior to socioeconomic status was again tested by the use of chi square. For the western sample seven items were found to differ significantly by socioeconomic status. "Skipped school" and "taken a car for a ride" were most frequently admitted in the lowest socioeconomic category, both in the boys' and in the combined boys' and girls' samples. "Purposely damaged or destroyed property" was most frequently admitted in the highest socioeconomic category, both in the girls' and in the combined boys' and girls' samples. "Heterosexual relations" were most frequently admitted by the boys in the lowest socioeconomic category. In all, 63 chi-square tests were made of the dichotomized

delinquency items—21 for girls, 21 for boys, and 21 for the combined western samples (boys and girls). Seven significant differences are somewhat in excess of the number expected by chance, but not all are consistent. Similarly, in the midwestern sample 63 tests were made with none significant at the 5 per cent level. Of the 126 tests made in the two samples, seven are significant, which is little if any in excess of the number that might occur by chance.

The possibility still remained that there were significant differences between some of the socioeconomic categories in their degree of delinquent involvement. A third test was therefore made. Percentages were computed from the dichotomized delinquency items, and significance of differences between proportions was computed.[17] Since with four socioeconomic categories, six comparisons are possible, for each item the total number of comparisons is 6×21, or 126 in each sample.

In the western boys' sample, of the 126 tests of significance of differences between proportions, six were found significant. For three delinquency items

---

[16] The combination of table cells serves to increase the n within each cell. *If* the distribution of responses of the two samples is similar in adjacent cells, the combination of such cells increases the n per cell without diminishing percentage differences between samples. As a result, differences previously not significant become significant. Total sample n is not increased, but, by decreasing the degrees of freedom, the end result is somewhat similar.

[17] Hovland and Linquest have cautioned against detailed tests following a general test which proved not significant. In each case, however, the caution appears to be directed against using such double tests in a search for support of a positive hypothesis. Hovland is particularly concerned about possible "false validities." We have guarded against false validities by discounting significant differences to the number of 5 per cent of the total tests made. As the tests are employed here, the analysis goes considerably beyond usual practice in exhausting every possibility for disproving our null hypothesis and providing support for the opposed traditional theory. For Hovland's and Linquest's discussions see Carl Hovland, A. A. Lumsdaine, and F. D. Sheffield, *Studies in Social Psychology in World War II*, Vol. 3: *Experiments on Mass Communication* (Princeton, N.J.: Princeton University Press, 1949), p. 297, and E. F. Linquest, *Statistical Analysis in Education Research* (Boston: Houghton Mifflin Co., 1940), pp. 296-297.

the offense was committed most frequently by the lowest socioeconomic category; for three, by the middle category. For the western girls' sample, five significant differences were found. Four of these delinquencies were committed most frequently by upper socioeconomic girls and one by lower socioeconomic girls. In the combined (boys' and girls') western sample, eight significant differences were found. Four were committed most frequently by upper and four by lower socioeconomic categories. For the western samples, 378 tests were possible, of which 19 (or 5 per cent) proved significant. At the 5 per cent level of significance this is about the percentage of differences that should appear significant by chance.

Since one category of the midwestern sample is very small, the analysis by significance of differences between categories was completed for the combined sample only. This test of 126 comparisons found two significant differences, one offense being committed most frequently by the lower and one by a middle category.

The third test involved a total of 504 possible tests of significance, of which 21 were found to be significant. At the 5 per cent level of significance this number might be expected to occur by chance. Furthermore, in only one-third of the cases was the act most frequently committed by the lowest socioeconomic status category. On the basis of this third test it must again be concluded that the evidence does not permit rejection of the null hypothesis.

Some patterning of significant dif-

Table 3

SUMMARY OF TESTS OF SIGNIFICANCE BETWEEN SOCIOECONOMIC STATUS AND DELINQUENT BEHAVIOR OF BOYS, GIRLS, AND COMBINED SAMPLES OF THREE WESTERN AND THREE MIDWESTERN TOWNS

| Sample and test | No. of possible differences | No. of differences significant | Socioeconomic status in which highest proportion committed delinquent act* | | |
			Lower	Middle two	Upper
4-4 Table χ^2:					
Midwestern girls	21	1	0	0	1
Midwestern girls	21	1	0	0	1
Midwestern combined	21	0	0	0	0
Western boys	21	1	1	0	0
Western girls	21	0	0	0	0
Western combined	21	1	0	0	1
2-4 Table χ^2:					
Midwestern boys, girls, and combined	63	0	0	0	0
Western boys	21	3	3	0	0
Western girls	21	1	0	0	1
Western combined	21	3	2	0	1
Significance of difference between proportions (t score):					
Western boys	126	6	3	3	0
Western girls	126	5	1	0	4
Western combined	126	8	4	0	4
Midwestern combined	126	1	1	1	0
Total	756	33	16	4	13

* Act that was significantly different by socioeconomic category.

ferences did occur. In all the tests made for the individual items, a total of 33 significant differences were found, as can be seen from Table 3. These differences were concentrated chiefly in the lower- and upper-class groups, and 26 of the 33 differences concerned five offenses. These offenses and the class groups reporting their higher incidence were: truancy (lower-class children); heterosexual relations (lower-class boys); car theft (lower-class boys); destroying property (upper-class boys); and gang fights (upper-class children). It seems likely that some of these differences are also spurious.

In addition to the tests of individual delinquent behavior items, the distribution of delinquency scale types by socioeconomic status was tested for significant differences.[18] Ten tests were made of distribution of scale types by socio-

[18] For a description of the construction of the delinquency scale see F. Ivan Nye and James F. Short, Jr., "Scaling Delinquent Behavior," *American Sociological Review*, 22 (June, 1957), 326-331.

economic status. Four samples were tested in both the western and the midwestern high-school populations: girls fifteen and younger, girls sixteen and older, boys fifteen and younger, and boys sixteen and older. One test was made in the boys' and girls' training schools of students sixteen and older. Of these ten tests, nine proved nonsignificant, with $P > .20$ in each case. (See Table 4.) The tenth test (western boys 16 and over) was significant at the 5 per cent level.

SELECTIVE FACTORS

Not all adolescents are in school. Since the "drop-outs" may be more delinquent than those in school and may be disproportionately recruited from the lower socioeconomic strata, a further test was considered necessary. In the western communities children are required to attend school until sixteen years of age. A check of census data in these towns shows that, in 1950, 97.5 per cent of children aged fourteen and

Table 4

DISTRIBUTION OF DELINQUENT BEHAVIOR SCALE TYPES FOR WESTERN BOYS TWELVE TO FIFTEEN YEARS OLD BY SOCIOECONOMIC STATUS

Socioeconomic level	Low*		Scale types intermediate†		High‡	
	N	Per cent	N	Per cent	N	Per cent
(High) 4	25	18	7	7	16	16
3	48	34	35	35	28	27
2	54	39	42	42	40	39
(Low) 1	13	9	16	16	18	18
Total	140	100	100	100	102	100
		$\chi^2 = 9.99$	$P < .20$			

* Scale Type No. 1 = no admitted offense.
  Scale Type No. 2 = admitted driving without driver's license.

† Scale Type No. 3 = admitted the above items plus defied parents' authority openly.
  Scale Type No. 4 = both the above plus petty larceny.
  Scale Type No. 5 = all the above plus taking automobile without permission.

‡ Scale Type No. 6 = all the above plus drank alcoholic beverages.
  Scale Type No. 7 = all the above plus heterosexual relations.
  Scale Types No. 8–15 = all the above plus some or all more than once or twice.

fifteen were attending school. Of those not attending, there were a number with extreme physical and mental handicaps presumably unrelated to the present analysis. "Drop-outs" were, therefore, so few proportionately that they could not affect (considerably) the findings in these age categories. The relationship of socioeconomic status to delinquent behavior was tested within this younger age group separately, and six significant differences were found. Two acts were committed less frequently by the upper-status group, three by the lowest, and one by the middle groups.

THE NON-CLASSIFIED CATEGORY

Not all respondents could be classified in terms of socioeconomic level (28 per cent of boys were "non-classifiable"). For example, "works on a newspaper" was deemed insufficient information for assignment to a particular category. These cases were necessarily omitted from the above analysis. It was considered desirable to know whether this non-classifiable group differed markedly from the group analyzed. A second measure of socioeconomic status—the education level of the father—was employed. Differences in education level of the father in the classified and non-classified groups were tested and found not significant. The two groups were then compared by delinquent behavior scale types, and again differences were found to be not significant. It was concluded, therefore, that the findings were not biased by the exclusion of the non-classified group.

SUMMARY

The null hypothesis was tested that there is no significant difference in delinquent behavior of boys and girls in different socioeconomic strata. The study was conducted in three western communities and three midwestern communities. The population included all pupils in Grades IX through XII. Delinquent behavior was measured by means of a delinquency check list and a delinquent behavior scale. Data were gathered anonymously by questionnaire under classroom conditions. Socioeconomic status was determined by the father's occupation, using a combination of the North-Hatt and Mapheus Smith occupational prestige scale.

The data were put to five tests: (1) The chi-square test was applied to the data in four-by-four tables for boys and girls separately and combined. (2) Delinquent behavior categories were dichotomized, and the chi-square test was applied to the data in two-by-four tables. (3) A test of significance of difference between proportions was applied to subgroups showing marked differences for the two-by-four tables. (4) A test was made of the distribution of delinquency scale types by socioeconomic status. (5) A separate test was made with adolescents of fourteen and fifteen years of age to minimize the effect of school "drop-outs." The tests employed failed to uncover enough significant differences to reject the null hypothesis.

This study does not attempt to explain the etiology of delinquent behavior, but the findings have implications for those etiological studies which rely upon the assumed class differential in delinquent behavior as a basis for a delinquency theory. Our data suggest that several *single* measures of socioeconomic status and delinquency are not highly correlated in rural areas and in small towns and cities.

Although present findings are negative, attention is called to the seemingly non-random distribution of significant differences in Table 3. The two middle socioeconomic categories are highest on delinquent behavior on only four tests in contrast to 29 for the highest and lowest categories combined. These seemingly non-random differences may be caused by underreporting of delinquent behavior by the middle classes or by slightly more effective social control and socialization by middle-class parents.

17.   Socio-economic Class and Area as Correlates of Illegal Behavior among Juveniles

JOHN P. CLARK AND EUGENE P. WENNINGER

Until recently almost all efforts to discover characteristics that differentiate juveniles who violate legal norms from those who do not have compared institutional and non-institutional populations. Though many researchers still employ a "delinquent" or "criminal" sample from institutions,[1] there is a growing awareness that the process through which boys and girls are selected to populate our "correctional" institutions may cause such comparison studies to distort seriously the true picture of illegal behavior in our society. Therefore, conclusions based upon such studies are subject to considerable criticism[2] if generalized beyond the type of

population of the particular institution at the time of the study. Although the study of adjudicated offenders is important, less encumbered studies of the violation of legal norms hold more promise for those interested in the more general concept of deviant behavior.

Though it, too, has methodological limitations, the anonymous-questionnaire procedure has been utilized to obtain results reflecting the rates and patterns of illegal behavior among juveniles from different social classes, ages, sexes, and ethnic groups in the general population.[3] The results of

* The total project of which this paper is a part was sponsored by the Ford Foundation and the University of Illinois Graduate Research Board. Professor Daniel Glaser was very helpful throughout the project and in the preparation of this paper.

[1] An outstanding example of this type of research design is Sheldon and Eleanor Glueck, *Unraveling Juvenile Delinquency*, New York: The Commonwealth Fund, 1950.

[2] See Marshall B. Clinard, *Sociology of Deviant Behavior*, New York: Rinehart, 1958, p. 124, for his assessment of the

validity of the study by Sheldon and Eleanor Glueck, *Unraveling Juvenile Delinquency*.

[3] Most outstanding are those by Austin L. Porterfield, *Youth in Trouble*, Fort Worth, Texas: Leo Potishman Foundation, 1946; F. Ivan Nye and James F. Short, "Scaling Delinquent Behavior," *American Sociological Review*, 22 (June, 1957), pp. 326–331; and Robert A. Dentler and Lawrence J. Monroe, "Early Adolescent Theft," *American Sociological Review*, 26 (October, 1961), 733–743; Fred J. Murphy, Mary M. Shirley, and Helen L. Witmer, "The Incidence of Hidden Delinquency," *American Journal of Orthopsychiatry*, 16 (October, 1946), pp. 686–696.

SOURCE. John P. Clark and Eugene P. Wenninger, "Socio-economic Class and Area as Correlates of Illegal Behavior among Juveniles," from *American Sociological Review*, Volume 27, December 1962, pp. 826–834. Reprinted with the permission of the American Sociological Association and the authors.

these studies have offered sufficient evidence to indicate that the patterns of illegal behavior among juveniles may be dramatically different from what was heretofore thought to be the case.

Some of the most provocative findings have been those that challenge the almost universally accepted conclusion that the lower socio-economic classes have higher rates of illegal behavior than do the middle or upper classes. For example, neither the Nye-Short study[4] nor that of Dentler and Monroe[5] revealed any significant difference in the incidence of certain illegal or "deviant" behaviors among occupational-status levels—a finding quite at odds with most current explanations of delinquent behavior.

Although most of the more comprehensive studies in the social class tradition have been specifically concerned with a more-or-less well-defined portion of the lower class (i.e., "delinquent gangs,"[6] or "culture of the gang," or "delinquent subculture"[7]), some authors have tended to generalize their findings and theoretical formulations rather specifically to the total lower class population of juveniles.[8] These

latter authors certainly do not profess that *all* lower class children are equally involved in illegal behavior, but by implication they suggest that the incidence of illegal conduct (whether brought to the attention of law enforcement agencies or not) is more pervasive in this class than others because of some unique but fundamental characteristics of the lower social strata. For example, Miller has compiled a list of "focal concerns" toward which the lower class supposedly is oriented and because of which those in this class violate more legal norms with greater frequency than other classes.[9] Other authors point out that the lower classes are disadvantaged in their striving for legitimate goals and that they resort to deviant means to attain them.[10] Again, the result of this behavior is higher rates of illegal behavior among the lower socio-economic classes.

Therefore, there *appears* to be a direct conflict between the theoretical formulations of Miller, Cohen, Merton, Cloward and Ohlin, and those findings reported by Nye and Short and Dentler and Monroe. This apparent discrepancy in the literature can be resolved, however, if one hypothesizes that the rates of illegal conduct among the social classes vary with the type of community[11] in which they are found. Were this so, it would be possible for studies which have included certain types of communities to reveal differential illegal

[4] James F. Short, "Differential Association and Delinquency," *Social Problems,* 4 (January, 1957), pp. 233-239; F. Ivan Nye, *Family Relationships and Delinquent Behavior,* New York: John Wiley, 1958; James E. Short and F. Ivan Nye, "Reported Behavior as a Criterion of Deviant Behavior," *Social Problems,* 5 (Winter, 1957–1958), pp. 207–213; F. Ivan Nye, James F. Short, and Virgil J. Olson, "Socio-Economic Status and Delinquent Behavior," *American Journal of Sociology,* 63 (January, 1958), pp. 381–389.
[5] Dentler and Monroe, *op. cit.*
[6] Richard A. Cloward and Lloyd E. Ohlin, *Delinquency and Opportunity: A Theory of Delinquent Gangs,* New York: The Free Press of Glencoe, 1961.
[7] Albert K. Cohen, *Delinquent Boys: The Culture of the Gang,* Glencoe, Ill.: Free Press, 1955.
[8] Walter B. Miller, "Lower Class Culture as a Generating Milieu of Gang Delinquency," *Journal of Social Issues,* 14 (No. 3, 1958), pp. 5–19.

[9] *Ibid.*
[10] Cohen, *op. cit.,* Cloward and Ohlin, *op. cit.,* and Robert K. Merton, *Social Theory and Social Structure,* Glencoe, Ill.: Free Press, 1957, pp. 146-149.
[11] In this report "type of community" is used to refer in a general way to a geographic and social unit having certain distinctive demographic qualities, such as occupational structure, race, social class, and size. Designations such as "rural farm," or "Negro lower class urban," or "middle class suburbia," have long been utilized to describe such persistent physical-social characteristics.

behavior rates among social classes while studies which have involved other types of communities might fail to detect social class differences.

Whereas the findings and formulations of Merton, Cohen, Cloward and Ohlin, and Miller are oriented, in a sense, toward the "full range" of social situations, those of Nye-Short and Dentler-Monroe are very specifically limited to the types of populations used in their respective studies. It is important to note that the communities in which these latter studies were conducted ranged only from rural to small city in size. As Nye points out, "They are thus urban but not metropolitan."[12] Yet, most studies of "delinquent gangs" and "delinquent subcultures" have been conducted in metropolitan centers where these phenomena are most apparent. Perhaps it is only here that there is a sufficient concentration of those in the extreme socio-economic classes to afford an adequate test of the "social class hypothesis."

In addition to the matter of social class concentration and size, there is obviously more than one "kind" of lower class and each does not have rates or types of illegal behavior identical to those of the others. For example, most rural farm areas, in which occupations, incomes, and educational levels are indicative of lower class status, as measured by most social class indexes, consistently have been found to have low rates of misconduct—in fact lower than most urban middle class communities.

Therefore, to suggest the elimination of social class as a significant correlate to the quantity and quality of illegal behavior before it has been thoroughly examined in a variety of community situations seems somewhat premature. Reiss and Rhodes concluded as a re-

sult of study of class and juvenile court rates by school district that "it is clear that there is no simple relationship between ascribed social status and delinquency."[13] In order to isolate the factor of social class, to eliminate possible effects of class bias in the rate at which juvenile misbehavior is referred to court, as well as to vary the social and physical environs in which it is located, we chose in this study to compare rates of admitted illegal behavior among diverse communities within the northern half of Illinois. Our hypotheses were:

1. Significant differences in the incidence of illegal behavior exist among communities differing in predominant social class composition within a given metropolitan area.

2. Significant differences in the incidence of illegal behavior exist among similar social class strata located in different types of community.

3. Differences in the incidence of illegal behavior among different social class populations within a given community are not significant.

THE STUDY

The data used to test the above hypotheses were gathered in 1961 as part of a larger exploratory study of illegal behavior (particularly theft) among juveniles and its relationship to socio-economic class, type of community, age, race, and various attitudinal variables, such as attitude toward law, feelings of alienation, concept of self, and feelings of being able to achieve desired goals. Subsequent reports will deal with other aspects of the exploratory study.

[12] Nye, Short, and Olson, *op. cit.*, p. 383.

[13] Albert J. Reiss and Albert L. Rhodes, "The Distribution of Juvenile Delinquency in the Social Class Structure," *American Sociological Review*, 26 (October, 1961), pp. 720–732.

A total of 1154 public school students from the sixth through the twelfth grades in the school systems of four different types of communities were respondents to a self-administered, anonymous questionnaire given in groups of from 20 to 40 persons by the senior author. Considerable precaution was taken to insure reliability and validity of the responses. For example, assurances were given that the study was not being monitored by the school administration; questions were pretested to eliminate ambiguity; and the administration of the questionnaire was made as threat-free as possible.

The four communities represented in the study were chosen for the unique social class structure represented by each. The Duncan "Socio-Economic Index for All Occupations"[14] was used to determine the occupational profile of each community by assigning index scores to the occupation of the respondents' fathers. The results are summarized in Table 1.

The overwhelming majority of the

[14] Albert J. Reiss, Jr., Otis Dudley Duncan, Paul K. Hatt, and Cecil C. North, *Occupations and Social Status,* New York: The Free Press of Glencoe, 1961, especially pp. 109–161 prepared by Otis D. Duncan.

respondents comprising the *rural farm* population live on farms, farming being by far the most common occupation of their fathers. Many of the fathers who were not listed as farmers are, in fact, "part-time" farmers. Therefore, though the Duncan Index would classify most of the residents in the lower class, most of these public school children live on farms in a prosperous section of the Midwest. The sixth, seventh, and eighth graders were drawn from schools located in very small villages. Grades 9–12 were drawn from the high school which was located in open-farm land.

The *lower urban* sample is primarily composed of children of those with occupations of near-equal ranking but certainly far different in nature from those of the rural farm community. The lower urban sample was drawn from a school system located in a very crowded and largely Negro area of Chicago. The fathers (or male head of the family) of these youngsters are laborers in construction, waiters, janitors, clean-up men, etc. Even among those who place relatively high on the Duncan Scale are many who, in spite of their occupational title, reside, work, and socialize almost exclusively in the lower class community.

Table 1

DUNCAN SOCIO-ECONOMIC-INDEX SCORES BASED ON OCCUPATION OF FATHER

| | Type of community | | | |
Score	Rural farm %	Lower urban %	Industrial city %	Upper urban %
(1) 0–23	75.9	40.4	36.4	5.7
(2) 24–47	9.9	15.5	19.3	4.8
(3) 48–71	4.7	12.5	22.9	43.9
(4) 72–96	1.5	4.2	10.0	34.6
(5) Unclassifiable*	8.0	27.4	11.4	11.0
Total	100 (N—274)	100 (N—265)	100 (N—280)	100 (N—335)

* This category included those respondents from homes with no father and those respondents who did not furnish adequate information for reliable classification. The 27.4 per cent figure in the lower urban community reflects a higher proportion of "fatherless" homes rather than greater numbers of responses which were incomplete or vague in other ways.

As Table 1 demonstrates, the occupational structure of the *industrial city* is somewhat more diffuse than the other communities, though consisting primarily of lower class occupations. This city of about 35,000 is largely autonomous, although a small portion of the population commutes daily to Chicago. However, about two-thirds of these students have fathers who work as blue-collar laborers in local industries and services. The median years of formal education of all males age 25 or over is 10.3.[15] The median annual family income is $7,255.[16] The population of this small city contains substantial numbers of Polish and Italian Americans and about 15 per cent Negroes.

Those in the *upper urban* sample live in a very wealthy suburb of Chicago. Nearly three-fourths of the fathers in these families are high-level executives or professionals. The median level of education for all males age 25 or over is 16 plus.[17] The median annual family income is slightly over $20,000 —80 per cent of the families make $10,000 or more annually.[18]

With two exceptions, representative sampling of the public school children was followed within each of these communities: (1) those who could not read at a fourth grade level were removed in all cases, which resulted in the loss of less than one-half per cent of the total sample, and (2) the sixth-grade sample in the industrial city community was drawn from a predominantly Negro, working class area and was, therefore, non-representative of the total community for that grade-level only. All the students from grades 6 through 12 were used in the rural farm community "sample."

MEASURE OF ILLEGAL BEHAVIOR

An inventory of 36 offenses was initially assembled from delinquency scales, legal statutes, and the FBI Uniform Crime Reports. In addition to this, a detailed list of theft items, ranging from candy to automobiles, was constructed. The latter list was later combined into two composite items (minor theft and major theft) and added to the first list, enlarging the number of items in this inventory to 38 items as shown in Table 2. No questions on sex offenses were included in this study, a restriction found necessary in order to gain entrance into one of the school systems.

All respondents were asked to indicate if they had committed each of these offenses (including the detailed list of theft items) *within the past year,* thus furnishing data amenable to age-level analysis.[19] If the respondents admitted commission of an offense, they so indicated by disclosing the number of times (either 1, 2, 3, or 4 or more) they had done so. The first four columns of Table 2 reveal the percentage of students who admitted having indulged in each specific behavior one or more times *during the past year.*

Specific offense items were arranged in an array from those admitted by the highest percentage of respondents to those admitted by the lowest percentage of respondents. Obviously the "nuisance" offenses appear near the top while the most serious and the more situationally specific fall nearer the end of the listing.[20] Several offenses are

[15] *U.S. Census of Population: 1960,* Final Report PC (1)–15C, p. 15–296.
[16] *Ibid.,* p. 15–335.
[17] *Ibid.,* p. 15–305.
[18] *Ibid.,* p. 15–344.

[19] Rates of illegal behavior were found to increase until age 14–15 and then to decrease.
[20] Ordinarily, not receiving 100 per cent admission to the first few offenses listed would have raised doubt as to the validity of those questionnaires on which these extremely common offenses were not admitted. In the Nye-Short study such questionnaires were discarded. However, since the

Table 2

PERCENTAGE OF RESPONDENTS ADMITTING INDIVIDUAL OFFENSES AND SIGNIFICANCE OF DIFFERENCES BETWEEN SELECTED COMMUNITY COMPARISONS

Offense	Community				Significance of differences*		
	(1) Industrial city N = 280	(2) Lower urban N = 265	(3) Upper urban N = 335	(4) Rural farm N = 274	(1–2)	(2–3)	(3–4)
1. Did things my parents told me not to do.	90	87	85	82	X	X	X
2. Minor theft (compilation of such items as the stealing of fruit, pencils, lipstick, candy, cigarettes, comic books, money less than $1, etc.).	79	78	80	73	X	X	X
3. Told a lie to my family, principal, or friends.	80	74	77	74	X	X	X
4. Used swearwords or dirty words out loud in school, church, or on the street so other people could hear me.	63	58	54	51	X	X	X
5. Showed or gave someone a dirty picture, a dirty story, or something like that.	53	39	58	54	1	3	X
6. Was out at night just fooling around after I was supposed to be home.	49	50	51	35	X	X	3
7. Hung around other people who I knew had broken the law lots of times or who were known as "bad" people.	49	47	27	40	X	2	4
8. Threw rocks, cans, sticks, or other things at passing car, bicycle, or person.	41	37	33	36	X	X	X
9. Slipped into a theater or other place without paying.	35	40	39	22	X	X	3

* Code: X = no significant difference.

1, 2, 3, or 4 = significant differences at .05 level or higher. The numbers indicate which of the communities in the comparison is higher in incidence of the offense.

n = too few offender cases to determine significant level.

Table 2—Continued

10. Major theft (compilation of such items as the stealing of auto parts, autos, money over $1, bicycles, radios and parts, clothing, wallets, liquor, guns, etc.).	37	40	29	20	X	2	3
11. Went into another person's house, a shed, or other building without their permission.	31	16	31	42	1	3	4
12. Gambled for money or something else with people other than my family.	30	22	35	26	X	3	3
13. Got some money or something from others by saying that I would pay them back even though I was pretty sure I wouldn't.	35	48	26	14	2	2	3
14. Told someone I was going to beat-up on them unless they did what I wanted them to do.	33	28	24	32	X	X	4
15. Drank beer, wine, or liquor without my parents' permission.	38	37	26	12	X	2	3
16. Have been kicked out of class or school for acting up.	27	28	31	22	X	X	3
17. Threw nails, or glass, or cans in the street.	31	29	21	17	X	X	X
18. Used a slug or other things like this in candy, coke, or coin machines.	24	35	18	12	2	2	3
19. Skipped school without permission.	24	36	18	11	2	2	3
20. Helped make a lot of noise outside a church, or school, or any other place in order to bother the people inside.	17	37	18	15	X	2	X
21. Threw rocks, or sticks or any other thing in order to break a window, or street light, or thing like that.	24	26	22	16	X	X	3
22. Said I was going to tell something on someone unless they gave me money, candy, or something else I wanted.	23	28	17	19	X	2	X
23. Kept or used something that I knew had been stolen by someone else.	29	36	15	16	X	2	X

Table 2—Continued

Offense	(1) Industrial city N = 280	(2) Lower urban N = 265	(3) Upper urban N = 335	(4) Rural farm N = 274	Significance of differences* (1–2)	(2–3)	(3–4)
24. Tampered or fooled with another person's car, tractor, or bicycle while they weren't around.	26	13	19	24	1	3	X
25. Started a fist fight.	26	22	15	18	X	2	X
26. Messed up a restroom by writing on the wall, or leaving the water running to run onto the floor, or upsetting the waste can.	18	33	14	17	X	2	X
27. Hung around a pool hall, bar, or tavern.	21	18	10	23	X	2	4
28. Hung around the railroad tracks and trains.	16	13	23	16	X	3	3
29. Broke down or helped to break down a fence, gate, or door on another person's place.	15	14	8	8	X	2	X
30. Took part in a "gang fight."	12	18	7	7	X	2	X
31. Ran away from home.	12	12	8	7	X	X	X
32. Asked for money, candy, a cigarette or other things from strangers.	12	12	6	7	X	2	X
33. Carried a razor, switch-blade, or gun to be used against other people.	8	16	3	4	2	2	X
34. "Beat up" on kids who hadn't done anything to me.	8	5	5	6	X	X	X
35. Broke or helped break up the furniture in a school, church, or other public building.	8	4	2	8	X	X	4
36. Attacked someone with the idea of killing them.	3	6	1	3	2	n	n
37. Smoked a reefer or used some sort of dope (narcotics).	3	4	1	3	X	n	n
38. Started a fire or helped set a fire in a building without the permission of the owner.	3	2	1	3	X	n	n

apparently committed very infrequently by school children from the sixth to twelfth grades regardless of their social environs.

FINDINGS

In order to determine whether significant differences exist in the incidence of illegal behavior among the various types of communities, a two-step procedure was followed. First, each of the four communities was assigned a rank for each offense on the basis of the percentage of respondents admitting commission of that offense. These ranks were totaled across all offenses for each community. The resultant numerical total provided a very crude over-all measure of the relative degree to which the sample population from each community had been involved in illegal behavior during the past year. The results were (from most to least illegal behavior): industrial city, lower urban, upper urban, and rural farm. However, there was little over-all difference in the sum of ranks between upper urban and rural farm and even less difference between the industrial city and lower urban areas.

In the second step the communities were arranged in the order given above and then the significance of the difference between adjacent pairs was determined by applying the Wilcoxon matched-pairs signed-ranks test. Only those comparisons which involve either industrial city or lower urban versus upper urban or rural farm result in any significant differences.[21] This finding is

compatible with the above crude ranking procedure.

On the basis of these findings the first hypothesis is supported, while the second hypothesis received only partial support. Lower urban juveniles reported significantly more illegal behavior than did the juveniles of the upper urban community, and the two lower class communities of industrial city and lower urban appear to be quite similar in their high rates, but another lower class area composed largely of farmers has a much lower rate, similar to that of the upper urban area.

Much more contrast among the rates of juvenile misconduct in the four different communities than is indicated by the above results becomes apparent when one focuses on individual offenses. As the last column in Table 2 reveals, and as could be predicted from the above, there are few significant differences in the rates on each offense between the industrial city and lower urban communities. The few differences that do occur hardly fall into a pattern except that the lower urban youth seem to be oriented more toward violence (carrying weapons and attacking persons) than those in the industrial city.

However, 16 of a possible 35 relationships are significantly different in the upper urban-rural farm comparison, a fact that could not have been predicted from the above results. Apparently, variation in one direction on certain offenses tends to be neutralized by variation in the opposite direction on other offenses when the Wilcoxon test is used. There are greater actual differ-

---

respondents were asked in this study to admit their offenses during the past year only, it was thought that less than 100 per cent admission would be highly possible when one considers the entire age range. Undoubtedly some of the respondents who did not admit these minor offenses were falsifying their questionnaires.

[21] Significance of differences were calculated between pairs of communities across *all* 38 offenses by using the Wil-

coxon matched-pairs signed-ranks test (described in Sidney Siegel, *Non-Parametric Statistics*, New York: McGraw-Hill Book Company, Inc., 1956, pp. 75–83). The results of this procedure were:

1–2—P .35	1–3—P .00006
2–3—P .0034	1–4—P .0006
3–4—P .90	2–4—P .016

ences in the nature of illegal behavior between these two communities than is noticeable when considered in more summary terms. (It might be pointed out here, parenthetically, that this type of finding lends support to the suggestion by Dentler and Monroe that the comparison of criterion groups on the basis of "omnibus scales" may have serious shortcomings.) [22]

Rural farm youngsters are more prone than those in the upper urban area to commit such offenses as trespassing, threatening to "beat up" on persons, hanging around taverns, and being with "bad" associates—all relatively unsophisticated acts. Although some of the offenses committed more often by those who live in the upper urban community are also unsophisticated (throwing rocks at street lights, getting kicked out of school classes, and hanging around trains), others probably require some skill to perform successfully and probably depend on supportive peer-group relationships. For example, these data reveal that upper urban juveniles are more likely than their rural farm counterparts to be out at night after they are supposed to be at home, drink beer and liquors without parents' permission, engage in major theft, gamble, skip school, and slip into theaters without paying. In addition to their likely dependence upon peer-groups, perhaps these offenses are more easily kept from the attention of parents in the urban setting than in open-farm areas.

The greatest differences between rates of illegal conduct occur between the lower urban and upper urban communities, where 21 of a possible 35 comparisons reach statistical significance, the lower urban rates being higher in all except five of these. Although the upper urban youngsters are more likely to pass "dirty pictures,"

gamble, trespass, hang around trains, and tamper with other people's cars, their cousins in the lower class area are more likely to steal major items, drink, skip school, destroy property, fight, and carry weapons. The latter offenses are those normally thought to be "real delinquent acts" while the upper urban offenses (with the exception of vehicle tampering) are not generally considered to be such.

To summarize briefly, when the rates of juvenile misconduct are compared on individual offenses among communities, it appears that as one moves from rural farm to upper urban to industrial city and lower urban, the incidence of most offenses becomes greater, especially in the more serious offenses and in those offenses usually associated with social structures with considerable tolerance for illegal behavior.

While most emphasis is placed here on the differences, one obvious finding, evident in Table 2, is that in most of the nuisance offenses (minor theft, lying to parents, disobeying parents, swearing in public, throwing objects to break things or into the streets) there are no differences among the various communities. Differences appear to lie in the more serious offenses and those requiring a higher degree of sophistication and social organization.

The Reiss-Rhodes findings tend to refute theories of delinquent behavior which imply a high delinquency proneness of the lower class regardless of the "status area" in which it is found.[23] In view of this report, and since Nye-Short and Dentler-Monroe were unable to detect inter-class differences, inter-class comparisons were made within the four community types of this study.

---

[22] Dentler and Monroe, *op. cit.*, p. 734.

[23] Reiss and Rhodes, *op. cit.*, p. 729. The concept of "status areas" is used here as it was used by Reiss and Rhodes to designate residential areas of a definite social class composition.

Following the technique employed by Nye and Short, only those students age 15 and younger were used in these comparisons in order to neutralize the possible effects of differential school dropout rates by social classes in the older categories.

With the exception of the industrial city, no significant inter-class differences in illegal behavior rates were found within community types when either the Wilcoxon test was used for all offenses or when individual offense comparisons were made.[24] This finding supports hypothesis 3. It could account for the inability of Nye-Short and Dentler-Monroe to find differences among the socio-economic classes from several relatively similar communities in which their studies were conducted. It is also somewhat compatible with the Reiss and Rhodes findings. However, we did not find indications of higher rates of illegal conduct in the predominant socio-economic class within most areas, as the Reiss and Rhodes data suggested.[25] This may have been a function of the unique manner in which the socio-economic categories had to be combined for comparison purposes in this study. These findings, however, are logical in that boys and girls of the minority social classes within a

---

[24] Because of small numbers in social classes within certain communities, categories were collapsed or ignored for comparison purposes as shown below. Refer to Table 1 for designation of categories. The Wilcoxon matched-pairs signed-ranks test was used.

Rural farm
category 1 versus 2, 3, 4   insignificant
Lower urban
category 1 versus 2, 3, 4   insignificant
category 1 versus 5   insignificant
categories 2, 3, 4 versus 5   insignificant
Industrial city
category 1 versus 2   significant
category 2 versus 3, 4   significant
category 1 versus 3, 4   insignificant
Upper urban
category 3 versus 4   insignificant

[25] Reiss and Rhodes, *op. cit.*, p. 729.

"status area" would likely strive to adhere to the norms of the predominant social class as closely as possible whether these norms were legal or illegal.

Within the industrial city the second socio-economic category (index scores 24–47) was slightly significantly lower than either extreme category when the Wilcoxon test was used. Since the largest percentage of the sample of the industrial city falls in the lowest socio-economic category (0–23) and since this category evidences one of the highest rates of misconduct, the finding for this community is somewhat similar to the Reiss-Rhodes findings.

CONCLUSIONS

The findings of this study tend to resolve some of the apparent conflicts in the literature that have arisen from previous research concerning the relationship between the nature of illegal behavior and socio-economic class. However, some of the results contradict earlier reports.

Our findings are similar to those of Nye-Short and Dentler-Monroe in that we failed to detect any significant differences in illegal behavior rates among the social classes of rural and small urban areas. However, in keeping with the class-oriented theories, we did find significant differences, both in quantity and quality of illegal acts, among communities or "status areas," each consisting of one predominant socio-economic class. The lower class areas have higher illegal behavior rates, particularly in the more serious types of offenses. Differences among the socio-economic classes within these "status areas" were generally insignificant (which does not agree with the findings of Reiss and Rhodes), although when social class categories were compared across communities, significant differences were found. All this suggests some extremely interesting relationships.

1. The pattern of illegal behavior within small communities or within "status areas" of a large metropolitan center is determined by the predominant class of that area. Social class differentiation within these areas is apparently not related to the incidence of illegal behavior. This suggests that there are community-wide norms which are related to illegal behavior and to which juveniles adhere regardless of their social class origins. The answer to the obvious question of how large an urban area must be before socio-economic class becomes a significant variable in the incidence of illegal behavior is not provided by this study. It is quite likely that in addition to size, other considerations such as the ratio of social class representation, ethnic composition, and the prestige of the predominant social class relative to other "status areas" would influence the misconduct rates. The population of 20,-000 of the particular upper urban community used in this study is apparently not of sufficient size or composition to provide for behavior autonomy among the social classes in the illegal behavior sense. There is some evidence, however, that an industrial city of roughly 40,000 such as the one included here is on the brink of social class differentiation in misconduct rates.

2. Though the juveniles in all communities admitted indulgence in several nuisance offenses at almost equal rates, serious offenses are much more likely to have been committed by lower class urban youngsters. Perhaps the failure of some researchers to find differences among the social classes in their misconduct rates can be attributed to the relatively less serious offenses included in their questionnaires or scales. It would seem to follow that any "subculture" characterized by the more serious delinquencies, would be found only in large, urban, lower class areas. However, the data of this study, at best, can only suggest this relationship.

3. Lastly, these data suggest that the present explanations that rely heavily on socio-economic class as an all-determining factor in the etiology of illegal behavior should be further specified to include data such as this study provides. For example, Cohen's thesis that a delinquent subculture emerges when lower class boys discover that they must satisfy their need for status by means other than those advocated in the middle class public schools should be amended to indicate that this phenomenon apparently occurs only in large metropolitan centers where the socio-economic classes are found in large, relatively homogeneous areas. In the same manner, Miller's theory of the relationship between the focal concerns of the lower class culture and delinquency may require closer scrutiny. If the relationship between focal concerns to illegal behavior that Miller has suggested exists, then those in the lower social class (as determined by father's occupation) who live in communities or "status areas" that are predominantly of some other social class, are apparently not participants in the "lower class culture;" or, because of their small numbers, they are being successfully culturally intimidated by the predominant class. Likewise, those who are thought to occupy middle class positions apparently take on lower class illegal behavior patterns when residing in areas that are predominantly lower class. This suggests either the great power of prevailing norms within a "status area" or a limitation of social class, as it is presently measured, as a significant variable in the determination of illegal behavior.

RESEARCH QUESTIONS

At least three general questions that demand further research emerge from this study:

1. What dimension (in size and other demographic characteristics) must an urban area attain before socio-economic class becomes a significant variable in the determination of illegal behavior patterns?

2. What are the specific differences between lower class populations and social structures located in rural or relatively small urban areas and those located in large, concentrated areas in metropolitan centers that would account for their differential illegal behavior rates, especially in the more serious offenses?

3. The findings of this study suggest that the criteria presently used to determine social class levels may not be the most conducive to the understanding of variation in the behavior of those who fall within these classes, at least for those within the juvenile ages. A substitute concept is that of "status area" as operationalized by Reiss and Rhodes. For example, the differentiating characteristics of a large, Negro, lower class, urban "status area" could be established and would seem to have greater predictive and descriptive power than would the social class category as determined by present methods. Admittedly, this suggestion raises again the whole messy affair of "cultural area typologies" but area patterns of behaviors obviously exist and must be handled in some manner. Research effort toward systematically combining the traditional socio-economic class concept with that of cultural area might prove extremely fruitful by providing us with important language and concepts not presently available.

18. Status Deprivation and Delinquent Behavior

ALBERT J. REISS, JR. AND A. LEWIS RHODES

The relationship between delinquent behavior and life style in the slums of London and Paris reported over a hundred years ago finds its counterpart in contemporary metropolitan America.[1] Evidence for the population of the present study shows that official delinquency rates vary inversely with socioeconomic status.[2] There are some who argue that differential enforcement of the law and handling of law violators from the socioeconomic levels of the population account for these observed differences in official rates of delinquency.[3] But assuming the relationship

between delinquent behavior and socioeconomic status to be valid, the question quite naturally arises, what is there about low socioeconomic status that generates high delinquency rates?

One explanation for this relationship is Albert K. Cohen's theory of subcultural delinquency. A too brief statement of his theory is that working class boys, to the degree that they value middle class status, experience status frustration when in status competition. Status frustration generates a problem of adjustment and places these boys in the market for a solution. Delinquency is often a collective subcultural solution to this status frustration because it provides criteria of status which these adolescents can meet.[4]

Cohen's theory necessarily postulates that adolescents have developed a conscious awareness or perception of differences in class status (presumably denoted by both deference and possession of material goods) which brings about status frustration and aggression. He remarks that the child in our society "learns to make the (class) distinction adults make, to apply the criteria they

[1] M. Hill and C. Cornwallis, "Two Prize Essays on Juvenile Delinquency" (1852), quoted in Alfred R. Lindesmith and Yale Levin, "The Lombrosian Myth in Criminology," *The American Journal of Sociology*, 42:659 (Mar., 1937).

[2] Albert J. Reiss, Jr. and A. Lewis Rhodes, "The Distribution of Juvenile Delinquency in the Social Class Structure," *American Sociological Review*, 26:720–732 (Oct., 1961).

[3] Austin L. Porterfield, *Youth in Trouble* (Fort Worth: Leo Potishman Foundation, 1946), p. 41; James S. Wallerstein and C. J. Wyle, "Our Law Abiding Law Breakers," *National Probation*, 107–112 (Mar.–Apr., 1947); F. Ivan Nye, James F. Short, and V. J. Olson, "Socioeconomic Status and Delinquent Behavior," in F. Ivan Nye, *Family Relationships and Delinquent Behavior* (New York: Wiley, 1958).

[4] Albert K. Cohen, *Delinquent Boys: The Culture of the Gang* (Glencoe, Ill.: Free Press, 1955), Chs. 4 and 5.

SOURCE. Albert J. Reiss, Jr. and A. Lewis Rhodes, "Status Deprivation and Delinquent Behavior," from *The Sociological Quarterly*, Volume 4, Spring 1963, pp. 135–149. Reprinted with the permission of *The Sociological Quarterly* and the authors.

apply and to evaluate their families and his own, relative to theirs, as adults do. He also learns to recognize and to value the signs of membership in social class: clothing and equipment, homes, neighborhood and cars. By the time he is eleven or twelve years old, his knowledge of the class system has grown quite sophisticated."[5] The consequence of this sophistication is an unfavorable social comparison where "out of all this there arise feelings of inferiority and perhaps resentment and hostility."[6] Robin Williams and others contend that while this structural strain exists in American society, there are compensatory elements such as equalitarian ideology and behavior patterns, residential segregation, and a generally high standard of living which reduce feelings of status frustration in the lower classes, particularly by insulating persons from invidious comparisons of life style.[7]

THE PROBLEM

This paper is concerned with the validity of these two postulates in Cohen's theory: (1) that lower class adolescents compare their own life style unfavorably with peers in higher classes; (2) that this unfavorable social comparison leads to feelings of frustration and deprivation which generate a higher rate of delinquent behavior.[8] Specifically, if Cohen is correct, the facts which support the postulate are: (1) lower class adolescents experience greater relative status deprivation; (2)

lower class delinquents experience the greatest relative deprivation. But if Williams and others are correct, then relative status deprivation will either be infrequent in the population or distributed in some other fashion in the class structure.

Perception of (and reaction to) differences in dress and housing should be affected by such factors as age, sex, race, and the character of the social milieu in which the comparison takes place. If maturity brings greater class consciousness and sensitivity to class symbols, as Cohen suggests, then the oldest adolescents should be most aware of differences in clothes and housing. Females should be more sensitive to these differences than males, however, because the feminine role emphasizes clothing style and personal attractiveness, particularly in dating competition.[9] Variation by race is complicated by residential segregation in that for a given income there is less variability in housing for Negroes than whites. There also are subcultural variations in life style along ethnic as well as economic lines. However, it is hypothesized that Negroes will be more sensitive to differences in life style and, therefore, more likely to experience relative deprivation than whites since our life style indicators of clothes and housing are highly visible symbols of status discrimination.

The social milieu in which social comparison is made should influence perception of status differences and feelings of status deprivation.[10] Deprivation should be greatest in schools where status distance is maximized, i.e., schools which crosscut the class struc-

---

[5] *Ibid.*, pp. 82–83.
[6] *Ibid.*, p. 112.
[7] Robin M. Williams, Jr., *American Society: A Sociological Interpretation* (2nd ed.; New York: Knopf, 1960), pp. 138–149.
[8] The same postulates may underlie the Cloward-Ohlin formulation, though the case is less clear since they differentiate between "life style" and "material success" goals. Richard Cloward and Lloyd E. Ohlin, *Delinquency and Opportunity* (New York: The Free Press of Glencoe, Inc., 1960), pp. 94–97.

[9] Cohen, *op. cit.*, pp. 140–145.
[10] Robert K. Merton and Alice S. Kitt, "Contributions to the Theory of Reference Group Behavior," in Robert K. Merton and Paul F. Lazarsfeld (eds.), *Studies in the Scope and Method of the American Soldier* (Glencoe, Ill.: Free Press, 1950), pp. 53–58.

ture, drawing their students from the highest to the lowest class.[11]

THE DESIGN

The Merton and Kitt definition of relative deprivation was followed in devising the empirical test for this study; i.e., one feels at a disadvantage or deprived when comparing oneself with one or more reference groups.[12] A single item measures relative status deprivation: "Would you say that most of the students in your school have better clothes and a better house to live in than you have? (Check one) (1) a lot better clothes and house; (2) a little better clothes and house; (3) about the same clothes and house; (4) poorer clothes and house; (5) I *never* thought about this before." The use of the double referent, clothes and housing, complicates interpretation of response data. The reference group "most students in your school" may not be the most salient one for status comparison; it was chosen because Cohen suggests that the school is the principal locus of status frustration for adolescents. Comparison is limited to clothes and housing. While other symbols of life style and material success might serve equally well or better, these have the advantage that they characterize all male and female subjects in the population. The response choice, "I *never* thought about this before" was included as a test of salience of the item. If the respondent checked this response, it was assumed that conscious unfavorable social comparison is unrelated to status frustration.

Questionnaires from 12,524 pupils in grades seven through twelve of forty-one county public schools of Davidson County, Tennessee, together with in-

formation from the attendance division, the Juvenile Court, and the student's cumulative record folder provide the data for the study. Three categories of socioeconomic status are used: (*a*) *bottom class,* including youths from homes of laborers, operatives, service (except protective service) workers, peddlers and door-to-door salesmen; (*b*) *middle class,* including those from homes of craftsmen, foremen, and kindred workers, protective service workers, managers and proprietors of small businesses, clerical workers, sales workers not in other categories, and technicians allied to professional services; (*c*) *top class,* including children of managers, officials, proprietors, professional and semi-professional workers, and sales workers in finance, insurance, and real estate. The percentage distribution for the occupational status of students' families is used to define the socioeconomic status structure of each school which then becomes a basis for classifying the school in a social class context. The social class context is based on a classification of schools, not of communities. There undoubtedly is social class segregation in the residential area which makes up the school community. Only four social class contexts are used in this study:[13]

UPPER-MIDDLE CONTEXT. Approximately 90 per cent of the pupils are from white-collar homes.

CROSSCUT-TOP CONTEXT. The pupils come from all class levels but there is an overrepresentation of students from the top classes since there are 15 per cent more students from the top occupational groups than in the occupational structure for all schools.

---

[11] *Ibid.* Merton and Kitt report that deprivation is greatest where social distance within the immediate environment is maximized.

[12] *Ibid.*

[13] These represent a modification of a more detailed classification of the social status contexts of schools previously published. For the more detailed classification, see Albert J. Reiss, Jr. and A. Lewis Rhodes, *op. cit.,* p. 722.

CROSSCUT-CENTER AND REPRESENTATIVE CONTEXT. Either 15 per cent more pupils are from the middle occupational groups than in the occupational structure for all schools or the occupational distribution for the school is similar to that for all schools.

CROSS-CUT BOTTOM AND LOWER CONTEXT. Either 15 per cent more pupils are from bottom class occupations than in the occupational structure for all schools or three-fourths of the student body are from blue-collar occupational levels.

A boy's or a girl's behavior is defined as delinquent if there is an official record of delinquency, chronic truancy, or a delinquent score on a seven-item scale based on self reports of delinquent behavior. The derivation of the scale and the other measures of delinquent behavior are discussed in a previous publication.[14]

The methods of statistical analysis were chi square test for association ($p < .05$) for two variables and partial association in which subjects were divided into homogeneous subgroups according to one or more control variables (in this case, race, sex, socioeconomic status, and school context). Each subgroup is treated as if it were an independent test of the relationship. The sign test is used to see if the pattern of signs in this series of tests exceeds chance expectation ($p < .05$).

THE FINDINGS

Among the several findings of the study, nothing stands out more than the observation concerning the salience of our life style indicator to adolescents. Approximately three out of ten adolescents respond that they never thought

[14] Albert J. Reiss, Jr. and Albert Lewis Rhodes, *A Sociopsychological Study of Conforming and Deviating Behavior among Adolescents* (Washington, D.C.: U.S. Office of Education Project 507, 1959).

about comparing their own clothes and housing with that of their peers. Zero-order comparisons with the dependent and each of the independent variables fail to disclose any important variation in salience, except by race (see Table 1). The proportion who say they never thought about the comparison is substantially the same for adolescents in all age, sex, social class context, and conforming-deviant subgroups, although there are small and statistically significant differences among them.

The only substantial difference in Table 1, then, is the difference between Negro and white youth. Negroes are more likely than whites to say they never thought about comparing their own clothes and housing with that of their peers. Although the fact is not presented in our tables, there is no socioeconomic status difference within the Negro population in the percentage who never thought about differences in clothes and housing. Negroes may pay less attention to social class differences within their group because the race difference overshadows it. The finding is puzzling, nevertheless, since it is generally assumed that Negroes are consumption oriented, with dress an important feature of life style. But perhaps the salient comparison level for Negroes is the white social classes. Our question does not tap this dimension.

Further examination of the relationship between salience of the life style indicator and social status is limited to whites because the number of Negroes in this population is too small to permit higher-order partialing of the relationship. Multivariate analysis for whites (shown in Table 2) shows that the salience of the life style indicator does not increase uniformly with socioeconomic status in all social class contexts. Apparently the social class context has some effect on whether or not adolescents perceive differences in life style,

Table 1

PERCENTAGE OF ADOLESCENTS WHO NEVER THOUGHT ABOUT COMPARING THEM-
SELVES WITH PEERS REGARDING CLOTHES AND HOUSING BY CONTROL VARIABLES

Control variable	Percentage	N	Chi squared	$P(\chi^2)$
Age				
16 and over	25	2,841	36.0	< .001
14 and 15	29	3,437		
10 through 13	32	2,946		
No age information	31	959*		
Sex				
Males	31	5,003	20.1	< .001
Females	27	5,180		
Race				
White	28	9,533	110.8	< .001
Negro	47	650		
Social class				
Top	25	2,554	52.4	< .001
Middle	28	4,520		
Bottom	34	2,747		
No information	30	365*		
Social class context (whites only)				
Upper Middle	24	2,056	20.	< .001
Crosscut-Top	28	2,880		
Crosscut-Center	29	1,967		
Crosscut-Bottom	30	2,633		
Conforming-deviating rating				
Delinquent	32	587	16.0	< .001
Conformer	28	7,109		
Overconformer	32	2,487		
All cases	29	10,183		

* Not included in computation for χ^2.

particularly when at all ages those within the predominant class are less likely to have thought about life style comparisons than are top class boys generally. Bottom class boys and girls in top class contexts are most likely to be aware of differences in clothes and housing, particularly at older ages. Only roughly one in ten of the bottom class boys and girls aged 16 and over in top class contexts said they had not thought about life style comparisons. In general, older boys and girls at each social-status level in a social class context are more likely to say they have made such comparisons than are younger ones. The subgroups with the least life style consciousness are young boys in the crosscut-center and bottom contexts.

These results show that a substantial proportion of the adolescent population never thought about differences in life style. The fact remains, nevertheless, that a majority of 70 per cent of our adolescents did make some evaluation.

DEPRIVATION AND SOCIOECONOMIC STATUS

Examination of the questionnaire responses of adolescents who have made some evaluation of our indexes of life style reveals that only a minority of 18 per cent give the deprivation response that most students in their school have better clothing and housing (see Table 3). There is a small but statistically significant difference in this proportion by age and race but none by sex status.

Bottom class adolescents are most

Table 2

PERCENTAGE OF WHITE MALES AND FEMALES WHO NEVER BEFORE COMPARED OWN CLOTHES AND HOUSING WITH THOSE OF PEERS BY AGE, SEX, SOCIAL CLASS, AND CLASS CONTEXT

| Sex and age | Social class and class context | | | | |
	Upper, upper middle	Crosscut-top	Crosscut-center	Crosscut-bottom	Subtotal
TOP CLASS					
Males					
10–13	25	26	33	41	28
14–15	24	24	18	37	25
16+	21	19	18	43	24
No age	9	(33)*	(57)	(25)	26
Total	23	24	25	40	26
Females					
10–13	27	29	24	21	27
14–15	26	21	27	25	25
16+	23	17	25	18	21
No age	20	(31)	(33)	(75)	29
Total	25	22	25	23	24
MIDDLE CLASS					
Males					
10–13	29	35	45	35	36
14–15	22	44	31	27	31
16+	18	28	35	19	29
No age	(25)	36	35	19	29
Total	29	34	37	30	32
Females					
10–13	30	33	24	26	29
14–15	22	24	26	28	26
16+	17	14	21	18	17
No age	(15)	11	40	19	19
Total	24	23	24	24	24
BOTTOM CLASS					
Males					
10–13	(29)	46	40	35	39
14–15	15	32	29	34	32
16+	13	30	32	34	32
No age	(67)	(33)	(44)	30	33
Total	24	35	32	34	34
Females					
10–13	(24)	34	34	38	35
14–15	23	25	23	32	28
16+	(8)	25	20	24	22
No age	(0)	(33)	(23)	(37)	31
Total	18	28	25	32	28
ALL CLASSES					
Males					
10–13	27	35	41	36	34
14–15	23	32	29	32	30
16+	20	27	31	34	28
No age	39	28	23	25	27
Total	24	31	33	33	30
Females					
10–13	28	32	27	30	29
14–15	25	24	25	29	26
16+	21	17	21	20	19
No age	17	27	33	33	28
Total	25	24	25	27	25

* Parentheses indicate that N is less than twenty.

likely to feel that they have poorer clothing and housing; the social class context differences are negligible, however. When the relationship between status deprivation and socioeconomic status is refined to include the effects of age, sex, and class context, it becomes apparent that the relationship is not altogether independent of age and sex (see Table 4), though it remains true that both bottom class boys and girls are most likely to experience feelings of status deprivation when sex and class context are controlled (the relationship holds for twenty of twenty-four comparisons; $p < .01$). What is unexpected is the fact that status deprivation apparently is not confined to any particular social class context. This result is somewhat disappointing for those who make the assumption that the status composition of the school affects adolescent competition for success goals. We shall turn then to the last two questions: are those who feel most status-deprived the more likely to be delinquent deviators? and, is any relationship between status deprivation and delinquency affected by the social class context of the school in which status comparisons are made?

STATUS DEPRIVATION, DELINQUENT BEHAVIOR, AND SOCIOECONOMIC STATUS

There is a significant positive relationship between delinquent behavior and the perception that peers have better clothes and housing (see Table 3). In view of the importance of this rela-

Table 3

PERCENTAGE OF SUBJECTS SAYING PEERS HAVE BETTER CLOTHES AND HOUSE BY EACH CONTROL VARIABLE

Control variable	Percentage	N	Chi squared	$P(\chi^2)$
Age				
16 and over	16	2,122	14.1	< .001
14 and over	18	2,449		
10 through 13	14	1,991		
No age information	20	659*		
Sex				
Males	16	3,445	2.5	< .20
Females	17	3,776		
Race				
White	16	6,878	21.0	< .001
Negro	25	343		
Social class				
Top	10	1,909	126.6	< .001
Middle	16	3,246		
Bottom	24	1,812		
No information	14	257*		
Social class context (whites only)				
Upper middle	14	1,557	10.4	< .02
Crosscut-top	15	2,084		
Crosscut-center	16	1,396		
Crosscut-bottom	18	1,844		
Conforming-deviating rating				
Delinquent	28	400	45.6	< .001
Conformer	16	5,125		
Overconformer	16	1,696		
All cases	18	7,221		

* Not included in computation for χ^2.

tionship in the theory, the size of the relationship is disappointing ($r_\phi = .07$). The majority of the delinquents (72 per cent) do not feel that their fellow students have better clothes and housing. Furthermore, somewhat more of the delinquents than of the conforming adolescents said that they had never thought about making this status comparison (see Table 1).

Perhaps the relatively low relationship between status deprivation and delinquent behavior can be attributed to the type of measurement used in the study. Feelings of status deprivation may not be easily measured by a paper and pencil test or by the specific operational measure we used. Holding the measure relative to the school context should not be viewed as an inadequacy of the measure, however, since then substantial differences should have been observed by type of school context. Given the size of the relationship, the more detailed analysis below is justified only on the presumption that more precise measurement of relative deprivation and of deviant behavior will produce a more substantial relationship than the negligible one reported for this sample.

The relationship between status deprivation and nonconforming behavior should be class-linked, according to Cohen's theory, i.e., the relationship should be maximized for bottom class male subjects. Furthermore, previous research suggests that the relationship will be complicated by cross-pressures operating differentially in positions in the social structure: race, sex, social class, and school context. It can be seen in Table 5 that, in fact, the relationship is not independent of these variables. The size and direction of the relationship fluctuates from one race-sex-class category to another. Negro male delinquents in the bottom class are less likely than their conforming peers (and also white delinquents) to respond that others have better clothes and housing, while Negro female delinquents in the bottom class are more likely to indicate deprivation than conforming peers (and delinquent or conforming whites). The reversal of the expected relationship for Negro males and the accentuation of the relationship for Negro females may be an artifact of the small sample size for Negroes, but further research is desirable to resolve this apparent contradiction.

A sex difference complicates the status deprivation–delinquency relationship for whites in the several social class categories. Both male and female white delinquents are more likely to express status deprivation than are conformers, but the difference in the percentage expressing deprivation is somewhat greater for females. When class level is added to the analysis, white bottom class male delinquents are most likely to say that others in the school have better clothes and housing, middle class male delinquents are next most likely, and top class male delinquents least likely to express status deprivation. This is what Cohen's theory would lead one to expect. For white females, on the other hand, there is no real difference between bottom class and middle class adolescents, although bottom class girls, and particularly the delinquents, are most likely to express status deprivation. This result is consistent with the argument by Cohen and others that girls are essentially in competition for boys and that in this competition sexual attractiveness involving the cultivation of a style of life is an important element in competitive success.[15] Girls, therefore, should be somewhat more self-conscious than boys about status comparisons involving clothes and housing since it is more crucial to the per-

[15] Albert K. Cohen, *op. cit.*, pp. 142–146.

Table 4

PERCENTAGE OF WHITE MALES AND FEMALES SAYING PEERS HAVE BETTER CLOTHES AND HOUSE BY AGE, SOCIAL CLASS, AND CLASS CONTEXT

Sex and age	Social class and class context				
	Upper, upper middle	Crosscut-top	Crosscut-center	Crosscut-bottom	Subtotal
TOP CLASS					
Males					
10–13	11	4	3	21	9
14–15	15	10	7	6	11
16+	12	8	7	13	10
No age	(10)*	(0)	(0)	(0)	(6)
Total	12	8	6	12	10
Females					
10–13	9	7	10	4	8
14–15	10	12	12	5	11
16+	11	12	10	13	11
No age	30	(9)	(25)	(0)	16
Total	11	11	11	7	10
MIDDLE CLASS					
Males					
10–13	13	13	16	13	13
14–15	15	8	14	18	14
16+	17	19	15	15	17
No age	(25)	17	(31)	27	24
Total	19	14	16	17	15
Females					
10–13	17	14	15	11	14
14–15	19	20	25	19	24
16+	28	13	14	15	16
No age	(36)	15	(17)	14	18
Total	21	16	18	15	17
BOTTOM CLASS					
Males					
10–13	(10)	22	17	18	18
14–15	(38)	22	27	28	26
16+	(29)	25	21	16	19
No age	(0)	(20)	(11)	43	32
Total	21	23	20	23	22
Females					
10–13	(31)	25	17	24	23
14–15	(30)	28	21	28	26
16+	(18)	25	21	20	21
No age	(0)	(42)	(40)	(25)	33
Total	25	27	21	24	24
ALL CLASSES					
Males					
10–13	9	12	13	16	13
14–15	16	12	17	20	17
16+	14	17	16	15	15
No age	(14)	9	12	12	16
Total	14	13	15	18	15
Females					
10–13	13	14	15	15	14
14–15	14	20	21	21	19
16+	17	15	16	17	16
No age	28	17	22	20	21
Total	15	17	17	18	17

* Parentheses indicate that N is less than twenty.

Table 5

PERCENTAGE OF SUBJECTS SAYING PEERS HAVE BETTER CLOTHES AND HOUSE BY CONFORMING-DEVIATING BEHAVIOR RATING, SEX, RACE, SOCIAL CLASS, AND CLASS CONTEXT

Sex, race, and social class context	Socioeconomic status and conforming-deviating behavior														
	Bottom class			Middle class			Top class			No information			Subtotal		
	Over conf.	Conv. conf.	Del.	Over conf.	Conv. conf.	Del.	Over conf.	Conv. conf.	Del.	Over conf.	Conv. conf.	Del.	Over conf.	Conv. conf.	Del.
WHITE MALES															
Upper middle	(13)*	(21)	(50)	16	14	27	6	13	14	(0)	(9)	(50)	11	14	21
Crosscut-top	23	23	20	10	13	29	5	7	15	(0)	(10)	(0)	11	13	21
Crosscut-center	8	25	31	13	15	22	8	4	(25)	0	14	(14)	9	16	25
Crosscut-bottom	22	20	41	14	15	31	14	11	(17)	0	13	(20)	17	16	34
Subtotal	18	22	31	13	14	28	8	10	15	(0)	12	14	12	15	26
WHITE FEMALES															
Upper middle	(31)	19	(50)	17	22	(67)	14	10	(0)	(50)	(0)	—†	16	14	(43)
Crosscut-top	33	23	(67)	15	16	(40)	15	10	(0)	(0)	(18)	(0)	19	15	(40)
Crosscut-center	13	23	(50)	18	18	(0)	12	11	(0)	(20)	(10)	—	16	18	(13)
Crosscut-bottom	29	20	45	14	14	(50)	10	4	(50)	(67)	(20)	(0)	20	15	46
Subtotal	26	22	50	16	17	43	13	9	(12)	24	15	(0)	18	16	41
WHITES															
All whites	23	23	38	15	16	31	11	10	15	10	14	12	16	15	28
NEGROES															
Negro males	11	29	(25)	27	20	(33)	(0)	(0)	—	(0)	(32)	—	16	26	(29)
Negro females	30	28	(60)	27	(6)	—	(0)	(0)	—	(0)	—	—	28	21	(60)
All negroes	25	28	(44)	27	15	(33)	(0)	(0)	—	(0)	(32)	—	25	25	42
ALL CASES															
All males	17	23	30	13	14	28	8	10	15	0	14	14	12	15	25
All females	26	22	51	16	17	43	13	9	(12)	22	15	(0)	19	16	42
All cases	23	23	38	15	16	31	11	10	15	10	14	12	16	16	28

* Parentheses indicate that N is less than twenty.
† Two periods indicate no cases in the subcategory.

formance of their competitive sex role.

The relationship between status deprivation and delinquency varies among social class contexts. There is a consistent difference in the predicted direction in the expression of status deprivation. Contrary to our deduction from Cohen's theory, the relationship between delinquency and status deprivation is greatest in the class contexts which are homogeneous in the social class background of boys (upper middle and bottom class schools), and the relationship is weakest for schools which crosscut the class structure (crosscut-top and crosscut-center contexts). For our measure of status deprivation, then, if one assumes the deprivation to be linked to status frustration that under certain circumstances leads to delinquency, such frustration is apparently greater when peers on the average are more like than unlike one. This finding is similar to others in reference group theory which show that the within status group comparison is more closely related to attitude and behavior than those across status groups.[16] The principal question for further investigation is why associates in one's own status group are taken as a frame of reference for evaluation.[17]

Since both status deprivation (the independent variable) and delinquency (the dependent one) increase with age, it would be desirable to examine the effects of age as well on the relationship. Unfortunately, the fifth-order partial, controlling race, sex, social class, class context of school, and age produces most subgroups with too few cases for statistically reliable comparison. Examination of this partial relationship, however, lends the over-all impression that the relationship between status deprivation and delinquency increases as age increases, especially for working class boys and girls in the bottom class school contexts. Part of the fifth-order partial table is shown in Table 6.[18]

DISCUSSION

The findings of this study indicate that the large majority of adolescents in American society do not experience status deprivation. Of the adolescents in our sample, 29 per cent maintained they never thought about differences in life style, and an additional 58 per cent maintain that their life style is equal to or better than that of their schoolmates. These findings are perhaps fairly consistent with the view of Williams and others that there are compensating factors for the structural strains generated by status differences in American society. Only a minority of 13 per cent responded that they felt others in their school had better clothes and housing than they. Nonetheless, this is a sufficiently large proportion of boys and girls expressing status deprivation to more than account for the volume of serious delinquency in our society.

When the social class context of schools, where comparisons of life style occur, and the socioeconomic status of the adolescent are simultaneously taken into account, there is a somewhat higher probability that bottom status boys and girls in bottom status contexts will experience status deprivation than that those in other social classes and contexts will. This finding lends some support to Cohen's theory in that reported experience of status deprivation is greatest in those positions of the social structure where subcultural delinquency and female delinquency are more prevalent, i.e., among bottom class adolescents in schools where the

[16] Robert K. Merton, *Social Theory and Social Structure* (rev. ed., Glencoe, Ill.: Free Press, 1957), pp. 227–232.

[17] *Ibid.*, p. 233.

[18] Copies of this table are available from the authors on request.

Table 6

PERCENTAGE OF BOTTOM CLASS, WHITE CONFORMERS AND DEVIATORS INDICATING THAT PEERS HAVE BETTER CLOTHES AND HOUSES BY AGE, SEX, AND SOCIAL CLASS CONTEXT OF SCHOOL

Sex and social class context of school	Age and conforming or deviating behavior								
	Age 10–13			Age 14–15			Age 16+		
	Over conf.	Conv. conf.	Del.	Over conf.	Conv. conf.	Del.	Over conf.	Conv. conf.	Del.
WHITE MALES									
Upper middle	(0)°	(20)	—†	(0)	(25)	(50)	(50)	(20)	—
Crosscut-top	17	(25)	(100)	(23)	21	(25)	(50)	25	(13)
Crosscut-center	37	29	(40)	(21)	29	(20)	(0)	20	(36)
Crosscut-bottom	11	27	(0)	(42)	20	48	13	18	(32)
Subtotal	10	27	(33)	30	23	39	(27)	18	23
WHITE FEMALES									
Upper middle	(38)	(20)	—	(50)	(20)	(50)	(0)	(25)	—
Crosscut-top	32	19	—	33	25	(50)	(36)	(21)	—
Crosscut-center	12	21	—	15	22	(50)	(12)	23	—
Crosscut-bottom	28	20	(40)	34	24	(43)	17	17	(50)
Subtotal	26	20	(40)	30	23	(47)	19	20	(50)

° Parentheses indicate that N is less than 20.
† Dash indicates no cases in the subcategory.

student body is predominantly bottom class. But the actual relationship between status deprivation and delinquency is so low that it makes the postulate of little value to the theory. A recent study by Rothstein comparing delinquent and nondelinquent perceptions of factors in high social status concluded: "the absolute magnitude of the per cent of delinquents selecting any one of the . . . attributes as one of the three most important in social status is under 15 per cent in every instance. . . . Thus some of the near axioms about the extent to which these represent universal or nearly universal key values among delinquents are placed in doubt. . . ."[19] The inference which might be drawn from the present study and that of Rothstein is that although delinquents and nondelinquents differ somewhat in the aggregate in their percep-

tion of factors in high social status and feelings of status deprivation, the differences are inconsequential, given the place accorded them in current theories of delinquency.

The failure to obtain results which strongly support the postulated relationship between status deprivation and delinquency can, however, be due to failures of operationalization and measurement as well as to flaws in theory, or to both. We have already suggested that other reference groups may be more important than the ones we selected or that other criteria of status are more relevant than those of life style which we chose to operationalize. Ohlin and Cloward, in particular, would have us distinguish between middle class life style and strictly material success goals.[20] Furthermore, we did not distinguish between subcultural delinquents and all others, as does Cohen's theory, though this should not be a serious

[19] Edward Rothstein, "Attributes Related to High School Status: A Comparison of the Perceptions of Delinquent and Non-delinquent Boys," *Social Problems*, 10:82 (Summer, 1962).

[20] Cloward and Ohlin, *op. cit.*, pp. 96–97.

limitation since we know that a substantial proportion of the bottom class delinquents in bottom class contexts are career-oriented delinquents. On the theoretical side, the Ohlin-Cloward hypothesis that the problem of adjustment for which delinquency is a solution arises from the disparity between the *opportunity* to achieve success and what lower class youth want rather than from the perception of status deprivation that leads per se to status frustration may provide the more fruitful hypothesis for future test.[21]

[21] For a test of this hypothesis, see Delbert S. Elliott, "Delinquency and Perceived Opportunity," *Sociological Inquiry,* 32: 216–227 (Spring, 1962).

19. Family Status and the Delinquent Child: A Reappraisal and Some New Findings

THOMAS P. MONAHAN

When a child loses a parent through death, desertion, divorce, or long separation, some form of deprivation is bound to result.[1] Where, as is generally the case, the male parent is missing, the child is placed under an obvious economic handicap. Absence of either parent may also cause a certain affectional loss for the child. In addition, the complementary control, example, and guidance given by both parents is wanting and complete socialization of the child is rendered more difficult.

At the death of a parent no cultural opposition is imposed upon the situation. Rather, social and economic assistance, both public and private, is readily forthcoming. Furthermore, the acquisition of a stepparent through remarriage of the remaining parent may even reestablish something of a family norm for the bereaved child.

But, in cases of desertion and divorce (and illegitimacy) we have an entirely different set of circumstances. Here we frequently find the child exposed to a highly emotionalized atmosphere of discontent and discord. The child most often remains with the mother only, financial support may be withheld by the father, or the parents may fight over the child's custody. In case of desertion no new father may legally become part of the child's home. And the subtle challenge of public disapproval of the family situation and the psychological impact of a seeming rejection by one's parents may becloud the child's outlook.

Divorce in many cases is indeed simply a formal recognition or acknowledgment of an already socially broken home, and it is generally appreciated that the home in constant discord might cause the child more harm than if the

---

° The assistance of Mr. Frank S. Drown, Statistician for the Philadelphia Municipal Court, in the preparation of this paper is gratefully acknowledged.

[1] As James H. S. Bossard and Eleanor S. Boll say in *Family Situations* (Philadelphia: University of Pennsylvania Press, 1943), p. 163, "But however specific the situation of the Incomplete Family, in the great average of broken homes the child loses more than he gains." For a treatment of deprivation from the psychiatric and mental health point of view, see John Bowlby, *Maternal Care and Mental Health* (Geneva: World Health Organisation, 1952) and G. E. Gardner, "Separation of the Parents and the Emotional Life of the Child," *Mental Hygiene*, 40 (January 1956), 53–64.

SOURCE. Thomas P. Monahan, "Family Status and the Delinquent Child: A Reappraisal and Some New Findings," from *Social Forces*, Volume 35, March 1957, pp. 251–258. Reprinted with the permission of the University of North Carolina Press.

parental relationship were severed. Such reasoning has merit, but, interestingly enough, this argument has been used to justify divorce rather than to plead for the rehabilitation or prevention of unhappy families. Such a viewpoint, it should also be noted, contradicts another social philosophy which holds that even a bad home is better than no home at all for the child.

There are many varieties of broken homes and many correspondingly different kinds of family relationships involved. Even the social disparateness in family structure which results from long-term hospitalization, military service, or employment of the breadwinner away from home may bring about some serious consequences for the members of a family. On the other hand, the conventional family structure may cloak a host of baneful influences or situations harmful to a child's wholesome development. To say it in another way, all broken homes are not bad ones, and all conventional types are not good ones.

This article is not concerned with a delineation of all possible types of homes and their effect on children, but rather it is restricted to a consideration of the more evident types of broken homes as they relate to children who are apprehended for committing delinquent acts.

DELINQUENCY STUDIES OF BROKEN HOMES

With the establishment of juvenile courts in the United States around 1900 and the compilation of social statistics on youth who were brought before these courts, observers were struck by the high proportion—40 to 50 percent —of all delinquent children who came from broken homes. Since it was far beyond normal expectancy that such a proportion of all youth was similarly disadvantaged, early writers saw broken homes to be an important, if not the greatest single proximate (causal), factor in understanding juvenile delinquency.[2]

There was no denial that the broken home was only one of a number of factors to take into account and that the age of the child and the quality of the home life, as well as the mere fact of a break, were important. A number of studies have shown, however, that abnormal or defective family relationships are much more prevalent among families of delinquent children than among families of comparable children who do not become delinquent.[3] This aspect of the matter is a subject unto itself.

Not counting the statistical tabula-

[2] G. B. Mangold, *Problems of Child Welfare* (New York: Macmillan Co., 1930), p. 406; Mabel Rhoades, "A Case Study of Delinquent Boys in the Juvenile Court of Chicago," *American Journal of Sociology*, 13 (July 1907), 3–25; S. P. Breckenridge and E. Abbott, *The Delinquent Child and the Home* (New York: Russell Sage Foundation, 1912); C. A. Ellwood, "The Instability of the Family as a Cause of Child Dependency and Delinquency," *Survey*, 24 (September 1910), pp. 886–889; Municipal Court of Philadelphia, *Annual Report* (1918), pp. 98–99.

[3] See, for instance, John Slawson, "Marital Relations of Parents and Juvenile Delinquency," *Journal of Delinquency*, 8 (September–November 1923), 280–283, and *The Delinquent Boy* (Boston: Gorham Press, 1926); Cyril Burt, *The Young Delinquent* (New York: D. Appleton and Co., 1925); Mabel Elliott, *Correctional Education and the Delinquent Girl* (Harrisburg, Pennsylvania State Department of Welfare, 1929); K. D. Lumpkin, "Factors in the Commitment of Correctional School Girls in Wisconsin," *American Journal of Sociology*, 37 (September 1931), 222–230; T. E. Sullenger, "Juvenile Delinquency, A Product of the Home," *Journal of Criminal Law and Criminology*, 24 (March–April 1934), pp. 1088–1092; W. Healy and A. Bronner, *New Light on Delinquency and Its Treatment* (New Haven, Connecticut: Yale University Press, 1936), pp. 29–30; A. M. Carr-Saunders, H. Mannheim, and E. Rhodes, *Young Offenders* (New York: Macmillan Co., 1944), p. 70; and Connecticut Public Welfare Council, *Needs of Neglected and Delinquent Children* (Hartford, Connecticut, 1946).

tions of many juvenile courts over the years, dozens of studies have been made which deal with the broken home and juvenile delinquency or crime. Some of the early studies attempted to estimate the proportion of broken homes in the population at large from existing census data, to use for a comparison with their special groups of delinquent or institutionalized children.[4] A common conclusion was that delinquent children had about twice the proportion of broken homes as did children in the general population. A few comparisons were made of boys in the same school or city area, revealing a greater prevalence of broken homes among the delinquent group; one such comparison of several groups of children in 1918 suggested that more orphans were found in the delinquent group.[5]

The first major attempt at a controlled comparison was made by Slawson in 1923, using delinquent boys in four state institutions and boys in three New York City public schools, from which he concluded that there were over twice as many broken homes in his delinquent group.[6] Concurrently, in England, Cyril Burt analyzed a group of misbehaving ("delinquent") children and public school children of the same age and social class. Although his classification of "defective family relationships" included other factors besides the broken home, he, too, found the problem children to be doubly disfavored.[7] And, in 1929, Mabel Elliott compared the family structure of her group of Sleighton Farm girls—mostly sex offenders—with that of a group of Philadelphia working-class, continuation school girls, revealing the respective proportions of broken homes to be 52 and 22 percent.[8]

Even greater refinement was introduced into the question by Shaw and McKay when they compared boys against whom official delinquency petitions were filed in the juvenile court of Chicago in 1929 with other boys drawn from the public school population of the same city areas.[9] They found that a rather high proportion (29 percent) of the school boys 10 to 17 years of age came from broken homes. After the school population data were carefully adjusted statistically for age and ethnic composition to make them comparable with the delinquent group, the propor-

---

[4] E. H. Schideler, "Family Disintegration and the Delinquent Boy in the United States," *Journal of Criminal Law and Criminology*, 8 (January 1918), 709–732; E. Bushong, "Family Estrangement and Juvenile Delinquency," *Social Forces*, 5 (September 1926), pp. 79–83; W. Roach, "Record of Juvenile Delinquency in Benton County, Oregon, 1907–1929," *Journal of Juvenile Research*, 14 (January 1930), 34–40; M. G. Caldwell, "Home Conditions of Institutional Delinquent Boys in Wisconsin," *Social Forces*, 8 (March 1930), pp. 390–397; S. B. Crosby, "A Study of Alameda County Delinquent Boys, with Special Emphasis upon the Group Coming from Broken Homes," *Journal of Juvenile Research*, 13 (July 1929), 220–230. For a recent study see New Jersey Department of Institutions and Agencies, Trenton, New Jersey, *The Welfare Reporter*, 5 (January 1951), 17.

[5] F. G. Bonser, *School Work and Spare Time*, Cleveland Recreation Survey (Philadelphia: William Fell, 1918), pp. 36–40; E. H. Johnson, "The Relation of Conduct Difficulties of a Group of Public School Boys to Their Mental Status and Home Environment," *Journal of Delinquency*, 6 (November 1921), p. 563; E. H. Sutherland, *Criminology* (Philadelphia: J. B. Lippincott Co., 1924), and study by Roy D. Young cited therein, p. 143.

[6] Slawson, "Marital Relations of Parents and Juvenile Delinquency," *loc. cit.*, p. 280.

[7] Burt, *op. cit.*, pp. 51, 90 ff.

[8] Elliott, *op. cit.*, p. 28.

[9] C. R. Shaw and H. D. McKay, *Report on the Causes of Crime, Vol. II, Social Factors in Juvenile Delinquency* (Washington, D. C.: National Commission on Law Observance and Enforcement, Government Printing Office, 1931), pp. 261–284, and Shaw and McKay, "Are Broken Homes a Causative Factor in Delinquency?" *Social Forces*, 10 (May 1932), pp. 514–524, and discussion pp. 525–533.

tion of broken homes rose to 36.1 percent for the school group, as compared to 42.5 percent for the delinquent boys. This result, as Shaw and McKay interpreted it, "suggests that the broken home, as such, is not an important factor in the case of delinquent boys in the Cook County juvenile court," while other writers further interpreted the findings as showing that broken homes generally are "relatively insignificant in relation to delinquency."[10] Even accepting the above figures for Chicago, mathematical exception has been taken to such interpretations.[11]

DISAGREEMENT AMONG AUTHORITIES

Thus there arose a sharp divergence of opinion among sociologists as to the importance of the broken home as a factor in delinquency. Standard references in criminology refer to this lack of agreement and "welter of conflicting opinion," but they offer no clarification of the question.[12] Indeed one senses somewhat of a partisan approach in the differing selection of references and the interpretations of extant information.

Rather significantly, Hodgkiss' study of Chicago girls, done at about the same time and in the same manner as the Shaw-McKay inquiry, disclosed that 67 percent of the delinquent girls and 45 percent of the controls came

from broken homes.[13] These figures were less readily dismissed. Again the high percentage of broken homes among the control group is remarkable. Probably because of difficulties surrounding the collection of such data from school children, the studies have not been repeated in Chicago.

OTHER STUDIES

Six other investigations published after the Shaw-McKay report deserve special mention. First, Cavan, in her study of school children in 1930, placed in opposition information on several classes of children in the same locality. The proportion of broken homes increased consistently from the control group of boys (21 percent) to the predelinquent boys (35 percent), to the institutionalized boys (49 percent), to the institutionalized girls (71 percent).[14] Second, in a study of Spokane, Washington, public school boys, 14 to 17 years of age, and delinquent boys in 1937, Weeks and Smith made a careful comparison only to find that broken homes among the delinquents (41 percent) were far more numerous than among the control group of boys (27 percent), even when refined according to a number of social categories.[15] Third, in the mid-1930's, Merrill matched 300 run-of-the-mill cases referred to the court of a rural California county with other children selected according to age, sex, and neighborhood (school). In this case 51 percent of the delinquents were found to come from broken homes versus 27 percent for the

---

[10] Shaw and McKay, *Report on the Causes of Crime, loc. cit.*, p. 392; and Sutherland, *Principles of Criminology* (Philadelphia: J. B. Lippincott Co., 1947), p. 159.

[11] J. B. Maller in Shaw and McKay, "Are Broken Homes a Causative Factor in Delinquency?" *loc. cit.*, pp. 531–533.

[12] Teeters in N. Teeters and J. O. Reinemann, *The Challenge of Delinquency* (New York: Prentice-Hall, 1950), p. 153. Compare Sutherland, *Criminology* 1924 ed. versus 1947 ed.; and H. M. Shulman's summarization, "The Family and Juvenile Delinquency," *Annals of the American Academy of Political and Social Science*, 261 (January 1949), pp. 21–31.

[13] M. Hodgkiss, "The Influence of Broken Homes and Working Mothers," *Smith College Studies in Social Work*, 3 (March 1933), pp. 259–274.

[14] R. S. Cavan, *The Adolescent in the Family* (New York: D. Appleton-Century Co., 1934), pp. 220–221.

[15] H. A. Weeks and M. G. Smith, "Juvenile Delinquency and Broken Homes in Spokane, Washington," *Social Forces*, 18 (October 1939), pp. 48–55.

control group.[16] Fourth, Wittman and Huffman's study of teen-aged youth in Elgin, Illinois, disclosed that a very high disproportion of the institutionalized delinquents came from broken homes as compared to high school students in the same area.[17] Fifth, the Gluecks carefully paired 500 boys from the general school population with 500 delinquent (correctional school) boys in the Boston area. They found that only 50 percent of the delinquent boys had been living with their own parents, whereas the control group of boys were living with both parents in 71 percent of the cases.[18] Sixth, a study of pre-war delinquents was made in England by Carr-Saunders and others, using an individual-matching technique (boys under 16 years), with the following results: delinquents had a much higher proportion of broken homes than the controls (28 percent versus 16 percent), and there was a greater amount of separation and divorce in the delinquent group of broken homes.[19]

A PARTIAL SUMMATION

Thus, in comparisons of delinquents with control samples, and in statistical adjustments of delinquency data for age, ethnic, and neighborhood biases, the children with intact families have shown a clear and persistent advantage over those from broken homes. This is especially true for the females. In addition to this, the home of the delinquent child appears to be much more "defective," "immoral," or "inadequate" than are homes in general. In broken homes one seems to find a conjunction of deprivations and positive influences toward criminal behavior.

From an over-all viewpoint it is well to remember that a large proportion of children from broken homes do not become delinquent, but this hardly refutes the inescapable fact that more children from broken homes, as compared to those from unbroken homes, become delinquent. Even among families having delinquents, siblings are more often delinquent in the broken family group.[20]

For the social analyst, the broken home may be regarded either as a symptom or as a consequence of a larger process, but for the child it becomes a social fact with which he has to abide. In a very real sense the abnormal structure of his family may impede his own normal adjustment and in some cases may bring him into conflict with the requirements of the larger society, more so than if he were surrounded by a conventional family milieu. That so many children surpass this handicap is an exemplification of their own resilience and a demonstration of the presence of other forces acting towards the child's socialization in the community, rather than a proof of the unimportance of normal family life in the development of norms of conduct or the unimportance of the handicaps experienced by the child in the broken home.

[16] M. Merrill, *Problems of Child Delinquency* (New York: Houghton Mifflin Co., 1947), pp. 66, 311.

[17] M. P. Wittman and A. V. Huffman, "A Comparative Study of Developmental, Adjustment, and Personality Characteristics of Psychotic, Psychoneurotic, Delinquent, and Normally Adjusted Teen Aged Youths," *Journal of Genetic Psychology,* 66 (June 1945), 167–182.

[18] S. Glueck and E. Glueck, *Unraveling Juvenile Delinquency* (Cambridge, Massachusetts: Harvard University Press, 1950), p. 88. However, if one includes prolonged absence of a parent because of delinquency, illness, and the like, 34 percent of the control group of children experienced a broken home prior to their inclusion in the study, versus 60 percent of the delinquent children (p. 122).

[19] Carr-Saunders et al., *op. cit.,* pp. 60, 149.

[20] N. D. Hirsch, *Dynamic Causes of Juvenile Crime* (Cambridge, Massachusetts: Sci-Art Publishers, 1937), pp. 66, 79.

In former years when divorce was less common and desertion less apparent perhaps, broken homes were probably thought to be largely a result of the death of a parent. The material and other losses to such children may not have been readily perceived. How such a simple event as death could wreak enduring havoc with the child's development was difficult to discern. Hence, disbelief in the importance of orphanhood as to delinquency causation, coupled with the very unsatisfactory nature of the early studies, no doubt led some sociologists to take exception to the prevailing beliefs and to question the whole relationship.

A convergence of information from the other disciplines as to the deleterious effects of divorce and desertion or family separations upon the child, as well as a psychological appreciation of the different nature of these types of family disruption, brought a more unanimous acknowledgment of the importance of the *socially* broken home. In some quarters the recent "wave" of delinquency has been interpreted to be a result of the growth of divorce and separation. However, information on the particular family relationships of children in the community and those who become delinquent are generally lacking. We know that over the past 50 years there has been a lessening of orphanhood through improvement in life expectancy, and an upward rise in family dissolutions through desertion and divorce, until now there seems to have been a reversal in the relative importance of the two factors of death and social discord in the breaking up of a child's family. Oddly enough, in spite of the change in the nature of broken homes, the high over-all proportion of delinquent children from broken homes apparently has not changed significantly.

A SIX-YEAR STUDY OF PHILADELPHIA RECORDS

In order to throw some additional light upon the subject of broken homes, some special tabulations were made of all delinquency charges—44,448 cases, of which 24,811 were first offenders— disposed of in the Philadelphia Municipal Court in the period 1949–1954.

METHODOLOGICAL PROBLEMS
Accuracy of Data

In cases which are adjusted before going to court or which receive no investigation, children are quite often the only source of some of the information recorded. The precision of the data suffers thereby, especially if one is interested in the details of family relationships. Erratic or unreasonable fluctuations in the statistics sometimes disclose the unreliability of information derived from court records, as Breckenridge and Abbott, for instance, suggest may have been the case for some early Chicago data.[21] A high degree of reliability may obtain in some jurisdictions, but one must always use particular sets of data with reservations.

Types of Data

The proportion and types of broken homes among juvenile offenders are known to vary greatly according to racial or ethnic group, sex and age, and certain offenses. As one proceeds from first offenders to the recidivists, from those dismissed to those adjudged delinquent, and from the probationary types to those who require institutionalization, it may be expected that one will find an increasing proportion of broken homes. Unfortunately, very little attention has been given to the correspon-

[21] Breckenridge and Abbott, *op. cit.*, p. 92.

dence between the degree of broken homes and the type of data being studied. A number of early studies, for instance, were concerned exclusively with special types of offenders, recidivists and institutionalized children.[22] Since chronic offenders represent a special class, and other cases may be institutionalized *because* they come from broken homes, there is a basic weakness in using such selective kinds of information to demonstrate a relationship between broken homes and unlawful behavior of juveniles.

Lack of Population Statistics

Perhaps the greatest stumbling block in all attempts to analyze and interpret statistics on delinquency has been the lack of population data which would show the family situation of children as a whole. For nearly 50 years this deficiency in census compilations has been bemoaned by many students of the subject, and a wide variety of crude estimates have been made. If such information were tabulated from census cards and classified according to governmental units for age, color, and neighborhood area (census tracts), we could begin to assess this problem with more certainty. Among different elements of the population the proportion and types of broken homes vary so greatly that one must be cautious in using particular kinds of data for comparative purposes. It should be recognized that the percentages of broken homes in some control groups (Shaw-McKay, Hodgkiss, and Glueck) do not purport to represent the condition prevailing among the population as a whole. In general, no more than 20 percent of all children of juvenile court age have broken homes, with the pro-

portion among the nonwhites being about twice that for the whites.[23]

FAMILY STATUS OF DELINQUENTS BY SEX AND COLOR

As shown in Table 1, the proportion of broken homes among Negroes is considerably greater than among the whites, and girls in each group are more often from broken homes than are boys in each class. The range of broken homes extends from about one-third of all cases of white boys to three-fourths of the cases of Negro girls, with white girls and Negro boys showing less than 50 percent with intact families.

The families of first offenders show a lesser degree of fragmentation, whereas those who offended in a prior year (Class I recidivists) are from families particularly marked by a greater degree of orphanhood, illegitimacy, and social disruption. Including children who are recidivists increases the proportion of broken homes in the whole.

The parents of Negro delinquents are less often legally separated and more often unmarried or living apart than are the parents of white children. Girls, of course, with a higher proportion of broken homes also show a higher degree of orphanhood; but, except for a moderate excess of orphanhood of Negro boys as compared to white boys, the impact of death is not an outstanding element of difference between the two classes. Initial disorganization and informal social disorganization of family status are most characteristic of Negro delinquent children.

RECIDIVISM BY FAMILY STATUS

Recidivism betokens not merely the frequency or probability of repetition of infractions of the law, but also the like-

[22] References available on request.

[23] References on population estimates available on request.

Table 1

PERCENTAGE DISTRIBUTION OF JUVENILE DELINQUENTS IN PHILADELPHIA BY TYPE OF FAMILY STATUS, ALL CASES, FIRST OFFENDERS, AND CLASS I RECIDIVISTS, 1949–1954*

| | Boys | | | | | | Girls | | | | | |
| | White | | | Negro | | | White | | | Negro | | |
	All cases	First offenders	Recidivists	All cases	First offenders	Recidivists	All cases	First offenders	Recidivists	All cases	First offenders	Recidivists
With whom child was living												
Number of cases	17,772	11,236	4,108	18,317	8,706	5,708	2,919	1,984	504	4,378	2,736	933
Total	100.0	100.0	100.0	100.0	100.0	100.0	100.0	100.0	100.0	100.0	100.0	100.0
With both own parents	67.5	72.4	58.6	41.7	47.2	37.8	43.6	48.4	31.4	24.6	27.3	19.8
Father only	3.1	2.6	4.4	4.0	3.8	4.2	5.1	4.6	6.3	4.4	5.2	2.8
Mother only	17.9	15.5	22.0	39.4	35.2	42.1	27.0	26.1	30.8	45.4	46.7	42.2
Mother and stepfather	4.9	4.2	5.9	2.8	2.8	2.8	7.1	7.0	7.1	2.7	2.7	2.7
Father and stepmother	1.6	1.3	1.7	1.4	1.4	1.4	3.3	3.1	2.4	1.8	2.0	1.3
Adoptive parents	0.1	0.1	0.2	†	†	†	0.2	0.3	—	0.2	0.1	0.5
Other family home	4.9	3.9	7.2	10.7	9.6	11.7	13.7	10.5	22.0	20.9	16.0	30.7
(Excluded: in institution)	(2.5)	(0.4)	(5.9)	(1.4)	(0.1)	(2.3)	(5.6)	(0.9)	(12.5)	(2.0)	(0.1)	(4.7)
Marital status of parents												
Number of cases	18,138	11,244	4,323	18,456	8,643	5,813	3,076	1,996	571	4,443	2,717	968
Total	100.0	100.0	100.0	100.0	100.0	100.0	100.0	100.0	100.0	100.0	100.0	100.0
Own parents living together	67.8	73.1	58.7	42.1	47.8	38.1	44.6	49.7	33.6	25.7	27.9	22.5
Parents unmarried	2.3	1.6	3.6	13.0	10.7	14.2	5.8	4.1	10.2	22.0	20.3	25.5
Mother dead	3.6	2.9	4.6	5.2	4.8	5.6	7.1	6.3	8.6	7.9	7.5	8.4
Father dead	8.3	7.7	9.5	10.4	9.8	11.0	12.2	11.0	12.6	10.4	10.4	10.8
Both parents dead	0.6	0.5	0.6	1.7	1.7	1.8	1.7	1.6	1.9	2.5	2.1	3.6
Father deserted mother	1.0	0.7	1.4	2.7	2.3	2.9	2.2	1.7	4.2	3.7	3.6	3.6
Mother deserted father	0.3	0.2	0.5	0.3	0.2	0.3	0.8	0.8	1.1	0.4	0.3	0.3
Both parents deserted	0.1	0.1	0.1	0.2	0.2	0.2	0.2	0.1	0.3	†	†	—
Parents living apart	9.6	7.9	12.9	22.2	20.1	24.0	15.0	14.0	18.4	24.8	25.4	22.5
Parents divorced	6.4	5.3	8.1	2.2	2.4	1.9	10.4	10.7	9.1	2.6	2.5	2.8

* Each time a child is dealt with on a new delinquency charge is called a case. Class I recidivists does not include second offenses in the calendar year for recidivist children. Cases not reporting as to family status or parental status are excluded from the percentage distribution.
† Less than 0.05 percent.

lihood of the development of a pattern of such behavior, or even a career of criminality in adulthood. It is a reasonable conjecture that if a broken home predisposes a child to commit a delinquent act, then it follows, to state it simply, that lacking the necessary parental guidance and control in the first place, this tendency toward misconduct will continue throughout the period of childhood and there will be a greater recurrence of offenses among children in broken homes. Some studies have, in fact, revealed a greater degree of recidivism among children in broken homes.[24] One cannot ignore this evidence by assuming that there is a selective apprehension of youth on the basis of their home conditions rather than a direct operation of the law.

The deleterious effect of broken homes upon children as regards the repetition of their delinquencies is portrayed in Table 2. In all sex and color groups children who are living with both parents are much less likely to appear again on charges of delinquency. Since family status is a changing thing for the child, the pattern cannot be delineated with perfect clarity, because a child living with both own parents in 1949 may have committed an offense after his home was broken in 1950 or later, thus blurring the picture. However, calendar year figures disclose essentially the same pattern and serve to show that further refinements would minimize the contrasts only moderately.

As between the types of marital status, further meaningful differences appear. The exceedingly high proportion of recidivism among institutional children is no doubt related to their

unusual background of deprivation and their likelihood of offending by running away. For white boys the percentage of all cases in the recidivist class increases from 32 where both parents are married and living together, to 38 where the father is dead and the boy is with his mother, to 42 where both parents are dead and the child is with a surrogate family, to 46 percent where the parents are living apart and the child is with the mother, to 49 where the parents are divorced, to 55 where the boy is living with his unmarried mother. In general the same pattern holds for both sex and color groups, except that the recidivism contrast among the types of broken homes for Negroes is not as well defined or as great. This could betoken a greater ambiguity or inaccuracy of Negro data, or a lesser significance to the Negro child as to the specific manner by which his home is broken.[25]

Interestingly enough, although girls more often come from broken homes, to an observable degree they are less likely to engage in repeated offenses, whatever the type of broken home. Explanation for this may lie in the fundamentally different nature of offenses of boys and girls.

Where the child, especially the girl, remains with the mother there appears to be less likelihood of recidivism. The death of the mother, as compared to the death of the father, also leads to somewhat greater recidivism; while the loss of both parents is particularly severe on the Negro girls. For the most part, a child living in another family home and not with one of his parents is more likely to commit repeated offenses.

DIFFERENTIAL TREATMENT BY FAMILY STATUS

In Philadelphia, except for the handling of complaints which are rather

[24] M. E. Kirkpatrick, "Some Significant Factors in Juvenile Recidivism," *American Journal of Orthopsychiatry*, 7 (July 1937), p. 356; Carr-Saunders et al., *op. cit.*, pp. 39, 99; Slawson, *The Delinquent Boy*, pp. 373–374.

[25] Cavan, *The Adolescent in the Family*, pp. 60, 63, 90.

Table 2

JUVENILE DELINQUENCY CASES IN PHILADELPHIA: REPEATED OFFENSES AS A PERCENTAGE OF TOTAL OFFENSES, OR RECIDIVISM BY FAMILY STATUS 1949–1954

Family status	Boys — Total	Boys — Own parents living together	Boys — Deceased Mother	Boys — Deceased Father	Boys — Deceased Both	Boys — Desertion	Boys — Parents living apart	Boys — Divorced	Boys — Not married	Girls — Total	Girls — Own parents living together	Girls — Deceased Mother	Girls — Deceased Father	Girls — Deceased Both	Girls — Desertion	Girls — Parents living apart	Girls — Divorced	Girls — Not married
Total																		
White	38	33	49	43	(46)	55	50	49	58	35	28	42	41	(38)	(47)	40	33	54
Negro	53	47	57	56	55	59	58	49	61	39	34	42	39	50	41	37	41	43
With both own parents																		
White	32	32							54	24	24							50
Negro	46	46								31	31							38
With father only																		
White	48		45				54	(38)	(63)	38		(32)				(23)		
Negro	56		53				59			26		(25)						
With mother only																		
White	45			38		56	46	51	55	34			34		35	30	(28)	
Negro	58			55		61	57	45	62	36			33			34		
With mother and stepfather																		
White	46			46				45		33			(39)				30	
Negro	52			54				48		37			(36)					
With father and stepmother																		
White	49		49					50		(36)		(40)						
Negro	53		53							(33)		(30)						

Table 2—Continued

Girls

		Total	Own parents living together	Deceased Mother	Deceased Father	Deceased Both	Desertion	Parents living apart	Divorced	Not married
In other family home	White	50	38	49	(56)	(42)	(54)	52	(53)	(66)
	Negro	57	54	60	59	54		59		46
In institution	White	91	96					(90)		
	Negro	98	(100)					(98)		

Boys

		Total	Own parents living together	Deceased Mother	Deceased Father	Deceased Both	Desertion	Parents living apart	Divorced	Not married
In other family home	White	48	(45)	(48)	(63)			(56)		
	Negro	52	(56)	51		47		48		55
In institution	White	89	(93)							
	Negro	98								

Note. Cells with less than 50 cases not calculated; cells with 50–99 cases shown in parentheses. Excluding children in institutions, the total-total and total-own parents living together become: whites—37, 32, 32, 25, and Negroes—53, 46, 38, 32, for boys and girls respectively.

trifling, law officers routinely deliver all children who are apprehended in the commission of delinquent acts into the hands of juvenile court authorities. They do not adjudicate or dispose of cases in the police station. Hence, in Philadelphia, as compared to other areas of the country, a much higher proportion of allegedly delinquent children receive treatment by the court, and the information on these cases approaches a completeness and representativeness as regards all children apprehended in the commission of delinquent acts. There does not seem to be any great tendency for policewomen, who arrest nearly 30 percent of the girls, to turn girls over to their parents rather than to charge them with delinquency. Indeed, girls show the same excessively high proportion of broken homes no matter what the type of offense may be.

The same proportion of broken homes appears in both the minor and major offense groups, as shown in Table 3. However, children who are living with both parents are much more likely to be dismissed by the intake interviewing staff, whereas the children from broken homes are more often held for court. The parentless child (one or both natural parents absent from home) is more often adjudged delinquent or in need of care, and a rather high proportion of them are committed to institutions for delinquents.

From these figures on first offenders it should be evident that the use of court arraignment and institutional statistics can give a rather distorted picture regarding the family status of delinquent children in general.[26]

26 Cf., P. M. Smith, "Broken Homes and Juvenile Delinquency," *Sociology and Social Research*, 39 (May–June 1955), pp. 307–311; and New Jersey, *op. cit.*, p. 18, fn. 4.

Table 3

PERCENTAGE DISTRIBUTION OF JUVENILE DELINQUENTS IN PHILADELPHIA FROM BROKEN HOMES AMONG APPREHENDED FIRST OFFENDERS FOR TOTAL AND MAJOR OFFENSES, MANNER OF REFERRAL AND DISPOSITION, 1949–1954*

	Boys		Girls	
Treatment stage	White	Negro	White	Negro
Total first offenders	27.7	53.0	52.0	73.2
Major offense group†	27.4	54.2	48.0	72.3
Source of referral				
Policeman	27.9	53.1	50.0	71.3
Policewoman	—	—	54.7	75.6
Railroad police	21.7	42.4	—	—
Initial action				
Adjusted by staff	21.6	45.0	43.9	59.6
Held for court	35.0	60.9	55.3	76.8
Disposition, all cases				
Dismissed	23.1	47.1	46.1	66.1
Adjudged "delinquent"	38.7	64.5	57.4	77.5
Placed on probation	35.2	63.1	52.3	74.9
Committed to institution for delinquents	49.8	68.3	59.9	83.8

* With both own parents, married and living together. In 19 out of 20 of these cases the illegitimate child (see Table 1) does not live with both his natural parents. The smallest figure represented by a percentage is 130 (Negro girls committed to an institution for delinquents).

† Major offenses include injury to person, carrying deadly weapons, arson, vandalism, robbery, burglary, theft, drug and liquor violations, and sex offenses.

POPULATION COMPARISONS

Some 14 percent of all Philadelphia children *under 16 years* of age were *not* in husband-wife families in 1934–1936 (11 percent of the white and 31 percent of the Negro children).[27] At that time, in about 30 percent of all cases of delinquent boys and 50 percent of all cases of delinquent girls under 16 years of age, the children were living with one parent only, and no stepparent, or in a substitute family. Delinquency cases for the same age group in 1940 showed the following proportions of such incomplete families: white boys 27 percent, Negro boys 55 percent, white girls 43 percent, and Negro girls 70 percent.

The 1950 Census for Philadelphia revealed that 7 percent of the white children and 33 percent of the nonwhite children *under 18 years* of age were *not* in census-classified husband-wife families. In 1940 the corresponding figures were 13 percent for the whites and 33 percent for the nonwhites.[28] Any adjustment for the age factor does not seem warranted because the proportion of broken homes among delinquent first offenders, 1949–1954, is practically the same for children of all ages.

With *incomplete* families among *first offenders* (1949–1954) under 18 years of age amounting to 22 percent for the white boys and 49 percent for the Negro boys, it should certainly be appar-

[27] United States Social Security Board, *Statistics of Family Composition in Selected Areas of the United States, 1934–1936*, Vol. 6, Philadelphia, Bureau Memorandum No. 45 (February 1942), pp. 3, 196–197; and Municipal Court of Philadelphia, *Annual Reports.*
[28] United States Bureau of the Census, *Population—Families, Types of Families, 1940* (Washington, D.C.: Government Printing Office, 1943), pp. 24, 90; and *General Characteristics of Families, 1950* Special Report P-E, No. 2A (Washington, D. C.: Government Printing Office, 1955), pp. 174, 180.

ent that in their respective groups broken homes predispose these boys to acts of delinquency. Among the females the proportions from incomplete families are so high (42 percent for white girls and 68 percent for Negro girls) that there can hardly be any doubt as to the importance of parental deprivation to them.

CONCLUSION

One large minority in the population consistently shows twice the average rate of socially broken homes and twice the average rate of delinquency. Other groups with strong family cohesiveness show below average rates of delinquency. Such apparent associations cannot be dismissed as happenstance.

On the whole very little disagreement has been expressed over the probable harmful influence of the socially broken home on the child. This does not gainsay, however, the deprivation consequent to the loss of a parent through death. Indeed, the same high proportions of delinquents were found to come from broken homes more than a generation ago when orphanhood loomed larger as the reason for family disruption. Of even more importance to the child than the nature of the break is the fact of a break in his home.

All in all, the stability and continuity of family life stands out as a most important factor in the development of the child. It would seem, therefore, that the place of the home in the genesis of normal or delinquent patterns of behavior should receive greater practical recognition. The relationship is so strong that, if ways could be found to do it, a strengthening and preserving of family life, among the groups which need it most, could probably accomplish more in the amelioration and prevention of delinquency and other problems than any other single program yet devised.

20. A New Theory of Delinquency and Crime

WALTER C. RECKLESS

Containment theory is an explanation of conforming behavior as well as deviancy.[1] It has two reinforcing aspects: an inner control system and an outer control system. Are there elements within the self and within the person's immediate world that enable him to hold the line against deviancy or to hew to the line of social expectations? The assumption is that strong inner and reinforcing outer containment constitutes an insulation against normative deviancy (not constitutional or psychological deviancy), that is, violation of the sociolegal conduct norms.

A MIDDLE RANGE THEORY

Containment theory does not explain the entire spectrum of delinquency and crime. It does not explain crime or delinquency which emerges from strong inner pushes, such as compulsions, anxieties, phobias, hallucinations, personality disorders (including inadequate, unstable, antisocial personalities, etc.), from organic impairments such as brain damage and epilepsy, or from neurotic

[1] For the complete statement on containment theory, see Walter C. Reckless, *The Crime Problem*, 3rd Ed. New York: Appleton-Century-Crofts, 1961, pp. 335–359.

mechanisms (exhibitionists, peepers, fire setters, compulsive shop lifters). All told these cases are minimal. And containment theory does not explain criminal or delinquent activity which is a part of "normal" and "expected" roles and activities in families and communities, such as the criminal tribes of India, Gypsy vocations and trades (very similar to the former), begging families, and certain phases of delinquency subculture and organized crime. Between these two extremes in the spectrum of crime and delinquency is a very large middle range of norm violation, perhaps as big as two thirds to three quarters of officially reported cases as well as the unreported cases of delinquency and crime. Containment theory seeks to explain this large middle range of offenders. According to its place on the spectrum of delinquency and crime, one might say that it occupies the middle position.

A QUICK REVIEW OF CRIMINOLOGICAL THEORIES

Before proceeding further, it might be a good idea to see in what directions theory in criminology is pointing at present. Since the early nineteenth century we have had a long succession

SOURCE. Walter C. Reckless, "A New Theory of Delinquency and Crime, from *Federal Probation*, Volume 25, December 1961, pp. 42–46. Reprinted with the permission of *Federal Probation*.

of theories, most of which have not stood the test of time. It is possible to assemble these theories into three main camps of schools: (1) biological and constitutional theory—often called the school of criminal biology—in which the mainsprings of deviancy are sought in the inherited physical and mental makeup of man; (2) psychogenic theory, in which the formation of antisocial character is traced to faulty relationships within the family in the first few years of life; and (3) sociological theory, in which the pressures and pulls of the social milieu produce delinquent and criminal behavior.

Mention should be made of some of the specific theories. The dominating theory in Europe today is still the all-inclusive one which falls into the school of criminal biology. It points to the inheritance of weaknesses or pronenesses toward crime and delinquency (plus pressure from a bad environment).[2] Many variants of this theory have shown up in recent years: The attempt to prove inheritance of proneness through the method of studying criminal twins (Lange);[3] the attempt to identify body-mind types (Kretschmer);[4] the general acceptance throughout Europe in the past 25 years of several criminally oriented types of psychopaths, based on inherited proneness (according to Kurt Schneider);[5] the attempt to identify and explain habitual (serious) offenders as contrasted with occasional offenders or offenders of opportunity, according to early onset which in turn points to

inheritance of proneness (Irwin Frey);[6] the specification of the mesomorphic somatotype (muscular) as the type of constitution which is most usually related to delinquency (first according to William Sheldon[7] and later to the Gluecks).[8]

The psychogenic school probably claims August Aichhorn as its fountainhead. According to Aichhorn,[9] faulty development in the first few years of life makes it impossible for the child to control his impulses. The child lingers on as a sort of aggrandizing infant, living in the pleasure principle and failing to develop the reality principle in life. Friedlander[10] indicates that this faulty development in the first few years of life adds up to an antisocial character structure, incapable of handling reality properly. Redl,[11] who is also a disciple of Aichhorn, calls attention to the failure of the child to develop a management system over his impulsivity; that is, fails to develop a good ego and super ego.

The sociologists, ever since Ferri[12] (Italy, c. 1885), have been calling attention to bad environmental conditions. This was echoed by Bonger,[13] who placed the blame for dispropor-

[2] Franz Exner, *Kriminologie*. Berlin, 1949, pp. 115–120.

[3] Johannes Lange, *Crime and Destiny*, translated by Charlotte Haldane. New York: C. Boni, 1930.

[4] E. Kretschmer, *Physique and Character*, translated by W. I. H. Sprott. New York: Harcourt, Brace and Co., 1925.

[5] Kurt Schneider, *Psychopathische Persönlichkeiten*, 6th Ed. Berlin, 1943.

[6] Irwin Frey, *Die Frühkriminelle Rückfallsverbrecher*. Basel, 1951, pp. 95–98, 103, 253.

[7] William H. Sheldon, *Varieties of Delinquent Youth*. New York: Harper and Brothers, 1949, p. 727.

[8] Sheldon and Eleanor Glueck, *Physique and Delinquency*. New York: Harper and Brothers, 1956, p. 219.

[9] August Aichhorn, *Wayward Youth*. New York, 1936.

[10] Kate Friedlander, *The Psycho-Analytic Approach to Delinquency*. New York: International Universities Press, 1947.

[11] Fritz Redl and David Wineman, *Children Who Hate*. Glencoe, Illinois: The Free Press, 1951.

[12] Enrico Ferri, *Criminal Sociology*. New York: Appleton and Co., 1896.

[13] W. G. Bonger, *Criminality and Economic Conditions*, translated by H. P. Horton. Boston: Little, Brown and Co., 1916.

tional crime and delinquency among the proletariat on the pressures of the capitalistic system. However, the American sociologists in the twenties pointed to conditions of social or community disorganization, rather than factors related to poverty. They became engrossed with identifying the location and characteristics of high delinquency areas of the city, specifying family disruption and conflict instead of broken home, and calling attention to the modal importance of companionship in delinquency.

It was not until around 1940 that a basic American sociological theory of delinquency and criminal behavior was propounded. This was done by Sutherland and it was called differential association.[14] According to this theory, delinquent or criminal behavior is learned as is most other kinds of behavior—learned in association with others, according to the frequency, intensity, priority, and duration of contacts. Sutherland's theory really is not basically different from the one announced by Tarde[15] 50 years earlier, which regarded criminal behavior as a product of limitation of circulating patterns. Glaser[16] fairly recently proposed differential identification as a substitute for differential association. One takes over the models of behavior from those (reference) groups with which one identifies. But this does not have to be a face-to-face or person-to-person identification. (One can identify with the Beatniks without having actual physical contact with them.)

Still more recently Albert Cohen,[17]

picking up the lead from Whyte's *Street-Corner Society,* contended that working class boys who turned their backs on middle class virtues and values found the solution for their status problems in the delinquency subculture of the gang. And most recent of all is the theory propounded by Cloward and Ohlin[18] that urban slum boys gravitate to delinquency subculture when they discover they do not have access to legitimate avenues of success.

COMMENT ON THE THEORIES

Working backward in commenting on these theories, one might say that Cloward's theory only applies to those forms of delinquency which are part and parcel of the role structure of delinquency subculture. Jackson Toby[19] makes the estimate that this might only be 10 percent of the whole spectrum of delinquency. Assuming that Cloward's focus is very restricted, his theory does not account for the boys who do not gravitate toward the fighting gang, the criminal gang, and the retreatist groups (drugs). It does not specify that the ones who do gravitate to the three types of subculture have internalized an awareness of inaccessibility to legitimate success goals. It does not indicate that there are degrees of participation in gangs and that delinquency involvement of some members might be nil.

Cohen's theory has somewhat more merit. Somewhere and somehow in the growing-up process, slum boys turn their backs on middle class values and look to street-corner groups to come to their aid. But Cohen is not able to specify the boys who do or do not

[14] Edwin H. Sutherland, *Principles of Criminology,* 4th Ed. Philadelphia: J. B. Lippincott Co., 1947, pp. 6–7.

[15] Gabriel Tarde, *Penal Philosophy,* translated by R. Howell. Boston: Little, Brown and Co., 1912.

[16] Daniel Glaser, "Criminality Theories and Behavioral Images," *American Journal of Sociology,* Vol. 61, 1956, p. 440.

[17] Albert K. Cohen, *Delinquent Boys:*

The Culture of the Gang. Glencoe, Illinois: The Free Press, 1955, pp. 128–133.

[18] R. A. Cloward and Lloyd Ohlin, *Delinquency and Opportunity.* Glencoe, Illinois: The Free Press, 1960.

[19] Private circulated comment on the Cloward and Ohlin book, 1961.

turn their backs on middle class virtues and opportunities and gravitate to the street corner. He does not indicate whether only some of the boys on the street corner get involved in delinquent acts, as Shaw and Thrasher did a generation ago. So we have two interesting sociological formulations here, but not much realistic applicability.

Sutherland's differential association theory was meant to be a general theory, applying to the entire spectrum of delinquency and crime, from low to high in the class structure and across the board in personality. The trouble with Sutherland's theory (as well as Tarde's and Glaser's) is that it does not explain who *does* and who *does not* take up with carriers of delinquent patterns or who internalizes and who does not internalize delinquent models of behavior.

Coming now to the contributors to theory in the psychogenic school (Aichhorn, Redl, et al.), one should observe that at the most they only occupy a small end of the total spectrum of delinquency and crime. It is granted that there are some individuals whose ego and superego development is too weak or poor to control impulses and to handle ordinary expectancies. But it is not at all clear just which children succumb to or are recipients of faulty socialization in the first few years of life. And it is not clear just which of the children, teen-agers, late adolescents, and adults who are supposed to have little control over their impulse system run afoul the laws and regulations of society and those who do not.

One certainly finds it difficult to specify just exactly what the proneness is that is supposed to be the mainspring of serious, habitual, and early-starting offenders (criminal biology). It seems to be a sort of weakness in character. The evidence for the inheritance of proneness is very skimpy and most un-impressive, a sort of unreliable family-tree assessment by clinicians.

William Sheldon was able to specify the different kinds of somatotypes much more definitely than Kretschmer was able to specify his body-mind types. A group of 200 problem youth in a Boston hostel, according to Sheldon, tended to have mesomorphic (athletic) body types along with several related forms of mental deviancy. The Gluecks discovered that among 500 delinquent and 500 nondelinquent boys the delinquents showed up very much more mesomorphic than the nondelinquents. The mesomorphs were found by the Gluecks to have a higher delinquency potential than other body types. Associated with mesomorphy were strength, social assertiveness, uninhibited motor responses, less submissiveness to authority. While mesomorphy does not explain all of delinquent behavior in the Gluecks' sample, it is certainly associated with a large segment of it and seems to reinforce many of the mental, emotional, and family traits connected with delinquency. Future studies will have to confirm the mesomorphic potential in delinquency.

GLUECKS: 4 TO 1 CAUSAL LAW

Out of their research on 500 delinquent and 500 nondelinquent boys, the Gluecks[20] proposed a five point causal law. According to this formulation, delinquents are distinguishable from nondelinquents (1) physically, in being essentially mesomorphic; (2) temperamentally, in being restless, impulsive, aggressive, destructive; (3) emotionally, in being hostile, defiant, resentful, assertive, nonsubmissive; (4) psychologically, in being direct, concrete learners; (5) socioculturally, in being

[20] Sheldon and Eleanor Glueck, *Unraveling Juvenile Delinquency*. New York: The Commonwealth Fund, 1950, pp. 281–282.

reared by unfit parents. This might be looked upon as a 4 to 1 law: four parts individual and one part situational. Items 2, 3, and 5 were chosen from among more than 100 overlapping traits, which distinguished delinquents from nondelinquents. The use of more sophisticated statistical methods would have enabled the Gluecks to find the two or three components within this maze of overlapping items which basically differentiate the delinquents from the nondelinquents. Nevertheless, the 4 to 1 causal law still stands as one of the few formulations which is worth attempting to confirm, qualify, or disprove by more rigorous research methods in the future. The law covers most of the spectrum of juvenile delinquency as we know it in the United States, certainly insofar as the full spectrum is represented by 500 boys from Boston who had been committed by juvenile courts to state schools in Massachusetts for delinquency.

INGREDIENTS OF INNER AND OUTER CONTAINMENT

In contrast to the buck-shot approach of the Gluecks, that is, shooting out in all directions to explore and discover, containment theory seeks to ferret out more specifically the inner and outer controls over normative behavior. It is attempting to get closer on the target of delinquency and crime by getting at the components which regulate conduct.

Inner containment consists mainly of self components, such as self-control, good self-concept, ego strength, well-developed superego, high frustration tolerance, high resistance to diversions, high sense of responsibility, goal orientation, ability to find substitute satisfactions, tension-reducing rationalizations, and so on. These are the inner regulators.

Outer containment represents the structural buffer in the person's immediate social world which is able to hold him within bounds. It consists of such items as a presentation of a consistent moral front to the person, institutional reinforcement of his norms, goals, and expectations, the existence of a reasonable set of social expectations, effective supervision and discipline (social controls), provision for reasonable scope of activity (including limits and responsibilities) as well as for alternatives and safety-valves, opportunity for acceptance, identity, and belongingness. Such structural ingredients help the family and other supportive groups contain the individual.

Research will have to ferret out the one or two elements in inner and outer containment which are the basic regulators of normative behavior. Undoubtedly in the lists cited above there are items which, if present, determine the existence of other items and cause most of the regulation of conduct. Likewise, research must indicate the way in which the inner and outer regulatory systems operate conjointly. How much self-strength must be present in a fluid world with very little external buffer? How much weakness in self-components is an effective external buffer able to manage?

SUPPORTING RESEARCH

The research and observations so far which give support to containment theory are the following:

1. According to Albert J. Reiss,[21] as a result of a study of Chicago delinquents who failed and succeeded on probation, the relative weakness of personal and social controls accounts for most cases of delinquency. Reiss found,

[21] Albert J. Reiss, Jr., "Delinquency as the Failure of Personal and Social Controls," *American Sociological Review*, Vol. 16, 1951, pp. 196–206.

however, that the personal controls had more predictive efficiency than the social controls as far as recidivism was concerned.

2. Nye[22] presented evidence to the effect that trends toward delinquent behavior are related to four control factors: (a) direct control which comes from discipline, restrictions, punishments; (b) internalized control which is the inner control of conscience; (c) indirect control which is exerted by not wanting to hurt or go against the wishes of parents or other individuals with whom the person identifies; and (d) the availability of alternative means to goals. Nye contends that his social control theory should not be applied to compulsive behavior or the behavior influenced by delinquency subcultures. He feels that the more indirect control is effective, the less need for direct control; the more internalized control is effective, the less need for any other type of control.

3. Reckless and Dinitz[23] found that a favorable concept of self insulated 12-year-old boys in the slum against delinquency, including perceptions about self, companions, home, and school. A poor concept of self, including perceptions that one is likely to get into trouble, his friends are in trouble, his family and home are unsatisfactory, that he will not finish school, and so on, was associated with delinquency vulnerability in 12-year-old slum boys. Four years later, followup contact revealed that the good self-concept group had pretty much held the line and the favorable direction, while the poor self-concept group had gravitated in unfavorable directions, 35 percent being involved with the law three times on an average. Reckless and Dinitz look upon a good or poor self-concept as an internalization of favorable or unfavorable socialization.

4. As a result of his observations on hyperaggressive, hostile children, Redl[24] identifies 22 functions of the ego in managing life situations. He conceives of the ego as the manager in the behavior control system, while the super ego is looked upon as the system which gives the signals to the ego. Redl, as is true of Aichhorn disciples, recognizes, particularly at the extremes, ego shortage and ego strength as well as a sick conscience and a healthy one.

Containment theory points to the regulation of normative behavior through resistance to deviancy as well as through direction toward legitimate social expectations. It may very well be that most of the regulation is in terms of a defense or buffer against deflection. At any rate, it appears as if inner and outer containment occupies a central or core position in between the pressures and pulls of the external environment and the inner drives or pushes. Environmental pressures may be looked upon as a condition associated with poverty or deprivation, conflict and discord, external restraint, minority group status, limited access to success

[22] F. Ivan Nye, *Family Relationships and Delinquent Behavior.* New York: John Wiley and Sons, Inc., 1958, pp. 3–4.

[23] Walter C. Reckless, Simon Dinitz, and Ellen Murray, "Self Concept as an Insulator against Delinquency," *American Sociological Review*, Vol. 21, 1956, p. 745; "The Self Component in Potential Delinquency and Potential Non-Delinquency," *ibid.*, Vol. 22, 1957, p. 569; Dimon Dinitz, Barbara Ann Kay, and Walter C. Reckless, "Group Gradients in Delinquency Potential and Achievement Score of Sixth Graders," *American Journal of Orthopsychiatry*, Vol. 28, 1958, pp. 598–605; Frank Scarpitti et al., "The 'Good' Boy in a High Delinquency Area: Four Years Later," *American Sociological Review*, Vol. 25, 1960, pp. 555–558.

[24] Fritz Redl and David Wineman, *Children Who Hate.* Glencoe, Illinois: The Free Press, 1951, pp. 74–140.

in an opportunity structure. The pulls of the environment represent the distractions, attractions, temptations, patterns of deviancy, advertising, propaganda, carriers of delinquent and criminal patterns (including pushers), delinquency subculture, and so forth. The ordinary pushes are the drives, motives, frustrations, restlessness, disappointments, rebellion, hostility, feelings of inferiority, and so forth. One notices at once that Bonger as well as Cloward fall into pressure theory, while Tarde, Sutherland, and Glaser fall into pull theory.

In a vertical order, the pressures and pulls of the environment are at the top or the side of containing structure, while the pushes are below the inner containment. If the individual has a weak outer containment, the pressures and pulls will then have to be handled by the inner control system. If the outer buffer of the individual is relatively strong and effective, the individual's inner defense does not have to play such a critical role. Likewise, if the person's inner controls are not equal to the ordinary pushes, an effective outer defense may help hold him within bounds. If the inner defenses are of good working order, the outer structure does not have to come to the rescue of the person. Mention has already been made of the fact that there are some extraordinary pushes, such as compulsions, which cannot be contained. The inner and outer control system is usually not equal to the task of containing the abnormal pushes. They are uncontainable by ordinary controls.

SEVEN TESTS OF VALIDITY

1. Containment theory is proposed as the theory of best fit for the large middle range of cases of delinquency and crime. It fits the middle range cases better than any other theory.

2. It explains crimes against the person as well as the crimes against property, that is the mine run of murder, assault, and rape, as well as theft, robbery, and burglary.

3. It represents a formulation which psychiatrists, psychologists, and sociologists, as well as practitioners, can use equally well. All of these experts look for dimensions of inner and outer strength and can specify these strengths in their terms. Differential association and/or pressure of the environment leave most psychiatrists and psychologists cold, and an emphasis on push theory leaves the sociologists for the most part cold. But all of the experts can rally around inner and outer weaknesses and strengths.

4. Inner and outer containment can be discovered in individual case studies. Weaknesses and strengths are observable. Containment theory is one of the few theories in which the microcosm (the individual case history) mirrors the ingredients of the macrocosm (the general formulation).

5. Containment theory is a valid operational theory for treatment of offenders: for restructuring the milieu of a person or beefing up his self. The most knowledgeable probation workers, parole workers, and institutional staff are already focusing to some extent on helping the juvenile or adult offender build up ego strength, develop new goals, internalize new models of behavior. They are also working on social ties, anchors, supportive relationships, limits, and alternative opportunities in helping to refashion a new containing world for the person.

6. Containment theory is also an effective operational theory for prevention. Children with poor containment can be spotted early. Programs to help insulate vulnerable children against delinquency must operate on internaliza-

tion of stronger self components and the strengthening of containing structure around the child.

7. Internal and external containment can be assessed and approximated. Its strengths and weaknesses can be specified for research. There is good promise that such assessments can be measured in a standard way.

Finally, it is probable that the theory which will best supplement containment theory in the future will be "damage theory," according to which a light to dark spectrum of damage produces maladjustment and deviancy. The problem here is to find measures to isolate the less serious and less obvious damage cases and to estimate how far into the middle range of delinquency and crime the lighter impairments go.

Section III THE EMPIRICAL STRUCTURE OF DELINQUENT GROUPS

There is considerable evidence that most juvenile delinquency is a group phenomenon. Because most delinquency occurs in groups, the structure of the gang is an important area for study by sociologists. Lack of empirical data, however, has led us to assume that the delinquent gang is virtually a closed social system, and that its influence on the gang member is pervasive. The selections in this section were included to provide the reader with some of the recent analyses of the empirical structure of delinquent groups.

The study of delinquent subcultures reported by Spergel was conducted largely within the framework of anomie and opportunity theories developed by Robert Merton, Richard Cloward, and Lloyd Ohlin. The contribution of this study is the increased understanding we have of delinquent conduct and the structure of delinquent gangs through a comparison of different neighborhoods and the patterns of delinquent conduct which are characteristic of the neighborhoods.

Yablonsky suggests an interesting conceptualization of the gang as a "near-group." He describes gangs as informal, short-lived, secondary groups without a clearcut, stable delinquent structure. According to his observations, their diffuse and malleable structure makes it possible for them to meet the varied and individual needs of the members.

Important issues concerning the structure and values of delinquent groups are also raised by observations of middle-class gangs. With the exception of the leadership role, the groups described by the Myerhoffs manifest all the characteristics given by Yablonsky as those of a near-group. Moreover, in comparing Negro and white lower-class gang boys with lower-class boys of the same race, Short, Rivera, and Tennyson found that gang members perceived legitimate opportunities as available less often than did nongang boys; lower-class boys less often than middle-class boys; and Negro boys less often than white boys.

The next selection reports data on behavior factors based on detached workers' ratings of gang boys in metropolitan Chicago. These data suggest that delinquent subcultures exist but are perhaps not as "pure" as we have been led to believe, and, further, that they become articulated in more complex ways than current theories of subcultures specify.

The crucial ways in which the structure of delinquent gangs may be a function of the culture are suggested by the few studies that have been made of delinquent groupings in other societies. The study by Vaz of teen-age gangs located in Paris suggests that gangs among Parisian youth differ from the subcultural varieties described by Cloward and Ohlin. These differences are explained by Vaz in terms of the structural and normative differences between American and French society. The way in which gangs may differ from one another is further emphasized by Scott's analysis of London street gangs. These gangs have characteristics that are in some respects both similar to and different from those of the American and French gangs described in this section.

21. An Exploratory Research in Delinquent Subcultures

IRVING SPERGEL

The purpose of the present paper is briefly to report an exploratory effort to develop a typology of gangs within a sociocultural framework. The research findings are presented as a beginning attempt to differentiate types of delinquent groups which appear to arise in certain kinds of neighborhoods under varying social conditions. The investigation focuses on a sociocultural system of variables. It does not deal primarily with other sets of variables such as personality, small-group factors, and situational pressures.

* The present article is an elaboration of a paper presented at the November 9, 1960, meeting of the Illinois Academy of Criminology and is based on "Types of Delinquent Groups" (D.S.W. dissertation, New York School of Social Work, Columbia University, 1960) and on additional research supported largely through grants from the National Institute of Mental Health (MF-10,083 and M-4351 [A]). For many of the key ideas in this article, the writer is indebted to Lloyd E. Ohlin, New York School of Social Work of Columbia University. A monograph more fully presenting the data here summarized is now in preparation.
[1] Numbers in parentheses refer to the numbered references in the Bibliography at the end of the article.

A great deal of attention has been directed to the problem of gang delinquency. Various theories about the genesis and development of delinquent behavior and delinquent subcultures have arisen (13).[1] An even larger number of ideas for solution of the problem have been proposed, of which some are currently being further elaborated and tested through diverse research programs.

The neighborhood street-club worker has served both in the collection of data for research and in the provision of services. He has influenced theory and practice by providing a broad group-oriented service to delinquents in a neighborhood setting. Some consensus has been reached on what is expected of the street-club worker. One agency described street-club work as follows:

Trained workers were sent out into the streets to seek out anti-social gangs at their hang-outs and to gain their acceptance and confidence. Once close relations were established, the workers were to try to influence the clubs along socially constructive lines. [It was] assumed that gang boys would respond positively to accept-

SOURCE. Irving Spergel, "An Exploratory Research in Delinquent Subcultures," from *Social Service Review*, Volume 35, March 1961, pp. 33–47. Copyright © 1961, University of Chicago Press. Reprinted with the permission of the University of Chicago Press.

ing, understanding adults, and that relationships with such adults would serve as a powerful force for personal and social growth [7, pp. 4–5].

While there is gross identification of the modified group work techniques involved in "reaching" and "serving" delinquent group members, there is still little clarity as to who gang youngsters really are. The criterion for working with a gang continues to be the vague standard of "troublesome" behavior. But specifically what is "troublesome" behavior and to whom is it irritating? What are the dimensions of delinquent behavior in personality and sociocultural terms? What goals should be emphasized for what groups? What is the range of problems to be solved? These are basic questions which have not been generally addressed, either by social scientists or by social workers dealing with delinquents. In order to understand the theoretical framework of the present research and the meaning of the data gathered, a short review of some relevant and current sociological thinking on the problem of delinquency is in order.

THE RELEVANT SOCIOLOGICAL LITERATURE[2]

The Cultural Tradition

One sociological tradition has emphasized the cultural processes and environmental circumstances associated with the condition of delinquency in the lower-class neighborhood. The ideas of culture conflict, transmission of culture, the learning of criminal behavior, and the ecological distribution of certain kinds of deviant behavior have provided the major framework for describing the criminal culture. Shaw (14, 15, 16, 17), McKay (18), Sutherland (19,

[2] For a complete and critical review of the current sociological literature, see (2), pp. 47–76.

20), Whyte (22), and Kobrin (10) have made eminent contributions in this tradition. More recently, Miller (12), an anthropologist, has added to this stream of understanding.

The Anomie Tradition

A second sociological tradition, stemming from the work of Durkheim (8) and Merton (11) on "anomie theory," has focused on the social structure, with stress on the institutional means available to achieve culturally induced goals. Deviant behavior in our society, according to Merton, occurs

when a system of cultural values extols, virtually above all else, certain *common* success-goals *for the population at large* while the social structure rigorously restricts or completely closes access to approved modes of reaching these goals *for a considerable part of the same population* [11, p. 146].

Partially in the same tradition, Cohen (4, 5) states that certain children in the lower class are denied status in the respectable middle-class society because they cannot meet the criteria of the respectable status system. The delinquent subculture or the "parent male subculture" (6) is the vehicle for the repudiation of middle-class standards and the adoption of their antithesis.

Cloward (1) contributes further to the development of the anomie tradition through his conception that there are "differentials in the availability of illegitimate means." Not only conventional means but illegitimate means are variously distributed in the social structure. Cloward utilizes the concepts of age-role integration (21) and the "meshing" of conventional and criminal systems in certain lower-class neighborhoods (10, 22) to develop his idea that not only legitimate but illegitimate opportunities are differentially available to persons situated at various locations in the social structure.

Following up a major integration of sociological theories, Cloward and Ohlin have theoretically located three distinct deviant patterns in lower-class areas: the "criminal," the "conflict," and the "retreatist" adaptations. They state that the criminal subculture is likely to arise in a neighborhood milieu characterized by close bonds or integration between different age levels of offender and between criminal and conventional elements. The criminal pattern stresses the achievement of the success goal through the means of the "big score," the "connection," and being a "right guy." The conflict pattern occurs in the disorganized urban area where adolescents are "cut off from institutionalized channels, criminal as well as legitimate." Thrown back on their own resources, adolescents "seize upon the manipulation of violence as a route to status." The conflict pattern stresses the normative attributes of "rep" and "heart" in the achievement of a modified or transmuted version of success status. The retreatist adaptation, characterized mainly by drug use, is essentially an adjustment to failure or "double failure." The retreatist adaptation is a response to the failure to overcome either internalized prohibitions regarding illegitimate means or the "socially structured barriers" to the acquisition of legitimate and illegitimate means. The retreatist subculture is characterized by the attributes of "kick," "hustle," and "cool" (2, 3). The conceptual schemes of anomie and differential opportunity theories provide the basis for the development of the research now to be described.

RESEARCH DESIGN

Theoretical Scheme

A major modification or development in the Cloward-Ohlin formulation was the division of the criminal pattern into a racket and a theft adaptation. Also, since focus in the research was to be on the values, norms, and beliefs shared by delinquents on a neighborhood basis, the drug addict pattern of the post-gang adolescent was conceived as a subtype for each of the delinquent subcultures. Stress was on the similarity of orientations of delinquents and drug addicts from each area.

The central hypothesis of the exploratory research was that delinquent subcultures had developed from the varying nature and extent of opportunities available to youth of lower-class neighborhoods by which to achieve culturally induced success goals. Different relationships between the internalized success goal and the legitimate and illegitimate opportunities present were expected to create the separate circumstances encouraging the rise of the three major kinds of delinquent subculture.[3]

The racket subculture was seen as arising within a social context of the ample availability of illegitimate means or opportunities in one type of neighborhood. The delinquent would be expected to have lofty aspirations for success and to be under pressure to utilize the criminal learning environments accessible to him in preparation for a career in a well-organized racket or

---

[3] The delinquent subculture was defined as the organized set of shared values, beliefs, and norms governing the behavior of youths in interaction with each other which is determined to be in serious violation of desirable modes of conduct and consequently is identified as delinquent by the official culture.

The success goal was described as inhering in a particular type of social status and as symbolized in the attributes of wealth, prestige, and power regarded as highly desirable by the official culture.

Means or opportunities were defined broadly to include the availability of appropriate learning environments for the acquisition of values and skills associated with the performance of a particular role as well as the condition permitting discharge of the role (1, p. 168).

criminal syndicate. The weakness of the conventional orientation in the neighborhood would set up little barrier to the acquisition of the "normative" deviant adaptation. In a sense, the delinquent from the racket subcultural area would be "socialized" into its criminal life-style, and the notion of a distinguishable youth subculture would be less relevant here than in the other areas.

The conflict subculture was viewed as a direct response to the extremely limited presence of both legitimate and illegitimate opportunities in a slum neighborhood. Delinquents with high aspirations would not find in this kind of area adequate opportunities, legitimate or illegitimate, by which to realize ambitions for prestige, power, and wealth. Delinquents in this type of lower-class neighborhood would create a substitute means system defined by a new set of criteria. The fighting or "bopping" subculture would provide a system of values and expectations, rules and regulations, rewards and punishments, which would make "rep" as a gang fighter equivalent to the achievement of the success goal. The conflict subculture was regarded as not integrated with neighborhood adult orientations, whether legitimate or illegitimate. However, it was thought that delinquents from this kind of area would tend to derive their normative values, if weakly, from the larger community culture.

The theft subculture, probably the most prevalent, if also the least noticeable kind of delinquent pattern, was regarded as growing out of a context of the partially limited availability of both legitimate and illegitimate opportunities. A highly organized racket system would not prevail in this type of neighborhood. Access to opportunities, generally, would not be so blocked off that the creation of an alternate means system, such as gang-fighting, was necessary. Yet it was expected that semiorganized, partially integrated opportunities for careers in thievery would exist. The delinquent who aspired to success goals could partially realize ambitions through the risky confiscation and appropriation of the symbols of success (cars, clothes, money) by such devices as burglary and shoplifting. The delinquent from the theft subcultural area would be controlled in part by the dominant and generally accepted commitment to a legitimate orientation.

The drug addict orientation of the older adolescent and young adult was seen as present in each kind of neighborhood investigated and as similar to local delinquent orientations. The retreatist orientations were regarded mainly as partial and transitional adaptations in each area. The older adolescent or young adult, no longer acceptable to the delinquent subculture by virtue of advancing age and unable through personal deficiencies or the absence of opportunities to make the transition to adult status, would utilize various narcotic drugs to maintain adolescent fantasies of wealth, power, and omnipotence. At the same time the level of aspirations of the drug addict would be lowered through pressures of the neighborhood reality to accord more with the level of existing opportunities, legitimate and illegitimate. Addicts would seek to approach a normative adult adjustment.

Methodology

Three kinds of neighborhoods were selected: two with reputations for high-level racket activity, a second type noted for the productivity of violent fighting gangs, and a third accepted as rather ordinary, except for the extensive but not alarming involvement of its delinquent youth in acts of car theft or "joy-riding" and burglary. Polar and clear-cut types of neighborhoods were preferred, of course, but were not entirely available. The racket neighborhoods contained some gang-fighting groups. The neighborhood with conflict groups was ridden with petty racket activity, and the area of the theft subculture had its limited share of adult racketeering and infrequent gang fights. The specific gangs selected were not typical in the sense that each represented some mean or median of qualities characterizing delinquent groups in each neighborhood selected. Rather, the worst or most delinquent groups were chosen in order that peculiar and characteristic forms of delinquent behavior would be clearly evident, even if in an exaggerated manner. It was not difficult to select such groups on the basis of social agency, police, and youth community consensus. There was general agreement about which group or groups in each area were most delinquent. However, the criteria for delinquent behavior appeared to vary from neighborhood to neighborhood. In the areas of the racket and conflict subcultures, the criterion was mainly aggressive behavior. In the areas of the theft subculture, the criterion was aggressive or theft behavior. The representativeness of such delinquent groups was not established through any systematic sampling process. Leaders and core members of delinquent groups were the subjects of the research procedures employed.

Drug addicts and non-delinquents were selected on a similar basis. Non-delinquents were chosen for their highly conforming behavior by recommendation of social agency (settlement house) and church officials. The drug addict sample comprised mainly the universe of patients from the three areas receiving treatment at a special drug treatment hospital and its after-care clinic during a six-week summer period.

Four types of procedure were employed to gather the data: a six-month observational process in two neighborhoods, followed a year later by a two-month period of observation in a third neighborhood;[4] formal interviews with 125 subjects, including non-delinquents, delinquents, and drug addicts mainly from the three types of areas; a content analysis of conversation of members of the three delinquent groups and of a drug addict group from the racket subcultural area; and, finally, an analysis of agency records.[5]

The following highly telescoped discussion provides a comparison of the three types of delinquent groups in relation to certain variables: neighborhood factors, types of delinquent behavior and delinquent subcultures, success goals and differential opportunities, and relationships to significant adults. However, it should be noted that this research is exploratory and that the data collected are not from a random selection of subjects. The groups studied are very small. The chief value of the analysis is illustrative.

RESEARCH FINDINGS

Neighborhood Factors

Certain generalizations about the three kinds of city areas were possible. The delinquent racket subculture in one case was found in an Italian lower-

[4] Observations were made by the researcher for each group, usually on an alternate-day basis, seven days per week, for periods of approximately two hours in the afternoon and three hours in the evening. Observations were electronically recorded directly following the time of observation or on the morning of the following day.

[5] The writer is greatly indebted to staff members of the Council of Social and Athletic Clubs of the New York City Youth Board for assistance in collection of data. Staff members at Riverside Hospital, Lenox Hill Neighborhood Association, and James Weldon Johnson Community Center were also especially helpful in this process.

class neighborhood. The indexes of social breakdown (public assistance case load, home relief case load, aid to dependent children, infant mortality, venereal disease, terminations from psychiatric clinics, and delinquency rates) were high but not as high as in the most deteriorated neighborhoods of the city. Adults, particularly parents of delinquents, had little formal education. Breadwinners were engaged in skilled and semiskilled occupations, primarily well-paying jobs that were highly unionized. Criminal and conventional adult orientations and activities were integrated. It was common knowledge that the "numbers" banker, the "big" loan shark, and the other syndicate racketeers worked closely with local businessmen and political and police officials. The racketeer played a variety of significant economic and social roles in the neighborhood. He was the sponsor and subsidizer of legitimate and illegitimate business enterprise. He was helpful when others were in trouble by raising bail money and making appropriate "payoffs." He was a parent surrogate for recalcitrant youth. He could establish direct controls over certain types of undesirable deviant behavior, such as prolonged or violent gang-fighting and drug-selling to local neighborhood youth. Integration of age levels existed. Older youths served as role models. Their seniority and influence were unquestioned. They played paternal and educative roles and exerted vigorous authority and control functions over the junior members of the neighborhood.

The delinquent conflict subculture developed in one of the worst slum areas of the city. The official indexes of social breakdown were the highest in the city. The adult population was composed mainly of immigrants from Puerto Rico with limited formal education. However, it was noteworthy that the parents of delinquents from this area had a higher level of school grade attainment than the parents of delinquents from the racket subcultural area. In general, adults were engaged in unskilled, low-paying jobs in factories and service industries. Nevertheless, there was evidence that gang delinquents in this area did not necessarily come from the most deprived families. The median family income and parental educational level was higher for delinquents than for nondelinquents. It was possible to speculate that there was more pressure for upward mobility for delinquents than for non-delinquents, as well as a greater sense of relative deprivation.

Conventional and criminal opportunities were less well integrated than in the other two areas. Major racketeers did not, in the main, operate in the area, although many types of petty racketeers and criminals, sometimes in conflict with each other, were present. The criminal did not appear to play a major or respected role in the structure of this lower-class neighborhood. Neither was there evidence of the significant influence of local conventional or legitimate leadership. The contacts of delinquents with criminals were either insignificant or antagonistic. Youth gangs in the area were in varying stages of war and peace with each other. The gangs and segments of gangs were enclaves related weakly to other youth and young adult sectors. In one instance, the relations between a junior and a senior segment of a gang became so strained that threats of violence and actual violence occurred. This disintegrative character of age-level relationships would have been inconceivable in the closely knit area of the racket subculture. In the conflict subcultural area relationships between conventionally and criminally oriented adults and between different age levels of offenders were not positively "meshed," and open conflict periodically arose.

The delinquent theft subculture developed in a heterogeneous nationality (Italian, Irish, German, Czech, etc.) and mixed-class neighborhood. The indexes of social breakdown were lower than in the other areas. Although family income averaged less for the lower-class population than in the racket subcultural area, occupational status was somewhat higher. Adults were engaged in skilled, semiskilled, and white-collar occupations. Adults in many cases had been born in the city and had obtained at least some high-school education. Conventional and criminal systems of opportunity were integrated only in part, especially in the disposal of stolen material. Some of the proprietors and workers in radio and television stores, automobile shops, and restaurants, as well as other adults, served as fences for stolen goods and even aided in planning juvenile burglaries. Members of delinquent groups were loosely integrated on an age-level basis. Older youths served as role models but did not exercise strong influence and control over younger delinquents.

Delinquent Behavior and Subcultures

The distribution of serious delinquent behavior and the collective lifestyles of gang members varied in each of the types of neighborhood. Delinquents from the racket subcultural area were more intensely involved, by their own reports, in policy and loan-shark rackets than were delinquents from the other areas. Delinquents from the conflict subcultural area reported the highest incidence of participation in gang-fighting. The difference was confirmed through an analysis of agency records and carefully compiled answer-

ing-service message units[6] on gang fights in the areas. In one of the racket neighborhoods, but not in the other, there was evidence of considerable gang-fighting, yet much less than occurred in the conflict subcultural area, and the character of such youth group-fighting tended to be defensive, growing out of collective neighborhood concerns of attack, real or imaginary, from a new and sizable non-Italian population in the area. In this particular racket neighborhood, gang-fighting was used sporadically as a means to prevent the derogation of neighborhood and personal status by the perceived incursion of a lower-status population.

For delinquents from the conflict subcultural area, organized and systematic gang-fighting was a full-time, pervasive way of life. It was an aggressive manifestation by which opportunities were developed to achieve "rep" and status as tough, daring, brave, and foolhardy fighters. To be called a "guy with a heart" was to be identified with the attributes of successful status. Since gang-fighting was the means by which the success goal was achieved, it was essential to create crises leading to combat and to guard against conditions which destroyed opportunities for achieving gang and individual "rep."

Delinquents from the theft subcultural area reported the highest incidence of car theft or "joy riding" and burglary. On the other hand, there was almost no evidence of car theft by delinquents from the conflict subcultural area and little car theft by delinquents from the racket subcultural area. The incidence

[6] The Council of Social and Athletic Clubs of the New York City Youth Board uses a telephone answering service between the hours of 5 P.M. and 9 A.M. on weekdays and day and night on weekends and holidays. All messages received are recorded and relayed to appropriate staff members.

of burglary of apartments and stores appeared to be lower in the other two areas. "Joy riding" for delinquents from the theft subcultural neighborhood signified a status of importance and indicated at least temporarily the sharing of a successful adult life-style. Car parts were stolen and sold. Material goods and cash obtained from burglaries were the symbols and the wherewithal for the achievement of the success goal. Expensive clothes, record players, portable radios, and jewelry were some of the items commonly appropriated.

In no subcultural area was there evidence that spontaneous aggression was more prevalent. The frequency of brawling and non-gang-related fighting, according to interview responses, was similar for delinquents from each of the areas.

An attempt was made to characterize and assess the criminal or illegitimate orientation in the three kinds of neighborhood. It was speculated that the delinquent value systems were related to future adult orientations. The delinquent orientations could serve to foreshadow the type of adult orientations to which young people aspired. A value-norm index was constructed on the basis of nineteen interview items, three directly reflecting values, i.e., whether racketeers are good or bad, whether it is all right to cheat, whether people should be honest; and sixteen items on norms of serious delinquent activity, used to assess subcultural expectancies as to whether subjects would be likely to "kill someone," "steal a car," "engage in policy operations," and so forth. When the responses were added, total scores indicated that delinquents from the racket subcultural area had the most extreme criminal value orientation. Seventy-three per cent of the total responses of all delinquents from the racket subcultural area indicated an illegitimate orientation, 46 per cent of

the total responses of all delinquents from the conflict subcultural area reflected illegitimate orientations, and 47 per cent of the total responses of all delinquents from the theft subcultural area indicated illegitimate orientations.

It was postulated that the kind of adult a young person aspired to be "like" was a manifestation of values which he esteemed highly and which might forecast his own adult orientation. Responses to the interview question, "What is the occupation of the adult in the neighborhood whom you would most want to be like ten years from now?" strongly suggested that delinquents from the racket subcultural neighborhood were most identified with the racketeer or "businessman," as he was alternately termed in one area. Delinquents from the conflict and theft subcultural areas mainly identified with conventional role models.

Subjects were asked to rank what they considered the most important attribute in "getting ahead." There were four categories: ability, good luck, "connections," or education (5). The term "connections" had a questionable connotation in each of the areas. The data were as follows: nine of ten delinquents from the racket subcultural area regarded "connections" as most important and education as least important; seven of ten delinquents each from the conflict and theft subcultural areas regarded ability and education, but mainly education, as most important in "getting ahead."

It was possible, particularly in the racket subcultural area, that the concepts of education and "connections" were antithetical. A strong value investment in the importance of "connections" precluded the possibility of emphasis on the educational orientation. In a larger sense the pursuit of education represented the pursuit of truth and that which was highly legitimate. The pervasive use of "connections" represented the rejection of truth and the pursuit of the deviant. The way of life in the racket subcultural area might be stated as, "It isn't what you know but who you know that counts, especially if the person you know is a racketeer." The conflict and theft subcultures still shared the dominant cultural theme of American society that education and formal schooling were a means of achieving success. This was true despite the fact that delinquents in each of the neighborhoods had left school at the minimum age permissible.

Success Goals and Differential Opportunities

It was assumed that success in our society was measurable by the amount of income and the kind of job the individual possessed. One indicator of the internalization of the success goal was considered income aspiration. The answer to the question, "How much money would you like to make, ideally, in ten years?" showed that in each area delinquents had higher income aspirations than non-delinquents. On the other hand, the expectations of actual income in ten years were higher for non-delinquents than for delinquents, except in the neighborhood containing the racket subculture. The gap or disjunction between aspiration and expectation levels was very large for delinquents from the conflict subcultural area, not quite so large for delinquents from the theft subcultural area, and smallest for delinquents from the racket subcultural area, who had most access to illegitimate means. In each of the areas, the disjunction between aspiration and expectation level was less for non-delinquents than for delinquents. Participation-observation revealed that perceived expectations in regard to future income and job status were closely related to the actual opportunities available in the different neighborhoods.

Also, questions on the interview schedule were designed to get at perceptions of subjects in regard to educational and employment opportunities currently available to young people. Subjects (delinquents, non-delinquents, and drug addicts) from the racket and theft subcultural areas tended to perceive that their opportunities were better than those of persons from the conflict subcultural area.

An effort was made to estimate the extent of organized criminal opportunities in an area. The response to the interview question on the number of racketeers and professional thieves found in the block and in the neighborhood confirmed the overwhelming presence of significant criminal adults and illegitimate opportunities in the neighborhood of the racket subculture. Only weak or partial criminal opportunities were to be found, respectively, in the conflict and theft subcultural areas.

In addition, the content of free-flowing group conversation—that is, verbal references to conventional and criminal adults and to peers—was recorded and analyzed.[7] It was assumed that adults generally controlled opportunities and that verbal allusions to adults grossly reflected access to them. The results showed a high degree of verbal reference and, presumably, integration with adults by delinquents from the racket subcultural area and an extremely low degree of integration with adults by the delinquents from the conflict subcultural neighborhood, who instead indicated a very strong orientation to peer associates. Delinquents from the theft

[7] A technique was devised whereby references by observed subjects to peers and to conventional and criminal adults were instantly noted by use of mechanical clickers or simple counts over successive time periods under relatively uniform conditions.

subcultural area fell between these two extreme types of orientation. The total verbal output of delinquents from each area did not vary significantly. Only the character of the verbal production differed. It suggested the varying accessibility of adult contacts and opportunities.

Relationships to Significant Adults

The nature of relationships to significan adults was explored in each area. A selected total of meaningful adult relationships by subjects was analyzed. The nature of relationships—to mother, father, teacher, employer, community center worker, policeman, probation/parole officer, street-corner worker, neighborhood adult, racketeer, and thief[8]—was examined through interview responses. It was assumed that close, positive relationships to adults constituted access to opportunities. The results indicated that delinquents from the racket subcultural area had positive and strong relationships with racketeers and neighborhood adults, but highly negative relationships with representatives of legitimate society—teachers, community center workers, and, in part, street-club workers. Delinquents from the conflict subcultural area had generally weak and negative relationships to adults. They appeared to be isolated from them. The delinquents from the theft subcultural area had the most positive relationships to conventional adults. They also had positive and close contacts with fences, burglars, and shoplifters.

Especially noteworthy was the finding that the relationships of delinquents from the theft subcultural area to their parents were least positive and co-

operative of all delinquents. This fact suggested the particular significance of a psychosocial variable of disturbed intra-family functioning. This was not to say that delinquents from the other areas did not have poor relationships with parents, too. It indicated only that the extent of the reported disturbance was much greater, according to their own reports, for the delinquents from the theft subcultural area. In each neighborhood, non-delinquents reported their relationships with parents to be at least slightly more positive and productive than did delinquents.

THE ADDICT ORIENTATIONS

The drug addicts studied were in their late teens and early or middle twenties. The major drug was heroin, which was used in varying quantities, on the average of from two to four times daily. There appeared to be a somewhat different drug use pattern in different neighborhoods. Addicts from the conflict subcultural area seemed to have employed more often in the past and still tended to use marijuana in addition to heroin, although not usually at the same time. Addicts from the theft subcultural area appeared most sophisticated in their use of a wide variety of drugs, including heroin, demerol, laudanum, benzedrine, and morphine. This in part could be accounted for by the slightly older median age of drug addicts in the theft subcultural area studied. However, it suggested the possibility of significantly different drug use patterns, related to opportunities for obtaining and using various drugs. Drug addicts from the racket subcultural area claimed that they had, at one time, access to the best-quality heroin available. It was possible that the lower cost and easy availability of marijuana had in part determined its relatively wider use in a conflict subcultural area.

In the main, drug addicts had

---

[8] The questions on the nature of relationships to adult thieves were included only in the interviews with a second sample of twenty-five delinquents from the theft subcultural area.

progressed through the delinquent subcultural orientation and behavioral system which characterized their neighborhoods and still shared the same values as the younger delinquents in the specific areas. Nevertheless, there seemed to be some convergence by narcotic addicts, regardless of neighborhood, in the commission of acts which yielded income for drug purchases. However, there was evidence that such money-yielding antisocial efforts were subculturally relevant. Some drug addicts from the racket subcultural area had access to certain organized criminal opportunities. They were involved in policy and upper-echelon drug-selling operations. Drug addicts from the conflict subcultural area were limited to petty theft, minor extortion, and small-time drug-peddling. Drug addicts from the theft subcultural neighborhood tended to obtain money to purchase drugs through sophisticated forms of burglary, shoplifting, and even forgery. It was not at all clear that drug use or addiction was always a vocational liability and a necessary handicap or that it impeded in every case the development of a highly proficient burglar or shoplifter. This did not gainsay the probability that most addicts were mainly engaged in petty but subculturally characteristic types of criminal behavior.

A major distinction between drug addicts and delinquents in each area was the level of aspiration. The evidence was that drug addicts had lower income-aspiration levels than delinquents. The addicts studied were, for the most part, former members of delinquent groups in their respective subcultural areas. They had gone through a phase of characteristic delinquent activity. They were older than the delinquents and probably were more fully socialized into acceptance of lower-class aspiration levels. The gap between aspirations and expectations for drug addicts was smaller than for delinquents in the conflict and theft subcultural areas. In these two neighborhoods, both legitimate and illegitimate opportunities appeared to become at least partially available to addicts. However, drug use appeared especially to handicap the addict in advancement in a criminal career in the racket area relatively more than in the other two areas.

The relationships of drug addicts to adults were reported to be more positive and productive than those of delinquents. They were more oriented to adult relationships, both conventional and criminal. They recognized more fully that opportunities, as they existed, were provided and controlled by adults, and they sought to exploit adult relationships as best they could. A significant and expected exception was that addicts had relatively poorer relationships to racketeers and neighborhood adults than delinquents in the racket subcultural area. The particularly close personal relationship of drug addicts to mothers confirmed the findings of another study (9).

Drug addicts from one type of neighborhood were rarely in contact with addicts from another type of area, except occasionally at the point of drug purchase, or in treatment hospitals or jails. They did not feel a strong sense of identity with addicts elsewhere. Their interactions, aspirations, values, and general life-style were rooted in the subcultural area in which they lived or to which they attached themselves.

The status of drug addict was neither desirable nor acceptable to either addicts or non-addicts. Much effort was exercised to conceal the fact of addiction, which was commonly recognized as indicative of personal weakness and failure. Addicts looked forward to the time when they would no longer be addicted or would be able better to control their drug intake. Drug addicts and users expected and sometimes were able to participate to varying degrees in the pursuit of some desired criminal or conventional adult career.

Summary

In summary, each neighborhood seemed to provide social pressures and different opportunities for the development of distinctive and characteristic types of delinquent subcultures. In one kind of area, the presence of an integrated and well-organized criminal system offered learning environments which eventuated in certain types of behavior in preparation for later careers in the rackets. In the second area, the extremely limited availability of legitimate and illegitimate means seemed to make for the development of a temporary adolescent alternate status-giving system—gang-fighting. In the third type of area, the presence of partial opportunities, legitimate and illegitimate, within the context of a neighborhood commitment to conventional norms seemed to make for a theft orientation, which could be useful preparation for later careers as professional and semi-professional thieves. The delinquent orientation of the drug addict was a specialized post-adolescent adaptation occurring in the three kinds of neighborhood and stemming in part from the same socioeconomic pressures which earlier had produced the delinquent adaptations and in part from socio-cultural pressures of transition from adolescence to adulthood.

DISCUSSION OF FINDINGS AND IMPLICATIONS FOR SOCIAL WORK

This has been a report of an exploratory research which requires replication and testing on a much larger scale. Until this testing is done the reliability and validity of the findings are open to question. Yet the results of the investigation do tempt one to speculate about applications to social work practice. It is possible that different emphases and limits in the social work role are found in each neighborhood.

The Racket Subculture

The neighborhood youth worker will probably be least effective in his efforts to change the behavior of the delinquent group from the racket subcultural area as long as the parent-neighborhood orientation with its criminal cultural and social structures continues to persist and spawn a youth subculture in its own image. Vigorous uncorrupted community action, mainly by law enforcement agencies, is required to curb the influence of the racketeer. Perhaps, as some have suggested in light of the experience of other countries, consideration should be given to making legitimate certain enterprises presently incorporated in the illegitimate opportunity structure, thus legalizing off-track betting, creating local, state, and national lotteries, and distributing narcotic drugs to addicts under specific conditions. The major strategy to be employed in modifying the criminal value system of this kind of subculture is the destruction of the illegitimate opportunity structure or at least the reduction of its influence.

It is unlikely that the cultural norms of the larger society have been completely eliminated in the racket dominated neighborhood. Some measure of the conventional value system remains and may induce "personality tensions and conflict" (11, p. 136, note 7). The social worker may find himself able to utilize his counseling skills and his understanding of the dynamics of human behavior under pressure of value conflicts to assist the troubled individual to resolve problems of personal and social adjustment in a manner that is both beneficial to himself and more useful to society. However, this can be only a secondary approach, which constitutes in no measure any major assault on the criminal system which supports delinquent values and behavior in this kind of neighborhood.

The Conflict Subculture

It is, perhaps, unlikely that social work, through either casework or group work (or street-club work) or combinations of these methods, even on a large scale, will affect substantially the character or reduce the incidence of gang-fighting in the neighborhood containing the conflict subculture. At best, the social worker's efforts are supplementary. They provide a measure of restraint or control on the rate of spread of this kind of antisocial behavior. Through its own body of skills and knowledge, social work probably cannot offer a significant program of prevention. Social service approaches alone do not constitute the addition of a major opportunity system in the neighborhood. Social caseworkers and social group workers strive primarily to enhance substantive opportunities which must be present already. To say this is not to deny the extreme importance for social workers to persist in their efforts, and indeed to augment them, in building bridges to the meager conventional means available. It points to the particular importance of community organization and developmental efforts encouraging maximum contribution of local and city-wide resources to the area. However, only as the larger conventional society opens the floodgates of opportunity and provides a massive program whereby adequate schooling, good jobs, better housing, and health and social services of a broad range and high quality are more fully available to low-status groups will delinquency of the conflict variety drastically be diminished or transformed.

The Theft Subculture

Perhaps social work can make its major contribution in efforts toward modification of the delinquent theft orientation. When a major campaign to eradicate a racket structure is not required, when at least partial access to conventional means exists, and when the dominant neighborhood orientation is legitimate, the task of rehabilitating the delinquent may fall more substantially within the scope of the ample deployment of a variety of social services. The social worker can be called on to reorient and redirect the delinquent, his group, his family, and his neighborhood in the most effective use and development of the inner resources of people and the external resources in the neighborhood. In particular, the delinquent and his group need intensive counseling and environmental support so that optimum use is made of the personality strengths, conventional interpersonal relationships, and the external structural means which exist.

Narcotic Addict Orientations

In the measure that the addict is a former delinquent, efforts directed at the alleviation of pressures producing different types of delinquent subcultures also reduce the incidence of this adaptation. However, it is unlikely that the problem of addiction for the post-adolescent gang member may be more than partially amenable to the influence of the social worker. It is possible that a recognition of the adjustive function of drugs will enable the worker to focus on and support the positive efforts made by the addict to get and hold a job, to stabilize marriage and family relationships, as well as to cut down on drug consumption. Perhaps further social breakdown and psychological deterioration may be mitigated through a rational and controlled system of medical distribution of drugs to addicts.

Finally, attention must be given by social workers to the improvement of the social and economic conditions of the delinquency-producing lower-class population on both an absolute and a relative basis. What is recommended is not merely the provision of legitimate opportunities as such, but the provision of legitimate opportunities in such a way that the expectations of individuals more closely accord with culturally induced aspirations. In other words, the race for success increasingly has to be equalized by the provision of adequate means to all the contenders for success. Lower-class persons must not only have more opportunity now or at a future time to achieve success goals, they must have as much opportunity as persons from other class locations to attain significant status in society. Also desirable is some redefinition of success goals with increased cultural emphasis on the goal of fulfillment of the intellectual, artistic, spiritual, and creative capacities of people and less emphasis on the goal of achievement purely in terms of money and material things.

Clearly implied in the present research is the possible future utilization of anomie and differential opportunity theories for the development of problem typologies that will ultimately be of use in prevention, treatment, and control programs. Anomie and differential opportunity theory may fruitfully be incorporated into the larger body of social work theory, alongside or integrated with psychoanalytic theory in order to achieve a fuller understanding of socially incapacitated neighborhoods, deviant social types, and disordered personalities.

Bibliography

1. Cloward, Richard A. "Illegitimate Means, Anomie, and Deviant Behavior," *American Sociological Review*, 24 (April, 1959), 164–176.

2. Cloward, Richard A., and Ohlin, Lloyd E. *Delinquency and Opportunity*. Glencoe, Ill.: Free Press, 1960.

3. ———. "Types of Delinquent Subcultures." New York: New York School of Social Work of Columbia University, December, 1958. Mimeographed.

4. Cohen, Albert K. *Delinquent Boys: The Culture of the Gang*. Glencoe, Ill.: Free Press, 1955.

5. ———. "Juvenile Delinquency and Social Structure." Unpublished Ph.D. dissertation, Harvard University, 1951.

6. Cohen, Albert K., and Short, James F., Jr. "Research in Delinquent Subcultures," *Journal of Social Issues*, 14, No. 3 (1958), 20–37.

7. Crawford, Paul L., Malamud, Daniel I., and Dumpson, James R. *Working with Teen Age Gangs*. New York: Welfare Council of New York City, 1950.

8. Durkheim, Emile. *Suicide: A Study in Sociology*. Trans. John A. Spaulding and George Simpson. Glencoe, Ill.: Free Press, 1951.

9. Gerard, Donald L., et al. *Post Hospitalization Adjustment: A Follow-Up Study of Adolescent Opiate Addicts*. New York: New York University Research Center for Human Relations, October, 1955.

10. Kobrin, Solomon. "The Conflict of Values in Delinquency Areas," *American Sociological Review*, 16 (October, 1951), 653–661.

11. Merton, Robert K. *Social Theory and Social Structure*. Rev. ed. Glencoe, Ill.: Free Press, 1957.

12. Miller, Walter B. "Lower Class Culture as a Generating Milieu of Gang Delinquency," *Journal of Social Issues,* 14, No. 3 (1958), 5–19.
13. Moles, Oliver, Jr., Lippitt, Ronald, and Withey, Stephen B. *A Selective Review of Research and Theories Concerning the Dynamics of Delinqueny.* Ann Arbor, Michigan: Institute for Social Research, University of Michigan, September, 1959.
14. Shaw, Clifford R. *Brothers in Crime.* Chicago: University of Chicago Press, 1938.
15. ———. *Delinquency Areas.* Chicago: University of Chicago Press, 1929.
16. ———. *The Jack Roller.* Chicago: University of Chicago Press, 1930.
17. ———. *The Natural History of a Delinquent Career.* Chicago: University of Chicago Press, 1931.
18. Shaw, Clifford R., and McKay, Henry D. *Juvenile Delinquency and Urban Areas.* Chicago: University of Chicago Press, 1942.
19. Sutherland, Edwin H. *The Professional Thief.* Chicago: University of Chicago Press, 1937.
20. Sutherland, Edwin H., and Cressey, Donald R. *Principles of Criminology.* 5th ed. rev. Philadelphia: Lippincott Co., 1955.
21. Thrasher, Frederic M. *The Gang.* Chicago: University of Chicago Press, 1936.
22. Whyte, William F. *Street Corner Society.* Enl. ed. Chicago: University of Chicago Press, 1955.

22. The Delinquent Gang as a Near-Group

LEWIS YABLONSKY

This paper is based on four years of research and direct work with some 30 delinquent gangs in New York City. During this period I directed a crime prevention program on the upper West Side of Manhattan for Morningside Heights, Inc., a community social agency sponsored by 14 major institutions including Columbia University, Barnard, Teacher's College, Union Theological Seminary, and Riverside Church.

Approaches used in data gathering included field study methods, participant observation, role-playing, group interaction analysis, and sociometry. The data were obtained through close daily interaction with gang boys over the four-year period during which I was the director of the project.

Although data were obtained on 30 gangs, the study focused on two, the Balkans and the Egyptian Kings. It was the latter which committed the brutal killing of a polio victim, Michael Farmer, in an upper west side park of

* This is a revised version of a paper delivered at The Eastern Sociological Meetings in New York City, April 11, 1959. The theory of near-groups and gang data presented in this paper is part of a forthcoming volume on gangs by the author.

New York City. The trial lasted over three months and received nation-wide attention. These two groups were intensively interviewed and contributed heavily to the formulation of a theory of near-groups. In addition to the analysis of the gang's structure, a number of delinquent gang war events produced vital case material.

There is a paucity of available theory based on empirical evidence about the structure of delinquent gangs. Two landmarks in the field are Thrasher's *The Gang* and Whyte's *Street Corner Society*. Some recent publications and controversy focus on the emergence of gangs and their function for gang members. Professor Cohen deals with gangs as sub-cultures organized by working-class boys as a reaction to middle-class values (1). In a recent publication Block and Nederhoffer discuss gangs as organizations designed to satisfy the adolescent's striving for the attainment of adult status (2).

Although partial group structuring has been extensively discussed in sociological literature on "groups," "crowds," and "mobs," my gang research revealed that these collectivity constructs did not seem to adequately describe and properly abstract the un-

SOURCE. Lewis Yablonsky, "The Delinquent Gang as a Near-Group," from *Social Problems*, Volume 7, No. 2, Fall 1959, pp. 108–117. Reprinted with the permission of the Society for the Study of Social Problems and the author.

derlying structural characteristics of the delinquent gang. Consequently, I have attempted here to construct a formulation which would draw together various described social dimensions of the gang under one conceptual scheme. I call this formulation Near-Group Theory.

NEAR-GROUP THEORY

One way of viewing human collectivities is on a continuum of organization characteristics. At one extreme, we have a highly organized, cohesive, functioning collection of individuals as members of a sociological group. At the other extreme, we have a mob of individuals characterized by anonymity, disturbed leadership, motivated by emotion, and in some cases representing a destructive collectivity within the inclusive social system. When these structures are observed in extreme, their form is apparent to the observer. However, in viewing these social structures on a continuum, those formations which tend to be neither quite a cohesive integrated group nor a disturbed malfunctioning mob or crowd are often distorted by observers in one or the other direction.

A central thesis of this paper is that mid-way on the group-mob continuum are collectivities which are neither groups nor mobs. These are structures prevalent enough in a social system to command attention in their own right as constructs for sociological analysis. Near-groups are characterized by some of the following factors: (1) diffuse role definition, (2) limited cohesion, (3) impermanence, (4) minimal consensus of norms, (5) shifting membership, (6) disturbed leadership, and (7) limited definition of membership expectations. These factors characterize the near-group's "normal" structure.

True groups may manifest near-group structure under stress, in transi-

tion, or when temporarily disorganized; however, at these times they are moving toward or away from their normative, permanent structure. The near-group manifests its homeostasis in accord with the factors indicated. It never fully becomes a *group* or a *mob*.

THE GANG AS A NEAR-GROUP PATTERN

Some recent sociological theory and discourse on gangs suffers from distortions of gang structure to fit a group rather than a near-group conception. Most gang theorizing begins with an automatic assumption that gangs are defined sociological groups. Many of these misconceived theories about gangs in sociological treatises are derived from the popular and traditional image of gangs held by the general public as reported in the press, rather than as based upon empirical scientific investigation. The following case material reveals the disparities between popular reports of gang war behavior and their organization as revealed by more systematic study.

The official report of a gang fight, which made headlines in New York papers as the biggest in the city's history, detailed a gang war between six gangs over a territorial dispute.* The police, social workers, the press, and the public accepted a defined version of groups meeting in battle over territory. Research into this gang war incident, utilizing a near-group concept of gangs, indicates another picture of the situation.

N. Y. DAILY NEWS

NIP 200—PUNK FIGHT NEAR
COLUMBIA CAMPUS
by Grover Ryder and Jack Smee

A flying squad of 25 cops, alerted by a civilian's tip, broke up the makings of one

* New York Newspaper Headlines—June 11, 1955.

of the biggest gang rumbles in the city's turbulent teen history last night at the edge of Columbia University campus on Morningside Heights.

N. Y. HERALD TRIBUNE

POLICE SEIZE 38, AVERT GANG BATTLE—RIVERSIDE PARK RULE WAS GOAL

Police broke up what they said might have been "a very serious" battle between two juvenile factions last night as they intercepted thirty-eight youths.

N. Y. TIMES

GANG WAR OVER PARK BROKEN BY POLICE

The West Side police broke up an impending gang fight near Columbia University last night as 200 teen-agers were massing for battle over exclusive rights to the use of Riverside Park.

N. Y. JOURNAL-AMERICAN

6-GANG BATTLE FOR PARK AVERTED NEAR GRANT'S TOMB COPS PATROL TROUBLE SPOT

Police reinforcements today patrolled Morningside Heights to prevent a teenaged gang war for "control" of Riverside Park.

WORLD-TELEGRAM AND SUN

HOODLUM WAR AVERTED AS COPS ACT FAST
38 to 200 Seized near Columbia
by Richard Graf

Fast police action averted what threatened to be one of the biggest street gang fights in the city's history as some 200 hoodlums massed last night on the upper West Side to battle over "exclusive rights" to Riverside Park.

Depth interviews with 40 gang boys, most of whom had been arrested at the scene of the gang fight, revealed a variety of reasons for attendance at the battle. There were also varied perceptions of the event and the gangs involved reported simply in the press

as "gangs battling over territory." Some of the following recurring themes were revealed in the gang boys' responses.

Estimates of number of gang boys present varied from 80 to 5,000.

Gang boys interviewed explained their presence at the "battle" as follows:

I didn't have anything to do that night and wanted to see what was going to happen.

Those guys called me a Spic and I was going to get even. [He made this comment even though the "rival" gangs were mostly Puerto Ricans.]

They always picked on us. [The "they" is usually a vague reference.]

I always like a fight; it keeps up my rep.

My father threw me out of the house; I wanted to get somebody and heard about the fight.

The youth who was responsible for "calling on" the gang war—the reputed Balkan Gang leader—presented this version of the event:

That night I was out walkin' my dog about 7:30. Then I saw all these guys coming from different directions. I couldn't figure out what was happening. Then I saw some of the guys I know and I remembered we had called it on for that night.

I never really figured the Politicians [a supposed "brother Gang" he had called] would show.

Another boy added another dimension to "gang war organization":

How did we get our name? Well, when we were in the police station, the cops kept askin' us who we were. Jay was studying history in school—so he said how about The Balkans. Let's call ourselves Balkans. So we told the cops—we're the Balkans—and that was it.

Extensive data revealed this was not a case of two organized groups meeting in battle. The press, public, police, social workers, and others · projected group conceptions onto a near-group activity. Most of the youths at the scene of the gang war were, in fact, participating in a kind of mob action. Most had no real concept of belonging to any gang or group; however, they were interested in a situation which might be exciting and possibly a channel for expressing some of their aggressions and hostilities. Although it was not necessarily a defined war, the possibilities of a stabbing or even a killing were high —with a few hundred disturbed and fearful youths milling around in the undefined situation. The gang war was not a social situation of two structured teen-aged armies meeting on a battle-field to act out a defined situation; it was a case of two near-groups in action.

Another boy's participation in this gang war further reveals its structure. The evening of the fight he had nothing to do, heard about this event, and decided that he would wander up to see what was going to happen. On his way to the scene of the rumored gang fight he thought it might be a good idea to invite a few friends "just to be on the safe side." This swelled the final number of youths arriving at the scene of the gang fight, since other boys did the same. He denied (and I had no reason to disbelieve him) belonging to either of the gangs, and the same applied to his friends. He was arrested at the scene of "battle" for disorderly conduct and weapon-carrying.

I asked him why he had carried a knife and a zip gun on his person when he went to the gang fight if he did not belong to either of the reputed gangs and intended to be merely a "peaceful observer." His response: "Man, I'm not going to a rumble without packin'." The boy took along weapons for self-defense in the event he was attacked. The possibilities of his being attacked in an hysterical situation involving hundreds of youths who had no clear idea of what they were doing at the scene of a gang fight was, of course, great. Therefore, he was correct (within his social framework) in taking along a weapon for self-protection.

These characteristic responses to the situation when multiplied by the numbers of others present characterizes the problem. What may be a confused situation involving many aggressive youths (belonging to near-groups) is often defined as a case of two highly mechanized and organized gang groups battling each other with definition to their activities.

In another "gang war case" which made headlines, a psychotic youth acted out his syndrome by stabbing another youth. When arrested and questioned about committing the offense, the youth stated that he was a member of a gang carrying out retaliation against another gang which was out to get him. He attributed his assault to gang affiliation.

The psychotic youth used the malleable near-group, the gang, *as his psychotic* syndrome. Napoleon, God, Christ, and other psychotic syndromes, so popular over the years, may have been replaced on city streets by gang membership. Not only is it a convenient syndrome, but some disturbed youths find their behavior as rational, accepted, and even aggrandized by many representatives of society. Officials such as police officers and social workers, in their interpretation of the incident, often amplify this individual behavior by a youth into a group gang war condition because it is a seemingly more logical explanation of a senseless act.

In the case of the Balkans, the societal response of viewing them as a group rather than a near-group solidified their structure. After the incident, as one leader stated it, "lots more kids wanted to join."

Another gang war event further reveals the near-group structure of the gang. On the night of July 30, 1957, a polio victim named Michael Farmer was beaten and stabbed to death by a gang varyingly known as the Egyptian Kings and the Dragons. The boys who participated in this homicide came from the upper West Side of Manhattan. I had contact with many of these boys prior to the event and was known to others through the community program I directed. Because of this prior relationship the boys cooperated and responded openly when I interviewed them in the institutions where they were being held in custody.*

Responses to my interviews indicated the near-group nature of the gang. Some of the pertinent responses which reveal this characteristic of the Egyptian King gang structure are somewhat demonstrated by the following comments made by five of the participants in the killing. (These are representative comments selected from over ten hours of recorded interviews.)

I was walking uptown with a couple of friends and we ran into Magician [one of the Egyptian King gang leaders] and them there. They asked us if we wanted to go to a fight, and we said yes. When he asked me if I wanted to go to a fight, I couldn't say no. I mean, I could say no, but for old time's sake, I said yes.

Everyone was pushin' and I pulled out my knife. I saw this face—I never seen it before, so I stabbed it.

He was laying on the ground lookin' up at us. Everyone was kicking, punching, stabbing. I kicked him on the jaw

* The research and interviewing at this time was combined with my role as consultant to the Columbia Broadcasting System. I assisted in the production of a gang war documentary narrated by Edward R. Murrow, entitled "Who Killed Michael Farmer?" The documentary tells the story of the killing through the actual voices of the boys who committed the act.

or someplace; then I kicked him in the stomach. That was the least I could do was kick 'im.

They have guys watching you and if you don't stab or hit somebody, they get you later. I hit him over the head with a bat. [Gang youths are unable to articulate specific individuals of the vague "they" who watch over them.]

I don't know how many guys are in the gang. They tell me maybe a hundred or a thousand. I don't know them all. [Each boy interviewed had a different image of the gang.]

These comments and others revealed the gang youths' somewhat different perceptions and rationale of gang war activity. There is a limited consensus of participants as to the nature of gang war situations because the gang structure—the collectivity which defines gang war behavior—is amorphous, diffuse, and malleable.

Despite the fact of gang phenomena taking a diffuse form, theoreticians, social workers, the police, the press, and the public autistically distort gangs and gang behavior toward a gestalt of clarity. The rigid frame of perceiving gangs as groups should shift to the fact of gangs as near-groups. This basic redefinition is necessary if progress is to be made in sociological diagnosis as a foundation for delinquent gang prevention and correction.

THE DETACHED GANG WORKER

The detached-worker approach to dealing with gangs on the action level is increasingly employed in large cities and urban areas throughout the country. Simply stated, a professional, usually a social worker, contacts a gang in their milieu on the street corner and attempts to redirect their delinquent patterns into constructive behavior.

Because of the absence of an adequate perceptual framework, such as the near-group concept, detached gang workers deal with gang collectivities as if they were organized like other groups and social organizations. The following principle stated in a New York City Youth Board manual on the detached gang worker approach reveals this point of view:

> Participation in a street gang or club, like participation in any natural group, is a part of the growing-up process of adolescence. Such primary group associations possess potentialities for positive growth and development. Through such a group, the individual can gain security and develop positive ways of living with other individuals. Within the structure of his group the individual can develop such characteristics as loyalty, leadership, and community responsibility (3, p. 107).

This basic misconception not only produces inaccurate reports and theories about gang structure but causes ineffectual work with gangs on the action level. This problem of projecting group structure onto gangs may be further illuminated by a cursory examination of detached gang-worker projects.

Approaching the gang as a group, when it is not, tends to project onto it a structure which formerly did not exist. The gang worker's usual set of notions about gangs as groups includes some of the following distortions: (1) the gang has a measurable number of members, (2) membership is defined, (3) the role of members is specified, (4) there is a consensus of understood gang norms among gang members, and (5) gang leadership is clear and entails a flow of authority and direction of action.

These expectations often result in a group-fulfilling prophecy. A group may form as a consequence of the gang worker's view. In one case a gang worker approached two reputed gang leaders and told them he would have a bus to take their gang on a trip to the country. This gang had limited organization; however, by travel-time there were 32 gang members ready to go on the trip. The near-group became more organized as a result of the gang worker's misconception.

This gang from a near-group point of view was in reality comprised of a few disturbed youths with rich delusional systems who had need to view themselves as leaders controlling hordes of other gang boys in their fantasy. Other youths reinforce this ill-defined collectivity for a variety of personal reasons and needs. The gang, in fact, had a shifting membership, no clarity as to what membership entailed, and individualized member images of gang size and function.

The detached worker, as an agent of the formal social system, may thus move in on a gang and give a formerly amorphous collectivity structure and purpose through the projection of group structure onto a near-group.

NEAR-GROUP STRUCTURE

Research into the structure of 30 groups revealed three characteristic levels of membership organization. In the center of the gang, on the first level, are the most psychologically disturbed members—the leaders. It is these youths who require and need the gang most of all. This core of disturbed youths provides the gang's most cohesive force. In a gang of some 30 boys there may be five or six who are central or core members because they desperately need the gang in order to deal with their personal problems of inadequacy. These are youths always working to keep the gang together and in action, always drafting, plotting, and talking gang warfare. They are the center of the near-group activity.

At a second level of near-group organization in the gang, we have youths who claim affiliation to the gang but only participate in it according to their emotional needs at given times. For example, one of the Egyptian Kings reported that if his father had not given him a "bad time" and kicked him out of the house the night of the homicide, he would not have gone to the corner and become involved in the Michael Farmer killing. This second-level gang member's participation in the gang killing was a function of his disturbance on that particular evening. This temporal gang need is a usual occurrence.

At a third level of gang participation, we have peripheral members who will join in with gang activity on occasion, although they seldom identify themselves as members of the gang at times. This type of gang member is illustrated by the youth who went along with the Egyptian Kings on the night of the Farmer killing, as he put it, "for old time's sake." He just happened to be around on that particular evening and went along due to a situational condition. He never really "belonged" to the gang nor was he defined by himself or others as a gang member.

The size of gangs is determined in great measure by the emotional needs of its members at any given point. It is not a measure of actual and live membership. Many of the members exist only on the thought level. In the gang, if the boys feel particularly hemmed in (for paranoid reasons), they will expand the number of their near-group. On the other hand, at other times when they feel secure, the gang's size is reduced to include only those youths known on a face-to-face basis. The research revealed that, unlike an actual group, no member of a near-group can accurately determine the number of its membership at a particular point in time.

For example, most any university department member will tell you the number of other individuals who comprise the faculty of their department. It is apparent that if there are eight members in a department of psychology, each member will know each other member, his role, and the total number of members of the department. In contrast, in examining the size of gangs or near-group participation, the size increases in almost direct relationship to the lack of membership clarity. That is, the second- and third-level members are modified numerically with greater ease than the central members. Third-level members are distorted at times to an almost infinite number.

In one interview, a gang leader distorted the size and affiliations of the gang as his emotional state shifted. In an hour interview, the size of his gang varied from 100 members to 4,000, from five brother gangs or alliances to 60, from about ten square blocks of territorial control to include jurisdiction over the five boroughs of New York City, New Jersey, and part of Philadelphia.

Another characteristic of the gang is its lack of role definition. Gang boys exhibit considerable difficulty and contradiction in their roles in the gang. They may say that the gang is organized for protection and that one role of a gang is to fight. How, when, whom, and for what reason he is to fight are seldom clear. The right duties and obligations associated with the gang member's role in the gang vary from gang boy to gang boy.

One gang boy may define himself as a protector of the younger boys in the neighborhood. Another defines his role in the gang as "We are going to get all those guys who call us Spics." Still other gang boys define their participation in the gang as involuntarily forced upon them, through their being "drafted." Moreover, few gang members maintain a consistent function or role within the gang organization.

Definition of membership is vague and indefinite. A youth will say he belongs one day and will quit the next without necessarily telling any other gang member. I would ask one gang boy who came into my office daily whether he was a Balkan. This was comparable to asking him, "How do you feel today?"

Because of limited social ability to assume rights, duties, and obligations in constructive solidified groups, the gang boy attaches himself to a structure which requires limited social ability and can itself be modified to fit his monetary needs. This malleability factor is characteristic of the near-group membership. As roles are building blocks of a group, diffuse role definitions fit in adequately to the near-group which itself has diverse and diffuse objectives and goals. The near-group, unlike a true group, has norms, roles, functions, cohesion, size, and goals which are shaped by the emotional needs of its members.

GANG LEADERSHIP CHARACTERISTICS

Another aspect of near-groups is the factor of self-appointed leadership, usually of a dictatorial, authoritarian type. In interviewing hundreds of gang members, one finds that many of them give themselves some role of leadership. For example, in the Egyptian Kings, approximately five boys defined themselves as "war counselors." It is equally apparent that, except on specific occasions, no one will argue with this self-defined role. Consequently, leadership in the gang may be assumed by practically any member of the gang if he so determines and emotionally needs the power of being a leader at the time. It is not necessary to have his leadership role ratified by his constituents.

Another aspect of leadership in the gang is the procedure of "drafting" or enlisting new members. In many instances, this pattern of coercion to get another youth to join or belong to the gang becomes an end in itself, rather than a means to an end. In short, the process of inducing, coercing, and threatening violence upon another youth, under the guise of getting him to join, is an important gang leader activity. The gang boy is not truly concerned with acquiring another gang member, since the meaning of membership is vague at best; however, acting the power role of a leader forcing another youth to do something against his will becomes meaningful to the "drafter."

GANG FUNCTIONS

In most groups some function is performed or believed to be performed. The function which it performs may be a constructive one, as in an industrial organization, a P.T.A. group, or a political party. On the other hand, it may be a socially destructive group, such as a drug syndicate, a group of bookies, or a subversive political party. There is usually a consensus of objectives and goals shared by the membership, and their behavior tends to be essentially organized group action.

The structure of a near-group is such that not only do its functions vary greatly and shift considerably from time to time, but its primary function is unclear. The gang may on one occasion be organized to protect the neighborhood; on another occasion, to take over a particular territory; and on still another, it may be organized in response to or for the purpose of racial discrimination.

The function of near-groups, moreover, is not one which is clearly understood, known, and communicated among all of its members. There is no consensus in this near-group of goals, objectives, or functions of the collectivity—much near-group behavior is individualistic and flows from emotional disturbance.

A prime function of the gang is to

provide a channel to act out hostility and aggression to satisfy the continuing and momentary emotional needs of its members. The gang is a convenient and malleable structure quickly adaptable to the needs of emotionally disturbed youths, who are unable to fulfill the responsibility and demands required for participation in constructive groups. A boy belongs to the gang because he lacks the social ability to relate to others and to assume responsibility for the relationship, not because the gang gives him a "feeling of belonging."

Because of the gang youth's limited "social ability," he constructs a social organization which enables him to relate and to function at his limited level of performance. In this structure norms are adjusted so that the gang youth can function and achieve despite his limited ability to relate to others.

An example of this is the function of violence in the near-group of the gang. Violence in the gang is highly valued as a means for the achievement of reputation or "rep." This inversion of societal norms is a means for quick upward social mobility in the gang. He can acquire and maintain a position in the gang through establishing a violent reputation.

The following comments by members of the Egyptian Kings illustrate this point:

If I would of got the knife, I would have stabbed him. That would have gave me more of a build-up. People would have respected me for what I've done and things like that. They would say, "There goes a cold killer."

It makes you feel like a big shot. You know some guys think they're big shots and all that. They think, you know, they got the power to do everything they feel like doing.

They say, like, "I wanna stab a guy," and the other guy says, "Oh, I wouldn't dare to do that." You know, he thinks I'm acting like a big shot. That's the way he feels. He probably thinks in his mind, "Oh, he probably won't do that." Then, when we go to a fight, you know, he finds out what I do.

Momentarily, I started to thinking about it inside: den I have my mind made up I'm not going to be in no gang. Then I go on inside. Something comes up den here come all my friends coming to me. Like I said before, I'm intelligent and so forth. They be coming to me—then they talk to me about what they gonna do. Like, "Man, we'll go out here and kill this guy." I say, "Yeah." They kept on talkin' and talkin.' I said, "Man, I just gotta go with you." Myself, I don't want to go, but when they start talkin' about what they gonna do, I say, "So, he isn't gonna take over my rep. I ain't gonna let him be known more than me." And I go ahead just for selfishness.

The near-group of the gang, with its diffuse and malleable structure, can function as a convenient vehicle for the acting out of varied individual needs and problems. For the gang leader it can be a super-powered organization through which (in his phantasy) he dominates and controls "divisions" of thousands of members. For gang members, unable to achieve in more demanding social organizations, swift and sudden violence is a means for quick upward social mobility and the achievement of a reputation. For less disturbed youths, the gang may function as a convenient temporary escape from the dull and rigid requirements of a difficult and demanding society. These are only some of the functions the near-group of the gang performs for its membership.

NEAR-GROUP THEORY AND SOCIAL PROBLEMS

The concept of the near-group may be of importance in the analysis of other collectivities which reflect and produce social problems. The analysis of other social structures may reveal similar distortions of their organization. To operate on an assumption of individuals in interaction with each other, around some function, with some shared mutual expectation, in a particular normative system as always being a group formation is to project a degree of distortion onto certain types of collectivities. Groups are social structures at one end of a continuum; mobs are social structures at another end; and at the center are near-groups which have some of the characteristics of both, and yet are characterized by factors not found fully in either.

In summary, these factors may include the following:

1. Individualized role definition to fit momentary needs.

2. Diffuse and differential definitions of membership.

3. Emotion-motivated behavior.

4. A decrease of cohesiveness as one moves from the center of the collectivity to the periphery.

5. Limited responsibility and sociability required for membership and belonging.

6. Self-appointed and disturbed leadership.

7. A limited consensus among participants of the collectivities' functions or goals.

8. A shifting and personalized stratification system.

9. Shifting membership.

10. The inclusion in size of phantasy membership.

11. Limited consensus of normative expectations.

12. Norms in conflict with the inclusive social system's prescriptions.

Although the gang was the primary type of near-group appraised in this analysis, there are perhaps other collectivities whose structure is distorted by autistic observers. Their organization might become clearer if subjected to this conceptual scheme. Specifically, in the area of criminal behavior, these might very well include adult gangs varyingly called the "Mafia," the "National Crime Syndicate," and so-called International Crime Cartels. There are indications that these social organizations are comparable in organization to the delinquent gang. They might fit the near-group category if closely analyzed in this context, rather than aggrandized and distorted by mass media and even Senate Committees.

Other more institutionalized collectivities might fit the near-group pattern. As a possible example, "the family in transition" may not be in transition at all. The family, as a social institution, may be suffering from near-groupism. Moreover, such standardized escape hatches as alcoholism, psychoses, and addictions may be too prosaic for the sophisticated intellectual to utilize in escape from himself. For him, the creation and perpetuation of near-groups requiring limited responsibility and personal commitment may be a more attractive contemporary form for expressing social and personal pathology. The measure of organization or disorganization of an inclusive social system may possibly be assessed by the prevalence of near-group collectivities in its midst. The delinquent gang may be only one type of near-group in American society.

References

1. Cohen, Albert K., *Delinquent Boys* (Glencoe: The Free Press, 1955).
2. Bloch, Herbert, and Arthur Niederhoffer, *The Gang* (New York: The Philosophical Library, 1958).
3. Furman, Slyvan S., *Reaching the Unreached* (New York: Youth Board, 1952).

23. Field Observations of Middle Class "Gangs"

HOWARD L. MYERHOFF AND BARBARA G. MYERHOFF

The sociological literature about gangs contains at least two sharply conflicting descriptions of the extent of gang structure and the nature of their values. In the most prevalent view, the gang is seen as a kind of primary group, highly structured, relatively permanent and autonomous, possessing a well-developed delinquent subculture which is transmitted to new members. The gang is interpreted as meeting strongly felt needs of its members and as providing a collectively derived solution to common problems of adjustment. Different writers who hold this view have stressed different problems, but nearly all have agreed that one of the most important functions of the gang is to establish close bonds of loyalty and solidarity between members of a tightly knit peer group.

Cohen[1] has identified the primary needs met by the gang as those of resolving status frustration for lower class boys, and providing an expression of masculine identification for middle class boys. Parsons[2] has also emphasized the achievement of sexual identity as a problem dealt with by delinquent behavior. Cloward and Ohlin,[3] following Merton's conception, have specified the discrepancy between aspirations toward success goals and opportunities for achieving them as the problem giving rise to gang behavior. Kvaraceus and Miller[4] have stressed the inherent

* The observations reported in this paper were carried out as part of a Youth Studies Center developmental project, which ultimately led to an action-research program concerned with the treatment of delinquent gangs. Both the developmental project and the action-research program, now in process, received support from the Ford Foundation. The authors would like to thank A. W. McEachern of the Youth Studies Center, University of Southern California, for his generous and valuable assistance, criticism, and encouragement. A shorter version of this paper was read at the annual meeting of the Pacific Sociological Association in Sacramento, April 1962.

[1] Albert K. Cohen, *Delinquent Boys: The Culture of the Gang* (Glencoe: Free Press, 1955).

[2] Talcott Parsons, "Certain Primary Sources and Patterns of Aggression in the Social Structure of the Western World," reprinted in Mullahy (Ed.), *A Study of Interpersonal Relations* (New York: Grove Press, Evergreen Edition, 1949).

[3] Richard A. Cloward and Lloyd E. Ohlin, *Delinquency and Opportunity: A Theory of Delinquent Gangs* (Glencoe: Free Press, 1961).

[4] William C. Kvaraceus and Walter B. Miller, *Delinquent Behavior: Culture and the Individual* (Washington, D.C.: National Education Association, 1959).

SOURCE. Howard L. Myerhoff and Barbara G. Myerhoff, "Field Observations of Middle Class 'Gangs,'" from *Social Forces*, Volume 42, March 1964 pp. 328–336. Reprinted with the permission of the University of North Carolina Press.

conflict between lower and middle class values and the delinquent's predisposition to the former in explaining gang behavior. Eisenstadt[5] and Bloch and Niederhoffer[6] have pointed to the gang as a collective response to the adolescent's striving toward the attainment of adulthood and the frustrations attendant on the transition from one age status to another. These authors identify different components of the gang subculture according to their interpretation of its function, but implicit or explicit in all these positions is the view of the gang as an integrated and relatively cohesive group.

A strikingly different interpretation of the structure of gangs describes them as informal, short lived, secondary groups without a clear-cut, stable delinquent structure. Lewis Yablonsky[7] has suggested a conceptualization of the gang as a "near-group," specifying the following definitive characteristics: diffuse role definitions, limited cohesion, impermanence, minimal consensus on norms, shifting membership, emotionally disturbed leaders, and limited definition of membership expectations. On a continuum of the extent of social organization, Yablonsky locates the gang midway between the mob at one end and the group at the other. The gang is seen as in a state of equilibrium, moving sometimes closer to one end of the continuum and sometimes the other, but never actually becoming completely disorganized like a mob or completely organized like a group. He contends that detached worker programs, by treating the gang as a true group, may actually make it one. When a detached worker acknowledges a gang's leaders, recognizes its territory, membership, name, and purpose, he crystallizes its organization, lending it a structure which it did not previously have. This Yablonsky calls the "group-fulfilling prophecy."

The gangs he has observed are, in actuality, quite different from groups. They are "near-groups" which have a diffuse and malleable structure that enables them to meet the varied and individual needs of the members. For many gang members who are unable to meet the demands and responsibilities of more structured social organizations, it is the gang's very lack of organization and absence of expectations which constitute its primary sources of satisfaction. Youths affiliate with a gang not for a feeling of belonging and solidarity but because it is an organization within which they can relate to others in spite of their limited social abilities. The flexibility of gang organization means that it can meet diverse, momentary needs of the members who, accordingly, participate in it with varying intensity. Yablonsky suggests that in a gang there are a few core members, surrounded by a large number of peripheral members to whom the gang is much less important and who are more loosely attached to it.

James F. Short, Jr. objects to Yablonsky's description of the gang as a near-group on the grounds that he has overstated the case,[8] but agrees, never-

[5] S. N. Eisenstadt, *From Generation to Generation: Age Groups and Social Structure* (Glencoe: Free Press, 1956).

[6] Herbert A. Bloch and Arthur Niederhoffer, *The Gang: A Study of Adolescent Behavior* (New York: Philosophical Library, 1958).

[7] Lewis Yablonsky, "The Delinquent Gang as a Near-Group," *Social Problems*, Vol. 7 (Fall 1959), pp. 108–117.

[8] In a recent article Pfautz raised the question of whether Yablonsky's "near-group" concept is necessary. He suggests that Yablonsky's findings could be more productively recast into the theoretical traditions of collective behavior in general and social movements in particular. Certainly, Pfautz's point that this would widen the theoretical relevance of Yablonsky's findings is well-taken. There are two reasons for the authors' preference for the near-group concept rather than a collective behavior orientation: first, an immediate concern with indicating the point by point similarity between these observations and

theless, that gangs do not have "the stability of membership, the tightly knit organization and rigid hierarchical structure which is sometimes attributed to them."[9] Most of the groups he has observed have the kind of shifting membership which Yablonsky described.

The supervisor of a large, long-lived detached worker program in Los Angeles with many years of gang experience there and in Harlem has given a description much like that of Yablonsky.[10] He observed that delinquent gangs seldom act as a corporate group and that most of their anti-social activities are committed in groups of two's or three's, or by a single person. He found communication between members to be meager and sporadic, reflecting the same limitations in social abilities that Yablonsky identified. In fact, one of the goals of his detached worker program is the structuring of gangs into social groups, encouraging cooperation and communication between members and a gradual assumption of social responsibilities. When successful, a detached worker is able to form a gang into a club which elects officers, collects dues, arranges activities, and eventually establishes non-delinquent norms and role expectations. Thus by substituting the satisfactions of membership in an organized social group for delinquent

activities, the program provides an aspect of socialization which gang members have not previously experienced. The program is able, in this way, to prepare gang members to meet the requirements and responsibilities of conventional, adult social life. The technique is apparently the self-conscious application of what Yablonsky has called "the group-fulfilling prophecy," and seems to be quite a successful one.

The field observations presented here are based on the experiences of a participant-observer who spent two weeks among several groups of deviant and non-deviant middle class youths in a suburb of Los Angeles. These observations are particularly pertinent to the prevailing conflicting interpretations of the extent of gang structure. The middle class youngsters described here were located through lists of "hangouts" provided by local police, school authorities, and probation officers. The observer "hung around" these places and when asked who he was, which was seldom, explained that he was a writer doing a series of articles on teenagers. The youngsters talked freely in front of and to the observer, and after a short time included him in many of their activities, such as house and beach parties, drag races, car club meetings, bull sessions, and bowling. Altogether, about eighty youngsters ranging in age between fifteen and eighteen were observed. All were Caucasian, most in high school, Protestant, and in appearance and manner readily distinguishable from the lower class boys and girls who occasionally mixed with them.

Impressions, activities, and conversations were recorded by the observer in a daily journal and roughly classified into the following categories: values and peer interactions, deviant activities, and group organization.[11] It should be

---

those reported by Yablonsky, regardless of the conceptual framework he uses in describing them, and second, the authors' feeling that in view of the fragmented and discontinuous state of the literature on the subject, it is at present more important to compare and relate studies of adolescent collective deviant activities to one another than to more general sociological issues and concepts. Harold W. Pfautz, "Near-Group Theory and Collective Behavior: A Critical Reformulation," *Social Problems*, Vol. 9 (Fall 1961), pp. 167–174.

[9] James F. Short, Jr., "Street Corner Groups and Patterns of Delinquency," A Progress Report from National Institute of Mental Health Research Grant, M-3301 (Chicago, March 1961), p. 20.

[10] Alva Collier, personal communication (Los Angeles, 1961).

[11] These field observations precisely conform to what Zelditch has called Type I information. This consists of incidents

kept in mind that these comments are observations, not findings. Many authors have lamented the dearth of speculation about as well as empirical observations of gangs, in both the middle and lower classes. Cohen and Short recently said about middle class delinquent subcultures: "The saddest commentary, however, is that we are faced with a poverty of speculation, without which there can be no meaningful research, without which, in turn, there can be no conclusions that are more than speculation."[12] These observations and comments lead to some of the speculation which must precede meaningful empirical research, and their greatest value may prove to be heuristic.

VALUES AND PEER INTERACTIONS

The youngsters observed, like most groups of teenagers, were rather uniform in dress and demeanor. Their self-possession and poise, along with elaborate grooming and expensive, well-tended clothes combined to give an impression of urbanity and sophistication beyond what would normally be expected of this age group. For most events, the girls wore tight capris, blouses or cashmere sweaters, silver fingernail and toenail polish, towering intricate coiffeurs, brush-applied iridescent lipstick, and heavy eye make-up. The boys, like the girls, were uniformly clean, and like them preferred their pants as tight as possible; levis were rarely seen. Usually an Ivy League shirt was worn outside the pants and over

this a nylon windbreaker. At beaches both boys and girls wore bikinis, and apparently no one without a deep and even tan ever dared appear. The overall impression fostered was one of careful, elegant casualness sustained in manner as well as appearance. The complete absence of the social and physical awkwardness usually associated with adolescence was indeed striking.

The content of conversation among these groups did not differ appreciably from what one would expect to find among most teenagers; it concerned clothes, dates, sex, school classes and activities, bridge, sports, and so forth. But no subject dominated the conversation as much as the car, which seemed an object of undying, one might say morbid, fascination. The majority of girls and boys owned their own cars and virtually all had access to a car, usually a late model American or foreign sports car. "Custom jobs" were not rare and cars were often "shaved," "chopped," "channeled," and "pinstriped." All were scrupulously clean and highly polished. The argot concerning the car was as elaborate and subtle as one might expect in view of its importance; such matters as "dual quads," "turning seven grand," "slicks," "3:7 trans ratio" were frequently discussed with great intensity. Driving skill and mechanical expertise were prized far above mere ownership of a desirable car.

The car, in fact, permeated every aspect of these youngsters' social life. The size of groups which gathered was usually limited by the number a single car could hold, and when several cars congregated, at drive-ins for example, youngsters demonstrated a distinct unwillingness to leave the car. Radios in cars were never off and all activities took place against a background of popular music. The car also affected

---

and histories, and treats as data the meanings assigned to and explanations given for activities as well as the behavior itself. Morris Zelditch, Jr., "Some Methodological Problems of Field Studies," *American Journal of Sociology,* Vol. 67 (March 1962), pp. 566–576.

[12] Albert K. Cohen and James F. Short, Jr., "Research in Delinquent Subcultures," *Journal of Social Issues,* Vol. 14, No. 3 (1958), p. 34.

the places frequented, with drive-in movies and restaurants preferred. After school and on weekends, many of these youngsters could be seen slowly cruising in their cars, up and down the neighborhood streets, greeting acquaintances, chatting, taking friends for short rides, all with an air of easy sociability. These cruises in manner and purpose were reminiscent of the Spanish late afternoon *Paseo,* in which young people stroll casually up and down streets closed off for that purpose. The cars were the location for nearly all social events engaged in by these youngsters. They were the site of bull sessions, drinking bouts, and necking parties. In all, the car provided a mobile parlor, clubhouse, dining room, and bedroom; it was at once the setting and symbol of much of adolescent deviant and non-deviant sociability and sexuality.

Several writers have emphasized the dominant role of the car in patterns of middle class deviance. Wattenberg and Balistrieri[13] found auto theft to be characteristic of "favored groups," older white boys who had better relations with peers and came from more desirable neighborhoods than did boys charged with other types of offenses. T. C. N. Gibbens[14] studied adolescent car thieves in London and also found them to be a "favored group," not because they lived in better neighborhoods but because they came from homes which were intact and affectionate. All these findings and impressions may be interpreted as supporting the contention of Parsons[15] and Cohen[16]

that the primary middle class problem to which delinquency is a response is the establishment of masculine identity. Indeed, the sexual significance of the car has been widely recognized. Gibbens comments that: "In the simplest cases joy-riding is of the common 'proving' type, in which an overprotected lad from a 'good' home commits an offense to prove his masculinity. . . . The daring act represents a bid for independence, and the car provides a feeling of power in which he feels so lacking. . . ."[17] Certainly, this view is corroborated by the observations of middle class youths offered here, among whom the car, if not a sufficient cause of masculinity, is at least a necessary condition for it.

In view of the importance of the car, it was not surprising to find that the only formal social organizations to which many of these youngsters belonged were car clubs, whose membership often transcended the class and age affiliations typical of the more informal gatherings. These clubs usually consist of about fifteen members and are devoted to the building and legal and illegal racing of cars. In order to be admitted, youngsters' cars must undergo rigorous police safety inspections and members may be expelled or excluded for too many traffic tickets. In marked contrast to the informal groups, these clubs are highly structured. Meetings are regular and frequent, membership is stable, leaders are elected for specified terms, and the clubs have names, plaques, and jackets. The meetings are conducted strictly according to Roberts' Rules of Order, fines are levied for infractions of rules, dues are collected, and events are planned in detail and in advance. A well-developed pattern of mutual aid and extensive cooperation has been established, and it is not

---

13 William W. Wattenberg and James Balistrieri, "Automobile Theft: A 'Favored Group' Delinquency," *American Journal of Sociology,* Vol. 57 (May 1952), pp. 575–579.

14 T. C. N. Gibbens, "Car Thieves," *British Journal of Delinquency,* 7–9 (1957–1959), pp. 257–265.

15 Parsons, *op. cit.*

16 Cohen, *op. cit.*

17 Gibbens, *op. cit.,* p. 262.

unusual for members to pool money, skills, and time to build a car which is entered in races and rallies by the entire group. It is obviously no accident that the only object around which spontaneous, unsupervised yet structured groups form is the car.

DEVIANT ACTIVITIES

The deviant behavior of the groups observed varied greatly in seriousness. Some of their activities may be considered deviant only because technically illegal, such as curfew violation and beer drinking, while more serious infractions such as theft and narcotics are less common. The more serious deviant activities seemed to involve the least number of people at one time; youngsters were alone or with a friend or two on these occasions. The less serious infractions were not usually the purpose of a gathering but were rather incidental to another activity. These included spontaneous drag racing, drinking, and much sexual activity.

Of the more serious violations, theft was certainly the most common. Many boys spoke of frequent and regular stealing, often from employers. Ready access rather than need or desire seemed to determine the choice of stolen objects. These items were seldom traded or converted into cash. Great pride was evidenced in the cleverness with which the thefts were executed and a good performance seemed more important than the acquisition of goods. Several boys boasted about never having been caught although they had been engaging in this activity for years. The stolen goods were by no means small, inexpensive, or easily portable, but included such items as tires, car radios, phonographs, tape recorders, and television sets. Great care was taken in order to ensure that stolen goods were not missed. Thefts were timed so as to coincide with events such as inventories, and the filling of orders.

It is not possible on the basis of these observations to estimate the frequency of these thefts, but one can say with certainty that they were by no means uncommon. This phenomenon appears to be very similar to "white collar crime" and as such raises questions as to the generalizability of theories of delinquency causation based solely on socio-economic variables. As Wattenberg and Balistrieri have pointed out: "The point of impact of the concept of [white collar crime] lies in its assumption that the form of anti-social or illegal conduct rather than its frequency varies from . . . class to class in our society."[18] It may well be that the "white collar delinquent" engages in as many anti-social activities as do lower class youngsters, but a combination of factors, particularly the form of delinquency, interact to prevent these activities from coming to the attention of the authorities, or if apprehended, prevent the middle class youngsters from being officially handled and recorded. Indeed, there is already much evidence to suggest this is the case.[19]

The same discretion, judgment, and self-possession which characterized thefts was observed in the homosexual, and to a lesser degree, the heterosexual gatherings. These events were held in private homes and occasionally included slightly older boys from nearby colleges. They were not events which were likely to attract the attention of police or even parents. The homosexual youngsters often met one another at

[18] Wattenberg and Balistrieri, op. cit., p. 575.

[19] A. L. Porterfield, "Delinquency and Its Outcome in Court and College," American Journal of Sociology, Vol. 48 (1943), pp. 199–208; Ivan F. Nye and James F. Short, Jr., "Scaling Delinquent Behavior," American Sociological Review, Vol. 22 (1957), pp. 326–331.

small cabarets, coffee houses, and bars in which few lower class teenagers or adults were to be seen. They also met in several private clubs whose members were primarily upper and middle class teenage homosexuals. These youngsters were typically inconspicuous and did not indulge in egregious displays of homosexuality either in dress or manner. While in the clubs, many were openly solicitous and flirtatious, but upon leaving, their more conventional manners were resumed. The same caution was apparent among those who purchased and used narcotics, usually marijuana. It was smoked at small, quiet parties, rarely while driving or in public places. It was not unusual to hear these poised, well-dressed youngsters speak of stealing, using narcotics, and the advantages and disadvantages of their respective college choices in the same tone of voice and conversation.

The middle class group anti-social activities which *do* come to the attention of the authorities are of a rather different nature than those just described. Several examples of these were provided by a local probation officer assigned to the neighborhood. On one occasion, he recalled, a group of about ten boys went back and forth across a busy intersection between 5:30 and 6:30 in the evening, effectively bringing traffic to a complete standstill until dispersed by the police. Another time, a car full of boys drove slowly down a main shopping street spraying the well dressed shoppers with the contents of a fire extinguisher. One incident involved a group of boys who stole an old car and took it to a vacant lot and while one boy drove the car around in circles, the others threw stones at it, until it was nothing but a battered corpse.

There is a mischievous, often amusing overtone to all these incidents; they are not the kind likely to be thought malicious or violent. Rather, they are spontaneous and gratuitous, proving nothing but providing "kicks." This behavior is not the kind which is likely to seriously alarm parents or police. It has none of the grim overtones usually associated, correctly or not, with the activities of lower class gangs. In general, the non-violent nature of the deviant activities of these youngsters is salient, and personal aggression rare. The anti-social activities observed among these groups rarely took the form of open defiance of authority; manipulation rather than rebellion appeared to be the preferred technique for handling trouble with authorities. Cohen and Short have postulated just such a difference between lower and middle class delinquency:

. . . we are persuaded that further research will reveal subtle but important differences between working class and middle class patterns of delinquency. It seems probable that the qualities of malice, bellicosity, and violence will be underplayed in the middle class subcultures and that these subcultures will emphasize more the deliberate courting of danger . . . and a sophisticated, irresponsible, "playboy" approach to activities symbolic in our culture, of adult roles and centering largely around sex, liquor, and automobiles.[20]

How closely that description fits the middle class groups observed is readily apparent.

Interestingly enough, even while engaging in flagrant, frequent infractions of the law, these youngsters sustained the opinion that their activities would in no way interfere with their future plans. They did not define themselves as delinquents or even trouble makers and did not expect others to do so. More likely than not, upon graduating from high school and entering college, as most planned to do, these youngsters

[20] Cohen and Short, *op. cit.,* p. 26.

will leave their deviant activities behind without a trace in the form of official records, self-definition, or residues of unpleasant experiences with authorities. The police seemed to share this expectation. An incident was observed in which a boy was picked up for drinking and curfew violation. In the patrol car he expressed his concern lest the occasion jeopardize his chances for entering college. The officer, who had until that point been rather surly, hastened to reassure the boy that such a possibility was quite unlikely, and implied that nothing would come of the visit to the station.

The same expectations were shared by the people who worked at the places where these youngsters congregated— waitresses, life guards, theater managers—who did not feel that even as a group they constituted a serious nuisance. Their tolerance is no doubt increased by middle class youngsters' liberal spending habits which make it worth their while to put up with an occasional annoyance. But in addition their attitudes are affected by the usually pleasant relations they have with these boys and girls, whose interpersonal experiences with adults and peers are more harmonious and extensive than those observed among the more socially inadequate lower class gangs observed by Yablonsky and the supervisor of the detached worker program in Los Angeles. This difference in social ability is hardly surprising in view of the middle classes' traditional specialization in entrepreneurial activities. The techniques of smooth social relations are the bread and butter of the middle classes, and middle class teenagers, deviant and non-deviant alike, demonstrate remarkable agility in the manipulation of social situations. Their interpersonal skills enable them to control their social environment to a much greater degree than possible for lower class teenagers who have not had the opportunity to acquire and perfect these techniques.

GROUP ORGANIZATION

It can be seen that the groups observed, with the exception of disturbed leadership, precisely conform to Yablonsky's description of a near-group. Certainly, they do not qualify for the term "gang" as it is usually used, nor do they have well-developed delinquent values. On the contrary, the similarity between these youngsters' values and those of the adult, dominant society is conspicuous. Such a continuity has been suggested by Matza and Sykes[21] in a recent article in which they contend that the values underlying much juvenile delinquency are far less deviant than commonly portrayed, due to a prevailing oversimplification of middle class values. The authors argue that existing alongside the official, dominant values in society is another conflicting set which they call subterranean. These are values which are frequently relegated by adults to leisure time pursuits and are not ordinarily allowed to interfere with the regular course of a conventional life. Matza and Sykes point out that the content of these subterranean values has been described by Veblen in his portrayal of the "gentleman of leisure"—disdain for work, identification of masculinity with tough, aggressive behavior, and the search for thrills and adventures. The authors feel that the delinquent emphasizes a society's subterranean values but instead of relegating them to after-hours activities, he makes them a way of life, a code of behavior. The delinquent, then, has not

[21] David Matza and Gresham M. Sykes, "Juvenile Delinquency and Subterranean Values," *American Sociological Review*, Vol. 26 (October 1961), pp. 712–719.

evolved an original set of values but has only taken over one aspect of those held by most people along with their publicly proclaimed, respectable middle class values.

J. A. Pitt-Rivers[22] has suggested the concept "infra-structure" to describe what Matza and Sykes have referred to as subterranean values. The infrastructure is a set of values which exists alongside and in opposition to the official beliefs and behavior required by the formal systems of authority. It is not merely a set of separate beliefs held by one segment of the community but is that part of the social structure consisting of the personal, internalized version of officially endorsed values. The two systems are seen by Pitt-Rivers as interdependent, representing the private and public morals held simultaneously by everyone in the social system. The opposition of the value systems creates a structural tension or ambivalence which, though never really sharp enough to seriously endanger the social order, nevertheless provides a predisposition to deviance from officially prescribed behavior. The relation between the two systems is continuous, and while certain people or groups are more influenced by one system than the other, both affect all behavior to some degree.

In the light of the observations presented here, one may postulate that just as certain individuals and social groups are closer to one set of these values than the other, so are different age groups. Adolescence may be understood as a period in the life span of the individual when he is closer to deviant or subterranean values than he will be as an adult or has been as a child. Several authors have conceptualized ado-

lescence as a period of license, a time for social and sexual exploration. Benedict[23] has pointed out the expectation that the adolescent will be irresponsible, though as an adult a few years later he can no longer be, and Erikson[24] has described adolescence as a psychosocial moratorium, set aside for experimentation in establishing an identity prior to the assumption of adult roles. One implication which can be drawn from these interpretations is that a teenager's "deviant behavior" may be in actuality a phase in his history when he is allowed and even expected to behave in accord with a set of subterranean values which do not disappear when he becomes an adult but instead are acted upon only on more appropriate occasions.

The adolescent in our culture, it is suggested, may be viewed as an aristocrat, a gentleman of leisure who, for a time, is not required to work but is allowed to play, explore, test limits, indulge his pleasures, and little else besides. This description of the delinquent as a kind of aristocrat closely resembles Finestone's characterization of the Negro teenage narcotic addict.[25] The "cat" is an individual who has developed an elaborate repertoire of manipulative techniques for dealing with the world, eschewing violence in favor of persuasion and charm. "He seeks through a harmonious combination of charm, ingratiating speech, dress, music, the proper dedication to his 'kick' and unrestrained generosity to make of his day to day life itself a gracious work of

22 J. A. Pitt-Rivers, *The People of the Sierra* (Chicago: University of Chicago Press, Phoenix Edition, 1961).

23 Ruth Benedict, "Continuities and Discontinuities in Cultural Conditioning," reprinted in Mullahy (Ed.), *A Study of Interpersonal Relations* (New York: Grove Press, Evergreen Edition, 1949).

24 Erik H. Erikson, *Childhood and Society* (New York: W. W. Norton, 1950).

25 Harold Finestone, "Cats, Kicks and Color," *Social Problems,* Vol. 5 (July 1957), pp. 3–13.

art."[26] The similarity between this depiction of the "cat" and the youngsters described here is indeed remarkable, especially in light of the differences between them in race, class, and circumstance.

There is, then, much reason to think that Matza and Sykes are justified in urging that delinquency might be better understood as an extension of the adult conforming world rather than as discontinuous with it. One advantage of this interpretation is that it allows for a single explanation of lower and middle class delinquency and thus avoids the inconsistency inherent in theories which specify the influence of socio-economic factors in the etiology of lower class delinquency and psychological factors in the etiology of middle class delinquency. It is likely that much may be gained by exploring the similarity between the delinquent and the rest of society rather than his deviance from it. Certainly these observations suggest that middle class deviants may differ from lower class delinquents not in the frequency of their anti-social activities, but only in the form which they take and the sophistication, social intelligence, judgment, and skill with which they are executed.

SUMMARY

These observations have raised several important issues concerning the structure and values of delinquent groups. It may be that the extent of gang structure is frequently exaggerated and that such groups may not be as cohesive, structured, and stable as they are commonly depicted. The groups described here manifested all but one of the characteristics (disturbed leadership) described by Yablonsky as those of a near-group. There is a coincidence of opinion based on

26 *Ibid.*, p. 5.

three sets of observations (Yablonsky's, the supervisor of a detached worker program in Los Angeles, and those reported in this paper) suggesting that the common conception of the gang as a highly organized primary group is not always accurate and may be the result of the gross exaggerations made possible by the dearth of empirical observations of gangs. Exaggeration may also have taken place in the extent of the differences between delinquent values and those of the dominant society. The observations reported in this paper are in accord with the suggestions of Matza and Sykes that the delinquent subculture is an extension of values held by most members of the society but indulged in less openly and less often. Certainly the behavior and beliefs of the middle class youngsters observed are not dramatically different from those of most conventional teenagers or adults.

In view of these three sets of observations, the following questions may be asked: (1) How often and to what extent are gangs primary groups with elaborate delinquent subcultures, and how prevalent are such groups when compared with the loosely structured, secondary, impermanent collectivities with little or no delinquent subculture such as those described here? (2) In view of the conflicting characterizations of the extent of gang structure and the nature of gang values, would not there be more scientific value in describing gangs in terms of at least these two variables rather than primarily on the basis of the content of their deviant activities? (3) To what extent, if any, does adult recognition, particularly in the form of the assignment of detached workers to gangs, legitimize and formalize these groups, lending them a cohesion and solidarity which they previously might not have had? (4) Has the emphasis on the deviant activities of these groups obscured their similarity to conventional teenagers and adults, thereby exaggerating the differences between delinquents and nondelinquents? And (5) would it not be more fruitful to examine the extent and nature of the similarities rather than differences between deviant and nondeviant teenagers and adults?

The action implications of these questions are far-reaching. If, as Yablonsky suggests, the gang meets different needs for different members, a uniform approach on a gang basis is inappropriate. More suitable would be an attempt to help individual members develop the interpersonal skills which would enable them to participate in structured, socially accepted groups. Or, by deliberately applying techniques such as Yablonsky's "group-fulfilling prophecy," gangs might be made into non-deviant clubs. And, if delinquent values are but a continuation of one aspect of the accepted value system subscribed to by most law abiding people, a program designed to integrate these values into a more appropriate place in deviant youngsters' lives (for example, by providing socially acceptable means of expressing aggression and seeking adventure) would be more honest and effective than attempts to eliminate them altogether.

At this stage, only one firm conclusion is justified. The variables in terms of which gangs can best be understood have not yet been identified and are not likely to be until widespread and systematic empirical observation is conducted. The impressions reported here suggest just how valuable and unsettling such observation may prove.

24.   Perceived Opportunities, Gang Membership and Delinquency

JAMES F. SHORT, JR., RAMON RIVERA, AND RAY A. TENNYSON

Not since the advent of psychoanalysis has a theory had such impact on institutionalized delinquency control as the theory, explicit or implied, in *Delinquency and Opportunity*.[1] Given the impetus of major foundation and federal support, the theory has been extensively adopted as a rationale for action programs in many areas of the country. There is some danger that, like psychoanalysis, "opportunity structure theory" may be rationalized and elaborated so rapidly and extensively as to discourage, if not render impossible, empirical testing, pragmatic validation, or demonstration of worth by any other criterion of "good theory." *Delinquency and Opportunity* has been widely praised for its theoretical integration, e.g., as "a logically sound deductive system that is rich in its implications for delinquency causation and control," but the same critic also notes that "examined in terms of its logical, operational, and empirical adequacy, the theory poses a number of questions concerning the accuracy of some of its postulates and theorems."[2] Our paper will bring data to bear on certain aspects of the opportunity structure paradigm as we operationalized it in a study of delinquent gangs in Chicago.

Figure 1 reproduces in paradigm

* This research is supported by grants from the Behavior Science Study Section of the National Institute of Mental Health (M-3301 and MH-07158); the Office of Juvenile Delinquency and Youth Development, Welfare Administration, U. S. Department of Health, Education, and Welfare in cooperation with the President's Committee on Juvenile Delinquency and Youth Crime (No. 62220); the Ford Foundation; and the Research Committee of Washington State University. We are grateful for this support and for the support and encouragement of staff members at the University of Chicago, Washington State University, and the Program for Detached Workers of the YMCA of Metropolitan Chicago, whose wholehearted co-operation makes the entire enterprise such an exciting "opportunity." An earlier version of this paper was read at the annual meetings of the Pacific Sociological Association, 1963.

[1] Richard A. Cloward and Lloyd E. Ohlin, *Delinquency and Opportunity: A Theory of Delinquent Gangs*, Glencoe, Ill.: The Free Press, 1960.

[2] Clarence Schrag, "Delinquency and Opportunity: Analysis of a Theory," *Sociology and Social Research*, 46 (January, 1962), pp. 167–175.

SOURCE. James F. Short, Jr., Ramon Rivera, and Ray A. Tennyson, "Perceived Opportunities, Gang Membership and Delinquency," from *American Sociological Review*, Volume 30, February 1965, pp. 56–67. Reprinted with the permission of the American Sociological Association and the authors.

Structural features	Type of subculture	
	Criminal	Conflict
I. *Independent Variable*		
A. Culturally prescribed success goals	(Integrated areas) Internalized	(Unintegrated areas) Internalized
B. Availability of legitimate means to success goals	Limited; hence intense pressures toward deviant behavior	Limited; hence intense pressures toward deviant behavior
II. *Intervening Variables*		
A. Institutional norms	Incomplete internalization	Incomplete internalization
B. Availability of illegal means to success goals	Available	Unavailable
1. Relations between adult carriers of conventional and criminal values	Accommodative; each participates in value system of other	Conflicted; neither group well organized; value systems implicit and opposed to one another
2. Criminal learning structure	Available; offenders at different age levels integrated	Unavailable; attenuated relations between offenders at different age levels
3. Criminal opportunity structure	Stable sets of criminal roles graded for different ages and levels of competence; continuous income; protection from detection and prosecution	Unarticulated opportunity structure; individual rather than organized crime; sporadic income; little protection from detection and prosecution
4. Social control	Strong controls originate in *both* legitimate and illegal structures	Diminished social control; "weak" relations between adults and adolescents
III. *Dependent Variable*		
A. Expected type of collective response among delinquents	Pressures toward deviance originate in limited accessibility to success goals by legitimate means, but are ameliorated by opportunities for access by illegal means. Hence, delinquent behavior is rational, disciplined, and crime-oriented	Pressures toward deviance originate in blocked opportunity by *any* institutionalized system of means. Hence, delinquent behavior displays expressive conflict patterns

FIGURE 1. Social context and modes of delinquent behavior: a paradigm

form the principal elements of "opportunity structure theory" concerning *criminal* and *conflict* subcultures. It subdivides the "Innovation" category of Merton's deviance paradigm, referring to acceptance (internalization) of culturally prescribed success goals and rejection (incomplete internalization) of institutional norms or culturally prescribed means, by those for whom legitimate means to success goals are restricted.[3] To this the paradigm adds Cloward's four sets of defining conditions for the relative availability of illegitimate means to success goals,[4] and the two hypothesized types of "collective response among delinquents" produced by the preceding conditions.[5]

In our research in Chicago we have attempted to measure variables specified in this paradigm and to investigate their interrelations. For this purpose we have studied lower-class "delinquent gangs" involved in a "detached worker" program of the YMCA of Metropolitan Chicago, control groups of lower-class nongang boys from the same neighborhoods as the gang boys, and middle-class nongang boys.[6] Elements of the

paradigm were operationalized in terms of the *perceptions* reported by the boys studied.[7] In this paper we direct attention to perceptions of legitimate and illegitimate opportunities by Negro and white lower-class gang and nongang boys and middle-class boys of both races, and to the relations among these perceptions. Detailed discussion of the relation of perceived opportunities and patterns of behavior derived from self-reports and, for gang boys only, from detached-worker ratings, is deferred for later presentation.[8]

Data reported elsewhere establish different levels of aspiration among the boys studied, but they show that regardless of race, class, or gang membership, mean levels of both occupa-

---

[3] Robert K. Merton, *Social Theory and Social Structure*, Glencoe, Ill.: The Free Press, 1956, Ch. 4.

[4] Richard A. Cloward, "Illegitimate Means, Anomie, and Deviant Behavior," *American Sociological Review*, 24 (April, 1959), pp. 164–176.

[5] Cloward and Ohlin use a different theoretical rationale to explain "retreatist" subcultures, but our data are not relevant specifically to this aspect of the theory. See Cloward and Ohlin, *op. cit.*, pp. 25–27, 178 ff.

[6] Selection and description of study populations and other characteristics of the research program are described in previous publications and in greatest detail in a forthcoming book. See, for example, James F. Short, Jr., Fred L. Strodtbeck, and Desmond Cartwright, "A Strategy for Utilizing Research Dilemmas: A Case from the Study of Parenthood in a Street Corner Gang," *Sociological Inquiry*, 32 (Spring, 1962), pp. 185–202; James F. Short, Jr., "Street Corner Groups and Patterns of Delinquency: A Progress Report," *Amer-*

ican Catholic Sociological Review, 24 (Spring, 1963), pp. 13–32; and James F. Short, Jr., and Fred L. Strodtbeck, *Group Process and Gang Delinquency* Chicago: University of Chicago Press, 1965, esp. Ch. 1.

[7] Cloward and Ohlin refer to "common perceptions" of opportunities, and Schrag explains that one of the basic postulates of the theory is that "perceived disadvantage, regardless of the accuracy of the perception, is for lower-class youth the functional equivalent of objectively verified disadvantage in that it has the same effect on overt behavior." (Schrag, *op. cit.*, p. 168.) This is not to deny the importance of *objective* opportunities, legitimate and illegitimate. The former can be demonstrated to be greater for whites than Negroes, and for middle- than for lower-class persons. It is more difficult to demonstrate gang-nongang differences in terms of the cumulative *effects*—school performance, relations with the police, etc.—which favor nongang boys. Differences in objective illegitimate opportunities are similarly difficult to demonstrate, though the illegal enterprises are more likely to be present in a lower-class than in a middle-class environment.

[8] Behavior factors based on detached-worker ratings of gang boys are reported in James F. Short, Jr., Ray A. Tennyson, and Kenneth I. Howard, "Behavior Dimensions of Gang Delinquency," *American Sociological Review*, 28 (June, 1963), pp. 411–428. Self-reported behavior factors are presented in Short and Strodtbeck, *op. cit.*, Ch. 7.

tional and educational aspirations considerably exceed fathers' achieved levels of occupation and education.[9] In this sense the independent variable—internalization of culturally prescribed success goals—may be said to have a positive value among all the boys studied. For the first intervening variable in the paradigm, however—internalization of institutional norms—our gang members are less positive than the other boys studied. With "values" data from semantic differential scales, we established the fact that all groups assign equally high value and degree of legitimacy to such "middle-class" images as "Someone who works for good grades at school" and "Someone who likes to read good books"—again indicating that certain values are common to all groups —but gang boys of both races hold more positive attitudes toward *deviant* images than do the other boys.[10] These deviant images represented hypothesized "delinquent subcultures;" e.g., conflict ("Someone who is a good fighter with a tough reputation"), criminal ("Someone who knows where to sell what he steals" and "Someone who has good connections to avoid trouble with the law"), and retreatist ("Some-

one who makes easy money by pimping and other illegal hustles" and "Someone who gets his kicks by using drugs"). Middle-class boys generally attribute to these deviant images a lower value and less legitimacy, as we expected.

This paper is concerned with other elements in the paradigm, based on data from one part of an extensive interview schedule administered by specially trained interviewers to more than 500 boys in the six categories (race by class status and gang membership) under study. Respondents were instructed to indicate whether each of a series of statements was true of the "area where your group hangs out." In this way we hoped to measure perceptions of relatively specific legitimate and illegal opportunities. Perceptions of legitimate means to success goals, for example, were sampled by a series of statements concerning the *educational* and *occupational* orientations, abilities, and prospects for "guys in our area." We hoped by the impersonal referent to avoid the personalized ambitions and expectations which were the subject of inquiry in another part of the interview and thus to obtain measures referring to the boys' perceptions of general opportunities for legitimate and illegal achievement in their respective areas.

Aspects of the availability of illegal means to success goals to which attention was directed concerned the relative integration of the carriers of criminal and noncriminal values (in terms of the respectability of persons making money illegally and the orientation of local police toward law violation); adult "connections" and opportunities for learning and abetting criminal activities; the availability of criminal role models; and the probability of successful criminal enterprise in the area. Finally, because Cloward and Ohlin

---

[9] See James F. Short, Jr., "Gang Delinquency and Anomie," in Marshall B. Clinard (ed.), *Deviant Behavior and Anomie*, New York: The Free Press of Glencoe, 1964; see also Jonathan Freedman and Ramon Rivera, "Education, Social Class, and Patterns of Delinquency," paper read at the annual meetings of the American Sociological Association, 1962. Elliott's study of "200 delinquent and nondelinquent boys attending two adjoining high schools in a large West Coast city" supports these findings. See Delbert S. Elliott, "Delinquency and Perceived Opportunity," *Sociological Inquiry*, 32 (Spring, 1962), pp. 216–227.

[10] The data are reported in Robert A. Gordon, James F. Short, Jr., Desmond S. Cartwright, and Fred L. Strodtbeck, "Values and Gang Delinquency: A Study of Street Corner Groups," *American Journal of Sociology*, 69 (September, 1963), pp. 109–128.

stress the importance of these matters for social control, perceptions of appropriate adult role models and their interest and sincerity concerning the problems of adolescents were also covered. The list of statements is in Table 1, together with the percentage of boys in each group answering "true."[11]

In most cases responses to the statements concerning open legitimate opportunities and adult helpfulness form a gradient: gang boys are least likely to answer "true," followed by nongang and then by middle-class boys of each race. For negatively stated legitimate opportunity questions, and for the two negative adult power ("clout") statements, this gradient is reversed.[12] White gang boys generally are more sanguine than Negro gang boys about occupational opportunities and adult "clout," while Negroes tend to be slightly more optimistic concerning education and adult helpfulness. For all these areas, white middle-class boys have the most *open* view of "opportunities."

Conversely, gang boys are more likely to perceive illegitimate opportunities as open than are other boys, and these perceptions are held by more Negro than white boys in each stratum. The latter finding is somewhat surprising, in view of the acknowledged white domination of organized crime in Chicago. Informal observation suggests that vice organized on a large scale does flourish in Negro communities, and that "independent entrepreneurship" in such

forms as small (and large) policy wheels, marijuana peddling, street-walking prostitutes, pool sharks, professional burglars and robbers, and the like, is more common in lower-class Negro than in lower-class white communities.[13] In any case, illegitimate opportunities appeared to be open to more Negro than white boys.

To reduce these data further, we assigned an opportunity structure score to each item. Except for items 17(A) and 18(A) answers were scored 2, 1, or 0, with 2 assigned to *open* opportunity perceptions, whether legitimate or illegitimate. Thus, for questions in Table 1 followed by (—), a "true" answer received a 0, "Don't know," a 1, and "False," a 2. The reverse procedure was applied to questions followed by (+).

Statements 17(A) and 18(A) are difficult to score. At first we assumed that a positive response to these questions indicated that illegitimate opportunities were perceived as closed. Boys were asked these questions only if they had already responded positively to questions 17 and 18. Thus, a "true" response to the statement that "A lot of these guys who make money illegally do not operate alone. They have to answer to people above them who are calling the shots," was taken to mean that the "really big" hoodlums were not available as role models; hence, to this extent illegitimate opportunities for "making it big" were perceived as closed. On the other hand, a boy might answer "false" to this statement on the grounds that those who were making money illegally were involved in such petty pursuits as not to warrant concern or control by the syndicate, or, particularly in the case of middle-class white boys, illegal pursuits might be in

---

[11] In the interview schedule the statements were not labeled according to which "opportunity structures" were being studied, and they were arranged in different order.

[12] Elliott, *op. cit.*, finds that delinquents consistently perceive lower opportunities for educational and occupational "success" than do nondelinquents. For evidence of other gradients among boys in the present study, see Gordon et al., *op. cit.*, and Short and Strodtbeck, *op. cit.*

[13] See Short and Strodtbeck, *op. cit.*, esp. Ch. 5, "Racial Differentials in Gang Behavior."

Table 1

PERCENTAGE OF BOYS ANSWERING "TRUE" TO OPPORTUNITY STRUCTURE QUESTIONS, BY RACE, CLASS, AND GANG STATUS

Interviewer: "Once again I want you to think about the area where your group hangs out. I'm going to read a few statements to you, and all you have to do is say 'True' or 'False' after each statement. If you think the statement is true about the area, say 'True'; if you don't think it's true, say 'False.'"

| | Per cent answering "True" | | | | | |
| | Negro | | | White | | |
	Lower-class gang N = 206	Lower-class nongang N = 89	Middle class N = 26	Lower-class gang N = 90	Lower-class nongang N = 79	Middle class N = 53
Legitimate Educational Opportunities						
1. In our area it's hard for a young guy to stay in school. (−)*	48.5	28.1	7.7	52.2	21.5	0.0
2. Most kids in our area like school. (+)	43.2	49.4	80.8	32.2	60.8	94.3
3. Most of the guys in our area will graduate from high school. (+)	30.6	44.9	96.2	32.2	65.8	100.0
4. In our area, there are a lot of guys who want to go to college. (+)	37.4	47.2	84.6	16.7	44.3	98.1
5. College is too expensive for most of the guys in the area. (−)	75.7	76.4	53.8	80.0	65.8	7.5
6. As far as grades are concerned, most of the guys in our area could get through college without too much trouble. (+)	46.6	43.8	50.0	43.3	40.5	73.6
Legitimate Occupational Opportunities						
7. It's hard for a young guy in our area to get a good paying honest job. (−)	77.2	62.9	46.2	56.7	31.6	9.4
8. Most of the guys in the area will probably get good paying honest jobs when they grow up. (+)	51.9	59.6	61.5	65.6	79.7	92.5

* Signs in parentheses indicate the "valence" of a "True" answer relative to the opportunity structure area indicated.

9. For guys in this area honest jobs don't pay very well. (−)	56.3	47.2	26.9	40.0	22.8	3.8
10. Guys in this area have to have connections to get good paying jobs. (−)	53.9	51.7	30.8	56.7	44.3	22.6
11. In this area it's hard to make much money without doing something illegal. (−)	54.9	38.2	23.1	37.8	13.9	0.0
Integration of the Carriers of Criminal and Noncriminal Values						
12. Some of the most respectable people in our area make their money illegally. (+)	44.2	19.1	15.4	24.4	10.1	3.8
13. The police in this area get paid off for letting things happen that are against the law. (+)	51.5	37.1	30.8	42.2	36.7	20.8
Criminal Learning Structures						
14. There are connections in this area for a guy who wants to make good money illegally. (+)	57.8	49.4	38.5	47.8	35.4	5.7
15. Young guys can learn a lot about crime from older people in the area. (+)	75.2	66.3	34.6	52.2	35.4	11.3
16. There are adults in this area who help young guys make money illegally. (+)	59.2	49.4	30.8	42.2	26.6	15.1
Visibility of Criminal Careers						
17. In this area there are some people who make their living by doing things that are against the law. (+)	83.0	73.0	69.2	70.0	60.8	30.2
18. Some of the young guys in our area will be making a living someday by doing things that are against the law. (+)	83.0	79.8	73.1	75.6	59.5	39.6

Table 1—Continued

Interviewer: "Once again I want you to think about the area where your group hangs out. I'm going to read a few statements to you, and all you have to do is say 'True' or 'False' after each statement. If you think the statement is true about the area, say 'True'; if you don't think it's true, say 'False.'"

	Per cent answering "True"					
	Negro			White		
	Lower-class gang N = 206	Lower-class nongang N = 89	Middle class N = 26	Lower-class gang N = 90	Lower-class nongang N = 79	Middle class N = 53
Elite Criminal Opportunities						
17.(A) A lot of these guys who make money illegally do not operate alone. They have to answer to people above them who are calling the shots. (−)	62.6	62.9	65.4	45.6	40.5	18.9
18.(A) A lot of these guys won't be operating alone either. They'll have to answer to people above them who'll be calling the shots. (−)	70.4	70.8	65.4	62.2	53.2	30.2
19. A guy from this area has a chance of really making it big in the rackets. (+)	45.1	30.3	34.6	35.6	24.1	3.8
20. None of the people who make big money in the rackets live in this area. (−)	54.4	66.3	38.5	56.7	75.9	60.4
Adult "Clout"						
21. Not many really successful people live in this area. (−)	63.6	59.6	19.2	42.2	26.6	0.0
22. Adults in this area haven't much clout (pull). (−)	55.3	42.7	23.1	48.9	48.1	13.2
Adult Helpfulness						
23. There are adults in this area who help young guys get jobs. (+)	82.5	93.3	92.3	78.9	89.9	94.3
24. Adults in the area do a lot to help young guys keep out of trouble. (+)	67.0	91.0	61.5	50.0	73.4	88.7

the nature of white-collar crime and so not subject to syndicate control. In the latter case, a "false" answer still would be consistent with an *open* perception of opportunity, while in the former it would not. Answers to "elite criminal opportunities" questions are the only exceptions to the observed gradient for perceptions of illegitimate opportunities, suggesting that boys within each class of respondents may have interpreted these questions less uniformly than they did the others.

Before answers to these questions are dismissed as invalid, however, they should be examined more carefully. Note that responses to questions 17(A) and 18(A) follow a pattern: more Negro than white boys say that people in their areas who make money illegally have to "answer to people above them." Unfortunately, the question did not specify where these "higher ups" lived or whether they were visible to the boys. We may infer, however, that a higher proportion of persons making money illegitimately in the white areas were among the "higher ups" in organized crime than was the case in Negro neighborhoods.

The middle-class boys' answers to the entire set of four "elite" questions are especially interesting. Negro middle-class boys are far more likely to indicate that local area people have "a chance of really making it big in the rackets" and far less likely to say that locals do not "make big money in the rackets." Drake and Cayton[14] and Frazier[15] have described important criminal and otherwise "shady" elements in the Negro middle class. Frazier, in particular, indicates that influential segments of the "black bourgeoisie" are "recruited from

the successful underworld Negroes, who have gained their money from gambling, prostitution, bootlegging, and the 'numbers.' "[16] Frazier attributes the flashy consumption patterns of the new Negro middle class to the influence of these elements and contrasts this way of life with that of the old upper and middle classes who "erected an impenetrable barrier between themselves and Negroes who represented the 'sporting' and criminal world."[17] The white middle-class boys, who were chosen precisely because they were the "cream" of YMCA Hi-Y clubs, are very unlikely to be exposed to this sort of community influence. Such differences as these, if they are real, should find expression in other data from these subjects.[18]

These ambiguities in interpretation led us to score "elite" criminal opportunities in two ways—with and without questions 17(A) and 18(A). When they were included, we followed our original assumptions, adjusting the scoring so that if either question was not asked, implying closed opportunities, the boy was scored zero for the ques-

---

[14] St. Clair Drake and Horace R. Cayton, *Black Metropolis: A Study of Negro Life in a Northern City*, New York: Harper and Row, 1962, Vol. 2

[15] E. Franklin Frazier, *Black Bourgeoisie*, New York: Collier Books, 1962.

[16] *Ibid.*, p. 109.

[17] *Ibid.*, pp. 109–110.

[18] We were first alerted to differences between our Negro and white middle-class boys when they came to our offices for testing, and later by analysis of semantic differential data. See Gordon et al., *op. cit.* It should be emphasized that primary data for this paper represent perceptions rather than objective measures of opportunities or of the communities in which these boys live. Other investigators have emphasized the extent to which middle-class Negroes are like their white counterparts in terms of the character and stability of their institutions and their community leadership, and in interracial situations. Life styles, interaction patterns with whites, and leadership among middle-class Negroes vary greatly, however. See, for example, the discussion in Robin M. Williams, Jr., et al., *Strangers Next Door: Ethnic Relations in American Communities*, Englewood Cliffs, N.J.: Prentice-Hall, 1964, esp. Chs. 7–10; also James Q. Wilson, *Negro Politics: The Search for Leadership*, Glencoe, Ill.: The Free Press, 1960.

Table 2

MEAN OPPORTUNITY STRUCTURE SCORES, BY RACE, CLASS, AND GANG STATUS

Aspect of opportunity structure*	Negro			White		
	Lower-class gang N = 206†	Lower-class nongang N = 89	Middle class N = 26	Lower-class gang N = 89	Lower-class nongang N = 75	Middle class N = 53
Legitimate educational (0–12)	4.8	5.7	9.0	3.8	6.4	11.2
Legitimate occupational (0–10)	4.2	5.2	6.6	5.4	7.3	9.1
Integration of carriers of criminal and noncriminal values (0–4)	2.1	1.4	1.2	1.5	1.0	0.5
Criminal learning structures (0–6)	4.0	3.6	2.3	3.0	2.2	0.7
Visibility of criminal careers (0–4)	3.4	3.2	3.0	3.0	2.5	1.4
Criminal opportunities (0–10)	4.7	4.0	4.6	4.7	4.3	4.6
Adult *Clout* (0–4)	1.5	1.9	3.0	2.0	2.4	3.7
Adult helpfulness (0–4)	3.0	3.7	3.2	2.6	3.2	3.7
Criminal opportunities (0–4)	1.8	1.2	1.8	1.5	1.0	0.9
Summary Scores						
Legitimate educational and occupational opportunities (0–22)	9.0	11.0	15.6	9.3	13.7	20.2
Illegitimate opportunities (0–24)	14.3	12.3	11.0	12.1	10.0	7.2
Illegitimate opportunities less inclusive (0–18)	11.4	9.5	8.2	9.0	6.7	3.5
Adult power and helpfulness (0–8)	4.5	5.6	6.2	4.7	5.6	7.4

* Figures in parentheses indicate the possible range for each score.
† Ns vary slightly for some scores, due to nomresponse. Scores are based in each case on the number of boys who actually gave meaningful responses.

tion; if the question was asked and a "true" answer recorded, a score of 1 was given; "undecided" was scored 2, and "false," 3.

Table 2 presents mean opportunity structure scores, by race, class, and gang status of respondents. The trends apparent in Table 1 appear here, also.

In addition, it is clear that for *legitimate* opportunities, gang-nongang and middle-class differences *within* racial categories are greater than the Negro-white differences for each of the three gang and class strata. For *illegitimate* opportunities, differences between races are greater than within-race differences.

PERCEIVED OPPORTUNITIES AND AN OFFICIAL DELINQUENCY RATE

In Table 3, ranking on each of the summary opportunity scores is compared with the official delinquency rates of the six race-by-class-by-gang-status groups.[19] As far as the *ordering* of the

[19] These rates refer to the mean number of offenses known to the police, per boy, in each group. Data are based on John M. Wise, "A Comparison of Sources of Data as Indexes of Delinquent Behavior," M.A. thesis, University of Chicago, 1962.

six groups is concerned, perception of *legitimate* opportunities is more strongly associated with delinquency rates than is perception of illegitimate opportunities. This is consistent with the assumption that perceived legitimate opportunities are independent variables, while perceived illegitimate opportunities intervene, after legitimate opportunities have been appraised and found wanting. Legitimate achievement tends to be the universal standard in our culture, highly valued even by very deviant individuals.[20] Note, however, that *within* racial categories, perception of illegitimate opportunities does order the groups according to official delinquency rates.

Official delinquency rates measure the hypothesized dependent variables only in a very gross sense. The gang-nongang distinction probably measures participation in delinquent subcultural activity, and adding the middle-class –lower-class division permits a test of the theory in terms somewhat broader than it was originally set forth. Here the theory holds up well: gang boys of

[20] See Gordon et al., *op. cit.*

Table 3

MEAN OPPORTUNITY STRUCTURE SCORES KNOWN TO THE POLICE, BY RACE, CLASS, AND GANG STATUS[*]

Legitimate educational and occupational opportunities (0 to 22)	Perception of illegitimate opportunities (less inclusive) (0 to 18)	Perception of adult power and helpfulness (0 to 8)	Total opportunities score[†] (−18 to 30)	Mean number of offenses known to police, per boy
NG (9.0)	NG (11.4)	NG (4.5)	NG (2.1)	NG (3.14)
WG (9.3)	NLC (9.5)	WG (4.7)	WG (5.0)	WG (2.73)
NLC (11.0)	WG (9.0)	NLC (5.6)	NLC (7.1)	NLC (0.47)
WLC (13.7)	NMC (8.2)	WLC (5.6)	WLC (12.6)	WLC (0.31)
NMC (15.6)	WLC (6.7)	NMC (6.2)	NMC (13.6)	NMC (0.06)
WMC (20.2)	WMC (3.5)	WMC (7.4)	WMC (24.1)	WMC (0.02)

[*] NG stands for Negro gang members, NLC for Negro lower-class boys, and so on.
[†] Total opportunities score is designed to reflect both legitimate and illegitimate pressures toward delinquency. It is obtained by adding together legitimate educational and occupational opportunities and adult power and helpfulness scores, and from this sum subtracting illegitimate opportunity scores. Hence it should be negatively correlated with delinquency.

both races perceive greater restrictions on legitimate opportunities than do nongang boys in the same neighborhoods or middle-class boys. Thus, the *negative* pressure toward deviance is greater for gang boys. Within each racial group, gang boys perceive better illegitimate opportunities; hence the greater "pull" toward deviance. While perceived adult power and helpfulness, combined, rank the groups very much as do official delinquency rates, adult power alone turns out, as predicted, to be negatively related to delinquency, while helpfulness, which may be exercised by carriers of criminal as well as noncriminal values, is related inconsistently to delinquency among Negro boys.

Adult power and helpfulness are both hypothesized by Cloward and Ohlin to be negatively related to the emergence and maintenance of conflict subcultures. "The term that the bopper uses most frequently to characterize his relationships with adults is 'weak'. . . . He views himself as isolated and the adult world as indifferent. The commitments of adults are to their own interests and not to his. Their explanations of why he should behave differently are 'weak,' as are their efforts to help him."[21] This description holds up well with respect to "clout." Gang boys score lower than the others and Negro gang boys—by far our most conflict-oriented[22]—score lowest of all. But helpfulness scores are

comparatively high for all groups, and they are lowest for the less conflict-oriented white gang boys.[23]

Differences between nongang and gang boys on both scores are sufficient to suggest that these factors are important in selection for gang membership, though their relation to a particular type of delinquent subculture—conflict—is inconsistent with the theory. The previously noted higher illegitimate opportunity scores registered by the Negro boys are also inconsistent, but the greater visibility and availability of petty criminal activities in lower-class Negro communities may account for this. Similarly, the comparatively low Negro middle-class scores on clout and helpfulness are consistent with Frazier's descriptions of the superficial show put on by Negro middle-class "society," which he regards as a somewhat futile attempt to compensate for status insecurities relative to whites.[24]

The hypothesis that perceived adult power is inversely related to gang conflict is essentially a social control argument. But helpfulness, when exercised by illegitimate adults, may be conducive to involvement in a criminal subculture. To investigate this possibility, we examined the relation *between* perceptions of various types of opportunities.

THE RELATION BETWEEN LEGITIMATE AND ILLEGITIMATE OPPORTUNITIES

The product-moment correlations between opportunity scores, for all boys

---

[21] Cloward and Ohlin, *op. cit.*, pp. 24–25.

[22] For documentation, see Short, Tennyson, and Howard, *op. cit.*, and Short and Strodtbeck, *op. cit.*, esp. Chs. 1, 5, and 9. It was in large part because they were involved in gang fighting that most of the Negro gangs received the attention of newspapers, police, and the Program for Detached Workers with which this research program was associated. Close observation of the gangs over periods ranging from several months to more than three years suggests that nearly all the Negro gangs had at one time been more involved in "conflict subcultures" than had any of

the white gangs. Finally, detailed analysis of behavior ratings by detached workers indicates greater conflict involvement by Negro than white gangs.

[23] These findings are consistent with boys' ratings of a series of adult roles in the same interview. See James F. Short, Jr., Ramon Rivera, and Harvey Marshall, "Adult-Adolescent Relations and Gang Delinquency: An Empirical Report," *Pacific Sociological Review* (Fall, 1964).

[24] Frazier, *op. cit.*

and for gang boys only, by race, are in Table 4. Legitimate opportunity scores tend to be positively correlated with one another, as are illegitimate opportunity scores, and between legitimate and illegitimate scores correlations are negative. There are exceptions to this general pattern, however; for example, perceptions of legitimate educational and occupational opportunities are significantly correlated for all groups except white gang boys. The low correlation in the latter group suggests that perceptions of legitimate educational and occupational opportunities often are not mutually reinforcing.

The relation between adult power and perceived illegitimate opportunities suggests greater "integration" of the carriers of criminal and conventional values in white neighborhoods: the correlations are low but *positive* among white boys, and *negative* among Negroes. For both races, adult helpfulness is negatively correlated with illegitimate opportunities.

Correlations between perceived illegitimate opportunities are higher for white boys, particularly those involving the criminal *elite* measures. Thus, while white boys perceive illegitimate opportunities as less available than do Negro boys, "integration" as we have operationalized it is actually more characteristic of white than Negro gang areas. Negro gang boys perceive illegitimate opportunities as relatively open, but they tend to perceive illegitimate adults as neither powerful nor helpful. White gang boys, however, tend to perceive illegitimate adults as powerful but not very helpful. A similar pattern occurs in data from another section of the interview, in which boys were asked to indicate four characteristics of several adult roles in their local areas. Among Negro gang boys, 38 per cent, compared with 53 per cent of white gang boys, felt that adults making money illegally have "a lot of clout," while only

about one boy in five in both racial groups felt that such adults are "interested in the problem of teen-agers." Lower-class nongang boys consistently rated legitimate adult roles higher than gang boys did on scales reflecting their interest in and degree of contact with teen-agers, their "clout," and the extent to which they are considered "right guys."[25]

In the present analysis, the relations between various opportunity scores reveal no significant or consistent differences that explain behavioral differences between gang and nongang lower-class boys. The most striking differences are between middle-class Negro boys and all other groups in the correlation between adult helpfulness and perceived elite criminal opportunities. This correlation is positive for both elite scores (.34 for the more inclusive measure, .20 for the less inclusive measure) among Negro middle-class boys, but both correlations are negative in all other groups. Adult clout was also correlated positively with the two elite criminal opportunity scores among Negro middle-class boys (.22 and .30), and among white gang members, but negatively in the other groups. Again, reference to Frazier's perceptive analysis is pertinent.[26]

SUMMARY

Legitimate occupational opportunities are perceived as available less often by gang than by nongang boys, and most often by middle-class boys. White boys are more likely than Negro boys to perceive such opportunities as available, in each of the strata examined. With respect to legitimate educational opportunities, the same pattern occurs, except that the racial difference does not occur among gang boys. Race- and class-by-gang-status gradients are both

25 A more detailed report of these data is in Short, Rivera, and Marshall, *op. cit.*
26 Frazier, *op. cit.*

Table 4

CORRELATIONS AMONG OPPORTUNITY STRUCTURE SCORES, BY RACE*

	Legitimate educational		Legitimate occupational		Adult clout		Adult helpfulness		Criminal, noncriminal integration		Criminal learning opportunities		Visibility of criminal careers		Criminal opportunities elite (less inclusive)		Criminal opportunities elite (inclusive)	
	W†	N‡	W	N	W	N	W	N	W	N	W	N	W	N	W	N	W	N
Legitimate educational	1.00	1.00	.48	.38	.45	.34	.35	.27	−.36	−.17	−.49	−.22	−.42	−.23	−.27	−.13	−.06	−.03
Legitimate occupational	.13	.34	1.00	1.00	.42	.35	.28	.28	−.26	−.32	−.31	−.37	−.26	−.30	−.25	−.23	−.10	−.08
Adult clout	.10	.22	.28	.37	1.00		.29	.29	−.14	−.25	−.13	−.23	−.19	−.23	.04	−.01	.10	.05
Adult helpfulness	.23	.32	.23	.35	.19	.32	1.00		−.23	−.26	−.19	−.15	−.26	−.14	−.27	−.21	−.19	−.13
Criminal, noncriminal integration	−.26	−.19	−.18	−.33	.05	−.23	−.27	−.29	1.00		.49	.51	.37	.32	.46	.32	.20	.14
Criminal learning opportunities	−.26	−.20	−.15	−.31	.16	−.22	−.20	−.19	.59	.52	1.00		.54	.43	.52	.27	.19	−.02
Visibility of criminal careers	−.28	−.27	−.17	−.39	.10	−.22	−.34	−.16	.37	.34	.46	.37	1.00		.38	.21	.00	−.14
Criminal opportunities elite (less inclusive)	−.21	−.18	−.24	−.25	.24	−.04	−.32	−.24	.60	.31	.64	.29	.49	.23	1.00		.73	.70
Criminal opportunities elite (inclusive)	−.03	−.05	−.15	−.07	.19	.01	−.23	−.15	.32	.08	.41	−.03	.16	−.10	.74	.66	1.00	

* Italicized coefficients below the diagonal represent gang boys only; coefficients above the diagonal represent all boys, including gang members.

† White: p < .05 = .13 (all boys) and .21 (gang boys); p < .01 = .18 (all boys) and .27 (gang boys).

‡ Negro: p < .05 = .11 (all boys) and .14 (gang boys); p < .01 = .14 (all boys) and .18 (gang boys).

present concerning adult clout, but not perceived adult helpfulness, among lower-class boys. These data are consistent with the apparently greater *protest* orientation of white as compared with Negro gang boys.[27] Gradients within racial groups are consistent with inferences from the Cloward and Ohlin theory.

Differences in perceptions of illegitimate opportunities reverse most of those found for legitimate opportunities, as expected. These differences are inconsistent with the greater conflict orientation of Negro gang boys, but when adult clout is correlated with criminal opportunity scores, and other data are introduced, "integration" of criminal opportunities and between criminal and legitimate opportunities is greater for white than for Negro boys. Even for white gang boys, however, the negative correlations between adult helpfulness and criminal opportunity scores, and their small positive correlations with adult clout suggest a low degree of "integration" between the carriers of criminal and conventional values.[28]

The logic of the theory clearly presumes that perceptions of opportunities *precede* involvement in delinquency, while our data reflect perceptions "after the fact." We cannot fully resolve this problem. Evidence concerning the relation of *individual* gang boys' perceptions of opportunities to their behavior as individuals is relevant, however, and its mention permits brief discussion of the somewhat different causal model that has emerged from the larger study of which this paper is a partial report. Correlations between opportunity scores and theoretically relevant behavior scores for individual gang boys are low. For example, *conflict factor scores*, consisting of a combination of individual and gang fighting (with and without weapons), assault, and carrying concealed weapons, are not systematically related to perceptions of either legitimate or illegitimate opportunity scores. That is, boys with high scores do not have lower opportunity scores.[29] It seems unlikely, therefore, that data reported in this paper reflect the boys' efforts to rationalize delinquent behavior by "blaming" the lack of opportunity. Although this does not solve the problem of temporal order, it is presumptive evidence against an alternative interpretation based on the assumption of "after-the-fact" (of delinquency or gang membership) influences on perception.

Our argument is not that the latter are unimportant. Other data from our study suggest that social structure influences the development of ethnic, class, life-cycle, and perhaps "delinquent" subcultures with relatively distinctive content. Social structural theories are therefore appropriately applied to the social distribution of many phenomena—to delinquency "rates" rather than to individual episodes or degrees of involvement in delinquency. It is to the question of "rates" or the social distribution of delinquent subcultures, that the Cloward and Ohlin theory is addressed—appropriately. To account for selection into subcultures—into gang membership, for example—from the youngsters available, and for individual behavior within the context of a subculture, requires reference to "levels" of explanation other than social struc-

[27] See Short, Tennyson, and Howard, *op. cit.*, and Short and Strodtbeck, *op. cit.*, Ch. 5.

[28] This, perhaps, explains why we had such difficulty locating criminal gangs. See Short and Strodtbeck, *op. cit.*, Chs. 1 and 9.

[29] Derivation of the scores is detailed in Short, Tennyson, and Howard, *op. cit.* Full presentation of the data concerning individual opportunity perception and behavior is beyond the scope of this paper.

ture.[30] We have found it necessary to invoke personality level variables, as Inkeles suggested,[31] and *group process* considerations, to explain delinquent behavior *within* our gangs.[32] The give and take of interaction among gang boys, and between gang boys and others; a variety of role relations within the gang and status considerations re-lated to these roles and to opportunities present in situations of the moment —these are prime determinants of what happens in the gang, of who becomes involved in what type of behavior, and with whom.[33] This *level* of explanation "washes out" variations in perceptions of opportunities related to social structure as a major determinant of individuals' behavior in the gang context.

[30] See David Bordua's critique of social structural theories in this regard. David Bordua, "Delinquent Subcultures: Sociological Interpretations of Gang Delinquency," *Annals of the American Academy of Political and Social Science*, 338 (November, 1961), and his "Sociological Theories and Their Implications for Juvenile Delinquency," Children's Bureau, *Juvenile Delinquency: Facts and Facets*, No. 2, Washington, D.C.: Government Printing Office, 1960. See also, Short and Strodtbeck, *op. cit.*, and James F. Short, Jr., "Social Structure and Group Process in Explanations of Gang Delinquency," paper read at the Fifth Social Psychology Symposium, University of Oklahoma, 1964, to be published in the Symposium volume.

[31] Alex Inkeles, "Personality and Social Structure," Ch. 11 in *Sociology Today*, Robert K. Merton, Leonard Broom, and Leonard S. Cottrell, Jr., (eds.), New York: Basic Books, 1959. From the present study,

see Robert A. Gordon and James F. Short, Jr., "Social Level, Social Disability, and Gang Interaction," Ch. 10 in Short and Strodtbeck, *op. cit.*

[32] See, esp., Short, "Gang Delinquency and Anomie," *op. cit.;* Short and Strodtbeck, *op. cit.*, and by the same authors, "The Response of Gang Leaders to Status Threats: An Observation on Group Process and Delinquent Behavior," *American Journal of Sociology*, 68 (March, 1963), pp. 571–579, and "Why Gangs Fight," *Trans-Action*, 1 (September–October, 1964), pp. 25–29; and Strodtbeck and Short, "Aleatory Risks v. Short-Run Hedonism in Explanation of Gang Action," *Social Problems* (Fall, 1964).

[33] The point is made in more general theoretical terms in Albert K. Cohen, "The Sociology of the Deviant Act: Anomie Theory and Beyond," *American Sociological Review*, 30 (February, 1965).

25. Behavior Dimensions of Gang Delinquency

JAMES F. SHORT, JR., RAY A. TENNYSON,
AND KENNETH I. HOWARD

Apparently the gang of today is not the gang of yesterday. The rich "natural histories" compiled by the "old Chicago school"—Shaw, McKay, Thrasher,[1] et al.—give accounts of gang behavior that differ in important respects from delinquency as it is hypothesized to exist today. For example, *specialization* of delinquency pattern has received considerable emphasis in current literature as compared with the past. Weapons and the intent of gang conflict are more lethal, and "kicks" more addicting. Theoretically, delinquency is seen as rooted less in community tradition and "fun," and more in frustration and protest or in the serious business of preparing for manhood, whether in the female-based households of an autonomous lower class or in the mysterious and powerful underworld of organized crime.[2]

* The research reported in this paper is made possible by grants from the National Institute of Mental Health (M3301) and the Ford Foundation. This is an expanded version of a paper read at the annual meetings of the American Statistical Association, 1962. See *Proceedings of the Social Statistics Section*, pp. 62–67. The authors wish to express their gratitude to Robert A. Gordon, Hanan C. Selvin, and Stanton Wheeler for critical review of earlier versions of the paper. Our thanks also to the program for Detached Workers of the YMCA of Metropolitan Chicago, without whose cooperation the entire research enterprise would be impossible.

[1] See Clifford R. Shaw, *The Jack Roller*, Chicago: University of Chicago Press, 1930; Clifford R. Shaw and Maurice E. Morre, *The Natural History of a Delinquent Career*, Chicago: University of Chicago Press, 1931; and F. M. Thrasher, *The Gang*, Chicago: University of Chicago Press, 1936. More recent, but unsystematically gathered and analyzed, data are reported in many sources, e.g., Donald J. Merwin (ed.), *Reaching the Fighting Gang*, New York: New York City Youth Board, 1960. Discussion of the extensive clinical literature on juvenile delinquency is omitted in this paper.

[2] Cf., in comparison with the references in footnote 1, the theoretical points of view set forth in Albert K. Cohen, *Delinquent Boys: The Culture of the Gang*, Glencoe, Ill.: The Free Press, 1955; Albert K. Cohen and James F. Short, Jr., "Research in Delinquent Subcultures," *The Journal of Social Issues*, 14, 3 (1958), pp. 20–37; Richard A. Cloward and Lloyd E. Ohlin, *Delinquency and Opportunity: A Theory of Delinquent Gangs*, Glencoe, Ill.: The Free Press, 1960; Walter B. Miller, "Lower Class Culture as a Generating Milieu of Gang Delinquency," *The Journal of Social Issues*, 14, 3 (1958), pp. 5–19; H. A. Bloch and Arthur Neiderhoffer, *The Gang: A Study in Adolescent Behavior*, New York: Philosophical Library, 1958.

SOURCE. James F. Short, Jr., Ray A. Tennyson, and Kenneth I. Howard, "Behavior Dimensions of Gang Delinquency," from *American Sociological Review*, Volume 28, June 1963, pp. 411–428. Reprinted with the permission of the American Sociological Association and the authors.

Resolution of theoretical differences, between the past and the present and among currently competing theories, requires greater precision, theoretically and empirically, in the delineation of the dependent variables. We shall group these under the term "gang delinquency," avoiding for the moment the knotty problem of specifying the nature of "subcultural delinquency" or the even greater problem of defining delinquent subcultures. We will limit our discussion largely to the measurement of individual *behavior*, rather than individual or group norms, values, or self-concepts.[3] We shall discuss first of all the setting of our research and our

methods of gathering data. This will be followed by discussion of the statistical model chosen for analysis of the data, its application in the present instance, and interpretations of the behavior patterns isolated by this procedure. Finally, individual gangs will be described in terms of the patterns found among all gang boys studied, and an assessment undertaken of the implications of findings for subcultural theory.

THE RESEARCH SETTING

Data were collected from 598 members of 16 "delinquent gangs" assigned detached workers by the Program for Detached Workers of the YMCA of Metropolitan Chicago. The gangs ranged in size from 16 to 68 members, on the basis of workers' judgments concerning who should and who should not be considered members. Initially, gangs were selected by the YMCA on the basis of their generally troublesome character to the community, as judged by police complaints and the reports of welfare agencies, and by field investigations of the Detached Worker staff. Later, in collaboration with the University of Chicago research program, gangs were selected to fulfill requirements of a research design which sought to study gangs representative of major "delinquent subcultures."[4]

The unknown and ever-changing characteristics of the gang population, and the difficulty of gaining research *entrée* to a gang without some "service" legitimation, made conventional sampling techniques inappropriate for our purposes.[5] Our gangs were deliberately

---

Bordua recently has remarked on the differences between past and present notions concerning the structural motivations of delinquency, and particularly on the greater strain. See David J. Bordua, "Some Comments on Theories of Group Delinquency," *Sociological Inquiry*, 32 (Spring, 1962), pp. 245–260, and "Delinquent Subcultures: Sociological Interpretations of Gang Delinquency," *Annals of the American Academy of Political and Social Science*, 338 (November, 1961), pp. 119–136.

[3] For discussion of personal values and self-concepts of the gang boys studied in this paper, see Robert A. Gordon, James F. Short, Jr., Desmond S. Cartwright, and Fred L. Strodtbeck, "Values and Gang Delinquency: A Study of Street Corner Groups," *American Journal of Sociology* 69 (September, 1963), pp. 109–128. Patricia Leavey Hodge, "Self-Descriptions of Gang and Non-Gang Teen-Age Boys," M.A. Thesis, Department of Sociology, University of Chicago, 1963; Fred L. Strodtbeck, James F. Short, Jr., and Ellen Kolegar, "The Analysis of Self-Descriptions by Members of Delinquent Gangs," *Sociological Quarterly*, 3 (October, 1962), pp. 331–356. Papers from the present project which attempt to specify group norms and some of their consequences are: James F. Short, Jr., Fred L. Strodtbeck, and Desmond S. Cartwright, "A Strategy for Utilizing Research Dilemmas: A Case from the Study of Parenthood in a Street Corner Gang," *Sociological Inquiry*, 32 (Spring, 1962), pp. 185–202; and James F. Short, Jr. and Fred L. Strodtbeck, "The Response of Gang Leaders to Status Threats: An Observation of Group Process and Delinquent Behavior," *American Journal of Sociology*, 68 (March, 1963), pp. 571–579.

[4] Initial research designs are discussed in James F. Short, Jr., "The Nature of Street Corner Groups: Theory and Research Design," unpublished paper, Youth Studies Program, Spring, 1960 (mimeographed).

[5] We are in agreement with Kobrin who argues that "Fruitful observation of such a group is possible only when the observer

chosen from the *delinquent* end of a delinquent-nondelinquent continuum, the primary effort being directed toward locating carriers of conflict, criminal, and retreatist subcultures.[6]

The search for gangs concentrated on the "criminal" and "drug use" types, principally because conflict-oriented gangs, particularly among Negroes, were abundant.[7] Additionally, it was hypothesized that both drug use and criminal patterns are *rare*, as compared with the occurrence of the parent and conflict patterns. This hypothesis is based upon the assumption that extensive drug use is not a generally supported gang activity; moreover, community areas where carriers of criminal and conventional values are integrated in such a way as to produce adolescent criminal subcultures occur relatively infrequently.[8] *Finding* gangs whose pri-

mary activities and norms were oriented around drug use or rational, systematic, economically motivated criminal activity proved to be a major problem. Much marihuana smoking was found in several groups, and heroin and "pills" were experimented with by many boys, always in concert with other boys; but these were not major activities or normative emphases of the groups. It took more than a year of extensive inquiries among police and local community adults, coupled with field investigations by detached workers and our own research personnel, to locate a drug-oriented group. Although much criminal activity was found in nearly all groups, criminally oriented gangs such as those hypothesized by Cloward and Ohlin were equally difficult to locate. The failure to locate a criminal group, or more than one drug-using group, despite our highly motivated effort to do so, is a "finding" of some importance, for it casts doubt on the generality of these phenomena, if not on their existence. Our subsequent search for gangs to fit a research design based upon the typology of conflict, criminal, and retreatist gangs, and the analysis which follows must be viewed against this background. We were led to seek groups not primarily oriented around fighting, but with extensive involvement in the pursuit of "kicks" or various forms of theft. We hoped that systematic study of these groups would permit more precise identification of the nature of delinquent subcultures, either on the basis of between- or within-group behavioral differentiation.

is accepted by the subjects in a role which they perceive as meaningful in relation to their needs and problems." Solomon Kobrin, "Sociological Aspects of the Development of a Street Corner Group: An Exploratory Study," *The American Journal of Orthopsychiatry*, 31 (October, 1961), pp. 685–702.

[6] Rather than concentrating wholly on one type, or on the more amorphous "parent delinquent subculture" which has been hypothesized as a general subculture from which specialized variants emerge. See Cohen and Short, *op. cit.*

[7] When the research project began, in June, 1959, one white and six Negro gangs were assigned workers by the YMCA. All of these had been chosen because of their involvement in conflict with other gangs, their harassment of local community institutions, or their reputations for toughness and troublemaking among police and agency representatives. Though we could not be certain, it appeared that each was to a considerable degree a carrier of "conflict subcultures." None of these groups was being worked with primarily because of their criminal or drug use activities, though one of the Negro gangs was known to smoke marihuana heavily and occasionally to experiment with heroin.

[8] Cf. Cohen and Short, *op. cit.*; Cloward and Ohlin, *op. cit.*; and Isidor Cheilm and Eva Rosenfeld, "Juvenile Narcotics Use," *Law and Contemporary Problems*, 22 (1957), pp. 52–68.

THE DATA

Dissatisfaction with official statistics as a basis for measuring delinquent behavior has led in recent years to experimentation with a variety of methods for obtaining better measures of such behavior. Combinations of a variety of public and private agency records,[9] anonymously completed self-reports,[10] survey-type interviews,[11] detailed clinical investigations,[12] and reports of field observers[13] confirm the suspicions of those who claim that official records are unreliable as a basis for determining either the extent or the nature of delinquent behavior.[14]

[9] Edward E. Schwartz, "A Community Experiment in the Measurement of Juvenile Delinquency," *Yearbook of the National Probation Association*, 1945, pp. 157–182; Alfred J. Kahn, *Police and Children*, New York Citizens' Committee on Children of New York City, 1951.

[10] Austin L. Porterfield, *Youth in Trouble*, Fort Worth: Leo Potishman Foundation, 1946; James F. Short and F. Ivan Nye, "Reported Behavior as a Criterion of Deviant Behavior," *Social Problems*, 5, 3 (Winter, 1957–1958), pp. 207–213.

[11] Albert J. Reiss, Jr. and Albert Lewis Rhodes, "The Distribution of Juvenile Delinquency in the Social Class Structure," *American Sociological Review*, 26 (October, 1961), pp. 720–733.

[12] The clinical literature is vast. Among the more research-oriented investigations are: Lester E. Hewitt and Richard L. Jenkins, *Fundamental Patterns of Maladjustment: The Dynamics of Their Origin*, Springfield, Ill., State of Illinois, 1947; and Fritz Redl and David Wineman, *Children Who Hate—The Disorganization and Breakdown of Behavior Controls*, Glencoe, Ill.: The Free Press, 1951.

[13] Fred J. Murphy, Mary M. Shirley, and Helen L. Witmer, "The Incidence of Hidden Delinquency," *American Journal of Orthopsychiatry*, 16 (October, 1946), pp. 686–696; Walter Miller's recent work and our own are the most extensive examples of the use of such methods of generating data.

[14] These same studies suggest that police and court data are likely to be more reliable and perhaps more valid as a basis for studying certain types of behavior than others. Cf., particularly Schwartz, *op. cit.*; Murphy, Shirley, and Witmer, *op. cit.*; James F. Short, Jr., and F. Ivan Nye, "The Extent of Delinquent Behavior: Tentative Conclusions," *Journal of Criminal Law, Criminology, and Police Science*, 49 (December, 1958), pp. 296–302; and from the present research program, John M. Wise, "A Comparison of Sources of Data as Indexes of Delinquent Behavior," M.A. Thesis, University of Chicago, 1962, unpublished. This matter is of the greatest significance for the large scale and long

Consideration of alternative methods of generating data on the behavior of the gang boys under observation led to the rejection of most of the usual methods; instead, a system of ratings by the detached workers seemed the most feasible and reliable method of obtaining the needed data.

We required, first of all, a method of gathering data on a wide variety of behaviors, including many which were both illegal and regarded by society as definitely undesirable. This, plus the unfavorable exposure of many of these boys to law enforcement agencies and the necessity of identifying the boys by name, led to the rejection of self-reporting by the boys as a primary method of data collection. Resources for extensive clinical investigation of individual boys were not available to us, and the widely scattered location of the gangs throughout the inner-city area made the inter-agency "clearing house" method impractical for our purposes.

The availability of detached workers as intimate observers of the boys, particularly in the gang setting, offered a rare opportunity to gain more complete and objective insights into the behavior of these boys than could be provided by any other method. Weekly interviews with the workers convinced us that they shared intimately in the on-going life of the gang.[15] Such behavioral information as was not known by direct contact with a boy could usually be inferred from conversations among the boys or directly with the worker in the endless "bull sessions"

term measurement of delinquent behavior because only official sources of data have the potential for objective, continuous collection of data from very large populations and subpopulations.

[15] See Ray A. Tennyson, "Detached Workers as Sources of Data," paper read at the annual meetings of the Society for the Study of Social Problems, August, 1960 (dittoed).

on the street corner. The nature of these contacts seemed particularly conducive to objective reporting of the type of behavior we were interested in measuring, i.e., street corner behavior.[16] This behavior could be described in concrete terms and it did not require abstract conceptualization by our informants.

What we needed was a "baseline" of information on the behavior of our population, information which could be statistically manipulated and related to other variables we were studying. Toward this end a list of 69 behavioral categories was drawn up. Because we were interested more in incidence of behaviors and their relative frequency, rather than absolute frequencies, and because workers' observations could not extend to actual counts of behavior, we asked only that each boy be rated in terms of whether he had *engaged* in a particular type of behavior only a few times or many times. Workers were asked to report only after they had been in contact with a group for at least six months, to restrict their reporting to boys whom they and the group recognized as group members, and to limit their reports to information in which they were confident. An item-by-item review of their reports was undertaken by the research staff to insure the most accurate reporting possible. Most gang members were rated by only one rater, though two gangs had more than one worker over the rating period, and members of these were rated by each worker having at least six months contact. A high degree of consensus was noted in these ratings. Comparison of worker reports with police records reveals no marked tendency for workers

to "under report" or "over report."[17] Length of contact with the gang, beyond the six-month minimum requirement, is unrelated to behavior ratings so far as "reliability" is concerned.[18] Our assumption is that obtained differences between gangs were due to differences in behavior rather than differences in rater characteristics.

The 69 behaviors, together with their reported incidence by Negro and white gang boys, are listed in Table 1.

There are great differences in the incidence of these behaviors among our gang boys, and apparently some of these are related to racial composition of the population. In this form, however, the data are not interpretable as behavior patterns. We turn next, therefore, to the reduction of these data.

THE DIMENSIONALITY OF DELINQUENT BEHAVIOR

Empirically, our problem was to determine the nature of behavioral patterns characterizing the boys and gangs studied. Theoretically, we wanted to relate observed to hypothesized patterns and to assess their significance for subcultural theory.

The dimensionality of delinquent and criminal behavior has been approached by a variety of clinical and statistical techniques, and occasionally by a combination of these.[19] Several investigators have found self-reported delinquency

---

[16] In contrast to information concerning the behavior of the boys twithin the context of family, school, employment, and other more conventional institutions. For the latter we have relied particularly upon survey methods.

[17] See Wise, *op. cit.*

[18] See footnote 27. The point here is that groups with which the program has had the longest contact are not necessarily the most delinquent. Our interpretation is that workers come to know a great deal about the boys in a relatively short period of time and that reported differences between groups outweigh any tendency for boys to become "more delinquent" (in a cumulative sense) with the passage of time.

[19] Hewitt and Jenkins, *op. cit.*; Albert J. Reiss, "Social Correlates of Psychological Types of Delinquency," *American Sociological Review,* 17 (December, 1952) pp. 710–718.

Table 1

INCIDENCE OF 69 BEHAVIORS AMONG NEGRO AND WHITE GANG BOYS, RANKED BY
PERCENTAGE OF REPORTED INVOLVEMENT

	Negro N = 464	White N = 134	Total N = 598
Hanging on the street	89.2	95.5	90.6
Alcohol (drinking)	85.6	89.6	86.5
Dancing	85.1	63.4	80.3
Loitering	72.0	84.3	74.7
Smooch, neck, petting	72.8	78.4	74.1
Sexual intercourse	78.9	57.5	74.1
Signifying (playing the dozens)*	79.1	53.7	73.4
Joy riding	67.5	93.3	73.2
Softball	71.1	67.9	70.4
Statutory rape	73.1	50.7	68.1
Playing cards (for money)	62.7	85.8	67.9
Playing cards (for fun)	66.6	70.1	67.4
Drunk	62.5	82.1	66.7
Working (on a job)	59.1	79.9	64.2
Individual fighting—without weapons	67.5	52.2	64.0
Pool	60.1	69.4	62.2
Basketball	61.6	51.5	59.4
Shooting dice	64.4	35.1	57.9
Gang fighting—without weapons	61.4	44.8	57.7
Boxing	59.5	38.8	54.8
Penny pitching	58.8	33.6	53.2
Buy and sell alcohol	52.8	70.9	53.0
Theft	50.9	58.2	52.5
Carry concealed weapons	55.8	40.3	52.3
Swimming	51.1	56.0	52.2
Gang fighting—with weapons	53.2	40.3	50.3
Truancy	48.3	53.7	49.5
Create public disturbance	44.6	64.9	49.2
Shoplifting	47.2	47.0	47.2
Vandalism	40.9	64.9	46.3
Assault	48.7	35.1	45.7
Being "shook down"	44.2	36.6	42.5
Smoke pot	42.5	33.6	40.5
Individual fighting—with weapons	45.0	23.9	40.3
Auto theft	35.1	57.5	40.0
Strong-arm	45.6	12.7	38.3
Burglary	30.0	53.7	35.3
Running errands (for parents)	37.7	23.1	34.4
Ping pong	26.5	48.5	31.4
Football	28.7	35.8	30.3
Driving without a license	24.4	44.0	28.8
Wrestling	30.6	19.4	28.1
Baby sitting	27.2	20.1	25.6
Baseball	23.7	28.4	24.7
Drunk driving	18.5	31.3	21.4
Runaway	17.7	29.1	20.2
Track and field	24.6	4.5	20.1
Buy and sell marihuana	19.8	19.4	19.7
Shakedown	22.4	6.0	18.7
Gang bang	18.3	17.2	18.1
Skating	20.3	9.0	17.7
Robbery	18.7	11.9	17.2

Table 1—Continued

	Negro N = 464	White N = 134	Total N = 598
Bowling	5.8	32.1	11.7
Use hard narcotics	7.3	23.1	10.9
Fathering an illegitimate child	17.0	3.7	10.7
Child or wife abandonment	11.9	6.0	10.5
Homosexuality	6.5	14.2	8.2
Offering "protection"	9.5	3.0	8.0
Buy and sell narcotics	6.0	14.9	7.9
Forgery	7.3	6.7	7.2
Bribery	2.6	18.7	6.2
Rape	5.0	5.2	5.0
Lottery	1.7	15.7	4.8
Common-law marriage	4.7	3.7	4.5
Pimping	5.6	.7	4.5
Playing horses (betting)	1.3	4.5	2.0
Homicide	1.7	.7	1.5
Arson	.2	2.2	.7
Suicide (attempt)	.2	1.5	.5

* Signifying is a form of systematic exchange of insults, ordinarily carried out in the presence of an audience. It serves as a social control mechanism and a device for displaying verbal virtuosity. "Playing the dozens" is a special form of signifying, concentrating in pornographic insults concerning family members of opponents. See Ralph F. Berdie, "Playing the Dozens," *The Journal of Abnormal and Social Psychology,* 42 (January, 1947), pp. 120–121.

to scale acceptably when unidimensional scaling methods are employed.[20] These methods tend to be arbitrary in assigning items to particular scales, however, and to select for study dimensions which are not especially relevant to theories of delinquency causation. Unfortunately, the theories are not very helpful in this matter, for they lack specificity in describing the patterns of behavior they purport to explain. Hence the problem: the theories regard delinquency as multidimensional, but they do not tell us precisely the nature of these dimensions. Our delinquent population consisted of boys who were members of gangs and who thereby presum-

ably met one of the principal criteria of subcultural delinquency. Furthermore, these gangs were selected on the basis of at least superficial similarity to the subcultural patterns we wanted to study. We therefore chose a model which would tell us how the behavior of these boys "hangs together"— whether in demonstrable packages which could be interpreted in the light of subcultural theory, or in a more or less undifferentiated way.

Because we wished not to have a large number of dichotomous "variables," the 69 behaviors were combined into 37 items on the basis of similarity of item content. These combinations are presented in Table 2.

Product-moment correlations were calculated for all 37 items (Table 3). The generally positive character of the resulting correlation matrix suggested that involvement in delinquency is to some extent a global phenomenon, the dimensions of which might lie along a

[20] F. Ivan Nye and James F. Short, Jr., "Scaling Delinquent Behavior," *American Sociological Review,* 22 (June, 1957), pp. 326–331; John F. Scott, "Two Dimensions of Delinquent Behavior," *American Sociological Review,* 24 (April, 1959), pp. 240–243; Robert A. Dentler and Lawrence J. Monroe, "Social Correlates of Early Adolescent Theft," *American Sociological Review,* 26 (October, 1961), pp. 733–743.

Table 2

RECLASSIFICATION AND SCORING OF BEHAVIORS FOR STATISTICAL PURPOSES

New classification	Old classification	Range of scores, new classification
Domestic chores	Baby sitting; running errands	0–2
Team sports	Baseball; basketball; football; softball	0–4
Individual sports	Bowling; boxing; ping pong; pool; skating; swimming; track; wrestling	0–8
Signifying (playing the dozens)	No change	0–2
Hanging on the street	No change	0–2
Joy riding	No change	0–2
Social activities	Dancing; singing; playing cards for fun	0–3
Gambling	Playing horses; lottery (numbers, etc.); penny pitching; playing cards for money	0–4
Petting	No change	0–2
Working (on a job)	No change	0–2
Sexual intercourse	No change	0–2
Fathering an illegitimate child	Abandonment; fathering illegitimate child	0–2
Arson	No change	0–1
Auto theft	No change	0–2
Bribery	No change	0–1
Theft	Burglary; shoplifting; theft	0–6
Alcohol (drinking)	Use of alcohol; buying and selling alcohol; drunk; drunk driving	0–11
Narcotics	Use of narcotics; buying and selling narcotics	0–3
Marihuana (pot)	Use of marihuana; buying and selling marihuana	0–3
Carry concealed weapon	No change	0–2
Common-law marriage	No change	0–1
Public nuisance	Loitering; creating a public disturbance; vandalism	0–4
Driving without a license	No change	0–2
Group fighting	Group fighting with weapons; group fighting without weapons	0–6
Individual fighting	Individual fighting with weapons; individual fighting without weapons	0–6
Forgery	No change	0–2
Gang bang	No change	0–2
Homicide	No change	0–1
Homosexuality	No change	0–2
Pimping	No change	0–1
Robbery	Armed robbery; strong-arming; offering protection; shakedown	0–7
Rape	No change	0–1
Statutory rape	No change	0–2
Run away from home	No change	0–2
Suicide (attempt)	No change	0–1
Truancy	No change	0–2
Assault	No change	0–2

Table 3

PRODUCT MOMENT CORRELATIONS BETWEEN 37 BEHAVIORS, FOR ALL GANG BOYS

	D. chs.	T. spts.	I. spts.	Soc. ac.	Gambl.	Il. chl.	Theft	Alcoh.	Pot	Narco.	Pub. n.	G. fight	I. fight	Robb.	Signi.	Hang.	J. ride	Pett.	Wrk. ex.
Domestic chores	—	28	26	32	17	08	18	16	07	—11	25	34	30	12	26	22	22	24	11
Team sports	—	—	58	37	27	06	16	06	01	—04	18	10	09	05	21	25	21	19	17
Individual sports	—	—	—	45	44	13	29	21	24	07	29	16	14	20	28	30	35	24	21
Social acts	—	—	—	—	44	09	20	18	09	—14	25	29	27	18	38	34	31	32	13
Gambling	—	—	—	—	—	09	35	33	24	02	36	29	22	33	28	33	23	28	12
Illegitimate child	—	—	—	—	—	—	16	25	25	16	12	18	20	23	06	05	10	13	12
Theft	—	—	—	—	—	—	—	06	44	27	66	48	47	56	25	31	38	25	07
Alcohol	—	—	—	—	—	—	—	—	48	31	60	54	54	49	27	36	33	39	21
Pot	—	—	—	—	—	—	—	—	—	48	35	30	35	49	18	18	16	18	09
Narcotics	—	—	—	—	—	—	—	—	—	—	21	08	11	26	—07	04	15	04	06
Public nuisance	—	—	—	—	—	—	—	—	—	—	—	53	51	40	20	34	47	28	11
Group fighting	—	—	—	—	—	—	—	—	—	—	—	—	77	45	37	27	24	35	09
Individual fighting	—	—	—	—	—	—	—	—	—	—	—	—	—	47	29	22	23	30	08
Robbery	—	—	—	—	—	—	—	—	—	—	—	—	—	—	18	16	12	18	—04
Signifying	—	—	—	—	—	—	—	—	—	—	—	—	—	—	—	48	23	50	17
Hanging	—	—	—	—	—	—	—	—	—	—	—	—	—	—	—	—	43	48	18
Joy ride	—	—	—	—	—	—	—	—	—	—	—	—	—	—	—	—	—	22	24
Petting	—	—	—	—	—	—	—	—	—	—	—	—	—	—	—	—	—	—	26
Work experience	—	—	—	—	—	—	—	—	—	—	—	—	—	—	—	—	—	—	—
Sex intercourse	—	—	—	—	—	—	—	—	—	—	—	—	—	—	—	—	—	—	—
Arson	—	—	—	—	—	—	—	—	—	—	—	—	—	—	—	—	—	—	—
Auto theft	—	—	—	—	—	—	—	—	—	—	—	—	—	—	—	—	—	—	—
Bribery	—	—	—	—	—	—	—	—	—	—	—	—	—	—	—	—	—	—	—
Concealed weapon	—	—	—	—	—	—	—	—	—	—	—	—	—	—	—	—	—	—	—
Common law marriage	—	—	—	—	—	—	—	—	—	—	—	—	—	—	—	—	—	—	—
Driving without license	—	—	—	—	—	—	—	—	—	—	—	—	—	—	—	—	—	—	—
Forgery	—	—	—	—	—	—	—	—	—	—	—	—	—	—	—	—	—	—	—
Gang bang	—	—	—	—	—	—	—	—	—	—	—	—	—	—	—	—	—	—	—

Table 3—Continued

	D. chs.	T. spts.	I. spts.	Soc. ac.	Gambl.	Il. chl.	Theft	Alcoh.	Pot	Narco.	Pub. n.	C. fight	I. fight	Robb.	Signi.	Hang.	J. ride	Pett.	Wrk. ex.
Homicide	—	—	—	—	—	—	—	—	—	—	—	—	—	—	—	—	—	—	—
Homosexual	—	—	—	—	—	—	—	—	—	—	—	—	—	—	—	—	—	—	—
Pimp	—	—	—	—	—	—	—	—	—	—	—	—	—	—	—	—	—	—	—
Rape	—	—	—	—	—	—	—	—	—	—	—	—	—	—	—	—	—	—	—
Statutory rape	—	—	—	—	—	—	—	—	—	—	—	—	—	—	—	—	—	—	—
Runaway	—	—	—	—	—	—	—	—	—	—	—	—	—	—	—	—	—	—	—
Suicide	—	—	—	—	—	—	—	—	—	—	—	—	—	—	—	—	—	—	—
Truancy	—	—	—	—	—	—	—	—	—	—	—	—	—	—	—	—	—	—	—
Assault	—	—	—	—	—	—	—	—	—	—	—	—	—	—	—	—	—	—	—

	Sex int.	Arson	Auto th.	Bribe	C. weap.	C. l. mar.	DWOL	Forge	Gng. bng.	Homicide	Homosex.	Pimp	Rape	St. rape	Runaway	Suicide	Truancy	Assault
Domestic chores	19	—05	08	02	30	—01	09	18	16	04	—06	00	—00	21	06	—04	24	22
Team sports	09	—07	07	01	00	01	16	05	06	02	—08	—00	—23	11	05	03	20	07
Individual sports	16	—05	12	09	10	04	15	—04	11	—04	08	01	06	13	14	03	26	19
Social acts	29	—01	07	—03	16	05	10	14	16	—02	—17	11	—16	25	09	—06	28	27
Gambling	24	10	18	14	26	11	23	16	19	—06	03	14	02	28	16	—01	35	25
Illegitimate child	21	05	09	06	17	39	16	02	24	14	20	16	07	24	06	16	02	16
Theft	25	05	62	24	47	14	50	23	33	16	28	18	14	30	46	09	43	58
Alcohol	42	08	52	24	50	13	56	25	37	08	28	20	15	47	37	07	30	53
Pot	28	—01	32	01	36	21	25	09	30	10	39	22	11	29	20	12	15	39
Narcotics	08	06	28	05	10	17	20	13	22	11	42	17	05	10	16	21	01	19
Public nuisance	20	05	51	22	44	11	43	28	38	04	19	17	13	31	38	08	54	56
Group fighting	43	03	36	14	64	12	32	26	35	09	10	13	17	53	27	04	28	60
Individual fighting	40	01	37	12	59	10	28	27	35	11	08	17	20	47	30	01	26	65

Table 3—Continued

	Sex int.	Arson	Auto th.	Bribe	C. weap.	C. l. mar.	DWOL	Forge	Gng. bng.	Homicide	Homosex.	Pimp	Rape	St. rape	Runaway	Suicide	Truancy	Assault
Robbery	25	08	44	16	50	12	36	27	36	12	30	20	21	34	31	09	24	51
Signifying	45	-04	17	-01	27	03	15	14	12	09	01	09	04	40	12	-01	19	22
Hanging	34	00	23	06	24	04	20	11	12	05	03	04	05	30	13	03	27	19
Joy ride	12	01	33	09	21	07	29	16	20	03	04	06	07	08	22	05	38	32
Petting	57	01	22	12	29	07	25	16	15	08	04	06	04	50	12	-03	19	17
Work experience	28	-01	09	10	08	06	13	06	06	-09	-00	08	-02	19	-00	-05	-00	06
Sex intercourse	—	-01	24	11	34	11	22	14	21	06	12	12	13	74	14	05	08	29
Arson	—	—	10	14	01	-02	05	06	15	-01	05	-02	07	02	02	-00	-03	02
Auto theft	—	—	—	16	36	08	60	34	32	08	22	16	11	26	33	06	30	44
Bribery	—	—	—	—	09	14	25	21	17	06	15	04	09	13	11	05	04	10
Concealed weapon	—	—	—	—	—	12	28	26	35	09	13	15	12	44	25	04	23	54
Common law marriage	—	—	—	—	—	—	09	07	10	01	16	18	-05	15	-00	23	01	11
Driving without license	—	—	—	—	—	—	—	24	33	02	15	17	12	27	32	10	28	30
Forgery	—	—	—	—	—	—	—	—	31	-02	11	20	-02	17	12	12	16	26
Gang bang	—	—	—	—	—	—	—	—	—	—	28	18	12	26	21	17	24	36
Homicide	—	—	—	—	—	—	—	—	—	—	06	03	02	06	13	-01	02	13
Homosexual	—	—	—	—	—	—	—	—	—	—	—	10	10	10	20	23	04	22
Pimp	—	—	—	—	—	—	—	—	—	—	—	—	16	16	06	14	09	17
Rape	—	—	—	—	—	—	—	—	—	—	—	—	—	13	15	-02	09	14
Statutory rape	—	—	—	—	—	—	—	—	—	—	—	—	—	—	20	06	15	34
Runaway	—	—	—	—	—	—	—	—	—	—	—	—	—	—	—	02	29	37
Suicide	—	—	—	—	—	—	—	—	—	—	—	—	—	—	—	—	01	05
Truancy	—	—	—	—	—	—	—	—	—	—	—	—	—	—	—	—	—	29
Assault	—	—	—	—	—	—	—	—	—	—	—	—	—	—	—	—	—	—

continuum of more or less delinquency involvement, regardless of the specific offenses committed. However, the considerable range in incidence of the several types of delinquency found in Table 1—together with variations in the seriousness with which these behaviors are regarded by the law and the wide variation in the size of correlations between behaviors—suggested that it might be possible to find clusters of related items which would prove to be theoretically interesting. A preliminary cluster analysis suggested that factor analysis was a promising model.[21]

The correlation matrix was factor analyzed, using the principal axis method and entering the highest column correlations in the main diagonal. Following a modification of Wrigley's criterion for when to stop factoring,[22] five factors were extracted and rotated using Varimax. The first unrotated factor accounted for much more of the common variance than did any succeeding factor, again pointing to the existence of a general delinquency trait; but there was ample evidence from the factor analysis that somewhat specialized adaptations also existed among our subjects. Communalities of the 37 behavior items and their loadings on each of the factors are presented in Table 4.

Factor 1 is essentially a *conflict* factor, its highest loading items being

individual fighting (.79), group fighting (.76), carrying concealed weapons (.67), and assault (.67). None of these behaviors loads highly on any other factor. Robbery, theft, public nuisance, and statutory rape also load fairly highly on this factor, ranging from .51 to .40, but these items have similarly high loadings on other factors. Factor 1 may be more precisely characterized as consisting of conflict offenses, both acquisitive and destructive. Note the negative (though low) loadings on this factor of work experience, team sports, attempted suicide, and narcotics involvement.

Factor 2 has highest loadings of individual sports (.71), team sports (.68), social activities (.60), and gambling (.48). Other loadings higher than .40 are obtained for joy riding, truancy, and hanging. The latter behaviors have similarly high loadings on other factors, however. This factor may be characterized as a configuration of *stable corner activities*. No seriously delinquent behavior loads highly, though several minor types of delinquency have moderate loadings.

Factor 3 is difficult to characterize. It has as its highest loading items sex intercourse (.77), statutory rape (.68), petting (.67), signifying (.53), hanging on the corner (.44), and the use, buying, and selling of alcohol (.39). It also has the only moderately high loading of any factor for work experience (.36), accounting for nearly all of this item's common variance. We have chosen to call this a *stable sex* pattern and to regard the loading of work experience as a further indication of a type of relatively adaptive behavior which is represented by the factor.

Factor 4 is characterized by high loadings for quite different sex behaviors, namely homosexuality (.53), fathering an illegitimate child (.50), and common law marriage (.48). Ad-

[21] Louis L. McQuitty, "Elementary Linkage Analysis for Isolating Orthogonal and Oblique Types and Typal Relevancies," *Educational and Psychological Measurement*, 17 (Summer, 1957), pp. 207–229; Louis L. McQuitty, "Hierarchical Syndrome Analysis," *Educational and Psychological Measurement*, 20 (Summer, 1960), pp. 293–304; Louis L. McQuitty, "A Method for Selecting Patterns to Differentiate Categories of People," *Educational and Psychological Measurement*, 21 (Spring, 1961), pp. 85–94.

[22] Kenneth I. Howard and Robert A. Gordon, "Empirical Note on the 'Number of Factors' Problem in Factor Analysis," *Psychological Reports*, 12 (February, 1963), pp. 247–250.

Table 4

LOADINGS ON ALL FACTORS AND COMMUNALITIES—FIVE-FACTOR SOLUTION

Item	Commu- nalities	Factor 1	Factor 2	Factor 3	Factor 4	Factor 5
Group fighting	73	76	13	—30	—06	—19
Individual fighting	72	79	10	—22	—09	—19
Sex intercourse	70	26	02	—77	—17	—08
Statutory rape	66	40	01	—68	—18	—09
Public nuisance	65	43	34	—05	—10	—58
Theft	62	44	32	03	—22	—53
Assault	61	67	17	—03	18	32
Alcohol	60	36	06	—39	—26	—49
Auto theft	58	26	07	—10	—14	—69
Concealed weapon	56	67	05	—22	—13	—21
Individual sports	56	01	71	—13	—17	—07
Petting	55	12	22	—67	—01	—18
Robbery	51	51	09	—04	—35	—33
Driving without license	50	13	11	—17	—14	—65
Social activities	48	22	60	—26	06	06
Team sports	48	—06	68	—11	—02	03
Pot	46	29	10	—11	—55	—23
Hanging	42	07	40	—44	03	—25
Narcotics	42	—01	—08	04	—56	—32
Signifying	42	21	31	—53	04	—05
Truancy	41	26	43	04	09	—39
Joy riding	39	09	45	—10	—01	—41
Homosexuality	37	05	—10	03	—53	—27
Gambling	35	19	48	—20	—10	—17
Gang bang	29	32	08	—08	—28	—32
Illegitimate child	29	14	06	—15	—50	04
Runaway	28	27	10	02	—06	—44
Domestic chores	27	31	36	—17	11	02
Common law marriage	25	06	06	—07	—48	05
Work experience	18	—09	17	—36	—06	—10
Forgery	16	24	03	—09	—06	—30
Attempted suicide	14	—02	00	03	—36	—06
Bribery	11	03	—02	—10	—10	—29
Pimping	11	14	02	—07	—27	—11
Rape	10	18	—16	—05	—04	—19
Arson	04	00	—11	—01	—04	—15
Homicide	03	12	—03	—01	—11	—03

ditionally, it has as its highest loading the use, buying, and selling of narcotics (.56) and of marihuana (.55). This factor accounts for virtually all of the low communalities of suicide and pimping, with loadings of .36 and .27, respectively. In contrast with Factor 3, work experience has a loading of only .06, sex intercourse .17, statutory rape .18, petting .01, hanging .00, and signifying .00 on Factor 4. The combination of narcotics involvement, the "deviant" sex behaviors, and attempted

suicide, leads us to identify this factor as *retreatist*.

Factor 5 includes the highest loadings of auto theft (.69), driving without a license (.65), public nuisance (.58), theft (.53), use, buying, and selling of alcohol (.48),[23] and running

[23] We note, parenthetically, that only about 7 per cent of alcohol's variance is accounted for by its interaction on Factor 4. It seems clear that only a small proportion of the buying, selling, and use of alcohol is related to the extreme emphasis placed on kicks which is represented by

Table 5

LOADINGS AND PROPORTION OF VARIANCE OF SEVEN CRIMINAL BEHAVIORS AC-
COUNTED FOR BY EACH OF FIVE FACTORS[*]

Criminal behaviors	Factor 1	Factor 2	Factor 3	Factor 4	Factor 5
Robbery	51 (26.0)	09 (.8)	—04 (.2)	—35 (12.3)	—33 (10.9)
Theft	44 (19.4)	32 (10.2)	+03 (.1)	—22 (4.8)	—53 (28.1)
Auto theft	26 (6.8)	07 (.5)	—10 (1.0)	—14 (2.0)	—69 (47.6)
Forgery	24 (5.8)	03 (.1)	—09 (.8)	—06 (.4)	—30 (9.0)
Pimping	14 (2.0)	02 (.0)	—07 (.5)	—27 (7.3)	—11 (1.2)
Bribery	03 (.1)	—02 (.0)	—10 (1.0)	—10 (1.0)	—29 (8.4)
Gambling	19 (3.6)	48 (23.0)	—10 (1.0)	—10 (1.0)	—17 (2.9)
$\bar{x}$	(9.1)	(4.9)	(0.7)	(4.1)	(15.4)

[*] Proportion of variance placed in parentheses.

away from home (.44). In addition, this factor includes moderately high loadings for joy riding (.41) and truancy (.39). The versatility of this combination of offenses within a variety of institutional contexts (e.g., the "institutions" of property, school, and family, and in general the maintenance of public order) leads us to characterize this factor as an *auto-theft-authority-protest* pattern. As an abbreviated description we shall refer to Factor 5 as representing *authority protest*.[24]

We note that no clearly "criminal subculture" factor was extracted by our procedures. The variance of criminal behaviors is spread over all of the factors to a greater extent than either conflict or retreatist behaviors. It is clear from an examination of the seven most "criminal" items in Table 5, however, that the five factors are not "equally criminal."

While there is much variation in the loadings of items on each factor as well as across factors, Factor 5 emerges as the most generally "criminal" ($\bar{x} = 15.4$), followed by Factors 1 ($\bar{x} = 9.1$), 2 ($\bar{x} = 4.9$), 4 ($\bar{x} = 4.1$),

Factor 4. Alcohol is virtually ubiquitous, loading on all but the nondelinquent Factor 2.

24 We note the similarity of authority protest to the delinquent subculture hypothesized in Cohen, *op. cit.*

and 3 ($\bar{x} = 0.7$). The means for these criminal items are deceiving, however, because they cover up variations which aid in the interpretation of the factors and of these specific criminal behaviors. For example, auto theft and bribery are relatively specific to Factor 5, pimping to Factor 4, and gambling to Factor 2.

Except for the high loadings of noncriminal behaviors on Factor 5 this might be considered an essentially criminal factor. Our characterization of this factor, however, suggests that such a designation is not appropriate; observation of gangs with the highest Factor 5 scores, below, confirms this decision. Thus, the criminal behaviors studied are associated with different configurations of offenses rather than as a factor themselves. No rationally directed effort to acquire money emerges in isolation from other factors. Instead, criminal activity is associated with conflict, retreatism, and general rebellious activity, and to some extent also with stable corner boy activity. Only the stable-sex factor fails to share at least 10 per cent of the variance of at least one of these "criminal" behaviors. This factor accounts for no more than 1 per cent of the variance of any of these behaviors. The behaviors loading high on Factor 4, strong-arm robbery, pimping, and petty thefts, seem most appropriately characterized as "hustles" toward the acquisition of money to finance drugs, alcohol, and other kicks. The motivation for criminal activity is less clear in their association with other factors. Further interpretation of the relation of criminal and other types of behavior is undertaken in the "Discussion" section of the paper.

To maximize the independence of factors for etiological inquiry, we decided to eliminate from factor scoring all items which were not relatively "pure" on a given factor, and to weight the contribution of each item to a factor score according to the proportion of the item's variance which was accounted for by interaction with other items on a given factor. Loadings of .40 or higher on more than one factor were considered sufficient to eliminate an item from scoring.[25] Table 6 lists the items utilized for factor scoring. Scoring involved summing of the standard score, weighted by the factor loading of each item, for each boy.

The list of items *eliminated* from scoring by our criteria is instructive theoretically as well as empirically. Table 7 lists the 10 most common of these items, together with their loadings on each of the factors.

Robbery and theft, two of the previously considered "criminal" offenses, are the only two relatively serious "delinquencies" on this list. Slightly

[25] Items with nearly equal (but smaller than .40) loadings on more than one factor were eliminated, as were several items which did not load highly on any factor. For the latter, very little of their variance could be accounted for by the factors extracted from the original matrix. In some instances these behaviors were so infrequently committed that the items had virtually no variance. Items eliminated by this criterion were homicide, arson, rape, bribery, and forgery. Fathering an illegitimate child was eliminated because it is an "outcome" rather than a behavior. See Short, Strodtbeck, and Cartwright, *op. cit.*

Table 6

ITEMS AND LOADINGS UTILIZED FOR SCORING OF FIVE FACTORS

Factor 1	
Individual fighting	79
Group fighting	76
Concealed weapons	67
Assault	67
Factor 2	
Individual sports	71
Team sports	68
Social activities	60
Gambling	48
Factor 3	
Sexual intercourse	—77
Petting	—67
Signifying	—53
Work experience	—36
Factor 4	
Narcotics	—56
Pot	—55
Homosexuality	—53
Common law marriage	—48
Attempted suicide	—36
Pimping	—27
Factor 5	
Auto theft	—69
Driving without license	—65
Runaway	—44

more than 10 per cent of robbery's variance in the original matrix is accounted for by Factors 4 and 5, and about 25 per cent by Factor 1. Virtually no robbery variance is accounted for by the "nondelinquent" Factors 2 and 3. The variance of theft, by contrast, is distributed more evenly over four of the five factors.

The behaviors listed in Table 7 are interesting from still another standpoint, i.e., their versatility and, with the exception of theft and robbery, what might be called their "low delinquency valence" relative to the more seriously delinquent items. This is not to say that these items are nondelinquent in a legal sense. But they tend to be "noncriminal" in character, in the sense that their commission by adults is not considered to be criminal, and the "norms" which they violate are of

Table 7

LOADINGS OF TEN NON-SCORED ITEMS ON EACH OF FIVE FACTORS

Behavior	Factor 1		Factor 2		Factor 3		Factor 4		Factor 5	
Domestic chores	31	(9.6)	36	(13.0)	—17	(2.9)	11	(1.2)	02	(.0)
Theft	44	(19.4)	32	(10.2)	03	(.1)	—22	(4.8)	—53	(28.1)
Alcohol	36	(13.0)	06	(.4)	—39	(15.2)	—26	(6.8)	—49	(24.0)
Public nuisance	43	(18.5)	34	(11.6)	—05	(.3)	—10	(1.0)	—58	(33.6)
Robbery	51	(26.0)	09	(.8)	—04	(.2)	—35	(12.3)	—33	(10.9)
Hanging	07	(.5)	40	(16.0)	—44	(19.4)	03	(.1)	—25	(6.3)
Joy riding	09	(.8)	45	(20.3)	—10	(1.0)	—01	(.0)	—41	(16.8)
Gang bang	32	(10.2)	08	(.6)	—08	(.6)	—28	(7.8)	—32	(10.2)
Statutory rape	40	(16.0)	01	(.0)	—68	(46.2)	—18	(3.2)	—09	(.8)
Truancy	26	(6.8)	43	(18.5)	04	(.2)	09	(.8)	—39	(15.2)
$\bar{x}$		(12.1)		(9.1)		(8.6)		(3.8)		(14.6)

a predominantly moral character (as in the case of the sex offenses) or they are concerned specifically with upbringing of children (truancy and alcohol connected offenses) or with keeping the peace (hanging, public nuisance, and joy riding). Joy riding may in some instances be directed toward economically utilitarian goals, but the fact that its highest loading is on the essentially nondelinquent Factor 2 suggests that this rarely is the case. Joy riding, like most of the other behaviors in Table 7, is delinquent in the sense suggested by the term "parent delinquent subculture," i.e., associated with the general problems of adolescence, accentuated in most cases for gang boys (e.g., problems of interpersonal relations and striving for status and recognition). Such problems involve adolescents' relations among themselves and with the institutions of adult authority— property and school—or adult-adolescent relations in the process of keeping the peace.[26]

[26] This usage of the term "parent delinquent subculture" does not imply rejection of adult or middle class values in the manner of "reaction-formation," as originally hypothesized by Cohen. It implies, rather, recognition of the moral validity and legitimacy of adult and middle-class prescriptive norms. See Gordon, Short, Cartwright, and Strodtbeck, *op. cit.*

BEHAVIOR FACTOR PROFILES OF 16 GANGS

We turn now to an examination of the mean factor scores of our 16 gangs presented in Table 8. The data are presented in standard-score form and from the highest to the lowest ranking gang on each factor in order to facilitate comparison of gangs and examination of the total range of each type of behavior which is found within our population. In Table 9 the 16 groups are *ranked* according to the size of their mean score on each of the factors.

Because of the method of sample selection we must be extremely cautious in "hypothesizing" relationships between variables within our population on the basis of competing theories of delinquent subcultures. In this section we limit ourselves to the relation of race to group mean factor scores. Following Cloward and Ohlin, we expected that Negro gangs would have higher conflict factor scores than would white gangs. That is, both legitimate and illegitimate economic opportunities seem objectively more limited for Negroes than for whites—hence, the expectation of greater conflict orientation among Negro than among white gangs. No inference from the various theoretical positions under examination

Table 8

MEAN BEHAVIOR FACTOR SCORES FOR 11 NEGRO AND 5 WHITE GANGS, RANKED BY SIZE OF GROUP MEANS

Group identification number and race

Behavior																
Factor 1 (Conflict)	03 Negro 2.24	15 Negro 1.97	20 Negro .41	05 Negro .33	09 Negro .25	02 Negro .01	24 White −.05	18 White −.43	13 White −.44	23 Negro −.51	01 Negro −.68	22 White −.78	21 White −1.02	10 Negro −1.44	17 White −1.71	11 Negro −1.94
Factor 2 (Stable corner boy activity)	23 Negro 1.43	20 Negro .90	09 Negro .85	21 Negro .75	13 White .51	15 Negro .39	17 White .23	10 Negro .09	03 Negro .08	02 Negro −.34	05 Negro −.48	22 White −.49	11 White −.62	18 White −.73	01 Negro −.78	24 White −.89
Factor 3 (Stable sex-maturity)	09 Negro .85	15 Negro .82	03 Negro .71	05 Negro .54	10 Negro .52	13 White .02	24 White .01	20 Negro −.03	02 Negro −.17	22 White −.24	18 White −.26	11 Negro −.31	01 Negro −.82	23 Negro −1.14	21 Negro −1.15	17 White −1.30
Factor 4 (Retreatist)	24 White 2.16	09 Negro .63	20 Negro .51	02 Negro .10	05 Negro .00	22 White −.04	23 Negro −.09	15 Negro −.10	03 Negro −.13	18 White −.23	01 Negro −.27	21 Negro −.31	13 White −.41	10 Negro −.45	11 Negro −.48	17 White −.49
Factor 5 (Authority protest)	24 White .80	15 Negro .75	18 White .42	13 White .39	11 Negro .30	20 Negro .26	03 Negro .24	22 White .12	02 Negro −.11	09 Negro −.13	23 Negro −.18	17 White −.21	05 Negro −.34	01 Negro −.45	21 Negro −.49	10 Negro −.65

Table 9

FACTOR SCORE RANKS OF 16 GANGS ON FIVE FACTORS

Gang name	Code no.	Factor 1	Factor 2	Factor 3	Factor 4	Factor 5
Negro gangs						
Midget Knights	01	11	15	13	11	14
Junior Knights	02	6	10	9	4	9
Vice Kings	03	1	9	3	9	7
Rattlers	05	4	11	4	5	13
Chiefs	09	5	3	1	2	10
Conservatives	10	14	8	5	14	16
Mighty Pewees	11	16	13	12	15	5
Southside						
Rattlers	15	2	6	2	8	2
Vandals	20	3	2	8	3	6
Midget Vandals	21	13	4	15	12	15
Navahoes	23	10	1	14	7	11
Mean rank		7.7	7.5	7.8	8.2	9.8
White gangs						
Amboys	13	9	5	6	13	4
Aces	17	15	7	16	16	12
Ravens	18	8	14	11	10	3
Pizza Grill	22	12	12	10	6	8
Pill Poppers	24	7	16	7	1	1
Mean rank		10.2	10.8	10.0	9.2	5.6

relative to the expected elevation on other factors among Negro and white gangs seemed clear enough to be included in this paper.

Several findings emerge:[27]

1. The most conflict-oriented gangs are Negro. All six gangs with mean scores above the total population mean are Negro. The *mean rank* of Negro gangs on Factor 1 is 7.7 (out of 16) as compared with 10.2 for white gangs. (There is much variation in conflict orientation among Negro gangs, how-

[27] The reliability problem referred to earlier in the paper may be assessed in part by examination of the mean months of contact with the groups, in terms of their mean factor scores. A crude measure is provided in the following table:

Mean Months of Worker Contact with Groups Ranking

Factor	1–8	9–16
1	13.0	12.8
2	12.5	13.5
3	13.8	12.0
4	12.3	13.5
5	11.5	14.3

ever. Three of the four least-conflict oriented gangs also are Negro.)

2. The range of between-group variation within this population is greatest for Factor 1 (conflict) and least for Factor 5 (authority protest).

3. The largest *difference* between contiguous groups in rankings occurs between the highest and next highest ranking groups on Factor 4 (retreatism). This difference is 1.53 standard units, while the difference between the second highest group on retreatism and the lowest is only 1.12 standard units. The magnitude of these differ-

The one factor which might be expected to show the greatest tendency for increased incidence with time, does so—that is, Factor 3—due primarily to the increase in work and heterosexual activity with age. The difference in mean months of contact between groups ranking 1–3 and 14–16 on Factor 3 is even more striking—14.7 months and 10.0 months, respectively. Age differentials in factor scores will receive further discussion in a later paper. Suffice to say that for both Negroes and whites Factor 3 is positively related to age.

Table 10

RANK ORDER CORRELATIONS BETWEEN GANG MEAN FACTOR SCORES, FOR 16 GANGS, BY FACTOR

	Factor 2 (Stable corner boy activity)	Factor 3 (Stable sex-maturity)	Factor 4 (Retreatist)	Factor 5 (Authority protest)
Factor 1 (Conflict)	.16	.71	.68	.40
Factor 2 (Stable corner boy activity)	—	.09	.04	—.22
Factor 3 (Stable sex-maturity)	—	—	.44	.29
Factor 4 (Retreatist)	—	—	—	.18

ences makes comparison of mean ranks of Negro and white groups relatively meaningless for this factor.

4. Negro gangs are, on the average, higher on Factors 2 and 3, with mean ranks of 7.5 and 7.8, respectively, compared with mean ranks of 10.8 and 10.0 for white gangs.

5. Only on Factor 5 do white gangs clearly rank higher than Negro gangs. Four of the five white gangs have positive groups means for this factor, and three of the four highest ranking groups are white. Mean rank for white gangs is 5.6, compared to 9.8 for Negro gangs.

6. With one exception, individual group profiles are positively correlated with one another, but vary greatly and inconsistently in the relative elevation of different factors. Rank order correlations between the ranks of the 16 gangs studied on each of the five factors are presented in Table 10.

Only Factor 2 rankings fail to correlate consistently in the positive direction with the rankings of other factors.[28] No positive correlation with Factor 2 rankings is high, and its highest correlation is negative, with Factor 5.

Groups high on conflict tend also to be high on stable sex, retreatism, and authority protest. The correlation between rankings on Factors 3 and 4 is moderately high; other correlations are comparatively low but positive. Despite these generally positive correlations, however, much variation in the relative elevation of any group on any given factor remains unexplained by its elevation on any other factor.

DISCUSSION

Data presented here are only indirectly relevant to the issue of the existence or the nature of delinquent subcultures. We have, after all, investigated the behavior of individuals rather than groups. To assess subcultural theory on the bases of these data, we must assume the relevance of the groups to which these individuals belong for understanding their behavior. Such an assumption seems warranted in view of the methods of selection of boys for study and the group context within which the raters (detached workers) know the boys.[29]

[28] When factor scores are intercorrelated for individual boys, the resulting matrix also is positive, with product-moment correlations ranging from .06 to .47. Differences appear also between Negroes and whites in this matrix. These findings will be developed further in another paper.

[29] Selvin and Hagstrom have suggested factor analyzing grouped data as a means of empirically classifying groups. The small number of groups (16) in our study is a problem, but an attempt will be made to look at our data in this way. See Hanan C. Selvin and Warren O. Hagstrom, "The Empirical Classification of Formal Groups," *American Sociological Review*, 28 (June, 1963), pp. 399–411.

Conflict and retreatism emerge as fairly distinct emphases in terms of factor structure, but criminal behavior does not. Observational data clarify the relation between various types of "criminal" behavior and other types of delinquency which were found in Table 5. We know, for example, that tough, conflict-oriented boys sometimes display and utilize their neighborhood "rep" by charging small amounts from younger boys for "protection" or by "shaking down" paper boys. Members of such gangs are known to purse-snatch, shoplift, and burglarize. The norms of the gang regard these as acceptable ways of acquiring a little "bread" to buy a bottle of wine, a bite to eat, one's share of the cost of a game of pool, and the like.

By contrast, these criminal activities are directed toward the acquisition of larger sums of money when related to drug use. Even a "nickel bag" of marihuana costs $5. Pills are less expensive but the habit requires a continuous supply, and heroin is very expensive. In addition to robbery and theft, pimping emerges as a retreatist related activity consistent with the joint emphasis on "kicks" and "hustles."[30]

Auto theft often is part of a complex which involves dressing up one's own auto, "souping up" the motor, etc. These things require money or appropriate auto parts. Groups highest on this factor are known also to sell parts of stripped autos. Forgery and bribery are also related to Factor 5. Observational data suggest that both are relatively petty among our boys, involving attempts to cash forged checks in small denominations and bribing policemen who apprehend them in various delinquencies. Gambling and theft, which are the only criminal items with

moderate loadings on Factor 2, are part of a recreational rather than a criminal pattern. No criminal item has even a moderate loading on Factor 3.

None of our gangs is properly characterized as a "criminal subculture" or a carrier of such a subculture. No clear separation between criminal and conflict emphases is apparent from the factor analysis or from observational data. The latter suggest, however, that various criminal activities may characterize *cliques* of *conflict* gangs. Data from a large white street corner group *without discernible delinquency specialization* (not included in this analysis because they were discovered too late) also suggest that "criminal cliques" may develop within such groups. In the observed case a clique of eight boys formed exclusively around rationally directed theft activities—auto stripping, burglary, shoplifting, etc. This clique did not hang together on the corner, but met in one another's homes. When on the corner they hung with other members of the larger group. They participated in the general hanging and drinking patterns, and in occasional altercations with various adults as part of this larger group, but not as a distinguishable clique. *Only in their pattern of theft activities were they a clique.* For at least two years they were reasonably successful in these activities, in terms of money and goods acquired, in fencing or selling directly to customers, and in avoiding arrest or "fixing" arrests when they were apprehended. Several members of the group eventually were arrested, however, and several thousands of dollars worth of stolen goods was found stored in one of their homes. Prior to this, the activities of the group had been considerably cramped by the "capture" of the leader by a Detached Worker from the YMCA.

On balance, the criminal data concerning our gangs, based on ratings

---

[30] Harold Finestone, "Cats, Kicks, and Color," *Social Problems,* 5, 1 (July, 1957), pp. 3–13.

and preliminary analysis of observational data, are consistent with descriptions of "semi-professional" theft as an emphasis of individuals and cliques developed within the context of a "parent delinquent subculture" rather than as a fully developed criminal subculture as described by Cloward and Ohlin.[31] The "criminal clique" referred to above has this character, as do other cases from our observational data. The absence of a clear-cut factor among our boys, or of a clearly criminal gang in no way demonstrates the nonexistence either of the criminal subculture or of criminal gangs such as those described in the Cloward-Ohlin typology. On the basis of our experience in Chicago, however, we are skeptical of the existence in this city of gangs of this type.

The evidence presented here argues for the existence of types of behavior which are common to all gangs. It has been suggested that these items may constitute a "parent delinquent subculture," out of which the more specialized delinquent adaptations emerge. Neither the validity nor the utility of such a concept can be assessed on the basis of data presented in this paper, but the data are consistent with such a formulation. The extent to which specific delinquency emphases come to characterize a gang at any point in time—and if they do, just how such specialization comes about—is unclear from these data. Hopefully, answers to such questions will be provided from further study of such variables and processes as (1) the reaction of these lower-class gang boys to a variety of institutional contexts (involving, for example, relations in the family and at school, and the values of private property and keeping the peace); (2) the study of interpersonal relations within the gang as well as between gangs, and relations between the gang and the external world; and (3) the study of other variables specified in competing theories attempting to account for subcultural delinquency.

From one point of view, the positive correlations between delinquency factor scores, both between individuals and groups, argues against the existence of delinquent subcultures. Two considerations give us pause in following this line of argument. The first of these concerns evidence supportive of subcultural differentiation drawn from our own observational data. The second concerns the nature of the rating data employed in the analysis. In short, the positive association of factor scores found in our data may be due to the operation both of a theoretical characteristic of delinquent subcultures *and* to a methodological artifact. Concerning the first point, theories of delinquent subcultures hypothesize that groups may move from one adaptation to another. This is particularly true of discussions of the evolution of more specialized varieties of delinquent subcultures from a more amorphous parent delinquent subculture, and of discussions of the development of retreatist adaptations as a consequence of failure in other adaptations such as conflict or crime.[32]

Observational data tell us that this is indeed what happens in some cases among our groups. The most retreatist group studied, it may be noted, also was the highest scoring *white* group on conflict and the highest of all groups on Factor 5. We know, however, that this group has not been involved in conflict at least as long as we have observed them.[33] Their conflict score results from knowledge of *prior* con-

---

[31] Cf. Cohen and Short, *op. cit.;* and Cloward and Ohlin, *op. cit.*

[32] *Ibid.* See, also, Bloch and Neiderhoffer, *op. cit.*

[33] For further evidence on this point, see Short and Strodtbeck, *op. cit.*

flict activities by this group. They had, at one time, been very much engaged in conflict, but during the past two years had turned completely from conflict to embrace drug use and other kicks. Although our documentation is incomplete, their sequence of delinquency adaptation could be characterized as beginning with parent delinquent subcultural involvement to which were added, successively, conflict and then retreatism. Conflict was given up as an activity either participated in by the group or serving as a status-giving activity of the group. Conflict was no longer normatively prescribed by the group, if indeed it ever was, as kicks and other esoteric experiences became highly valued in terms of the individual and collective experiences of these boys. At the same time, the activities represented by Factor 5 (auto theft, driving without a license, runaway, etc.) were not given up, but continued in forms consistent with their other delinquency adaptations. The observational materials are rich and complete enough in this instance to encourage considerable confidence in labeling the retreatist phase of the group's behavior as subcultural in nature. This is true, also, of the criminal clique described above. Our difficulty in locating groups such as these, however, suggests that they were rare in Chicago, at the time of our investigation, relative to conflict gangs and gangs without discernible specialization.

The methodological artifact which inhibits interpretation of these findings as contra-indicative of the existence of delinquent subcultures is related also to the phasing hypotheses of subcultural adaptation. Recall that the raters were asked whether a boy ever had engaged in a particular type of behavior and how frequently. Thus, the data are cumulative and not sensitive to changing adaptations over time. A related consideration concerns the problem of the reliability of behavioral ratings based upon past as opposed to present behavior. Data on past activities are less reliable than reports of current activities.

Despite these limitations of the data, we believe that the data are useful in introducing greater precision in the measurement of the behavior of individuals and groups studied and that further analyses of data from the several phases of our research program will permit more complete documentation and modification of hypotheses concerning the subcultural nature of gang delinquency.

CONCLUSION

The full implications of our findings for subcultural theories of juvenile delinquency cannot be assessed until the data are viewed in combination with observational data from detached workers and our own staff, and in terms of analyses of their relation to etiological variables specified by the theories. The former add the richness and detail of situational and group-process determinants which the ratings employed in the factor analysis miss entirely. At the same time, without the more systematic and "objective" ratings, one can never be certain as to the representativeness of his observations or his own objectivity in recall and choice of behavior reported. Our tentative conclusion is that delinquent subcultures exist, but that they are not as "pure" as they have been pictured, and they become articulated in ways much more complex than existing theories specify. Further study is needed of within- as well as between-group variations in behavior. These, in turn, must be related to assumed causal variables within the group, community, and larger social system; and to variations in individual abilities, motivations, values, and personality characteristics.

26. Juvenile Gang Delinquency in Paris

EDMUND W. VAZ

A traditional deficiency in American studies of juvenile delinquency is the lack of concern with data from non-English speaking cultures. This shortcoming has recently been deplored by Albert K. Cohen: "The sad truth . . . is that the comparative study of juvenile delinquency does not exist. The acquaintance of American students of delinquency with the facts of delinquency in non-English speaking countries is negligible."[1] The sociology of juvenile delinquency must extend its research and observations beyond its immediate cultural horizons. The present report is a preliminary step in this direction.

The use of comparative statistics is risky; to grasp what gang delinquency "looks like" in other countries (much less our own), it is preferable to contact the gangs themselves. Such is not always possible however, and under restricted circumstances we must make do with second-hand information.

This paper is primarily a comparative, descriptive account of selected aspects of French anti-social adolescent gangs located in Paris. In this way a diversity of gangs in France, the present account deals largely with teenage gangs located in Paris. In this way a more legitimate comparison can be made with data on juvenile gangs found principally in large American cities. The research was conducted in Paris during a seven-week period in the spring of 1961. Thirteen interviews with research sociologists, psychologists, police commissioners, and éducateurs—men and women working directly with juvenile gangs—were conducted. Two visits were made to the research center at Vaucresson and recent research reports were studied. Interviews were informal and varied in length from thirty minutes to two hours. All interviews but one were conducted in French.

* Appreciation is expressed to the Ford Foundation for a grant in support of this research conducted in England and France, and to Professor Albert K. Cohen who made this work possible.

[1] Albert K. Cohen, "Sociological Research in Juvenile Delinquency," *The American Journal of Orthopsychiatry*, 27 (October, 1957), p. 783.

SOCIO-ECONOMIC CONDITIONS

American studies highlight the emergence of delinquent gangs among the most depressed socio-economic areas of the city. In Paris, parallel socio-economic conditions tend to generate similar anti-social groups. Eco-

SOURCE. Edmund W. Vaz, "Juvenile Gang Delinquency in Paris," from *Social Problems*, Volume 10, No. 1, Summer 1962, pp. 23–31. Reprinted with the permission of the Society for the Study of Social Problems and the author.

nomic deprivation, inferior housing, and the lack of adequate living space have long been perennial problems in the French capital. Disorganized family life, contact with criminal behavior patterns, isolation from contact with anti-criminal patterns, and the lack of adequate recreational facilities are traditional accompaniments of poverty. Such is the situation in Paris. Referring to the housing conditions in the French capital, one worker remarked:

[They] want a place to live where there is a little space because the big trouble in Paris is that there is nowhere to live and a large percentage of the people live in very cramped quarters. That is why so many people live and spend so much time in the cafés. It is the home of the poor, you know what I mean.

Harrison Salisbury has written that American gang boys live in disorganized families, "have a horror of home" where there often exists a "procession of 'uncles' moving in and out."[2] Parisian gang boys also emanate from aggravated family circumstances. In almost identical terms our data reflect Salisbury's words:

We find that these boys come from what we call multi-problem families. You know, families where the parents are divorced, where there is another man in the house every month or so, and where the parent is sick and the other works irregularly . . . where they are unable to manage their affairs.

While the development of relatively new, low-rent housing projects in Paris has improved the living standards of lower-class families, it has often done so at the expense of social organization and social cohesion within the community. An unanticipated result has been the emergence in these areas of anti-

[2] Harrison E. Salisbury, *The Shook-Up Generation,* Greenwich: Fawcett Publications, 1959, p. 16.

social gangs whose activities have contributed in many instances to a chronic state of violence.[3] A French psychologist sees the failure of these projects in Paris in this way:

You have heard of our large building sites . . . the H.L.M.'s. Here there is a lot of trouble with gangs. These families have very many children and they form into gangs. We were shortsighted in the construction of these buildings, we removed these people from their surroundings and housed them in places without a social setting.

Hence in major American and French cities the appearance of antisocial, often violence-prone adolescent gangs tends to emerge under (*a*) traditional slum conditions, and (*b*) deteriorating conditions (new slums) of newly developed, low-rent housing blocks. Unless greater awareness is given to effective planning for a satisfying community life in the development of low-rent housing, such reconstruction does not augur well for the future.

Schooling

Parisian gang boys, like their counterparts in American and English cities, show little enthusiasm for schooling and tend to leave school as early as the law will allow. One worker remarked: "They all quit school at 14 years of age. Of all the boys I know only one has his school-leaving certificate." In view of the impoverished living conditions of the Parisian slum boy, it is not surpris-

[3] The eruption of anti-social gangs on new housing estates is not confined to French and American cities. In an interview with the police chief of Speke, a relatively new housing estate located in the suburbs of Liverpool, he deplored the growth of violent gangs in this area. See also the report on French gang delinquency in *Rapport Annuel à M. le Garde des Sceaux,* Ministère de la Justice, Direction de l'Education Surveillée, 1960, pp. 84–108.

ing that so few look upon school with concern. The lack of encouragement given able students from such families is a theme common to both French and American observers.[4] One respondent remarked:

. . . for the others, the gifted ones, if you tell the parents that their children can get scholarships and that they should remain in school, they will not listen. They know that if the boy goes out to work he can earn 60,000 francs. And what is a scholarship worth? Maybe, say, 20,000 francs. They will not understand.

Parents from slums have seldom understood. Life conditions among these families breed attitudes which cannot contribute much towards a "deferred gratification" perspective. The occasion for higher wages and growing employment opportunities must appear as a boon to these boys, heightening their desire to quit school, leave home, take work, and earn "big money." Under such circumstances lower-class attitudes and behavior patterns complement, in part, the structural needs of an expanding economy.

Work

Chronic unemployment is a major problem among delinquent gang boys in Paris. One study found that upwards of 40 per cent of juvenile gang members were irregularly employed.[5] Our data suggest a similar situation. Parisian boys begin work at 14 or 15 years of age, as soon as they quit school. Poorly educated, they are inadequately prepared for work and are likely to engage in unskilled work which is neither challenging nor remunerative. The familiar movement from one poorly paid job to another

persists till the boys are called into military service.

When I first contacted the gang about a third of the boys were working. The other boys did odd jobs or made money through stealing . . . work for almost all of them was very irregular. Work for three months and then off for a while. [What kinds of work did they do?] Manual labor usually, or some of them were messenger boys on bicycle. Some of them had regular jobs, but very few.

Yet all the goals of these youths are not cut from the same aspirational weave, nor are they especially oriented towards a middle-class style of life. Like American gang youths, they tend to focus on the here-and-now, displaying an equal disregard for the future and the pursuit of long-term goals. With little sense of career development and minimum planning for the future, their conception of success sometimes takes a more tangible, immediate, and grandiose character. "Many had ambitions of having a lot of money, a big car, a Cadillac, of not working and living well." Others, more perceptive or maybe simply older, "would like maybe to be a mechanic or something like that. They want something stable with a steady income." Still others drifted about without direction, while a few engaged in fantasy. One worker recalls his experiences with a gang in these words:

. . . one boy who was very intelligent . . . wanted to become a journalist. Another wanted to be an airplane pilot, and I recall another who wanted to be a singer. These were fantastic, but later the boy who wanted to become a journalist . . . changed his ambitions and took courses in a technical trade.

DELINQUENT GANGS

Juvenile delinquent gangs in Paris have never reached the accentuated proportions that they have in the

---

[4] P. M. Smith, "The School as a Factor," in Joseph S. Roucek, editor, *Juvenile Delinquency*, New York: Philosophical Library, 1958, pp. 168–169.

[5] *Rapport Annuel, op. cit.*, p. 97.

United States. The pronounced subcultural varieties reported in large American cities[6] are not evident in Paris.

Drug-Addiction

The adolescent drug-addict subculture might well be a peculiarly American phenomenon.[7] Drug-addiction in France is reportedly non-existent among lower-class adolescents. Teenage gangs whose central activities highlight taking drugs do not appear on the Parisian scene. When drug-taking does occur among adolescents it is found among middle-class youth, predominantly in the student and bohemian sections of Paris. Confirming all our reports from gang workers, a police commissioner had this to say:

There is absolutely no [drug] problem in France among juveniles. We have not had a single case of a juvenile under 21 arrested for drug offenses. There are of course some people, maybe even a few juveniles, who smoke hashish, we are certain of this. But this is no problem. There are about maybe 500 drug cases in all of France. . . . As for juveniles, probably in X area where there are students there is, maybe, a bit of drugs, but that is all.

Two conditions help account for this situation: (a) the level of juvenile gang development in Paris, and (b) the absence of major criminal institutions in areas where juvenile gangs are located. In Paris there is no recognized community of adolescent gangs with its network of rules, codes, and norms of conduct, where the struggle for a reputation is rife, often violent. Conflict, competition, and the

rivalous display for status among gangs, although not unknown, are infrequent. The relatively loose organization and small membership of the majority of Parisian teenage gangs are not likely to generate an inordinate quest for status among adolescent groups or their members. Socially structured motivation towards innovating behavior and "operating inventions" in the daily behavior of these boys are, therefore, likely to be of a low order.

Moreover, since there is a marked absence of adult drug-taking subcultures in the slum areas of Paris, the illicit demand for drugs is limited, and the conjunction between criminality and lower-class adult drug-users is correspondingly weak. Under such circumstances the opportunity for gang boys to come in contact with drug-addict milieux—socially charged situations where pressures to experiment with drugs are often coercive upon the newcomer—is rare. And while many Algerians and "North Africans" are known to take hashish, they are not likely to find Parisian gang youths easy recruits. Speaking from knowledge with a large gang, one worker said, "The Algerians were disliked . . . one of the things the boys liked was to beat up the face of an Algerian." On the other hand, where wine and liquor are easily available, and where the custom of drinking is historically imbedded in the national culture, it occupies a large part of the boys' activities.

And the boys drink. They drink a lot. They drink beer and they drink till they get drunk. It is something which all the boys do. . . . And on weekends they drink and then go with the girls, and to the dance.

Criminal Associations

There exists in the literature on lower-class delinquency a recurrent emphasis on the integration between juve-

[6] Richard H. Cloward and Lloyd E. Ohlin, *Delinquency and Opportunity: A Theory of Delinquent Gangs*, Glencoe: The Free Press, 1960.

[7] See Harold Finestone, "Cats, Kicks and Color," *Social Problems*, 5 (1957), pp. 3–13; and "Narcotics and Criminality," *Law and Contemporary Problems*, 22 (1957), pp. 69–85.

nile delinquency and adult criminality. Contemporary theories suggest the structural connections between adolescent delinquents and criminal institutions, institutions which allegedly provide alternative avenues to higher status within the community,[8] support the integration of different delinquent age-groups, and strengthen their association to the adult criminal world. The reported absence of large criminal and gambling syndicates in Paris (like those alleged to operate in America) likely thwarts the development of structural connections between criminal and teen-age delinquent groups. At the same time, parents are known to encourage and abet their children in delinquencies, while occasionally criminals will work in conjunction with delinquent boys; but these relationships are not underscored in our data.

Yet the presence of a gang of older, sophisticated boys in a neighborhood attracts the younger element and strengthens the integration among multiple, juvenile age-groups. This association transmits values, knowledge and skills in the area, while older boys serve as models of prestige and objects of identification. The following quotation illustrates younger boys seeking "to dramatize their eligibility for membership" in a group by trying to conform "to the norms of a group to which they aspire but do not (quite) belong."[9]

[Did the younger boys look up to the older boys?] Oh yes, they did. You know, often when they first belonged to the gang they would try and show the older boys that they could steal a car or carry out some other act. Also, I knew of a gang of school boys between 12–14 years in the area who wanted nothing more than to belong to the gang.

If the harnessing of different age levels lends coherence and stability to a delinquent milieu, the absence of major criminal groups in the area likely stunts its maturity. One study suggests that criminals in France tend to have little confidence in delinquent gangs and prefer that they cease their activities.[10]

Because criminal models as objects of identification are likely to be scarce for these delinquent juveniles, they are unlikely to envisage easily a meaningful criminal career for themselves. This suggests why the vast majority of these boys, according to our data, do not aspire towards a criminal future. Yet some do engage in a "little traffic" while others, usually unsuccessfully, manage a few girls who hustle for them on weekends. The impaired socioeconomic conditions and the social organization of the areas in which they live probably offer them the knowledge and contacts, and, therefore, the opportunities for participating in small-time, partially organized illegal activities.

The ambition among some of the boys for a tidy, remunerative hustle mirrors an "only suckers work" philosophy, and suggests the influence of the black market ethic, with its concomitant attitudes and sub rosa practices, which spread throughout many major European cities after the last war. Survivals of this illicit subculture continue to persist among lower-class gang boys.

But really, what a lot of them want is to have a little deal, maybe two, three, four girls working for them bringing them money, something small and steady like that. But nothing large and nothing with any risk to it. Because in Paris even now there are all kinds of little "traffic"; American cigarettes—a couple of years ago it was transistor radios, there are gramophone records, No. 45 records, all kinds of little things like that. They buy them in order to sell them to someone else. They make a little money. Nothing big, mind you, but they make enough to get by.

[8] Cloward and Ohlin, *op. cit.*
[9] *Ibid.*, pp. 166–167.

[10] *Rapport Annuel, op. cit.*, p. 105.

A LARGE PARISIAN GANG

Much has been written about adolescent fighting gangs in major American cities, yet there is little consensus regarding their structure. Juvenile gangs in Paris vary considerably in size, age, organization, and delinquent activities. Yet none approaches the highly organized "warrior" gangs suggested in the American literature. The usual run of Parisian gangs range in size from five to eight members, while others, it is said, vary between ten and twenty boys.[11] The very large French gang (albeit rare) is nevertheless complex. A worker reported his experiences in these words:

The gang was extraordinary for Paris, even for France, I believe, because there were 60 members in the gang. . . . within the gang there were several cliques or nuclei. These were boys who were more closely associated, more friendly. These boys would commit delinquencies together, and know where to get rid of the goods. [Leader?] No, there was no recognized leader . . . there was one boy who was more intelligent, who had more ideas and seemed to lead some of the others, but there was no leader. [Were the nuclei specialized in any way?] Yes, they were. There was one group which was specialized in stealing cars. Another group seemed to specialize in other kinds of thefts, and another group seemed tougher than the others. [Ages?] The boys ranged in ages from 14 to 25 years. [Did they mix together?] Oh yes. There were 14's and 15's and boys of 17 and 20 and some of 25 . . . one thing was that a new boy had to be introduced by another member of the gang . . . they were suspicious of everyone . . . they considered adults to be working for the police.

The wide age range in this gang

suggests a hierarchically knit structure, yet the absence of any acknowledged leadership betrays a less cohesive group and more likely reflects a variety of younger cliques in pursuit of status, tenuously affiliated with one or more cores of older boys. While group boundaries seem ill-defined and the gang appears loosely organized, it possesses its own hangout where the members enjoy recognition and status. A worker remarked, "They had their own café which they went to every night and they did not like members of other gangs to enter the café. But they really didn't have any territory." The daily routine of these boys is consistent, unplanned, monotonous.

What do they do? Well, they go to the movies. They go three, four, five, no, they go seven times a week sometimes. And they go to the same movie too. They go to one of the four cinemas around the district. They never go elsewhere. . . . Or every night they come down to the café and they sit about, and they smoke and talk. And they play cards a little and play dice. [For money?] Oh yes, for money, but not for high stakes you know. They sit about till sometimes twelve, one or two o'clock in the morning.

While their sartorial elegance did not match that of the English "Teddy-Boys" they nevertheless paid conspicuous attention to their clothes, which became marks of identification for them.

. . . they didn't have nice clothes, but they all wore their hair long and wavy in the back of their necks. This was important . . . and at that time they wore bluejeans. They wore them frequently so they would become used and shaded. They were no longer bluejeans but a mélange of colors . . . it also indicated that they were part of the gang. The gang didn't have any uniforms so this, in a way, identified them.

The ethnic composition of the gang largely mirrored the ethnic population

[11] Cf. *Rapport Annuel, op. cit.*, p. 88. See also, "Le Phénomène des Bandes, Manifestation Actuelle de la Délinquance Juvénile," *Extrait de la Revue Pénitentiaire et de Droit Pénal* (Avril-Juin, 1961), pp. 20–21.

of the district; however, non-French boys never became full-fledged gang members and at least one ethnic group was altogether excluded from the gang.

Most of the area was French. There were some Armenians and a few Italians who were part of the gang but they never really became part of the inner gang, they remained on the outside all the time. In the area there were also Algerians and North Africans. The Algerians were disliked but there was never any trouble with the blacks.

Parisian gang boys engage in a wide variety of delinquencies including sex offenses, assaulting adults, armed holdups and, among older boys, even bank robbery. And drunkenness, gambling and vandalism were often routine activities.[12] Yet the majority of offenses committed by French gangs is against property. However, motivation for theft may well have changed since the war, and the period of economic need (when stolen objects are often sold for financial gain) might no longer be as urgent. A gang worker remarked:

There is more theft today for pleasure or other reasons than before. Right after the war boys used to steal food in order to eat. Even I stole too. Today this has changed.

When there is economic plenty the quest for social status may be uppermost and stolen objects, in the eyes of the boys, serve as indices of status. "The nature of the stolen objects closely correspond to the needs of the youth: liquor, pastry, transistor radios, records, phonographic equipment, etc."[13] Along

with automobile theft, theft of these objects clearly suggests a concern with success symbols, objects of conspicuous consumption.

There is no evidence of a fighting "gang world" in Paris.[14] The sensational warlike nomenclature and its "nom de guerre," popular among members of American gangs, is rare among Parisian boys. Nevertheless, the large French gang is a dangerous and mobile entity; skirmishes among lethally-armed boys with revolvers, knives, bicycle chains, iron bars, etc., were at one time not alien to their routine. Fighting, when it does erupt, is fierce.

I know of some cases of boys being badly hurt. One boy had his thigh cut with a knife. Another suffered a broken leg in a fight. Another boy was picked up and thrown through a window and had all one side of his face ripped up. Another was sent to the hospital with a fractured skull, and of course many were beaten about the head and things like that. One time there was a fight in a café and they fought each other with tables and chairs. This was the time when the boy was thrown through the window.

Although an extreme case, the use of a machine-gun suggests the limits to which these boys will resort when in conflict with a rival gang.

Once they even used a machine-gun. They went to a dance hall . . . and at the point of the machine-gun they made all the members of another gang and their girls leave the dance hall and line up outside. Nothing more happened, however, because the owner called the police and the boys had to run to escape the police.

In some cases girls associate with

---

[12] Mays reports that vandalism and outbursts of aggression among boys in Liverpool are committed by larger groups, of 15–20 boys. John Barron Mays, *Growing Up in the City*, Liverpool: The University Press of Liverpool, 1954, pp. 112–113. Similarly in France, acts of vandalism, uproars and public disturbances are committed principally by the larger gangs. See *Rapport Annuel, op. cit.,* p. 88.

[13] "Le Phénomène des Bandes," *op. cit.,* p. 29.

[14] Gang violence is rarely a deliberately organized event in Paris. There are two exceptions, however: (*a*) when a boy's pride or reputation is at stake, and (*b*) when a gang's neighborhood has been impugned by a rival gang. In these circumstances the gang mobilizes and seeks revenge. See *Rapport Annuel, op. cit.,* pp. 93–94.

teenage gangs. Some girls are hustlers, but non-hustlers also hang about with gangs. Within the gang itself their association with boys is usually temporary, and they move from one boy to the other. However, the norms of temporary fidelity during each association tend to prevent the eruption of sexual anarchy, and contribute to the effective functioning of the group.

And with regards sexuality they did not mind if a boy went from one girl to another, or that a girl eventually changed boyfriends. But they disliked and were against a girl if, while she were going or sleeping with one boy, she went to bed with another. This they were against . . . the girls seemed to remain with the gang. And of course they would change boyfriends within the gang.

The female role in this instance might be said to follow traditional adult lines: girls contribute to the sex activities of the boys, while they gain status among their own sex by successfully encouraging boys into special activities—in this case, delinquency. A woman worker reported her experiences this way:

Some [girls] are leaders and lead the boys on. Others simply hang about with the boys. Oh, it is prestige for them. [How do you mean?] Well, if they go about with some boys and can get one to beat up everyone in a café, then, oh, it is really something for them. But they will not do anything themselves.

ROLE TRANSITION

In the United States 18 or 19 is the age when "routine" lower-class delinquency begins to taper off.[15] At this age the teenage delinquent sheds his adolescent demeanor and begins to wear the behavioral and attitudinal apparel of the adult. Job, wife, and family take on added importance for him. In Liverpool, Mays reports a "graduation" out of delinquency occurring at 14 years, the time when many English lower-class boys leave school and begin work.[16]

Often it is military service which steers the Parisian gang boy away from what otherwise might be a permanent criminal career, since it occurs at a stage where delinquency often changes direction or persists into crime. Yet, the prospect of having to serve abroad enables the juvenile to procrastinate justifiably from pursuing vocational training, which he knows will soon have to be postponed. Moreover, his difficulty in perceiving for himself a meaningful career upon his return from military service precludes the likelihood of his discontinuing his present delinquent ways for the sake of an obscure future.

If then the *prospect* of military service does not encourage delinquency, it likely increases the difficulty of rehabilitation at this time. Yet the *age* (20 years) at which military service calls these boys probably contributes to the change in role already taking place. The critical period is when they return from military service. At this point the future direction of a boy's life is analogous to that of a released prisoner on parole. One worker remarked that this was the best period for rehabilitation because the boys were open to advice and assistance. For the majority

[15] David Bordua, *Sociological Theories and their Implications for Juvenile Delinquency*, Washington, D.C.: U.S. Department of Health, Education and Welfare, Children's Bureau, 1960, pp. 18–19.

[16] Mays, *op. cit.*, p. 115. Recent work by the writer with an adolescent gang in East London suggests a slightly different pattern. Although these boys left school at 14 years of age, "graduation" from nightly gang activities, which included delinquencies, occurred at 17–19 years of age.

"graduation" seems assured. Work, wife, and the future take on new meanings. The above worker replied to our enquiry in these words:

[What happens when the boys return from military service?] This is really the crucial time for the boys. It is here that they will either return to their previous conduct or change and live normal lives. I know some of the boys returned to the gang immediately. Some of them returned to the gang even before going home to see their parents. I know of another boy who went to see the gang before he went to see his wife. Most of them settle down and get married. . . . They will have a girl . . . and this will influence them. . . . Of course some of them, when they return still think they are in the war. . . . Still others . . . the war makes things even worse. They break up altogether.

DISCUSSION

Given the limitations of these data, how may we account for the relative absence of delinquent subcultural varieties (drug-addict, "bopping" gangs, etc.) among Parisian youth? Certain structural and normative differences between the two societies, and the differential development of major, adult criminal institutions, may help explain the distinctions in juvenile gang delinquency in French and American cities.

American theories of juvenile delinquency seem particularly appropriate in explaining such behavior in societies with an open class system, a strong democratic ideology (equality of opportunity, universally high success aspirations, etc.), adequate knowledge of which is widely transmitted throughout the class structure.[17] In contrast, the open class system of France, emerging from feudal, traditionalist values and, therefore, likely

[17] See Cloward and Ohlin, *op. cit.*

to be of a mixed variety, still contains strong support for social distinctions based on birth.[18] Moreover, the existing democratic ideology in France has probably never existed in as "pure" form as it has in the United States, and the communication of the dominant value system is probably not as effective among the lower classes in France. Under such circumstances lower-class adolescents are not likely to experience strongly felt discrepancies between aspirations and opportunity, nor will they be inclined to define their position vis-à-vis others as unfavorably as allegedly do lower-class boys in America. It may be that the likelihood of a "collective challenge to the legitimacy of the established rules of conduct" is thereby weakened.

We cannot say to what extent criminal and conventional value systems are integrated in depressed socio-economic areas in Paris. However, the absence of highly organized, criminal institutions in the French capital likely limits the development of structured opportunities for illegitimate careers among adolescents. Such structural differences might also preclude the collective emergence of teenage drug-addict subcultures. The absence of an illicit demand for drugs among adults stunts the growth of addict associations and value systems, and therefore both the availability of drugs and the opportunities for adolescents to use drugs are severely restricted.

CONCLUSION

Data gathered in interviews with French experts and workers in the field of juvenile delinquency suggest that anti-social teenage gangs in Paris tend

[18] Bernard Barber, *Social Stratification: A Comparative Analysis of Structure and Process*, New York: Harcourt, Brace and Company, 1957, pp. 346–349.

to be associated with recurrent indices of social disorganization: poverty, over-crowding, slum housing, disruption of family life, and the lack of recreational facilities. At the same time gangs of delinquents are evident among the newly developing slums of low-rent housing estates located in the "ban-lieues" of Paris.

The delinquent gang problem has never reached the dimensions in Paris that it has in some cities in the United States. An adolescent world of warring gangs is not evident in Paris, and teen-age drug-taking gangs are unknown to the French capital. Parisian teenage gangs are smaller, less formally or-ganized with limited cohesion, and often without clearly designated lead-ership. Yet gang members from both cultures reflect similarities in their be-havior: early termination of schooling, irregular employment, regular drink-ing habits, and a wide range of delin-quent activities. However, when a large Parisian gang does evolve, it partially resembles in structure and design American teenage fighting groups.

27. Gangs and Delinquent Groups in London

PETER SCOTT

Most of the early descriptions of juvenile gangs come from the United States. Jacob Riis (1890) wrote of the numerous antisocial gangs, the plankton of society, to be found at every street corner of the East Side of New York. "They have their calls, whistles, signs, rally suddenly from no one knows where, and vanish in the alleys, basements, roofs and corridors they know so well. . . . They have their own ideality and a gaudy pinch-beck honour." Gulick, at about the same time, gives a description which is reminiscent of Mark Twain's stories or perhaps of the actual experience of some who may read this article. "The manners and customs of the gang are to build shanties or 'hunkies,' hunt with sling shots, build fires before huts in the woods, cook their squirrels and other game, play Indian, build tree platforms, where they smoke or troop about some leader who may have an old revolver. They find or excavate caves, or perhaps roof them over. . . . The more plucky arrange fights beforehand; rifle unoccupied houses; set ambushes for gangs with which they are at feud; perhaps have secrets and initiations where new boys are triced up by old

boys and butted against trees and rocks. When painted for their Indian fights, they may grow so excited as to perhaps rush into the water or into the school-room." The gang either of village or city "is composed of these same footloose, prowling, predaceous adolescents who herd and hang together after the manner of the undomesticated male everywhere" (Pank, 1927).

In these and other descriptions can be seen the several basic characteristics of gangs and the purposes which they serve for their members. Thrasher (1927), whose book is the classic on the subject, gives these characteristics —the gang is a structured group whose social order is natural and crescive rather than enacted, whose leaders strive to keep their place, having a strong group loyalty, capable of planned action, having a definite meeting place and territory usually in a transitional area, often a tradition, initiation procedure, secret signs and an identity which may outlive the membership of its individuals. "The nuclei of most gangs can be traced back to early boyhood. . . . The gangs grew up on the corner and remained there with remarkable persistence from

SOURCE. Peter Scott, "Gangs and Delinquent Groups in London," from *British Journal of Delinquency*, Volume 7, July 1956, pp. 4–21, and 25–26. Reprinted with the permission of Routledge and Kegan Paul Ltd.

early boyhood until the members reached their late 20s or early 30s" (Whyte, 1943). An important point is made by Thrasher who points out that the real beginning of the gang is when someone looks upon it with hostility, "for now it starts to draw itself more closely together."

Not every gang of course is antisocial; Healy (1915) writes of a "jolly crowd of buccaneers, provisioned and armed . . . while together they enjoyed democracy and independence." Healy, incidentally, takes account of another motivation of gangs, the sexual one: "There can be no doubt that in many instances the influence of one person on another rests on a basis of overt or perhaps even unconscious sex relationship. This is true between persons of the same sex as well as the opposite. . . . The same is true for women or girls." And again, considering specifically a boys' gang, "They had gradually initiated one another into the mysteries of sex life and, while they did not ostensibly gather for this, at their meeting places they spent much time in discussing these things, and sometimes mutually engaging in bad sex habits."

Man is a social animal and for this very reason gangs are perhaps inevitable. Rather along these lines Hall (1904) and Puffer (1912) put forward the recapitulation theory, that in forming gangs the young person is repeating an evolutionary phase and in so doing gains companionship, recognition, status and a sense of belonging, "the zest and thrill of common purpose," "the quest for new experience." We need to know, however, what causes one group to engage in antisocial activities while another does not. There are two main answers to this query. First the sociological one, that a gang once formed reacts to the environment in which it finds itself, absorbing what is vicious from it. "The gang develops as a response to society. The social group of which the young boy is a member has failed to provide organized and supervised activities adequate to absorb his interests and exhaust his energies" (Thrasher, 1927, p. 251). The standard works, Thrasher's in Chicago, Whyte's in New York, Shaw and McKay's (1931) in Chicago, certainly leave the impression of gangs existing amidst slums, unemployment, racial problems, and great social inequality, but as these factors have receded, antisocial group activities have not. Furthermore, workers such as Crane (1952) conclude that preadolescent gangs are not the product exclusively of subnormal or borderline environments; they occur where there is no lack of space or of recreational facilities; indeed, these very recreational facilities may provide the focus for the gang. The second theory turns to factors within the child, and especially as determined by his early experience within the family. A mass of studies contribute to this theory. Miriam van Waters (1927) pointed out that the other gang members are likely to fill psychological needs not met by the individual's own parents. Bromberg (1942) goes further in stating that gangs need to express antiparental or antisocial tendencies and that their activities are likely to express a reversal of adult social values. Rosenthal (1942) confirmed psychoanalytical theory in finding that spontaneous gangs, formed by children aged 7 to 14, had the function of resolving conflicts arising from intrafamilial tendencies, by breaking the law, thus relieving unconscious guilt feelings and gaining secondary status. Beckham (1933) elaborated the sequence of events: a broken or disturbed home, retardation in school, willingness to join in truancy, and gang induction. Topping (1943) applied to gang boys

Alexander's concept of aggressiveness arising from a compensation for a sense of inadequacy or effeminacy, and noted their characteristic dependence on mother and resentment of father. She thought that these boys had experienced sufficient family acceptance to promote socialization but insufficient supervision and influence to build a strong sense of values. Her findings conform with those of Healy and Bronner (1936) and of Hewitt and Jenkins (1946) in seeing these children "as coming out of the family situation with a weak super-ego structure and ready to identify with the delinquent patterns found among their older siblings or playmates." These writers thus tend to combine the two theories, and the same may be said of an important paper by Wattenberg and Balistrieri (1950), who conclude that "the family picture of the gang boys is less like neglect and more like low tension or easy-goingness. More significant, the way in which the non-gang boys appeared to show evidence of emotional upset due to strong tensions or deprivations at home suggests that the two sets of influence, familial and socio-economic, are not equal in effect but are dynamically related. It looks as though the social forces are limited in their play upon the individuals by the previous effects of the family factors." Or, as Piaget (1932) wrote, "If the adult pattern placed before the child is sound, then there is little danger that gang membership will be anything but helpful to the child." The matter is well summed up by Trenaman (1952): "The gang may vary from a harmless holiday group to a fanatical secret society exacting lifetime loyalties. Though it usually led to pranks or mischief, and sometimes to serious trouble, it also offered the disgruntled youngster an outlet for his energies, a rudimentary social discipline, a sense of comradeship, and a substitute for a defective home." All these factors will clearly have to be taken into account in considering how gang antisocial activities can be reduced.

For the moment, however, it would be well to consider the various sorts of groups which have been described. Many terms have been used, playgroups ("gangs in embryo"), righteous gangs, bad gangs, semi-delinquent gangs, cliques, mobs, crowds, clubs, bunches, intimacies (Thrasher's term for the two-boy gang), parties (usually a police term), rings, syndicates, networks. Both boys and girls have their gangs. Thrasher finds girls' gangs everywhere, Burt (1925) finds none. Crane found that two-thirds of a group of thirty women, and four-fifths of a group of ninety men claimed in retrospect to have belonged to gangs; the female gangs were reported as better organized, less predatory, and occupied more with socially approved aims. Many gangs or groups have mixed membership or allow girls to participate to some degree. Healy firmly stated that the gang spirit is an age phenomenon; he agreed with Sheldon that predatory organizations are strongest between 11 and 15 years, and held that there is "a strong tendency to disband in late adolescence so that the gang spirit undoubtedly does reach its maximum intensity somewhere about 14 to 15." Rosenthal (1942) found that in spontaneous groups of children, at above the 7-year level self-preservation was the main objective, whilst at about the 11-year level the children were primarily seeking status. Wolman (1951), studying spontaneous groupings of children and adolescents in Israel, found no correlation between participation in gangs of younger children and social maladjustment; gangs formed later were usually composed of maladjusted individuals, whereas bright and well-adjusted adolescents preferred officially recognized organizations. Age, sex, environment, and degree of social adjustment clearly have their effect not only on gang formation, but on the type and activity of the gang when formed. The latter factors could usefully be considered according to their degree of diffuseness or organization, and the extent to which their activities are conventional or antisocial.

While we classify gang members they no doubt classify us. According to Dumpson (1952) they think of society as either authorities, hoodlums, or suckers—those, presumably, who are antagonistic and powerful, those who can be exploited, and those who abide by conventional rules and work!

Mention may now be made of some British findings. Hall (1904) stated that in London the groups were better organized and even more numerous than in America. ". . . war is often waged between them, weapons are used and murder is not so very infrequent." Such statements are a useful antidote to the modern scare-mongering of some sections of the Press, which erroneously tend to link up violent crime with an old problem in a new guise—the so-called Teddy Boy.

Figures, since at least 1920, consistently show that the great majority of juvenile crime, i.e., between 8 and 17 years, is committed in company of others. In that year the Board of Education estimated that 63 per cent of delinquent boys were "working in gangs." In Scotland (1923), again, 63 per cent were said to be working in "batches." Burt's (1925) figures were 11.4 per cent of his 123 boys, and 0 per cent of his 74 girls, but he has arbitrarily defined a gang as necessarily being of three or four members. In 1930 the London County Council school medical officer reported that 50 per cent of thefts by boys were in gangs. The annual report for 1951 of the Commissioner of Police for the Metropolis states that 67 per cent of persons under 21 arrested for crimes were operating in groups. Of this percentage, 91 per cent of the groups had members all under 21, 72 per cent all under 17, and 52 per cent all under 15 years of age. Only 9 per cent of young persons associated in their crimes with persons over 21, which confirms the clinical impression that, except for some parents who encourage their children to steal (often "scrounging" fuel) and some receivers of stolen goods, adults rarely use young people as cat's paws or confederates. This 1951 report concludes: "As usual, nearly ¾ of the young people in the groups were working in 2's or 3's, 45 per cent in pairs, 29 per cent in groups of only 3." These figures seem very general and can be confirmed from many sources. Carr Saunders, Mannheim, and Rhodes (1942) state that 71.6 per cent of all boy crimes in the London area were gang offences, and 74 per cent in six typical provincial towns; "It is obvious that the majority of offences are committed when boys are in company." Bagot and McClintock (1952) studying children remanded in custody found an increasing tendency to act alone as their age increased; thus 16 per cent of the 8- to 11-year-olds and one-third of the older boys acted alone. Norwood East and his collaborators (1942), in their notable study of 4,000 adolescent offenders, have a section on "associates" in which some interesting findings are given; the majority of companions were of an equal age; there was no evidence of a general tendency to graduate from "lone" offences to "company" offences, or vice versa. J. B. Mays (1954) gives a vivid and revealing account of the gangs of Liverpool, stressing the social and economic factors.

LONDON GROUPS

From experience with juvenile delinquents over a period of ten years in juvenile courts, remand homes, psychiatric clinics, a residential school, and a boys' club, some ideas have been gathered about the sort of groups in which these young people commit offences. Essentially the classification is into three: adolescent street groups, structured gangs, and loosely structured (diffuse) groups. The first (adolescent street groups) are not really much concerned with delinquency, but have been included here because many people seem to think they are. The members of such groups admittedly sometimes get into trouble, but not usually as members of these groups, which in the great majority of cases bear no more relation to the actual offence than would any youth club or evening class which the individuals happen to attend together. This adolescent street group is left out of the brief statistical analysis for the reason that none of the series studied offended as part of such a group. In short, they look very fearsome, and may behave abominably, but they are not often actually charged with offences.

The diffuse groups seem to fall under three subheadings: the fleeting, casual groups; the groups of customary friends and siblings; the loose antisocial groups. In spite of a number of intermediate stages between these groups and in spite of the fact that one group may evolve or degenerate into one of the others, they may possess some descriptive and perhaps clinical value.

ADOLESCENT STREET GROUPS

The uniformity of adolescent behaviour is often overestimated, for every surviving person must pass through this phase, and, carrying his psycho-logical peculiarities with him, will react variously to the new stresses. It is therefore not surprising that all adolescents do not belong to the sort of groups described here, and that the groups vary considerably one from another. Many youths, however, typically between 14 and 18 years of age, gather in the evenings and at week-ends into loosely structured street groups, of about five to thirty members, perhaps mixed in sex or, more likely, with girls occasionally tolerated. They occupy themselves in strolling along well-lighted thoroughfares, gossiping at street corners and coffee-stalls, or frequenting cafes and dance-halls dressed in characteristic fashion (Scott, 1954). "Foremost" among the purposes of such groups are self-display and mutual support in the difficult business of extricating themselves from an uncomfortably close emotional dependence at home, into a self-determined existence. When the home carapace is shed the group offers a shelter in which a new skin may harden—a breathing space for the acquisition of confidence. They gain a sense of security from contiguity in the group rather than from real confluence. Their very number seems to protect them from the necessity of making close relationships (especially with girls) for which they are not ready. Insofar as the members gradually begin to join the other, recognized groups of the community, and break up to make close relationships with the opposite sex, there is progress. Insofar as they take part in aggressive gang fights (an activity more appropriate to the ages of 8 to 12 years), and break up to commit offences, there is regression. It is obviously extremely important not to judge all by the few who cannot manage to grow out of this stage. The majority of such street groups are quite innocuous and, indeed, perhaps necessary and useful. It is by no means al-

324 THE EMPIRICAL STRUCTURE OF DELINQUENT GROUPS

ways incumbent upon us to go out and work upon them or "socialize" them.

The more severely disturbed adolescents (those who emerge from the home with marked resentfulness as well as with underlying feelings of inadequacy) are likely to congregate in separate groups whose members may actively seek opportunities of boosting their tender self-regard and of expressing their aggressiveness. Although weapons may be carried for their symbolic and prestige value, they are rarely used. Occasionally one or two individuals may break away from the group to commit offences, but planned crime, as opposed to group rowdyism, is very exceptional. There may be one or, not unusually, more than one nominal leader, but he or they will have little or no responsibility and their presence or absence scarcely makes any difference to the activity of the group. Indeed it is characteristic of such groups to be averse to the very concept of firm leadership. There is little loyalty, no firm control or persistence of membership, never a den, and no secret activities. In all these respects such groups are quite different from the gang proper. On the other hand, there is usually a territory, some sense of "we-ness," and a considerable degree of opposition to conventional standards. The following extract from a letter between two lads from such a "mob" or "click," as they call themselves, illustrates their inconclusive, poorly organized activities, the blending of different groups, and their need to appear "big" and tough among themselves.

. . . last Saturday we all went down to the A. . . . dance, T. . . . was there with all his mates, C. T. . . . was down there with all his Q. . . . boys, there was a few fights, X. . . . got his head kicked in and we all rushed outside to get the Q. . . . boys, everybody was breaking bottles but there wasn't a big fight, we decided to meet up at the T. . . . D. . . . (public house) on Wednesday, all the Q. . . . boys and all of us, our little click went up there, about 23 of us, and there was nobody up there so we went down D. . . . and then came home.

The situation has been observed in which a youth, who had belonged to a succession of such adolescent groups for an unusually long time, was gradually abandoned by his maturing mates until finally left with a small group whom he terrorized into supporting him; the group then superficially looked like a gang, but in fact lacked nearly all the real gang qualities. It is very important to diagnose such a group accurately, for it is useless to try and work with such a group and essential to remove the "leader" as quickly as possible, for he will not be amenable to psychiatric or social work while he remains at home, and is likely to wreck the efforts of field workers in the area.

GANGS PROPER

In view of the consistency of the literature, it is surprising that delinquent gangs with a leader, definite membership, persistence in time, a den, initiation procedure, and criminal objectives, are so unusual. An obvious possibility is that they are sufficiently clever or well-organized not to get caught, or, if they are caught, that loyalty prevents their disclosing information. These arguments are not strong, for, though delinquent gangs may remain hidden, their depredations would be known to the social workers and police of the area, who state that the existing delinquent gangs are known and that they are few. Further, of those boys who commit offences in groups, and are examined psychiatrically, nearly all disclose precisely what sort of association they had formed, in a manner so detailed and forthright, and so consistently with their colleagues, that it can be determined by a process of exclusion that true delinquent gang members comparatively rarely come before the juvenile courts.

It is indeed difficult to find good examples of gangs, nor do the few that are found conform with the picture of healthy devilment, adventurousness, pride of leadership or loyal lieutenancy that is often painted. Gang members who come before the courts usually have a gross antisocial character defect and come from homes in which the emotional atmosphere has been obviously disturbed and detrimental.

D. N., aged 14 years, was a determined and experienced delinquent from an extremely emotionally unsatisfactory home. Though both parents were present they rejected the boy through their callous indifference towards him. He had associated over a period of months with two boys from the same locality and of similar age; these two had similar, over-controlling, "managing" mothers and inadequate fathers. He was found guilty of breaking into an unoccupied house and systematically stealing readily convertible valuables. He was accustomed to meeting his accomplices by arrangement in a definite place. He planned the project, paid the fares to a distant suburb where they went round from house to house asking for "jobs" until an unoccupied house was found.

One explanation for the rarity of proper delinquent gangs is that, with the ever-decreasing waste sites and vacant lots, the gangs are quickly broken up. The following partnership, together with many of those subsequently described under the heading "unstructured antisocial" groups, might develop into gangs proper if allowed to continue.

H. (16¾₁₂) had excellent school reports and gave a superficially friendly, intelligent impression (I.Q. 100). There was no record of delinquency in his family but an older brother was "simple," easily influenced, and unfit on this account for army service; a younger brother had given up excellent educational opportunities without adequate reason. H. was unable to make friends, he indulged in childish fantasy of himself doing great things, he loved weapons and guns, and readily associated with delinquent companions. He seemed genuine in saying (quite cheerfully) that he often thought of suicide. He described typical *déjà vu* experiences. He seemed to have an ineffective, dreamy, poorly integrated personality, capable of adjusting comfortably under a cut and dried régime as he had done in an approved school, but not at home. His companion in crime, R. (15½), was equally abnormal but in a commoner and more understandable manner. He had been sent away from home between 3 and 5 years and never thereafter gained a welcome. He became a restless, talkative, "unattached" little boy, displaying at the age of 12 delinquent tendencies and wanting to get away from home. When this was arranged he was reported by his foster parents as mischievous, plausible, stubborn, and persistently enuretic. Both these boys had spent two years in an approved school but R. had never settled satisfactorily in it. After release R. sought out H. and they were soon found guilty of breaking into a shop together and stealing £ 30. H. was found armed with a knife and airgun just as he had been before committal to his approved school. H. and R. hardly constitute a gang yet do bear a definite leader-follower relationship to one another, plan their crime to some extent, have a definite antisocial purpose and some loyalty to one another. Their association seems to lie between a gang proper and an unstructured antisocial group.

Firm leadership, which is an absolute necessity for a proper gang, is best raised at this point. Thrasher says that "gang leaders hold sway like barons of old . . . ," and Healy that "a boy may initiate dozens of others especially if he has experience in courts and correctional schools." He adds that occasionally he found "the younger to be the more influential, but always because of superior mental and physical activity." This superiority according to Dumpson may be in physique, prowess, dash and daring, cleverness and cunning, impetuousness to act and dominate. The psychology of leader and led has also received attention. Topping states that "Leaders are far more aloof and uncompromising than followers," and Deutschberger (1947) finds them rigid, inflexible, tense and suspicious, while the followers, in submitting to the leader, are relieved of responsibility, and by a denial of the demands of society are relatively relaxed in conscience and free from guilt; the leader's anxiety and conflict is raised and externalized in hostility to society thus apparently tending to perpetuate the antisocial activities of the gang. He found that, in non-antisocial groups, no such stable centre of leadership existed and activities were proposed and executed by various individuals within the group.

The delinquent gangs of this series and of the writer's experience are quite different from those of Thrasher. The leader rarely "holds sway" (except in the occasional 8- or 9-year-old groups) over more than three henchmen, and Healy's process of initiation is more common in the unstructured groups and is not only carried out by a leader. The aloofness and tension of the leader is appreciable, as illustrated above in the case of H. and R., and the frequently gross accompanying antisocial character defect seems to obliterate the sense of guilt. It will be seen later that the absence of a "stable centre of leadership" is by no means confined to "non-antisocial" groups, but is also very obvious in many of the loosely structured groups to be described. The leaders are certainly boys of relatively superior intelligence, much less commonly of superior physique. It is noticeable, however, that a state of gross insecurity, with long-standing behaviour and conduct disorders, does not necessarily incapacitate them from leadership, though it does invariably mean that the followers will be even more handicapped in one way or another.

A 9½-year-old boy was the undoubted leader of a well-established gang which had a name, an initiation procedure involving the recording of members' names in a book, a cleverly chosen den, a highly delinquent purpose in which the leader directed operations and afterwards shared out the spoils. The leader was a very intelligent, active but physically weak boy whose superficial friendliness and charm covered chronic insecurity. He was an habitual bed-wetter and nailbiter, had truanted regularly for many years. He was the illegitimate child of an unstable and sexually promiscuous mother. There had been many changes of residence, two of them necessitated by the stepfather's action in "throwing them out." When there was a home, quarrels were constant. When held in custody for investigation, he was reported by all who observed him to be helpless and unable to hold his own with other boys. The followers in his gang were all handicapped in some way; either in being much younger or of much lower intelligence; one, though two years older and very much bigger, had a very defective level of intelligence.

In general the degree of emotional disturbance among the followers in this gang, as in the others studied, seemed to vary inversely with intelligence level. This rather suggests that unless they are handicapped in some way they cannot be tolerated by, or will not submit to, the leader, and that the double handicap of low intelligence plus severe emotional disturbance renders a boy unsuitable for gang membership, unless temporarily utilized by the gang as a "cat's paw." When held under observation the true leader sinks into obscurity; another member, often the least disturbed, then acts as mouthpiece and is usually mistaken for the leader. It is a regular finding that even the most determined and successful leader of a delinquent gang can only manage to dominate those who are relatively handicapped. This seems to apply to all age groups.

FLEETING, CASUAL DELINQUENT ASSOCIATIONS

A 13-year-old boy, reluctantly doing an errand for his mother, chanced upon another (from the same school but not well known to him) excitedly showing a bag of coins and relating how he had filched them from a stationary bus at the terminus. A third boy, also from the neighborhood but not well known to either, joined them. The first and third boys immediately went to the terminus and were caught attempting to repeat the crime. It was impossible for them or for anyone else to decide who was the leader—there wasn't one in the accepted sense of the term. The first boy had attended a child-guidance clinic for behaviour disorders and the third showed evidence of emotional disturbance (chronic truanting and a wide discrepancy between educational attainment and intelligence quotient). Both were considered predisposed by their home environments to delinquency, and of course both had been very much tempted.

The boys in these groups are often between 10 and 13, and tend to be physically immature for their age, excitable and overactive. The predisposition to delinquency must be considerable before a boy would join with a relative stranger in delinquency, and such associations are not common. These groups shade imperceptibly into the other unstructured, much commoner, delinquent groups. They differ from the loose antisocial groups in not having a history of repeated delinquency and in having a better prognosis.

S. A., a healthy intelligent 13-year-old boy, who had been under treatment at a child-guidance clinic, was discouraged and depressed by his parents' renewed rejection of him. They had both gone on a day's outing, leaving him at home. He sought out a boy, not his friend, but known to S. A. to have stolen in the past, and with his aid, took the back off the wardrobe (the usual repository for family savings) in his own home. With this fleeting acquaintance he then made a determined effort, aided by his father's £50 savings, to dispel his gloom and express his resentment. He asked to be sent from home.

Sometimes a boy will be carried along through a casual contact with a little group of more determined or experienced delinquents, so that the one delinquent escapade can have very different meanings for various members of the group. It is important to recognize the casual "inclusion" lest he be made to suffer unduly for the behaviour of others. A very obvious instance of this was N., a rubicund little boy of Frolich type, astonishingly charged with indecent assault of a girl. The circumstances were that P. (14) grabbed something belonging to a 12-year-old girl—the sort of activity which constantly goes on between restless children when they are unoccupied. She took fright and ran away, thus stimulating P.'s longings to be powerful and dominant; he gave chase and tongue; others, including N., joined in. The girl was run to earth, P. tugged at her clothing, sexual aggressive and exploratory instincts were released, some joined in and others stood round fascinated but doing nothing to help the frightened girl.

GROUPS OF FRIENDS AND SIBLINGS

Most group offences are committed in the company of friends or of siblings, whose usual activities are not delinquent. The delinquency may be primarily a matter of opportunity but in most cases predisposition is high. There is a leader but, if delinquency occurs, the initiative and direction may not have been taken by him. Although there may be a nucleus of "regulars" in the group, membership is not controlled as it is in gangs and there are no initiation procedures or secret signs. Such groups may develop into well-structured gangs or, more frequently, degenerate into distinctly antisocial, poorly structured "mobs"; they can, however, hover between the two for periods of many years. The members are often aware of having common difficulties at home and give the impression of trying to fend off unhappiness and a frankly antisocial existence through mutual support and shared legitimate activities. It is quite possible in these groups for some of the members to abstain from the occasional delinquent activities without losing face with the others—a situation which would be unthinkable in a gang.

Two intelligent boys of 14 and 15 years had been found guilty of snatching an elderly lady's handbag and sharing the contents, staying out over-night afterwards. One had no previous offence, while the other had been involved in a very minor stealing a year earlier. They had been friends since the age of 6 years and had been at the same schools, had often been camping together and recently had attended the same evening classes. This offence occurred when, in both cases, the home problem had flared up considerably. Separately examined, each showed accurate insight into the problem of the other. In one case the mother had, for a long time, been seeking to "send him away" and father said that he didn't hit the boy because "I might kill him." This boy had always been unwanted (an attempt was made to abort the pregnancy) and the marriage was a most unstable one. In the other case circumstances were equally unsatisfactory and complicated by mother's alcoholism. The basis of the association was genuine friendship and the sympa-

thetic sharing of a similar problem. The delinquency was a very secondary terminal development, but a definite indication that the situation was becoming intolerable.

The home backgrounds are not always rejecting. The following two 14-year-olds, belonging to a group of seven boys, were charged with stealing. R. T. had poor vision, bitten nails and was emotionally childish and with a strong sense of inferiority; he cried very easily and was unnaturally dependent on his over-protective mother. She was a pale anxious woman who could not bear quarrelling or scenes; she did not get on well with her husband who constantly criticized the boy. D. C.'s parents worried because he was undersized, childish and easily led. Mother tried to belittle her husband and held the family reins, over-indulging the boy as regards material comforts. Father was very lenient in reaction to his own strict upbringing. The seven boys had been friends for three years. Six months ago R. T. and D. C. had gradually defaulted from their club, from the Boys' Brigade and from the Army Training Corps. Neither had committed offences until two months ago when they were placed under probationary supervision for house-breaking. They were reintroduced to their clubs but only attended once. The other five boys, with whom they still maintained friendship, were not delinquent, although two of them would wait outside while a "job" was being done. The other three stayed at home when they thought delinquent activities were likely.

A more typical example is provided by four boys aged 14, 13, 12 and 11 years, who "lifted" a pineapple. On the day of the offence, three of them met on the pavement as was usual, and waited for the fourth. They intended to go to the park to play football, but decided to make a detour via the market to see what could be "knocked off." All the boys lived near one another and attended the same school, two of them in the same class. Each had belonged to youth recreational organizations and two still attended. Two of them, the 12- and 13-year-olds, independently stated that they had been stealing from shops and stalls, singly and as a group, when the opportunity presented itself, for years and without previously being caught. They met regularly for other purposes than delinquency, usually football. Two were living under great tension at home, the pattern being similar in both cases— only children of parents who did not get on well together, mother being dissatisfied and father discouraged and disinterested in the boy. The third was a boy with a history of epileptic fits and a mother who rejected him. The fourth was not studied.

Where little groups of siblings are involved in stealing useful things, the possibility of parental direction should be held in mind.

K. had been in trouble for stealing fuel and stores from shops and barges on five occasions between 9 and 12, on each occasion accompanied by a sister (two years older) or a brother (two years younger). He said there had been a great many other undetected offences. Psychiatric examination showed no abnormality of the children and no earlier history of emotional troubles. Investigation confirmed that the parents had encouraged the stealing and that both parents had criminal records.

Such findings of multiple stealings of valuables by several children of the family in the absence of other offences or of evidence of emotional difficulties is very typical of parental direction.

Sometimes very disturbed and jealous boys or girls will take with them, on their delinquent escapades, the young sibling who is the object of their jealousy, in order to involve him also in trouble, danger and parental disapproval. Indeed this sometimes seems to be the outstanding motive of the delinquency or running away.

The friendships, sometimes leading to delinquency, in which the basis of the relationship is the need of the older boy to protect and lead a younger and very passive boy who enjoys the dependent relationship, needs to be mentioned. Such relationships are clearly closely allied to homosexuality, but, as Healy suggested, can exist without any question of overt practices.

LOOSE ANTISOCIAL GROUPS

These groups are composed of very antisocially inclined children or youths, who combine promiscuously in loosely structured, unorganized, fluid groups. They are so unhappy and disturbed in relation to their homes and to society at large as to be careless of the consequences of their actions, often hoping to be removed from home, and regularly looking for or initiating delinquent openings in an indiscriminate and unplanned manner. They often appear to be bent on a headlong delinquent phase which is not interrupted by court appearance, so that even while on remand they may continue to offend.

Three boys, aged 7, 8 and 9 years, entered premises and in a few minutes did £100 worth of damage; they did not steal anything. Two of them were brothers. Their mother is an epileptic and her sister asthmatic. She is erratic and harsh but capable of affection to the young members of this large family. Recently she impulsively left home because she was "fed-up." The home atmosphere is chaotic and the older children driven out on to the street. These two lads were healthy, of average intelligence, restless, sensitive and distrustful of everybody—two highly frustrated, emotionally immature youngsters, one of whom frankly wanted to join a brother already in an approved school. The third boy also had a brother just licensed from an approved school, and his mother was an embittered, shrewish woman with little warmth of affection for the boy. Erratic and unstable in her own affairs, she was incapable of controlling her children. She found this boy "restless like a caged lion at home." She has long been separated from her husband so that this boy has been shuttled between two homes for most of his life. He also is healthy, intelligent, but distrustful and resentful. He wanted to get away from his frustrating and disappointing home. Such a combination of boys is particularly predisposed to embark on some orgy of destruction which expresses their resentment, releases their frustration and ensures that they be sent away. The more determined member makes the opportunity and is then himself stimulated by the uncontrolled excitement of the others.

H. A., W. M. and A. E. were found guilty of stealing from a parked motor car. Each had a considerable record of offences and had taken part in numerous undetected crimes over a period of many years, with a variety of different groups of boys. They were not organized as a gang and had little or no loyalty one to another. Table 1 shows the similarity and seriousness of their positions.

Another group of three boys who offended together had each taken part in other group offences involving fifteen other boys from the district.

In these groups the rôle of leader means very little. A boy may be the follower in one offence in the morning and the leader of a different group in the afternoon. As Emanuel Miller (1944) wrote, "I could find no sense of community between them, no feeling of a common end dominating or animating the group as such, and little sense of honour of the group. What held them together, on close examination, was the fact that each one of them needed some form of psychological outlet which could only be found through the temporary aggregation." Often it

Table 1

H. A. ($12\frac{3}{12}$)	W. M. ($12\frac{1}{12}$)	A. E. ($10\frac{7}{12}$)
Previous record		
at 9 Unlawful possession. 10 Stealing bicycle. 11 Stealing bicycle. 11 Suspected person.	at 11 Stealing. 11 Stealing. 12 Stealing.	at $8\frac{1}{2}$ Beyond control. 10 Stealing.
Other members of family with criminal record		
Father and brother.	Father and brother.	Two brothers.
Parental relationships		
Separated since F.'s last imprisonment. Mother cohabiting.	Father alcoholic and shirks responsibility. Mother "superior," well-spoken, tense, unaffectionate.	F. deserted just before this boy's birth, returning when he was 9. History of insanity in three near paternal relations. P.G.M. alcoholic.
Early history		
Unwanted baby. M. soon returned to work. Grandmother cared for him. Day nursery at first opportunity. Much illness. Away from home between 6 and 7.	Removed from home before 2. Fretted severely. Back at 5, but has remained "odd man out."	No separation from home till 8, when he went into a residential school for two years.
Boy		
Healthy, I.Q. 107. Aggressive, hostile and distrustful. Doesn't want to go home.	Healthy, I.Q. 92. Can't settle or concentrate. Covers his feelings beneath a superficial friendliness. No regret or sense of guilt.	Healthy, I.Q. 102. Anxious and insecure. Wants to go home.

is the most excitable and poorly self-controlled individual who acts as catalyst to the group, yet afterwards, when the group is examined as a whole, that member shows little or no powers of leadership.

P. had to be removed from home at 6½ because of his mother's continual neglect of him. He and some of his siblings were illegitimate and his mother was an ex-approved school girl. Father was passive, inadequate and avoided parental responsibilities. P., who has a long history of offences, is a pale, thin, backward boy, with many fears, yet can be willful and fiery tempered and seems quite irresponsible. He became involved with a younger boy who resembled him very closely even to the content of his drawings and phantasy. He was, if anything, the leader of the pair, but when the second boy was sent away from home because of offences as part of a different group, P. joined another, older, delinquent lad, and was then clearly a follower.

A 15½-year-old boy of immature physi-cal development, very weak character but good intelligence, acted as "catalyst" to his group. Shifted about as a child, and spending much of his time in hospitals and residential schools, he has never been able to make a satisfying personal relationship, least of all with his mother. He tries to impress people and to boost his self-regard, by being tough, but he dissolves into tears if threatened. He is extremely bitter and unhappy. He does not offend very often and then only with much older boys. But he acts as a spur to them, and, once entry into a building is gained, he feels powerful, excited and proceeds to wreck the place in wanton fashion.

STATISTICAL STUDY

Boys between the ages of 8 and 17 years, under investigation for present proved offences carried out in the company of other juveniles, were studied as regards age, type of association, composition of the group, damage done; they were compared (Table 2) in cer-

Table 2

Type of association		
	Uncertain	4
Structured	Proper gangs	17
	Fleeting associations	18
Unstructured (86 per cent)	Usual companions	69
	Loose antisocial groups	43
		151

Damage done
Estimated on a three-point scale: (1) Trivial and none
(2) Considerable
(3) Serious

	Rating			Number of offenders
	1	2	3	
Gangs proper	3 17.6%	5 29.4%	9 52.9%	17
Fleeting	8 44.4%	6 33.3%	4 22.2%	18
Usual companions	27 39.1%	27 39.1%	15 21.7%	69
Loose antisocial	16 37.1%	9 20.9%	18 41.8%	43
Solitary recidivists	36 56.2%	24 37.5%	4 6.2%	64
Solitary first offenders	73 67%	26 23.8%	10 9.1%	109

Table 3

Average ages in years

	Age	Number
Gang	13	17
Fleeting associations	12.4	18
Usual companions	13	69
Loose antisocial	13.1	43
Solitary	14	140

Composition

In 131 group offences
$\left\{\begin{array}{l}\text{349 individuals involved (av. 2.6)}\\ \text{3 offences included one girl each}\\ \text{39 siblings were involved in 32 cases}\end{array}\right.$

Gangs	average membership 2.5	no sibs. no girls
Fleeting associations	average membership 3.6	2 offences included 1 sib. each 1 offence included 2 sibs.
Usual companions	average membership 2.2	3 offences included 1 girl each 21 offences included 1 sib. each 7 offences included 2 sibs. each
Loose antisocial	average membership 2.9	1 offence involved 1 sib.

Order of offences

The first of 2 offences—53 as group member, 35 alone.
The first of 3 or more offences—35 as group member, 37 alone.

---

tain respects with boys under investigation for present proved offences but never known to have offended in company with others. It is recognized that these samples are not likely to be representative of delinquents as a whole. Elaborate study has not therefore been considered justifiable.

A gang does most damage per offence, then in decreasing order a loose antisocial group, a usual companion group, a fleeting group, with solitary offenders last (Table 3).

There is thus little indication as to whether, in those who commit both solitary and mixed offences, the solitary or group offence breaks the ice.

In an attempt to determine differences between those who offend in company and those who do not, forty-nine juveniles who had been found guilty of two or more lone offences and no group offences were compared with fifty-seven juveniles who had been found guilty of two or more group offences and no lone offences, in respect of the following five factors (each rated on a three-point scale): constitutional, organic, adverse social forces, neurotic conflicts, antisocial personality disorder. Adverse social forces are not significantly different for the two groups. Neurotic conflicts are not diagnosed in either group. Lone offenders show slightly greater constitutional handicap, a slightly higher incidence of antisocial personality disorder, and a slightly greater incidence of organic factors (organic here includes epilepsy and psychosis). Lone offenders also show a very much higher incidence of any of the five factors acting in high degree (i.e., scored three on the rating scale) even though the total score for all five factors may not be greater.

The handicap of group offenders is more evenly spread over the five possible areas. Lone offenders did not appear to be more neurotic than group offenders.

References

Bagot, J. H., and McClintock, F. H. (1952). "Detention in Remand Homes." *English Studies in Criminal Science,* Vol. VIII. Ed. L. Radzinowicz and J. W. C. Turner. London: Macmillan.

Beckham, A. S. (1933). "Oversuggestibility in Juvenile Delinquents." *J. Abn. and Soc. Psychol.,* 28, 172–178.

Bernstein, D. R. (1953). "Group Work on Our Corner." *Group,* 15(4), 19–24.

Brew, J. Macalister (1955). In "Social Group Work in Great Britain." Ed. P. Kuenstler. London: Faber and Faber, p. 73.

Bromberg, W. (1947). "Emotional Immaturity and Antisocial Behaviour." *J. Clin. Psychopathol.,* 8, 1.

Burt, Sir Cyril (1925). *The Young Delinquent.* London: Univ. Lond. Press.

Carr Saunders, Mannheim, and Rhodes (1942). *Young Offenders.* Cambridge: Cambridge Univ. Press.

Chazal, J. "Unruly Gangs of Children and Their Readjustment to Society." UNESCO Vagrant Children 26:5741, 44–59.

Cohen, A. K. (1955). *Delinquent Boys: The Culture of the Gang.* Glencoe, Ill.: Free Press.

Crane, A. R. (1952). "Preadolescent Gangs." *J. Genetic Psychol.,* 81, 113–123.

Deutschberger, Paul (1947). "The Structure of Dominance." *Am. J. Ortho-Psychiat.,* 17, 343–351.

Dumpson, J. (1952). "Gang and Narcotic Problems of Teen-Age Youth." *Am. J. Psychotherap.,* 6, 312–346.

East, Norwood, and collaborators (1942). *The Adolescent Criminal.* London: J. & A. Churchill.

Hall, Stanley (1904). *Adolescence, its Psychology.* New York and London: Appleton.

Harding, J. (1952). "A Street-Corner Gang and Its Implications for Sociological and Psychological Theory." In Hulett, J. E., and Stagner, R. (Eds.) *Problems in Social Psychology.* Urbana, Ill.: Univ. of Ill. Press.

Healy, W. (1915). *Honesty.* Indianapolis: Bobbs Merrill.

Healy, W. (1915). *The Individual Delinquent.* London: Heinemann.

Hewitt, L. E., and Jenkins, R. L. (1946). *Fundamental Patterns of Maladjustment.* Springfield, Ill.

Jones, Howard (1948). "Group Sentiment and Delinquency." *Mental Health, London,* 8, 41–44.

Mays, J. B. (1954). *Growing up in the City.* University Press of Liverpool.

Miller, Emanuel (1944). In *Mental Abnormality and Crime.* Ed. Radzinowicz and Turner. London: Macmillan, 220–227.

Mitchell, R. (1951). "Capturing Boys' Gangs." *Hum. Organiz'n.,* 10(2), 26–31.

Pank, R. (1927). Editor's preface to Thrasher's *The Gang.* Chicago: Univ. of Chicago Press.

Piaget, Jean (1932). *The Moral Judgment of the Child.* London: Kegan Paul.

Puffer, I. Adams (1912). *The Boy and His Gang.* Boston.

Riis, J. (1890). *How the Other Half Lives.* New York.

Rosenthal, Pauline (1942). "Group Studies of Preadolescent Boys." *Am. J. Ortho-Psychiat.,* 12, 115–126.

Scott, P. D. (1954). *The Roots of Crime.* Ed. Sir Norwood East. London.

Scott, P. D. (1955). "The Natural History of the Spiv." *Biology and Human Affairs,* 20, 3.

Shaw, C. (1931). *The Natural History of a Delinquent Career.* Chicago: Univ. of Chicago Press.

Shaw, C., and McKay, H. D. (1942). *Juvenile Delinquency and Urban Areas.* Chicago: Univ. of Chicago Press.

Spaulding, C. B. (1948). "Cliques, Gangs and Networks." *Sociol. and Soc'l. Res.* 32, 928–937.

Thrasher, F. W. (1927). *The Gang.* Chicago: Univ. of Chicago Press.

Topping, Ruth (1943). "The Treatment of the Pseudo-Social Boy." *Am. J. Ortho-Psychiat.*, 13, 353–360.

Trenaman, J. (1952). *Out of Step.* London: Methuen.

Turner, M. L. (1953). *Ship Without Sails.* London: Univ. of London Press.

Turner, M. L., and Spencer, J. C. in *Spontaneous Youth Groups.* Ed. P. H. Kuenstler. Chap. 4. "Spontaneous Youth Groups and Gangs," 56–59.

Waters, Miriam van (1927). "The Child Who Is a Leader." *Survey,* 58, 498–505.

Wattenberg, W. W., and Balistrieri, J. J. (1950). "Gang Membership and Juvenile Misconduct." *Am. Sociol. Rev.,* 15, 744–752.

Whyte, W. F. (1943). *Street Corner Society.* Chicago: Chicago University Press.

Wolman, Benjamin (1951). "Spontaneous Groups of Children and Adolescents in Israel." *J. Soc'l Psychol.,* 34, 171–182.

Section IV   LEGAL PROCESSING OF
DELINQUENCY

The materials of this section were selected to give the student a conception of the nature and practice of the juvenile court movement, as well as some of the sociolegal problems that have developed since the first law defining juvenile delinquency was passed by the Illinois legislature in 1899. The juvenile court movement grew out of the conviction that youthful offenders should not receive the same treatment as adults. The fundamental idea of this first juvenile court law was that the state, with a judge acting in the role of a parent, should extend its protective arm to children in order to "cure" and "save" rather than to punish. The court was to recognize the individuality of the child and adapt its procedure accordingly.

Since that time, many problems have arisen about the relation of the juvenile court to other courts, the legality of its procedure, and the rules of evidence. Part of this difficulty may be seen to be due to the diversity, jurisdiction, and functioning of the juvenile court systems in the various states.

Dunham's article presents two idealized conceptions of the juvenile court, the social agency and the legalistic, and discusses the nature of the conflict between these two contradictory orientations. Caldwell's article reviews the history and characteristics of the juvenile court; it discusses the events and forces that produced it and the consequences for the court's philosophy and operation. Basic questions are raised concerning the future of the court, with particular emphasis placed on the need to differentiate clearly the judicial function of the court from the casework function.

The selection by Tappan reflects the concern that many authorities have expressed regarding the functions of the court. Tappan accepts the basic goals of the juvenile court movement but opposes the continuing expansion of the functions of the juvenile court. He strongly objects to the vagueness of the definitions of offenses for which the courts may try children, for this factor makes possible serious interference with the individual's liberties. He enumerates what he con-

335

ceives to be minimal protections of due process, and refers to the dangers involved in practices such as informal probation and the unofficial handling of cases.

In a realistic appraisal of the juvenile court, Francis A. Allen discusses the problems that arise from inaccurate or mistaken conceptions of the court's roles and its ability to contribute to the solution of delinquency prevention and control.

As for the functions of the court, the question is often raised why probation is administered by the court whereas other forms of correctional treatment are administered by separate agencies. The administrative, casework, and welfare functions associated with adjudication are performed directly by probation personnel as a part of the court. The current practice is for the court to make the decision how the juvenile is to be processed—between placing the juvenile on probation or committing him to an institution.

Diana discusses present-day probation in contrast to what in his view are some unsubstantiated claims made about the way probation operates in practice. A significant discrepancy which emerges is that experienced workers in the field do not have as well-defined views of what constitutes probation as do those who are writing in this area.

General issues are raised by Rubin about procedural due process of law in probation in reference to presentence investigation and to the rules governing the legal status and supervision of the probationer.

The results of Cohn's study revealed that the probation officer was unaware of the meaning and importance of the criteria he was using in making recommendations that a juvenile be placed on probation, institutionalized, discharged, or recommended for psychiatric examination. Moreover, there was a stress on reporting only the more objective data which can be quickly and accurately recorded. Recommendations to probation were based on limited and rather nebulous criteria.

Not all youths who commit delinquent acts come to the attention of the courts and correctional agencies. Police officers are often permitted considerable latitude in deciding which juveniles come to the attention of the courts and are thereby officially identified as delinquents. The study by Piliavin and Briar shows that the social judgment made by police officers to label a juvenile a delinquent is influenced by race, prior offense records, grooming, and demeanor rather than by the kind of offense he has committed.

28. The Juvenile Court: Contradictory Orientations in Processing Offenders

H. WARREN DUNHAM

EVENTS AND FORCES FORMING THE JUVENILE COURT

The historical origin of the juvenile court is, no doubt, sufficiently familiar to the readers of this symposium to warrant but a brief recapitulation. While the first law defining juvenile delinquency was passed by the Illinois legislature in April 1899,[1] and the juvenile court itself began functioning in June of that year, its founding had been amply anticipated by certain legalistic precedents in equity and criminal law. More specifically, from the English courts of chancery or equity, the principle of *parens patriae* had evolved in the case of *Eyre v. Shaftsbury* in 1772.[2] This principle, which enabled the court to act in lieu of parents who were deemed unwilling or unable to perform their proper parental functions, paved the way for the juvenile court to assume jurisdiction of dependent and neglected children. Even before this decision, however, the doctrine that the

state under certain conditions had to act as a protector of minors had long been a part of the common law.[3]

But it is in dealing with delinquent children that the criminal-law origins of the juvenile court are of significance. It had long been an accepted principle of the common law that a child under seven years of age could not commit a criminal act because he could not have *mens rea*, a guilty mind.[4] From here, it was logical next to question the responsibility of children above seven years of age, and in so doing, the juvenile court law has been regarded merely as extending the application of a common-law principle.

Another development anticipating the juvenile court was the inauguration of probation as a device for dealing with offenders. This practice, initiated in Boston in 1841,[5] which included from the beginning adult as well as juvenile

[1] Ill. Laws 1899, p. 131.
[2] 2 P. Wms. 103, 24 Eng. Rep. 659 (Ch. 1722).

[3] See H. H. Lou, *Juvenile Courts in the United States* 3 (1927).
[4] See Rollin M. Perkins, *Criminal Law* 729–732 (1957).
[5] See Helen D. Pigeon, *Probation and Parole in Theory and Practice* 85 (1942).

SOURCE. H. Warren Dunham, "The Juvenile Court: Contradictory Orientations in Processing Offenders," from *Law and Contemporary Problems*, Volume 23, No. 3, Summer 1958, pp. 508–527. From a symposium, *Sentencing*, Copyright © 1958, Duke University. Reprinted with permission.

offenders, early highlighted some of the special protections that a child needed when brought before a court of law.

One other development which paved the way for the juvenile court was the establishment of special institutions for confining child offenders. The first institution for juvenile delinquents, the House of Refuge, in New York City, opened on January 1, 1825, and by 1860, sixteen of such institutions had been opened in the United States.[6] These responded to the need long felt by the reform element in American society that a child who had been convicted of violating a law should not be confined with hardened adult criminals in jails and penitentiaries, where, it was believed, only further demoralization and corruption could ensue. Even so, up to the first quarter of the twentieth century, children were still being punished by incarceration in institutions designed for adults.

Thus, it is seen that early legal precedents, the development of probation, and the establishment of special institutions for juvenile offenders anticipated the first juvenile court in Illinois, which was to become the prototype for legal tribunals dealing with children whose behavior or situation indicated positive state intervention. The concept of the juvenile court spread quickly and was favorably received throughout the country. Indeed, by 1923, all states, with the exception of Connecticut and Wyoming, had enacted legislation defining a juvenile delinquent and establishing a special court for hearing children's cases; and by the early 1940's, even the two hold-out states had come into compliance with this trend.

While these historical events define the establishment of the juvenile court, in a broader cultural sense it can be regarded as the product of such social forces as our humanitarianism, on the one hand, and the growth of cities, on the other. The force of humanitarianism is well symbolized in the personalities of those women, Jane Addams and Julia Lathrop in Illinois, who agitated for the first juvenile court law. The high principles and unselfish motives which fired these women played a positive role in giving to the juvenile court, from its inception, the stamp of a social agency for dealing with a maladjusted child, rather than that of a punitive court attempting to exact retribution.

The rapid growth of cities, which characterized not only the United States, but the world in the nineteenth century, was also a significant factor. In 1800, there was no city with a population of 100,000 in the United States, but by 1900, there were thirty-seven.[7] This urbanization was a product of the factory system plus improvements in agricultural technology. The cities grew not so much through natural increase, as through vast movements of people thereto from rural areas and from various European countries seeking jobs, opportunities, and a new life.

Most of these European migrants faced new and untested situations in the slum environments of our large cities. Their children, often caught in the conflict between European peasant values and the values reflected in American institutions, responded in delinquent ways and began to flood the jails, reformatories, and courts. Their parents, handicapped by language difficulties, were unable to comprehend or cope with these situations, and this tended

---

[6] See N. K. Teeters and J. O. Reinemann, *The Challenge of Delinquency* 429–447 (1950).

[7] See U. S. Dep't of State, Census Office, Second Census of the United States (1801); U. S. Dep't of Commerce, Bureau of the Census, Statistical Abstract of the United States (1957).

to foster certain unforeseen functions of the emerging juvenile court, such as aiding the process of immigrant family adjustment, serving as an educational agency in American values, and often protecting the child from demoralizing home situations.

Definitions

Some difficulty has been experienced in determining exactly what the juvenile court is and what a juvenile delinquent is. The difficulty in defining the juvenile court stems from the fact that it is usually attached to a probate or county court and is generally of limited jurisdiction. Thus, while each state now has a juvenile court, its organization and the policies governing it vary markedly throughout the country. While most large cities have a court presided over by a special judge that is devoted exclusively to the processing of cases involving children, many rural counties merely have the probate judge change hats when hearing children's cases. In some jurisdictions, the juvenile court judge is appointed; in many other jurisdictions, he is an elected official. A few judges have looked upon the juvenile court judgeship as a career; others have seen it merely as a step in an upward political climb. Some judges take a human, personal interest in the children brought before them; others merely handle the cases within the framework of the law. Some juvenile courts, particularly those in large cities, have a staff of trained professionals, probation officers, social workers, psychologists, statisticians; others have hardly any. In some juvenile courts, the probation officers are trained social workers; in others, their professional training is minimal. In some juvenile courts, these professionals are under civil service and have tenure; in others, they are largely personal and political appointments. Some juvenile courts

work closely with the numerous social agencies dealing with children; others have little or no contact with such agencies.

Three types of juvenile courts which have emerged in the various states have been identified. First, in most counties, other courts have jurisdiction over juvenile cases as well, and when hearing such cases they are referred to as juvenile courts. Second, there are some juvenile courts which are separate and divorced completely from other courts; these are usually found in counties with large cities. Finally, some juvenile courts are tied to special courts that handle selected social-problem cases, such as divorce and truancy, although there also has been a tendency to place such social-problem cases in juvenile courts which have an independent organization—a practice that has engendered certain support for a so-called family court.

A recent survey shows that in some forty states, jurisdiction is overlapping between the general criminal and juvenile courts. It is noted that the provision for alternate authority is related to the seriousness of the offense and/or the maturity of the child-defendant. The interpretive remarks on this matter are most relevant:[8]

Practice belies the motives which have supported the child welfare movement, revealing the limitations of our humanitarianism. More specifically, it points up the emphasis which our legal system continues to place upon incapacitation and deterrence—the protection of the public even at the expense of the child. In part, it may reflect too, the feeling that a fuller and more careful hearing should be given to serious cases than the juvenile court ordinarily provides.

When one turns to the definition of

[8] Tappan, "Children and Youth in the Criminal Court," 261 *Annals* 128, 132 (1947).

a juvenile delinquent, there is not so much variation as in the case of the juvenile court. All states have laws which, although varying in wording, show a common core of agreement in this regard. Thus, a child is uniformly considered delinquent if he acts in such a way as to violate a local ordinance or state law. In addition, most states further include such acts or conditions as "habitual truancy from school," "knowingly associating with thieves, vicious or immoral persons," "incorrigibility," "beyond control of parent or guardian," and "growing up in idleness and crime." These are only a few of the thirty-four items commonly found in the laws defining juvenile delinquency in the several states.[9]

In general, state laws defining delinquency have moved from the specific to the generic. Accordingly, the legislation that established the juvenile court in Illinois defined a delinquent as "any child under the age of sixteen years who has violated any law of the state or any city or village ordinance."[10] This concise statement contrasts markedly with the later New York legislation which defines a delinquent as:[11]

. . . a child over seven and under sixteen years of age (a) who violates any law of . . . this state or any ordinance of the city of New York, or who commits any act which if committed by an adult would be an offense punishable otherwise than by death or life imprisonment; (b) who is incorrigible, ungovernable, or habitually disobedient and beyond the control of his parents, guardian, custodian or other lawful authority; (c) who is habitually truant; (d) who without just cause and without the consent of his parent, guardian or other custodian deserts his home or place of abode; (e) who engages in any occupation which is in violation of the law; (f) who begs or who solicits alms or money in public places; (g) who associates with immoral or vicious persons; (h) who frequents any place the maintenance of which is in violation of law; (i) who habitually uses obscene or profane language; or (j) who so deports himself as wilfully to injure or endanger the morals or health of himself or others.

Another observable trend has been the strengthening of the role of the juvenile court by assuring it wider jurisdiction over children's cases and by emphasizing that the child is not on trial for a specific crime. But some decisions contain language to the effect that the child's constitutional rights are to be assured through right of appeal —even though this right is seldom exercised in the juvenile court;[12] and this matter has provided one of the principal foci for criticism of the juvenile court. Some judges and lawyers have maintained that the juvenile court in operation practically subverts the "due process" clause of the constitution in its zeal to apply the doctrine of *parens patriae*.

In addition to the generally diffuse manner in which they define delinquency, state laws differ markedly with respect to fixing the maximum legal age of a delinquent, varying from sixteen to twenty-one, with seventeen being the most common.

In summary, then, it should be noted that juvenile delinquency is a broad generic term which embraces many diverse forms of antisocial behavior of the child and which is defined somewhat differently in the various states, even though a converging tendency may be observed in the various laws.

It is only to be expected that these differences in court organization and

---

[9] See Frederick B. Sussman, *Law of Juvenile Delinquency: The Laws of the Forty-Eight States* 20 (1950).

[10] Ill. Laws 1899, p. 137.

[11] N.Y.C. Dom. Rel. Ct. Act § 2(15).

[12] Herbert A. Bloch and Frank T. Flynn, *Delinquency: The Juvenile Offender in America Today* 353 (1956).

in the definition of delinquency have made for wide variations in juvenile court policies and practices. Some juvenile courts are rigid, others are flexible; some are authoritarian, others are permissive; some are dictatorial, others are democratic. These contrasts are reflected in the number of cases heard unofficially in comparison with those heard officially, as well as in the use of various dispositions and the differences among juvenile court judges in the use of the dispositions available to them. But above all, they are reflected by the dominance of the image, as either a legal or social agency, that the juvenile court has of itself.

THE SOCIAL-AGENCY IMAGE OF THE COURT

Juvenile courts in the United States run the gamut from the authoritarian legalistic tribunal at one extreme to the permissive, social-agency type of organization at the other. While there is no one juvenile court which coincides completely with either of these idealized poles, it could probably be demonstrated that those which are an adjunct to another court correspond more closely to the legalistic image and those which have a completely independent organization, with a full-time judge, tend to adhere to the social-agency image. In this part, an attempt will be made to delineate the ideal social-agency image of the juvenile court. In so doing, those influences that were crucial in molding this image, the general character of this image, and some of its unanticipated consequences will be identified.

In the social-agency image, the purposes of the juvenile court are to understand the child, to diagnose his difficulty, to treat his condition, and to fit him back into the community. These purposes are held, to a greater or lesser degree, by the personnel that constitutes the juvenile court organization. More difficult, however, is the unraveling of all the tangible and intangible influences that have gone into constructing this social-agency image. In this connection, five influences have been selected which, in the judgment of the writer, have been primarily responsible for the evolution of this image and for its development at the expense of the juvenile court's more legalistic role. These are and have been: (1) the aggressive social-work orientation of the United States Children's Bureau; (2) the broadening jurisdiction of the juvenile court to include not only neglected and dependent children, but all matters of a legal nature involving children; (3) the gradual professionalization of social work; (4) various court decisions involving delinquency; and (5) the growing prospects of treatment through the increased acceptance by social workers of psychoanalysis, which has provided techniques for getting at the roots of conflict which supposedly produce delinquency. While each one of these influences has played its specific role, it would be quite difficult to assess their respective weights. It is sufficient merely to note that collectively they interacted and mutually reinforced an image of the juvenile court as a social-agency institution of independent status.

Thirteen years after the first juvenile court was established in Illinois, the Children's Bureau was created and lodged in the United States Department of Labor.[13] The appointment of Julia Lathrop, an early proponent of the first juvenile court law, as its first head was a significant factor in enabling the emerging profession of social work to exercise a powerful influence

[13] 37 Stat. 79 (1912), 42 U.S.C. § 191 (1952); 37 Stat. 737 (1913), 5 U.S.C. § 616 (1952).

over the development of the juvenile court. This influence has been reflected in the collection of statistics, the development of model juvenile court laws, the promulgation of standards for measuring juvenile court operation, the initiation of studies of juvenile court cases, the encouragement of juvenile courts to institute treatment services, the calling of national conferences of practicing professionals dealing with the problem, the emphasis on the need of probation officers with case-work training, and the attempts to construct educational and experience standards for those persons who would enter juvenile court work. All of these efforts and others have helped so to orient the juvenile court as to enable it to construct an image of itself as a social-work agency, designed primarily to meet the needs of the child. When Julia Lathrop left the Bureau in 1921, the high standards which she had set and the high ideals of child care and welfare for which she strived were carried forward by the distinguished social workers that followed her—Grace Abbott, 1921–1933, Katherine Lenroot, 1934–1951, and Martha Eliot, 1951–1956.

In short, the Children's Bureau, during its comparatively short history, has been most successful in shaping the image of the juvenile court as an agency for seeking the welfare of the child. Its failures, if they may be so termed, have been primarily of a negative nature— that is, it has failed to recognize that high ideals without sufficient knowledge are not enough, with the consequence that the social-agency image, which is at present the dominant image, has led to certain unanticipated consequences and unresolved dilemmas which have often placed the child in situations that are harmful rather than helpful to him. One commentator probably had these matters in mind when he noted that

"the plight of the youngster has been increased by the deprivation of these [public hearings, trial by jury, right of appeal] and other ordinary elements of due process that are assured in the criminal court."[14]

The second influence, the broadening jurisdiction of the juvenile court, was a natural outgrowth of the reform spirit which dominated its founding. This helped, again, to emphasize the often-quoted characteristic of the juvenile court—that the child before it is not being tried for a crime, but rather that the court is acting in lieu of the parent and, as a benevolent one, by inquiring into the development and circumstances surrounding his maladjustment in order to determine the course of action that will best meet his needs and insure his continued welfare. This tendency of the juvenile court to deal with all cases involving children, however, has resulted in an obscuring and sloughing over of the differences between the delinquent and the dependent or neglected child and in a dealing with every child as if he were maladjusted or presented some kind of problem. Social workers, in fact, in their conception of juvenile courts, unwittingly reflect this obscuring tendency:[15]

The purpose of the juvenile court is not to inflict a penalty on a child but to save him from further delinquency and from neglect. Its success, therefore, depends upon a comprehensive understanding of all significant aspects of the case.

. . . If treatment is to be directed to causes and adapted to the needs of the individual, the child himself must be studied—his physical condition, his mental capacities, his personality and the driving forces of his conduct.

14 Tappan, *supra* note 8, at 130.
15 K. F. Lenroot and E. O. Lundberg, *Juvenile Courts at Work—A Study of the Organization and Method of Ten Courts* 88, 94 (U.S. Children's Bureau, Dep't of Labor Pub. No. 141, 1925).

It seems only too clear. The purpose of the juvenile court is not to determine whether the child has committed any act for which he should be held; rather it is to get at the causes of his misbehavior in order that he can be given treatment appropriate to his needs.

The growth and establishment of social-work practice on a professional level has been a third influence that has helped to strengthen the social-agency image of the juvenile court. During the forty years following the birth of the juvenile court, the growth of social work was rapid. In the colleges and universities, social work, often lodged in sociology departments, gradually broke away to form independent departments; in some universities, it emerged as a full-fledged, degree-granting graduate professional school. The professional organizations for social workers kept pace. The American Association of Social Workers, an outgrowth of the National Social Workers Exchange, was founded in 1921, the American Association of Medical Social Workers in 1918, the National Association of School of Social Workers in 1919, the American Association of Psychiatric Social Workers in 1926, the American Association of Group Workers in 1946, and the Social Work Research Group in 1949. Within the last three years, all of these groups have joined to form the National Association of Social Workers. These professional organizations not only have helped to support the hands of those strategically placed workers in the Children's Bureau, but also have served as pressure groups in various communities to bring about the appointment of the type of juvenile court personnel that would strengthen the social-agency image of the court.

The fourth influence here—certain court decisions—have also helped to move the juvenile court toward a so-cial-agency image. The constitutionality of the legislation creating the juvenile court was quick to be tested. In one of the earliest of these cases, *Commonwealth v. Fisher,* the defendant attacked the juvenile court and its procedures, claiming that he had been deprived thereby of certain of his constitutional rights. The court stated in part:[16]

The last reason to be noticed why the act should be declared unconstitutional is that it denies the appellant a trial by jury. Here again is the fallacy that he was tried by the court . . . and no act of the legislature can deny this right to any citizen, young or old, minor or adult, if he is to be tried for a crime against the commonwealth. But there was no trial for any crime here, and the act is operative only when there is to be no trial. The very purpose of the act is to prevent a trial. . . .

And so it went. Decision after decision helped to mold an image of the juvenile court that departed farther and farther from traditional legal principles. At the time, various criticisms were leveled at these decisions. One charge was "socialism"; another, more reasoned, was that they were merely in keeping with a certain popular support that the new laws enjoyed. In any event, these decisions provided solid support for interpreting the laws to the end of converting the juvenile court into a kind of social agency.

Perhaps the most outstanding influence impelling the juvenile court towards its social-agency self-image has been the early recognition that a child brought before the court must be treated for his problem, rather than be punished for his crime. This attitude supposedly opened the door for "scientific justice," where the child before the juvenile court would be studied in a total fashion—biological, psychological, and sociological; a diagnostic judgment

[16] Commonwealth v. Fisher, 213 Pa. 48, 53, 62 Atl. 198, 200 (1905).

made; and a treatment prescribed which would meet unfulfilled needs, secure his protection, and insure his return to social and psychological health. Thus, individualization of treatment was to be achieved in the juvenile court by the convergence of the enthusiastic support of reformers, the scientific advances in psychology and psychiatry, and the dominant individualistic theme of our culture.

With this initial treatment-orientation, the medical analogy was quick to appear in the literature, aided and abetted particularly by the development of psychoanalysis, with its varieties and the application of its insights into the delinquent child.[17] From the study of neuroses and their emotional manifestations, it was, then, but a short jump to the viewing of delinquent behavior as a symptom of some underlying emotional conflict.[18] When this occurred, it followed that each case must be studied carefully and completely to reach the source of the conflict in the child's personality that could account for the "acting-out"— even though socially disapproved—behavior, and adequate provisions, psychiatric and/or case-work, made for its correction. As the doctor restores the physically sick child to health, so, it was urged, would the clinical team of psychiatrist, psychologist, and social worker restore the delinquent child to behavioral health, where those unpleasant "acting-out" symptoms would disappear.

[17] See, e.g., A. Aichhorn, *Wayward Youth* (1935).
[18] It should be emphasized that the claim is not advanced that delinquency is *never* the outgrowth of some emotional condition. It cannot, however, *explain* all delinquent behavior, as some of the uncritical adherents of the medical analogy seem to imply. The sole purpose here is to show the manner in which "treatment" philosophy has molded the social-agency image of the juvenile court.

As has been pointed out above, this treatment viewpoint has been present from the very beginning, despite the fact that no technique for treating delinquent behavior had been adequately formulated and tested. Even today, with the many advances of the basic sciences, such techniques are but imperfectly understood and do not, as many sophisticated therapists have recognized, meet expectations.[19] In study after study, this fact has been demonstrated. The fact remains, however, that during the fifty-nine years since the founding of the juvenile court, the clamor concerning the need for treatment, nature of treatment, correct treatment procedure, and treatment facilities has continued to fill the pages of the professional journals, newspaper supplements, and professional lectures on delinquency to various community groups.

While treatment has been discussed here primarily in terms of the application of psychiatric and case-work techniques, the inference should not be drawn that these are the only activities regarded as treatment by the juvenile court. The fact of the matter is that under the impact of the treatment philosophy held by professionals, every action that the juvenile court takes is regarded as "treatment." Whether the juvenile court sends the child to the reformatory or the clinic, places him on probation or in a foster home, dismisses him with a lecture or without a lecture—all is rationalized as treatment, especially by those professionals who have a deep need to view the juvenile court as an agency for treatment and never for punishment of the child.

[19] See Peck, "Why Does a Young Delinquent Resist Treatment?" *The Child*, Nov. 1951, p. 35; Lippman, *Treatment of Juvenile Delinquents*," in *National Conference of Social Work, Proceedings* 317 (1945).

The social-agency image of the juvenile court has had a dynamic quality—that is, it has been growing and expanding since the birth of the juvenile court in Illinois—and it is reflected in annual reports of various juvenile courts, in numerous publications of the Children's Bureau, in certain court decisions, and in many articles in professional and semiprofessional social-work journals. For example, here is a statement from an annual report of 1925:[20]

Or as the statute now reads, "The court from time to time may adjourn the hearing and inquire into the habits, surroundings, conditions and tendencies of the child so as to enable the court to render such order or judgment as shall best conserve the welfare of the child and carry out the objects of this act." As a result of this enactment the justices have been enabled to scrap once and for all the old legal trial of children with its absurd and obsolete limitations of testimony and to inquire into the causes of the children's neglect or delinquency untrammelled by narrow rules of evidence.

It is significant to note that the writer has no difficulty in considering delinquency and neglect together and is perfectly willing to throw out the "narrow rules of evidence" and the "absurd and obsolete limitations of testimony" in order to get at the "real causes" of the child's difficulty. It is difficult to refrain from observing, however, that it seems extremely relevant, if only in the interest of fair play, to establish the fact as to whether or not the child committed a particular act that would make him delinquent under the existing statute.

In this same report, the judge writes of the future of the court:[21]

We prefer to think of it as a definite arm of the government engaged in the task of protecting and correcting the handicapped children of the community and of supervising their social adjustments, but not extending its functions over matters which could be administered by other departments of state or even by semi-public agencies without invoking judicial action. . . . Even now the court is seeking to treat every case, in which its assistance is invoked, to the end that the cause of the disease or disorder complained of may be removed and that its patients may be restored to perfect moral health. As time goes on its facilities for helping its patients and of achieving their social adjustments will be developed and improved. . . . In short the court of tomorrow, as we picture it, will resemble in many respects the ideal which we are struggling, more or less imperfectly, to obtain today. It will administer the law faithfully and conscientiously but at the same time its emphasis will be laid more and more on the exercise of social justice by which alone the children who come before it may be readjusted, safeguarded and developed into future assets for the State.

This judge, only too clearly, has been willing to have his legal training modified or supplemented, as the case may be, by certain conceptions and values derived from a social-work point of view.

Perhaps no clearer formulation of this social-agency image of the juvenile court is provided than a statement by the Wayne County Juvenile Court made over fifteen years ago:[22]

The average citizen thinks of the Juvenile Court in terms of a criminal court for young boys and girls, and believes that the Detention Home is a jail to which these boys and girls are sentenced.

These misconceptions overlook the great progress which society has made in the past one hundred years in dealing with delinquent children. For it is as recent as that, that children of tender years who violated the criminal laws were locked

---

[20] Children's Court of the City of New York, Ann. Rep. 16 (1925).

[21] *Id.* at 31.

[22] The Wayne County Juvenile Court 1–2 (n.d.),

up in the same jails, were tried by the same prosecutors and judges, and in many cases received the same punishment, as hardened adult criminals. Often the punishment consisted of many years' imprisonment, and even, in a few instances, death. The protest by socially-minded people against this treatment by the criminal courts of juvenile offenders on the same basis as adult offenders, resulted in the Juvenile Court movement. Progressive people realized that the administration of social justice, at least so far as children are concerned, should not be based on theories of retribution and revenge, but rather on the principles of reformation and correction. They felt that children, by the very reason of their immature years, cannot and should not be held as strictly accountable for their acts as are adults.

The Juvenile Court is the outcome of this agitation for social justice for children. It is the first legal tribunal where the law works side by side with the sciences which deal with human behavior. The Court adopted the social case-work method, by which the child is treated individually in relation to his whole environment. It is in this procedure that the Juvenile Court differs from the criminal courts, where an accused person is sought to be convicted of and punished for having committed a particular crime. The juvenile delinquents who are brought before the Juvenile Court are not regarded as criminals, irrespective of the misconduct or offense with which they are charged. They are considered to be boys and girls who have become maladjusted and, perhaps through no fault of their own, have expressed their normal feelings and emotions in delinquent ways. The Court recognizes that these children need its special care, protection and understanding; and through proper supervision and guidance, it endeavors to divert the forces of delinquent behavior into normal and satisfactory channels.

This statement, which appears to be largely for public-relations purposes, epitomizes the spirit and aspirations of the juvenile court set in a social-agency framework. It goes almost without saying that there will be great disparity between actual practice and this pollyanna view of what the juvenile court aspires to be.

Within this social-agency framework, the juvenile court ideally should function in the following manner: A complaint would be made to the juvenile court's intake desk by the police, a social agency, a neighbor, a parent, or a socially minded citizen. If the behavior difficulty could not be resolved with the complainant, process would issue and the child would be brought in. The child and its parents would be questioned by a social worker, and if the child could be released to its parents, this would be done; otherwise, the child would be held at a detention home pending a thorough social study of the case. In this latter event, the child himself would be variously viewed as maladjusted, having a problem, in trouble, or an example of need frustration or a type of "acting-out" behavior. A social worker then would be assigned to the case to make the required social study.

Preliminary study of the case might indicate to the worker that the child's difficulty was not very deep-seated and that the case could be handled unofficially with a preliminary hearing and dismissed to the best interests of the child and others who were involved. On the other hand, preliminary inquiry might indicate the need for a complete social study; and, if so, the study would continue and might include thorough physical, psychiatric, and psychological examinations, as well as a thorough developmental picture of the child in his family and/or other social situation. The social investigation would logically lead to some diagnostic formulation involving the nature of the problem and the probable roots of the difficulty. On the basis of this formulation, some plan of treatment would be outlined which, of course, might include "institutional treatment." At this point, again, a decision would be made as to whether the case could be handled unofficially and recommended treatment carried out by the juvenile court clinic, child-guidance agency, a family agency, or a private psychiatrist, or whether the case should be handled officially and brought before the juvenile court judge, with the understanding that he would see that the recommended treatment was carried out. In either case, treatment would continue if the subject proved willing to accept it. If, however, he did not, more stringent measures would probably be recommended; in fact, the plan might include any one of the several dispositions, euphemistically called "treatments," that have been traditionally open to the juvenile court judge—namely, dismissal, supervised probation, foster-home place-ment, or institutional commitment. The juvenile court might also insist that the child be given psychiatric treatment by some independent agency. At this point, social-work supervisors, now termed probation officers, would take over and follow the child through the prescribed course. In the ideal social-agency-type juvenile court, however, the great majority of the cases would tend to be handled "unofficially."

As the juvenile court has moved in the direction of perfecting its social-agency image, several unforeseen consequences have emerged. For example, court decisions have helped mold this image as, one after another, they have affirmed that private hearings, the introduction of social-study material, the absence of a defense attorney, and the lack of trial by jury do not constitute a denial of due process because the child is not being tried for a crime. Accordingly, those legal safeguards which have been the cornerstone of Anglo-Saxon jurisprudence for centuries are not available to the child in the juvenile court because he is considered not to be responsible for his act up to a specified age, depending upon the state law, but rather is regarded as "having a problem." The disposition of the child in the juvenile court is, thus, almost entirely dependent upon the wisdom of the judge.

Another consequence of this emerging social-agency image of the juvenile court has been an attempt, particularly noticeable in the first six postwar years, to hold parents responsible for the delinquent acts of their child. The underlying reasoning is this: Social workers, via their varieties of psychoanalytic orientations, have regarded the home as the fundamental source of the love and security necessary to shape the child into a mature adult. When the child is not given this love and security, he experiences a feeling of frustration and unfulfilled needs, which leads to distorted and ambivalent reactions to one or both parents, and some resultant deep-seated conflict or splintering of his ego. The parents, in turn, owing to their own inadequacies or because of the emotional state of the child, are able to provide nothing but the most erratic and inconsistent discipline and supervision. In such a family atmosphere, accordingly, the child may begin to "act out" his conflicts in delinquent ways. Now, this all-too-brief statement of the asserted psychological roots of delinquency in the family setting has been sold to certain juvenile court judges, with the result that schools for parents have been started, and parents have been summoned into juvenile court and, in some instances, given jail sentences because they have, from this perspective, been adjudged responsible for the delinquencies of their child.[23]

Another consequence of the juvenile court's assumption of the role of a social-work agency is that the original differences among the conditions of dependency, neglect, and delinquency have gradually become obscure, and the juvenile court has approached each child as a young person who has a problem and needs help, regardless of his basic condition. It is but a step from this obfuscation to the general notion that the underlying cause of these diverse conditions is the same, despite the lack of evidence to support such a position.

A final consequence of this adherence to a social-agency orientation by the juvenile court—and perhaps the most telling one—is the moral confusion it occasions in both the child and his parents. In the popular mind, a court is an instrument for securing justice between persons and for securing the rights of the person charged with a specific criminal act by the state. When, however, the juvenile court fails directly to advert to the fact that a particular illegal act has been committed by the child and, in its zeal to "treat" the child, completely glosses over this matter, the final disposition of the child's case is very likely to seem to him confusing and even unjust. And his parents, in turn, will reflect this confusion, because on their social level, they cannot very easily accept the view that the child by virtue of his behavior is "sick" and needs "treatment," but rather are committed to the view that

the court is there for justice and for punishing a person who has done something that is wrong.

One critic perceives this situation very clearly when he notes the lack of understanding of parents as to the function of a psychiatric clinic to which the juvenile court referred their children's cases. He points out that when cases brought before the juvenile court on charges of incorrigibility were referred to the clinic, the parents and the child considered the clinic action a part of the punishment for the offense instead of a means of treatment.[24] Moreover, this attitude on the part of the child and his parents will continue to exist and plague the "treatment" process, because it will generally be impossible for the juvenile court to convey its "scientific" orientation to people whose morality is framed exclusively in terms of right and wrong.

It is also cogent to inquire how far we can carry certain theories of treatment of criminal behavior, on both juvenile and adult levels, without undermining the concept of legal responsibility; for it should be clear that a popular acceptance of the idea that no one is responsible for what he does would lead to chaos. Here, confusion is attributable to the deterministic character of science—the attempt to explain given behavior by isolating the interrelated factors antecedent to it—under which the doctrine of scientific responsibility replaces that of legal responsibility.[25] So, when the juvenile court attempts to help the child by "treating" his "disorder," it is literally using the child to collect data to substantiate certain theories of child be-

---

[23] Space does not permit consideration of this problem in greater detail. The statutes have generally given judges authority to proceed against a parent or other adult where it can be shown that he has directly contributed to the delinquency of the child. See Teeters and Reinemann, *op. cit. supra* note 6, at 200–206.

[24] O'Keefe, "Mental Hygiene Facilities for the Juvenile Delinquent," *Federal Probation,* June 1948, pp. 31–35.

[25] See Green, "The Concept of Responsibility," 33 *J. Crim. L. & Criminology* 392–394 (1943).

havior and to foist on him some inadequately tested notions about treatment of juvenile misconduct, while, at the same time, chipping away at the concept of legal responsibility.

THE LEGAL IMAGE OF THE COURT

It has been observed that the true social-agency image of the juvenile court tends to emerge only in those few highly organized, independent juvenile courts to be found in large cities. The juvenile court as established by law in the great majority of states, however, is a part of a court of general jurisdiction and, as such, is part of a county court system. With such legal status, therefore, one can well appreciate the furious character of the conflict that has been occasioned by efforts to convert the juvenile court into a type of social agency, with traditional legal procedures de-emphasized or eliminated and various treatments introduced in order "to cure" the child. The conflict has, in fact, been continuous, and in recent years it has become even sharper as various studies have indicated both that many basic legal rights are being denied the child and his parents and that there may be a great gap between conception and execution of successful treatment of a "maladjusted" child. Thus, it has been observed that "measured by any reasonable standards the juvenile courts have failed to live up to the high expectations held by the early reformers."[26]

The conventional response to such observations has been that the juvenile court fails precisely because the community cannot or is unwilling to provide the necessary resources and facilities to do a first-rate job. Statements to the effect that there are not enough

[26] Bloch and Flynn, *op. cit. supra* note 12, at 317.

properly trained probation officers, the judge is only part-time and has failed to grasp the juvenile court idea, detention facilities are inadequate, there are not sufficient treatment facilities in the juvenile court or community, there is a need for more psychiatric time, the people comprising the community must be educated to the function of the juvenile court, and the salary scale is inadequate are to be found scattered throughout the literature. While any one or all of these shortcomings may exist with respect to any particular juvenile court, however, there is no evidence convincingly to show that if these defects were remedied, juvenile courts in general would be able to do a better job in preventing recidivism in children who had once been found to be delinquent. In fact, much of the evidence appears to be exactly to the contrary.[27] Even so, ameliorative measures might still be justified on the ground that the juvenile court would be able to perform its social-control function more adequately and more humanely.

What, then, are some of the central issues in this conflict between the social-agency and the legalistic orientations of the juvenile court?

First, the problem of the extent of jurisdiction of the juvenile court has been debated on two fronts: what

[27] See W. Healy and A. Bronner, *Treatment and What Happened Afterward* (1939); E. Powers and H. Witmer, *An Experiment in the Prevention of Juvenile Delinquency: The Cambridge Somerville Youth Study* (1951); Dunham and Knauer, "The Juvenile Court and Its Relation to Adult Criminality," 32 *Social Forces* 290 (1954); Diana, "Is Casework in Probation Necessary?," *Focus*, Jan. 1955, p. 1; Adamson and Dunham, "Clinical Treatment of Male Juvenile Delinquency: A Case Study in Effort and Result," 21 *Am. Socio. Rev.* 312 (1956); R. W. England, "What Is Responsible for Satisfactory Probation and Post Probation Outcome?," 47 *J. Crim. L., C. & P.S.* 667 (1957).

relationship does it bear to other courts; and what type of cases should legitimately come before it? The problem of the relationship of the juvenile court to other courts was considered in the often-quoted case of *People v. Lattimore*. There, the Illinois Supreme Court reviewed and affirmed the criminal court conviction of the defendant while she was still a ward of the juvenile court, upholding the lower court's jurisdiction in these words:[28]

The Juvenile Court is a court of limited jurisdiction. The legislature is without authority to confer upon an inferior court the power to stay a court created by the constitution from proceeding with the trial of a cause jurisdiction of which is expressly granted to it by the constitution. . . . It was not intended by the legislature that the juvenile court should be made a haven of refuge where a delinquent child of the age recognized by law as capable of committing a crime should be immune from punishment of violating the criminal laws of the state, committed by such child subsequent to his or her being declared a delinquent child.

The problem is still widely debated, however, and generally arises in one form or another when a child of juvenile-court age commits a capital offense. One solution has been to make the juvenile court independent by creating state-wide juvenile courts systems, as has been done in Connecticut, Rhode Island, and Utah. But it will take more time to determine where this system has improved the administration of juvenile justice.[29]

With respect to the types of cases that should come before it, there has been a tendency throughout its history for the juvenile court to assume jurisdiction over most cases involving children—often, it is asserted, more than it could satisfactorily handle. Thus, adoption, unmarried mothers, mother's pension, and sometimes divorce cases have been lodged in the juvenile court, as it has extended its aegis over cases of dependency and neglect as well as delinquency. As noted above, this tends to confuse the juvenile court's function.

The practice of handling cases unofficially is another matter about which much controversy has raged over the years. This practice is extremely variable among juvenile courts, as certain juvenile courts handle no cases unofficially, while others may handle the bulk of their cases in this manner. The arguments advanced in support of the practice is that it is in keeping with the juvenile court's basic treatment philosophy; it keeps the child from having a court record; it enables professional opinion other than that of the judge to influence the case; and it saves the time and energy of the judge for the more serious cases. On the other hand, it is argued that the practice conduces inefficiency in that it diverts judicial attention to cases that should be handled by other agencies; it weakens the juvenile court's authority in the more serious cases; and it confuses any criteria which attempt to distinguish between court and noncourt cases and discourages other agencies from developing and devoting their resources to the prevention of delinquency. It almost goes without saying that the practice makes meaningless any attempt to report statistical comparisons between communities as to the frequency of delinquency.

Another problem confronting every juvenile court judge is that of balancing the welfare of the child, in accordance with the juvenile court's basic philosophy, against the protection of the community. This issue has not been

---

[28] People v. Lattimore, 119 N.E. 275, 362 Ill. 206 (1935).
[29] See Rubin, "State Juvenile Court: A New Standard," *Focus,* July 1951, p. 103.

articulated very clearly in the past, but recently it has received greater attention as it has been brought more sharply into focus.[30] While it might be argued, in the spirit of Adam Smith's economic theory, that securing the welfare of the child will insure best the welfare of the community, this is not likely to have much appeal to those persons who have been injured in some fashion by the acts of a child. They may demand retribution and even revenge, which to them is justice. In fact, it is extremely doubtful that the aims of protecting and securing the welfare of the child can ever be completely realized until a sizable majority of the people in any community understands and accepts the basic philosophy of the juvenile court. This widespread lack of public rapport accounts for the perennial charge that the juvenile court is "coddling young criminals." Even if the necessary public understanding were brought about, however, the issue would still have to be faced as to how to deal most effectively with delinquent behavior in achieving both the welfare of the community and that of the child.

Another problem, as yet not adequately explored, concerns the limitations of individualized treatment within an authoritative court setting. While it has been accepted by many enlightened persons that punishment per se secures no beneficial results to the person or to the community, it is also becoming increasingly clear that our treatment techniques do not accomplish what we would like. In this area, however, our knowledge is quite deficient. We cannot well distinguish between those cases that might benefit from some form of psychotherapy and

those cases that will not. Nor can we distinguish between those cases in which delinquency will, in any event, be arrested and those in which help is needed. Then, too, no matter what "treatment" disposition the court may use—probation, foster-home placement, referral to a treatment clinic, or commitment to an institution—the fact remains that it is likely to be viewed by the child and his parents as punishment and not treatment, although these devices probably afford a more individualized and progressive scheme of punishment than various kinds of treatment per se. There is, finally, some doubt as to the validity of one assumption of treatment philosophy seldom mentioned in the literature—the assumption that the child facing the therapist is either not thinking or, if he is, he is freely entering into cooperation with the therapist to achieve a cure. With delinquents, nothing could be farther from reality. For quite often, the delinquent "patient" is not only thinking, but thinking of how he can beat this "rap"; and in trying to do so, he will not hesitate to attempt to manipulate the therapist, who will have to be steeped in a knowledge of the delinquent's world if he is not to be duped.

These issues must all be resolved if the juvenile court is to fulfill a valid legal function.[31] Ideally, the juvenile court would be independent of other courts, with its jurisdiction carefully defined by law. The law would, for the guidance of the juvenile court, carefully and precisely define the specific acts for which a child could be held as a delinquent. At the intake desk, a complaint would be registered with the appropriate evidence to sup-

[30] See *Standards for Specialized Courts Dealing with Children* 2 (U. S. Children's Bureau, Dep't of Health, Education and Welfare Pub. No. 346, 1954).

[31] In constructing this legal image, the focus here is primarily on delinquency cases and excludes other kinds of cases handled by juvenile courts.

port the contention that an act of delinquency had been committed. The gathering of such evidence would be primarily a police task, in which assistance might perhaps be rendered by a probation officer of the juvenile court. The probation officer, the police, and the juvenile court referee would decide whether or not the evidence was sufficient to warrant a delinquency petition. If not, the child would be dismissed with a warm, friendly attitude; if the evidence was sufficient, however, the child would be held either in the custody of his parents or guardian or in a detention home for a juvenile court appearance.

When brought before the juvenile court, after a very short detention period, the first task of the judge would be to inform the child and his parents of all their legal rights according to law, particularly their right to legal counsel and appeal. The judge would then hear the evidence and find whether or not the child had committed a delinquent act. The judge, before determining the disposition of the case, would then confer with those professional members of his staff who had worked on the case to determine if some consensus had been reached among them as to which available disposition would serve best to secure both the welfare of the child and protection for the community. He would then pronounce the disposition that had been decided in consultation. Such dispositions, even though mild and humane, would bear a punishment and not a treatment label. The atmosphere of the juvenile court at all times would be formal, dignified, and authoritative. The judge, as representative of community authority, would always attempt to impress the child and his parents with the gravity of the situation and the consequences that would likely ensue if such act or acts were repeated. Such a juvenile court would

have no facility for clinical treatment of the child, for it would be recognized that treatment can be carried on only when a case is not being adjudicated. Nor would it indulge in the unofficial handling of cases. For it should be clear that if no delinquent act has been committed, the taking of any action with reference to the child is a violation of his rights, unless the child and/ or his parents request help—and in that event, he and/or they would be referred to the most appropriate available agency.

CONFLICT OF IMAGES—A NEW OPPORTUNITY

The proponents of these two images —the social-agency and the legalistic —which have here been delineated have been engaged in ideological battle over the juvenile court during its sixty years of existence. To be sure, the social-agency image has been the more dominant and aggressive, although in recent years, the balance has swung back somewhat toward the legalistic image.[32] The conflict of these images, however, still clearly appears in juvenile court attitudes and the decisions of the various judges as they seek to cope with the cases before them. A slight ironical twist may be seen when an eminent judge describes the juvenile court as comparable to a hospital or clinic where the "sick" patient is diagnosed, hospitalized, treated, and discharged,[33] while a well-known

[32] See, e.g., Paul W. Tappan, Comparative Survey on Juvenile Delinquency (1952); Killian, "The Juvenile Court as an Institution," 261 Annals 89 (1949). Over thirty years ago, Eliot saw the need to separate judicial and treatment functions. See Eliot, "The Project Problem Method Applied in Indeterminate Sentence, Probation, and Other Re-educational Treatment," in The Child, the Clinic and the Court 102 (1925).
[33] P. W. Alexander, "Of Juvenile Court Justice and Judges," in N.P.P.A. Yearbook 187, 192 (1947).

social worker states that the juvenile court is first a court where legal responsibility is established specifically by law with respect to certain behavior and conditions of children and adults.[34]

The clash of these two images in the history of the juvenile court has been of crucial significance, because it tends to force a re-examination of all theories concerning the etiology of delinquent behavior, as well as theories concerning the most effective ways of handling delinquents to produce the desired results. It has brought the juvenile court to what one critic, drawing an analogy from the field of mechanics, has termed "dead center," where no force can move it either way and it slowly grinds to a dead stop![35] Whether "dead center" or some other phrase best describes the present situation of the juvenile court, however, is beside the point; the fact still remains that the juvenile court has not demonstrated the accomplishments which would justify the faith of its founders. But the present situation of the juvenile court might well afford a unique opportunity —that is, the opportunity to sponsor and encourage scientific research inquiries to answer some of the pressing questions that this clash of images has produced. Both the spirit and tradition of the juvenile court make it possible to do this.

Lack of space limits a detailed discussion here, and so only a few problems suitable for research can be suggested. There is a great need to determine how the juvenile court can be made most effective, both as an instrument of social control in the community and as an instrument for arresting delinquent behavior in youth. Let us consider this experiment: We hear from many sources that a delinquent child needs psychological treatment and not punishment. Therefore, let us set up a well-equipped clinic, with the best-qualified personnel that it is possible to obtain, even at the expense of paying them salaries somewhat higher than the prevailing scales in the community. When such a clinic is established, from the signed complaints coming to the juvenile court, one child would go to the clinic for appropriate treatment and one would go to the juvenile court, which would function exclusively as a legal tribunal, using the dispositions available to it. The clinic would only take enough cases to insure an adequately sized sample, previously agreed upon. Two to three years after treatment, a follow-up study would be made on both juvenile court and clinic cases, primarily to determine if the subjects still continued their delinquent behavior or were in any way dependent problems for the community. The writer strongly suspects that there would be no significant differences in outcome between the juvenile court and clinic cases because of the almost universally overlooked fact that clinic treatment may be useful in only certain types of cases. If the clinic succeeded with certain kinds of cases, they might be hidden in the figures and would be balanced by those cases in which a favorable adjustment would have been effected regardless of the disposition made. This suggests that successfully treated cases are those that would recover if nothing were done.

There is need also to determine the relative merits of the different disposals available to the juvenile court and the kind of cases that might respond most appropriately to each. Similarly, there is need to determine, if possible, the significance of the impact of the court experience upon the child: Will it be more crucial to certain children coming

[34] Alice Scott Nutt, *The Juvenile Court and the Public Welfare Agency in the Child Welfare Program* (U. S. Children's Bureau, Dep't of Health, Education and Welfare Pub. No. 327, 1949).

[35] McCrea, "Juvenile Courts and Juvenile Probation," 3 *N.P.P.A.J.* 385 (1957).

from some segments of society than to other children from other segments? In evaluating each study, a two-faceted standard would be employed: does the child continue his antisocial behavior as an adult; and/or does the child continue to have a socially unacceptable dependent status as an adult?

These research suggestions are only a few of the tacks that the juvenile court might pursue to help ease itself from its present static position. Research might also promote the divestiture of the built-in egocentric protective mechanisms that are found in certain juvenile courts and direct attention once again to the problem of the child and the task of transforming the juvenile court into an effective agency for the social control of youth.

There would hardly seem to be any dispute among professionals in the criminological field that a philosophy of treatment and reformation is of a morally higher order than is a philosophy of punishment; there is less certainty, however, about the views of the general public on this matter. But regardless of public attitudes, the question of how far and under what circumstances the reward-penalty system of a society can be modified is most crucial. For it would seem that in any kind of social structure, there will always be certain persons who cannot and will not be accommodated. Some of these persons will be so-called criminals, and the central sociological task is to discover, if possible, what their minimum number should be and then to determine the best social arrangements to keep their number at this level. With respect to juvenile delinquents, this probably represents the

"hard core" which fails to respond to any therapeutic approach.

The juvenile court, most markedly of all our agencies for handling socially aberrant individuals, has adhered to the philosophy of treatment and reformation, with the lofty ideal of safeguarding, almost at any cost, the welfare of the child. While this ideal is eminently praiseworthy and expressive of the humanitarian quality of American culture, the question can, however, and should be raised as to whether the existing social-agency-type juvenile court has succeeded in creating the most appropriate conditions for arresting a child's misconduct and for providing him with those personality strengths that will enable him to adjust to the community in a socially acceptable manner. This is a question, it is submitted, that merits the most careful and thoughtful examination.

In this paper an attempt has been made to portray two idealized conceptions of the juvenile court—the social-agency and the legalistic—the nature of the conflict between them, and the resultant state of rigidity into which it has become frozen. While the social-agency image has been the most dominant and aggressive, the legalistic image still remains with us in many juvenile courts, hidden in the traditions of the criminal law. The future of the juvenile court hinges upon our capacity to analyze carefully the issues in this conflict in order that we may devise the type of institutional procedure—in conformity with our existing knowledge—that will best insure both protection for the community and essential personality strengths for our youth.

29.   The Juvenile Court: Its Development and Some Major Problems

ROBERT G. CALDWELL

On July 1, 1899, the first juvenile court in the world[1] began its legal existence in Chicago, Illinois.[2] This event has been widely acclaimed as a revolutionary advance in the treatment of delinquent and neglected children and as the beginning of a new era in the co-operation of law, science, and social work in the field of child welfare. In fact, according to some writers, it foreshadows the time when all offenders, both juvenile and adult, will be treated individually through scientific and case work processes instead of punished by the methods of criminal law.[3]

LEGAL ROOTS OF THE COURT

The juvenile court owes a great deal to American ingenuity and enterprise, but it also has legal roots that can be traced back to principles that are deeply embedded in English jurisprudence. These principles are to be found in the differential treatment which was given to children by the English courts through the application of common law and equity doctrines for the protection of innocence and dependency.

One of the legal roots of the juvenile court is the principle of equity or chancery that originated because of the rigidity of the common law and its failure to provide adequate remedies in

[1] There is some difference of opinion as to whether the first juvenile court was established in the United States. It is said, for example, that children's courts were introduced by ministerial order in South Australia in 1889 and later legalized under a state act in 1895, but it is generally agreed that the United States should be given credit for having the first real juvenile court. There is also some dispute as to whether Chicago, Illinois, or Denver, Colorado, had the first juvenile court in the United States, but preference is generally given to Chicago, since the law approved in Colorado on April 12, 1899, was essentially a truancy law although it did contain some of the features of a juvenile court law. See Lou, *Juvenile Courts in the United States* 13–23 (1927); Lindsey, "Colorado's Contribution to the Juvenile Court," *The Child, the Clinic, and the Court* 274–289 (Addams ed. 1925); Clarke, *Social Legislation* 375–377 (1957).

[2] For easy reference to the first juvenile court act, see 2 Abbott, *The Child and the State* 392–401 (1938).

[3] Lou, *op. cit. supra* note 1, at 2; Pound, "The Juvenile Court and the Law," *Yearbook*, 1944, 1–22 (Nat'l Prob. Ass'n, 1945); Chute, "Fifty Years of the Juvenile Court," *Yearbook*, 1949, 1–20 (Nat'l Prob. and Parole Ass'n, 1950); Winnet, "Fifty Years of the Juvenile Court: An Evaluation," 36 A.B.A.J. 363–366 (1950).

SOURCE. Robert G. Caldwell, "The Juvenile Court: Its Development and Some Major Problems," from *Journal of Criminal Law, Criminology and Police Science*, Volume 51, January-February 1961, pp. 493–511. Copyright © 1961, The Williams and Wilkins Company, Baltimore, Maryland.

deserving cases. Eventually the chancellor, who was the head of England's judicial system, was held responsible for giving greater flexibility to the law in such cases and for balancing the interests of litigants in a more equitable manner as measured by the merits of the individual case. Since equity was thus dispensed by the Council of Chancery, the terms "equity" and "chancery" came to be used interchangeably. Through this system of equity the king acted as *parens patriae*, or as "father of his country," in exercising his power of guardianship over the persons and property of minors, who were considered wards of the state and as such entitled to special protection. Although originally equity was used chiefly to protect dependent or neglected children who had property interests, its action prefigured the protective intervention of the state through the instrumentality of the juvenile court in cases of delinquency.

The other legal root of the juvenile court is the presumption of innocence thrown about children by the common law. According to its doctrines a child under the age of 7 is conclusively presumed incapable of entertaining criminal intent and therefore of committing a crime. Between the ages of 7 and 14, a child is presumed to be incapable of committing a crime, but the presumption may be rebutted by showing that the offender has enough intelligence to know the nature of his act. After the age of 14, children, like adults, are presumed to be responsible for their actions. Thus the creation of the juvenile court involved the extension of the principle that children below a certain age cannot be held criminally responsible—a principle that has a long history in the common law.[4]

HISTORICAL BACKGROUND OF THE COURT

In America, where English jurisprudence was introduced by the early colonists, such tendencies as the increase in the complexity of social relationships, the growth of humanitarianism, and the rise of the social sciences contributed to the expansion of the area in which the child received differential treatment by law.[5] Thus in order to protect children from confinement in jails and prisons, institutions for juvenile offenders were opened in New York in 1825, in Boston in 1826, and in Philadelphia in 1828. Gradually such institutions were constructed in other parts of the country. The foster-home movement, originating in New York in 1853 with the establishment of the Children's Aid Society, which specialized in the placement of destitute and deserted children, soon spread to other states. Chicago as early as 1861 provided for a commission to hear and determine petty cases of boys from 6 to 17. Suffolk County (Boston) in 1870 and New York in 1877 instituted separate hearings for children, and then in 1892 New York created separate dockets and records as well as separate trials for juveniles under 16. By the enactment of a statute in 1869, Massachusetts stipulated that an agent of the State Board of Charities should attend the trials of children, protect their interests, and make recommendations regarding them to the judge. Between 1878 and 1898 Massachusetts established a state-wide system of probation and thus initiated a movement that eventually carried this method of correction into every state in the United States. The years of the nine-

---

[4] Lou, *op. cit. supra* note 1, at 1–12; Clarke, *op. cit. supra* note 1, at 372–374; Sussman, *Law of Juvenile Delinquency* 15,

16 (1959); Pound, *op. cit. supra* note 3, at 4–8. See also Pound, "The Rise of Socialized Criminal Justice," *Yearbook,* 1942, 1–22 (Nat'l Prob. Ass'n, 1942).

[5] Caldwell, *Criminology* 360 (1956).

teenth century also saw the enactment of laws for the regulation of child labor, the development of special services for handicapped children, and the growth of public education.[6]

As this brief summary of some of the important changes in the field of child welfare indicates, there was a growing acceptance of public responsibility for the protection and care of children, but as yet there was no legal machinery by which juvenile offenders could be handled, not as criminals according to the regular procedure of the criminal court, but as wards of the state who were in need of special care, protection, and treatment. Meanwhile, however, Chicago welfare and civic organizations, notably the Chicago Woman's Club and the Catholic Visitation and Aid Society, were setting the stage for the appearance of exactly this kind of machinery. As a result of their persistent agitation, a spirited campaign was begun for the establishment of a juvenile court, and under the leadership of such organizations as the State Board of Charities and the Chicago Bar Association, this campaign was eventually successful in creating the world's first juvenile court.[7]

An examination of the historical background of this court shows that many varied influences helped to produce the climate in which it had its origin. In fact, its establishment may well be considered a logical and exceedingly important development in a much broader movement for the expansion of the specialized treatment given to children in an increasingly complex society. Although the idea of the juvenile court combined the already existing elements of institutional segregation, probation supervision, foster-home placement, separate judicial hearings, and an approach that emphasized the rehabilitation of the juvenile offender, even so, as Tappan explains, it did constitute a significant achievement in judicial integration by providing for a more systematic and independent handling of children's cases.[8]

THE FIRST JUVENILE COURT

The Juvenile Court of Cook County, the first of its kind in the world, was established in Chicago by a state law approved on July 1, 1899. This law, entitled "An Act to Regulate the Treatment and Control of Dependent, Neglected, and Delinquent Children," provided for the establishment of a juvenile court in all counties with a population of over 500,000, but since only Cook County had a population of that size, it alone received such a court. In other counties circuit and county courts were to handle cases arising under the law. The juvenile court was given jurisdiction over children under the age of 16 years who were adjudged to be dependent, neglected, or delinquent, and it was to have a special judge (chosen by the circuit court judges from among their number at such times as they should determine), a separate court room, separate records, and an informal procedure, which meant that such important parts of the

---

[6] Chute, *op. cit. supra* note 3, at 2, 3; Sussman, *op. cit. supra* note 4, at 11–14; Teeters and Reinemann, *The Challenge of Delinquency* 282–286 (1950); Tappan, *Comparative Survey of Juvenile Delinquency* (Part I, North America) 14–16 (United Nations Department of Economics and Social Affairs, 1958); Block and Flynn, *Delinquency: The Juvenile Offender in America Today* 307–312 (1956).

[7] Lathrop, "The Background of the Juvenile Court in Illinois," and Hurley, "Origin of the Illinois Juvenile Court Law," *The Child, the Clinic, and the Court* 290–297, 320–330 (Addams ed. 1925); 2 Abbott, *op. cit. supra* note 2, at 330, 331; Chute, *op. cit. supra* note 3, at 3, 4; Lou, *op. cit. supra* note 1, at 20, 21; Sussman, *op. cit. supra* note 4, at 13, 14.

[8] Tappan, *op. cit. supra* note 6, at 14, 15.

criminal court trial as the indictment, pleadings, and jury (unless the jury was demanded by an interested party or ordered by the judge) were to be eliminated. A summons, unless it proved to be ineffectual, was to be used instead of a warrant in all cases, and the court was given authority to appoint probation officers, who were to serve without compensation. The juvenile court act was to be construed liberally so that the care, custody, and the discipline of the child should approximate as nearly as possible that which should be given by his parents.[9]

If one bears in mind the following facts about the first juvenile court law, it may help him to acquire a better perspective of the juvenile court movement in the United States:

1. The first court was not to be a new or independent tribunal but merely a special jurisdiction in the circuit court.

2. The juvenile court was to be a special court and not an administrative agency. As Dean Pound has said, "It was set up as a court of equity, with the administrative functions incidental to equity jurisdiction, not as a criminal court, and not, as might have happened later, as an administrative agency with incidental adjudicating functions."[10]

3. The law did not stipulate that juvenile delinquents should be "treated" and not punished. It merely provided that the child should receive approximately the same care, custody, and discipline that his parents should give to him.[11]

4. A juvenile delinquent was simply defined as "any child under the age of 16 years who violates any law

of this State or any city or village ordinance."[12]

5. In all trials under the law any interested party might demand, or the judge might order, a jury of six to try the case.[13]

In effect, then, the first juvenile court law established the status of delinquency as "something less than crime."[14] In doing this it made two fundamental changes in the handling of juvenile offenders that are especially noteworthy. First, it raised the age below which a child could not be a criminal from 7 to 16 and made a child who was alleged to be delinquent subject to the jurisdiction of the juvenile court. Secondly, it placed the operation of the court under equity or chancery jurisdiction and thereby extended the application of the principle of guardianship, which had been used to protect neglected and dependent children, to all children, including juvenile delinquents, who were in need of protection by the state. These two changes, in modified form, remain as essential characteristics of all juvenile court legislation.[15]

TRENDS IN THE JUVENILE COURT MOVEMENT

Geographical Expansion

After Illinois had taken the initiative, other states soon followed her example and established juvenile courts. In fact, within ten years twenty states and the District of Columbia enacted juvenile court laws. By 1920 all except three states had done so, and in 1945, when Wyoming took action, the list of states having juvenile court laws was finally complete. Today

[9] 2 Abbott, op. cit. supra note 2, at 392–401.

[10] Pound, op. cit. supra note 3, at 5.

[11] 2 Abbott, op. cit. supra note 2, at 400, 401.

[12] Id. at 393.

[13] Ibid.

[14] Tappan, op. cit. supra note 6, at 14.

[15] Caldwell, op. cit. supra note 5, at 360, 361.

all states, the District of Columbia,[16] and Puerto Rico have some kind of juvenile court legislation,[17] and the movement has had considerable success in other countries.[18]

Jurisdictional Extension

While the juvenile court movement was spreading, the jurisdiction of the court itself was being extended. In general, the definition of juvenile delinquency was broadened, and the types of nondelinquency cases (such as those involving illegitimacy, mental and physical defectives, etc.) under the jurisdiction of the court were increased. Furthermore, the tendency was to raise the upper age level of the children subject to the authority of the court from 16 to 17 or 18, and for some cases in a few states, to 21. In addition, the juvenile court was given jurisdiction over adults in certain cases involving children—for example, in cases in which an adult had contributed to the delinquency of a juvenile.[19]

Increase in Court's Influence

Then, too, after the creation of the juvenile court, it began to exert an increasing influence on the principles and methods used in the adjustment of many other family problems and in the handling of adolescent and adult offenders. For example, some cities, like Cincinnati, Philadelphia, and Wilmington, Delaware, established special courts, called family or domestic relations courts, with jurisdiction over cases involving all kinds of family problems, such as delinquency, dependency, neglect, adoption, illegitimacy, nonsupport, and crimes by members of a family against one another. In effect, the operation of these courts means that many of the principles and methods of the juvenile court are being applied to an increasing variety of social problems. Moreover, special courts for adolescents have been set up in certain cities, like Chicago, Philadelphia, and New York, in which an attempt is being made to combine some of the principles and methods of the juvenile court with those of the criminal court in proceedings against youthful offenders who are above the juvenile court age but below the age of 21. A much more systematic and inclusive program for dealing with this type of offender is represented by the various youth authorities that have been created in such states as California and Minnesota. In their emphasis upon individual diagnosis and treatment these programs, too, reflect to some extent the spreading influence of the philosophy of the juvenile court. Finally, it may be said that this influence can also be seen in the use of presentence investigation and probation in the cases of adult offenders in our criminal courts.[20]

[16] There are no federal juvenile courts. Children under 18 who violate a federal law not punishable by death or life imprisonment may be transferred to a state juvenile court or proceeded against as juvenile delinquents in a federal district court. Sussman, *op. cit. supra* note 4, at 76.

[17] Sussman, *op. cit. supra* note 4, at 15, 65–76; Caldwell, *op. cit. supra* note 5, at 361.

[18] See Smith, *Juvenile Court Laws in Foreign Countries* (U. S. Children's Bureau Publication No. 328, Washington, D.C.: U. S. Government Printing Office, 1951); Clarke, *op. cit. supra* note 1, at 377–383; *Int'l Com. of the Howard League for Penal Reform, Lawless Youth: A Challenge to the New Europe* (London: George Allen and Unwin, Ltd., 1947); Watson, *British Juvenile Courts* (London: Longmans, Green and Co., 1948); Henriques, "Children's Courts in England," 37 *J. Crim. L. & C.* 295 (1946); Sellin, "Sweden's Substitute of the Juvenile Court," 261 *Annals* 137 (Jan. 1949); Pihlblad, "The Juvenile Offender in Norway," 46 *J. Crim. L., C.&P.S.* 500 (1955).

[19] Caldwell, *op. cit. supra* note 5, at 361.

[20] No attempt will be made in this article to discuss the development of family and adolescent courts and the various youth

The increasing complexity of American society has contributed significantly to these trends in the juvenile court movement. Such interrelated factors as industrialization, urbanization, the unprecedented movement of populations, the amazing utilization of natural resources, the rapid accumulation of inventions and discoveries, and the acceleration of transportation and communication have tended to undermine the family and the neighborhood and, forcing our communities to find additional sources of social control, have given considerable impetus to the establishment of juvenile courts and sent into them an increasing number and variety of cases. In the meantime, other influences have more specifically affected the philosophy and methods of the juvenile court. Thus social workers, under the aggressive leadership of such organizations as the United States Children's Bureau, the National Probation and Parole Association, and various other associations now united into the National Association of Social Workers, have joined with psychiatrists in stressing the importance of case work training and treatment services in the operation of the juvenile court, and the efforts of a comparatively few well-organized, big-city juvenile courts at conventions and conferences have served to focus and intensify these in-

fluences. The resulting tendency has been to picture juvenile delinquency as symptomatic of some underlying emotional condition, which must be diagnosed by means of the concepts and techniques of psychiatry, psychology, and social work, and for which treatment, not punishment, must be administered through the efforts of a team of psychiatrists, psychologists, and social workers. Surprisingly enough, the legal profession, also, has contributed to this tendency through important court decisions regarding the juvenile court that have stressed its social service functions and minimized its legal characteristics. The total effect of all this has been to place increasing emphasis on the treatment of the individual and to give decreasing attention to his legal rights and the security of the community. Thus the balance between rights, on the one hand, and duties and responsibilities, on the other, which every court must seek to maintain, has been upset as the juvenile court has been pushed more and more into the role of a social work agency.

CHARACTERISTICS OF THE JUVENILE COURT

Although the juvenile court has had an uneven development and has manifested a great diversity in its methods and procedures, nevertheless, certain characteristics have appeared which are considered essential in its operation. As early as 1920, Evelina Belden of the United States Children's Bureau listed the following as the essential characteristics of the juvenile court: (1) separate hearings for children's cases, (2) informal or chancery procedure, (3) regular probation service, (4) separate detention of children, (5) special court and probation records, and (6) provision for mental and physical examinations.[21] Of course, many so-called

authorities. However, a considerable bibliography about these subjects now exists. See for example, Teeters and Reinemann, *op. cit. supra* note 6, at 344–383, 762–765; Block and Flynn, *op. cit. supra* note 6, at 459–507; Caldwell, *op. cit. supra* note 5, at 378–385; Tappan, *Delinquent Girls in Court* (1947); Beck, *Five States* (1951); Ludwig, *Youth and the Law* (1955); Tappan, "The Young Adult Offender under the American Law Institute's Model Penal Code," 19 *Fed. Prob.* 20 (Dec. 1955); Youngdahl, "Give the Youth Corrections Program a Chance," 20 *Fed. Prob.* 3 (March 1956); Tappan, "Young Adults under the Youth Authority," 47 *J. Crim. L., C.&P.S.* 629 (1957); Melson, Delinquency and the Family Court," 23 *Fed. Prob.* 13 (March 1959).

[21] Beldin, *Courts in the United States Hearing Children's Cases* 7–10 (U. S.

juvenile courts have few of these characteristics, and others possess them in varying degrees. However, in the opinion of many observers, if a court does not have them, it cannot claim to be a juvenile court.

A few years ago, Katharine Lenroot, then chief of the United States Children's Bureau, presented a summary of standards for the juvenile court which indicate the characteristics that many now believe the court should have. These standards call for the following:

1. Broad jurisdiction in cases of children under 18 years of age requiring court action or protection because of their acts or circumstances.

2. A judge chosen because of his special qualifications for juvenile court work, with legal training, acquaintance with social problems, and understanding of child psychology.

3. Informal court procedure and private hearings.

4. Detention kept at a minimum, outside of jails and police stations and as far as possible in private boarding homes.

5. A well-qualified probation staff, with limitation of case loads, and definite plans for constructive work in each case.

6. Availability of resources for individual and specialized treatment such as medical, psychological, and psychiatric services, foster family and institutional care, and recreational services and facilities.

7. State supervision of probation work.

8. An adequate record system, providing for both legal and social records and for the safeguarding of these records from indiscriminate public inspection.[22]

These standards form much of the basis of the *Standard Juvenile Court Act,* the latest edition of which was issued by the National Probation and Parole Association in 1959,[23] and to a great extent they have been incorporated in the *Standards for Specialized Courts Dealing with Children,* which was prepared by the United States Children's Bureau in 1954.[24]

THE PRESENT STATUS OF THE COURT

In the United States the juvenile court varies greatly from one jurisdiction to another, manifesting at present all stages of its complex development. And it should not be overlooked that its philosophy, structure, and functions are still in the process of evolution. Rarely is the court a distinct and highly specialized one, and in the more rural counties it is largely of a rudimentary nature. Usually it is part of a court with more general jurisdiction, the judges holding sessions for juveniles at regular or irregular intervals.[25] Since there is this great diversity, no simple description of the juvenile courts of the United States can be given. However, it is possible to indicate in general terms their present status with respect to certain important features.

---

[22] Lenroot, "The Juvenile Court Today," 13 *Fed. Prob.* 10 (Sept. 1949).

Children's Bureau Publication No. 65, Washington, D.C.: U. S. Government Printing Office, 1920).

[23] *A Standard Juvenile Court Act* (rev. ed.; New York: Nat'l Prob. and Parole Ass'n, 1959). This act is the product of the efforts of the National Probation and Parole Association and the United States Children's Bureau together with others who want to promote greater uniformity and higher standards in the juvenile courts of America. Its various editions have been published in the hope that they might be used as models in the preparation and amendment of state laws. For the provisions of the 1959 edition of this act and comments on its various sections see 5 *Nat'l Prob. and Parole Ass'n Jour.* 323–391 (1959).

[24] *Standards for Specialized Courts Dealing with Children* (U. S. Children's Bureau Publication No. 346, Washington, D.C.: U. S. Government Printing Office, 1954).

[25] Tappan, *op. cit. supra* note 6, at 15, 24.

Philosophy of the Court

In the words of Tappan, the juvenile court and its methods are "by no means a mere direct borrowing from chancery and common law," but, on the contrary, have emerged largely from "the philosophy and techniques of modern casework and, more particularly, the ideologies of the child-welfare movement concerning the rights of children and the devices that should be used to meet their needs." In fact, "the operations of the specialized juvenile court reflect the contemporary impact of case-work oriented probation officers, administrative social agency procedures, and other non-legal (if not distinctly anti-legal) forces far more than they do the influence of either chancery or common law, modern or ancient."[26]

Although generalizations about anything as complex as the juvenile court are always hazardous, it appears that the following are important elements in the court's philosophy:

1. THE SUPERIOR RIGHTS OF THE STATE. The state is the "higher or ultimate parent" of all the children within its borders. The rights of the child's own parents are always subject to the control of the state when in the opinion of the court the best interests of the child demand it. If the state has to intervene in the case of any child, it exercises its power of guardianship over the child and provides him with the protection, care, and guidance that he needs. This is an adaptation of the ancient doctrine of *parens patriae*, by which all English children were made wards of the Crown.[27]

2. INDIVIDUALIZATION OF JUSTICE. A basic principle in the philosophy of the juvenile court is the recognition that people are different and that each must be considered in the light of his own background and personality. The court, therefore, must adapt its actions to the circumstances of the individual case by ascertaining the needs and potentialities of the child and coordinating the knowledge and skills of law, science, and social work for the promotion of his welfare. This means the balancing of interests in an equitable manner by administrative rather than adversary methods within a flexible procedure such as that provided by chancery. Dean Pound has called this "individualized justice."[28]

3. THE STATUS OF DELINQUENCY. The state should try to protect the child from the harmful brand of criminality. In order to accomplish this the law created the status of delinquency, which is something less than crime and is variously defined in different states. However, this still does not satisfy some students of the court who advocate the removal of even the "delinquency tag," which they claim is just another harmful label, and assert that delinquency acts have no significance except as symptoms of conditions that demand investigation by the court.[29]

4. NONCRIMINAL PROCEDURE. By

---

[26] *Id.* at 9. There is a difference of opinion regarding the extent to which the principles of equity and the criminal law contributed to the origin of the juvenile court. See Mack, "Legal Problems Involved in the Establishment of the Juvenile Court," *The Delinquent Child and the Home* 181 (Breckinridge and Abbott eds. 1912); Pound, *Interpretations of Legal History* 134, 135 (1923); S. and E. T. Glueck, "Historical and Legislative Background of the Juvenile Court," *The Problem of Delinquency* 258, 259 (Glueck ed. 1959); Lou, *op. cit. supra* note 1, at 2–7.

[27] Mack, *op. cit. supra* note 26, at 181–187; Lou, *op. cit. supra* note 1, at 2–9; Schramm, "Philosophy of the Juvenile Court," 261 *Annals* 101 (June 1949).

[28] Pound, "The Future of Socialized Justice," *Yearbook*, 1946, 6 (Nat'l Prob. Ass'n 1947); Schramm, *op. cit. supra* note 27, at 103, 104; Lou, *op. cit. supra* note 1, at 2–5; Block and Flynn, *op. cit. supra* note 6, at 317, 318; *Standards for Specialized Courts Dealing with Children, op. cit. supra* note 24, at 1, 2.

[29] Mack, *op. cit. supra* note 26, at 189; Sussman, *op. cit. supra* note 4, at 20; Tappan, *op. cit. supra* note 6, at 14, 15.

means of an informal procedure the juvenile court functions in such a way as to give primary consideration to the interests of the child. In general the courts have held that the procedure of the juvenile court is not criminal in nature since its purpose is not to convict the child of a crime, but to protect, aid, and guide him, and that, therefore, it is not unconstitutional if it denies him certain rights which are guaranteed to an adult in a criminal trial.[30]

5. REMEDIAL, PREVENTIVE, AND NON-PUNITIVE PURPOSE. The action of the juvenile court is to save the child and to prevent him from becoming a criminal. It seeks to provide him with about the same care and protection that his parents should give him. Although, as we have explained, the first juvenile court law did not stipulate that the child should not be punished, many subsequent court decisions and most of the literature on the subject insist that the substitution of treatment for punishment is an essential element in the philosophy of the court.[31]

Geographical Area Served by the Court

The county is the geographical area served by most juvenile courts in the United States, but for some the jurisdictional unit is the town, the city, the borough, or the judicial district. Since the county is the conventional unit of state government and of many private organizations, its use as the jurisdic-

tional area for the court has obvious advantages in the coordination of the court's work with that of other agencies interested in child welfare. However, most counties cannot afford to maintain courts at modern standards, and even if they could, the volume of work would not justify the necessary expense.[32] In some states this problem could be solved by making the area served by the juvenile court the same as the judicial district served by other courts in the state and thereby enable one juvenile court to take care of the cases of two or more counties. Utah, Connecticut, and Rhode Island have pushed beyond this and, establishing state systems of juvenile courts, have created larger jurisdictional districts within their borders.[33]

Types of Juvenile Courts

There are about 3000 juvenile courts in the United States, although actually many are only slightly different from criminal courts. In referring to the inferior quality of many juvenile courts, Lowell Carr has said, "In well over 2000 counties in the United States nobody has ever seen a well-staffed, modern juvenile court in action."[34] Even New York City, a wealthy community with relatively high welfare standards, has fallen considerably short of the ideal level of performance set for the juvenile court.[35]

Juvenile courts in the United States may be classified into these three types: (1) "designated courts," such as municipal, county, district, and circuit courts which have been selected or

---

[30] Clarke, *op. cit. supra* note 1, at 410; Lou, *op. cit. supra* note 1, at 10. For a convenient digest of some of the important cases regarding the constitutionality of the juvenile court, see *The Problem of Delinquency* 334–506 (Glueck ed. 1959).

[31] Mack, *op. cit. supra* note 26, at 190; *Int'l Com. of the Howard League for Penal Reform, op. cit. supra* note 18, at 9–21; *Standards for Specialized Courts Dealing with Children, op. cit. supra* note 24, at 1; Chute, *op. cit. supra* note 3, at 1; Lou, *op. cit. supra* note 1, at 7; Hurley, *op. cit. supra* note 7, at 328; Clarke, *op. cit. supra* note 1, at 410–415.

[32] Carr, "Most Courts Have To Be Substandard," 13 *Fed. Prob.* 29 (Sept. 1949).

[33] Sussman, *op. cit. supra* note 4, at 25; Larson, "Utah's State-Wide Juvenile Court Plan," 13 *Fed. Prob.* 15 (June 1949).

[34] Carr, *op. cit. supra* note 32, at 31. See also Dobbs, "Realism and the Juvenile Court," 31 *Focus* 104 (July 1952).

[35] Tappan, *op. cit. supra* note 6, at 15, 16. For a careful study of New York's juvenile courts, see Kahn, *A Court for Children* (1953).

designated to hear children's cases and while so functioning are called juvenile courts; (2) independent and separate courts whose administration is entirely divorced from other courts; and (3) coordinated courts, which are coordinated with other special courts such as domestic relations or family courts. The great majority of the juvenile courts are "designated courts," and even many of the separate and independent ones are presided over by judges from other courts so that their separateness and independence may be more nominal than real.[36]

Jurisdiction of the Court

All juvenile courts have jurisdiction in delinquency cases, and almost all of them have jurisdiction in cases of dependency and neglect as well. In addition, some have authority to handle other problems such as feeble-mindedness, adoptions, illegitimacy, and guardianship. Although the definition of delinquency varies from state to state, in most states the violation of a state law or municipal ordinance (an act which in the case of an adult would be a crime) is the main category of delinquency. Yet in all states delinquency is more than this, including such items as habitual truancy, incorrigibility, waywardness, and association with immoral persons.

Juvenile court laws differ also with respect to the age of the children over whom the court has jurisdiction. The laws of most states do not specify any lower age limit, merely providing that children under a certain age are subject to the jurisdiction of the court. Most states make 18 the upper age limit; some set it at 16 or 17; and a few put it as high as 21. In some states the upper age limit differs according to the sex of the child. Many states permit the juvenile court, after it has once acquired jurisdiction over the child, to retain jurisdiction until he has reached 21.

In many states the juvenile court does not have exclusive jurisdiction over all delinquency cases but has only concurrent jurisdiction with the criminal court, delinquency cases being handled by either court. Often, however, such concurrent jurisdiction is limited by law to cases of children above a specified age or to cases involving certain offenses or to certain counties. Furthermore, in many states certain offenses, for example, murder, manslaughter and rape, are entirely excluded from the jurisdiction of the juvenile court, and in these states children charged with such offenses are tried in the criminal court.

The jurisdiction of the court is affected in still another way by the provision in most states that it may exercise authority over adults in certain cases involving children. Thus in many states the juvenile court may require a parent to contribute to the support of his child, or it may try adults charged with contributing to the delinquency, neglect, or dependency of a child.[37]

The Judge and the Probation Officer

Although the effectiveness of the juvenile court depends to a very large degree upon the efficiency of its personnel, relatively few courts have staffs that are especially qualified for their work. In most juvenile courts the judges have been appointed or elected on the basis of their general qualifications for judicial work, and they divide their time between adult and juvenile cases. Only in a very few courts has the judge been selected because he has some specialized training or experience in the handling of children's problems. Often,

[36] Teeters and Reinemann, op. cit. supra note 6, at 295–297.

[37] Sussman, op. cit. supra note 4, at 18, 19, 26–28.

however, a referee is appointed to assist the judge in the performance of his juvenile court duties. Although considerable progress has been made in improving the quality of probation in some parts of the country, the great majority of courts are still without the services of a sufficient number of well-qualified and adequately paid workers.[38]

Procedure of the Court

Police action initiates the procedure in most delinquency cases, but often it begins with action by a parent or other private person or with a referral by a social agency or another court. In recent years, about 50 percent of the delinquency cases have been handled informally or unofficially, that is, without an official record or hearing, but with the judge or someone else, such as a probation officer, taking the necessary steps to dispose of the case. The types of cases that are handled in this way vary greatly from court to court, but the tendency seems to be to reserve official hearings for older children and those brought before the court on serious charges.

When a case is handled officially, a petition (which is merely a statement containing important facts of the case, such as the names and addresses of the child and his parents or guardian and the cause of the action) is filed in the court, and the case is then scheduled for a hearing. If the child is not being held in detention and his presence is required, a summons ordering him to appear, or in some cases a warrant for his arrest, is issued. In most jurisdictions a prehearing investigation is conducted so that both the hearing and the disposition of the case can be based on the facts so obtained. Some jurisdictions, however, require that the child must be adjudged delinquent before his case is investigated. In these jurisdictions the hearing is held first, and if the child is found to be delinquent, the court is adjourned, the investigation is completed, and the information is then used by the court in the disposition of the case. Unfortunately, inadequacy of personnel and excessive case loads often prevent the investigation from being more than a superficial inquiry.

Juvenile court hearings are usually less formal than trials in the criminal court, but the degree of informality varies considerably throughout the country. Privacy, however, characterizes most hearings; only persons who are definitely connected with the case are permitted to attend. Seldom is a prosecuting attorney or a counsel for the defense present during the hearing, and although jury trials are permitted in many jurisdictions, usually juries are not used. However, the right of appeal in one form or another is available in most jurisdictions.[39]

Disposition of Cases

After the hearing, the case may be disposed of in one of several ways. The case may be dismissed; a court order may be issued stipulating that the child be examined and treated by a physician, psychiatrist, or psychologist or placed in a hospital or some other institution or agency for whatever care may be necessary; the child may be placed on probation or in a

[38] Lenroot, *op. cit. supra* note 22, at 14, 15; Killian, "The Juvenile Court as an Institution," 261 *Annals* 92 (Jan. 1949); Teeters and Reinemann, *op. cit. supra* note 6, at 313–319; Tappan, *op. cit. supra* note 6, at 13; Davis, "The Iowa Juvenile Court Judge," 42 *J. Crim. L., C.&P.S.* 338 (1951).

[39] Sussman, *op. cit. supra* note 4, at 29–37; *Nat'l Conference on Prevention and Control of Juvenile Delinquency, Report on Juvenile Court Laws* 6, 7 (Washington, D.C.: U. S. Government Printing Office, 1947).

foster home; or he may be committed to a correctional institution. According to the United States Children's Bureau, almost half of all delinquency cases disposed of by the juvenile courts during 1957 were dismissed, adjusted, or held open without further hearing, and about one-fourth were placed on probation.[40]

Cooperation with Other Agencies

The success of the juvenile court depends to a great extent upon the work of other agencies, such as the police, schools, clinics, churches, welfare organizations, and correctional institutions, and it in turn can significantly contribute to the success of these other agencies. It should be obvious, then, that the court should play an important part in promoting greater coordination among the law-enforcement and welfare agencies of the community and in the establishment of a delinquency prevention program. Some courts have coordinated their work very closely with other agencies, but many have done very little to foster this relationship.[41]

CRITICISMS OF THE JUVENILE COURT

Ever since the juvenile court was established over sixty years ago, it has been severely criticized by both its friends and its enemies.[42] At first much of the criticism questioned the constitutionality of the court, but as one judicial decision after another supported the court, the attack against it shifted toward its modification or improvement. In fact, today few critics would have the temerity to advocate the abolition of the court, and it seems, as Dr. William Healy has said, that "the juvenile court is here to stay."[43] However, since so many well-informed persons have joined in the criticism, several of the important questions raised by them require our examination.

1. *Has the juvenile court dealt effectively with juvenile delinquency?* This question is so complex that perhaps any discussion of it can succeed in only raising other perplexing questions. It is true that various statistical attempts have been made to evaluate the effectiveness of the juvenile court. Several of these show that from about one-fourth to over two-fifths of older juveniles and adult offenders have previously been dealt with by the court.[44] Another study, made by the Gluecks, revealed that 88.2 percent of the juveniles included in their analysis again became delinquent within five years after the end of their official treatment by the juvenile court of Boston, and that 70 percent of them were actually convicted of serious offenses.[45]

However, studies such as these have not been conclusive. Not only have comparatively few courts been carefully studied, but also the findings of the investigations have not been con-

[40] Sussman, *op. cit. supra* note 4, at 45–50; *United States Children's Bureau, Juvenile Court Statistics,* 1957, 2 (Statistical Series, No. 52, 1959).

[41] Schramm, *op. cit. supra* note 27, at 104, 105; *Nat'l Conference on Prevention and Control of Juvenile Delinquency, Report on Juvenile Court Administration* 18–20 (Washington, D. C.: U. S. Government Printing Office, 1947); Breckinridge, *Social Work and the Courts* 231–240 (1934).

[42] Much of the discussion of the criticisms of the juvenile court presented here is an adaptation of that contained in the author's text, *Criminology,* published by the Ronald Press Co. in 1956. See pp. 370–378.

[43] Healy, "Thoughts about Juvenile Courts," 13 *Fed. Prob.* 18, 19 (Sept. 1949).

[44] Sutherland, *Principles of Criminology* 316, 317 (1947).

[45] S. and E. Glueck, *One Thousand Juvenile Delinquents* 167 (1934). For opposing views regarding this study, see Sheldon Glueck's and Harry L. Eastman's articles in *Yearbook,* 1934, 63–103 (Nat'l Prob. Ass'n, 1934).

sistent. Besides, there are all kinds of juvenile courts, many being such in name only, and an evaluation of one is hardly a fair appraisal of others. Then, too, the cases covered by the investigations often do not constitute a representative sample of those coming before the court, and the recidivism noted is only that of which there is a record. Actually no one knows how much undetected delinquency and crime there is among those who have been previously handled by the court. Furthermore, the court is only one part of a very complex culture, with which it is inextricably and functionally related, and no one, therefore, knows to what extent influences other than (and perhaps even in spite of) that of the court caused the improvement in those who subsequently did not become recidivistic.

But suppose it could be proved that the juvenile court has failed, should delinquents be tried in the criminal court? Certainly no informed person would be in favor of this. Is the solution, then, "bigger and better" juvenile courts? To this question no simple answer can be given. Most counties have too few people to justify, others too little wealth to afford, better juvenile courts. Besides, large segments of our population are already restive under the burden of heavy taxation. Should taxpayers be asked to contribute more for the improvement of our juvenile courts? Should some of the funds that are now being spent for other purposes, for example, for the operation of public schools, be diverted to the development of the juvenile courts?[46]

But even the "biggest" and the "best" court could do little to change the conditions that are causing crime and delinquency. No systematic science

[46] Caldwell, *op. cit. supra* note 5, at 371.

of human behavior exists, and the knowledge that we do have requires the support of public opinion if it is to be used most effectively. Furthermore, how much judicial regulation will a community tolerate? If a community is to preserve certain rights and privileges, how much regulation should it tolerate? Obviously, questions of this kind can be considered only as they are related to other values in our culture.

Still other questions must be raised. What is meant by a "better" or the "best" juvenile court? What criteria should be used to measure the quality of a court? There is considerable disagreement regarding these questions. Some claim that the provisions of the *Standard Juvenile Court Act* should be used as the criteria for evaluating a juvenile court, but others would refuse to endorse such a proposal. However, in spite of the fact that so many difficulties interfere with attempts to evaluate the effectiveness of the juvenile court, certain steps can be taken now to improve the quality of its work. Some of these will be mentioned later in the discussion of the problems of the court.

2. *What types of cases should be handled by the juvenile court?* Like the first question, this one is too broad to be examined thoroughly in an article of this kind, but reference to a few specific situations will indicate why it has been raised.

After the juvenile court was established it became the one agency in most communities which could provide some kind of social service for the increasing number of children who needed care and protection, and so it tended to assume responsibility for a growing volume of cases. Moreover, this tendency was accelerated by the passage of laws that stipulated that certain types of children were to be cared for at public expense. In general the court did not resist this tendency, and in some communities court officials actually encouraged it so that they might gain in power and influence. And once the court had assumed responsibility for certain cases, it tended to keep this responsibility even after the need for doing so had disappeared. As a result, the juvenile court has become a catchall for a great variety of cases requiring public attention.

As educational facilities and child welfare services have developed throughout the country, there has developed an increasing demand for the transfer of certain cases from the jurisdiction of the court to that of the schools and welfare agencies. However, it is difficult to determine just what criteria could be employed in dividing the cases between the court and other agencies. Some who speak for the welfare agencies say that the juvenile court could exercise functions that are primarily judicial and pertain to law enforcement, while the welfare agencies could exercise functions that are primarily administrative.[47] But this suggested standard is not sufficiently precise to indicate exactly where the line is to be drawn. Undoubtedly it would mean the transfer of many neglect and dependency cases to welfare agencies, but opponents have stressed the complexity of the situation. Neglect, dependency, and delinquency are often interrelated, and delinquency cases involve much administrative work. Besides, many neglect and dependency cases require the exercise of authority supported by the law. In many instances only the court has sufficient authority to enforce decisions and to protect the rights of children and parents, and depriving the court of its administrative duties would unnecessarily complicate the handling of every delinquency case.

The suggestion that certain cases, such as truancy and incorrigibility, be transferred from the juvenile court to the school has likewise stirred up a controversy. Those in favor of the transfer have argued that schools are in close contact with children and their families, have a great deal of information about them, and are already doing a considerable amount of work with them through the efforts of visiting teachers, counselors, clinicians, and parent-teachers' associations; that children should not be exposed to court experience, with its stigmatizing and traumatic implications, except as a last resort; and that the schools would develop more effective programs for the prevention of delinquency if they were not permitted to shift so many of their responsibilities to the court. On the other side of the controversy, many have contended that the personnel of the schools are already overworked and underpaid and should be relieved of some of their responsibilities instead of being given more; that schools do not have enough authority to handle many of the cases; that the stigma of a law-enforcement agency would be attached to the schools if they had to handle delinquency cases; and that many children are not attending school or are in private and parochial schools and thus beyond the authority of public educational officials.

Actually there is much merit in the arguments on both sides of this controversy. Some of the work of the

[47] See, for example, Nutt, "The Responsibility of the Juvenile Court and the Public Welfare Agency in the Child Welfare Program," Yearbook, 1947, 206 (Nat'l Prob. and Parole Ass'n, 1948). See also Nutt, "The Future of the Juvenile Court as a Case Work Agency," Yearbook, 1939, 157 (Nat'l Prob. Ass'n, 1939); Nutt, "Juvenile Court Function," Yearbook, 1942, 94 (Nat'l Prob. Ass'n 1942); Geiser, "The Court as a Case Work Agency," Yearbook, 1942, 105 (Nat'l Prob. Ass'n, 1942); Mead, "The Juvenile Court and Child Welfare Services," Yearbook, 1947, 224 (Nat'l Prob. and Parole Ass'n, 1948).

court can be safely transferred to educational and welfare agencies, but many administrative duties must be retained by it. Just where the line will be drawn will probably have to be worked out on a local basis through the judicious balancing of needs and resources and the development of greater cooperation among courts, schools, and welfare agencies.[48]

Apart from this, however, other critics of the court have insisted that older juveniles who commit serious crimes, such as murder, manslaughter, rape, and robbery, should not be dealt with in the juvenile court but should be tried in the criminal court. In fact, many states have laws giving the criminal court either original or exclusive jurisdiction over such cases. Opponents of this policy have branded it as reactionary and in violation of the philosophy of the court. According to this philosophy, they explain, the court should have exclusive jurisdiction over all children requiring judicial action, should guide and protect those who come before it, and should not stigmatize or punish them or hold them up as examples for others.

In reply to this argument, those who believe that older juveniles charged with serious offenses should be tried in the criminal court contend: (1) that the upper age limit of children, especially those charged with serious crimes, over whom the juvenile court should have jurisdiction is a debatable subject; (2) that although the juvenile court uses words like "guidance," "care," and "protection," the fact is that it, too, resorts to punitive methods in handling children; (3) that the public, regardless of what the philosophy of the court may be, looks upon the court as a place where violators of the law are sentenced and punished; (4) that one measure of the support that courts and the law receive is the intensity of the feeling that law-abiding citizens have against law violators; and (5) that failure to punish serious violators not only encourages others to commit crimes but also discourages law-abiding citizens from supporting law-enforcement agencies.

In this controversy, also, there is much to be said in favor of both sides. Certainly no court can exist apart from the community in which it functions and to which it must look for support, and to hold that the court should try to ignore the deep feelings and strong desires of the people whose values it is called upon to enforce is a highly unrealistic and arbitrary attitude. It is partly because of this fact that the *Standard Juvenile Court Act* includes a provision that juveniles 16 years of age or older charged with serious crimes may be tried in the criminal court if the juvenile court deems this to be in the best interest of the children and the public.[49] However, if the case of a youthful serious offender is heard in a juvenile court, then this should be done according to clearly defined rules of procedure, and he should be protected from arbitrary action and abuse of authority just as the adult felon is in the criminal court.

There has also been some recognition of the limitations of the juvenile court for dealing with older and more

[48] Eliot, "Case Work Functions and Judicial Functions: Their Coordination," *Yearbook*, 1937, 252 (Nat'l Prob. Ass'n, 1937); Pound, *op. cit. supra* note 3, at 14, 15; Schramm, "The Juvenile Court Idea," 13 *Fed. Prob.* 21 (Sept. 1949); *Controlling Juvenile Delinquency* (U. S. Children's Bureau Publication No. 301, Washington, D. C.; U. S. Government Printing Office, 1943); Hyatt, "The School, the Juvenile Court, and the Social Attitude," *Yearbook*, 1931, 49 (Nat'l Prob. Ass'n, 1931); Harper, "School and Court Relationships Concerning Behavior Problems," *Yearbook*, 1932 and 1933, 163 (Nat'l Prob. Ass'n, 1933); Taber, "The Judge and the Schools," *Yearbook*, 1944, 41 (Nat'l Prob. Ass'n, 1945).

[49] *A Standard Juvenile Court Act, op. cit. supra* note 23, § 13.

serious offenders in states where the pressure has been to raise the upper age limit of the court and to give it exclusive jurisdiction over all children. For example, in California where the court had exclusive jurisdiction to the age of 18 and concurrent jurisdiction to the age of 21, a special study commission in 1949 recommended that the juvenile court judge should be required to decide specifically whether a juvenile over 16 charged with a crime could be better handled by the juvenile court or by a criminal court.[50]

3. *Are the rights of the child and his parents protected in the juvenile court?* As the juvenile court has developed it has become increasingly dominated by the ideas and methods of child welfare and case work authorities. Contributing to this tendency have been the occupancy of many juvenile court positions by persons who have been trained in social work or who are in agreement with its principles, the very infrequent presence of attorneys in the court, the inadequate legal training of many of its judges and referees, the general exclusion of the public and the press from its hearings, and the rarity of appeals from its decisions. As a result of this departure of the juvenile court from some of the most basic concepts of justice in our culture, there has appeared a growing controversy over whether the rights of the child and his parents are being endangered by the increase in the authority and administrative functions of the court.[51] In this controversy, criticism has been directed especially

against (1) broad definitions of delinquency, (2) unofficial handling of cases, (3) prehearing investigations, and (4) extreme informality of procedure.[52]

In general these aspects of the court have been defended by the claim that they facilitate preventive and nonpunitive action by the court. Thus advocates of a broad definition of delinquency contend that it permits the court to act in situations which warrant its intervention without becoming entangled in technical disputes over the meaning of terms. In conformance with this point of view, some states have broadened the definition of delinquency by substituting a few general categories of delinquency for a number of specifically defined acts. The laws of some other states and the *Standard Juvenile Court Act*[53] have gone beyond this and do not define delinquency at all. Instead, without using the term delinquency, they merely describe certain situations and classifications of children over which the court has jurisdiction. This avoidance of the "delinquency tag," it is argued, enables the court to help and protect the child without stigmatizing him in any

---

[50] Tappan, *op. cit. supra* note 6, at 8.

[51] *Id.* at 2. Administrative functions of the court include such activities as investigation of cases, planning for the care of children, supervision of probationers, and foster-home placement. These are to be contrasted with the court's judicial functions, which refer to such matters as adoption and guardianship and decisions regarding custody and commitment.

[52] See Tappan, *Juvenile Delinquency* 195–223 (1949); Schramm, *op. cit. supra* note 48, at 19–23; Pound, *op. cit. supra* note 4, at 1–22; Waite, "How Far Can Court Procedure Be Socialized without Impairing Individual Rights?" 12 *J. Crim. L. & C.* 339 (1921); Rubin, "Protecting the Child in the Juvenile Court," 43 *J. Crim. L., C.&P.S.* 425 (1952); Kahn, *op. cit. supra* note 35, at 95–135; Nunberg, "Problems in the Structure of the Juvenile Court," 48 *J. Crim. L., C.&P.S.* 500 (1958); Herman, "Scope and Purposes of Juvenile Court Jurisdiction," 48 *J. Crim. L., C.&P.S.* 590 (1958); Diana, "The Rights of Juvenile Delinquents: An Appraisal of Juvenile Court Procedure," 47 *J. Crim. L., C.&P.S.* 561 (1957); Allen, "The Borderland of the Criminal Law: Problems of 'Socializing' Criminal Justice," 32 *Soc. Serv. Rev.* 107 (1958).

[53] *A Standard Juvenile Court Act, op. cit. supra* note 23, at 8.

way. The unofficial handling of cases has been justified on the grounds that official court action is not needed in many situations, that it enables the court to assist children who, although not yet within its jurisdiction, are in danger of becoming so, and that the official label of delinquency should be avoided as much as possible. Prehearing investigations should be used, it is asserted, because they provide important facts for the hearings and thus allow the hearings themselves to be utilized as part of the treatment process. Extreme informality of procedure is favored by those who believe that only by minimizing all rules can the philosophy of the juvenile court gain full expression. They maintain that rules are not important anyway since the state is not bringing action against a defendant, as it would in a criminal trial, but is rather acting as a guardian of the child, and that therefore we need not be concerned about protecting the child from possible harm.

However, a number of important points have been stressed on the other side of the controversy, and an examination will now be made of some of these. Broad definitions of delinquency and the unofficial handling of cases, it is contended, channel an increasing number of children not having serious problems into courts which, by general admission, are overloaded, understaffed, and inadequately equipped for preventive work. Handling by these courts not only gives such children the appearance of being seriously delinquent in the eyes of the public, and thus actually defeats the alleged purpose of this practice, but also exposes them to the danger of being treated as if they were serious delinquents or, what is worse, of being indiscriminately committed to correctional institutions when perhaps they are suffering only from neglect or dependency. More-

over, even when the court can engage in extensive preventive work, this activity may discourage the development of other agencies better organized and equipped to do this work.

Besides, it is argued, where is the child who does not have a problem? With little effort hundreds of children who have problems can be found in any community and brought into court. And if the court is not vigilant, it may be used by parents as a weapon against children in situations where the parents themselves are to blame. Thus the family is given a crutch at a time when it should be encouraged to strengthen itself through its own efforts—and other agencies can assist the family to do this far more effectively than can the court.

Furthermore, it is asserted, the situation is not improved by the use of the prehearing investigation. Too often this tends to become the hearing itself—a process during which the facts are gathered and the decision regarding disposition is reached even before the court has determined whether the child is delinquent. Indeed, his mere presence in court may be interpreted as presumptive evidence of his delinquency, and this may be easily inflated to conclusive evidence if some personal problem in his history can be discovered and dilated upon by the probation officer. If the hearing has been conducted with an extremely informal procedure, the child will find that the decision can be overturned only with great difficulty. If, as its advocates claim, the prehearing investigation is not to be used to acquire evidence against the child, then there is no sound reason why the investigation should not be postponed until after the child has been adjudged delinquent. Here another point needs to be stressed. The court cannot be certain that a problem child will become a delinquent child, and besides, its own ineptitude may convert a problem into delinquency.

Moreover, it is urged, the rights of the child and his parents are especially endangered if the case is handled with extreme informality, because then there is no attorney to guard against the abuse of authority, no set of rules to ward off hearsay and gossip, no way of breaking through the secrecy of the hearing, and often no appeal from the court's decision. The child and his parents have even less protection if the case is handled unofficially, for in such a procedure very few legal checks limit the court's discretion, and redress at law becomes difficult since no official record exists upon which the child can plead his case. The situation can be worse if broad definitions of delinquency are used, because these leave the term vague and fuzzy, and under them all children tend to be pooled indiscriminately as wards of the state without an opportunity to marshal evidence against a specific charge. If these children are then processed through unofficial handling or informal hearings from which many, if not most, of the limitations of due process have been removed, they are largely at the court's discretion, which too frequently may be only the expression of the judge's prejudice. How ironical it is that this situation is justified in the name of equity, especially since the court of equity has always had its rules and formality for the same reason that rules and formality should be present in the juvenile court, that is, to check the abuse of power and to protect the rights of the individual.

Finally, it is protested, euphemistic terminology, such as "hearing" instead of "trial," or "disposition" instead of "sentence," should not be allowed to conceal the fact that the nature of the entire procedure in the juvenile court may be little different from that of a criminal court. In fact, it may be worse, for it may abandon the principles upon which justice is based under the guise of promoting a superior justice. It is understandable, therefore, why Carr has said, "No man is wise enough or good enough to be trusted with arbitrary power—even the arbitrary power to prejudge the case of some delinquent child in the juvenile court."[54]

These, then, are some of the points that have been stressed by those who are opposed to broad definitions of delinquency, unofficial handling of cases, prehearing investigations, and extreme informality of procedure. That they are impressive ones is evidenced by the fact that an increasing number of thoughtful writers have demanded greater protection for the child and his parents in the juvenile court. And Tappan, in dismay over the seriousness of the situation, has asked, "Who is to save the child from his saviors?"[55]

This analysis of the criticisms of the juvenile court clearly shows that we are dealing with questions of emphasis and fine distinctions in a process which involves the balancing of the best interests of both the individual and society. It also indicates some of the social, philosophical, legal, and operational problems that confront the juvenile court. In the consideration of these problems, we shall be able to maintain a better sense of proportion if we remember these facts: (1) Although the general tendency has been toward the operation of the juvenile court as an administrative agency with great emphasis on social service functions, this type of operation has not been achieved to any great extent except in the comparatively few highly-organized, independent courts in our large cities; but,

[54] Carr, *Delinquency Control* 240 (1950).

[55] Tappan, *op. cit. supra* note 52, at 208.

it must be added, these courts have been exerting a disproportionate influence in the establishment of standards and goals in the juvenile court movement. (2) Many courts, instead of taking action themselves, are already referring a large number of cases to schools and welfare agencies. (3) Many courts that have few of the essential characteristics of the juvenile court are nevertheless effectively handling cases because of the wisdom of the judge and the support of interested citizens. (4) Many courts, regardless of what can be done in their behalf, will remain "substandard courts" even when measured by the most moderate criteria—a fact which becomes increasingly apparent since these courts have shown little improvement despite the unprecedented prosperity of this country. (5) Many communities will have to continue to send their neglect and dependency cases and some of their truany cases to the juvenile court simply because they do not now have, and may never have, any other agency able to assume this responsibility. (6) The majority of the alleged delinquents appearing in the juvenile court do not contest the allegations brought against them and are actually delinquent, although, of course, this does not mean that these children are not entitled to all necessary legal protection.

Since the juvenile court in the United States is a functioning part of an increasingly complex culture, it must share in all the social problems, including delinquency, that this type of society tends to produce. To the extent that the juvenile court operates effectively to rehabilitate juvenile offenders and to deter others from becoming delinquent, it functions as an agency of prevention and contributes somewhat to social reorganization. But obviously it can remove only some of the conditions that are causing the delinquency

with which it is dealing, and it has virtually no control over industrialization, urbanization, and other such powerful forces that are transforming and disorganizing American society— including the juvenile court itself—and piling up social problems faster than we can handle them.

Although there has been considerable debate about how the juvenile courts can improve their staffs, lower their case loads, and reduce their other operational problems, most students of the court agree that certain changes can be made now to accomplish these objectives. Many communities can and should spend more money on their courts, and others should use their present expenditures more effectively. Many courts should have judges who are better trained in both the law and the social sciences, larger jurisdictional areas, and a stronger position in their state's judicial system.[56] All courts should closely coordinate their operations with those of welfare and law-enforcement agencies. And everywhere the public should be told more about the court and encouraged to support its work.

It is recognized, of course, that all the problems of the court are interrelated and interacting and that many of them are beyond its control. However, there are major problems of a philosophical and legal nature with which the court can deal directly and which are contributing materially to

[56] The way in which the position of the juvenile court in the state's judicial system is to be strengthened will be affected by the surrounding social and political conditions. According to the Standard Juvenile Court Act, if the court is not part of a state system of juvenile courts, it should be set up within the existing judicial structure as a separate division at the level of the highest court of general trial jurisdiction. Sussman, *op. cit. supra* note 4, at vii. See also Rubin, "State Juvenile Court: A New Standard," 30 *Focus* 103 (July 1951).

its operational difficulties. The juvenile court, like all courts, must try to balance the interests of the individual and society in the adjudication of its cases. In the United States social relationships are being torn apart by conflicts, and agencies of social control subverted by divisive influences. The ensuing confusion is blurring the sense of right and wrong, diluting basic loyalties, endangering many cherished rights, and sweeping away duties and responsibilities essential for the security of the community. The juvenile court can help to reduce this confusion if its philosophical and legal foundations are strengthened. The proposals advanced below are designed to do this by casting the court in a more realistic role, protecting the rights and clarifying the duties of those coming before it, and enabling it to effect a better balance between the rights of the child and his parents and the security of the community.

PROPOSALS REGARDING THE COURT'S PHILOSOPHY AND LEGAL BASIS

Philosophy of the Court

The roots of most of the controversy over the juvenile court are to be found in the dual role that it plays in attempting to function both as a court of law and as a social service agency. In fact, many writers on the subject believe that the basic problem confronting the court involves a decision as to which of its two functions, the legal or the social service, is to predominate.[57]

The juvenile court was established

as a court, albeit a special one, and in structure, function, and procedure it remains essentially a court.[58] Therefore, efforts should be made to strengthen its true, or judicial, nature and to retain and develop only that part of its social service function that is necessary for the administration of individualized justice.

As a court, even in the administration of this type of justice, it must not only express the values of the society in which it functions but also reinforce these values. Dean Pound, a friend of the juvenile court, clearly recognized this when he said:

> If we work out a system of making penal treatment fit the crime, we risk losing sight of the individual delinquent in pursuit of system. If we look only at the individual delinquent, we risk losing system in pursuit of individual treatment and lose objectivity which is demanded when we are constraining the individual by the force of politically organized society. It comes down to the reconciling of the general security with the individual life, which as I have said, is a fundamental problem of the whole legal order.[59]

In other words, no court, not even the juvenile court, can be just a therapeutic agency. It is, and must be, a moral agency as well. And when a child is adjudicated a delinquent by the court, he is, and of necessity must be, stigmatized as a violator of the moral values of his society. This is what the people want and expect of any agency such as a court which is established to protect and strengthen their values. In fact, the court must act in this way if it is to promote the rehabilitation of the child. If it did otherwise, it would flaunt the very values to which the child must learn to adjust and for which he

---

[57] See for example, Baker, "The Functions of the Juvenile Court," 24 *Case and Con.* 449 (Nov. 1917); Long, "The Juvenile Court and Community Resources," *Yearbook*, 1940, 24 (Nat'l Prob. Ass'n, 1940); Eastman and Cousins, "Juvenile Court and Welfare Agency: Their Division of Function," 38 *A.B.A.J.* 575–577, 623 (1952); Nunberg, *op. cit. supra* note 52, at 500.

[58] Both legal scholars and social welfare authorities have recognized this fact. See, for example, Pound, *op. cit. supra* note 3, at 5; Nutt, *op. cit. supra* note 47, at 212.

[59] Pound, *op. cit. supra* note 4, at 15.

must develop a loyalty. This is not to ignore the fact that values change and that considerable confusion regarding moral standards exists in the United States. The point is that the court cannot avoid its responsibility as a moral agency. It must do what it can to reduce this confusion. It must devote itself to the interests of the delinquent and respect his rights, but it must also take its stand with the community and insist that he learn to discharge his duties and assume his responsibilities as a member of society, thus giving encouragement and support to law-abiding citizens and helping to maintain the public sense of justice. The way in which the court does this will, of course, depend upon the facts of the case as they are revealed and evaluated in the process of "individualized justice."

Furthermore, in the disposition of the delinquency case the court forces the child to submit to its authority by placing him on probation, by committing him to a correctional institution, or by dealing with him in some other similar way. And by no stretch of the imagination can what actually happens to the child during this process be called merely treatment. Thus the action of the court involves both community condemnation of antisocial conduct and the imposition of unpleasant consequences by political authority—the two essential elements of punishment.[60] It is, therefore, highly unrealistic to say that the court treats, but does not punish, the child. What it really does is to emphasize treatment in a correctional process which includes, and of necessity must include, both treatment and punishment.

This conclusion tends to be supported by several other facts. There is no systematic science of human behavior,

and the concepts and techniques of treatment are still largely inadequate. Moreover, as Dunham has explained, neither the child nor his parents are inclined to view his behavior as symptomatic of a sickness that needs treatment, but instead "are committed to the view that the court is there for justice and for punishing a person who has done something that is wrong."[61] Besides, the stipulation that the court should act as a parent in protecting and caring for the child does not rule out the necessity and desirability of punishment. Here again Dean Pound had a clear understanding of the nature of the court. "Juvenile probation," he said, "is not a mode of penal treatment nor a substitute for punishment. It is a mode of exercising the authority of the state as *parens patriae*. It may be conceded that the parent may have at times to administer what common law called reasonable correction to the child. No doubt there is often a corrective element in judicial treatment of juvenile offenders. But the spirit is that of the parent rather than that of the ruler."[62]

This modification of the philosophy of the juvenile court is superior to that generally accepted in several important respects. First, it clearly recognizes the necessity of balancing the interests of the delinquent and the community in the process of "individualized justice." Second, it provides a practical basis of action which can be accepted without conflict by both law-enforcement officers and court personnel. Third, by honestly admitting that the court must not only treat but also punish, this modified philosophy dispels the cloud of hypocrisy now enveloping the juvenile court, and gives it a position in society

[60] Hart, "The Aims of the Criminal Law," 23 *Law and Contemp. Prob.* 401 (1958).

[61] Dunham, "The Juvenile Court: Contradictory Orientations in Processing Offenders, 23 *Law and Contemp. Prob.* 520 (1958).

[62] Pound, *op. cit. supra* note 4, at 16.

where it can be respected by all law-abiding citizens. Finally, by revealing the true nature of the court, this modified philosophy brings the possibility of the abuse of power out into the open where it can be clearly understood and effectively controlled.

Jurisdiction of the Court

The jurisdiction of the juvenile court should be limited to (1) delinquency cases, and (2) those dependency and neglect cases in which a decision must be made affecting the legal status of the child, his custody, or the rights of his parents. All other dependency and neglect cases should be handled by administrative agencies without court action, and truancy should be dealt with by the schools.[63] This proposal is made in recognition of the fact that the juvenile court is essentially a court and not an administrative agency, and that, therefore, it suffers from inherent limitations in welfare work. Furthermore, the considerable increase in the number of welfare agencies and public services during the past few decades not only makes this transfer of responsibilities possible but also leaves the court with a greater capacity to handle the growing volume of delinquency cases.

The court should deal with children who can be shown to be delinquent by the application of specific, sharply defined criteria, and not with children who have problems according to the opinions of teachers, clergymen, and social workers—however sincere these beliefs may be. Juvenile delinquency, therefore, should be defined as the violation of a state law or city or town ordinance by a child whose act if committed by an adult would be a crime. This simple, specific definition eliminates all the references to such vague conditions as "being ungovernable" or "growing up in idleness" which clutter up our statutes on delinquency and invite loose interpretation and abuse of authority. Thus it will prevent the juvenile court from moving into areas where other agencies can render more effective service, and at the same time it will protect children and their parents from indiscriminate handling by the court without regard for the cause of action in the case.

The juvenile court should have original and exclusive jurisdiction over all children between the ages of 7 and 18 who are alleged to be delinquent, except in cases where a child is charged with a minor traffic offense or where a child of 16 or over is charged with a serious felony, such as murder, armed robbery, or rape. In the cases involving minor traffic offenses, there is no need of special handling. They can be adequately dealt with by a police or traffic court, and thus the burden on the juvenile court can be reduced.[64] In the cases where children 16 or over are charged with serious felonies the criminal court should have original jurisdiction but with authority to transfer such cases to the juvenile court if in the opinion of the judge this would be in the best interests of both the child and the community. The criminal court should have the authority to act first in these cases, because it, more than the juvenile court, is held responsible for the security of society and is organized and administered especially for this purpose. As Ludwig has emphasized, "Making treatment of all criminal behavior of young offenders, regardless of its seriousness or triviality, depend

---

[63] This is essentially the proposal made by Sol Rubin in his book, *Crime and Juvenile Delinquency* 60–63 (1958). See also Nutt, *op. cit. supra* note 47, at 213; Hanna, "Dependency and Neglect Cases in the Juvenile Court," *Yearbook*, 1941, 136 (Nat'l Prob. Ass'n, 1941).

[64] See *Standards for Specialized Courts Dealing with Children, op. cit. supra* note 24, at 29, 30.

solely upon the individual need of the offender for rehabilitation may well lead our impressionable young community to conclude that fracturing someone's skull is no more immoral than fracturing his bedroom window."[65] This point is particularly important since a large and increasing percentage of serious crimes are being committed by young people. Thus the handling of a large percentage of these young offenders in the juvenile court—a court which is not primarily concerned with the public sense of justice and security —will make the criminal law increasingly inoperative and cause additional confusion regarding our code of morality and the importance of vigorous law enforcement. This in turn may contribute to the growth of indifference and cynicism regarding the duties and responsibilities of citizenship and to an already alarming trend toward the centralization of power in the hands of a few who, under the guise of science and treatment, often seek to impose their own values upon an increasingly disorganized people. To make matters worse, what is hailed as humanitarianism is frequently just public indifference regarding the way in which delinquents and criminals are handled.

The case of an adult charged with an offense against a child should be handled not in the juvenile court but in the criminal court. This will place these cases in a court better designed to assure protection of all fundamental rights in a criminal proceeding[66] and will help the public to understand that the juvenile court is a special court for children and not in any sense of the word a criminal court.

Procedure of the Court

Through its intake procedure the juvenile court should carefully screen all cases brought to its attention so as to eliminate those that do not require the attention of the court or any other agency and to insure the referral of as many other cases as possible to agencies that are better equipped than the court to provide curative and preventive treatment. The cases that are accepted by the court should receive official handling. If a case is not in need of official handling, it should not be handled by the court at all, but should be referred to some other agency. Too often unofficial handling is merely the haphazard, ineffective disposition of cases by understaffed, overloaded courts, which is justified under the guise of avoiding the "delinquency tag."[67]

The court should establish the fact of delinquency in a case before an investigation of the case is made. Prehearing investigations are not only an encroachment upon the rights of the child who has not yet been proved delinquent, but are costly in time, energy, and money in the cases of those who are discharged as not delinquent.

The procedure during the hearing should be informal but based upon sufficient rules to insure justice and consistency. The child and his parents should be fully informed regarding their legal rights. These should include the right to be represented by counsel, to have a clear explanation of the allegations against the child, to cross-examine hostile witnesses, to summon witnesses in the child's defense, to have protection against irrelevant and hearsay testimony and compulsory self-incrimination, to have a hearing before a jury if this is desired, to have proof of delinquency by at least a preponderance

---

[65] Ludwig, *op. cit. supra* note 20, at 311.
[66] *Id.* at 151.

[67] Tappan, "Unofficial Delinquency," 29 *Neb. L. Rev.* 547 (1950); Herman, *op. cit. supra* note 52, at 596; Sussman, *op. cit. supra* note 4, at 29, 30; Rubin, *op. cit. supra* note 63, at 66–68; *Standards for Specialized Courts Dealing with Children, op. cit. supra* note 24, at 43–45.

of convincing evidence, and to have access to a higher court for the purpose of an appeal. In addition, every juvenile before the court should be given the opportunity to have a public hearing if he so desires, and if he prefers a private one, members of the press should be admitted to the hearing but should not be permitted to publish the name of the child or any identifying data regarding him without the permission of the court. Their mere presence, however, should exert a wholesome and restraining influence on the court's operations.[68]

Disposition of Cases

The disposition of the case should be made by the judge after a study of the investigation report and consultation with the probation officer and other specialists who have worked on the case. However, simply because the judge must turn to specialists for assistance in his disposition of the case does not mean that it might be better to have the disposition made entirely by a panel of "experts." In the first place this incorrectly suggests that there is a type of knowledge that the judge does not have, cannot understand, and can never acquire. This not only grossly exaggerates the amount of knowledge we now have regarding human behavior but also greatly underestimates the intelligence and skill of the majority of our judges. If a particular judge is so incompetent or stubborn that he cannot, or will not, benefit by having the assistance of specialists, then the solution lies in his removal from office, not in unnecessarily complicating the machinery of the court by the creation of a panel of "experts." And if the judge

is so overworked that he does not have time to analyze carefully the facts contained in the investigation report and to consult with specialists about the various aspects of the case, then the answer is to be found in the appointment of more judges. There is no short cut or cheap way to "individualized justice," and the mere existence of a juvenile court does not insure its achievement.

Furthermore, the facts of adjudication and disposition cannot be examined as if they existed apart from each other. These facts exist in the life of a single child who must be seen in his entirety —developing from what he was to what he will be. They must be assembled creatively in the mind of one person who has the authority to balance the interests of both the individual and the community and who is held responsible by the community for this function. The facts of a case can be seen in a variety of ways, depending upon the relation of the examiner to the facts, and the mind is easily misled into seeing only one side of this picture. The judge who decides that a child is a delinquent should make this decision to intervene in the child's life not only in full knowledge of what will happen to the child as he is subjected to the available social services but also in deep awareness of being held responsible for the entire procedure. Only in such a process of sober deliberation can the knowledge of the facts be creatively transformed into a wise decision. The division of authority among the members of a panel fragmentizes the facts of the case and dilutes the sense of responsibility regarding the interests of the child and his relationship to the community.[69]

[68] Tappan, "Treatment Without Trial," 24 Social Forces 308 (March 1946); Cappello, "Due Process in the Juvenile Court," 2 Catholic U. L. Rev. 90 (1952); Geis, "Publicity and Juvenile Court Proceedings," 30 Rocky Mt. L. Rev. 101 (1958).

[69] Kahn, op. cit. supra note 35, at 277; Hall, "The Youth Correction Authority Act, Progress or Menace," 28 A.B.A.J. 317 (1942); Frank, Courts on Trial ch. 4 (1949).

These proposals are not advanced with any desire to convert the juvenile court into a criminal court but rather with full recognition of both its great potentialities and its inherent limitations. The juvenile court must be seen as a court—not as an administrative agency, but as a court—designed to protect the child from the traumatic experiences of a criminal trial and to provide more flexible machinery for balancing the interests of the child and the community in the light of the most recent knowledge regarding human behavior. It is not, however, especially equipped to do welfare work, and so wherever possible it should be divested of jurisdiction over cases in which the child is simply in need of aid. On the other hand, it is a court, and its action does necessarily stigmatize the child. Therefore, its jurisdiction and procedure should be governed by simple, specific rules so that while the child is receiving guidance and protection, his rights and the security of the community are not neglected.

The foregoing proposals have sought to strip away those excrescenses that have interfered with the expression of the true nature of the juvenile court, but they have left it with all the characteristics which are essential to its functioning and growth. Delinquency as a status different from that of crime, judges carefully selected on the basis of both their legal and social science training and knowledge, separate hearings as informal and private as are consistent with the protection of rights, availability of resources, such as medical, psychological, and psychiatric services, that can be used to make the investigation of cases more effective, regular probation service by an adequate number of well-trained officers, separate detention of children, special and confidential court and probation records—all these and more remain intact and are given a deeper meaning by a more realistic philosophy.

It is recognized that not all these proposals can immediately be put into effect everywhere. It is believed, however, that they do represent desirable goals toward which all juvenile courts should be directed so that they will become more effective agencies of social control.

But, as Dean Pound wisely counseled, "the law is not equal to the whole task of social control. Delinquency presents a problem far too complex to be dealt with by any single method. Hence in this field cooperation is peculiarly called for and is called for in a very wide field. If a socialized criminal justice is to achieve all that it may, we must be thinking about more than cooperation of judge and probation officer and social worker. These must cooperate, or at least be prepared to cooperate with the community organizer, the social engineer, the progressive educator, the social coordinator, the health officer, the clergyman, and the public-spirited promoter of legislation."[70]

[70] Pound, *op. cit. supra* note 4, at 13, 14.

30. Treatment Without Trial

PAUL W. TAPPAN

During the past generation there have developed in the court procedures of this country a series of novel institutional devices breaking with legal tradition and looking toward a more "socialized" processing of offenders. These devices are largely a hybrid product of court and case work methods. Some of them it is the purpose of this paper to consider. In general they are characterized by one or both of the following: (1) informal, unofficial probation supervision or institutional remand before a hearing is held, and (2) hearings in which there is no determination as to guilt of an offense, where personality factors and the "total situation" determine adjudication.

The purposes behind the emerging procedural methods appear fairly clear and, on their face at least, "progressive" and laudable. The desire is to avoid the stigma which grows out of court contact and adjudication and, particularly where the offense involved is of no great seriousness, to prevent the sentencing to an offender's status and to formal correction. The aim, too, is to break with the legal approach of adjudging defendants on the proof of a given criminal act, holding it more scientifically appropriate to determine through social and biological information whether a case needs treatment and, if so, what sort is required. To the socially minded it may appear absurd to concentrate attention upon a criminal act when it is itself merely a symptom or end product of character drives conditioned through extended experience. The need, it may be claimed, is to view rather the area of true significance—the defendant's total personality —in order to deal correctly with the case. Statutes which define the elements of a crime and establish a fixed penalty conceived by a legislature as punishment appropriate to the seriousness of that act appear as absurd relics of a classical criminology in an age when social science points toward individualization, prevention, and rehabilitation. Furthermore, the experimental courts of today rest largely on the shoulders of probation departments which have fostered the development of the new procedures. They would extend the philosophy and practice of case work in dealing with what are basically conduct problems, avoiding the "legal technicalities" which may slow or prevent the application of

SOURCE. Paul W. Tappan, "Treatment Without Trial," from *Social Forces*, Volume 24, March 1946, pp. 306–311. Reprinted with the permission of the University of North Carolina Press.

needed therapy based on social diagnosis and prescription for the peculiar needs of the case. The prevailing philosophy of these courts has been expressed ably by its advocates.[1]

The growth of an idea and its institutional entrenchment are well illustrated by the continuing crystallization in our courts of these new procedures. The methods used are rather numerous and varied in detail, but they fall into one or the other of the two general categories referred to above. For the most part they have originated in nonstatutory or extra-legal procedures, avoiding therefore the hazard of invalidation by appellate decisions. Some have received statutory formulation. By and large, however, the legal specifications under which the experimental courts operate do not sanction that full flowering of novel procedure which case work philosophy has brought into actual court custom. Indeed, under the statutes many of the existing practices are invalid; some of the informal administrative procedures are clearly violative of due process.

Let us review briefly the evolution of some of these devices employed to circumvent the traditional methods of criminal trial (wherein the issue of guilt is determined by the court and penalties are graded to the offense). Their origins lie in the children's court movement in which has developed a series of peculiarities in processing, today quite generally diffused throughout the country at this level of tribunal. Their emergence may be understood in part as a result of the rationalizing principle of the state as *parens patriae,* protector to the child, associated with the belief that deprivation of proce-

dural rights is unimportant when the court is attempting to treat and protect the child. Its purpose is clinical and rehabilitative. There has been small danger of defendant's contesting the validity of the procedural methods employed: neither the naive child nor his distraught parent are wont to challenge the procedures, and no attorney or prosecutor is present generally to raise the issue. If the right of review is permitted, it is discouraged and often condemned as a legal device to undo the progressive work of the court.[2] Chiefly the following differentiating characteristics mark the children's court methodology:

1. *Intake.* Basic information is sought by a probation officer at intake on the background of the case—family data; educational, economic and recreational history; conduct of the child; and other germane matters.

2. *Unofficial treatment.* Probation personnel (known in the New York Children's Court as the Adjustment Bureau) may apply informal supervision to cases in which the intake officer believed that social therapy was needed but which did not appear to require court hearing and adjudication. (It should be noted that an extremely elastic discretion may be employed at intake in directing the case to unofficial treatment or to court. When—as is the widely prevailing condition today —the operative philosophy of probation departments favors informal case work without a hearing, this "treatment without trial" becomes a popular practice.)

3. *Pre-adjudication investigation.* Reversing the procedure traditional in our criminal courts, at the juvenile level a social investigation on each case is undertaken by a probation officer *prior to*

---

[1] See, for example, Pauline V. Young, *Social Treatment in Probation and Delinquency* (1937); Herbert H. Lou, *Juvenile Courts in the United States* (1927); Belle B. Beard, *Juvenile Probation* (1934).

[2] See Benedict S. Alper, "Forty Years of the Juvenile Court," *American Sociological Review* (April, 1941), p. 230.

a hearing, and the information obtained therefrom is made available later at the hearing. This is unorthodox procedure in two chief respects: It applies to all cases whether or not the defendant is later adjudicated. (It tends, of course, to lead to adjudication in commonly establishing the foundation therefor in the discovery of social problems deemed to need treatment.) Also, in preceding the hearing, it allows in evidence matters which would be considered prejudicial, incompetent, and irrelevant for purposes of proof in the usual criminal trial.

4. *Interim dispositions.* During the period of social investigation a temporary disposition of the case must be made by adjourning to a later date and either paroling the defendant to home or agency or remanding him to an institution. The period of interim disposition is usually several weeks. In effect it constitutes a phase of treatment without trial when the child is either incarcerated (often with others already found to be delinquent, sometimes with convicted adult criminals[3]) or held under the restricted liberty of probation-scrutiny.

5. *Adjudication based on the total situation.* As noted above, the information from reports of probation investigation is available at the hearing. Thereby social data come to determine not only the treatment methods to be employed (as in the criminal court) but very largely whether or not the defendant is to be adjudicated a delinquent. Hence his guilt of a specific offense comes to be considered irrelevant, court decision being predicated upon the social and personal problems appearing in the history of the defendant and his family.

6. *Omnibus statutes.* The wide lati-

tude of discretion possible in adjudication is supported and extended by the statutes defining the recalcitrant child so broadly as to facilitate the easy status-fixing of delinquency.[4] Where, in accordance with the provisions of the statutes, a hearing is held before treatment is applied, it is scarcely a "trial" in the usual sense since guilt of specific enumerated offenses need not be proven to adjudicate. Rather, rumor of the needs of the defendant and/or his family may be a matter of primary moment to the children's court's decision. Again it is treatment without trial.

The procedures which evolved in the children's courts have come to be applied in the more recently emerging tribunals for adolescents. The variations in age-coverage of the children's court statutes in different jurisdictions are significant here. A large proportion of the states provide for children's court control over the delinquent up to the age of 18, some as high as 21. A few, including New York, end jurisdiction at 16. The trend has been generally upward throughout the country.

The result has been a drive to develop special facilities for the adolescent who otherwise must traverse the trial routes taken by adult criminals. New York City in its Adolescent Courts in Brooklyn and Queens, its citywide Wayward Minor Court for girls, and its Youthful Offender divisions of the County Courts, has provided special tribunals and methods of processing for the recalcitrant youth over 16. Similarly,

[4] Under the Federal Juvenile Court Act which has now been in operation for six years, such pre-hearing investigations are also conducted and reports submitted to the court at the hearing. As in the state courts, the procedures used are largely extra-legal in permitting adjudication based in part upon untested hearsay of probation reports. In the federal courts, however, many protections to the defendant's interests exist which are absent in the courts of the states.

[3] See Leonard V. Harrison and Pryor M. Grant, *Youth in the Toils* (1938).

Chicago, Philadelphia, and other cities have established courts to deal particularly with young offenders over the juvenile age.[5] For the most part these tribunals apply procedures comparable to those previously developed in the children's courts and they justify their use by analogy. It should be noted in passing, however, that there are several clear differences which should distinguish adolescent from juvenile procedures: The children's courts are often —as in New York—civil, whereas the adolescent courts are a part of the criminal court system. Also, the same standards of behavior cannot justifiably be applied to adolescent and child. Too, the facilities of the children's courts for treatment are generally more numerous, varied, and qualitatively superior to those of the adolescent courts—a significant matter in determining the sorts of cases in which jurisdiction should be taken by a court.

These courts for adolescents, too, operate under broad statutes which define the recalcitrant or wayward youth in most general fashion, thus facilitating adjudication when the court may wish to apply treatment to the case before it.[6] Pre-hearing investigations, interim procedures—often with temporary institutional disposition—and adjudication based on general hearsay information concerning personality and social background appear again at this

[5] See particularly the following: *Young People in the Courts of New York State*, Leg. Doc. 55 (1942); Paul W. Tappan, *Court for Wayward Girls* (1946); Worthington and Topping, *Specialized Courts Dealing with Sex Delinquency* (1925).

[6] See New York Statutes: the Wayward Minor Act, chapter 873, laws of 1945, recently expanding the terms of the original statute and permitting, particularly, remands without consent. See also the Youthful Offender Act, chapter 549, laws of 1943, recently repealed in its application to the Special Sessions Court, chapter 873, laws of 1945.

level—though somewhat more fearfully than in the children's courts. Here the individuals processed are adults under the criminal law and the large variations from due process could more easily lead to invalidation of the court methods. "Consent" of the defendant to the investigation before hearing has usually been required. There is formal statutory enunciation of defendant's rights, including the provision that his statements during investigation may not be used against his interest at the trial. Yet these matters are taken as a most *pro forma* matter. Indeed, under the new Wayward Minor Act in New York the requirement of consent for interim remands of two weeks has been abandoned so that such commitments may be made automatically. In some of the experimental courts the adolescent's consent to investigation and special hearing virtually assures adjudication of the status of offender but with more lenient treatment than could be expected from the criminal court to which the case would otherwise go. Thus the defendant is presented with a choice of consenting to an investigation by an officer of the court on the basis of which adjudication is most probable, to be followed by probation supervision; or, protesting his innocence, he risks conviction in an ordinary criminal court where the judge may impose a harsher penalty of commitment. This selection would test severely the preferences of many defendants innocent of law-violation.

These recent experimental methods of treatment without trial outlined above which have taken hold at the children's level and entered the adolescent range somewhat tentatively have come to appear in our adult criminal courts as well. Here they have emerged in at least two forms. The idea of "pre-adjudication conciliation" has been applied unofficially in the Magistrates' Courts of New York City, though never very largely used. It has been chiefly a matter of attempting informal probation treatment of social problems and conciliatory efforts between defendants and complainants when the offense alleged was minor and/or no complaint would issue. Considerably more formalized has been the device adopted elsewhere of applying probation where certain offenses are alleged without the requirement of arraignment or of adjudication.[7] The accused party is confronted with an option not unlike that of the defendant in the adolescent courts: he may accept unofficial treatment, without however going through trial and conviction for an offense at all, or he may stand trial with the danger of conviction and possible incarceration. One would dislike to be "taken in" "on suspicion" and confronted with this choice.

These various methods of applying court treatment without a full and fair judicial trial of the issue of guilt of a particular offense, despite their seductive rationale, appear to the writer to be peculiarly hazardous and unnecessary. Though criticism of methods used in experimental courts has sometimes been attacked as "technical" and reactionary, nevertheless the techniques which develop crescively through unthoughtful adoption in our social institutions do need careful inspection to test their effectiveness and their wider consequences. Novel experimental devices must be tried to be sure, yet permanent crystallization is to be avoided of methods which are based on error or which lead to excessive in-

[7] See *Attorney General's Survey of Release Procedures*, Vol. II, pp. 113–115, for the development of assorted practices of this sort under the statutes of Massachusetts, Rhode Island, Kentucky, and Maine.

justice. Existing or developing institutions may be "progressive" or "reactionary" depending upon the directions of their development and their effects.

In general denial of the validity of the current procedures, the writer maintains that they resemble too closely in some respects the philosophy of the Star Chamber. For their greatest fault is in failing to give to the defendant some of the most basic protections of due process which inhere in our modern legal system. Under our constitutions and laws the defendant deserves at very least (1) a definite charge of a particular offense, (2) the right to be confronted by the witnesses from whom is derived the evidence on which he is convicted, (3) a (real) right to counsel and appeal, and (4) conviction only upon a preponderance of credible, competent, relevant evidence. (In a criminal court such evidence should, of course, be convincing beyond a reasonable doubt.) These rights are assured even in the administrative tribunals of today; their disappearance from our criminal and quasi-criminal courts should not be tolerated.

The view is expressed by some criminologists that the issue of a particular criminal act is unimportant, particularly in dealing with the young where the general objective is to accomplish preventive and rehabilitative results; that general conduct, personality, and social problems are sufficient to justify adjudication and/or treatment at this level; and that broad statutes are needed to give the necessary latitude, the free play to court discretion. The difficulties with this approach are basic: Where no specific and clear-cut offense categories are established most anyone can be adjudicated to a status carrying stigma and potentially damaging treatment by the correctional agencies of criminal and quasi-criminal courts. The utmost of discretion is left in the hands of judicial and probation personnel unhampered by statutory definitions or limitations, undirected save by a very general principle of treating, reforming, rehabilitating. Unfortunately the personnel of our courts cannot be omniscient or omnicompetent. Indeed, they vary tremendously in their views on conduct, morality, treatment methods, and in their personal biases. Too they tend to lean toward punitive and correctional treatment and, in the experimental courts, toward broadening their functions to treat all manner of social problems. The result may often be damaging when individuals innocent of any serious wrongdoing or real law violation are subject to the rather crude tools of correctional treatment such as those available to our courts. As the author has said elsewhere:

. . . the court system is not designed to deal with problems which are not directly associated with law violation. The philosophies of courts, commitment institutions and probation bureaus are preponderately correctional and punitive. Their rôles have been clearly assigned in the mind and reactions of the defendant by the stereotypes of the cop, the criminal court, the reform school, and the probation officer. Similarly the public attitude toward these institutions and the adolescents subjected to them renders it wholly unrealistic for the courts to attempt to operate as general social agencies: they bear the indelible stamp of public stigma and ostracism. *Thus the frame of reference within which the court may legitimately and effectively operate is narrowly limited by public and institutional definition.* Attempts therefore at comprehensive social work are sheer folly; the problems of domestic relations, psychological pathology, occupational maladjustments, etc. are not within the sphere of appropriate function. This is the more obviously true when no offense has been shown—haphazard manipulation by the unskilled or partially trained probation officer in areas of specialized therapy adds

misapplied treatment to the injustice of court and institutional contact. Even when an offense has been proven, far greater success in treatment could be achieved by the referral of problems requiring trained and non-correctional specialized assistance to proper public and private agencies. (Yet, the adolescent courts are far from attaining a nice integration with the varied social agencies of the city, though the fault is not wholly their own.) In addition to the inappropriateness of crimino-legal handling of general social problems, the absurdity of this trend is enhanced by the insufficiency of personnel in the courts. Where, for optimum results, they should work experimentally and intensively on a carefully selected sample of favorable probation risks to insure creative individualization and reformation, the expansive drive in some courts toward problem-solving for all-comers has resulted in attenuated, inexact, and ineffectual service. The proper sphere of social agencies and behavior clinics should not be usurped by the courts, however benevolent the motivation. It appears clear that the work of crime prevention must be performed, if at all, *before* court contact and by non-court agencies. *The personnel of correctional court and institution is not equipped to do a non-correctional job.*[8]

Within the present limitations of our knowledge in the fields of psychology, sociology, and biology, our guesses must be quite tentative concerning treatment methods. Nevertheless we can and should use the training of specialists in these fields to recommend and apply therapy to the unadjusted who go through our courts. It is a different matter entirely, however, to attempt to apply these still-infantile sciences through non-specialists, who make up our court personnel for the most part, to determine on the basis of personality or total situation whom the court should adjudicate, whom it should treat. The idea that the function of law is

[8] Paul W. Tappan, *The Adolescent in Court* (1946).

to provide officials with convenient and general tools by which they may convict and treat those known to be criminals, or believed to require treatment, is a very cynical notion. Held by a few officials of our criminal courts, it is even more out of place at the children's or adolescents' level. The best and safest criterion justifying court action is the commission of an act in violation of a rule of law specifically defining the conduct to be avoided. Such a criminal act expresses—as no vague standard of recalcitrance or "moral depravity" can—a clear, definite, and relevant foundation for court action. It may well be argued that the offense categories should be increased to include specific forms of misconduct appearing in youth which, if untreated, would lead into crime of a more serious nature. If so, these must come into legal definition and delimitation so as to avoid the injustices flowing from an uninstructed judicial latitude. The present law and practice encourage abuse by the generality and variability of principles applied. The result is that these experimental courts appear either to operate on a presumption of guilt or to assume guilt to be irrelevant. A most progressive step, then, for the courts desiring to deal as effectively as possible with the young would be the clear statutory enunciation of the conduct-categories to be tabooed. This would mean that adjudication should occur only if and when such conduct is clearly shown by legitimate evidence.

Closely associated with the problem of the general statutes and free discretion which now obtain in these courts is the method so widely use of holding pre-adjudication investigations with reports to the court at the hearing. If adjudication of the offender status should be based—as the author has maintained—on proof of guilt of a particular offense, there is no sound reason for requiring an investigation until after the hearing—and then, of course, only for those cases which are adjudicated. This more traditional procedure would provide at least three distinct advantages over the present method:

1. It would save from court correctional devices those cases which do not merit adjudication legally, cases which are now treated with inappropriate methods due to the expansionist drives within these tribunals toward general social problem-solving.

2. It would make unnecessary the use of parole and remand during rather extended periods of social investigation when no hearing has been held. It is certainly impossible in good law or sound sense to assume a defendant to be guilty of an unproven charge or to justify his treatment without trial during an interim disposition. Errors can be and frequently are made in these courts, as in adult criminal courts, through arrests of and complaints against innocent parties. Too, often when the complaint is made by parents, the fault and problem lies with them not their child; in these cases to impose institutional remands or to adjudicate, as we often do, and apply treatment that is at least partially correctional, punitive, and non-specialized does unnecessary injustice.

3. It would result in a considerably more efficient utilization of the all-too-limited probation resources available in these courts. Under the suggested procedure numerous investigations would not be required: the time thus saved could be devoted to the more creative and rehabilitative work of supervision in cases that had been carefully selected by legal process for social treatment. To reiterate, social investigations should be made *after* adjudication in order that the court may apply therapy as

nicely adjusted to the individual requirements of the cases as possible. To be sure, the suggested change in procedure would require that more witnesses be used at hearings to determine the relevant facts and adjudication would be made more difficult. However, difficulty in eliciting proof of specific offenses is no justification for holding as offenders all who are brought into court. Rather, the elimination of many who do not deserve adjudication could be a great positive gain in preventing that development of delinquencies which occurs so often among the young who have been exposed to the correctional facilities of our courts.

Since the adoption in our adolescent courts of the procedures referred to has been rationalized by their prior institutionalization at the children's court level, it is significant to note that these devices have come under serious criticism by the judiciary of that children's court system. Chief Justice W. B. Cobb of the Domestic Relations Court in New York City has recently attacked with vehemence the unofficial treatment of the adjustment bureau, the use of prehearing investigations for purposes of adjudication, and extended remands without a hearing. He condemns them as legally and socially invalid.[9] The reasoning which denounces them must apply as vigorously in the adolescent and adult courts where mild misconduct or complete innocence may lead today to criminal court treatment.

In conclusion it should be noted that our system of law as it is constituted

today and within its appropriate methods of application does permit of full and sound individualization of treatment based on the findings and theories of the social sciences. Just treatment of the alleged offender requires this sort of processing. (1) The charge of a specific, statutorily defined offense. (2) A hearing of the issue at the earliest meeting of the court at which witnesses may be summoned with full protection of the defendant's rights of due process (including an attorney, relevant and competent testimony in his presence, adjudication only on convincing proof, and appeal). (3) Where court contact with a case indicates that the individual is not guilty of an offense but does require treatment, he should be referred to those public or private social agencies which may deal in a specialized way with his problem, thereby assuring most effective treatment without stigma. Much of this could be done at Intake. (Indeed, one of the most useful functions of these specialized tribunals could well be to act as agencies of referral to more specialized social facilities in order that individual and community problems may be met more effectively.) (4) A probation investigation into the background of the adjudicated offender to determine on the basis of his prior history, conduct, and character what methods of therapy may best be applied to re-condition him and protect society. (5) In the case of adjudicated offenders after receipt of the probation report and any other information available which is relevant to disposition, the court should dispose of the case with careful attention to adjusting treatment methods to the needs of the case, avoiding institutionalization wherever possible.

9 W. Bruce Cobb, Address delivered on February 6, 1945 before a Joint Meeting of the Committees of the Court of Domestic Relations, of the Association of the Bar, and the County Lawyers Association.

31. The Juvenile Court and the Limits of Juvenile Justice

FRANCIS A. ALLEN

The years since World War II have brought about a revival of interest in the American juvenile court. Following the burst of enthusiasm in the early years of the century that led to widespread adoption of juvenile court legislation, the institution in many localities suffered the consequences of public apathy and neglect. This neglect and its consequences are still being felt; but in recent years the court has again become the subject of discussion and debate, and this to a degree not approached for a half-century. Not all supporters of the juvenile court movement have welcomed the new attention, for some modern critics have subjected basic assumptions of the movement to challenge and doubt. Fortunately, however, most persons who wish well for the court recognize the recent discussion as a source of strength. Indeed, unless one assumes that the little band of creative reformers who launched the juvenile court at the turn of the century was possessed of revealed truth, final and unassailable, it must be recognized that criticism and analysis are essential to the proper evolution of the institution and its adaptation to current realities.

The modern reappraisal of the juvenile court, however, has not proceeded far. We have only begun to make use of the techniques and insights that have been acquired in the study of other social institutions.[1] We are only beginning to obtain systematic information on what, in reality, the juvenile court is and does. Certainly we are far from formulating secure principles to direct its future development. These are formidable tasks and require more thought and effort than have thus far been devoted to them, even in this period of increasing interest in the court and its functions.

The juvenile court, both in theory and practice, is an institution of re-

[1] Compare examples of "organizational analysis" as applied to prisons and other custodial institutions: Clemmer, *The Prison Community* (1940); Sykes, *The Society of Captives* (1958); Social Science Research Council, *Theoretical Studies of Social Organization of the Prison* (Pamphlet 15, 1960).

SOURCE. Francis A. Allen, "The Juvenile Court and the Limits of Juvenile Justice," from *The Borderland of Criminal Justice*, Chicago: University of Chicago Press, 1964, pp. 43–61. Reprinted with the permission of the University of Chicago Press.

markable complexity. It is called upon to perform a bewildering variety of functions. On the one hand, it administers what are essentially welfare functions, such as the exercise of its dependency jurisdiction. On the other hand, it may be required to provide a forum for criminal prosecution, as in cases of adults alleged to have contributed to the delinquency of minors. The juvenile court is a court; but it is also a governmental agency charged with manifold administrative responsibilities and, in some localities, the performance of clinical services. Not only does the court perform a variety of functions and assume a variety of roles; it must also inevitably express a wide range of values and aspirations. But functions conflict and values collide; hence, there must be some sort of mediation or accommodation of the various goals and values if the institution is to function at all. This accommodation and compromise may result from intelligent deliberation or it may be the product of caprice and indifference.

But the complexity which obstructs understanding and reappraisal of the juvenile court involves more than the proliferation of functions or the conflict of conscious goals and values. We have come to realize that understanding an institution requires that we know more than the motives and aspirations of those who created it and of those who operate it. In the language of Merton, we must be concerned not only with its manifest functions but with its latent functions;[2] not only with what the institution consciously attempts to do but with what it does in fact. And we may expect to discover in looking closely at the juvenile court that its operations result in certain unintended and unanticipated consequences, consequences

no less real because they are unintended and unanticipated.

In short, it is clear that wisdom and understanding in this area cannot be purchased cheaply. The inquiry and critical analysis required demand the contributions of many disciplines and much time, ingenuity, and resources. They also demand a willingness to subject cherished presuppositions to the hazards of inquiry and analysis. This is not to deny that there are short-term goals of practical reform worthy of support; but it is to suggest that our fundamental need is knowledge and understanding. Accordingly, I am concerned less with the immediate reform of the juvenile court and more with a few general questions which, it has seemed to me, may have some relevance to a modern reconsideration of the court.

Perhaps the search for understanding can best begin with a consideration of the history and antecedents of the juvenile court movement. No institution as complex as the juvenile court emerges suddenly and fully formed. On the contrary, the juvenile court can properly be regarded as the culmination of certain ideas and tendencies of thought that had their origins at least as early as the eighteenth-century Enlightenment. Throughout the century that followed many of these distinctive ideas were given practical application, so that by the time the first juvenile court legislation became effective in Illinois on July 1, 1899, many of its assumptions were familiar and well tested. Thus the nineteenth century saw the beginnings of the effort to segregate juveniles from adult offenders in detention and correctional institutions and the establishment of cottage-type schools for children. Separate courts or divisions of courts for children were put into operation in several localities, and systems of probation were

---

[2] Merton, *Social Theory and Social Structure* 60–64 (rev. ed. 1957).

devised and administered.[3] These reforms were part of a broader effort to advance the welfare of children, evidenced both in the United States and western Europe, which included the rise of public education, the development of protective services for dependent and neglected children, and agitation against child labor and other abuses of children in industry. All these activities were in some degree influenced by new theories of human behavior which sometimes challenged the validity of such basic concepts of the legal order as the concept of criminal responsibility and resulted, among other things, in the formation of the schools of positivist criminology.[4]

It is never possible to explain completely the rise of an elaborate system of thought and practice such as that given expression in the juvenile court movement. But most social movements can be understood, in part, as reactions against older modes of thought and practice. There is no doubt that the juvenile court represents to a significant degree a reaction against the older methods of dealing with children which were employed by the legal order. That some of these methods were and are properly the subject of protest is also clear. Historical examples of the inhumanity of criminal justice in confronting the problem of the misbehaving child and the insensitivity of public attitudes that supported these practices still possess the power to shock and startle. Thus, in the first half of the last century the diarist, Charles

Grenville, in describing a hanging at Tyburn gaol, expressed astonishment at the incomprehensible attitude of the boys about to be hanged. "Never," he is reported as saying, "did I see boys cry so."[5] But the demonstration that the old days were in many respects the bad old days does not depend upon the collection of historical examples. The badness of much of the older practices is demonstrated by such as have persisted to the present day. For at least two centuries thoughtful persons have recognized the danger of detaining juveniles in facilities that bring them into contact with older offenders. And yet, in many parts of the country our detention practices have not taken this small first step in the direction of decency and rationality.[6] At the adult level, American corrections have rarely been capable of making the elementary distinction between the accused person charged with crime and the convicted offender. In most of our jails both classes of persons are indiscriminately confined together and subjected to basically the same regimen.[7] We know that many of the old ways are bad ways because we can observe their effects in present practice; we are able thereby to gain some appreciation of the intensity of the reaction which is expressed in efforts at reform like the juvenile court movement.

The juvenile court may thus be regarded as a response to problems that are real and important. There is no doubt that the juvenile court movement was founded on strong and ex-

---

[3] See Caldwell, "The Juvenile Court: Its Development and Some Major Problems," 51 *J. Crim. L., C.&P.S.* 493 (1961); Rosenheim, "Perennial Problems in the Juvenile Court," in *Justice for the Child* 1–16 (Rosenheim ed. 1962).

[4] Consult Jeffery, "The Historical Development of Criminology," in *Pioneers in Criminology* 364 *et seq.* (Mannheim ed. 1960).

[5] Quoted in Bevan, *In Place of Fear* 177 (1952).

[6] See, e.g., Norman, "The Detention Home," 241 *Annals* 161 (January, 1949).

[7] See Foote, "Forward: Comment on the New York Bail Study," 106 *U. Pa. L. Rev.* 685, 689 (1958). And note the comments in chapter 3 of the *Attorney General's Committee on Poverty and the Administration of Federal Criminal Justice Report* (1963).

plicit dissatisfaction with conditions then generally prevailing and was intended to effect a radical and thoroughgoing reform. Not only were conditions in juvenile custodial institutions to be improved, but separate and distinctive judicial proceedings were to be established and the benefits of probation services to be extended. A whole new view of juvenile misbehavior as essentially non-criminal was propounded and a completely non-punitive course of treatment was to be substituted for the old criminal sanctions. Writing in 1909, Judge Julian Mack described the ideal and responsibility of the juvenile court in the following terms: ". . . to find out what [the child] is, physically, mentally, morally, and then if it learns that he is treading the path that leads to criminality, to take him in charge, not so much to punish as to reform, not to degrade but to uplift, not to crush but to develop, not to make him a criminal but a worthy citizen."[8] The juvenile court thus represents the most important and ambitious effort yet undertaken by our law to give practical expression to the rehabilitative ideal.

It reveals, I believe, no hostility toward the rehabilitative ideal to suggest that the effort to give it expression is attended by certain distinctive problems and that the tendency to view the court in exclusively rehabilitative or therapeutic terms imposes its own characteristic limitations. Nor should this be regarded as surprising. We are not blessed with a capacity to view human problems in all their infinite complexities, and any posture assumed in the presence of large social issues is likely to express its own particular bias and be vulnerable to its own forms of pathology. In reacting against old errors we are constantly in danger of

being enslaved by our emancipation. This is not to say that progress is impossible because we are doomed simply to exchange old errors for new. It is to say that in the process of reform we may encounter new and distinctive problems. To insure that progress will result from reform, we must be continually vigilant in order to detect the unanticipated consequences of our action.

With these matters in mind we may now inquire whether the concept of the juvenile court as expressed by its founders and frequently repeated in various forms of language by later proponents provides a theory adequate to describe what the court is and to define what its role ought to be now and in the future. In his eloquent essay entitled "Philosophy of the Juvenile Court," the late Judge Schramm of Pittsburgh remarked: "Juvenile courts are the least understood and the most misunderstood of the courts of our land."[9] Anyone who has observed the juvenile court over any considerable period of time has sensed, on occasion, a tension between the court and the community. Most supporters of the court are disposed to explain this tension by the persistence of an impulse for retribution in the public at large and by a lack of whole-hearted commitment to the rehabilitative ideal. It would be difficult to deny that this explanation contains a large element of truth. But is it a complete and adequate explanation? The tension to which I refer is sometimes made explicit in the juvenile court legislation itself. In the first section of the Michigan juvenile court act, the legislature declared that the law should be liberally construed so as to advance "the child's welfare and the best interest of

---

[8] Mack, "The Juvenile Court," 23 *Harv. L. Rev.* 104, 107 (1909).

[9] Schramm, "Philosophy of the Juvenile Court," 241 *Annals* 101 (January, 1949).

the state."[10] Are these objectives in all cases the same? Are there instances in which the best interests of the community, if not inconsistent with the welfare of the child, are at least to some degree separate and distinct? Is it possible that the traditional view of the court as exclusively or largely a therapeutic or rehabilitative agency has obstructed the identification of areas of legitimate community interest that the court may properly be expected to serve? These are large and difficult questions, and the remarks that follow represent only a tentative effort to explore the issues as they relate to the court's delinquency jurisdiction.

The typical, indeed almost automatic, reaction to the issues posed, on the part of those imbued with the classic theory of the court, is to deny the possibility of any community interest separate from, and certainly any community interest adverse to, the welfare of the child brought before the juvenile court. If, it is argued, we are able to provide the delinquent child with therapy and treatment that will profoundly change his motivations and behavior so that in the future he will be able and disposed to live in harmony, rather than at war, with the community, we shall not only have advanced the welfare of the child but at the same time have made a most fundamental contribution to the "interest of the state." That this response has genuine force and cogency ought to be recognized. A community which fails simply for want of vision or energy to provide its children with the means of therapy and rehabilitation will inevitably suffer the effects of self-inflicted wounds. Moreover, this response gives expression to an aspiration and an ideal that have supplied the impetus for much of the juvenile court's soundest

10 Mich. Comp. Laws § 712 A.1 (1948).

achievement. And yet, it must be concluded by those seeking understanding of the court that the response is insufficient. We still need to inquire whether, assuming full capability to achieve the objectives of rehabilitation, the court has purposes to serve that involve more than the interests and welfare of the particular children coming before it. We need also to inquire about the purposes of the court in those cases in which the court is incapable of achieving its rehabilitative objectives, either because of the limits of scientific knowledge or because of the inadequacies of the facilities and personnel available to it or because the particular problems of adolescent misconduct are of the sort that give rise to issues no court can adequately confront or resolve.

It is the point last mentioned which perhaps best exposes the inadequacy of any theory of the juvenile court that views the institution wholly as a therapeutic or rehabilitative device. For it is an unfortunate fact that the juvenile court of every large urban community is confronted by significant numbers of adolescents whose behavior cannot be ignored because it imperils the basic security of the community, and who, as a class, elude the reformative capabilities of the court. These are adolescents who are not mentally ill in any sense of the term that meaningfully distinguishes this group of young persons from the population as a whole. On the contrary, these are children alienated from the legitimate institutions of society, lacking in opportunities for employment and goal satisfactions, victims of discrimination and cultural deprivation. The behavior of such children, even that which contributes most to community concern and insecurity, may often reflect normal adaptation to the conditions of life to which they are subjected. Some modern writers have suggested that much violent group behavior on the part of adolescents reflects an effort to obtain prestige or to force themselves onto the attention of the community.[11] However this may be, it appears clear that such behavior is in some measure the product of conditions not within the control of the court, conditions which create the environment to which the child must return after the program of treatment instituted by the juvenile court has come to an end.

There is surely nothing new in this statement. It constitutes no revelation to anyone acquainted with the operations of the American juvenile court to be told that it is regularly required to act in cases of children whose prognosis for rehabilitation at the hands of the court is highly unfavorable. What are the implications of this observation? Surely not that such cases should be excluded from the jurisdiction of the juvenile court; for the processes of the court, with all their limitations, may still represent the best and least harmful method that our civilization has devised to handle these problems. But it is, in my judgment, both inaccurate and deceptive to describe the operation of the juvenile court in this area as the exercise of a rehabilitative or therapeutic function. These cases are being adjudicated by the court for one principal reason: because they involve disturbing and dangerous behavior on the part of adolescents which the community must respond and attend to, for it is behavior that threatens the security and well-being of the community. The primary function being served in these cases, now and for what is likely to be an extended period in the future, is the temporary incapacitation of chil-

[11] See, e.g., Cloward and Ohlin, *Delinquency and Opportunity* (1960).

dren found to constitute a threat to the community's interest. In short, the value advanced is not primarily that of the welfare of the child adjudicated a delinquent. This is due not so much to the court's lack of commitment to the rehabilitative ideal as to the incapacity of the court and its instrumentalities to deal effectively with the conditions giving rise to delinquent behavior.

Thus if our concern is to understand what the juvenile court is and what in significant measure it is likely to be in the years ahead, these facts cannot be ignored. In a great many cases the juvenile court must perform functions essentially similar to those exercised by any court adjudicating cases of persons charged with dangerous and disturbing behavior. It must reassert the norms and standards of the community when confronted by seriously deviant conduct, and it must protect the security of the community by such measures as it has as its disposal, even though the available means may be unsatisfactory when viewed either from the standpoint of the community interest or of the welfare of the delinquent child. These propositions do no more than describe a situation which is familiar to all those who have observed the work of the juvenile court. What is remarkable is how rarely such observations have been included in what might be called the "official" literature of the court.

It may be objected, of course, that the theory of the court ought to emphasize those elements that distinguish it from, rather than identify it with, other agencies of justice. Moreover, the rehabilitative ideal, the aspiration to advance "the best interests of the child," has provided impetus and inspiration for the important effort to improve and render more rational our methods of dealing with children who have run afoul of the community's standards and expectations. The importance of preserving the ideal and invigorating the dynamics of reform cannot, I believe, be seriously doubted. Yet this does not justify a refusal to recognize candidly the realities that confront us. Theory is important because, among other reasons, it affects our conduct; a theory that is partial and incomplete is likely to produce unsatisfactory results. Insofar as the juvenile court is concerned, the bad results of inadequate theory are not merely a matter of speculation and conjecture. They are tangible and can be readily identified.

First, the failure to perceive that the juvenile court is often called upon to protect the community from acts of violence or depredations of property and to do this by the use of means that may in no sense advance the welfare of the delinquent child has, on occasion, encouraged laxness and unfairness in the procedures employed by the court in executing its charging, adjudicatory, and dispositional functions. Even today many persons professionally involved in the processes of juvenile justice conceive of the court as a large welfare agency blessed by some mysterious gift of Providence with access to the coercive powers of the state. Various factors combine to strengthen this impression. These include a widespread failure to communicate to members of the court's social staff the legal presuppositions of the system, the fact that the court deals with many matters that are essentially of a welfare character, and the circumstance that some juvenile court legislation, particularly the older statutes, defines the delinquency concept in terms so vague and flexible as to allow an assertion of jurisdiction in almost any case in which the intervention of the court is thought to be helpful to the child.[12] Nevertheless, the jurisdictional principle on which the court properly proceeds in the delinquency area is not the presumed ability of the court to be of service to the particular child, but the existence of behavior on the part of the child that is dangerous to the community's security or that imminently threatens such danger. Since the intervention of the court can only be justified by the existence of certain behavioral facts, it is of the highest importance that the procedures of notice and adjudication be adapted to careful and reliable fact-finding. Fair and reliable fact-finding procedures are, of course, essential in all cases, including those in which the court's disposition of the case may be expected to result in a genuine rehabilitative effort. But the importance of fair procedures may be more readily perceived when it is noted that in many delinquency proceedings the rehabilitative effort is at best a matter of secondary concern and that the juvenile court is performing a function in many respects similar to that of courts of criminal justice. This surely suggests that the essence, if not the precise content, of the fair procedures required to be provided in other courts should also be respected in the juvenile court. These points warrant further attention; but since the problems of fair procedure in the juvenile courts have been canvassed so frequently in recent years, this limited reference may perhaps be sufficient.[13]

Other difficulties arise from an insufficient conception of the court's role and the court's capabilities. Thus, the

[12] An interesting discussion of related problems may be found in Paulsen, "The Delinquency, Neglect, and Dependency Jurisdiction of the Juvenile Court," in *Justice for the Child* 44 *et seq.* (Rosenheim ed. 1962).

[13] See discussion pp. 16–23 *supra*.

tendency to describe the court only by reference to its therapeutic or rehabilitative potential creates the peril of unrealistic and unrealizable expectations. In more than one American locality friends of the juvenile court, particularly when seeking to recruit larger financial support from the public, have advanced insupportable claims as to the court's capabilities in the control of juvenile delinquency through the processes of treatment and supervision of delinquent children. Such claims are rarely, if ever, made with the conscious purpose to deceive. On the contrary, they are born of enthusiasm and devotion, and they reflect the normal human tendency to confuse wish for reality, aspiration for existing fact. Yet one wonders whether in the long run more cautious and responsible public representations might serve better the juvenile court movement. Disillusionment is the product of disappointed expectations; and the resulting public apathy, or even hostility, to the court may obstruct its achieving those goals experience has shown clearly to be within its competence.

But the more serious problems are those that arise from confusion as to the nature of the court and its capabilities on the part of those directly engaged in the work of the court and those charged with developing a program of care and custody of children brought within the court's jurisdiction. Such confusion militates against sound judgment in determining what the needs of the institution are, assigning priorities, and making proper allocation of limited and often inadequate resources. That the welfare of many delinquent children has been advanced as a result of their contacts with the juvenile court and that more substantial gains in this respect could be made in many localities through more generous governmental support of the

court's program are facts that demand acknowledgment in any appraisal of the court and its work. Nevertheless, if one views the processes of American juvenile justice as a whole, one is compelled to conclude that in a broad spectrum of cases the immediate need and the immediate goal are less the rehabilitation or changing of children for the better and more the altering of conditions and practices that render children worse and more dangerous as a result of their contacts with the official agencies. In few localities have we fully achieved the basic objectives of decency and humanity in dealing with the misbehaving child. The attainment of these objectives, although sometimes obstructed by formidable difficulties, is surely not impossible. One difficulty may be that our larger ambitions may sometimes divert us and prevent us from achieving the more modest goals. Perhaps this phenomenon can be illustrated by a concrete example. Several years ago the legislature of an American state established at considerable expense a diagnostic center for children committed by the juvenile courts of the state. An elaborate facility was erected and manned. The children were subjected to interviews and batteries of tests before being assigned to the state training schools. Inquiry soon revealed, however, that the intensive programs of therapy and treatment recommended for the children by personnel of the diagnostic center were being largely ignored in the training schools, and this for the very good reason that the training schools lacked the facilities and skills essential to carry the recommendations into effect. To my knowledge, the situation has not materially changed in the intervening years. This incident is, of course, by no means unique, and it demonstrates that the ambition to achieve, or appear to achieve, important therapeutic objectives may on occasion distort judgment and a sense of priorities. For in the case described, however valuable the diagnostic center may one day prove to be, it is clear that it was established at the expense of less spectacular measures—measures urgently required to advance the rationality and decency of the system. These measures included such mundane matters as the improvement of the physical environment of the training schools and the enhancement of the quality of institutional programs of academic and vocational instruction.

One other set of problems arising from inaccurate or mistaken conceptions of the court's roles and capabilities should be mentioned. These relate to the nature and extent of the contribution the court may be expected to make to the solution of the larger problems of delinquency prevention and control. Whatever may have been the hopes of early supporters of the juvenile court movement, there must surely be few persons today who fail to recognize that effective confrontation of seriously disturbing adolescent behavior requires much more by way of techniques and resources than the court alone can command or provide. Since, however, the juvenile court presumably has a contribution to make, one of the most pressing modern concerns has come to be that of defining the role of the court in relation to other community agencies and programs aimed at minimizing serious juvenile misconduct. It is no more than just to say that progress in this respect has not been impressive. Indeed, the typical situation, even in communities in which the problems of delinquency are most urgent, is one in which the efforts of the various interested agencies are almost wholly uncoordinated, with the result that the efforts of one agency not only do not gain strength and support from those of other agencies but may sometimes be frustrated and rendered largely ineffectual by the efforts of other agencies. The complexities here are almost infinite; but it must be apparent that sound integration of the court's efforts into community programs of delinquency prevention and control must be preceded by a realistic appraisal of the court's role and its capacity to make effective contributions to a total effort.

Until events provide a basis for more sanguine hopes, however, a healthy skepticism seems appropriate. Although the various functions of the juvenile court are important and are, in fact, indispensable, and even though a significantly large fraction of the nation's adolescent population makes contact each year with the juvenile court,[14] it seems likely that the court's contributions to the eradication of delinquency will be limited and peripheral. Indeed, insofar as the delinquency phenomenon is associated with patterns of life in the subcultures of our large cities, it may be doubted whether fundamental gains can be achieved by any program directed to ends more limited than the radical alteration of the patterns of life that prevail in such areas. If this be true (and no assertions on this subject can confidently be offered), fundamental solutions appear to lie in the direction of integrating our alienated populations into full participation in the social, economic, political, and cultural life of our communities. The difficulties involved hardly need to be itemized, for such measures run afoul

---

[14] "The United States Children's Bureau has estimated that as many as 12 per cent of all American youth—and roughly 20 per cent of all our country's boys—will be referred to juvenile courts on delinquency charges at some time between the ages of ten and seventeen." Shireman, *Foreword* in Rosenheim, *op. cit. supra* note 12, at v.

of the interests, attitudes, and prejudices of the dominant segments of our population. It is precisely at this point that the juvenile court may provide an obstacle to fundamental reform unless great care is taken. For it may be true that the tendency to attribute capabilities to the court that it does not possess represents in some degree a largely unpremeditated effort to evade the necessity of accepting more fundamental and less comfortable alternatives. Surely we shall be confronted by the ultimate irony if the juvenile court, itself the product of a radical and creative movement of reform, should today be permitted to serve as an obstruction to the basic reforms required in mid-twentieth-century America.

I have attempted to suggest and demonstrate that a full and accurate conception of the work of the juvenile court and its potential is of the greatest importance to its proper functioning and to its future development. In suggesting that traditional conceptions of the court are deficient in certain important respects, I have not challenged the importance of the rehabilitative ideal that has played such a vital role in the court's history and development. The court has contributed significantly to the welfare of children and its capacities in this respect have never been fully exploited. Moreover, the court and its allied institutions provide valuable laboratories for acquiring new knowledge and the testing of new rehabilitative techniques. The court, however, is not simply a laboratory or a clinic and the tendency to conceive of it in these terms, largely to the exclusion of the other functions it is called upon to perform, contributes neither to a sound understanding of the institution nor to its proper use in serving the public interest. Self-knowledge is as vital to the proper growth of institutions as it is to the moral and intellectual development of individuals. The perils to sound development are also similar. We need the capacity to distinguish between wish and reality and to determine with reasonable accuracy the limits of our powers and capabilities. Given these capacities, the juvenile court may long extend its useful career and reach levels of achievement not yet attained.

32.   What Is Probation?

LEWIS DIANA

SUMMARY OF HISTORICAL DEVELOPMENT OF PROBATION

Some authorities trace the roots of probation to the middle ages when such devices as the benefit of clergy and the law of sanctuary made it possible either to avoid or at least to postpone punishment.[1] It is more likely that there was not any continuous linear development of probation, although one can point to various forerunners such as the judicial reprieve, by which the court suspended the imposition or execution of a sentence, and the practice of releasing an offender on his own recognizance. Consequently, probation was probably more directly an outgrowth of the different methods in England and America for suspending sentence.

Under the common law the courts of England had for many years bound over petty offenders to sureties or released them on their own recognizance even without sureties.[2] Such practices were also common in some of the American colonies, especially Massa-chusetts, which in 1836 recognized by law the releasing of minor offenders with sureties. In 1869 this same state also authorized the placement, after investigation, of youthful offenders in private homes under the supervision of an agent of the state.

Credit for the first use of the term probation goes to John Augustus, a Boston shoemaker, who apparently became interested in befriending violators of the law, bailed many of them out of jail, and provided them with sympathetic supervision. This was as early as 1841. It was not until 1878, however, that the first probation law was passed, Massachusetts again taking the lead. In that year the mayor of Boston was given the power to appoint probation officers, and only two years later, in 1880, the law was extended to apply to other communities within the state. Then in 1891 Massachusetts passed a second law, which required the extension of probation to the criminal courts. By 1900, though, only five states—Massachusetts, Missouri, Rhode Island, New Jersey, and Vermont—recognized probation legally.[3] By 1933 all states

[1] Halpern, "Probation," *Encyclopedia of Criminology* 388 (Philosophical Library, New York, 1949).

[2] United Nations, Department of Social Affairs, *Probation and Related Measures* 16 (1951).

[3] Barnes and Teeters, *New Horizons in Criminology* 760 (2d ed., Prentice-Hall, New York, 1955).

SOURCE. Lewis Diana, "What Is Probation?", from *Journal of Criminal Law, Criminology and Police Science*, Volume 51, July-August 1960, pp. 189–204, Copyright © 1960, The Williams and Wilkins Company, Baltimore, Maryland.

except Wyoming had juvenile probation laws, and all but thirteen states had adult probation laws. This latter group had been cut to five states by 1950: Mississippi, Nevada, New Mexico, Oklahoma, and South Dakota.[4]

The variety of legislation governing probation in the United States may have stemmed (1) from the Supreme Court's denial in the *Killits* case that there existed any inherent judicial power to suspend sentence or any other process in the administration of the criminal code and (2) from the different points of view which developed concerning the practice of probation. The result, in the United States at any rate, has been to give to the courts a fairly wide discretion in the use of probation.

It remains to be said that with the creation of the Cook County Juvenile Court in 1899, probation as a principle and as a practice received great momentum. Great hopes have since been pinned upon it.

DEFINITIONS OF PROBATION

Probation as a Legal Disposition Only

One point of view sees probation simply as a suspension of sentence by the court. Since sentence is not imposed, the offender remains in the community until the length of the sentence has expired, unless, of course, in the meantime he has engaged in any conduct that would warrant carrying out the sentence. This system leaves everything to the probationer and makes of probation a simple policing procedure. Therefore, it implies two things to the probationer: another chance, and the threat of punishment should he fail to improve his behavior.

In point of time this view has been expressed by authors, mostly with a legal background, writing in the first

decade of the twentieth century. I have found no references to it after 1908 when Judge McKenzie Cleland put it this way: probation is a plan "of suspending over offenders the maximum sentence permitted by law" and of allowing them "to determine by their subsequent conduct whether they should lose or retain their liberty . . . with the full knowledge that further delinquency meant . . . severe punishment."[5]

Probation as a Measure of Leniency

In a review of the literature I found but one author who took this approach to probation.[6] However, it probably best represents the general lay point of view, as well as that of most probationers. This fact presents a basic problem to professional personnel, who view probation as a form of treatment. Many offenders, however, especially among juveniles, feel their acts are unfortunate slips, and while possibly inexplicable, they are, in the final analysis, choices between right and wrong, choices which the offenders feel capable of controlling. Consequently, in their own minds they are not sick persons or necessarily even the products of undesirable environments and so certainly in no need of treatment.

Probation as a Punitive Measure

This again represents a view which has found little acceptance in the literature, especially during the last fifty years. I discovered only one writer who made punishment the *dominant* note in his theory of probation. According to Almy, probation must be presented to the probationer as a form of punishment, one which permits him to escape

---

[4] *Ibid.*

[5] Cleland, "New Gospel in Criminology; Municipal Court of Chicago," 31 *McClure's* 358–362 (June 1908).

[6] Smith, A. C., "Does Probation Aid or Prevent Crime?," 125 *Annals* 242 (1926).

commitment and its stigma but one which also makes other demands. If these demands are not met, then the probationer can expect to receive the same type of punishment as other offenders.[7] The assumption underlying such a view is that it is the certainty of punishment which deters.

Probation as an Administrative Process

It is likely that the earlier ideas of reform and rehabilitation attached to probation came about as a reaction to the various abuses associated with the imprisonment of children. As a result, a great deal of sentiment was tied to the concept of probation in its beginnings. This sentiment, together with the goal of reform or rehabilitation, formed the nucleus of the conception of probation as an administrative process. Essentially what probation consists of under this conception is the execution of concrete measures aimed at helping the offender stay out of further trouble. The ultimate goal of complete rehabilitation in this approach, however, was something which was more hoped for than worked for. In this respect it is a fairly negative approach consisting mainly of things done for the offender in the *hope* that they will *somehow* deter him from a further career in crime. Thus, arranging for medical treatment, making appointments for the administration of tests, effecting school transfers, seeking employment for the offender, checking on his activities, and so on constitute the major content of probation under this viewpoint.

Slightly more than thirty per cent of the authors writing in this field have seen the administrative process as the major framework of probation.[8] Most of these, however, date from 1902 to 1920. Since 1935, only two writers have espoused this concept. This fact may indicate the close identification of the correctional field with social work, which was largely administrative in the earlier years. Later, changing concepts and techniques in social work quickly found their way into child welfare and juvenile court probation services. The newer approaches represented by casework and its psychoanalytic foundations have not found unanimous approval, however.

Thus, Dr. Philipp Parsons of the Department of Sociology, University of Oregon, has stated:

> In the rehabilitation field . . . research and administration become the all important factors. Research consists in getting the facts of a given situation, and administration consists in devising programs adapted to the facts and in carrying out these programs by whatever techniques the conditions may make practical. . . .
>
> . . . changing conditions, economic, political, and social, have shifted the major emphasis in remedial work from individuals and families to groups and conditions. Training for remedial work, therefore, must be built upon a base of research, organization, and administration rather than upon the case work which was the foundation of social work training in the past generation.
>
> . . . rehabilitating convicted persons in connection with a scientific system of penology . . . is primarily an administrative job and also primarily a job for men.[9]

The process of probation which follows an administrative pattern is illustrated in an article by Jessie Keys. Writing in *World's Work* in 1909, Miss Keys stated that the search for ultimate causes is not the least important work

---

[7] Almy, "Probation as Punishment," 24 *Survey* 657 (1910).

[8] All of the available literature since 1900 has been reviewed.

[9] Parsons, P. A., "Qualifying Workers for the Correctional Field," *Yearbook, Nat'l Probation and Parole Ass'n* 66–86 (1938).

of the juvenile court. These causes were usually felt to be parental neglect or parental vice or both. To illustrate she cited the case of a boy who had a mania for stealing pocket knives:

His father and paternal grandfather had been master mechanics. After his father died his mother led an irregular life and neglected the boy. His hereditary instincts came to the surface. Since his mother refused to help him gratify his desire for mechanics, he undertook to gratify it in any way he could.[10]

Unlike modern casework, no attempt was made during the boy's probation to help him "verbalize" and express his feelings and so come to a personal solution based on the untapped resources of his deeper personality. Instead: "We went to his mother and she awoke to her responsibility. We talked to the boy firmly and found him willing to work. Finally, we found a position for him."[11]

The probation process not only included finding work for the boy but also included telling the mother how to keep her house clean and giving her other directives. It literally forced the boy into a certain mold, by the use of pressure, and sometimes intimidation, to do what he was told was right. Thus the probation officer attempted to produce what was not ordinarily a part of the boy's pattern of behavior.

In 1910 Maude E. Miner, Secretary of the New York Probation Association, reported that probation for the convicted girl consisted of a process of character building through discipline and correction. These were applied by obtaining employment for the girl, visiting her home, getting the cooperation of her parents, providing needed medical care, and bringing her into contact with beneficial influences such as churches and clubs.[12]

In 1911 the Illinois law on adult probation provided that certain categories of first offenders could be placed on probation. The court was obliged to impose certain conditions designed both to protect the community and to give the probationers some "sensible practical aid." These conditions included paying court costs, supplying bond, supporting dependents, and making regular reports to the probation officer.[13] Obviously, under such circumstances probation could be little else than administrative.

From a figure well known in corrections, C. L. Chute:

The probation officer must investigate all offenders and must keep himself informed concerning their conduct and condition. He must report on each case at least once every month to the court and must use all suitable methods not inconsistent with the conditions imposed by the court, to aid persons on probation and to bring about improvement in their conduct and condition.[14]

Or:

The probation officer helps a man to get and keep a job, finds him wholesome amusement, looks after his leisure hours and generally backs him up to playing a man's part in the world much as the special war agencies kept up the morale of the army.[15]

The supposed therapeutic effects of administrative techniques are illustrated in an article by Platt:

[10] Keys, "Cases of the Children's Court," 18 *World's Work* 11612 (1909).
[11] *Ibid.*

[12] Miner, "Probation Work for Women," 36 *Annals* 27 (1910).
[13] "New Illinois Law on Adult Probation," 26 *Survey* 18 (1911).
[14] Chute, "Probation a Federal Need," 43 *Survey* 775 (1920).
[15] "Emptying the Jails: Probation System in New York City," 100 *The Independent* 40 (1919).

Get a boy into a good club, give him duties and see what happens—interest, pride, loyalty, ambition, cooperation, social teamwork, social sense, all will probably soon follow.[16]

In 1919 no less an authority than the sub-committee of the National Conference of Social Work summed up this point of view by reporting that the office of the probation officer is administrative. It may have its authority beyond the court but accountability to the court is, in the final analysis, the foundation of probation service.[17]

Probation as Social Casework Treatment

Reinemann has defined probation as follows:

Legally, in the case of an adult offender, probation is the suspension of sentence during a period of freedom, on condition of good behavior. In the case of a delinquent child, the juvenile court uses probation as a form of *case disposition* which allows the child to live at liberty in his own home or in the custody of a suitable person, be it a relative, a friend of the family, or a foster home, under supervision of an agent of the court and upon such conditions as the court determines. *Socially, probation is a form of treatment* administered by probation officers on a case work basis."[18] (Emphasis added.)

The dichotomy between adult and juvenile probation seemingly is disappearing. In any event definitions of probation as a legal disposition are rarely found in current literature. On the contrary, the bulk of the literature —between eighty-five and ninety per cent of it since 1940—views probation

as some form of treatment, more often than not as casework treatment.

Casework and its foster parent, psychiatry, have had extensive influence in the juvenile court movement. This influence is illustrated by the broad scope of many of our juvenile court laws, by the shunting aside, in the rising tide of a clinical ideology, of legal precedents in favor of loose and informal procedures, by the indeterminate sentence, by the emphasis on the total situation of an offender, by the absorption with emotional problems, and by the prevailing adherence to a psychoanalytic theory of causation.

The point of view which identifies probation with casework treatment is difficult to analyze. It cannot be presented as a consistent or well-defined approach and appears, rather, to represent an attitude or state of mind in lieu of a technique or substantive theory. In any event the literature presenting probation as casework treatment generally defines probation as the *application* of casework principles and techniques in dealing with the offender. But what is casework?

Taber describes it this way:

Case work . . . may be defined as a process of attempting to understand the needs, impulses and actions of an individual and of helping him to recognize these in a way that is satisfying to himself and yet in accord with the demands of social living.

. . . treatment cannot be forced upon another person . . . . To help another person we must accept him as he is with an honest respect for his capacity as well as regard for his need to solve his own problem with whatever help the worker can give him. The case worker is concerned with assisting the individual to realize his own capacities to the fullest extent, as well as to orient him to the resources existing within his environment which will provide a satisfying outlet. In short, change

---

[16] Platt, "Does Punishment Pay?," 55 *Survey* 605–607 (1926).

[17] Parsons, H. C., "Probation and Parole; Report of the Sub-Committee," *Nat'l Conference of Social Work* 113 (1919).

[18] Reinemann, "Probation and the Juvenile Delinquent," 261 *Annals* 109 (1949).

to be effective depends upon the individual's willingness to help himself. . . . He must be assisted in finding his own way at his own pace. . . .

Every phase of behavior has a different meaning for each individual, and treatment if it is to be effective must be differentiated according to the individual's need. . . . There are no formulas which we can readily apply . . . but we can sharply define in a warm but objective manner the alternatives which confront a delinquent in order that he may redirect his behavior if he has the strength and will to do so.[19]

Most concepts of casework also include assumptions concerning the nature and causes of delinquent behavior:

Delinquent behavior and other forms of conflict are generally compensating substitutes for experiences and impulses which the individual fears to recognize and dares not express. The tension resulting creates frustration and fear. Whether or not the release takes the form of a criminal act is purely fortuitous and is dependent upon the attitudes and tensions operating at the time. . . .

If we accept the fact that the probation officer's work concerns itself with helping the man under supervision to bring to conscious expression his underlying emotional conflicts and thus rid those deep-seated unknown drives of their tension and potency, and if we recognize that the probationer's moral decisions must be his own, not the probation officer's, then is the generic problem of interpretation with which the probation officer is faced any different from that which must be met by the case worker?[20]

Miss Genevieve Gabower, formerly Director of Social Work in the Juvenile Court, Washington, D. C., refers to casework in this way:

The worker sees a need for giving service in the case of a child where either the solicitude or the indifference of the parents, or a combination of extremes of the two operates as a barrier to his growth and development. He can be of service by developing and maintaining a relationship of continuing interest and acceptance and thus assisting in establishing stability. Case work . . . through this kind of relationship . . . may operate as a medium through which the youth can find that he has ability to conform to community standards.[21]

In other words, from Miss Gabower's point of view, the relationship which by some is described *as* casework is here presented only as an instrument of casework. But what casework is, is still not explained.

One thing is certain, however: the casework point of view represents a shift in emphasis from the social conditions of behavior to individual behavior itself, especially such behavior as can be approached from the standpoint of the "dynamics" of psychoanalytic mechanisms. The shift has been from a social to a clinical frame of reference. Crime and delinquency are acts containing social implications, but it is chiefly the individual personality which interests the caseworker. Thus, Miss Louise McGuire, also one-time Director of Social Work in the Juvenile Court, Washington, D. C., states: "Back of the overt acts are the motives. These latter are our concern and the basis of case work treatment."[22]

Miss McGuire's article represents an attempt to delineate casework into three phases: (1) social inquiry into the total situation of the client; (2)

---

[19] Taber, "The Value of Casework to the Probationer," *Yearbook, Nat'l Probation and Parole Ass'n* 167–179 (1940).

[20] Reeves, "Administrative Procedures and Case Work Services," *Yearbook, Nat'l Probation and Parole Ass'n* 180–192 (1940).

[21] Gabower, "Motivating the Delinquent to Accept Treatment," *Yearbook, Nat'l Probation and Parole Ass'n* 207–219 (1940).

[22] McGuire, "Essentials of Case Work with Delinquents," *Yearbook, Nat'l Probation and Parole Ass'n* (1935).

social diagnosis, that is, inquiry into the relationships and attitudes of the client; and (3) social casework treatment. In this last phase there are three objectives: (1) to induce right notions of conduct (responsible behavior) in the client; (2) to induce motives which will assure loyalty to good norms of conduct; and (3) to develop the client's latent abilities.

To achieve these objectives casework treatment is divided into two sections: mechanistic devices and deep therapy. The former consist in the utilization of the resources of community agencies. The latter, deep therapy, refers to the process of changing the attitudes of the probationer, giving him insight through interpretation.[23]

This essentially clinical approach is supported by most other writers outside the academic disciplines of criminology and sociology. Hagerty, for example, has said, "We offer as our major premise that solution of the crime problem involves chiefly the study and personality treatment of the individual offender."[24] He goes on to define casework as an aid in the restoration of self-support and self-respect in the "client."

More recently Hyman S. Lippman, Director of the Amherst H. Wilder Child Guidance Clinic, St. Paul, Minnesota, has declared that casework on the part of the probation officer is the essential ingredient in his "treatment" of delinquency.[25] While not defining casework, Lippman does specify *relationship* as the major contribution of a probation officer and the interview as his main tool. The unconscious conflicts

of the neurotic delinquent of course, "are deeply imbedded, and can *only* be brought to light by the psychiatrist trained in psychoanalytic techniques."[26] (Emphasis added.)

David Crystal, Executive Director, Jewish Social Service Bureau Rochester, N. Y., sees probation as a treatment process of the entire family. But the process is curiously enough still described in clinical terms as the focus of casework is:

1. How does the probation officer help the probationer accept the conditions of his current reality?
2. How does and can the family relate to the probationer in terms of the new experience?

(*a*) Can they express honestly their feelings of guilt, of anticipated reprisal, of uncertainty about the impact this will have on their future lives?

(*b*) Will they require special help from a worker other than the probation officer, in a different kind of agency in the community? Can they now or later accept the need for help?

(*c*) Is the total responsibility for change to be lodged exclusively on the offender, or can the family see change as a reaction not to one but multiple causes and that they too are part of the change, externally and internally, by their physical presence and concrete offering of shelter and food and job and by the attitude with which these visible and tangible things about the family are given?[27]

Henry J. Palmieri, Director of Social Services of the Juvenile Court of the District of Columbia, declares probation is a casework service and a method of treatment which "is no longer an ideal" but "a reality."[28] However, he defines neither casework nor treatment but assumes their identity with probation.

[23] *Ibid.*
[24] Hagerty, "The Delinquent as a Case Problem," *Yearbook, Nat'l Probation and Parole Ass'n* (1935).
[25] Lippman, "The Role of the Probation Officer in the Treatment of Delinquency in Children," 12 *Federal Probation* 36 (1948).

[26] *Id.* at 37.
[27] Crystal, "Family Casework in Probation," 13 *Federal Probation* 47–53 (1949).
[28] Palmieri, "Probation Is Treatment," 13 *Federal Probation* 20 (1949).

Glover outlines four basic principles of treatment without, however, specifying how they are effected: (1) treatment based on consent of the offender; (2) treatment planned for the individual; (3) treatment planned around the offender's own situation; and (4) treatment planned to redirect the offender's emotions.[29]

The strong clinical orientation of casework seeking to induce proper motives, to aid in the achievement of insight and self-respect, and to change attitudes of the offender may be worthwhile and desirable. But the aims and the orientation do not define the process of casework. *How* is insight produced? *How* are interpretations given? *How* are attitudes changed? *How* is relationship established? The answers to these questions are rarely mentioned in the literature, and casework continues to be defined in broad and general terms as, for example, "an art in which knowledge of the science of human relations and skill in relationship are used to mobilize capacities in the individual and resources in the community appropriate for better adjustment between the client and all or any part of his total environment."[30]

One of the most recent and well-known texts defines casework as follows: "Social casework is a process used by certain human welfare agencies to help individuals to cope more effectively with their problems in social functioning."[31]

The elements, then, which are said to comprise the principles of casework invariably stamp it as a clinical process for the most part. It is often stated, for example, that casework implies that the probation officer has a respect for individual differences and that he should have not only a natural desire to serve others but also an understanding of the processes that develop personalities. The probation officer *accepts* and the client then may show "movement" because for the first time he is seen able to talk freely and naturally to another person about himself and how he feels. The worker understands and conveys that understanding to the "client," thereby relieving the "client's" anxieties and stimulating a more constructive outlook.

Biestek explains a casework relationship on the basis of seven needs of the client. "The caseworker is *sensitive* to, *understands,* and appropriately *responds* to these needs" and "the client is somehow *aware* of the caseworker's sensitivity, understanding, and response."[32] The seven needs of the client embody corresponding principles:[33]

The need of the client	The name of the principle
1. To be treated as an individual.	1. Individualization.
2. To express feelings.	2. Purposeful expression of feelings.
3. To get sympathetic response to problems.	3. Controlled emotional involvement.
4. To be recognized as a person of worth.	4. Acceptance.
5. Not to be judged.	5. Nonjudgmental attitude.
6. To make his own choices and decisions.	6. Client self-determination.
7. To keep secrets about self.	7. Confidentiality.

[29] Glover, "Probation: The Art of Introducing the Probationer to a Better Way of Life," 15 *Federal Probation* 8 (1951).

[30] Bowers, "The Nature and Definition of Social Casework: Part III," 30 *J. Soc. Casework* 417 (1949).

[31] Perlman, *Social Casework, A Problem-Solving Process* (Chicago, University of Chicago Press, 1957).

[32] Biestek, *The Casework Relationship* 17 (Chicago, Loyola University Press, 1957).

[33] Reproduced from Biestek, *op. cit. supra* note 32, at 17.

Casework thus attempts to formalize, standardize, and professionalize the display and exercise of warmth, sympathy, respect, and understanding, all of which are considered to be basic elements in therapeutic treatment of the individual. In probation, also, any punitive quality in the process has been removed, and the goal has become not merely the elimination of the probationer's anti-social conduct but, whenever possible, the improvement of his personality and the achievement of a more nearly perfect total adjustment. What probation is, therefore, must include the means by which those goals are realized. This casework usually does by simply stating casework *as* the means or process. There have been attempts at clarification, but the field defies synthesis.

Miss Witmer has pointed out that:

. . . social work is a very specific system of organized activities based on a body of values and technical rules which are becoming increasingly well-formulated. . . . it has a definite function to perform. It is not a vague, indeterminate method of doing good or promoting welfare, or even of helping people out of trouble, indistinguishable from psychiatry at one end and uplift work at the other. . . .

. . . social case work centers around helping individuals with the difficulties they encounter in a particular group relationship. . . .[34]

Miss Witmer also suggests that while probation presently involves the use of casework, it is mainly executive and diagnostic, centering on changes in the environment of the offender. Such casework "lacks the sharpness of focus and precision of method which perception of specific function has given to case work in other fields."[35] But in my ex-

perience, at least, this "sharpness of focus and precision of method" of casework in other fields is more an attribute of casework in the literature than of casework in the field. What is specific and precise in any other agency is not mentioned. It appears that it is the field or area of operation of these other agencies that is more or less precise and not necessarily their techniques.

Miss Witmer denies the similarity of casework and psychiatry or therapy but nevertheless states its aims in therapeutic terms: "Modern case work works with the client rather than on his behalf" since the sources of difficulty are supposedly known only to the "client."[36] However, the caseworker assumes the existence of underlying or unconscious conflicts and so is practically committed to a psychotherapeutic point of view. Where this is denied, superficial distinctions are usually drawn between casework and therapy, such as the fact that in therapy it is the "client" himself who seeks the therapist, or that in therapy one delves more deeply into the unconscious and there is a more intense emotional involvement of "client" and therapist. There is convincing evidence, however, that points to the emergence of casework, and certainly of psychiatric social work, as another therapeutic profession.

The dominant theoretical note in casework is sounded by psychoanalysis. Acceptance of a psychoanalytic view will, of course, influence notions of what makes a criminal a criminal or a delinquent a delinquent. The major assumptions fall back on the emotional problems of the individual offender; consequently, illegal behavior is seen primarily as a symptom of an emotional illness, and the offense itself is not considered to be very important, especially in delinquency. Parallel with this as-

[34] Witmer, "Social Case Work in the Field of Juvenile Probation," *Yearbook, Nat'l Probation and Parole Ass'n* 153–166 (1941).
[35] *Ibid.*
[36] *Ibid.*

sumption, which is accepted by many caseworkers as a sound and accurate summary of the facts, is the habit of looking for emotional problems in all cases before the court. This ignores the real possibility that many of the problems of offenders arise from the hazards common to all people in learning to live with themselves and others. Also, to most people, appearing before a court of law is a new experience. When a person has not had time to cope with such a new situation, it is conceivable that he may present the appearance of maladjustment. In any event, life is such that most, if not all, people have emotional and other problems, and whether or not they are offenders, they generally adjust without services based on any nebulous clinical ideology.

Casework must be numbered among the victims of much of the epidemic dogma and naïveté that is psychoanalysis. Too many correctional workers have become dizzy on a diluted psychoanalytic approach. They allow its glib and fanciful formulations to explain difficult problems. It is all neatly done, since little thought and no proof are necessary. Ready-made proof exists: whatever the problem, it is the result of emotional conflicts originating in the oral, anal, phallic, and other erotic stages of development, and the dynamic interplay of id, ego, and superego. The criminal and the delinquent, too, as each and all of us, end up as the appendage to the penis. It is the tail that twirls the tiger.

As matters now stand the probation officer or caseworker grounded in a psychoanalytic approach tends to look at a case through the lenses of his "trained" preconceptions of the client's emotional life. He is likely, therefore, to ignore the group processes from which that emotional life is nourished. Obeisance and abject devotion to the illusory and presumptuous claim of psychoanalytic theory to absolute knowledge of the dynamics of human behavior may lead to a great deal of dialectical ingenuity but not to much progress in the treatment of the problem of crime and delinquency.

In conclusion, probation as casework concentrates not so much on crime and delinquency as on criminals and delinquents, and not so much on criminals and delinquents as on criminals and delinquents with emotional problems. In general, as Sutherland has pointed out,[37] casework in probation follows psychiatric conceptions in that insight by the probationer into the reasons for his behavior is the chief goal of treatment. A person with such insight is felt to be unlikely to repeat his delinquent activities. The primary method consists of intensive interviews through which the probation officer not only comes to understand the probationer but the probationer, to understand himself. An identification with the probation officer then helps the offender emulate his behavior until finally the point is reached where the probationer becomes independent of this identification and can carry on normal and socially acceptable behavior on his own.

Probation as a Combination of Casework and Administration

This point of view regarding probation does not, as it might suggest, constitute a catch-all for those approaches which do not fit the categories discussed thus far. From this standpoint probation is represented both by casework functions and by administrative or executive procedures. Where casework is paramount, administrative functions are supplementary. Where administrative duties are indicated as the primary plan of approach, casework skills and tech-

[37] Sutherland, *Principles of Criminology*, 399–400 (Philadelphia, J. B. Lippincott Co., 4th ed., 1947).

niques, however defined, must be utilized in the performance of those duties. In other words, some cases may be felt to require intensive interviews more than anything else. But in the course of most cases there are, practically without exception, other things to be done as well: arranging a transfer of schools, scheduling medical and other appointments, and so on. Other cases may be felt to call for mainly administrative functions, such as those just mentioned, plus limited and superficial contacts with the probationers. But in performing those functions and in making those contacts, a casework approach must be applied. In this respect the utilization of casework techniques is usually manifested in the attitude taken toward the probationer.

Murphy illustrates this school of thought:

Probation officers have another task, that of controlling, guiding and rehabilitating probationers. Here they are called upon to make accurate personality diagnoses and plan comprehensively to improve the probationers' environment and economic life, to adjust delicate family problems, find employment, provide for necessary medical treatment and health assistance, determine recreational needs and social needs, stimulate spiritual and moral improvement. . . . Patterns of behavior can be changed only when attitudes, loyalties and group relationships can be altered or recreated.[38]

In summary, then, this point of view sees probation as the simultaneous application of casework and administrative functions, but in specific cases it is more one than the other. Whichever is paramount in any particular case, the other is complementary. About twenty per cent of the literature reviewed supports this approach to probation.

[38] Murphy, "Training For and On the Job," *Yearbook, Nat'l Probation and Parole Ass'n* 93–108 (1938).

WHAT IS PROBATION?

With the exception of the first three categories (legal, punitive, merciful), all views emphasize the treatment aspects of probation. In the literature reviewed only five per cent of the writers thought of probation wholly as a legal disposition or as a measure of either punishment or leniency. In fact, in the literature of the past thirty years such views receive no mention at all. Therefore, notions of probation as either casework or administration, or a combination of the two, are prominent. These leading approaches overlap considerably so that their differentiation consists almost solely in their respective points of emphasis. Thus, all three would agree that probation is a legal disposition and that probation is not to be thought of as mere leniency or as mere punishment; but in the first instance, it is viewed as basically casework treatment; in the second, administrative supervision; and in the third, both of these. Each, however, contains elements of the other. So in all cases probation is seen as a social as well as a legal process, as a method of supervision and guidance in which all available community resources are used, and as a process which should aim at the total adjustment of the offender. The casework approach overshadows the rest by far, so that in phrasing a composite definition derived from the literature it should receive its obvious prominence.

As culled from the professional literature, then, probation may be thought of as the application of modern, scientific casework to specially selected offenders[39] who are placed by the courts

[39] It is standard practice to accept for probation only those offenders whose cases have been investigated and found to meet the requirements of favorable prognosis set up by the individual courts. Therefore, offenders placed on probation may be thought of as specially selected.

under the personal supervision of a probation officer, sometimes under conditional suspension of punishment, and given treatment aimed at their complete and permanent social rehabilitation.

Probation in Reality

What is depicted in the literature does not often represent a very real or accurate representation of what exists in reality. The result of abject worship at the holy shrine of psychoanalysis has not been the development of scientifically validated techniques for the treatment of offenders on probation.[40] In fact, few probation officers, either in the literature or in the field, give a clear and specific description of what they mean by treatment, casework or otherwise. Probation officers, whether trained in schools of social work or not, frequently express the opinion that just about anything that is done in the way of investigation of cases, bringing into play any of the skills one may have acquired in training or by his experiences, comes under the heading of casework treatment. This would include any service, advice, counseling, or surveillance.

Undoubtedly part of the difficulty lies in the fact that the field of social work seems to have no well-defined and consistent theory which it can call its own. Casework can mean anything from "working with an offender" to helping a "client" to "grow" or to achieve insight, helping him to help himself, a form of therapy, or a "method which recognizes the individual's inner capacity as to the key to his adjustment, and the necessity of his participating in the process of rehabilitation."[41]

How these things are accomplished, however, is rarely specified except in

terms of an *administrative* process. So the probation officer will be told, ideally, that he must have a plan of treatment, that his attitude toward the offender must be non-punitive, and that he will try to "win the confidence" of the probationer and overcome the resistance of parents, or of husband or wife, as the case may be. The constructive kind of relationship that the probation officer thus aims for apparently is to be gained through frequent and periodic contacts at the office of the probation officer or at the offender's home or even school, in the case of a juvenile. In addition, the probation officer will be acquainted with most, if not all, of the resources of the community and will hold frequent conferences with the offender's employer, school principal, teacher, or school social worker and refer the offender to any one of a number of other agencies which might help him on his road to readjustment.

It is interesting, then, to compare such a description of probation as casework treatment with what probation officers actually do. At the Juvenile Court of Allegheny County in Pittsburgh, Pennsylvania, it was found that more than half the probation officers did active work with only thirty to forty per cent of their caseload. Even if telephone conversations and correspondence with an offender, members of his family, and others are counted as contacts, sixty-four per cent of the staff had fewer than six contacts with a child over a period of one year.[42] As a matter of fact more than half the probation officers considered that the most important part of their work consisted of their contacts with a child and others during the investigation period prior to the hearing.

[40] See Cressey," The Nature and Effectiveness of Correctional Techniques, 23 *Law & Contemp. Prob.* 754-771 (1958).

[41] Taber, *op. cit. supra* note 19.

[42] All the figures and information in this section were obtained from the Juvenile Court, Pittsburgh, Pa., in 1951, when the author was a probation officer of the court.

Half of the probation officers reported they did no planning on *any* of their cases, one-fourth indicated that they approached from five to ten per cent of their caseload with a plan in mind, and the remaining fourth said this was true in forty to fifty per cent of their cases. Thirty-five per cent of the probation staff felt that many of the children under their supervision at any one time could probably get along *without any* probation service at all, and ninety-five per cent felt that some of the children under their supervision could adjust without it.

Analysis of a sample of 540 probation records for this court (up to 1951) showed that the total number of personal contacts with each probationer averaged less than five in an average probation period of sixteen and one-half months. In other words, each probationer generally got to see his probation officer about once every three months. Only six per cent received more than five visits at home during the probation period, and nearly eighty-four per cent received only *one* home visit. Similarly, seventy-eight per cent of the probationers had but one interview in the probation office during the average probation period of sixteen and one-half months. Yet the number of delinquents on probation who later became criminals was less among those who had the *fewest* contacts with their probation officers. Since the majority of the delinquents received a minimum of attention while they were on probation and yet did not later become criminals (as of ten years later), this apparent adjustment must be attributed to factors other than treatment received on probation.

Supervision in seventy-six percent of the cases consisted *entirely* of routine reporting, and only ten per cent of the cases were handled with a definite plan of treatment. How it could be other-

wise would be difficult to conceive after a glance at the duties of the probation officers of this court (Table 1).

The duties outlined in Table 1 take, on an average, from three and one-half to four and one-half days of a five-day week. The time remaining *may* then be devoted to supervising offenders placed on probation, i.e., checking on their activities either by conducting personal interviews or by having the probationer and his parents fill out forms sent by mail; getting progress reports from school or place of employment or institution; and helping the offender get employment, club membership, and so on.

To what extent such a system as this applies to other courts I cannot say, except for the dozen or so with which I am personally familiar and among which, for the most part, a similar situation exists. As late as 1957 members of the staff of the juvenile court in Pittsburgh, Pennsylvania, informed me that the situation at that time remained the same as presented here. The Family Court of the State of Delaware is one exception. The counselors of that court prepare no pre-hearing or pre-sentence reports as such, nor do they usually appear in court at the initial hearing. On the contrary, the judges refer cases which they continue for ninety days to members of the probation staff for counseling. The results of the counseling then help the judges make a final disposition at the end of the ninety-day period.

However, even with such a procedure the offender who is referred to the staff receives, on the average, one-half hour per week of counseling, or a total of six hours for the ninety-day period.

Returning to the juvenile court in Pittsburgh, Pennsylvania, it is significant that only fourteen per cent of probationers in the sample studied received what their probation officers called

Table 1

Duties		Details
Pre-hearing investigations.	Average five per week, consuming about two-thirds of probation officer's time.	Get statements from: complainants, offender, offender's mother and father, and any other interested party. Compile personal history of offender. Describe offender's environment—home visit. Get reports from school, other agencies active, past or present, with offender or family. Arrange for physical examination of offender.
Prepare report for judge.		Dictation.
Conference with supervisor.		Diagnose behavior and personality of offender. Plan of treatment, if any.
Prepare case summaries for psychologist, psychiatrist, other agencies, institutions. Arrange institutional, foster home placement.	Involves about 20% of cases.	Correspondence. Phone calls.
Make appointments for testing, clothing issue, medical care, etc. Release assigned cases from detention home.		
Presentation of cases in court.	One day per week set aside for this.	Notify by letter all persons to appear; file petitions; prepare old cases continued and those reappearing on new charges.

casework treatment. A comparison of the results of their work with those of the officers not qualified for casework showed no difference in the recidivism rates of their charges. It is also interesting to note that in the two courts with which I have been associated the probationers who were referred to psychiatrists for treatment had the highest recidivism rate of all!

It is fairly certain that most probation, however it may be conceived in the literature or in the field, still amounts to little more than administrative supervision. But in order to compare the views of the professional personnel represented in the literature with the views of those whose work actually determines what is probation, I asked twenty of the most experienced probation officers from eight courts, including officers both trained and not trained in schools of social work, to write me their answers to the following questions:

1. How would you define probation? Generally speaking, of what does it consist in practice?

2. Is casework an essential part of probation? If so, how would you define casework?

3. What are the aims of probation?

4. What do you believe probation *should* be ideally?

The following are the verbatim replies to question (1) which I received:

1. Probation is a kind of status the child obtains as a result of the court hearing.

2. Probation is a suspended sentence to begin with, as a basis for providing

supervision. In practice it is a continuation of a suspended case, to see if the child does all right. There is no intention of doing anything, though most probation officers won't admit it. Probation is putting a threat over the head of a child. Authority puts weight back of probation. You can see this with our success with neglected and delinquent cases which other agencies have given up. We're the policemen back of the agencies.

3. What it simmers down to is police work. There is no planning, but giving supervision to prevent violations or repetition of delinquent behavior.

4. Probation is an instrument of the court. The child is under the jurisdiction of the court. There are certain areas in which he is expected to function in a certain way. This consists of periodic reports made by the youngster or his family to the probation officer, or the probation officer's contacts with the family and the child, or any collateral contacts, the purpose of the contacts being to determine the child's ability to adjust in the community and to offer additional assistance in a supportive way to help the child adjust.

5. Probation is to help instill in a boy enough confidence in himself to make an adjustment in society, with the knowledge that he can always call on the probation officer for information and advice when needed.

6. Probation consists of the contacts which a probation officer has with a boy after the court hearing. It is also supervision to see how the boy adjusts in the home and the community. Through probation we try to select what boys have to abide by and to explain to them the negative and the positive sides of a situation, explaining limitations and the need to face them.

7. Probation means that the court feels that whatever a child has done he can adjust at home under the supervision of his parents. We look the parents and the home over and decide whether they can handle the supervision. The probation officer merely gives support to that supervision, like a doctor who prescribes. He isn't going to go to your home and make

you take the medicine, but if he feels the patient needs to go to the hospital, he goes.

8. Probation is comparable to commitment; that is, it is handled through a court order. But it is not leniency. Probation can be as severe as commitment. Probation is not only law but also a mutual relationship in which we are trying to get children to accept limits.

9. Probation is a period of time during which a child is expected to realize he has made a mistake and that he must be careful to avoid repetition while he is on probation. This realization may or may not be with the help of the probation officer.

10. Probation is using the material brought out by investigation, the causes as well as the effects of antisocial or asocial behavior on the part of delinquents brought to the court. It is taking that and trying to determine from it the particular mores or standards that have been operating in the growing period of the delinquent and trying to arrive at standards or mores which will fit that child and his family and be satisfactory to society, and using all these in a plan thought best in terms of adjustment.

Probation is not something which comes after the court hearing. When a child becomes known to us, he is thought of as being on probation. There is no reason to wait for the hearing. We try to work with a child as soon as we get him. Finally, probation can only be successful if the basic family make-up is considered. What caused a child to be delinquent must be changed.

11. Primarily we are a court of rehabilitation when it comes to the delinquent. When we put a child on probation we are saying to him, "You have run afoul of the rules of society and this is the court's offer to you to try to prove you can live in society without continuing that type of behavior. It is not only probation on the part of the child but also on the part of the parents, because adult behavior often lies behind a child's behavior. The child has to show he no longer needs supervision other than his own family.

12. Probation has a Latin derivation and means the act or process of giving a chance or trial. It is comparable to repairing damage done to an automobile. You repair it and give it another trial rather than let it run in its poor condition.

13. Probation is the period after a child has been brought to the court's attention as a result of a behavior problem. During this period there is an opportunity to see whether, with the help of the worker, his attitudes and activities can be reorganized so that he can make a better adjustment and conduct himself in a more acceptable manner.

It is a two-way thing. It is not just a period. The child must have someone interested in him, to guide him. Interviews with him may be of a general nature or be related to his specific behavior.

14. Probation is working with a child and his family on the problems presented at the court hearing. For the worker it is almost the role of confidant and adviser.

15. Probation is a helping service to a person with a problem. The problem itself may be adjusted or the person is helped to make an adjustment to the problem. Probation is also a means of keeping in touch with a person in order to prevent further difficulty.

16. Probation has its legal aspects. But it is also helping a child adjust to society and its requirements, which is the chief aim of probation. It should be a constructive experience.

17. Probation is helping a child fit into the school, home and community, fitting him into their standards.

18. In practice probation consists in meeting emergencies as they arise instead of routine treatment, which time doesn't allow.

19. When a child comes to the court and a problem is presented, you are not putting him on probation for punishment but to find causes and remedies. Probation means not only working with a child but also considering all the surrounding factors.

20. Probation is helping the individual to adjust. You utilize your own skills and the community resources within the scope and functions of the agency.

Only one of the above statements mentions the idea that punishment is even an aspect of probation, and the concept of leniency is omitted by all twenty probation officers, though it is implied by some. Four offer a partly legal definition, while none specifically presents the view that probation is essentially either an administrative process or a combination of administrative and casework. Partly this may be attributed to the fact that most personnel in the field probably do not express themselves in the same way as do professional authors who are not primarily workers but administrators and teachers. In this respect perhaps the most significant thing of all is the fact that, although certain cliches appear, *in not one definition is casework itself mentioned.* Yet in reply to the second question, "Is casework an essential part of probation?", fourteen probation officers gave an unqualified *yes.* Five of the others felt casework was essential to probation but limited time precluded its use. Only one answered *no.*

Definitions of casework itself were even more general and vague than the definitions of probation. The explanation which was offered most contained such phrases as "helping people to help themselves," "helping a person make an adjustment," "changing a person's attitudes," "establishing a mutual relationship," "working with a person," and "the ability to work with people." Sixteen of the twenty responses fell into such a classification. Two probation officers felt probation *is* casework and that the definition of casework is about the same as the definition of probation. The remaining two expressed the opinion that almost anything that is done in the way of investigation of cases can be thought of as casework.

Obviously there is no consensus or standardization of opinion concerning probation among these twenty experienced workers, nor have they any clear conception of what casework is. I suspect such a situation is general.

When the aims of probation were considered, half the probation officers said the "total adjustment" of the offender was the chief goal. Five believed "complete rehabilitation" was the end pursued, and four th ight that adjustment with respect to the particular problem presented was the purpose of probation. Only one officer stated that supervision alone was the real aim of probation. If the two terms "total adjustment" and "complete rehabilitation" are considered synonomous for all practical purposes, then fifteen of the twenty probation officers concurred on this, the highest goal of probation.

With respect to what probation *should* be, thirteen probation officers felt probation should consist of casework treatment. The remaining seven believed casework is not a general process and therefore should be applied only to those cases which indicate a need for that type of treatment. (Yet in answer to the second question all but one believed casework *is* essential to probation.)

It may well be that few correctional personnel are really aware of whatever techniques they use, and it is very highly probable that only a small percentage of the total are qualified caseworkers. It is also highly probable, and certainly seems to be the case from this writer's experience, that the image that many probation officers have of themselves is a picture of a warm and understanding though objective person, a kind of watered-down or embryonic clinician. In any event the influence of a clinical, casework ideology, along with its confused and contradictory elements, has been pervasive. Convention papers, the literature and supervisors are filled with this ideology, so that it is constantly before the probation officer. It

is no more than could be expected, then, if the probation officer feels that whatever he does and however he does it, it *is* treatment.

CONCLUSION

A review of the literature reveals the predominance of the view that probation is a process of casework treatment, and this point of view seems to be shared by probation personnel in the field. However, casework is usually described in general, vague and nebulous language characterized by an abundance of cliches and a lack of clarity and specificity.

Seen from an operational point of view probation appears to be quite different from its ideal, casework conceptions. Probation varies from rare instances of intensive individual treatment, however defined, to simply non-commitment.

Actually, then, probation may be defined as a legal disposition which allows the offender his usual freedom during a period in which he is expected to refrain from unlawful behavior. Operationally, probation is primarily a process of verifying the behavior of an offender (1) through periodic reports of the offender and members of his family to the probation officer and (2) by the incidence or absence of adverse reports from the police and other agencies. Secondarily, probation is a process of guiding and directing the behavior of an offender by means of intensive interviewing utilizing ill-defined casework techniques.

Finally, it can be said that probation in practice is a gesture toward conformity to the school of thought which combines administrative and casework procedures. For the most part, however, probation remains an administrative function with the statement Healy and Bronner made thirty-four years ago still quite accurate: "probation is a term that gives no clue to what is done by way of treatment."[43]

Beyond the Clinical Horizon

Current conceptions of the causation, prevention, and treatment of crime and delinquency center almost exclusively on the offender himself, in spite of the fact that, logically, the offender himself is only part of the problem. Most contemporary thinking is based upon observations made only under certain highly selective conditions—in courts, institutions and schools. Behavior related to other less accessible, though perhaps more important situations—for example, family behavior, behavior in the gang, in the play group, and an analysis of the societal setting of such behavior—are relegated to an academic and professional purgatory in the current craze and obsession with psychodynamics. Whatever the merits of psychodynamics, the picture remains unbalanced. Correctional workers and littérateurs have an obligation to examine *and question* the basic assumptions of a psychoanalytically ridden and prejudiced clinical profession. They ought to consider, for example, whether the social system itself should be investigated as a basic variable in anti-social behavior and whether the correctional workers should become active in promoting fundamental social reform or reorganization. These and other pertinent questions are largely ignored and most likely will continue to be ignored so long as those in corrections are held in an apparently hypnotic grip of obsession with behavior problems and psychodynamics.

The theories which have dominated, and continue to dominate, practitioners are psychiatric in origin. Insight by the

[43] Healy and Bronner, *Delinquents and Criminals, Their Making and Unmaking,* 82 (New York, The Macmillan Co., 1926).

probationer into the reasons for his behavior is the major goal of treatment. A person with such insight is considered to be unlikely to repeat his deviant behavior as he becomes independent of his identification with the probation officer. At that point, supposedly, the offender can carry on normal and socially acceptable behavior on his own.

Concerning the nature and causes of delinquent behavior, most casework concepts include assumptions involving emotional tensions which result in maladjustment. However, the resolution of the inner conflicts which generate such tensions offers no guarantee of relief from criminality. Neither does the existence of such tensions invariably lead to criminal or delinquent behavior.

Despite an apparently increasing emphasis in psychiatry upon group processes in treating individual cases, the focus still remains the resolution of the individual's disorder or conflicts. As yet there exists no theory or technique for treating the *group* relationships of the individual. The New York City Youth Board's Street Club Project is a step in that direction but with the disadvantage, perhaps, of channeling the energies of gang members into strictly middle-class pursuits. There is also an underlying assumption that *all* members of the individual's relevant group need treatment or assistance.

The conclusion must be that an exclusively clinical approach to the criminality of behavior, relying as it does on the dynamics of intrapsychic phenomena, will continue to yield disappointing results. So, too, will any approach favoring a group etiology if it fails to make the basis of its approach an appraisal of the total society.

The clinical approach of psychiatry and casework views the individual offender, or his behavior, as abnormal when in fact such behavior may accurately reflect the character of group life. Given certain particular patterns of life, criminal and delinquent behavior may be the type of adjustment to those patterns one would expect.

It may be the character of our societal organization itself that produces personalities which cannot assume responsible attitudes.[44] And such personalities need not take shape only as criminals and delinquents but may be reflected in other types of irresponsibility of which the law takes little or no notice. In fact the more perverse and dangerous forms of personality deviation symbolized by aggression and an irrepressible urge to dominate others are those which reach their ultimate forms of expression *within* the existing institutional structure. Since positions of power attract such aggressive and egocentric types, we often view the spectacle of criminals prosecuting criminals! It is a matter of what types of anti-social or abnormal behavior the society will tolerate. Excesses of power and avarice are in conformity with our standards if displayed by those on the way up, or by those already there. It might be profitable, or at least interesting, to put some promising doctoral candidate on the track of executives in business, labor, religion, and government, and of professional caseworkers, psychiatrists, and psychoanalysts. How do they compare in personality and background with our delinquents and criminals? In many cases I should venture to guess that the similarities would be remarkable indeed!

The problems we face today, in this and in other fields, may be the result of a number of factors which we will never be able to put together into a meaningful theory. We must try at any rate. We may start at almost any point, perhaps with the observation that many of the

individual's functions in life have been passed onto the state. The modern American is materially relatively secure, but he is personally insecure and anxious. With the tremendous ballooning of authority, he has been compelled to submit to a complex form of institutional control, and he finds many of his once acceptable outlets for aggression effectively taken away. His is a situation of maximum stimulation of aggressive drives and minimum outlet for their expression. Such a condition deprives individual energies of much constructive force. On the contrary, our contemporary condition intensifies anxiety, enhances the development of dominant attitudes which are themselves abnormal and irrational, and encourages individually irresponsible behavior which may nonetheless be socially acceptable. For in America there is no organized protest against an asocial condition. Instead there are orgies of random activities, of lust for sex and payola, of ambitions tuned to success, the special talent, as someone put it, of those who have no talent, or of crime—all manifestations of boundless energy, but with no real power within.

The American character is essentially egotistical and asocial, ever striving to find its own peculiar niche, a spot which, in the end, may prove to be inimical to his very nature. His social relations are fluid and formless. No one is more addicted to the concept "community" and yet so indifferent to it in reality, no one so willing and ready to separate himself from every social mooring, to run wherever the fortunes of dollars and status happen to drag him. Freedom in America is the right to break away. And when he is not climbing up in society, or running away from it, he is taking the criminal's path of running straight into it. The tantalizing promises of success are still held out to him, his appetites keyed up to

[44] Comfort, *Authority and Delinquency in the Modern State* (London, Routledge and Kegan Paul, 1950).

the breaking point by the hucksters' din, only to be disappointed and disillusioned by the stark realities. Crime may often be his revenge for the dashing of hopes, promises, and ambitions bred from and nourished in a criminal philosophy of life.

The American temperament is a criminal temperament sprung from an undisciplined individualism. The exaltation, the deification of success selects those who can manipulate, "put one over" on someone, who can circumvent the law, who can literally "get away with murder."

The American temper also continues to persist in the illusion of classlessness so that social energy among us is wasted either in aimless, diffuse, excess sociability or, with no social ideal or movement to give conscious direction to our frustrations and discontents, in anti-social behavior. Rather than becoming socially conscious or revolutionary, we become Masons or criminals. This inability to identify oneself consistently with one's particular class results in a sociological dualism that casts doubt in one's own mind as to what he really is and disrupts the achievement of balance and stability of character. The conflict deepens, too, when, unaware of his fundamental class relationship to his society, he feels drawn to it directly. But that society, dedicated to a bourgeois existence, has never been imbued with and has never produced a real spirit of solidarity among its people. It has produced little that is socially substantial; it has produced only a philosophy of every man for himself.

But the clinician will, I suspect, for some time to come continue to see the anti-social man as a sick man. He will urge more and better clinics and more and better trained caseworkers, psychologists, and psychiatrists. It would be worthwhile to investigate to what extent the clinical professions attract people with a basic impulse to direct and control the lives of others. It is certainly not improbable that, in many cases, the therapist or counselor gains a great deal more in ego support from the therapeutic situation than does the patient! In fact, what has been said above may apply to clinical personnel in whom hostility and the compulsion to dominate others may appear as the other side of the coin. And the remainder of us will probably continue to rely on the very institutions which threaten to, or already have, eclipsed the possibility of much more enlightenment. It may be time to look to extra-institutional means by which individual behavior may be rationally developed and controlled, for institutions alone, I suspect, have not all the power we have attributed to them. In any event, in the final analysis, as Comfort has said, ". . . a statement of the desirable pattern of individual conduct makes nonsense without an extension of the description to cover the type of society in which such conduct is possible."[45]

Social scientists apparently fear the prospect of viewing their fields in political terms. But if the institutional ethics of power are not examined and attacked, if need be; if, instead of disentangling ourselves from the decayed and decaying elements of our society we, on the contrary, continue to identify with them and invest our future in their fortunes, then our prospects are dark indeed.

[45] *Ibid.*

33. Probation and Due Process of Law

SOL RUBIN

In 1941 the Illinois Supreme Court said: "Any person indicted stands before the bar of justice clothed with a presumption of innocence, and, as such, is tenderly regarded by the law. Every safeguard is thrown about him. . . . After a plea of guilty . . . instead of being clothed with a presumption of innocence they are naked criminals, hoping for mercy but entitled to justice."[1] I doubt that such a statement would be made today. The fact is that after conviction there are a number of safeguards, not only around the defendant but also against error by the court. These things are better understood today, partly because of new decisions and statutes. The safeguards fall into two categories, procedural due process and substantive due process.

PROCEDURAL DUE PROCESS OF LAW

Procedural due process of law in probation refers (1) to those procedural elements in the presentence investigation which are requisite to a valid proceeding and (2) to the rules governing probation status and supervision.

Presentence Investigation

One of the due process elements is the statutory requirement, in nine states and in the federal courts, that a presentence investigation be made before sentence is pronounced. A sentence passed without the investigation would be invalid. It has been so held;[2] and it would seem to follow from the cases litigated under statutes by which the investigation is *not* mandatory. In these cases it is held that the judge's refusal to order the investigation is not a violation of due process or an abuse of discretion.[3] However, the results would undoubtedly be different under the mandatory statute, which makes it clear that a sentence shall not be pronounced without the investigation.

This is an interesting development. I

---

* Adapted from a speech presented at the Annual Conference of the Probation Association of New Jersey, March 21, 1962.
[1] People v. Riley, 376 Ill. 364, 368, 33 N.E.2d 872, 875, *cert. denied*, 313 U.S. 586 (1941).

[2] State v. Culver, 23 N.J. 495, 129 A.2d 715, *cert. denied*, 354 U.S. 255, 77 Sup. Ct. 1387 (1932).
[3] People v. Roveano, 130 Cal. App. 222, 19 P.2d 506 (1933); People v. Bailey, 328 Ill. App. 584, 66 N.E.2d 477 (Ill. 1946); People v. Sudduth, 14 Ill. 2d 605, 153 N.E.2d 557 (1958).

SOURCE. Sol Rubin, "Probation and Due Process of Law," from *Crime and Delinquency*, Volume 11, January 1965, pp. 30–38. Reprinted with the permission of the National Council on Crime and Delinquency.

do not interpret it as merely strengthening probation. Many statutes formerly said, and some still do, that a defendant could not be *placed on probation* without a presentence investigation. However, he could—and still can—be *committed* without one. In its origin, then, the presentence investigation was related to probation, but the ordering of the investigation in relation to *all* sentencing constituted a real jump in jurisprudence, so altering the sentencing process that the presentence investigation became an essential part of it. That is why we no longer talk about a "probation investigation" as we used to; it is a *presentence* investigation.

A second element of due process in connection with the presentence investigation is its development (both in jurisdictions where it is mandatory and in those where it is not) as something more than the mere authorization of an officer of the court to supply the court with information. Some of the statutes require certain qualities in the report. For example, some declare that the report shall be "accurate," or "fair," or "made promptly." These are not merely administrative admonitions; they are requirements that underlie the very validity of a sentence imposed. In an Illinois case the state supreme court reversed a commitment on a plea of guilty where the defendant sought to withdraw the plea because of the quality of the probation officer's report. The court sent the matter back for a new arraignment because, in its words, "It cannot be said in this condition of the record that the report of the probation officer was either of that accurate or prompt character which the statute requires."[4]

In a Pennsylvania case this happened: The presentence report was incorrect in what it said about the defendant's past conduct and the extent of his participation in the crime to which he had pleaded guilty. In Pennsylvania the defendant does not have a right to see the report, so that the man was committed before he discovered the misinformation in it. He was held to be entitled to a writ of habeas corpus. The appellate court said:

> If unknown to this prisoner or his counsel he was sentenced on assumptions concerning his past criminal activity which were untrue or upon misinformation as to other facts, "such a result [in the language of *Townsend v. Burke,* 334 U.S. 736, 68 Sup. Ct. 1252], whether caused by carelessness or design, is inconsistent with due process of law."[5]

Not just the quality of the report is involved in this case. Here, and in other cases and statutes, the content of the report is involved also.

Investigations commonly report on the defendant's prior criminal record. One interesting statutory development is found in Massachusetts, where a statute provides that records of arrest eventuating in a not guilty verdict may not be included in the report. In the absence of a statute, the cases are not in agreement.[6]

---

[4] People v. Adams, 379 Ill. 323, 40 N.E.2d 730 (1942). See also Klingstein v. United States, 217 F.2d 711 (1954).

[5] *Ex parte* Hoopsick, 172 Pa. Super. Ct. 12, 91 A.2d 241 (1952). To the same effect, Commonwealth v. Cater, 396 Pa. 172, 152 A.2d 259 (1959) (reversing murder convictions).

[6] "Counsel might not have changed the sentence, but he could have taken steps to see that the conviction and sentence were not predicated on misinformation or misreading of court records, a requirement of fair play which absence of counsel withheld from this prisoner." (The errors in this case were the defendant's prior record and admission of arrests for charges that had been dismissed or of which the defendant had been found not guilty.) Townsend v. Burke, 334 U.S. 736 (1947), discussed in "Due Process and Legislative Standards in Sentencing," 101 *U. Pa. L. Rev.* 257, 265 (1952). On previous charges

A few decisions mention other content and indicate what would be deemed irrelevant or prejudicial, but sometimes without considering the error sufficient for reversal. In a California case, for example, the appellate court declared that the probation officer had gone "far afield" (1) in obtaining from a state board an estimate of the amount of property stolen but not indicating the source of his data, (2) in informing the judge that employers in the oil industry were watching the case with interest and that "the attitude of the general public and more particularly of the oil industry should be considered," and (3) in taking these things into account in his recommendation against probation by making "an apparent effort to influence the court by argument, which is not to be approved." However, it affirmed the commitment, declaring:

We must reject the contention the court was influenced by the improper statements and arguments in the reports. While the matter was being discussed, the court expressed criticism of the report in these particulars and we think it is reasonable to suppose that the recommendation against probation was weakened in the mind of the court, by some of the faulty reasoning upon which it was based.

The court also said:

In other respects the reports were fair. They spoke highly of the appellant's past record and . . . closed with the statement that the officer did not believe that ap-

pellant, if granted probation, would commit any further offense.[7]

The probation officer's recommendation is part of the report and must conform to the requirements of fairness. In a New Jersey case the probation officer's recommendation of the maximum sentence was held to be "of doubtful propriety." On this and other grounds the court reversed, and ordered a new presentence investigation.[8]

Although the observations regarding the report's "fairness," "promptness," etc., and some of the developments regarding its content are derived in part from the statutes, these statutes evidently express propositions of such elementary fairness that they would seem to be inherent requirements in *any* investigation, even one made under a statute that said nothing about the quality or content of the report; and several courts have said as much. If a court relies on a report for guidance in forming the sentence, the report must satisfy the elementary attributes required of any information the court might use, if the sentence is to be valid. If the contents of the report do not have these attributes, the court must either disregard such parts or obtain other information.

Finally there is the controversial question of whether a defendant has a right to see the presentence investigation report. I have argued that it is good casework for defendants to have this right;[9] most administrators argue that for various reasons it is inadvisable for the defendant to see it. Whether he has the right to see it as a matter of law (aside from statute)—that is, whether seeing the report is a matter of such

---

admissible, see People v. Escobar, 264 P.2d 571 (Calif. 1953); Taylor v. United States, 179 F.2d 690 (1950). On reversal for misuse of police records, see State v. Pohlabel, 61 N.J. Super. 242, 160 A.2d 647 (1960). The Connecticut Sentence Review Division does not take into account arrest records and nolle contenderes in reviewing sentences; see "Appellate Review of Primary Sentencing Decisions: A Connecticut Case Study," 69 *Yale L.J.* 1453, 1457 n.73 (1960).

[7] People v. Fenton, 141 Cal. App. 2d 357, 296 P.2d 829 (1956).

[8] State v. Pohlabel, *supra* note 6.

[9] Rubin, *Crime and Juvenile Delinquency: A Rational Approach to Penal Problems* Ch. 13 (1961).

elementary fairness (i.e., due process) that any proceeding in which the right is denied would be void—has not yet been ruled on by the U. S. Supreme Court, although state courts have upheld denial of access.[10]

Williams v. New York[11] has received a certain fame in connection with the issue of use of the presentence investigation. But the view that it deals with, let alone disposes of, this issue is erroneous. The issue in the Williams case was not the defendant's access to the report. That matter was never raised.[12] Rather the issue was confrontation of informants and their cross-examination.[13] The U. S. Supreme Court has not passed on the question of access. Considering some of the comments of the court in the *Williams* case and the court's record on due process, the defendant's right of access to information in the hands of the police and the prosecutor, and the general test of fairness, I believe that, if the issue arose there, the U. S. Supreme Court would be likely to hold that the defendant does have a right of inspection. In a case in Canada (where the defendant has the right to see the report) the court made the following statement:

[10] United States v. Schwenke, 221 F.2d 356 (1955); State v. Moore, 49 Del. 29, 108 A.2d 675 (1954); State v. Benes, 16 N.J. 389, 108 A.2d 846 (1954); Smith v. United States, 223 F.2d 750 (1955).

[11] Williams v. New York, 337 U.S. 241 (1949).

[12] See Williams v. Oklahoma, 358 U.S. 576, 3 L. Ed. 2d 516 (1959), *rehearing denied*, 359 U.S. 956, 3 L. Ed. 2d 763 (1958). The court had ruled that the defendant had no right to cross-examine the informants.

[13] The statements made by the judges as to Williams' background "were not challenged by appellant or his counsel, nor was the judge asked to disregard . . . or discredit any of them by cross-examination or otherwise." (The implication was that if the defendant *were* to raise these challenges, his right to do so might be upheld.)

I would be loath to believe the Supreme Court of the United States intended to hold that while a trial judge has a wide latitude as to information he may ask for and receive in a presentence report without being hedged about by the procedural formalities of strict proof of the facts alleged therein he may read this material in the privacy of his own chambers and then take his place on the bench and allowing such material to influence him against the prisoner, sentence that prisoner thereon without disclosing a word of what has been placed before him by an official acting pursuant to the provisions of a statute.[14]

In some of the cases that have been reversed as a matter of law because of inaccuracy or unfairness in the presentence investigation report, the defendant and the appellate court came to know about the report almost accidentally. If the defendant has the right to have an appellate court pass on the validity of his sentence and, in so doing, consider the presentence investigation on which the sentence was based, how can this process operate intelligently unless the defendant knows enough about the report to challenge it where necessary and unless the court has the report in front of it? The fact is that some appellate courts *have* called for the reports.[15] Certainly if the defendant can raise issues about the report, he has a right to examine it to see whether it is legally adequate in his case.

Probation Status and Supervision

If the defendant is placed on proba-

[14] Rex v. Benson, 3 West. Weekly R. (n.s.) 29 (1951) (Ct. App. B.C.).

[15] People v. Adams, Klingstein v. United States, *supra* note 4; also Commonwealth v. Cater, *supra* note 5; People v. Guiden, 172 N.Y.S.2d 640 (1958). By statute, the Review Division of the Superior Court in Connecticut may call for the report—Conn. Gen. Stat. § 51-196. See "Appellate Review of Primary Sentencing Decisions," *op. cit. supra* note 6. *Contra*, Hurt v. Commonwealth, 333 S.W.2d 951 (Ky. 1960).

tion he is subject to the supervision of the court and probation service, which, in turn, are also subject to certain legal requirements—the defendant's consent to probation, the limiting rules of law governing the validity of the conditions of probation, the procedures of supervision and revocation, and the administration of the probation service.

CONSENT. A defendant has a right to refuse probation.[16] At first blush the right to prefer imprisonment to freedom does not seem like much of a "right." But in some situations the right may well have practical significance. A man may be offered probation for two or three years—or a short term in prison; he may choose the latter. In a jurisdiction that attaches a term in jail as a condition of probation, probation is *not* an offer of freedom.

A defendant may refuse probation where the conditions would, in his opinion, be too onerous.[17] Accordingly, the better practice—and it is required under some statutes—is for the court to obtain consent to probation and to the conditions of probation.[18]

CONDITIONS. Does requiring the conditions to be subject to the defendant's consent produce sufficient control over the nature of the conditions? Because of the defendant's status, consent is, except in rare cases, automatic. However, the law itself exercises some controls. Some cases state that a condition of probation may not require behavior

which would be illegal, immoral, or impossible.[19] A court may not impose, through a condition of probation, a punishment not otherwise authorized. For example, it may not impose an unwarranted fine[20] or suspend a driver's license for longer than authorized by the Motor Vehicle law.[21] The pecuniary conditions, such as restitutions, may not be unreasonable or unrelated to the crime or other responsibility of the probationer.[22] Probation conditions specifying religious behavior probably could be questioned.[23] The legal rule enunciated in *Logan v. People* sounds like good casework to me:

Since the purpose of probation is educational and reconstructive rather than primarily punitive or oppressive, the program of probation should envisage only such terms and conditions as are clearly and specifically spelled out in the statutes, and such other conditions as fit the probationer by education and rehabilitation to take his place in society.[24]

When we examine the rulings pertaining to conditions of probation, we see that the courts protect the probation status, consistently with one of the

---

[16] Lee v. Superior Court, 8 A.C.A. 801, 201 P.2d 882 (1949); Marks v. Wentworth, 199 Mass. 44 (1908); *In re* Osslo, 334 P.2d 1 (Calif. 1958); State v. Cole, 241 N.C. 576, 86 S.E.2d 203 (1955). *Contra*, Cooper v. United States, 91 F.2d 195 (1937).

[17] People v. Caruso, 345 P.2d 282 (Calif. 1959).

[18] Required by statute, D.C. Code § 24-102; S.D. Code § 34.3708-2; Vt. Public Laws § 8878 (1933); 2 *United States Attorney General, Survey of Release Procedures* 254 (1939).

[19] State v. Harris, 116 Kans. 387, 226 Pac. 715 (1924).

[20] People v. Labarbera, 201 P.2d 584 (1949).

[21] People v. Williams, 144 C.A.2d 144, 30 P.2d 734 (1956).

[22] Karrell v. United States, 181 F.2d 981 (1950); People v. Funk, 193 N.Y. 202, 117 Misc. 778 (1921). See State v. Scherr, 9 Wis. 2d 418, 101 N.W.2d 77 (1960). An order for restitution for injuries to the person was held improper where the crime was leaving the scene of an accident—People v. Becker, 349 Mich. 476, 84 N.W.2d 833 (1957); State v. Barnett, 110 Vt. 221, 3 A.2d 521 (1939).

[23] Jones v. Commonwealth, 38 S.E.2d 444 (1946), declared unconstitutional a juvenile court order requiring regular attendance at Sunday School and church: "No civil authority has the right to require anyone to accept or reject any religious belief or to contribute any support thereto."

[24] Logan v. People, 332 P.2d 897 (1958).

guiding principles of American law, the protection of individual liberty. Since the courts are leaning in the direction of narrowing the conditions of probation that may be imposed, I would suggest as a proper general rule that the authorized conditions should be only those necessary for protection of the public or rehabilitation of the defendant, and not peripherally those devised to induce the defendant to behave like a gentleman, or even like a good husband, father, or worker.

SUPERVISION. Does supervision include the right to intervene in the offender's life in such matters as control of his finances? It would not seem so except insofar as a condition spells out a monetary obligation by the offender, whether by restitution, fine, or support—and even then, a probationer has rights of privacy. How far does the officer's right of visitation extend? Does it include the right to search the residence of the offender? Probably not (unless the officer has a search warrant). I know of few cases which deal with these points, but probation practice does present these questions.

REVOCATION. The cases and many statutes clearly hold that a probationer is entitled to a hearing on notice of a charge of violation. Some reasonable quantum of evidence must be submitted to sustain a revocation.

SUBSTANTIVE DUE PROCESS OF LAW

The procedural requirements have given rise—perhaps unintentionally—to substantive rights. For example, as a matter of procedure, probation may not be revoked unless a violation is alleged, notice is given, a hearing held, and so on. All this implies a corresponding *right*. A probationer has the right to remain on probation until satisfactory proof is submitted and a finding made that he has violated a condition of probation. When probation is said to be a matter of grace, what is being referred to is the sentencing stage, *not* the status of a man on probation. His continuance on probation is a matter of right, not grace. Probation cannot be terminated by judicial fiat. Practically every statute upholds this proposition, and the courts almost uniformly adhere to it.

In a Maryland case a few years ago the state supreme court reversed a revocation for a very petty offense, saying:

> To hold that merely because a man attaches a poster to an unoccupied building he thereby ceases to be law-abiding and must be locked up for three months is, on its face, somewhat shocking. . . . A [probationer] is not expected or required at once to achieve perfection. If his conduct is that of the ordinary well-behaved person with no more lapses than all people have, with no serious offenses charged against him, and with no indication that he intends in the future to pursue the course which led to his original conviction, the courts and probation officers should not seek for unusual and irrelevant grounds upon which to deprive him of his freedom.[25]

One can infer from this the suggestion that no condition of probation is an absolute and that a violation must be of sufficient seriousness to return a man to prison.

Presentence Investigation and Substantive Due Process

We seem to be more aware of procedural and substantive rights pertaining to probation status and supervision than of the substantive rights that have developed in connection with the presentence investigation. Many judges—most, for all I know—believe that the sentence they choose to impose is within their absolute discretion, provided it is authorized by statute. Their

[25] Swan v. State, 90 A.2d 690 (1952).

discretion has, in fact, been modified by the effect of the probation statutes.

Some courts have expressed the belief that denial of probation may not be arbitrary, may not be in contradiction to the presentence report.[26] In a recent California case the defendant had waited in a car while her companion killed a man in a store holdup. She pleaded guilty and was sentenced to life imprisonment, with the judge indicating in advance of the sentence hearing that he would not consider probation. The state supreme court reversed on the grounds that the California statute requires that consideration be given to the presentence investigation and to the desirability of probation in the light of the presentence investigation report. The court held that a judge may not commit a defendant, even on a murder charge, without considering probation as a possible disposition.[27]

A federal court has held that sentences against co-defendants must be consistent, considering their backgrounds—a holding that, in effect, required the trial court to grant probation.[28]

Cases like these may promise some very important developments. In all the centuries of sentencing defendants, the courts and the constitutional conventions and the legislatures have not developed working criteria to guide judges in sentencing. That is why the range of sentences for similar offenses committed by defendants not very

much different from one another is ridiculously broad. Even under the best statutes some judges use probation in 5 per cent of their cases; others, in the same jurisdiction, use it in 70 per cent. Some commit defendants for long maximum terms; others, in the same situation, suspend sentence.

No criteria have been developed to control this chaotic exercise of discretion. Yet the California case mentioned above says that *every* offender must be assessed for his *suitability for probation*. It may be a great step from that decision to a practical rule by which probation will actually be a defendant's right, under the proper circumstances —a right, not a matter of utter "grace" by the court. If that leap seems great and impossible, we ought to bear in mind that in several cases in New York the Appellate Division of the Supreme Court has ordered probation where the trial judge had committed a defendant. (New York is one of the fairly large number of jurisdictions in which a defendant may appeal from the sentence.)

Another of the few criteria supportive of probation is the holding that a court may not reject probation or increase a sentence because of the jury's action,[29] or because the defendant had put the state to the trouble of a jury trial by pleading not guilty.[30]

Finally, the sentencing judge should be required to place on record the reasons for the sentence. The Arizona supreme court recently reviewed the commitment of a defendant convicted

[26] People v. Cooper, 123 Cal. App. 2d 353, 266 P.2d 566 (1954); State v. Ivan, 33 N.J. 197, 162 A.2d 851 (1960); People v. Silver, 10 App. Div. 2d 274, 199 N.Y.S.2d 254 (1960); People v. Walker, 5 Cal. Rptr. 283 (1960); State v. Pohlabel, *supra* note 6. *Contra,* People v. Stover, 317 Ill. 191, 148 N.E. 67 (1925).

[27] People v. Wade, 1 Cal. Rptr. 683, 348 P.2d 116 (1959).

[28] United States v. Wiley, 278 F.2d 500 (1960).

[29] State v. Mitchell, 77 Idaho 115, 289 P.2d 315 (1955); United States v. Wiley, 267 F.2d 455 (1959). The jury had been charged on involuntary manslaughter as well as reckless driving. It brought a verdict of manslaughter. Despite the defendant's clear record and good reputation, the judge refused to consider probation because the jury had convicted on the more serious charge.

[30] People v. Guiden, *supra* note 15.

of manslaughter in the second degree. His previous record was immaculate. The issue raised on review was the denial of probation. Holding that denial was not an abuse of discretion, the court said:

Nor can we agree that because other judges have suspended sentence and granted probation in cases where the prisoner at the bar was apparently less worthy of mitigation of punishment than was the defendant in the instant case, that this amounts to a denial of the constitutional rights of due process or equal protection of the laws.

(The court added—though it was no consolation to the defendant: "We do agree with counsel that there is room for improvement in the rationalization of the standards of sentencing."[31])

This decision is very unsatisfactory. I do not suggest that identity of treatment can or should be sought; with all of the differences in human beings, that is impossible. But—especially in view of the other criteria for discretion discussed above—the sentencing judge has an obligation to explain his sentence in terms of either equality or individualization. The matter is not too different from the problem of equality in law enforcement, on which a considerable volume of law has been written. Although the writers do not all take the same stand, there are numerous cases to the effect that a conviction based on discriminatory law enforcement is invalid.[32] It seems to me that nondiscrimination in sentencing is just as mandatory.

[31] State v. Douglas, 87 Ariz. 182, 349 P.2d 622 (1960).
[32] Comment, "The Right to Nondiscriminatory Enforcement of State Penal Laws," 61 Colum. L. Rev. 1103 (1961).

In Pennsylvania the supreme court reversed two death sentences because the sentencing judge had failed to individualize, and it sustained a third, saying:

The court erred in stating that "all three [defendants] went to Cater's house to procure the gun before the holdup." The fact is that there is no evidence in the record to support this statement against either Cater or Rivers. Similarly, the court was mistaken in its belief that as to Cater and Rivers the motive for the crime was "the discharge of aggressive hatred."[33]

It is not difficult to see that the presentence investigation is the basic soil for the kind of individualization this supreme court calls for.

In New Jersey the judge is required to state the reason for his sentence. In many of the cases that have made law in sentencing, the judges who were reversed had put on the record their reason for the sentence—and the reason turned out to be wrong. If the judges had said nothing, in many cases the ground of appeal would have been undetected and the legal fiction would operate that the mute judge was most wise. The law assumes (where the judge does not demonstrate the contrary) that his mental process is consistent with law. The New Jersey rule corrects this.

We have a long way to go to develop working criteria in sentencing, but there are some straws, and it is clear that the development of probation and the presentence investigation have played and will continue to play a big part in it.

[33] Commonwealth v. Cater, supra note 5.

34. Criteria for the Probation Officer's Recommendations to the Juvenile Court Judge

YONA COHN

The purpose of this study is to analyze the underlying criteria used by the probation officers of the Bronx (New York) Children's Court in recommending dispositions to the judge at the end of their presentence investigation reports. In other probation settings where the officer's basic assumptions about the delinquent child, the court's philosophy about the role of the probation officer, the officer's professional background, and the community's attitude toward juvenile delinquency may vary, the criteria will, of course, differ from the ones we shall present.

Although a probation officer's recommendation is common practice in the juvenile court, it is not always a formal part of the presentence investigation report. Williamson refers to the formal recommendation in her statement that "the report may or may not contain a recommendation. Some judges desire recommendations; others do not permit them, or else do not request them."[1]

Much has been written about the causes of delinquency, but whether these writings focus on the delinquency itself, on the individual juvenile, his social background, or on any combination of the three, a suitable disposition is required. For example, as far back as 1922, John W. Houston considered it inappropriate to give probation treatment to juveniles who had committed serious delinquent acts.[2] Other authors investigated the child's previous convictions, his intelligence, personality make-up, and seriousness of emotional pathology as elements to be considered in recommending probation. Dressler conducted special research on the "probation risk" presented by the "lone wolf" as compared with the gang member.[3] Many, such as Flexner and Baldwin[4] and Teeters and

[1] Margaretta A. Williamson, *The Social Worker in the Prevention and Treatment of Delinquency* (New York: Columbia University Press, 1935).

[2] John W. Houston, "The Right Selection of Probation Cases," *Journal of Criminal Law and Criminology*, Feb. 1922, p. 577.

[3] David Dressler, *Probation and Parole* (New York: Columbia University Press, 1951).

[4] Bernard Flexner and Roger N. Baldwin, *Juvenile Courts and Probation* (New York: Century Co., 1914), p. 73.

SOURCE. Yona Cohn, "Criteria for the Probation Officer's Recommendations to the Juvenile Court Judge," from *Crime and Delinquency*, Volume 9, July 1963, pp. 262–275. Reprinted with the permission of the National Council on Crime and Delinquency.

Reinemann,[5] stressed family cohesiveness; while early prediction tables like Monachesi's emphasized interaction of the various social, psychological, and legal criteria as a means of foretelling the successful outcome of a probation period. One of Monachesi's findings was that "no single factor may be important in determining probation behavior" and that "outcome of probation depends upon the accumulative effect of all pre-probation factors."[6]

THE STUDY

Our study analyzes the broad background information presented by the probation officer in his presentence investigation report, with concentration on the four major recommendations he may make: probation, institutionalization, psychiatric examination, or discharge. As a means of obtaining a picture of some general trends, we shall try to isolate the criteria on which his investigation and recommendations are based.

For our study, we examined, in chronological order, 175 presentence investigation reports presented to the judge of the Bronx Children's Court from January 1, 1952 to about the middle of that year. Of these 175, 50 recommended probation, 50 recommended institutionalization, 50 recommended psychiatric examination, and 25 recommended discharge. (This last group was limited to 25 because relatively fewer such recommendations are made to the court. In the tables that follow, these 25 cases were multiplied by two to make comparison with the other

groups more convenient.) In addition to the 175 cases selected, another 500 cases were reviewed—about one-third of the yearly total. The following factors were tabulated for each case:

1. sex
2. age
3. religion
4. race
5. type of delinquent act
6. seriousness of delinquent act
7. child's role in delinquent act
8. number of previous prosecuted offenses
9. number of previous unprosecuted offenses
10. number of parents or guardians
11. economic situation
12. type of neighborhood
13. father's personality
14. mother's personality
15. degree of marital stability of parents
16. mother's relationship with child
17. father's relationship with child
18. church attendance
19. school/job attendance
20. school/job conduct
21. school/job performance
22. personality difficulties (including physical handicaps)
23. child's relationship with father
24. child's relationship with mother
25. child's relationship with sibling
26. child's relationship with peers
27. child's relationship with neighbors
28. child's group affiliation
29. child's cooperation with probation officer
30. parents' cooperation with probation officer

The statistical results for cases in each recommendation group were then tabulated and compared with the results for the other groups.

Let us examine the major tables—the distributions for sex, race, and per-

[5] Negley K. Teeters and John Otto Reinemann, *The Challenge of Delinquency* (New York: Prentice-Hall, 1950).

[6] Elio D. Monachesi, *Prediction Factors in Probation* (Minneapolis: The Sociological Press, 1932), p. 110. The Gluecks also stress a multidimensional interpretation. Sheldon and Eleanor Glueck, *Unraveling Juvenile Delinquency* (New York: Commonwealth Fund, 1950), p. 281.

sonality of the child and the type and seriousness of his delinquent act—so that we may compare the characteristics of each recommendation group with the others in order to determine the criteria used by the probation officers in selecting these groups.

DISTRIBUTION ACCORDING TO SEX

Table 1 shows a large number of girls recommended for institutionalization and a small number of girls recommended for discharge and probation. While girls made up only one-sixth of the total, they constituted nearly half the group recommended to an institution; restated as a proportion, this means that three times as many girls as boys were recommended for institutionalization.

Table 1

DISTRIBUTION ACCORDING TO SEX

	Male	Female	Total
Probation	47	3	50
Institutionalization	29	21	50
Psychiatric examination	41	9	50
Discharge	48	2	50
Total	165	35	200

For 30 out of 35 girls, the probation officer recommended psychiatric examination (diagnosis) or institutional treatment. Cross-tabulation of data for the 21 girls recommended to an institution reveals that most of them had committed delinquent acts against sexual taboos—acts which were generally con-sidered decisive factors in arriving at the recommendation they received.

DISTRIBUTION ACCORDING TO RACE

The racial distribution of the total group of 200 was three white children to one Negro child (Table 2). Of these, fewer Negroes were recommended for psychiatric examination or discharge than for institutionalization. The number of Negro children who were recommended for institutional commitment was cross-tabulated with the kind and seriousness of delinquent act committed, the number of parents or guardians in the home, the mother's relationship with the child, the child's school attendance and personality difficulties, and parental cooperation with the probation officer. The only significant correlation found from this cross-tabulation referred only to the type and seriousness of the delinquent acts committed, which, for these Negro children, were primarily acts against sexual taboos.

The eleven unrecorded cases refer mainly to Puerto Rican children whose race the probation officer could not identify.

PERSONALITY AS A CRITERION

The following classifications of the child's personality were inferred from examination of a number of investigation reports: "No Difficulties," "Disturbed Behavior," "Neurotic Symptoms," "Undiagnosed Symptoms," and "Psychotic Symptoms."

A child was classified under the "No

Table 2

RACIAL DISTRIBUTION

	White	Negro	No record	Total
Probation	36	13	1	50
Institutionalization	25	20	5	50
Psychiatric examination	37	8	5	50
Discharge	44	6	—	50
Total	142	47	11	200

Difficulties" heading under the following three conditions: (1) when the probation officer merely said so, (2) when the officer indicated that the child's behavior problems were not attributed to any emotional disturbance, and (3) when the officer discussed a rehabilitation plan, implying that the child had no personality difficulties.

A child was classified as having "Disturbed Behavior" when the probation officer stated it in his report or when he expressed agreement with the school report's description of disturbed behavior. This classification was also used when the rehabilitation plan set forth by the probation officer seemed to suggest the presence of disturbed behavior. The probation officer's report never contained a clinical description of a child's behavior disorder.

The classification "Neurotic Symptoms" was listed in those instances where the probation officer was quoting from the psychiatric examination report.

"Undiagnosed Symptoms" were reported when the probation officer did not expressly state that the child evidenced neurotic symptoms but merely implied that certain undiagnosed personality difficulties existed. The following descriptions were illustrative of this group: "an occasionally enuretic, nervous, high-strung youngster"; "[has] fear of school boys, unexpressed hostility to mother, [is] not facing responsibility, depressed"; "sullen, uncooperative, unreliable, uncommunicative, [has] temper tantrums, [is] enuretic"; "a quiet child, thumbsucker . . . mixed up, could use psychiatric help"; "a nervous bed-wetting hoodlum"; "the girl seems dazed, sad, hysterical, giggles constantly."

A child was classified as "Psychotic" when a psychiatric diagnosis of psychosis was quoted by the officer.

Personality criteria were recorded by probation officers in slightly more than two-thirds of 200 cases (see Table 3). The high number of unrecorded descriptions of personality for the group recommended to an institution may indicate either the officer's indifference or his hesitation in attaching diagnostic labels to the child when recommending referral to an institution.

The discharge group showed a clear picture of "No Difficulties." In the probation group, two-thirds of those recorded were also classed under this heading; only one was described as showing neurotic symptoms, and none as showing psychotic symptoms. Probation was recommended, however, not only in cases having no difficulties, but also in cases with disturbed behavior or undiagnosed symptoms.

This picture is reversed in the group recommended to an institution, where only one-fourth of the recorded cases

Table 3

THE PERSONALITY OF THE CHILD

	No difficulties	Disturbed behavior	Neurotic symptoms	Undiagnosed symptoms	Psychotic symptoms	No record	Total
Probation	25	5	1	5	—	14	50
Institutionalization	8	5	5	11	1	20	50
Psychiatric examination	2	10	7	16	1	14	50
Discharge	32	—	1	1	—	16	50
Total	67	20	14	33	2	64	200

were classified under "No Difficulties" and one-third under "Undiagnosed Symptoms." The *same* number of cases with disturbed behavior appeared in the group recommended for institutionalization as well as in the group recommended to probation; but *more* cases with neurotic symptoms were recommended for institutionalization than for probation. The proportional difference is striking: of the 36 recorded cases recommended to probation, only one was diagnosed under "Neurotic Symptoms"; but of the 30 recorded cases recommended for institutionalization, five were so diagnosed.

The "Psychiatric Examination" group contained the highest number of children with undiagnosed symptoms and only two children with no difficulties. But even this particular group shows a smaller number of recorded judgments than the probation and discharge groups. Half of the "Disturbed Behavior" cases, half of the "Neurotic Symptoms" cases, half of the "Undiagnosed Symptoms," and one of the two "Psychotic Symptoms" cases were recommended for psychiatric examination, thus leading to the conclusion that the probation officer recommended psychiatric examinination on general grounds —the presence of some sort of personality problem—rather than on the presence of a specific sort of personality problem. He tended to throw all difficult personality cases into the psychiatrist's lap instead of examining each case individually.

From the tabulation it is evident that personality difficulties were important criteria in the probation officer's recommendations; yet the relatively high number of cases in which no personality assessment had been recorded indicates some lack of perceptiveness on the probation officer's part.

THE DELINQUENT ACT AS A CRITERION

Delinquent acts were classified according to whether they were committed against life or property, against sexual taboos, and against parents (Table 4). Delinquent acts against parents usually were reflected in petitions made by parents or guardians against "ungovernable" children—children (especially girls) accused of such acts as running away from home, stealing from home, or destroying furniture. Often, cases of truancy were included in this group (the accusation being that the child was refusing his parents' *legal* demand to go to school).

Type of delinquent act committed was a significant factor in the probation officer's recommendation. Among the three types of acts designated, those against life or property constituted 88 per cent of the recommendations to probation and 84 per cent of the recommendations for discharge. Sexual delinquencies, which constituted a very small number in all groups, were completely absent from the group recommended for probation.

Delinquent acts against parents are

Table 4

KIND OF DELINQUENT ACT

	Against life or property	Against sexual taboos	Against parents	Total
Probation	44	0	6	50
Institutionalization	17	6	27	50
Psychiatric examination	30	7	13	50
Discharge	42	2	6	50
Total	133	15	52	200

usually referred to the court by the parents. The conflict in the home, evidenced by both the child's delinquent act and his parents' referral, seemed to lead the probation officer to the decision that removal of the child to an institution would be the best solution to the problem. In these "Delinquency against Parents" cases, the officer recommended a psychiatric examination only half as often, and probation or discharge only one-quarter as often, as he did institutionalization. The recommendations for probation and discharge show many similarities on this table. Although the "Institutionalization" and the "Psychiatric Examination" groups are similar in their high number of sexual delinquencies, they are dissimilar in their distribution of delinquent acts against parents and against life or property. Only one-eighth of all children committing delinquencies against life or property were recommended for institutionalization, but one-half of those committing delinquent acts against parents were so recommended.

SERIOUSNESS OF DELINQUENT ACT

The following acts against life or property were regarded as serious delinquencies: a robbery with an assault which resulted in the victim's death, a serious stabbing in a gang fight, sodomy, possession of loaded firearms, an attack on a girl that caused a fracture of her skull, an armed robbery, an auto theft, a forcible rape. Serious delinquent acts against parents included

suicide attempts and severe damage of the home; illegitimate births constituted a serious violation of sexual taboos (among girls), when the babies' whereabouts were unknown.

Moderate delinquency included burglary with forced entry into a building; purse-snatching; participation, in a minor role, in a group car theft; minor thefts; assembling for a gang fight; forced entry into a school and theft of valuables there; forgery. Girls' delinquencies against their parents involved staying away from home a few nights.

Mild delinquency included kicking a boy during a fight and attempts at thefts. Delinquency against parents in this category included some truancy cases and cases of coming home late in the evening (see Table 5).

The seriousness of the delinquent act appears to have been of only secondary significance to the probation officer in making his recommendation. The officer who may have hesitated in putting on probation a child who committed a serious delinquent act often did not hesitate at all in recommending a discharge or a psychiatric examination.

THE CHILD'S FAMILY RELATIONS

Most mothers of children recommended for probation and psychiatric examination had treated them with "some rejection," as recorded by the probation officers. In the discharge group, the majority of mothers were classified as evidencing "no rejection" of the child, while those children rec-

Table 5

SERIOUSNESS OF THE DELINQUENT ACT

	Serious	Moderate	Mild	Total
Probation	5	35	10	50
Institutionalization	9	39	2	50
Psychiatric examination	14	34	2	50
Discharge	10	26	14	50
Total	38	134	28	200

ommended to an institution suffered from "severe rejection" by their mothers.

A similar pattern can be discerned in the less frequently recorded relationship of father and child. (While the maternal relationship was recorded in 157 of the 200 cases, the paternal relationship was recorded in only 96 instances.)

Children in each of the four recommendation groups showed distinctively different types of relationships with their parents. The children recommended to an institution usually had tense relations with both parents; the children recommended for discharge usually had good relations with both; and those recommended for probation or psychiatric examination had fair relations with them. But despite the rather distinctive differences in those cases where such information was recorded, a high number of presentence investigation reports completely omitted this information. Of the 200 reports studied, 86 did not include information on the child's relationship with his mother, and 116 did not include information on his relationship with his father.

A similar trend can be observed when one studies the factor of marital stability of the parents, which was recorded in only about half the 200 presentence reports (104 cases). The highest number of stable marital relations was recorded for parents of the discharge group, the next highest for parents of the groups recommended to probation and psychiatric examination (the figures for both of which were only slightly less than those for the first group), and the lowest number for parents of those in the institution group.

The large number of unrecorded cases—three-quarters of the 200—indicates that the probation officers did not consider the personality of the parents an important factor in arriving at a recommendation for the child. Hence, no pattern could be traced because of the limitations of the sample.

Economic level affected the officers' recommendations in much the same manner as did the familial relationships; high economic level appeared most often among those in the discharge group, least often among those in the institution group.

All data about a child's family background should be significant in determining one or another recommendation. The probation officers in our study, however, were not completely aware of this and so they only partially investigated the family background of the children, frequently omitting some vital information. As noted above, the child's personality difficulties were also frequently ignored in the investigation report.

DESCRIPTION OF EACH GROUP

Children Recommended for Probation

What kinds of children were most likely to be recommended for probation? Rarely were they girls. Girls who appeared before the court usually had committed delinquent acts against their parents or against sexual taboos—acts which the probation officer generally considered products of social background and personality make-up beyond the range of effective probation treatment. Indeed, sexual delinquents were *never* recommended to probation. Racial or religious affiliation was not considered a factor in recommending, or not recommending, probation. The child most often recommended to probation was the one with no personality difficulties; a child with behavior difficulties or undiagnosed symptoms was only rarely recommended. Children suffering from a physical handicap were practically never in this group. Age, gang membership, and delinquent neighborhood made no difference to the probation officer. Where parents were more cooperative with him, probation was recommended slightly more often. Economic status was not considered significant.

The child recommended to probation had both his original parents in more instances than did the child recommended for institutionalization; but marital stability was no more frequent among parents of those in the probation group than among parents of those in the other groups.

The child's school attendance, his conduct at school, and his achievements there neither qualified nor disqualified him for a recommendation to probation. Even church attendance, although it was more frequent in this group than among the institution group, was not a significant criterion for the probation officer. Neither the child's group affiliation nor his good or bad relationship with siblings, neighbors, relatives, and even his mother was significant. (The child's relationship with his peers went practically unrecorded, although more followers than leaders, more "group" delinquents than "lone wolf" delinquents were recommended for probation.) With regard to his mother's relationship with him, he did not differ from the children in the other groups. Interestingly, though, his father less frequently treated him with "severe rejection" than did the fathers of those in the psychiatric examination and institution groups. The parents' personalities, however, were not considered important criteria to the probation officer—and were seldom recorded.

Few children who had committed serious delinquent acts were recommended for probation; to the probation officer, commission of an act against the parents evidenced a family background and personality structure too disturbed to warrant probation. Thus, delinquents who had committed acts against life or property were more often recommended to probation.

Number of previous convictions was not an important criterion, but the group recommended to probation differed significantly from the others in that a larger number had previously committed delinquent acts that had not been prosecuted. If the child cooperated with the probation officer during the presentence investigation, he had a slight edge in his chances of being recommended to probation; this was also true of his parents' cooperation with the officer.

Children Recommended for Institutionalization

Age was not considered significant in the officer's recommendations for institutionalization. As to religious affiliation, the child recommended for commitment was less likely to be Catholic than either Protestant or Jewish. He was slightly less cooperative than the child recommended for probation, and relatively more often handicapped than those in the other groups—but mental deficiency was not a significant criterion.

With respect to personality difficulties, he differed markedly from the other groups and usually had undiagnosed personality problems. A smaller number of those recommended for commitment had behavior difficulties or neurotic symptoms; few were rated as having no difficulties.

The child's family structure revealed factors important enough to influence the probation officer's recommendation. The child had only one original parent in more instances than did those in the other groups. (The number of children with one or both parents who were substitutes was not deemed an important criterion.) His economic status was the lowest of those in the four groups, but the others were just as frequently found in a delinquent neighborhood as he.

Most mothers, but slightly fewer fathers, of these children had severely rejected them, and their relationship with both parents was usually bad. The parents' marital relations were very unstable, although the symptoms characteristic of an unstable personality were found slightly less often among the mothers than among the fathers. The parents were not cooperative with the probation officer. Curiously, the sibling relationship of children in this group was not exceptionally bad.

In other social areas, the child recommended to commitment presented a less clear-cut picture. Although his attendance at church and school was the most sporadic of the four groups, he did not differ in his behavior or achievements at school. His group affiliations were not in any way distinctive, and his relationship with his peers, neighbors, or relatives was too infrequently recorded to show any trend in the probation officer's process of selection.

As to his delinquent acts: those against sexual taboos or against parents more frequently resulted in the child's being recommended to an institution than to any other disposition—a fact which explains the disproportionately high number of girls recommended for institutionalization, even when their social background was better than that of boys committing the same kind of delinquent act.

While the seriousness of the delinquent act was not significant, very few "mild" cases were recommended to an institution. The fact that most children in this group had committed their delinquent acts alone is consistent with the two kinds of delinquencies (i.e., against parents and against sexual ta-

boos) most frequently found in this group. To the probation officers, previous convictions had some significance for this recommendation group, but previous *unprosecuted* delinquent acts had none. The same applied to gang membership. In spite of the high number of Negroes in this group, the kind of delinquent act, rather than a child's race, was what brought him into the institution.

Children Recommended for Psychiatric Examination

What makes the probation officer deem his investigation insufficient in determining a child's difficulties or the proper treatment to be used so that he decides to recommend a psychiatric examination? According to the reports the officers filled out, the answers cannot be found in the child's family background. With respect to family structure and to the economic situation and marital stability of the parents, *all* children recommended for psychiatric examination resembled those recommended for probation. A slightly greater number of families of children in this group, however, lived in a delinquent neighborhood, but no significant differences were reported in the familial relationship—mother to child, child to mother, father to child, child to father. There was a very slight tendency for the father to have an unstable personality, but nothing of note was reported about the mother's personality or the child's relationship with his siblings. Parental cooperation with the probation officer was slightly better in the probation group. Thus, those children recommended for psychiatric examination have family backgrounds very similar to that of the probation group.

With respect to this group's ability to socialize—and this refers to their church and school attendance, school conduct and performance, their relationship with neighbors, relatives, and other groups—no significant trends distinguished the child in the psychiatric examination group from the child in the probation group. Peer-group relationships were unrecorded in so many cases that no conclusion about them could be made. Neither age nor religious affiliation was deemed of any significance.

What *did* distinguish the child in this group from those in the others was his personality structure, which showed a major and marked difference. Here, he had every manner of severe personality disorder. But the probation officer, it is interesting to note, did not attempt to distinguish between various kinds of difficulties. Instead, he recommended to psychiatric examination an equally high number of children with neurotic or undiagnosed symptoms, disturbed behavior, and psychotic symptoms, and did not presume to diagnose certain kinds of disturbances himself. The fact that a disturbance existed was sufficient evidence for him to recommend a psychiatric examination.

Children in this group also differed significantly in their cooperativeness with the probation officer—a difference that was especially outstanding when compared with the probation group, which these children resembled for the most part. When no working relationship was established, the probation officer would ask for a psychiatric examination in hopes that this would make for a better relationship.

The relatively large number of girls recommended for examination (large when compared with those recommended to probation or discharge) could not be analyzed further because the number studied (only nine) was in such small proportion to the total. The fact that girls committed acts against sexual taboos or against parents

was enough, apparently, to lead the probation officer to assume that psychiatric help was needed.

The eight Negro children in this group, although as thoroughly investigated, did not show as many personality difficulties as the white children, despite the striking similarities in many other areas—a feature which served to emphasize the importance of the child's relationship with the probation officer (rather than any extrapersonal or social factors) in selection for examination.

As to the importance of the delinquent act, previous conviction or previously committed, unprosecuted delinquent acts were obviously not significant criteria for psychiatric examination. Gang membership was, however, as was the fact that a serious act had been committed. Leadership in a group committing delinquent acts against property also had some significance for the probation officer making this recommendation. The large number of "lone wolf" delinquents corresponded to the high number of sex delinquencies and delinquencies against parents characteristic of this group, for whom the probation officer recorded a greater number of combined personality disorders. But there is no evidence that the *kind* of delinquent act alone determined the recommendation for psychiatric examination.

Children Recommended for Discharge

Contrary to what might be expected, children were not recommended for discharge because of the mildness of their delinquent acts. However, this group did show fewer unprosecuted previously committed delinquent acts and slightly fewer previous convictions. In kind of delinquency committed, this group resembled the probation group in that their delinquencies were usually against life or property; very few were against parents or sexual taboos. But this group differed in its delinquency pattern—fewer children involved in group delinquency against life or property were recommended for discharge than were those involved in solo delinquent acts. Gang membership, however, was not any different in this group than in the others.

Slightly more indicative criteria for the discharge group were those pertaining to the child himself. Neither sex nor age of these children differed meaningfully from the sex and age of those recommended for other dispositions; but fewer Protestant and fewer Negro children were recommended for discharge than expected, considering their proportion to the total. In the incidence of physical handicaps, children in the discharge group resembled those of the other groups, although no child with a mental deficiency was recommended for discharge. Outstanding in all these cases was the fact that, by and large, the probation officer did not record any personality difficulties; the discharge group included a great number of children whom he rated "stable." These children were also more cooperative than the others.

The children's family background and superior social adjustment are the major areas which distinguish this recommendation group from the others. Most of the children had both their original parents, who were of good economic status and who had a good relationship with their child. Their marital relations were more stable than those of the parents in the other groups; and, although the father was more stable than those in the other groups, the mother did not differ. Both, however, were conspicuously cooperative with the probation officer. The child's relationship to his siblings was not too different from that of the children in the other groups (an observation seldom recorded for

any group, however). These children lived in slightly less delinquent neighborhoods, attended church more frequently, and were comparatively outstanding in school attendance, conduct, and achievement. They did not differ in their spontaneous association with other children. Their relationships with neighbors, relatives, and peers were too rarely recorded to be interpreted.

CONCLUSIONS

Certain salient features emerge from analysis of the criteria for each recommendation. Seriousness of the delinquent act had only secondary significance to the probation officer in making his recommendation; of primary significance were the child's personality, his family background, and his general social adjustment. But the number of items omitted from the presentence investigation report indicates that the probation officer was unaware of the importance of the criteria he was actually using. Items most often recorded were objective in nature: identification of the child (by age, sex, religion, race), the delinquent act (kind, seriousness, role, previous conviction), the family composition and economic situation, and church and school attendance. Omitted were the more subjective, broader criteria: the various personal relationships in the family, the personalities of the parents and, especially, of the child. (The psychiatric examination group, with its highest number of children with personality difficulties, did not show more pathogenic relationships, so that no connection can be made between a child's disturbance and his pathogenic family.) This stress on reporting only the more objective data was extended to school adjustment as well—a child's attendance was much more completely recorded than were his conduct and actual achievement.

Obviously, these objective data can

be more quickly and accurately recorded; but on analysis a number of these heavily recorded criteria proved to be quite useless to the probation officer in his choosing among the four kinds of recommendations. Modern casework practice considers the other kind of criteria—often obscured or lost in the records—more important to understanding the social and emotional pathology of the child and his family and crucial to his successful supervision and rehabilitation. Data on the child's personality and family situation, no matter how meagerly recorded, proved their own worth when they were actually used by the officer in distinguishing among the four groups.

More detailed records on the child's social adjustment outside the family would also be helpful. His relationship with his peers is especially important for our cases, since most of these children are in their adolescence—a period of life when peer groups have an important function in the youngster's maturation. The dynamic relationships between parent and child, child and sibling, carry over into the child-peer relationships as well. Therefore, information about the specific character of this relationship is important not only as a diagnostic tool but also as a means by which the probation officer can help effect the youngster's social rehabilitation.

The results of this study show not only a lack of application of these important criteria, but also the use of certain rather inconsequential criteria (sex, age, race, etc.) rather than consideration of the individual child. The high number of Negro children who committed delinquent acts against parents and sexual taboos and were recommended to institutions and the low number of girls who committed the same types of acts and were recom-

mended to probation exemplify this trend.

As to the specific recommendation groups, the following can be said:

PROBATION. Recommendation to probation, as shown in our research sample of 200, was based on rather nebulous and limited criteria. The overwhelming majority of the cases recommended to probation did not have the personality difficulties which would require the personal and social rehabilitation that probation offers. A shift in criteria—reducing the number of cases with no personality difficulties who are recommended to probation and increasing the number of children with behavior disturbances and undiagnosed or neurotic symptoms—would bring more disturbed, but still curable, children to probation and would change the kind of delinquency "needed" to become a member of this group. Children committing sexual delinquencies or delinquencies against their parents could then receive the benefits of casework treatment. Membership in an unstable family would not necessarily mean a child's removal from home and community to an institution, but would allow instead for his inclusion in the probation caseload. This latter disposition would be especially appropriate since probation is an individual treatment situation, built on the relationship between the probation officer, the child, and the child's family. Many of those cases now recommended for probation showed adjustment difficulties that a well-conducted group program would help solve if the child were prepared by the probation officer to participate in it.

INSTITUTION. Institutional treatment is a group experience within a relatively controlled setting, but a child's need for such a group experience should be evaluated before he is sent to an institution.

PSYCHIATRIC EXAMINATION. If the family and the broader social background of the child were investigated in more detail, the group recommended for psychiatric examination would be more carefully selected by type and severity of personality difficulty and would include more children with severe pathology, with neurosis, and with undiagnosed symptoms. There would be no change in the use of the delinquent act as a criterion for recommending an examination.

DISCHARGE. The criteria used in deciding on this recommendation are fully justified; disregard of the delinquent act is, it should be stressed, a constructive approach. The probation officer should concentrate on the juvenile delinquent's general social maladjustment rather than on its particular expression.

The proposed change in selecting children for probation would mean that a number of cases now recommended for probation would become candidates for discharge. But this shift of cases would not affect the criteria now used for this recommendation.

35. Police Encounters with Juveniles

IRVING PILIAVIN AND SCOTT BRIAR

As the first of a series of decisions made in the channeling of youthful offenders through the agencies concerned with juvenile justice and corrections, the disposition decisions made by police officers have potentially profound consequences for apprehended juveniles.[1] Thus arrest, the most severe of the dispositions available to police, may not only lead to confinement of the suspected offender but also bring him loss of social status, restriction of educational and employment opportunities, and future harassment by law-enforcement personnel.[2] According to some criminologists, the stigmatization resulting from police apprehension, arrest, and detention actually reinforces devi-

ant behavior.[3] Other authorities have suggested, in fact, that this stigmatization serves as the catalytic agent initiating delinquent careers.[4] Despite their presumed significance, however, little empirical analysis has been reported regarding the factors influencing, or consequences resulting from, police actions with juvenile offenders. Furthermore, while some studies of police encounters with adult offenders have been reported, the extent to which the findings of these investigations pertain to law-enforcement practices with youthful offenders is not known.[5]

* This study was supported by Grant MH-06328-02, National Institute of Mental Health, U. S. Public Health Service.

[1] Richard D. Schwartz and Jerome H. Skolnick, "Two Studies of Legal Stigma," *Social Problems,* 10 (April, 1962), 133–142.

[2] Sol Rubin, *Crime and Juvenile Delinquency* (New York: Oceana Publications, 1958); B. F. McSally, "Finding Jobs for Released Offenders," *Federal Probation,* 24 (June, 1960), 12–17; Harold D. Lasswell and Richard C. Donnelly, "The Continuing Debate over Responsibility: An Introduction to Isolating the Condemnation Sanction," *Yale Law Journal,* 68 (April, 1959), 869–899.

[3] Richard A. Cloward and Lloyd E. Ohlin, *Delinquency and Opportunity* (Glencoe, Ill.: Free Press, 1960), pp. 124–130.

[4] Frank Tannenbaum, *Crime and the Community* (New York: Columbia University Press, 1936), pp. 17–20; Howard S. Becker, *Outsiders: Studies in the Sociology of Deviance* (New York: Free Press of Glencoe, 1963), chaps. i and ii.

[5] For a detailed accounting of police discretionary practices, see Joseph Goldstein, "Police Discretion Not To Invoke the Criminal Process: Low Visibility Decisions in the Administration of Justice," *Yale Law Journal,* 69 (1960), 543–594; Wayne R. LaFave, "The Police and Non-enforcement of the Law—Part I," *Wisconsin Law Review,* January, 1962, pp. 104–137; S. H. Kadish, "Legal Norms and Discretion in the Police and Sentencing Processes,"

SOURCE. Irving Piliavin and Scott Briar, "Police Encounters with Juveniles," from *The American Journal of Sociology,* Volume 70, September 1964, pp. 206–214. Copyright © 1964, University of Chicago Press. Reprinted with the permission of the University of Chicago Press.

The above considerations have led the writers to undertake a longitudinal study of the conditions influencing, and consequences flowing from, police actions with juveniles. In the present paper findings will be presented indicating the influence of certain factors on police actions. Research data consist primarily of notes and records based on nine months' observation of all juvenile officers in one police department.[6] The officers were observed in the course of their regular tours of duty.[7] While these data do not lend themselves to quantitative assessments of reliability and validity, the candor shown by the officers in their interviews with the investigators and their use of officially frowned-upon practices while under observation provide some assurance that the materials presented below accurately reflect the typical operations and attitudes of the law-enforcement personnel studied.

The setting for the research, a metropolitan police department serving an industrial city with approximately 450,000 inhabitants, was noted within the community it served and among law-enforcement officials elsewhere for the honesty and superior quality of its personnel. Incidents involving criminal activity or brutality by members of the department had been extremely rare during the ten years preceding this

study; personnel standards were comparatively high; and an extensive training program was provided to both new and experienced personnel. Juvenile Bureau members, the primary subjects of this investigation, differed somewhat from other members of the department in that they were responsible for delinquency prevention as well as law enforcement, that is, juvenile officers were expected to be knowledgeable about conditions leading to crime and delinquency and to be able to work with community agencies serving known or potential juvenile offenders. Accordingly, in the assignment of personnel to the Juvenile Bureau, consideration was given not only to an officer's devotion to and reliability in law enforcement but also to his commitment to delinquency prevention. Assignment to the Bureau was of advantage to policemen seeking promotions. Consequently, many officers requested transfer to this unit, and its personnel comprised a highly select group of officers.

In the field, juvenile officers operated essentially as patrol officers. They cruised assigned beats and, although concerned primarily with juvenile offenders, frequently had occasion to apprehend and arrest adults. Confrontations between the officers and juveniles occurred in one of the following three ways, in order of increasing frequency: (1) encounters resulting from officers' spotting officially "wanted" youths; (2) encounters taking place at or near the scene of offenses reported to police headquarters; and (3) encounters occurring as the result of officers' directly observing youths either committing offenses or in "suspicious circumstances." However, the probability that a confrontation would take place between officer and juvenile, or that a particular disposition of an identified offender would be made, was only in part determined by the knowledge that an offense

Harvard Law Review, 75 (March, 1962), 904–931.

[6] Approximately thirty officers were assigned to the Juvenile Bureau in the department studied. While we had an opportunity to observe all officers in the Bureau during the study, our observations were concentrated on those who had been working in the Bureau for one or two years at least. Although two of the officers in the Juvenile Bureau were Negro, we observed these officers on only a few occasions.

[7] Although observations were not confined to specific days or work shifts, more observations were made during evenings and weekends because police activity was greatest during these periods.

had occurred or that a particular juvenile had committed an offense. The bases for and utilization of non-offenses related criteria by police in accosting and disposing of juveniles are the focuses of the following discussion.

SANCTIONS FOR DISCRETION

In each encounter with juveniles, with the minor exception of officially "wanted" youths,[8] a central task confronting the officer was to decide what official action to take against the boys involved. In making these disposition decisions, officers could select any one of five discrete alternatives:

1. Outright release.
2. Release and submission of a "field interrogation report" briefly describing the circumstances initiating the police-juvenile confrontation.
3. "Official reprimand" and release to parents or guardian.
4. Citation to juvenile court.
5. Arrest and confinement in juvenile hall.

Dispositions 3, 4, and 5 differed from the others in two basic respects. First, with rare exceptions, when an officer chose to reprimand, cite, or arrest a boy, he took the youth to the police station. Second, the reprimanded, cited, or arrested boy acquired an official police "record," that is, his name was officially recorded in Bureau files as a juvenile violator.

Analysis of the distribution of police disposition decisions about juveniles revealed that in virtually every category of offense the full range of official disposition alternatives available to officers was employed. This wide range of discretion resulted primarily from two conditions. First, it reflected the reluctance of officers to expose certain youths to

8 "Wanted" juveniles usually were placed under arrest or in protective custody, a practice which in effect relieved officers of the responsibility for deciding what to do with these youths.

the stigmatization presumed to be associated with official police action. Few juvenile officers believed that correctional agencies serving the community could effectively help delinquents. For some officers this attitude reflected a lack of confidence in rehabilitation techniques; for others, a belief that high case loads and lack of professional training among correctional workers vitiated their efforts at treatment. All officers were agreed, however, that juvenile justice and correctional processes were essentially concerned with apprehension and punishment rather than treatment. Furthermore, all officers believed that some aspects of these processes (e.g., judicial definition of youths as delinquents and removal of delinquents from the community), as well as some of the possible consequences of these processes (e.g., intimate institutional contact with "hard-core" delinquents, as well as parental, school, and conventional peer disapproval or rejection), could reinforce what previously might have been only a tentative proclivity toward delinquent values and behavior. Consequently, when officers found reason to doubt that a youth being confronted was highly committed toward deviance, they were inclined to treat him with leniency.

Second, and more important, the practice of discretion was sanctioned by police-department policy. Training manuals and departmental bulletins stressed that the disposition of each juvenile offender was not to be based solely on the type of infraction he committed. Thus, while it was departmental policy to "arrest and confine all juveniles who have committed a felony or misdemeanor involving theft, sex offense, battery, possession of dangerous weapons, prowling, peeping, intoxication, incorrigibility, and disturbance of the peace," it was acknowledged that "such considerations as age, attitude and prior criminal record might indicate that a different disposition would be more appropriate."[9] The official justification for discretion in processing juvenile offenders, based on the preventive aims of the Juvenile Bureau, was that each juvenile violator should be dealt with solely on the basis of what was best for him.[10] Unofficially, administrative legitimation of discretion was further justified on the grounds that strict enforcement practices would overcrowd court calendars and detention facilities, as well as dramatically increase juvenile crime rates—consequences to be avoided because they would expose the police department to community criticism.[11]

In practice, the official policy justifying use of discretion served as a demand that discretion be exercised. As such, it posed three problems for juvenile officers. First, it represented a departure from the traditional police practice with which the juvenile officers themselves were identified, in the sense that they were expected to justify their juvenile disposition decisions not simply by evidence proving a youth had committed a crime—grounds on which police were officially expected to base their dispositions of non-juvenile offenders[12]—but in the character of the youth. Second, in disposing of juvenile offenders, officers were expected, in effect, to make judicial rather than ministerial decisions.[13] Third, the shift from the offense

to the offender as the basis for determining the appropriate disposition substantially increased the uncertainty and ambiguity for officers in the situation of apprehension because no explicit rules existed for determining which disposition different types of youths should receive. Despite these problems, officers were constrained to base disposition decisions on the character of the apprehended youth, not only because they wanted to be fair, but because persistent failure to do so could result in judicial criticism, departmental censure, and, they believed, loss of authority with juveniles.[14]

DISPOSITION CRITERIA

Assessing the character of apprehended offenders posed relatively few difficulties for officers in the case of youths who had committed serious crimes such as robbery, homicide, aggravated assault, grand theft, auto theft, rape, and arson. Officials generally regarded these juveniles as confirmed delinquents simply by virtue of their involvement in offenses of this magnitude.[15] However, the infraction committed did not always suffice to determine the appropriate disposition for some serious offenders;[16] and, in the case of minor offenders, who comprised over 90 per cent of the youths against

---

[9] Quoted from a training manual issued by the police department studied in this research.

[10] Presumably this also implied that police action with juveniles was to be determined partly by the offenders' need for correctional services.

[11] This was reported by beat officers as well as supervisory and administrative personnel of the Juvenile Bureau.

[12] In actual practice, of course, disposition decisions regarding adult offenders also were influenced by many factors extraneous to the offense per se.

[13] For example, in dealing with adult violators, officers had no disposition alter-

native comparable to the reprimand-and-release category, a disposition which contained elements of punishment but did not involve mediation by the court.

[14] The concern of officers over possible loss of authority stemmed from their belief that court failure to support arrests by appropriate action would cause policemen to "lose face" in the eyes of juveniles.

[15] It is also likely that the possibility of negative publicity resulting from the failure to arrest such violators—particularly if they became involved in further serious crime—brought about strong administrative pressure for their arrest.

[16] For example, in the year preceding this research, over 30 per cent of the juveniles involved in burglaries and 12 per cent of the juveniles committing auto theft received dispositions other than arrest.

whom police took action, the violation per se generally played an insignificant role in the choice of disposition. While a number of minor offenders were seen as serious delinquents deserving arrest, many others were perceived either as "good" boys whose offenses were atypical of their customary behavior, as pawns of undesirable associates or, in any case, as boys for whom arrest was regarded as an unwarranted and possibly harmful punishment. Thus, for nearly all minor violators and for some serious delinquents, the assessment of character—the distinction between serious delinquents, "good" boys, misguided youths, and so on—and the dispositions which followed from these assessments were based on youths' personal characteristics and not their offenses.

Despite this dependence of disposition decisions on the personal characteristics of these youths, however, police officers actually had access only to very limited information about boys at the time they had to decide what to do with them. In the field, officers typically had no data concerning the past offense records, school performance, family situation, or personal adjustment of apprehended youths.[17] Furthermore, files at police headquarters provided data only about each boy's prior offense record. Thus both the decision made in the field—whether or not to bring the boy in—and the decision made at the station—which disposition to invoke—were based largely on cues which emerged from the interaction between the officer and the youth, cues from

which the officer inferred the youth's character. These cues included the youth's group affiliations, age, race, grooming, dress, and demeanor. Older juveniles, members of known delinquent gangs, Negroes, youths with well-oiled hair, black jackets, and soiled denims or jeans (the presumed uniform of "tough" boys), and boys who in their interactions with officers did not manifest what were considered to be appropriate signs of respect tended to receive the more severe dispositions.

Other than prior record, the most important of the above clues was a youth's *demeanor*. In the opinion of juvenile patrolmen themselves the demeanor of apprehended juveniles was a major determinant of their decisions for 50–60 per cent of the juvenile cases they processed.[18] A less subjective indication of the association between a youth's demeanor and police disposition is provided by Table 1, which presents the police dispositions for sixty-six youths whose encounters with police were observed in the course of this study.[19] For purposes of this analysis, each youth's demeanor in the encounter was classified as either co-operative or unco-operative.[20] The results clearly

---

[17] On occasion, officers apprehended youths whom they personally knew to be prior offenders. This did not occur frequently, however, for several reasons. First, approximately 75 per cent of apprehended youths had no prior official records; second, officers periodically exchanged patrol areas, thus limiting their exposure to, and knowledge about, these areas; and third, patrolmen seldom spent more than three or four years in the juvenile division.

[18] While reliable subgroup estimates were impossible to obtain through observation because of the relatively small number of incidents observed, the importance of demeanor in disposition decisions appeared to be much less significant with known prior offenders.

[19] Systematic data were collected on police encounters with seventy-six juveniles. In ten of these encounters the police concluded that their suspicions were groundless, and consequently the juveniles involved were exonerated; these ten cases were eliminated from this analysis of demeanor. (The total number of encounters observed was considerably more than seventy-six, but systematic data-collection procedures were not instituted until several months after observations began.)

[20] The data used for the classification of demeanor were the written records of observations made by the authors. The classifications were made by an independent judge not associated with this study. In classifying a youth's demeanor as

Table 1

SEVERITY OF POLICE DISPOSITION BY YOUTH'S DEMEANOR

Severity of police disposition	Youth's demeanor		Total
	Co-operative	Unco-operative	
Arrest (most severe)	2	14	16
Citation or official reprimand	4	5	9
Informal reprimand	15	1	16
Admonish and release (least severe)	24	1	25
Total	45	21	66

reveal a marked association between youth demeanor and the severity of police dispositions.

The cues used by police to assess demeanor were fairly simple. Juveniles who were contrite about their infractions, respectful to officers, and fearful of the sanctions that might be employed against them tended to be viewed by patrolmen as basically law-abiding or at least "salvageable." For these youths it was usually assumed that informal or formal reprimand would suffice to guarantee their future conformity. In contrast, youthful offenders who were fractious, obdurate, or who appeared nonchalant in their encounters with patrolmen were likely to be viewed as "would-be tough guys" or "punks" who fully deserved the most severe sanction: arrest. The following excerpts from observation notes illustrate the importance attached to demeanor by police in making disposition decisions.

1. The interrogation of "A" (an eighteen-year-old upper-lower-class white male accused of statutory rape) was assigned to a police sergeant with long experience on the force. As I sat in his office while we waited for the youth to arrive for questioning, the sergeant expressed his uncertainty

---

co-operative or unco-operative, particular attention was paid to: (1) the youth's responses to police officers' questions and requests; (2) the respect and deference—or lack of these qualities—shown by the youth toward police officers; and (3) police officers' assessments of the youth's demeanor.

as to what he should do with this young man. On the one hand, he could not ignore the fact that an offense had been committed; he had been informed, in fact, that the youth was prepared to confess to the offense. Nor could he overlook the continued pressure from the girl's father (an important political figure) for the police to take severe action against the youth. On the other hand, the sergeant had formed a low opinion of the girl's moral character, and he considered it unfair to charge "A" with statutory rape when the girl was a willing partner to the offense and might even have been the instigator of it. However, his sense of injustice concerning "A" was tempered by his image of the youth as a "punk," based, he explained, on information he had received that the youth belonged to a certain gang, the members of which were well known to, and disliked by, the police. Nevertheless, as we prepared to leave his office to interview "A," the sergeant was still in doubt as to what he should do with him.

As we walked down the corridor to the interrogation room, the sergeant was stopped by a reporter from the local newspaper. In an excited tone of voice, the reporter explained that his editor was pressing him to get further information about this case. The newspaper had printed some of the facts about the girl's disappearance, and as a consequence the girl's father was threatening suit against the paper for defamation of the girl's character. It would strengthen the newspaper's position, the reporter explained, if the police had information indicating that the girl's associates, particularly the youth the sergeant was about to interrogate, were persons of disreputable character. This stimulus seemed to resolve the sergeant's uncertainty. He told the reporter, "unofficially," that the youth was known to be an undesirable person, citing as evidence his membership in the delinquent gang. Furthermore, the sergeant added that he had evidence that this youth had been intimate with the girl over a period of many months. When the reporter asked if the police were planning to do anything to the youth, the sergeant answered that he intended to charge the youth with statutory rape.

In the interrogation, however, three points quickly emerged which profoundly affected the sergeant's judgment of the youth. First, the youth was polite and co-operative; he consistently addressed the officer as "sir," answered all questions quietly, and signed a statement implicating himself in numerous counts of statutory rape. Second, the youth's intentions toward the girl appeared to have been honorable; for example, he said that he wanted to marry her eventually. Third, the youth was not in fact a member of the gang in question. The sergeant's attitude became increasingly sympathetic, and after we left the interrogation room he announced his intention to "get 'A' off the hook," meaning that he wanted to have the charges against "A" reduced or, if possible, dropped.

2. Officers "X" and "Y" brought into the police station a seventeen-year-old white boy who, along with two older companions, had been found in a home having sex relations with a fifteen-year-old girl. The boy responded to police officers' queries slowly and with obvious disregard. It was apparent that his lack of deference toward the officers and his failure to evidence concern about his situation were irritating his questioners. Finally, one of the officers turned to me and, obviously angry, commented that in his view the boy was simply a "stud" interested only in sex, eating, and sleeping. The policemen conjectured that the boy "probably already had knocked up half a dozen girls." The boy ignored these remarks, except for an occasional impassive stare at the patrolmen. Turning to the boy, the officer remarked, "What the hell am I going to do with you?" And again the boy simply returned the officer's gaze. The latter then said, "Well, I guess we'll just have to put you away for a while." An arrest report was then made out and the boy was taken to Juvenile Hall.

Although anger and disgust frequently characterized officers' attitudes toward recalcitrant and impassive juvenile offenders, their manner while processing these youths was typically routine, restrained, and without rancor. While the officers' restraint may have been due in part to their desire to avoid accusation and censure, it also seemed to reflect their inurement to a frequent experience. By and large, only their occasional "needling" or insulting of a boy gave any hint of the underlying resentment and dislike they felt toward many of these youths.[21]

PREJUDICE IN APPREHENSION AND DISPOSITION DECISIONS

Compared to other youths, Negroes and boys whose appearance matched the delinquent stereotype were more frequently stopped and interrogated by patrolmen—often even in the absence of evidence that an offense had been committed[22]—and usually were given

[21] Officers' animosity toward recalcitrant or aloof offenders appeared to stem from two sources: moral indignation that these juveniles were self-righteous and indifferent about their transgressions, and resentment that these youths failed to accord police the respect they believed they deserved. Since the patrolmen perceived themselves as honestly and impartially performing a vital community function warranting respect and deference from the community at large, they attributed the lack of respect shown them by these juveniles to the latters' immorality.

[22] The clearest evidence for this assertion is provided by the overrepresentation of Negroes among "innocent" juveniles accosted by the police. As noted, of the seventy-six juveniles on whom systematic data were collected, ten were exonerated and released without suspicion. Seven, or two-thirds of these ten "innocent" juveniles were Negro, in contrast to the allegedly "guilty" youths, less than one-third of whom were Negro. The following incident

more severe dispositions for the same violations. Our data suggest, however, that these selective apprehension and disposition practices resulted not only from the intrusion of long-held prejudices of individual police officers but also from certain job-related experiences of law-enforcement personnel. First, the tendency for police to give more severe dispositions to Negroes and to youths whose appearance corresponded to that which police associated with delinquents partly reflected the fact, observed in this study, that these youths also were much more likely than were other types of boys to exhibit the sort of recalcitrant demeanor which police construed as a sign of the confirmed delinquent. Further, officers assumed, partly on the basis of departmental statistics, that Negroes and juveniles who "look tough" (e.g., who wear chinos, leather jackets, boots, etc.) commit crimes more frequently than do other types of youths.[23] In this sense, the police justified their selective treatment of these youths along epidemiological lines: that is, they were concentrating their attention on those youths whom they believed were most likely to commit delinquent acts. In the words of one highly placed official in the department:

If you know that the bulk of your delin-

___

illustrates the operation of this bias: One officer, observing a youth walking along the street, commented that the youth "looks suspicious" and promptly stopped and questioned him. Asked later to explain what aroused his suspicion, the officer explained, "He was a Negro wearing dark glasses at midnight."

[23] While police statistics did not permit an analysis of crime rates by appearance, they strongly supported officers' contentions concerning the delinquency rate among Negroes. Of all male juveniles processed by the police department in 1961, for example, 40.2 per cent were Negro and 33.9 per cent were white. These two groups comprised at that time, respectively, about 22.7 per cent and 73.6 per cent of the population in the community studied.

quent problem comes from kids who, say, are from twelve to fourteen years of age, when you're out on patrol you are much more likely to be sensitive to the activities of juveniles in this age bracket than older or younger groups. This would be good law-enforcement practice. The logic in our case is the same except that our delinquency problem is largely found in the Negro community and it is these youths toward whom we are sensitized.

As regards prejudice per se, eighteen of twenty-seven officers interviewed openly admitted a dislike for Negroes. However, they attributed their dislike to experiences they had, as policemen, with youths from this minority group. The officers reported that Negro boys were much more likely than non-Negroes to "give us a hard time," be uncooperative, and show no remorse for their transgressions. Recurrent exposure to such attitudes among Negro youth, the officers claimed, generated their antipathy toward Negroes. The following excerpt is typical of the views expressed by these officers:

They (Negroes) have no regard for the law or for the police. They just don't seem to give a damn. Few of them are interested in school or getting ahead. The girls start having illegitimate kids before they are sixteen years old and the boys are always "out for kicks." Furthermore, many of these kids try to run you down. They say the damnedest things to you and they seem to have absolutely no respect for you as an adult. I admit I am prejudiced now, but frankly I don't think I was when I began police work.

IMPLICATIONS

It is apparent from the findings presented above that the police officers studied in this research were permitted and even encouraged to exercise immense latitude in disposing of the juveniles they encountered. That is, it was within the officers' discretionary authority, except in extreme limiting cases, to decide which juveniles were to come to the attention of the courts and correctional agencies and thereby be identified officially as delinquents. In exercising this discretion policemen were strongly guided by the demeanor of those who were apprehended, a practice which ultimately led, as seen above, to certain youths (particularly Negroes[24] and boys dressed in the style of "toughs") being treated more severely than other juveniles for comparable offenses.

But the relevance of demeanor was not limited only to police disposition practices. Thus, for example, in conjunction with police crime statistics the criterion of demeanor led police to concentrate their surveillance activities in areas frequented or inhabited by Negroes. Furthermore, these youths were accosted more often than others by officers on patrol simply because their skin color identified them as potential troublemakers. These discriminatory practices—and it is important to note that they are discriminatory, even if based on accurate statistical information —may well have self-fulfilling consequences. Thus it is not unlikely that frequent encounters with police, particularly those involving youths innocent of wrongdoing, will increase the hostility of these juveniles toward law-enforcement personnel. It is also not unlikely that the frequency of such encounters will in time reduce their significance in the eyes of apprehended juveniles, thereby leading these youths to regard them as "routine." Such responses to police encounters, however, are those which law-enforcement personnel perceive as indicators of the serious delinquent. They thus serve to

vindicate and reinforce officers' prejudices, leading to closer surveillance of Negro districts, more frequent encounters with Negro youths, and so on in a vicious circle. Moreover, the consequences of this chain of events are reflected in police statistics showing a disproportionately high percentage of Negroes among juvenile offenders, thereby providing "objective" justification for concentrating police attention on Negro youths.

To a substantial extent, as we have implied earlier, the discretion practiced by juvenile officers is simply an extension of the juvenile-court philosophy, which holds that in making legal decisions regarding juveniles, more weight should be given to the juvenile's character and life-situation than to his actual offending behavior. The juvenile officer's disposition decisions—and the information he uses as a basis for them —are more akin to the discriminations made by probation officers and other correctional workers than they are to decisions of police officers dealing with non-juvenile offenders. The problem is that such clinical-type decisions are not restrained by mechanisms comparable to the principles of due process and the rules of procedure governing police decisions regarding adult offenders. Consequently, prejudicial practices by police officers can escape notice more easily in their dealings with juveniles than with adults.

The observations made in this study serve to underscore the fact that the official delinquent, as distinguished from the juvenile who simply commits a delinquent act, is the product of a social judgment, in this case a judgment made by the police. He is a delinquent because someone in authority has defined him as one, often on the basis of the public face he has presented to officials rather than of the kind of offense he has committed.

---

[24] An unco-operative demeanor was presented by more than one-third of the Negro youths but by only one-sixth of the white youths encountered by the police in the course of our observations.

Section V   TREATMENT AND PREVENTION

The treatment and prevention of juvenile delinquency is a difficult process. The difficulty stems from the fact that there is no consensus about what to prevent and treat, or how to accomplish these objectives. In terms of the psychiatric approach, Hakeem points out that delinquency is not viewed as behavior that is learned in the process of association, facilitated by certain self-conceptions and social processes, and supported by the definition of the situation. Rather, delinquency is but a *symptom* of psychopathology or some deeply embedded personality disturbance, although the literature reveals many contradictory statements and little data to substantiate the claims made by those advocating the psychiatric approach to delinquency treatment and prevention. In assessing the contradictions of psychiatry to delinquency prevention, Hakeem concludes that the limitations on data should be kept in mind.

Cressey, on the other hand, maintains that behavior, attitudes, beliefs, and values are not only the products of groups but also the properties; therefore attempts to change individual behavior should be directed at groups, and he discusses the application of Sutherland's theory of differential association to treatment.

A pioneering example of environmental change that was structured to achieve both preventive and rehabilitative goals is the Chicago Area Project. This program was begun in 1932 as an outgrowth of the "area" studies of Clifford Shaw and his associates. The basic purpose of the project is to develop an interest and involvement in welfare activities and organization on the part of noncriminal citizens in slum areas, concentrating especially on enlisting the aid and support of indigenous leaders. Kobrin examines the accomplishments of the program over a twenty-five-year period and expresses his opinion concerning the effectiveness of the project to reduce delinquency, although there is little objective evidence available.

The importance of a local community approach to delinquency prevention is discussed by Martin. Another approach which is at present widely used in New York City and elsewhere is the detached-worker movement. This movement began in Chicago in the late 1920s, and was advanced by Thrasher in his study of gangs. The workers present themselves as friendly adults who provide guidance and assistance to adolescent groups. The worker must offer his services within a framework of values that reflects the adolescent group's orientation to the world—one that may be in conflict with the larger society. Walter Miller describes a detached-worker program which was carried out in Boston between the years 1954 and 1957 and evaluates the impact of this stratagem to achieve a significant reduction in delinquency.

The Highfields Project illustrates an attempt by an institutional correctional system to develop and articulate connections between formal group therapy activities and other aspects of the total operation of the institution. Empey and Rabow discuss the effects of using group counseling as the strategy for inducing behavioral change in delinquent probationers in Provo, Utah. This interesting experiment was guided by a behavioral theory that views delinquency as a group phenomenon and sees the task of rehabilitation as one of changing the shared delinquent characteristics. Treatment strategy is concerned with the total social system in which treatment must operate.

Apart from custody, another important goal of correctional institutions is that of treatment and prevention. Zald and Street analyze the problems that juvenile correctional institutions have in regard to their goals, particularly those institutions that have attempted to convert organizational goals from a custodial to a treatment-oriented emphasis. In addition to the impediment to treatment which may occur as a consequence of conflict within single institutions, delinquency prevention goals may also be blocked because of interinstitutional conflict over the issue of proper procedure. Miller indicates how conflict among different groups responsible for delinquency prevention results in a lack of coordination and mutual blocking of efforts. The eventual consequence is a stalemate in achieving a community-supported program.

36. A Critique of the Psychiatric Approach to the Prevention of Juvenile Delinquency

MICHAEL HAKEEM

THE POWERFUL INFLUENCE OF PSYCHIATRY

Psychiatrists, psychologists, social workers, and other psychiatrically oriented personnel have been powerfully influential in the work on the prevention of juvenile delinquency. The ideology of the psychiatric approach has had widespread acceptance. Psychiatrists and others who share their persuasion are much sought after for help with the problem. Their counsel is attended to eagerly. In turn, these practitioners have been more than generous with their advice.

To illustrate how widely the psychiatric approach has permeated public thinking, reference can be made to the final report of the New York Temporary State Commission on Youth and Delinquency. A large number of hearings were held by this body. All aspects of delinquency were discussed. Participants were from many walks of life. Psychiatrists, judges, school officials, social workers, legislators, and representatives of the general public testified. Hundreds of people were heard. The report concludes: "The emphasis placed on personality development, with its related problems of physical health, as the major immediate causative factor in delinquent behavior emerges as a striking characteristic of this inquiry." It is pointed out that the psychiatric orientation predominated also in the deliberations on prevention. The influence of this approach was likewise observed in the discussions on the correction of delinquents, where the emphasis was on "psychiatrically oriented treatment whether in clinic, hospital or training school" (39).

THE MODEST INFLUENCE OF SOCIOLOGY

The influence of sociology in policies and practices relating to the prevention of delinquency has been modest in comparison with that of psychiatry. As a matter of fact, sociologists, especially those in criminology and corrections, have, in the main, subscribed to the psychiatric ideology. Furthermore, when sociologists have joined in deliberations looking toward the institution

SOURCE. Michael Hakeem, "A Critique of the Psychiatric Approach to the Prevention of Juvenile Delinquency," from *Social Problems*, Volume 5, No. 3, Winter 1957–1958, pp. 194–205. Reprinted with the permission of the Society for the Study of Social Problems and the author.

of practical measures for the prevention of delinquency, they have advocated, more often than not, the selfsame proposals which psychiatrists put forth. Sociologists have not often made recommendations distinguishable from those of the adherents of the psychiatric approach. It seems that sociologists have just not been able to convert their theories and research findings into propositions usable in the prevention of delinquency.

It is true that there have been some notable exceptions to this generalization, but they remain exceptions. Now, here is a discipline, psychiatry, which represents a portentous challenge to both the theory and practice of sociology in the prevention of delinquency. How have sociologists reacted? Generally speaking, they have not critically examined this alternative approach. Instead, they have frequently hailed and promoted its emergence and dominance almost as vigorously as have the psychiatrists. It is not surprising, incidentally, that an examination of psychiatric literature on delinquency reveals a negligible influence of sociological thinking.

Sometimes it is argued that social caseworkers, who work so intimately with psychiatrists, represent the sociological frame of reference in work with delinquents, and therefore sociologists are not needed. But social caseworkers do not represent sociology. Social caseworkers are almost completely committed to the psychiatric approach. Kahn, a social work educator, has noted that social work is not substantially influenced by social science and makes limited use of its knowledge (24).

Psychiatrists and social workers view the social case history through the frame of reference provided by the psychiatric, particularly the psychoanalytic, approach. They do not interpret social factors sociologically. Social data are viewed as the raw material for incorporation into psychological explanations. For example, Friedlander, who holds that the primary factors leading to antisocial behavior are "purely psychological" ones, sees environmental factors as important only insofar as they affect the parents' psychological rearing of the child (13). Schmideberg views social conditions as "the trigger or catalyst which brings into play various psychological phenomena which have their origin largely in the period of infantile development" (32). Most commonly, there is an even more clear-cut adherence to the fallacy of reductionism, as illustrated in the following statement by Bovet: "If a social factor is to become a criminal force, it must set in motion a number of psychological processes" (6, p. 20).

The point is that cultural conflict, group affiliations, social interaction, role, status, cultural norms, self-conception, and dozens of other sociological concepts are not viewed as providing, in their own right, a framework for analyzing behavior. They are most often seen, if they are seen at all, only as phenomena which may affect the psychological processes and psychopathology of the individual.

THE CONCEPT OF
PRE-DELINQUENCY

Psychiatry, in its approach to the prevention of delinquency, proceeds on the basis of a number of assumptions. The claim is made that there exists a condition variously designated "pre-delinquency," "potential delinquency," or, in the psychoanalytic jargon, "latent delinquency." The position is taken that children afflicted with this condition will become delinquent unless there is remedial intervention. The contention is that such children can be identified at a very early age—even in earliest infancy—by psychiatrists and associated personnel. Once detected, they should be psychiatrically treated. Such treatment, preferably in a clinic, will prevent future delinquency. That is the series of assumptions subscribed to by the International Group of Experts on the Prevention of Crime and the Treatment of Offenders (30), the United Nations European Social Welfare Seminar (37), the United Nations itself (28), the Senate Subcommittee to Investigate Juvenile Delinquency (23), the United States Children's Bureau (19, p. 9), and the World Health Organization (6, pp. 55–56).

These agencies are taking their cues from psychiatrists and psychiatrically oriented specialists. For the assumptions are precisely the ones which these practitioners have been proclaiming. A typical example is provided by Banay, a psychiatrist who has long worked in corrections. He gives the following advice, referring to the prevention of delinquency:

If children were intelligently examined and treated [only under the supervision of a qualified psychiatrist] during the course of their school attendance it would be no difficult matter to predict which ones, upon graduation, would be likely to continue to have emotional difficulties resulting in deviant behavior. The most seriously disordered children could be treated and trained in special clinics (4).

The principle has been put in countless ways and it has been promulgated by countless psychiatrists. But only rarely has psychiatric zeal in this matter reached as high a pitch as it did in a declaration made by a renowned British psychiatrist and psychoanalyst, Dr. Edward Glover. He submitted a memorandum to the Royal Commission on Capital Punishment, on behalf of the Institute for the Scientific Treatment of Delinquency, which averred:

"If sufficient trouble were taken pathological cases liable to commit murder could be detected during early childhood; in other words pathological murder is potentially preventable . . ." (27, p. 492). Following is an excerpt from the dialogue between the chairman of the Commission and Dr. Glover on this point:

Do you think that that is only theoretically true, or do you think there is also some practicable way of setting about doing it?—I am quite convinced that there is a practicable way. It may require elaborate organisation [of psychiatric facilities] but it is practicable, that is beyond doubt . . . . I have no hesitation in saying that the crux of the whole approach to the problem of murder and the problem of prevention or punishment lies in an adequate attack at the right point. The right point is theoretically at any age, from birth upwards, but in practice between the ages of 2½ and 8. There should be an adequate service of child guidance, including the use of batteries of tests; and we feel fairly convinced that although you would not recognise all the potential murderers, that would be a foolish claim, you would strike seriously to the root of the problem of murder and its prevention.

You mean that by means such as those you could at least to a large extent eliminate that class of murderers who are murderers because they suffer from some form of mental disease?—From that age, yes. I could not say that would apply to all cases of murder, because mental stress is a thing which operates at all times of life.

Can you at that age identify those who have these potentialities in them?—That can now be done quite rapidly. There are so-called projective techniques of examination which are valuable, because they eliminate subjective bias on the part of the examiner and of the case examined. They have now arrived at a state of, not perfection, but adequacy, so that it is possible to take a child who is to all appearances merely an inhibited child, without any history of bad behaviour, and discover that he is potentially violent. I do not myself use these projective techniques, but I would like to see them widely employed to enable the diagnosis of potentially delinquent children to become effective (27, p. 501).

How did the Commission react to this attribution of extraordinary prescience to the projective tests? Did it probe skeptically for evidence? It did nothing of the sort. Rather, it asked for more details on the proposed procedures for carrying out the recommendations of Dr. Glover. And he obliged with a vast scheme for examining children in the schools, for "screening" the potential pathological murderers, for certifying suspected cases to local health officials, and for referring them to clinics for psychiatric observation, treatment, and surveillance (16).

Dr. Glover would place heavy emphasis on projective tests, and he cited the Rorschach as an example. This, of course, is the most widely used projective test. Now, it happens that the status of the Rorschach test—its usefulness, its reliability, and its validity— continue to be subjects around which swirls endless controversy. These are so far from being settled matters that the results of the Rorschach test should not be used as a basis for reaching decisions about people, and they should not be allowed to enter in any serious way into deliberations looking toward the disposition of cases.*

---

* Clinicians are quick to point out that they use the Rorschach results only as one part of a large array of information. Even if this were true, there are no scientific conclusions on the relative weight which should be assigned to them. In the deliberations of clinicians on any given case, scientifically standardized and demonstrable controls are not used to ensure that the Rorschach will not play a greater or lesser role than is thought desirable. Actually, it has been reported that some practitioners do depend exclusively on the Rorschach (12, p. 221). In either event, if the Rorschach is unreliable and invalid, its use as a basis for disposition of cases is unjustified.

Psychologists' evaluations of the Rorschach test range from unquestioning acceptance to outright rejection. It might be revealing to cite authorities whose views are at odds with Dr. Glover's enthusiasm. A psychologist, who is a specialist in the construction and evaluation of personality tests, recently stated that the Rorschach is "very unreliable and almost completely lacking in validity as far as the measurement of good or poor adjustment and emotional stability are concerned" (12, p. 134). Indeed, he takes as jaundiced a view of the Rorschach as he does of graphology, palmistry, and astrology and rules them all out as methods for determining personality characteristics. He even goes so far as to impugn the "critical acumen and scientific outlook" of psychiatrists and psychologists who would accept the Rorschach test, so certain is he that it is not a scientifically valid instrument (12, p. 225).

In an elaborate and comprehensive survey of statistical research on the Rorschach, Cronbach concluded:

So widespread are errors and unhappy choices of statistical procedures that few of the conclusions from statistical studies of the Rorschach test can be trusted. . . . Perhaps ninety per cent of the conclusions so far published as a result of statistical Rorschach studies are unsubstantiated . . . (9).

Wallen has described what he regards as severe defects in the Rorschach. He points out that examiners vary in their interpretation of the same record, that different examiners may obtain different records from the same client, and that any given record is only one of the possible records that a subject could produce (38). Finally, Benton, in a review of experimental and clinical data on the Rorschach, found that "current Rorschach practice is built on extremely shaky foundations." The use of the Rorschach test proceeds on the basis of assumptions which are largely unverified, according to him. His review led him to conclude that "the basic validity of the Rorschach personality sketch as an indicator of the important personality trends in the individual is yet to be established." As a matter of fact, Benton found that the personality of the examiner may play a decisive role in the subject's performance on the test (5).

THE SYMPTOMS OF PRE-DELINQUENCY

It is one of the basic tenets of the psychiatric approach that delinquent acts are symptoms. Delinquency is not viewed as behavior that is learned in the process of association, that is facilitated by certain self-conceptions, that is the outcome of social processing, that is supported by the definition of the situation. Delinquency is not explainable in its own right, according to the explicit or implicit psychiatric view of the matter. Delinquency is but a symptom—a surface symptom of psychopathology or some deeply hidden personality disturbance. Not only is it a symptom; it is "the hurt child's cry for help" (10). Children, clinicians say, do not, of course, consciously seek psychiatric treatment or other help when they are disturbed enough to need or want it. Their delinquency "is often their way of indirectly pointing up their need for help" (29).

Pre-delinquency, according to psychiatric reasoning, fits into the same framework. The child manifests certain personality traits and behavior that are taken for portents of delinquency. As has been mentioned, the psychiatrists insist that they can identify and treat such children and thereby stem the impending misfortune.

To illustrate the psychiatric ideology in the prevention of delinquency, the personality traits and behavior regarded as symptomatic of maladjustment and oncoming delinquency, and the operation of a program calculated to identify and treat potential delinquents, reference can be made to a demonstration project sponsored by the United States Children's Bureau (35). This project covered one area in St. Paul, Minnesota, and was conducted from 1937 to 1943. It was directed by a psychiatrist, and the staff included caseworkers, group workers, psychologists, and others. A total of 1,466 children were registered for service. Of these, 739 received group work services and 727 received individualized services. However, casework permeated the whole treatment program (35, p. 57). The range in age was from three to twenty-two years and the median age was twelve. The project staff worked closely with community agencies. Parents, schools, churches, neighborhood organizations, parent-teachers associations, playground associations, the police, and social agencies were urged to refer children to the project. These groups were told that "any behavior exaggerated beyond what was normal for the child's age and sex might prove the forerunner of difficulty and should be weighed as a possible indication that some of the child's needs were not being satisfactorily met" (35, p. 47). Such behavior was regarded as a sign that the child "had called for help" (35, p. 13). That the project aimed squarely at the prevention of delinquency can be seen from the following rationale:

Service before the child has firmly established a pattern of behavior that is socially unacceptable . . . has a much greater opportunity to meet his needs than service brought to him at the point when, because of some antisocial act, the whole community is aroused (35, p. 13).

Four hundred and thirty-two cases were selected for a detailed analysis of the causes of maladjustment and of the treatment needed. These cases received intensive or limited treatment. The staff judged the outcome of treatment in these cases and found that 18 per cent showed "major improvement," 65 per cent, "partial improvement," and 17 per cent, "no improvement" (35, p. 72).

A long list of personality traits and types of behavior regarded as symptoms calling for the referral of children for expert diagnosis and treatment was prepared. Each symptom was described in a sentence or two, usually containing nothing more than examples of the behavior referred to (35, pp. 178–182). This list is presented below (35, pp. 47–48).

Bashfulness
Boastfulness
Boisterousness
Bossiness
Bullying
Cheating
Cruelty
Crying
Daydreaming
Deceit
Defiance
Dependence
Destructiveness
Disobedience
Drinking
Eating disturbances
Effeminate behavior (in boys)
Enuresis
Fabrication
Failure to perform assigned tasks
Fighting
Finicalness
Gambling
Gate-crashing
Hitching rides
Ill-mannered behavior
Impudence
Inattentiveness
Indolence

Lack of orderliness
Masturbation
Nailbiting
Negativism
Obscenity
Overactivity
Over-masculine behavior (in girls)
Profanity
Quarreling
Roughness
Selfishness
Sex perversion
Sex play
Sexual activity
Shifting activities
Show-off behavior
Silliness
Sleep disturbances
Smoking
Speech disturbances
Stealing
Stubbornness
Sullenness
Tardiness
Tattling
Teasing
Temper displays
Tics
Timidity
Thumbsucking
Truancy from home
Truancy from school
Uncleanliness
Uncouth personalities
Underactivity
Undesirable companions
Undesirable recreation
Unsportsmanship
Untidiness
Violation of street-trades regulations
Violation of traffic regulations

NORMALITY AND DEVIATION IN PRE-DELINQUENT BEHAVIOR

A large number of criticisms could be leveled at the St. Paul study. It violates some of the most elementary canons of research design. It does not even utilize a control group. That this is a crucial error in a research purporting to experimentally test the merit of a particular sort of treatment has been demonstrated amply in researches that have found mental patients, delinquents, and other types of subjects to show essentially the same kind and amount of improvement whether or not they receive treatment. For example, a recent survey of a large number of reports involving several thousand cases of neurotic children concluded that those who did not receive psychotherapy improved just as much as those who did (25). In regard to delinquents, Adamson and Dunham have shown that the general outcome for those receiving and those not receiving psychotherapy is the same (2). The point is that there is no evidence that it is the treatment which brought about the alleged changes in the children of the St. Paul project. There is certainly good reason to believe that the children would have "improved" without treatment. And there is no evidence that simpler and less costly methods could not have yielded whatever results are claimed to have accrued from the methods used.

Ignoring other defects and turning to the items of behavior designated as precursors of delinquency, it must be said that it is at this point that the ideology of the psychiatric approach to the prevention of delinquency collapses. The kinds of behavior which are generally supposed to indicate predelinquency and which are said to require clinical treatment have not issued from valid research operations. Rather, they rest on the untested preconceptions of the adherents of the psychiatric ideology. Furthermore, research has not yet reduced these personality traits and behavior to reliably and validly measurable units. And it certainly has not been scientifically determined which traits, at what ages, in what degree, for what duration, in relation to what other traits, in what

configurations, and under what conditions, are indicative of future delinquency.[*]

That the staff of the St. Paul project was itself confused about the gravity of the behavior which should necessitate professional attention is shown by its discrepant references on this point. In one place, it is stated that the concern is with personality and behavior problems "however mild" (35, p. 3). Elsewhere, concern is expressed if these problems are "exaggerated" (35, p. 47). In another place, the reference is to "faint signals," and there it is noted in passing that these should be rated as equal in importance to behavior whose seriousness would be too great to ignore (19, p. 9). Whether mild or serious, faint or exaggerated, there have not been established scientific standards of normality in these characteristics and no objectively formulated yardstick for gauging their deviations has been developed. The St. Paul study provides no evidence whatsoever that

[*] *Unraveling Juvenile Delinquency,* the study by the Gluecks in which delinquents and non-delinquents are compared, has been widely pointed to as evidence of the attainment of the state of knowledge which is here denied. This study does not constitute refutation of the position taken here. The Gluecks' predictive attempts have not been satisfactorily validated to date. Further, the strong bias of the Gluecks in favor of a psychological explanation of delinquency led them to minimize some of the most significant findings of their study, namely, the operation of sociological factors, and to exaggerate the impact of psychological factors which their findings indicate to be of far less significance. Reckless has rearranged the factors in the study by the Gluecks and has shown that their own data provide evidence of the overwhelmingly greater importance of sociological than of psychological factors. See Walter C. Reckless, *The Crime Problem* (New York: Appleton-Century-Crofts, 2nd ed., 1955), 74–78. See also the two critical evaluations of the Glueck study, one by Rubin, and the other by Reiss, in the *American Journal of Sociology* for September, 1951.

would dispel any suspicion which one might be disposed to entertain that referral could have taken place on the basis of the referring adult's prejudices, peculiarities, whims, or private philosophy regarding children's behavior.

Even if deviations were measurable with complete scientific objectivity and were fully treatable, this would still be almost completely irrelevant to the prevention of delinquency. For example, suppose a child were discovered to evince a bothersome quantum of aggression, a characteristic which many clinicians insist is one of the cardinal signs of pre-delinquency. Should measures be taken to reduce the aggression? But aggression is not a trait that eventuates only in wanton rape and plunder. It can be quite handy in managing a corporation. Some generals have been aggressive. Some aggressive people have become noted explorers. Some have gone into medicine and law. Some have specialized in psychiatry. Some have entered teaching, as any student and any faculty member could attest. Aggression can find many happy uses.

THE PSYCHIATRIC "TOWER OF BABEL"

There is no better way to illustrate that labeling some children "pre-delinquent" is arbitrary and even whimsical and that the designation is dependent on the biases and preconceptions of the psychiatric personnel than to point to the vast confusion and conflict which prevail in psychiatry when it comes to a consideration of children's behavior and personality traits.

Some psychiatrists are fully aware of this state of affairs and have been frank in discussing it. Ackerman has dubbed the subject of diagnosis in child psychiatry a "Tower of Babel." He says that even within the same clinic there are differences in diagnostic concepts and practices (1). Balser has written, "We have no exact data or scientific standards relating to norms and deviations in adolescent behavior" (3, p. 265). Josselyn has pointed out that "in this era of microscopic evaluation of personality, and particularly of childhood, there is a tendency to establish a yardstick for normalcy so finely calibrated no child can be measured by it and be adjudged psychologically healthy" (21). Senn has called attention to the existence of differences among psychiatrists in judging a child's normality and need for treatment and explains this by saying that psychiatry is "relatively young and unscientific" (33).

To be more specific, consider the long list of behavioral and personality traits which were given sinister significance in the St. Paul project. Practically every one of these items has been regarded as perfectly normal by some psychiatrists and other reputable experts on the development and rearing of children. Some regard them as normal even when exhibited in extreme form. Some, who do not designate them as normal or abnormal, simply state that they are worthy of nothing more than indifference.

Take "bashfulness," for example. A psychiatrist recently felt impelled to make an eloquent defense of a child's right to be bashful. Further, she makes it clear that a child's chances of winning out in any argument about the matter are nil: "If a child is not sufficiently shy he is considered unpleasantly bold, a state indicative of problems. If he is shy, something is wrong" (21). While she decries this dilemma, she devises one of her own which is bound to prove equally ensnaring. In discussing "truancy from school," another item which appears in the above list, she takes a dim view of the emotional condition of a child who truants. But she has an equally gloomy perspective of the child who does not: "The child's acceptance of school attendance and of returning to his home at prescribed hours indicates how fearful he is of giving up what little security he has and how dangerous the world beyond his immediate environment seems" (22). Take "masturbation," as a third example. A psychiatrist has advised parents that "almost all children should be permitted to set their own pace concerning masturbation" (20, p. 101). Take the matter of "overt homosexual practices," which is included under "sex perversion." One psychiatrist says that the period from roughly ten to fifteen years of age is a "homosexual phase." He further advises that the overt homosexual activities of this period may be thought of as rehearsals for heterosexuality (17).

Take "bullying," as a fifth example. One psychiatrist interprets this as a normal aspect of the group activity of children. "They will pick on one individual, and they are merciless." Instead of seeing this as requiring the psychiatric therapy of the bullies, he recommends that parents of the hapless victim explain to him that "these things do happen, that he must learn to take it, and that, if he does, they will respect him" (3, p. 267). Take "daydreaming," as an additional illustration. Clothier reports that "typical daydreams of the adolescent girl are phantasies of being raped, of acting as a prostitute, or of having a baby like the Virgin Mary without sex relations"* (8). Take "shifting activities." One psychiatrist

* These daydreams, which would appear bizarre to most people, are considered to be normally characteristic of the adolescent girl by Clothier. On the other hand, the daydreams that aroused concern in the St. Paul study are a most innocuous variety, as can be seen from the description of them: "Indulgence in pleasant reveries characterized by withdrawal of attention more or less completely from external sources" (35, p. 178).

maintains, referring to adolescent behavior, that the only predictable thing about it is its unpredictability (20, p. 56). Consider together such items as "ill-mannered behavior," "uncouthness," "roughness," "defiance," and "indolence." One psychiatrist claims, as do many others, that the adolescent may normally become "greedy, sloppy, disorderly, rough, impolite; he may lose interest in active work, become difficult in school, unsocial, moody, withdrawn" (36).

Take "stealing," to push the point still further. This has been viewed as "practically normal" for the child of eight or nine (18). Take "overactivity." Gesell and his associates, in their well-known studies on the development of normal children, found that the eleven-year-old boy is characterized by "incessant bodily activity and expenditure of energy." They noted that even when he was seated the activity of a boy at this age is "so constant that one almost becomes seasick watching him" (14, p. 73). Take "obscenity." To again draw on Gesell's observations, it was discovered that the twelve-year-old boy greatly enjoys "dirty jokes." "He not only understands them, but tells them with great relish, and laughs uproariously" (14, p. 123). Take "untidiness." It is unmistakably clear from Gesell's descriptions that children between ten and sixteen are extraordinarily messy, and there is only very slow, and most of the time very spotty, improvement during this period (14, pp. 322–323). Take "temper displays." Gesell found the boy of ten to exhibit unexpected periods of "frenzy." "He verily yells, strikes out, kicks furiously, and even bites!" (14, p. 332). Even in boys eleven years of age, Gesell observed "undercurrents of irritability, belligerence, and argumentativeness . . . . His anger has new intensity and depth" (14, p. 332). Take, finally, "sex perversion," which is said to apply to adolescents. Markey, a psychiatrist in a juvenile court, lists a number of sex perversions ranging from voyeurism to incest. In discussing these, he asserts that "any of these acts can appear in adolescents who give promise of good psychosexual health." He further takes the position that "any act which is expressed while growth is taking place is in itself relatively unimportant" (26).

Certainly these citations, drawn from a much larger number that could be assembled, incontrovertibly show that if the psychiatrically oriented staff of the St. Paul project was worried about the traits listed above, other specialists do not share their concern; if some psychiatrists see these traits as deviations, others see them as normal; if some see them as symptoms of pre-delinquency, others see them as signs of healthy personality development.

THE CACOPHONY IN CHILD-REARING ADVICE

While some psychiatrists are threatening parents with the horrendous eventualities in store for children who exhibit traits that other psychiatrists regard as eminently normal, still others are engaged in urging parents to take a view toward these traits that is diametrically opposed to that counseled by the alarmists. English, a well-known child psychiatrist, for example, presents a list of various types of behavior, all of which have been repeatedly implicated as symptoms of pre-delinquency and all of which were used in the St. Paul project, and tells parents that they should "certainly not worry" about them. He reassures parents that these are "entirely natural manifestations of childhood" (11, p. 275). But no sooner does he proffer this consoling reassurance than he, as have many other psychiatrists, calls attention to a kind of behavior which he apparently regards

as *really* ominous, namely, good behavior—in fact, exemplary behavior. The child who actually merits the parent's concern, according to English, is not the child who manifests the traits that have been so often viewed as calling for psychiatric treatment at the earliest possible moment. Rather, it is the "extremely good child" who should prove disquieting. This is the child, who, in the words of English, "always obeys [his father] without protest, strives to please him in every way, is meticulous about his clothes and belongings, and delights in bringing home an all A report card" (11, p. 276).

Not only do some psychiatrists advise parents to ignore or at least not to worry about the behavior and characteristics that other psychiatrists insist should occasion apprehension; some harshly rebuke parents for being concerned about the very traits that others have painstakingly instructed and warned them to get exercised about. For example, Senn thinks a parent who would worry about such behavior in a child is himself in need of assistance or therapy (34, pp. 45–46). Another psychiatrist makes his impatience with parents who worry about such behavior perfectly plain in the following angry outburst: "We cannot be too harsh against parents who become unduly alarmed over such symptoms" (31).

While parents are thus being buffeted about; while "pre-delinquents" are increasingly being summoned to the clinics and hospitals; while the clinicians are haranguing parents with their value judgments, which they commonly mistake for scientific dicta, regarding children's behavior; and while practically every tenet about child rearing held by some psychiatrists is being opposed by others, the voices of those few authorities who plead for caution, restraint, and the exercise of professional responsibility get all but lost in the raging din.

A fundamental postulate underlying the mental health movement, which, in the psychiatric scheme of things, encompasses the prevention of delinquency, is that if children were reared and handled in accordance with the recommendations and advice of psychiatry, they would be spared delinquency, maladjustment, mental illness, and other misfortunes. This rests on the premise that knowledge of what child-rearing practices will lead to this end has been scientifically established and is agreed upon by the experts. The evidence adduced here should go a long way in showing this to be largely an illusion.

More than this, some psychiatrists, the unheard voices already referred to, have frankly and explicitly disclaimed any such knowledge and agreement. Bruch, for example, denies that the three assumptions she considers to underlie the education of parents on child rearing have been validated. She lists these unvalidated assumptions as follows:

(1) That there is a body of knowledge about best techniques of child care, (2) that they can and should be taught to parents (and this has been done with the fervor and intensity of advertising and publicity campaigns), and (3) that their application will prevent the development of emotional maladjustment and produce good mental health in the coming generation (7).

Senn, reviewing the trends in research on child development since the turn of the century and examining the research of the past ten years, finds that the various child-rearing practices that have been widely disseminated and advocated "did not develop from the appearance of large bodies of scientific data which had been arrived at by careful research" (34, p. 43). Ginsburg,

reviewing the present status of the mental hygiene movement, observes that it has "flowered . . . without benefit of a sound body of scrutinized and validated facts." He further concludes: ". . . we do not have an adequate definition of mental health . . . . The notion of normality (the 'normal mind,' the 'healthy personality,' etc.) is based to a large degree and often solely on the value system of the author using the term . . ." (15). Finally, Bovet, who surveyed the psychiatric aspects of juvenile delinquency for the World Health Organization, and whose report has already been referred to, sets forth the following reflection:

It must be rare for decisions with serious coercive consequences to be taken with so little supporting evidence as in the case of juvenile delinquency. The inquirer who seeks by reading or discussion to ascertain current opinions on juvenile delinquency must be struck by the following two facts: first, each point of view, whether calmly or forcibly expressed, is based on a deep-rooted conviction; and secondly, it is impossible to demonstrate objectively the validity of any one opinion* (6, pp. 10-11).

CONCLUSIONS

Certain conclusions are inescapable. Psychiatry has great prestige and power in the work on the prevention of juvenile delinquency. This status is not justified if it is assumed to rest on psychiatry's positive contributions to this work. Nor is it justified if it is assumed to emerge from the demonstrated reliability and validity of psychiatric knowledge and premises.

Psychiatric knowledge regarding personality development has not been em-

---

* Bovet himself forgets all this in the remainder of his report and makes the same kind of incautious and unsubstantiated recommendations and statements that motivated his bleak observation. All of the "unheard voices" quoted above likewise forget their reservations in other writings.

pirically verified to the point where it can be applied to the prevention and therapy of juvenile delinquency. On the other hand, the zealousness of psychiatrists in making unsubstantiated claims and their success in winning support and in implementing their views seem boundless.

Sociologists should examine the claims of psychiatry more cautiously than they have been prone to do. There is reason to believe that correctional sociologists have done almost as much as psychiatrists and their adherents to advance the claims and practices of psychiatry, as much by their reluctance to view it critically as by their eagerness to support it actively.

Sociologists should explore their own concepts and research and determine how best these can contribute to practical programs in the understanding and prevention of delinquency and in the correction of delinquents. They should view psychiatric theories, research, and claims with the same scientific caution and sophistication that they are increasingly applying to their own discipline. Certainly they should resist the psychiatric aura that has come to dominate practical measures in corrections and before which many laymen, correctional administrators, legislators, and members of welfare boards stand agape.

References

1. Ackerman, Nathan W., "Psychiatric Disorders in Children—Diagnosis and Etiology in Our Time," in Paul H. Roch and Joseph Zubin, eds., *Current Problems in Psychiatric Diagnosis* (New York: Grune and Stratton, 1953), 220–221.

2. Adamson, LaMay, and H. Warren Dunham, "Clinical Treatment of Male Delinquents: A Case Study in Effort and Result," *American Sociological Review*, 21 (June, 1956), 312–320.

3. Balser, Benjamin H., "The Adolescent," in John P. Hubbard, ed., *The Early Detection and Prevention of Disease* (New York: McGraw-Hill, 1957).

4. Banay, Ralph S., *Youth in Despair* (New York: Coward-McCann, 1948), 186, 196.

5. Benton, Arthur L., "The Experimental Validation of the Rorschach Test," *British Journal of Medical Psychology*, 23 (Parts I and II, 1950), 55.

6. Bovet, Lucien, *Psychiatric Aspects of Juvenile Delinquency*, Monograph Series, No. 1 (Geneva: World Health Organization, 1951).

7. Bruch, Hilde, "Parent Education or the Illusion of Omnipotence," *American Journal of Orthopsychiatry*, 24 (October, 1954), 724.

8. Clothier, Florence, "The Unmarried Mother of School Age as Seen by a Psychiatrist," *Mental Hygiene*, 39 (October, 1955), 639.

9. Cronbach, Lee J., "Statistical Methods Applied to Rorschach Scores: A Review," *Psychological Bulletin*, 46 (September, 1949), 425.

10. Dorsey, John M., "The Use of the Psychoanalytic Principle in Child Guidance Work," in K. R. Eissler, ed., *Searchlights on Delinquency: New Psychoanalytic Studies* (New York: International Universities Press, 1949), 137.

11. English, O. Spurgeon, and Constance J. Foster, *Fathers Are Parents, Too: A Constructive Guide to Successful Fatherhood* (New York: G. P. Putnam's Sons, 1951).

12. Eysenck, H. J., *Sense and Nonsense in Psychology* (Middlesex: Penguin Books, 1957).

13. Friedlander, Kate, *The Psycho-Analytical Approach to Juvenile Delinquency: Theory: Case-Studies: Treatment* (New York: International Universities Press, 1947), 274–275.

14. Gesell, Arnold, Frances L. Ilg, and Louise Bates Ames, *Youth: The Years from Ten to Sixteen* (New York: Harper, 1956).
15. Ginsburg, Sol W., "The Mental Health Movement and Its Theoretical Assumptions," in Ruth Kotinsky and Helen L. Witmer, eds., *Community Programs for Mental Health: Theory, Practice, Evaluation* (Cambridge, Mass.: Harvard University Press, 1955), 6.
16. Glover, Edward, "Section II. A Method of Prevention of Pathological Crimes of Violence Including Murder" (Research and Methodology), *British Journal of Delinquency*, 2 (October, 1951), 147–149.
17. Gottlieb, Bernhardt S., *Understanding Your Adolescent* (New York: Rinehart, 1957), 51.
18. Hadfield, J. A., *Psychology and Mental Health: A Contribution to Developmental Psychology* (London: George Allen and Unwin, 1950), 98, n.1.
19. *Helping Children in Trouble* (Washington, D.C.: U. S. Children's Bureau, 1947).
20. Joseph, Harry, and Gordon Zern, *The Emotional Problems of Children: A Guide for Parents* (New York: Crown, 1954).
21. Josselyn, Irene Milliken, *The Happy Child: A Psychoanalytic Guide to Emotional and Social Growth* (New York: Random, 1955), 48.
22. ———, *Psychosocial Development of Children* (New York: Family Service Association of America, 1948), 82–83.
23. *Juvenile Delinquency* (Report of the Committee on the Judiciary, United States Senate, 85th Congress, 1st session) (Washington, D.C.: Government Printing Office, 1957), 115.
24. Kahn, Alfred J., "The Nature of Social Work Knowledge," in Cora Kasius, ed., *New Directions in Social Work* (New York: Harper, 1954), 199–200.
25. Levitt, Eugene E., "The Results of Psychotherapy with Children: An Evaluation," *Journal of Consulting Psychology*, 21 (June, 1957), 189–196.
26. Markey, Oscar B., "A Study of Aggressive Sex Misbehavior in Adolescents Brought to Juvenile Court," *American Journal of Orthopsychiatry*, 20 (October, 1950), 720.
27. *Minutes of Evidence Taken Before the Royal Commission on Capital Punishment* (London: His Majesty's Stationery Office, 1949).
28. "The Prevention of Juvenile Delinquency" (Report prepared by the Secretariat of the United Nations), *International Review of Criminal Policy* (Published by the United Nations), Nos. 7–8 (January–July, 1955), 44.
29. *Reaching Adolescents Through a Court Clinic*, Monograph No. 3 (New York: New York City Youth Board, June, 1955), 33.
30. *Report of the International Group of Experts on the Prevention of Crime and the Treatment of Offenders* (New York: Economic and Social Council, United Nations, August 9, 1949), 3.
31. Ritey, Hector J., "On the Etiology of Juvenile Delinquency," *Journal of Criminal Law and Criminology*, 41 (November-December, 1950), 441.
32. Schmideberg, Melitta, "The Psychoanalysis of Delinquents," *American Journal of Orthopsychiatry*, 23 (January, 1953), 13.
33. Senn, Milton J. E., "The Child," in John P. Hubbard, ed., *The Early Detection and Prevention of Disease* (New York: McGraw-Hill, 1957), 252.
34. ———, "Fads and Facts as the Bases of Child-Care Practices," *Children*, 4 (March-April, 1957), 43–47.
35. Stone, Sybil A., Elsa Castendyck, and Harold B. Hanson, *Children in the Community: The St. Paul Experiment in Child Welfare* (Washington, D.C.: U. S. Children's Bureau, 1946).
36. Teicher, Joseph D., *Your Child and His Problems: A Basic Guide for Parents* (Boston: Little, Brown, 1953), 22.
37. *United Nations European Social Welfare Seminar* (New York: United Nations, 1950), 64.

38. Wallen, Richard W., *Clinical Psychology: The Study of Persons* (New York: McGraw-Hill, 1956), 211–212.
39. *Youth and Delinquency* (Summary Report on Regional Hearings and Statewide Conference) (Albany, N.Y.: Temporary State Commission on Youth and Delinquency, 1956), 78.

37. Changing Criminals: The Application of the Theory of Differential Association

DONALD R. CRESSEY

Sociological theories and hypotheses have had great influence on development of general correctional policies, such as probation and parole, but they have been used only intermittently and haphazardly in reforming individual criminals. Since sociology is essentially a research discipline, sociologist-criminologists have devoted most of their time and energy to understanding and explaining crime, leaving to psychiatrists and others the problem of reforming criminals. Even the sociologists employed in correctional work have ordinarily committed themselves to nonsociological theories and techniques of reformation, leading the authors of one popular criminology textbook to ask just what correctional sociologists can accomplish which cannot be accomplished by other professional workers.[1]

Perhaps the major impediment to the application of sociological theories lies not in the nature of the theories themselves but, instead, in the futile attempt to adapt them to clinical use. Strictly speaking, the now popular policy of "individualized treatment" for delinquents and criminals does not commit one to any specific theory of criminality or any specific theory of reformation, but, rather, to the proposition that the conditions considered as causing an individual to behave criminally will be taken into account in the effort to change him. An attempt is made to diagnose the cause of the criminality and to base the techniques of reform upon the diagnosis. Analogy with the *method* of clinical medicine (diagnosis, prescription, and therapy) is obvious. However, by far the most popular interpretation of the policy of individualization is that the *theories*, as well as the methods, of clinical medicine must be used in diagnosing and changing criminals. The emphasis on this clinical principle has impeded the application of sociological theories and, it may be conjectured, success in correctional work.

The adherents of the clinical principle consider criminality to be an individual defect or disorder or a symp-

[1] Harry Elmer Barnes and Negley K. Teeters, *New Horizons in Criminology* (New York: Prentice-Hall, 1951), p. 644.

SOURCE. Donald R. Cressey, "Changing Criminals: The Application of the Theory of Differential Association," from *The American Journal of Sociology*, Volume 61, September 1955, pp. 116–120. Copyright © 1955, University of Chicago Press. Reprinted with the permission of the University of Chicago Press.

tom of either, and the criminal as one unable to canalize or sublimate his "primitive," antisocial impulses or tendencies,[2] who may be expressing symbolically in criminal behavior some unconscious urge or wish arising from an early traumatic emotional experience,[3] or as a person suffering from some other kind of defective trait or condition.

In all cases the implication is that the individual disorder, like a biological disorder, should be treated on a clinical basis. An extreme position is that criminality actually is a biological disorder, to be treated by modification of the physiology or anatomy of the individual. However, the more popular notion is that criminality is analogous to an infectious disease like syphilis—while group contacts of various kinds are necessary to the disorder, the disorder can be treated in a clinic, without reference to the persons from whom it was acquired.

Sociologists and social psychologists have provided an alternative principle on which to base the diagnosis and treatment of criminals, namely, that the behavior, attitudes, beliefs, and values which a person exhibits are not only the *products* of group contacts but also the *properties* of groups. If the behavior of an individual is an intrinsic part of groups to which he belongs, attempts to change the behavior must be directed at groups.[4] While this principle is generally accepted by sociologists, there has been no consistent or organized effort by sociologist-criminologists to base techniques or principles of treatment on it. Traditionally, we have emphasized that sociologists can make unique contributions to *clinical* diagnoses, and we have advocated the development of a "clinical sociology" which would enable us to improve these diagnoses.[5] But here we reach an impasse: if a case of criminality is attributed to the individual's group relations, there is little that can be done *in the clinic* to modify the diagnosed cause of the criminality. Moreover, extra-clinical work with criminals and delinquents ordinarily has merely extended the clinical principle to the offender's community and has largely ignored the group-relations principle. For example, in the "group work" of correctional agencies the emphasis usually is upon the role of the group merely in satisfying the needs of an individual. Thus the criminal is induced to join an "interest-activity" group, such as a hiking club, on the assumption that membership in the group somehow will enable him to overcome the defects or tendencies considered conducive to his delinquency.[6] Similarly, in correctional group therapy the emphasis is almost always on the use of a group to enable the individual to rid himself of undesirable psychological disorders, not criminality.[7] Even

---

[2] Sheldon and Eleanor T. Glueck, *Delinquents in the Making* (New York: Harper and Bros., 1952), pp. 162–163; see also Ruth Jacobs Levy, *Reductions in Recidivism through Therapy* (New York: Seltzer, 1941), pp. 16, 28.

[3] Edwin J. Lukas, "Crime Prevention: A Confusion in Goal," in Paul W. Tappan (ed.), *Contemporary Correction* (New York: McGraw-Hill Book Co., 1951), pp. 397–409.

[4] Cf. Dorwin Cartwright, "Achieving Change in People: Some Applications of Group Dynamics Theory," *Human Relations,* 4 (1951), 381–392.

[5] See Louis Wirth, "Clinical Sociology," *American Journal of Sociology,* 27 (July, 1931), 49–66; and Saul D. Alinsky, "A Sociological Technique in Clinical Criminology," *Proceedings of the American Prison Association,* 64 (1934), 167–178.

[6] See the discussion by Robert G. Hinckley and Lydia Hermann, *Group Treatment in Psychotherapy* (Minneapolis: University of Minnesota Press, 1951), pp. 8–11.

[7] See Donald R. Cressey, "Contradictory Theories in Correctional Group Therapy Programs," *Federal Probation,* 18 (June, 1954), 20–26.

in group-work programs directed at entire groups, such as delinquent gangs, emphasis usually is on new and different formal group activities rather than on new group attitudes and values.

The differential association theory of criminal behavior presents implications for diagnosis and treatment consistent with the group-relations principle for changing behavior and could be advantageously utilized in correctional work. According to it, persons become criminals principally because they have been relatively isolated from groups whose behavior patterns (including attitudes, motives, and rationalizations) are anticriminal, or because their residence, employment, social position, native capacities, or something else has brought them into relatively frequent association with the behavior patterns of criminal groups.[8] A diagnosis of criminality based on this theory would be directed at analysis of the criminal's attitudes, motives, and rationalizations regarding criminality and would recognize that those characteristics depend upon the groups to which the criminal belongs. Then, if criminals are to be changed, either they must become members of anticriminal groups, or their present pro-criminal group relations must be changed.[9]

The following set of interrelated principles, adapted in part from a more general statement by Dorwin Cartwright,[10] is intended as a guide to specific application of the differential association theory to correctional work. It is tentative and directs attention to areas where research and experimentation should prove fruitful. Two underlying assumptions are that small groups existing for the specific purpose of reforming criminals can be set up by correctional workers and that criminals can be induced to join them. The first five principles deal with the use of anticriminal groups as *media* of change, and the last principle emphasizes, further, the possibility of a criminal group's becoming the *target* of change.

1. If criminals are to be changed, they must be assimilated into groups which emphasize values conducive to law-abiding behavior and, concurrently, alienated from groups emphasizing values conducive to criminality. Since our experience has been that the majority of criminals experience great difficulty in securing intimate contacts in ordinary groups, special groups whose major common goal is the reformation of criminals must be created. This general principle, emphasized by Sutherland, has been recognized and used by Gersten, apparently with some success, in connection with a group therapy program in the New York Training School for Boys.[11]

2. The more relevant the common purpose of the group to the reformation of criminals, the greater will be its influence on the criminal members' attitudes and values. Just as a labor union exerts strong influence over its members' attitudes toward management but less influence on their attitudes toward say, Negroes, so a group organized for recreational or welfare purposes will have less success in influencing criminalistic

---

[8] Edwin H. Sutherland, *Principles of Criminology* (Philadelphia: J. B. Lippincott Co., 1947), pp. 6–9, 595, 616–617.

[9] Cf. Donald R. Taft, "The Group and Community Organization Approach to Prison Administration," *Proceedings of the American Prison Association,* 72 (1942), 275–284; and George B. Vold, "Discussion of *Guided Group Interaction in Correctional Work* by F. Lovell Bixby and Lloyd W. McCorkle," *American Sociological Review,* 16 (August, 1951), 460–461.

[10] Cartwright, *op. cit.*

[11] Sutherland, *op. cit.,* p. 451; Charles Gersten, "An Experimental Evaluation of Group Therapy with Juvenile Delinquents," *International Journal of Group Psychotherapy,* 1 (November, 1951), 311–318.

attitudes and values than will one whose explicit purpose is to change criminals. Interesting recreational activities, employment possibilities, and material assistance may serve effectively to attract criminals away from pro-criminal groups temporarily and may give the group some control over the criminals. But merely inducing a criminal to join a group to satisfy his personal needs is not enough. Probably the failure to recognize this, more than anything else, was responsible for the failure of the efforts at rehabilitation of the Cambridge-Somerville Youth Study workers.[12]

3. The more cohesive the group, the greater the members' readiness to influence others and the more relevant the problem of conformity to group norms. The criminals who are to be reformed and the persons expected to effect the change must, then, have a strong sense of belonging to one group: between them there must be a genuine "we" feeling. The reformers, consequently, should not be identifiable as correctional workers, probation or parole officers, or social workers. This principle has been extensively documented by Festinger and his co-workers.[13]

4. Both reformers and those to be reformed must achieve status within the group by exhibition of "pro-reform"

[12] See Margaret G. Reilly and Robert A. Young, "Agency-initiated Treatment of a Potentially Delinquent Boy," *American Journal of Orthopsychiatry,* 16 (October, 1946), 697–706; Edwin Powers, "An Experiment in Prevention of Delinquency," *Annals of the American Academy of Political and Social Science,* 261 (January, 1949), 77–88; Edwin Powers and Helen L. Witmer, *An Experiment in Prevention of Delinquency—the Cambridge-Somerville Youth Study* (New York: Columbia University Press, 1951).

[13] L. Festinger et al., *Theory and Experiment in Social Communication: Collected Papers* (Ann Arbor: Institute for Social Research, 1951).

or anticriminal values and behavior patterns. As a novitiate, the one to be reformed is likely to assign status according to social position outside the group, and part of the reformation process consists of influencing him both to assign and to achieve status on the basis of behavior patterns relevant to reformation. If he should assign status solely on the basis of social position in the community, he is likely to be influenced only slightly by the group. Even if he becomes better adjusted, socially and psychologically, by association with members having high status in the community, he is a therapeutic parasite and not actually a member until he accepts the group's own system for assigning status.

5. The most effective mechanism for exerting group pressure on members will be found in groups so organized that criminals are induced to join with noncriminals for the purpose of changing other criminals. A group in which criminal A joins with some noncriminals to change criminal B is probably most effective in changing criminal A, not B; in order to change criminal B, criminal A must necessarily share the values of the anticriminal members.

This process may be called "retroflexive reformation"; in attempting to reform others, the criminal almost automatically accepts the relevant common purpose of the group, identifies himself closely with other persons engaging in reformation, and assigns status on the basis of anticriminal behavior. He becomes a genuine member of this group, and at the same time he is alienated from his previous pro-criminal groups. This principle is used successfully by Alcoholics Anonymous to "cure" alcoholism; it has been applied to the treatment of psychotics by McCann and Almada; and its usefulness in criminology has been demonstrated by

Knopka.[14] Ex-convicts have been used in the Chicago Area Projects, which, generally, are organized in accordance with this principle, but its effect on the ex-convicts, either in their roles as reformers or as objects of reform, appears not to have been evaluated.

6. When an entire group is the target of change, as in a prison or among delinquent gangs, strong pressure for change can be achieved by convincing the members of the need for a change, thus making the group itself the source of pressure for change. Rather than inducing criminals to become members of pre-established anticriminal groups, the problem here is to change antireform and pro-criminal subcultures, so that group leaders evolve from among those who show the most marked hospitality to anticriminal values, attitudes, and behavior. Neither mere lectures, sermons, or exhortations by correctional workers nor mere redirection of the activities of a group nor individual psychotherapy, academic education, vocational training, or counseling will necessarily

change a group's culture. If the subculture is not changed, the person to be reformed is likely to exhibit two sets of attitudes and behaviors, one characteristic of the agency or person trying to change him, the other of the subculture.[15] Changes in the subculture probably can best be instigated by eliciting the co-operation of the type of criminal who, in prisons, is considered a "right guy."[16] This principle has been demonstrated in a recent experiment with hospitalized drug addicts, whose essentially antireform culture was changed, under the guise of group therapy, to a pro-reform culture.[17] To some extent, the principle was used in the experimental system of prison administration developed by Gill in the Massachusetts State Prison Colony.[18]

[14] Freed Bales, "Types of Social Structure as Factors in 'Cures' for Alcohol Addiction," *Applied Anthropology,* 1 (April-June, 1942), 1–13; Willis H. McCann and Albert A. Almada, "Round-Table Psychotherapy: A Technique in Group Psychotherapy," *Journal of Consulting Psychology,* 14 (December, 1950), 421–435; Gisela Knopka, "The Group Worker's Role in an Institution for Juvenile Delinquents," *Federal Probation,* 15 (June, 1951), 15–23.

[15] See Edwin A. Fleishman, "A Study in the Leadership Role of the Foreman in an Industrial Situation" (Columbus: Personnel Research Board, Ohio State University, 1951) (mimeographed).

[16] See Hans Riemer, "Socialization in the Prison Community," *Proceedings of the American Prison Association,* 67 (1937), 151–155.

[17] James J. Thorpe and Bernard Smith, "Phases in Group Development in Treatment of Drug Addicts," *International Journal of Group Psychotherapy,* 3 (January, 1953), 66–78.

[18] Howard B. Gill, "The Norfolk Prison Colony of Massachusetts," *Journal of Criminal Law and Criminology,* 22 (September, 1937), 389–395; see also Eric K. Clarke, "Group Therapy in Rehabilitation," *Federal Probation,* 16 (December, 1952), 28–32.

38. The Chicago Area Project—A Twenty-five-Year Assessment

SOLOMON KOBRIN

The Chicago Area Project shares with other delinquency prevention programs the difficulty of measuring its success in a simple and direct manner. At bottom this difficulty rests on the fact that such programs, as efforts to intervene in the life of a person, a group, or a community, cannot by their very nature constitute more than a subsidiary element in changing the fundamental and sweeping forces which create the problems of groups and of persons or which shape human personality. Declines in rates of delinquents —the only conclusive way to evaluate a delinquency prevention—may reflect influences unconnected with those of organized programs and are difficult to define and measure.[1]

For two reasons the simple and satis-

fying laboratory model of the controlled experiment is difficult to achieve in measuring the effects of a program. First, it is virtually impossible to find groups which are identical in all major respects save that of participation in a given program. Second, there exists a widespread and understandable reluctance to deny to systematically selected segments of homogeneous groups the putative benefits of programs, a procedure which does produce an approximation to a control group.[2]

The present assessment of the Chicago Area Project will have to rest, therefore, on an appraisal of its experience in carrying out procedures assumed by its founders and supporters to be relevant to the reduction of delinquency. To this end, the theory of delinquency causation underlying the Area Project program will be presented.

---

[1] For example, rates of delinquents among nationality groups whose children at one time figured prominently in juvenile court statistics declined as these groups improved their economic and social position and moved out of neighborhoods of high rates of delinquents. See Clifford R. Shaw and Henry D. McKay, *Juvenile Delinquency and Urban Areas* (Chicago: University of Chicago Press, 1942), pp. 151–157.

[2] See Edwin Powers and Helen Witmer, *An Experiment in the Prevention of Delinquency* (New York: Columbia University Press, 1951), as a distinguished and solitary example of one program which, in the interest of advancing knowledge, denied hypothesized benefits of a program to a control group.

SOURCE. Solomon Kobrin, "The Chicago Area Project—A Twenty-five-Year Assessment," from *The Annals of the American Academy of Political and Social Science*, Volume 322, March 1959, pp. 20–29. Reprinted with the permission of the American Academy of Political and Social Science and the author.

This will be followed by a description of the procedures regarded as essential to the modification of conditions which produce delinquency. Finally, the adaptations and modifications of these procedures will be described and evaluated.

CONCEPTION OF THE DELINQUENCY PROBLEM

A distinctive feature of the Area Project program is that at its inception it attempted explicitly to relate its procedures in a logical manner to sociological postulates and to the findings of sociological research in delinquency. Under the leadership of the late Clifford R. Shaw, founder of the Area Project and its director during virtually all of its existence, a series of studies completed between 1929 and 1933 brought to the investigation of this problem two heretofore neglected viewpoints: the ecological and the socio-psychological. The first was concerned with the epidemiology of delinquency in the large city; the second with the social experience of the delinquent boy in the setting of his family, his play group, and his neighborhood.[3]

[3] Studies in the first category include Clifford R. Shaw and others, *Delinquency Areas* (Chicago: University of Chicago Press, 1929); certain sections of Clifford R. Shaw and Henry D. McKay, *Social Factors in Juvenile Delinquency* (Washington, D.C.: U. S. Government Printing Office, 1931); and a final volume in which the geographic distribution of rates of delinquents in a number of American cities was analyzed in great detail, Clifford R. Shaw and Henry D. McKay, *Juvenile Delinquency and Urban Areas*. While the last volume was published a decade after the earlier ones much of its data were available to the authors at the time of the founding of the Area Project. Studies of the social experience of delinquent boys include Clifford R. Shaw, *The Jack-roller* (Chicago: University of Chicago Press, 1930); Clifford R. Shaw, *The Natural History of a Delinquent Career* (Chicago: University of Chicago Press, 1931); and Clifford R. Shaw, Henry D. McKay, and

With respect to the first problem, it was found that certain areas of the large city produced a disproportionately large number of the delinquents. The high-rate areas were characterized as "delinquency areas" and subsequently an effort was made to define their major social features. In the American city of the period, the populations of these communities were made up of predominantly recent migrants from the rural areas of the Old World. As a group they occupied the least desirable status in the economic, political, and social hierarchies of the metropolitan society and in many ways showed an acute awareness of their position. Their efforts to adapt their social institutions to the urban industrial order were at the most only partly successful. The generation of immigrants, in their colonies in the decaying heart of the city, adapted with moderate success only those institutions which preserved customary forms of religious practice, mutual aid, and sociability.

However, the immigrant generation was notably unable to preserve the authority of the old institutions, including the family, in the eyes of the rising generation and was quickly confronted with a problem of conflict with their children. Disruption of cross-generational control produced the conditions for the emergence of a variant species of youth subculture in these communities marked by a tradition of sophisticated delinquency. At the same time this tradition was sustained and fostered by the anonymity of much of the population of slum areas, by the presence of a young adult element which engaged in crime both as an occupation and a way of life, and by the extraordinary harshness of the competitive struggle which arises when the controls of

James F. McDonald, *Brothers in Crime* (Chicago: University of Chicago Press, 1938).

social usage decay. The distribution of official delinquents pointed firmly to the conclusion that the high-rate areas constituted the locus of the city's delinquency problem, both as to number of delinquents and seriousness of offenses.

THE DELINQUENT AS A PERSON

With respect to the second problem, these investigations suggested that, given the conditions of social life in the delinquency areas, delinquency in most cases was the product of the simple and direct processes of social learning. Where growing boys are alienated from the institutions of their parents and are confronted with a vital tradition of delinquency among their peers, they engage in delinquent activity as part of their groping for a place in the only social groups available to them. From investigations of the type reported in *The Jack-roller, Natural History of a Delinquent Career,* and *Brothers in Crime,* the conclusion was drawn that with significant frequency, delinquency in the slum areas of our cities reflects the strivings of boys in a social rather than an antisocial direction. These studies focused attention on the paradoxical fact that no matter how destructive or morally shocking, delinquency may often represent the efforts of the person to find and vindicate his status as a human being, rather than an abdication of his humanity or an intrinsic incapacity to experience human sentiment.

This view formed something of a contrast to notions of human nature and delinquency which were, and still are, somewhat more widely accepted. These beliefs, which generally represent delinquent conduct as a manifestation of pathology or malfunction of personality, rest implicitly on an image of man as quick to lose his distinctively human capacities under adverse conditions. The image implied in the Area Project conception of the delinquency problem is that man tends always to organize his behavior in the service of his human identity. To what extent this view is supported by the research of Shaw and his associates, and to what extent the research proceeded from this view is, of course, a difficult question to answer. The fact remains, however, that from the beginning the Area Project program rested on a conception of human nature which was optimistic concerning the prevention of delinquency and the rehabilitation of the delinquent. Delinquency was regarded as, for the most part, a reversible accident of the person's social experience.

Thus, the theory on which the Area Project program is based is that, taken in its most general aspect, delinquency as a problem in the modern metropolis is principally a product of the breakdown of the machinery of spontaneous social control. The breakdown is precipitated by the cataclysmic pace of social change to which migrants from a peasant or rural background are subjected when they enter the city. In its more specific aspects, delinquency was seen as adaptive behavior on the part of the male children of rural migrants acting as members of adolescent peer groups in their efforts to find their way to meaningful and respected adult roles essentially unaided by the older generation and under the influence of criminal models for whom the inner city areas furnish a haven.

SOCIALIZATION AND COMMUNITY ACTION

Research in the problem of delinquency formed one of two major sources of suggestion for the Area Project program. The second was furnished by what may best be regarded as a set of sociological postulates concerning, first, the processes by which persons come under the influence and control of social groups and take over their values; and, second, those affecting communal or collective action in the solution of social problems.

It is a commonplace of sociological observation that the source of control of conduct for the person lies in his natural social world. The rules and values having validity for the person are those which affect his daily nurturance, his place in primary groups, and his self-development. He is responsive as a person within the web of relationships in which his daily existence as a human being is embedded.

The inference seemed unavoidable, therefore, that to succeed delinquency prevention activities must somehow first become activities of the adults constituting the natural social world of the youngster. Or, put another way, a delinquency prevention program could hardly hope to be effective unless and until the aims of such a program became the aims of the local populations. Thus, an indispensable preliminary task of delinquency prevention is to discover effective methods of inducing residents of the disadvantaged city areas to take up the cause of prevention in a serious manner. The disposition of the founders of the Area Project was to regard this element of the program as so indispensable that if these populations proved unable to act in relation to the problem, the prevention of delinquency was a lost cause.

A second postulation concerned the problem of developing collective action toward delinquency. Here another commonplace of sociological observation suggested that people support and participate only in those enterprises in which they have a meaningful role. The organized activity of people everywhere flows in the channels of institutions and organizations indigenous to their cultural traditions and to the system of social relationships which defines their social groups. Consequently one could not expect people to devote their energies to enterprises which form part of the social systems of groups in which they have no membership. The relevance of this observation is that there had always existed an expectation that people residing in the high delinquency rate areas could somehow be induced to support the welfare agencies established there. A basic assumption of the Area Project program was that under prevailing conditions it was illusory to expect this to happen.

Thus, in view of the primacy of the local social life in the socialization and control of the young person, all effort, it was felt, should be devoted to helping residents of high delinquency rate areas to take constructive action toward the problem. The interest of the wider society in winning the rising generation of these communities to orderliness and conformity had first to become a vital interest of the local society.

ORGANIZATION OF THE DELINQUENCY AREA

A final assumption necessary to the rationale of the Area Project program had to do with the social and institutional organization of the high delinquency rate neighborhood and with the related issue of the capacity of residents of these areas to organize and administer local welfare programs. It was observed that despite the real disorder and confusion of the delinquency area, there existed a core of organized communal life centering mainly in religious, economic, and political activity. Because the function of the slum area is to house the flow of impoverished newcomers and to furnish a haven of residence for the multitudes who, for various reasons, live at the edge of respectability, the nucleus of institutional order actually present is sometimes difficult to discern. There seemed further to be strong evidence that the residents most active in these local institutions were, in terms of interest, motivation, and capacity, on their way up the social class ladder. With respect to these elements of the population it was assumed, therefore, that they represented forces of considerable strength for initiating delinquency prevention activities.[4] There being no evidence of a deficiency of intelligence among them, it was taken for granted that with proper guidance and encouragement they could learn how to organize and administer local welfare programs.

In summary it may be said, then, that the Area Project program regards as indispensable to the success of welfare activity in general and delinquency prevention in particular the participation of those who form a significant part of the social world of the recipients of help. This is seen not as a prescription or a panacea, but as a condition for progress in finding a solution. The program has remained experimental in the sense that it has continued to explore the question: What kind of participation is necessary on the part of which kinds of persons in terms of social role in the local society? But it has rested firmly and consistently on the conviction that no solution of a basic and lasting character is possible in the absence of such participation.

PROCEDURES IN NEIGHBORHOOD ORGANIZATION

It follows that the basic procedure in the program is the development of local welfare organization among residents of high delinquency rate neighborhoods. This undertaking called for skill of the

organizer in identifying the residents holding key positions of influence and the ability to arouse their interest in youth welfare activities. The first phase requires a knowledge of the local society; the second a capacity for sympathetic identification with the local resident. Knowledge of the local society implies familiarity with its culture and history, in the case of ethnic groups; with the local institutions; with the structure of power through which decisions are made and executed; and with the conflicts and cleavages which orient and align the population.

Initial organization in several of Chicago's delinquency areas was undertaken by sociologists employed jointly by the Behavior Research Fund, now dissolved, the Chicago Area Project, and the Illinois Institute for Juvenile Research. The Institute, an agency of state government, until recently has furnished a major share of the salaries of the staff engaged in this program.[5]

It became quickly evident, however, that, for cogent reasons, the employment of qualified local residents offered advantages in the establishment of such programs. In the first place the indigenous worker usually possessed a natural knowledge of the local society. Second, he was hampered by none of the barriers to communications with residents for whom the nonresident, especially those identified with "welfare" enterprise, tended to be an object of suspicion and hostility. Third, his employment was a demonstration of sincere confidence in the capacity of the area resident for work of this sort. Fourth, he was more likely than the nonresident to have access to the neighborhood's delinquent boys and therefore to be more effective in redirecting

---

[4] It should be observed in passing that some of the economic and political leadership of these communities did not always fit philistine specifications of respectability, and that on this score the Area Project program came under criticism during its early days.

[5] A recent reorganization of these services shifted much of this staff to the administrative jurisdiction of the Illinois Youth Commission.

their conduct. Fifth, his employment represented a prime means of initiating the education of the local population in the mysteries of conducting the welfare enterprise. Hence, virtually from the first, one of the most distinctive features of Area Project procedure was the employment, in appropriate categories and under the tutelage of staff sociologists of the Institute, of local residents to aid in the organization of the approximately dozen community or civic "committees" which were established in Chicago over the course of two decades.[6]

A second major procedural feature of the Area Project program is represented by efforts to preserve the independence of the neighborhood groups after they become established as functioning units. This turned out to be mainly an exercise in self-restraint, for the easier and in many ways more natural course would have been to maintain a close supervision and control of their activities. However, since it was the aim of the program to foster the development of knowledge and competence in the conduct of youth welfare activities and to encourage among residents of delinquency areas confidence in their own capacities to act with respect to their problems, the policy was followed of insisting upon a formal, structural autonomy of the organization. The problem in this connection was to maintain full support and help without rendering the independence of the group an empty formality.

[6] Sharp question has been raised by leaders of the social work profession regarding the competence of such persons, whose qualifications rested on assets of character and personal trait rather than on formal training and education. Leaders of the Area Project have always encouraged talented workers in this field to obtain as much training in the group work and social work fields as they could. However, they have regarded the talent for this work as the primary value.

MAINTAINING AUTONOMY

Three devices were found to be useful in dealing with this problem. First, neighborhood groups either exercised the power of veto in the assignment of Area Project staff to function as their executives or, more frequently, nominated a qualified local resident as their executive who was then employed as an Area Project staff member. Second, staff members were required to function as representatives and spokesmen of the local groups rather than as representatives of the Area Project central office or of the Sociology Department of the Institute for Juvenile Research. This served to foster an identification of the worker with the point of view and the needs of the local group. Third, policy decisions of neighborhood groups which appeared to Area Project staff to be unsound were nonetheless accepted and acted upon by them. Since staff members exercised much informal influence with the groups to which they were assigned, this problem arose infrequently. However, when it did arise, the autonomy of the neighborhood group was scrupulously respected.

These, then, are the procedural principles of the Area Project program: development of youth welfare organizations among residents of delinquency areas; employment of so-called indigenous workers wherever possible; and the fostering and preservation of the independence of these groups.

TYPES OF NEIGHBORHOOD GROUPS

Before moving to an evaluation of the Area Project as a delinquency prevention program, some indication ought to be made of the specific activities and forms of organization found among these neighborhood groups. The founders of the Area Project were always mindful of variety in the forms of social life and of the necessity, therefore, of adapting the approach to problems of organization as well as the content of program to conditions existing in each work location. In consequence each neighborhood organization within the Area Project differs somewhat from the others in both these respects.

Generally these differences are related to the patterns of social organization existing in their areas of operation and to the degree of unity and co-ordination among local institutions. On this axis, delinquency areas may be classified as structured and stable, structured but unstable, and unstructured and unstable.[7]

In the structured and stable communities, Area Project neighborhood organizations reflect a direct expansion in interests and functions of established neighborhood institutions. In some cases in this category, the dominant local church sponsors the organization, encouraging influential lay leaders to assume responsibility in the development of its program. However, there are few urban neighborhoods in which a single institution exercises complete dominance of the life of the residents. The more usual case in this class is represented by the local organization in which a number of important neighborhood institutions participate. These may include one or more churches, local political bodies, businessmen's groups, and lodges and fraternal groups. However, the representation is always informal, and membership belongs to participating persons as individuals. This informal mode of representation has come to be preferred, probably because

it permits the inclusion of important groups which are not formally constituted. Such, for example, are extended kinship groups, friendship cliques, and aggregations of persons temporarily unified around specific problems or issues. In unstructured or unstable communities the member usually represents only himself.

REASONS FOR JOINING GROUPS

Differences of this order among Area Project groups seem also to be accompanied by differences in motivation for participation. Members of all Area Project groups share a responsiveness to slogans of youth welfare. However, members of groups operating in the relatively well-organized neighborhoods tend to find in this activity a means for realizing their aspiration for upward mobility. A related need is served in those communities where the framework of institutional life fails to furnish a satisfactory place for certain age or sex groups. In these situations young adults and women, for example, may find in the Area Project neighborhood organization a means of gaining recognition.

The second major motivation is found most frequently in communities with few or no organizations (unstructured), and in those that have no fixed pattern of integration of the activities of organizations which may exist (unstable). Here the dominant motives for participation in the Area Project group are, first, a simple concern with the tragedies attending youthful law violation; and second, a desire to break down social isolation through organized contact with neighbors. These constitute the motivations most frequently sanctioned in official representations of Area Project doctrine because they are most apt to evoke a positive response to promotional appeals.

[7] These terms are relative. From the vantage point of an orderly and integrated middle-class residential community the structured and stable delinquency area might appear to be both excessively disorderly in terms of delinquency, crime, and other social problems and excessively controlled and dominated by religious or political organizations.

VARIETY IN PROGRAM CONTENT

Area Project neighborhood organizations all include, with varying emphasis and elaboration, three elements in their programs. The first is the sponsorship of a standard kind of recreation program for the children of the neighborhood, including in some instances programs of summer camping of considerable scope. Such recreation programs are likely to have two distinctive features: the use of residents, usually active memers of the Area Project group, as volunteers assisting in carrying on the recreation program; and the improvisation of store-front locations or unused space in churches, police stations, and even basements of homes for recreational use.

The second element of the program is represented by campaigns for community improvement. These are usually concerned with such issues as school improvement, sanitation, traffic safety, physical conservation, and law enforcement.

The third element of the program is reflected in the activity directed to the delinquent child, gangs of boys involved in delinquency, and, in some cases, adult offenders returning to the neighborhood from penal institutions. The activity includes helping police and juvenile court personnel develop plans for the supervision of delinquent youngsters; visiting boys committed to training schools and reformatories; working with boys' gangs in the informal settings of the neighborhood; and assisting adult parolees in their problems of returning to the community.

Specific program content in each of the local groups varies in relation to a number of factors. Among these are the facilities available for recreation or camping; the character and intensity of problems of safety, physical maintenance, or law enforcement in the area; and the staff's ability to arouse enthusiasm and effort from the leaders of the local organization in carrying on direct work with delinquents. Some groups are committed to an extensive program of recreation, including the development and operation of summer camps. Others, located in neighborhoods well equipped with such facilities, carry on no recreation work at all.[8] Some have labored strenuously in programs of neighborhood conservation; others have not concerned themselves with such issues. All have been continuously encouraged and helped by state-employed Area Project staff to maintain direct work with delinquent children and with street gangs, and with virtually no exception all local groups have done so.

ACHIEVEMENTS OF THE AREA
PROJECT

The achievements of the Area Project may best be assessed in relation to its theory of delinquency causation in the social setting of the high-rate neighborhoods. In this theory, delinquency is regarded as a product of a local milieu (a) in which adult residents do little or nothing in an organized public way to mobilize their resources in behalf of the welfare of the youth of the area; (b) in which the relative isolation of the adolescent male group, common throughout urban society, becomes at its extreme an absolute isolation with a consequent absolute loss of adult control; and (c) in which the formal agencies of correction and reformation fail to enlist the collaboration of persons and groups influential in the local society. Leaders of the Area Project

[8] Contrary to popular impression those of our big city neighborhoods which have been centers of social problems, including delinquency, for many decades sometimes acquire more than a just share of recreational facilities. This has resulted, quite simply, from their long-time status as objects of society's solicitude and philanthropy.

assume that progress in the prevention of delinquency cannot be expected until these three problems are well on their way to solution. Since progress in the solution of these problems comes only slowly, permanent declines in delinquency are not expected even after years of effort.

First among the accomplishments claimed by the Area Project is its demonstration of the feasibility of creating youth welfare organizations among residents of delinquency areas. Even in the most unlikely localities capable persons of good will have responded to the challenge of responsibility and have, with help and guidance, operated neighborhood programs. On the whole these organizations have exhibited vitality and stability and have come to represent centers of local opinion regarding issues which concern the welfare of the young. Above all, they have justified the assumption made by Clifford Shaw and his associates that persons residing in these localities have the capacity to take hold of such problems and contribute to their solution.

The Area Project has made an equally distinctive contribution respecting the problem of the isolation of the male adolescent in the delinquency area. From the beginning it called attention to the fact that the recreational and character-building agencies in these areas were unable, through their established programs, to modify the conduct of boys caught up in gang delinquency. In all probability the Area Project was the first organized program in the United States to use workers to establish direct and personal contact with the "unreached" boys to help them find their way back to acceptable norms of conduct. The adoption of this pattern in many cities during recent years may be regarded as in part, at least, a contribution of the Area Project to the development of working methods in the delinquency prevention field. At the

same time, it should be indicated that from the viewpoint of Area Project assumptions and procedures such work, to be effective, must be carried on as an integral part of a more general program sponsored by residents of the locality.

Finally, the Area Project has pioneered in exploring the problem of tempering the impersonality of the machinery which an urban society erects to control and correct the wayward child. Leaders of the Area Project have tended to regard the procedures of juvenile courts, school systems, police departments, probation and parole systems, training schools, and reformatories as inescapably bureaucratic. That is, the procedures of these organizations tend to become set ways of dealing with persons as members of categories. While it is both rational and efficient as a way of processing human problems, of doing something about and hence disposing of cases, this mode of operating results in serious loss of control of the conduct of the young person. The young person in particular is regarded as responsive mainly to the expectations of his primary groups. Thus, to enhance the effectiveness of the corrective agencies of society, it is necessary to enlist the disciplining power of such groups. This is a difficult and complex undertaking, since the customary primary groups for the child, namely family and peers, are often, in the disorder of the delinquency area, unable or undisposed to exercise the needed discipline.

However, it has been found that in no area is the disorder so unmitigated as to be devoid of persons, whether residents or staff employees of the local organization or both, who staunchly represent the values of conformity, many of whom have or can gain the trust of the wayward. Such relationships capture the essential element of the primary group. The Area Project effort has been to discover an effective pattern through which the good offices of these persons may be used by teachers, police, social workers, and court officials to formulate and execute for the supervision of delinquent children jointly conceived plans designed to meet the specific problems and needs of the person. In this exploration the Area Project has found that there are natural primary relationships with delinquents which may be used effectively for delinquency prevention and that they are best utiliized in collaboration with the agencies having formal responsibility for the welfare of the children and the protection of the community.

CONCLUDING OBSERVATIONS

In all probability these achievements have reduced delinquency in the program areas, as any substantial improvement in the social climate of a community must. However, the extent of the reduction is not subject to precise measurement. The effects of improvement in the environment of children are diffuse, cumulative, and intertwined with trends and forces which have their origin outside of programs of this character. In the final analysis, therefore, the Area Project program must rest its case on logical and analytic grounds.

No assessment of this program can be complete without defining its historically unique character. The genius of its founder, Clifford Shaw, lay in his sharp perception of delinquency as human behavior and in his sense of the naturalness or inevitability of violative activity in the youngster who, whether singly or in groups, is neglected, despised, or ignored as a person. This is the spirit which has animated the Area Project program and which has made it distinctive among delinquency prevention programs. This image of the delinquent and this notion of the delin-

quency-making process have led to the program's insistence on centering the operation within the milieu directly productive of delinquency, upon drawing into the operation as many as possible of the persons involved in the basic socializing experiences of youngsters, and upon dealing with delinquents or incipient delinquents as persons worthy of consideration and respect.

Not uncommonly, programs of prevention, whatever their initial intention or resolve, understandably tend to move away from direct contact with the delinquent and his milieu. Distance is achieved by interposing institutional forms between workers and delinquents, as in programs of formal and official treatment, or by dealing with the delinquent as a person arbitrarily abstracted from his social environment, as in programs based on individual therapy. This kind of evolution is comprehensible in the former type of retreat because the delinquent arouses anger and resentment in the law-abiding person, who consequently is hard put to form a sympathetic identification with him. Retreat from the milieu of the delinquent is even more understandable, for nothing would seem more unrewarding than to attempt to put aright the social disorder of the delinquency area.

It may well be that in perspective the Area Project's distinctive contribution to delinquency prevention as a field of practice and technique will be seen in its development of a method designed to keep preventional work focused upon its proper object, the delinquent as a person in his milieu. Central to this method is not only a view of the problem which stubbornly refuses to uncouple the delinquent from the social world which has created him, but a set of procedures which have demonstrated a capacity to draw into the preventional process itself the inhabitants of this world.

39. Three Approaches to Delinquency Prevention: A Critique

JOHN M. MARTIN

Aside from punishment and strict repression, delinquency prevention is usually defined in these three different ways:

1. Delinquency prevention is the sum total of all activities that contribute to the adjustment of children and to healthy personalities in children.

2. Delinquency prevention is the attempt to deal with particular environmental conditions that are believed to contribute to delinquency.

3. Delinquency prevention consists of specific preventive services provided to individual children or groups of children.[1]

GENERAL DESCRIPTION

The logic underlying preventive activities of the first type is disarmingly simple: anything that contributes to the adjustment of children and to their healthy personality development pre-

vents delinquency. Basically this approach links delinquency prevention with general improvements in the institutional fabric of our society, particularly as these affect child welfare. In large part this approach rests on a continuation and extension of measures, now commonplace on the American scene, which are designed to reduce the economic inequities of our social system. Such activities include procedures for raising the income levels of poverty stricken families, better low-rent housing, improving job tenure and work arrangements, and other means for reducing the rigors of poverty and economic insecurity. The approach also embraces attempts to reduce prejudice and discrimination against minority group people, increase the educational achievements of oncoming generations, improve marital relations by premarital counseling and family social work, and increase the impact of religious doctrines on both adults and children.

Preventive activities of the second type, by and large, aim to overcome factors in the immediate environment of children that seem to contribute to their delinquency. Such activities in-

---

* Adapted from the author's book, *Juvenile Vandalism: A Study of Its Nature and Prevention*, Charles C Thomas, Springfield, Ill., 1961.

[1] H. A. Bloch and F. T. Flynn, *Delinquency: The Juvenile Offender in America Today*, New York, Random House, 1956, p. 512.

SOURCE. John M. Martin, "Three Approaches to Delinquency Prevention: A Critique," from *Crime and Delinquency*, Volume 7, January 1961, pp. 16–24. Reprinted with the permission of the National Council on Crime and Delinquency.

clude attempts at community organization, such as the Chicago Area Projects (to be discussed later in this article); work by "coordinating councils" for harmonizing the efforts of welfare and child care agencies in delinquency prevention; the work of recreational and character-building agencies of all types; and attempts to reduce the commercial activities of adults which are clearly illegal and detrimental to the welfare of children who may get caught up in such traffic as, for example, the sale of liquor to minors, dope peddling, and receiving stolen goods.

Preventive activities of the third type include probation and parole services to children and youths, the programs of residential institutions and special schools for delinquents, child guidance clinics insofar as they are concerned with the diagnosis and treatment of delinquents, direct work with antisocial street gangs, and a variety of other services whose principal purpose is the adjustment of individual children or groups of children.

RELATIVE MERITS

It would be enormously difficult, if not impossible, to measure the effectiveness of these three types of preventive activities in terms of their ability actually to reduce delinquency, and no attempt will be made to do so here. However, general comment will be made about the relative merits of the three approaches.

In the main it is correct to conclude that improvement in the collective welfare, particularly in the welfare of depressed minority people, will reduce delinquency. In areas such as metropolitan New York the reduction of juvenile delinquency is most intimately linked with the successful assimilation of low-status groups, in particular the ever increasing number of migrant and uprooted Negroes and Puerto Ricans.[2] Whatever contributes to the welfare and assimilation of these people reduces the delinquency rate among their children and, correspondingly, in the communities in which they live; conversely, whatever impedes their progress inflates the delinquency rate in those areas.

But the relationship between delinquency and improvement in the general welfare is more complicated than it appears at first glance. For example, although it is tempting to claim that improved housing and the reduction of poverty will reduce both crime and delinquency, evidence that delinquency is highest during periods of extreme prosperity and *not* during depressions, as well as awareness of the variety and number of offenses committed by middle- and upper-class persons, should warn us against the facile assumption that the elimination of poverty is the Rosetta stone of crime prevention.

The relationship between delinquency, at least in terms of official statistics, and poverty and poor housing has, of course, long been noted by students of social problems. However, it is erroneous to conclude that the abolishment of these living conditions will also abolish delinquency among low-status children. As Bernard Lander pointed out in his study of differential juvenile delinquency rates by census tracts in Baltimore,[3] delinquency appears to be fundamentally related to social instability or *anomie* and not basically to poverty and poor housing.

[2] For an excellent discussion of this point, see O. Handlin, *The Newcomers*, Cambridge, Mass., Harvard University Press, 1959, especially chap. 4.

[3] See B. Lander, *Towards an Understanding of Juvenile Delinquency*, New York, Columbia University Press, 1954, especially p. 89.

It is within this context that we can best understand the disillusionment of those who expected too much by way of delinquency prevention from public housing. Their disappointment is well reflected in the pungent remark reportedly made by one student of New York's slums: "Once upon a time we thought that if we could only get our problem families out of those dreadful slums, then papa would stop taking dope, mama would stop chasing around, and Junior would stop carrying a knife. Well, we've got them in a nice apartment with modern kitchens and a recreation center. And they're the same bunch of bastards they always were."[4]

Emphasis upon *anomie* or social disorganization as a basic contributing factor to the high delinquency rates characteristic of some urban areas, with a concomitant de-emphasis of the obvious poverty of these areas as the underlying factor in their high delinquency rates, would, then, appear to be of cardinal importance for understanding and preventing delinquency in such places.

ANOMIE AND DELINQUENCY

Useful as Lander's statistical analysis of census tracts in Baltimore may be for destroying the myth that poverty and inadequate housing are the root causes of delinquency, the relationship between *anomie* and delinquency may also be more complicated than it seems. Lander emphasized the "internal" disorganization characteristic of high delinquency areas. Yet relatively *stable* neighborhoods may also be characterized by comparatively high rates of delinquency. A good example of just such a neighborhood is the tightly knit Italian slum of "Eastern City" examined by William Foote Whyte in his classic, *Street Corner Society.*[5]

The existence of stable but delinquent neighborhoods suggests that there are at least two kinds of areas that produce delinquency:

One is the rapidly changing and thoroughly chaotic local area of the kind isolated by Lander, perhaps best illustrated by New York City's racially mixed and tension-ridden Spanish Harlem so well described by Dan Wakefield in *Island in the City.*[6]

The other is the rather well-organized neighborhood such as the Italian ethnic community studied by Whyte, "disorganized" primarily in the sense that the way of life there is judged "out of step" when contrasted with the essentially middle-class culture of the greater society.[7]

It is in the second kind of area particularly that well-developed relationships are likely to exist between criminally precocious adolescents, corrupt politicians, and the seemingly inevitable racketeers. These relationships go far in explaining the easy transition many delinquents make from juvenile misbehavior to the more sophisticated forms of adult criminality. It is in this type of area, too, that personality and family structures are less likely to split and disintegrate under the stresses and strains characteristic of more chaotic and tension-ridden neighborhoods.

But distinctions of this sort, important as they may be for understanding differences in the social structure of

[4] D. Seligman, "The Enduring Slums" in The Editors of Fortune, *The Exploding Metropolis*, Garden City, N.Y., Doubleday, 1958, pp. 111–132.

[5] W. F. Whyte, *Street Corner Society*, enlarged edition; Chicago, University of Chicago Press, 1955.

[6] D. Wakefield, *Island in the City*, Boston, Houghton Mifflin, 1959.

[7] For a further discussion of these two kinds of delinquency areas, see W. F. Whyte, "Social Organization in the Slums," *American Sociological Review*, February, 1943, pp. 34–39.

delinquency areas, must not obscure a more basic fact: quite aside from the stability or instability of social relations in delinquency-prone areas, the traditions, standards, and moral sentiments of such areas are notoriously delinquent and criminal in "complexion" and "tone." This peculiar cultural climate has long been recognized by students of urban life, particularly by the ecologists and social psychologists of the "Chicago School" of American sociology.[8]

Recently this recognition has linked up with a more general discussion of social-class subcultures and particularly with more detailed analyses of lower-class culture as a breeding ground for delinquency. A good example of this is found in an article by Walter B. Miller which called attention to the delinquency proneness of lower-class culture in a discussion of the "focal concerns" of the urban lower-class way of life.[9] Miller's emphasis is not upon the so-called "subculture of the delinquent gang" as discussed by Albert K. Cohen,[10] but upon the content of the whole mode of existence of urban lower-class people. Miller believes that in the lower class, in contrast with the middle class, people are likely to have commitments to focal concerns such as physical "toughness," "smartness" interpreted as the ability to "con" or dupe others, and "excitement" in terms of seeking thrills, taking risks, and courting danger. When these commitments are combined with the intense need for

"in-group" membership and status or "rep" so characteristic of lower-class adolescents, Miller feels that conditions are especially ripe for the development of juvenile misconduct, particularly gang delinquency.

Thus the concept of social disorganization can be used to describe both stable and unstable delinquency areas. If we accept such disorganization as basic to an understanding of law violation in both kinds of areas, then we must question the value of other delinquency prevention methods besides those aimed at the reduction of poverty. In particular we should examine the limitations inherent in current attempts to prevent delinquency by the use of "individual-centered" techniques, such as social casework and related psychological-psychiatric services.

"INDIVIDUAL-CENTERED" TECHNIQUES

Practitioners of such techniques work toward individual adjustment, not social change. Seldom do they try to reduce the delinquency-producing features of the delinquent's environment, especially his extrafamilial environment; instead they emphasize adjustment to prevailing environmental conditions. For most delinquents, who are generally without emotional disturbance and who reflect the patterned deviancy so often found in their lower-class neighborhoods,[11] this means that they are expected to make a nondelinquent adjustment to a highly delinquent life situation. Our recidivism rates testify that at best this adjustment is precarious. Furthermore—and this is perhaps the more basic point—because such efforts fail to come to grips with

[8] For an excellent survey of studies in the "social ecology" of crime conducted during the past 150 years, see T. Morris, *The Criminal Area*, London, Routledge and Kegan Paul, 1958, chaps. 1–6.

[9] W. B. Miller, "Lower Class Culture as a Generating Milieu of Gang Delinquency," *The Journal of Social Issues,* Vol. 14, No. 3, 1958, pp. 5–19.

[10] See A. K. Cohen, *Delinquent Boys: The Culture of the Gang*, Glencoe, Ill., The Free Press, 1955.

[11] For a recent discussion of this crucial point, see W. C. Kvaraceus et al., *Delinquent Behavior: Culture and the Individual*, Washington, D.C., National Education Association of the United States, 1959, chap. 7.

the underlying social and cultural conditions giving rise to delinquency, they do little to prevent the outcropping of delinquency in the first instance. Most try to take hold only after maladjustment, even delinquency itself, has become manifest in the lives of the youngsters they seek to help.

This, however, should not be taken as a rejection of probation and parole, of training schools and reformatories, of child guidance clinics, and of other kinds of institutions and agencies given over to the care and "correction" of delinquents. Far from abandoning this line of approach, we must work hard at improving existing facilities of this sort and act imaginatively regarding the "invention" of new ones. Furthermore, we must, as we have seldom paused to do in the past, rigorously test and verify the effectiveness of various approaches aimed at the rehabilitation of individual delinquents. In this regard the basic question still to be answered is: To what extent and under what conditions do our correctional agencies really correct?

But despite all of this, we must not be so carried away by our desire to rehabilitate delinquents that we fail to see individual treatment in a proper perspective, lose sight of its limitations, and ignore the fundamental proposition that *the prevention of delinquency should include both individual treatment and general or social prevention.* Unfortunately this is just what has happened. To a truly remarkable degree public and private delinquency prevention agencies have spent comparatively little money or energy on community-centered programs of social prevention. For decades most of these agencies have put their effort into establishing various kinds of facilities for rehabilitating delinquents on a case-by-case basis, with the "model" and most prestigeful approach in recent

years being that of the psychiatrically-oriented child guidance clinic.

In sum, if we grant the primary role social disorganization plays in the development of delinquency, then the prevention of delinquency is not fundamentally a problem of bettering the general welfare of children or rehabilitating individuals, although the wisdom of continuing our attempts at both seems obvious. Nor for that matter is delinquency prevention essentially a problem of coordinating the activity of welfare agencies, although, like the application of "individual-centered" techniques, this too has an important role to play in prevention. (The coordination of agency activity is particularly valuable insofar as it enables accurate statistics on reported delinquency to be gathered in various jurisdictions, for it is only on the basis of such statistics that a community can determine the trend of its delinquency and measure the effectiveness of its preventive efforts. Agency coordination is even more valuable when it serves to bring various preventive programs and techniques to bear on potential delinquents before their deviancy becomes well established.)

Basically, the problem of delinquency prevention is a problem of social organization or reorganization, and other approaches have merit only to the degree that they contribute to such reorganization.

SOCIAL REORGANIZATION

How can social reorganization best be accomplished? Although we may be both unable and unwilling to reduce substantially the drift toward *anomie* that Robert K. Merton[12] and others have suggested is a pervasive characteristic of American society, we may be

[12] See R. K. Merton, *Social Theory and Social Structure*, Glencoe, Ill., The Free Press, 1949, chap. 4.

able to make partial inroads upon such disorganization, particularly insofar as it is related to the problem of juvenile delinquency, if we focus directly on the local areas in which delinquency is most pronounced. The logic underlying this proposal is that a local area "does not need to control the entire culture of a nation (which would be impossible) in order to control its delinquency rate. The things that need to be done are local and relate to personal interaction rather than to the larger institutions."[13] The essence of this approach to social reorganization, then, is to stimulate social change in delinquency-prone neighborhoods.

Unfortunately we have no rich arsenal of tried and proven techniques for accomplishing such change. Much needs to be learned and many innovations need to be developed toward this end. Despite these difficulties, however, we do know much about stimulating change in delinquency areas. The framework within which the reorganization of such neighborhoods can be accomplished has been well described by Frederic M. Thrasher in his outline of a proposal for coordinating neighborhood activity for delinquency prevention.[14]

This proposal envisions that any attempt to prevent delinquency in local areas must fix responsibility for social change at the neighborhood level where such changes can be implemented by local community leaders assisted by experts. Implicit in this approach is the assumption that in even the most delinquency-prone neighbor-

hoods not all the residents are criminals or delinquents, and that in such areas there is actually a duality of conduct norms—one favoring law-abiding behavior, the other favoring delinquency.[15]

Although Thrasher's plan utilizes, as subsidiary techniques, the best services offered by the usual community agencies—especially those of school, court, training institutions, and child guidance clinic—his proposal "represents a radical departure from the methods of social work and community organization as formerly conceived."[16]

This comment made almost three decades ago is nearly as applicable now as it was then. When one surveys current social work efforts at community organization, it becomes abundantly clear that, far from being focused in local areas, this activity is largely county- or city-wide in scope. Furthermore, all too often "community organization" in social work means that professional social workers meet with one another and with upper- and middle-class laymen for the purposes of mapping fund-raising campaigns, educating the public, coordinating agency activity, and similar objectives. Even when particular neighborhoods are the targets for such organization, seldom is the basic responsibility for such work placed in the hands of leaders who are truly representative of the people living in such areas.

Fundamentally the difference between the kind of plan outlined by Thrasher and traditional social work proposals for community organization is that in the former the real work is

[13] E. H. Sutherland, "Prevention of Juvenile Delinquency" in A. Cohen et al. (eds.), *The Sutherland Papers*, Bloomington, Indiana University Press, 1956, pp. 131–140.
[14] F. M. Thrasher, "Some Principles Underlying Community Co-ordination," *The Journal of Educational Sociology*, March, 1945, pp. 387–400.

[15] For a discussion of the duality of conduct norms in delinquency areas, see S. Kobrin, "The Conflict of Values in Delinquency Areas," *American Sociological Review*, October, 1951, pp. 653–661.
[16] F. M. Thrasher, *The Gang*, second revised edition; Chicago, University of Chicago Press, 1936, p. 538.

done by local residents who, banded together in a committee or council, act to (1) get the facts about delinquents and delinquency in their neighborhood; (2) organize existing preventive forces serving their neighborhood; (3) stimulate the development of new programs and services as required; and (4) in cooperation with professional agencies, look to the adjustment of their own delinquents, organize the leisure-time activities of their own children and young people, and improve the neighborhood environment, particularly by encouraging the enforcement of laws outlawing the activities of "slum landlords," petty racketeers, and other adults that are clearly detrimental to the welfare of their neighborhood and their children.

Other sociologists besides Thrasher have also foreseen the urgency of organizing the local community for delinquency prevention. Thus Edwin H. Sutherland, for example, endorsed local community organization as the most effective means for preventing delinquency, emphasized the need for placing responsibility for such organization in the hands of those whose children are the most likely to become delinquent, and cited the necessity of including juveniles themselves as participants in such organization.[17]

The inclusion of children and youths in neighborhood organizations for delinquency prevention is most vital. Too often they are simply left out of the planning and management phases of such activity. As a result, the isolation of their adolescence is compounded and a real opportunity for establishing closer ties between the generations is overlooked.

CHICAGO AREA PROJECT

Perhaps the best known of the relatively few delinquency prevention pro-

grams predicated on local community organization that are actually in operation are the Chicago Area Projects developed by Clifford R. Shaw and his associates.[18] Basically these projects aim at producing internal cohesiveness and conventional behavior in delinquency areas through the development of *indigenous leadership.* Outside professional leadership is minimal. Chiefly it is used to interest and develop local talent. Program activities are not ends in themselves but are used to achieve local unity. Some direct work is done with children and adolescents on a one-to-one counseling basis, and psychiatric and other types of referrals are made when needed. But the central aim is to draw local youngsters into various project activities so that they will identify with conventional rather than with delinquent groups and cultural patterns.

Outside leaders have a definite but limited role. This approach to area reorganization places principal emphasis on the role of natural community leaders who are carriers of conventional conduct norms. Not only do such leaders serve as nondelinquent models for emulation by youngsters attracted to programs offered by projects of this type, but because these indigenous leaders have prestige in the local area, they easily attract adults, as well as children and youths, to project programs in the first instance. It is around natural community leaders, then, that legitimate social structures can be germinated and multiplied in delinquency-prone areas. And it is in relationship

---

[17] Sutherland, "Prevention of Juvenile Delinquency," *op. cit.*

[18] For detailed descriptions of the Chicago Area Projects, see A. Sorrentino, "The Chicago Area Project after Twenty-five Years," *Federal Probation,* June, 1959, pp. 40–45; S. Kobrin, "The Chicago Area Project—A Twenty-five-Year Assessment," *The Annals of the American Academy of Political and Social Science,* March, 1959, pp. 20–29.

with such leaders and within such structures that youngsters can develop the close and intimate attachments with conventional models, achieve the satisfactions, and acquire the sense of personal worth and purpose necessary to counter the drift toward delinquency characteristic of their life situations.

SOME BASIC QUESTIONS

Two basic questions arise relative to preventive programs like the Chicago Area Projects: First, *can they be established, and once established will they last?* Second, *do they actually prevent delinquency?*

In regard to both parts of the first question, the answers seem to be definitely affirmative. Thus, in their recent evaluation of the Chicago Area Projects, Witmer and Tufts found that:

1. Residents of low-income areas can organize and have organized themselves into effective working units for promoting and conducting welfare programs.

2. These community organizations have been stable and enduring. They raise funds, administer them well, and adapt the programs to local needs.

3. Local talent, otherwise untapped, has been discovered and utilized. Local leadership has been mobilized in the interest of children's welfare.[19]

A definite answer to the second question is much more difficult to obtain. However, two types of evidence tentatively suggest that it too may be affirmative. First, statistics from 1930 to 1942 indicate that delinquency rates declined in three out of four of the communities in which projects were then being carried on; second, in some of the projects, work with men and

boys on parole from institutions has been very successful, with one project noting that out of forty-one parolees worked with between 1935 and 1944, only one was recommitted to an institution.[20] However, evidence such as this, without comparable controls, must obviously remain inconclusive. As has been remarked elsewhere, "the role of any preventive agency is likely to be most difficult to assess."[21] The Chicago Area Projects are no exception.

Another question that arises with respect to delinquency prevention programs geared to local leadership is: *How can they best be originated?* In this regard Walter C. Reckless has warned against waiting for the "spontaneous generation of experimental action"; outside help must get such programs started by stimulating local leaders to action.[22] Likewise it seems necessary that outside assistance should also include sufficient money, at least in the beginning, to help defray costs. Again and again programs of this type have foundered because the few hundred dollars raised by raffles, cake sales, thrift shops, and local donations were simply not enough to meet day-to-day expenses.

Who should provide such assistance? To this there are a number of answers. The potential role of private foundations, boards of education, fraternal organizations, and private industry and labor unions in supporting or initiating such activity is enormous. Of special significance is the potential but presently underdeveloped role urban churches can play in this field. The force of organized religion in the prevention of delinquency will be more fully realized if, and only if, more

[19] H. L. Witmer and E. Tufts, *The Effectiveness of Delinquency Prevention Programs*, Children's Bureau, United States Department of Health, Education and Welfare, Publication 350, Washington, D.C., Government Printing Office, 1954, p. 15.

[20] *Ibid.*, p. 16.
[21] Bloch and Flynn, *op. cit.*, p. 514.
[22] W. C. Reckless, *The Crime Problem*, New York, Appleton-Century-Crofts, 1950, pp. 524–525.

churches make realistic financial appropriations for such purpose and if, on the personal level, more churchmen base their approach to delinquency on love, direct service, intimate communication, and example, instead of on benign indifference, social distance, and exhortation.[23]

Assistance should also be available from other sources. For example, communities in states with Youth Authority plans might well call upon such authorities for help insofar as these state agencies actually make provision for realistic assistance to local communities; and in New York the new State Youth Division, one purpose of which is to stimulate communities to take action with regard to delinquency, should be a prime source of both money and advice, as should the Youth Board in New York City. Although the Federal Youth Corrections Act makes no provision for rendering assistance to local communities, the capacity of the federal government in this and other

[23] For excellent descriptions of religious programs in which churchmen have established intimate relationships with gang members and other residents of delinquency-prone neighborhoods, see C. K. Myers, *Light the Dark Streets*, Greenwich, Conn., Seabury Press, 1957, and H. J. Rahm and J. R. Weber, *Office in the Alley: Report on a Project with Gang Youngsters*, Austin, University of Texas, Hogg Foundation for Mental Health, 1958.

facets of community programs for delinquency prevention is tremendous. Finally, professional social workers themselves, as citizens, as agency representatives and educators, and as spokesmen for their highly influential professional associations, might become less remiss about endorsing, inaugurating, and experimenting with community-centered crime prevention programs.

In any event, if neighborhood programs run by residents are to develop to their full potential, it seems almost axiomatic that outside assistance must be provided.

IN SUMMARY

Students of delinquency are becoming increasingly aware of the necessity of reaching out beyond the child and his family in their efforts at prevention. It is submitted that the most efficacious approach for modifying the operating milieu of the bulk of our delinquents is through the widespread establishment of community-centered programs of prevention. Supported by continued improvement in the collective welfare —particularly in terms of the successful assimilation of low-status groups— and incorporating the best of "corrections" and individual treatment, the community-centered approach offers the most hope for reducing law-violation by our children and adolescents.

40. The Impact of a "Total-Community" Delinquency Control Project

WALTER B. MILLER

THE MIDCITY PROJECT: METHODS AND CLIENT POPULATION

The Midcity Project conducted a delinquency control program in a lower-class district of Boston between the years 1954 and 1957. A major objective of the Project was to inhibit or reduce the amount of illegal activity engaged in by resident adolescents. Project methods derived from a "total community" philosophy which has become increasingly popular in recent years and currently forms the basis of several large-scale delinquency control programs.[1] On the assumption that delinquent behavior by urban lower-class adolescents, whatever their personality characteristics, is in some significant degree facilitated by or actualized through certain structural features of the community, the Project executed "action" programs directed at three of the societal units seen to figure importantly in the genesis and perpetuation of delinquent behavior—the community, the family, and the gang.

The community program involved two major efforts: (1) the development and strengthening of local citizens' groups so as to enable them to take direct action in regard to local problems, including delinquency, and (2) an attempt to secure cooperation between those professional agencies whose operations in the community in some way involved adolescents (e.g., settlement houses, churches, schools, psychiatric and medical clinics, police, courts and probation departments, corrections and parole departments). A major short-term objective was to increase the possibility of concerted action both among the professional agencies themselves and between the professionals and the citizens' groups. The ultimate objective of these organizational efforts

[1] The principal current example is the extensive "Mobilization for Youth" project now underway in the Lower East Side of Manhattan. Present plans call for over 30 separate "action" programs in four major areas of work, education, community, and group service. The project is reported in detail in "A Proposal for the Prevention and Control of Delinquency by Expanding Opportunities," New York City: Mobilization for Youth, Inc. (December 1961), and in brief in "Report on Juvenile Delinquency," Washington, D.C.: Hearings of the Subcommittee on Appropriations, 1960, pp. 113–116.

SOURCE. Walter B. Miller, "The Impact of a 'Total-Community' Delinquency Control Project," from *Social Problems*, Volume 10, No. 2, Fall 1962, pp. 168–191. Reprinted with the permission of the Society for the Study of Social Problems and the author.

was to focus a variety of diffuse and uncoordinated efforts on problems of youth and delinquency in a single community so as to bring about more effective processes of prevention and control.[2]

Work with families was conducted within the framework of a "chronic-problem-family" approach; a group of families with histories of repeated and long-term utilization of public welfare services were located and subjected to a special and intensive program of psychiatrically-oriented casework.[3]

Work with gangs, the major effort of the Project, was based on the detached worker or area worker approach utilized by the New York Youth Board and similar projects.[4] An adult worker is assigned to an area, group, or groups with a mandate to contact, establish relations with, and attempt to change resident gangs. The application of this method by the Midcity Project incorporated three features not generally included in earlier programs: (1) All workers were professionally trained, with degrees in casework, group work, or both. (2) Each worker but one devoted primary attention to a single group, maintaining recurrent and intensive contact with group members over an extended time period. (3) Psychiatric consultation was made available on a regular basis, so that workers

were in a position to utilize methods and perspectives of psychodynamic psychiatry in addition to the group dynamics and recreational approaches in which they had been trained.

Between June 1954 and May 1957, seven project field workers (five men, two women) maintained contact with approximately 400 youngsters between the ages of 12 and 21, comprising the membership of some 21 corner gangs. Seven of these, totaling 205 members, were subjected to intensive attention. Workers contacted their groups on an average of 3.5 times a week; contact periods averaged about 5 or 6 hours; total duration of contact ranged from 10 to 34 months. Four of the intensive service groups were white males (Catholic, largely Irish, some Italians and Canadian French); one was Negro male, one white female, and one Negro female. All groups "hung out" in contiguous neighborhoods of a single district of Midcity—a fairly typical lower-class "inner-city" community.[5]

[5] The term "lower class" is used in this paper to refer to that sector of the population in the lowest educational and occupational categories. For the purposes of Project statistical analyses, those census tracts in Midcity were designated as "lower class" in which 50% or more of the adult residents had failed to finish high school, and 60% or more of resident males pursued occupations in the bottom five occupational categories delineated by the 1950 United States Census. Nineteen of the 21 census tracts in Midcity were designated "lower class" by these criteria. Within lower class, three levels were distinguished. "Lower-class 3" included census tracts with 80% or more of adult males in the bottom five occupational categories and 70% or more of the adults in the "high-school non-completion" category; "Lower-class 2" included tracts with 70–80% males in low occupations and 60–70% adults not having completed high school; "Lower-class 1," 60–70% low occupation males, 50–60% high-school non-completion. Of the 6,500 adolescents in Midcity, 17.5% lived in Lower-class 3 tracts; 53.1% in Lower-class 2, and 20.4% in Lower-class 1. The remaining 8.8% were designated "middle class." Project gangs de-

[2] See Lester Houston and Lena DiCicco, "Community Development in a Boston District," Boston: on file United Community Services of Boston, 1956.

[3] See David M. Austin, "The Special Youth Program Approach to Chronic Problem Families," Community Organization Papers, New York City: Columbia University Press, 1958. Also, Joan Zilbach, "Work with Chronic Problem Families: A Five-Year Appraisal," Boston: on file Judge Baker Guidance Center, 1962.

[4] A brief description of the background of this method appears on p. 406 of Walter B. Miller, "The Impact of a Community Group Work Program on Delinquent Corner Groups," The Social Service Review, 31 (December 1957), pp. 390–406.

The average size of male groups was 30, and of female nine. All intensive service groups, as well as most of the other known groups, were "locality-based" rather than "emergent" or "situationally organized" groups.[6] This meant that the groups were indigenous, self-formed, and inheritors of a gang tradition which in some cases extended back for 50 years or more. This kind of gang system in important respects resembled certain African age-class systems in that a new "class" or corner-group unit was formed every two or three years, recruiting from like-aged boys residing in the vicinity of the central "hanging" locale.[7] Thus the

total corner aggregate in relatively stable residential areas generally consisted of three to five age-graded male groups, each maintaining a sense of allegiance to their corner and/or traditional gang name, and at the same time maintaining a clear sense of identity as a particular age-graded unit within the larger grouping.

Girls groups, for the most part, achieved their identity primarily through their relations with specific boys' units, which were both larger and more solidary. Each locality aggregate thus included several female groups, generally bearing a feminized version of the male group name (Bandits-Bandettes; Kings-Queens).

ACTION METHODS WITH CORNER GANGS

The methods used by Project workers encompassed a wide range of techniques and entailed work on many levels with many kinds of groups, agencies, and organizations.[8] Workers con-

---

rived primarily from Lower-class 2 and 3 areas; studied gangs comprised approximately 16% of the adolescent (13–19) Lower-class 2 and 3 population of the study area—roughly 30% of the males and 4% of the females.

[6] Beyond this crude distinction between "locality-based" gangs and "other" types, a more systematic typology of Midcity gangs cannot be presented here. Karl Holton also distinguishes a locality-based gang ("area gang") as one type in Los Angeles County, and includes a classic brief description which applies without modification to the Midcity type. Karl Holton, "Juvenile Gangs in the Los Angeles Area," in *Hearings of the Subcommittee on Juvenile Delinquency,* 86th Congress, Part 5, Washington, D.C.: (November 1960), pp. 886–888. The importance of the "locality-based" typological distinction in this context is to emphasize the fact that Project gangs were *not* "emergent" groups organized in response to some common activity interest such as athletics, or formed around a single influential "magnetic" youngster, or organized under the influence of recreational or social work personnel. The gang structure pre-existed the Project, was coordinate with and systematically related to the kinship structure, and was "multi-functional" and "versatile" in that it served as a staging base for a wide range of activities and served a wide range of functions, both practical and psychological, for its members.

[7] The age-class system of Midcity closely resembles that of the Otoro of Central Sudan as described by Asmarom Legesse; "[Some East African Age-] Class Systems," Special Paper, Graduate School of Education, Harvard University, May 1961, and

S. F. Nadel, *The Nuba,* London: Oxford University Press, 1947, pp. 132–146. The Otoro age-class system, "one of the simplest . . . in eastern Africa" is in operation between the ages of 11 and 26 (in contrast to other systems which operate during the total life span), and comprises five classes formed at three-year intervals (Class I, 11–14; II, 14–17; III, 17–20; IV, 20–23; V, 23–26). The Midcity system, while less formalized, operates roughly between the ages of 12 and 23, and generally comprises four classes with new classes forming every two to four years, depending on the size of the available recruitment pool, density of population, and other factors. (Class I [Midgets] 12–14; II [Juniors] 14–16; III [Intermediates] 16–19; IV [Seniors] 19–22.) Otoro age classes, like Midcity's, are "multi-functional" in that they form the basis of athletic teams, work groups, and other types of associational unit.

[8] Project "action" methods have been described briefly in several published papers; David M. Austin, "Goals for Gang Workers," *Social Work,* 2 (October 1957), pp. 43–50; Ethel Ackley and Beverly Fliegel, "A Social Work Approach to Street-Corner Girls," *Social Work,* 5 (October

ceptualized the process of working with the groups as a series of sequential phases, on the model of individual psychotherapy. Three major phases were delineated—roughly, relationship establishment, behavior modification, and termination. In practice workers found it difficult to conduct operations according to the planned "phase" sequence, and techniques seen as primarily appropriate to one phase were often used during another. There was, however, sufficiently close adherence to the phase concept as to make it possible to consider specific techniques as primarily associated with a given phase.

Phase I: Contact and Relationship Establishment

During this phase workers sought out and located resident corner gangs and established an acceptable role-identity. Neither the location of the groups nor the establishment of a viable basis for a continued relationship entailed particular difficulties.[9] This phase included considerable "testing" of the workers; the youngsters put on display a wide range of their customary behaviors, with particular stress on violative forms—watching the worker closely to see whether his reactions and evaluative responses fell within an acceptable range. The workers, for their part, had to evince suffi-

cient familiarity with and control over the basic subcultural system of lower-class adolescents and its component skills as to merit the respect of the groups, and the right to continued association.

A major objective in gaining entrée to the groups was to establish what workers called a "relationship." Influenced in part by concepts derived from individual psychotherapy, Project staff felt that the establishment of close and meaningful relationships with group members was a major device for effecting behavior change, and was in fact a necessary precondition of all other direct service methods. The workers' conception of a "good" relationship was complex, but can be described briefly as a situation in which both worker and group defined themselves as contained within a common orbit whose major conditions were mutual trust, mutual affection, and maintenance of reciprocal obligations. The workers in fact succeeded in establishing and maintaining relationships of just this type. Considering the fact that these alliances had to bridge both age (adult-adolescent) and social status (lower class-middle class) differences, they were achieved and maintained with a surprising degree of success.[10]

Phase II: Behavior Modification via Mutual Activity Involvement

The behavior modification phase made the greatest demands on the skills, resourcefulness, and energy of the workers. Workers engaged in a wide variety of activities with and in behalf of their groups. The bulk of these activities, however, centered around three major kinds of effort: (1) Organizing groups and using these

---

1960), pp. 27–36; Walter B. Miller, "The Impact of a Community Group Work Program on Delinquent Corner Groups," *op. cit.*; and "Preventive Work with Street-Corner Groups: Boston Delinquency Project," *The Annals of the American Academy of Political and Social Science*, 322 (March 1959), pp. 97–106, and in detail in one unpublished report, David Kantor and Lester Houston, *Methods of Working with Street Corner Youth*, 1959, mimeo, 227 pp., on file Harvard Student Volunteers Project.

[9] Extensive discussion of the specific techniques of contact, role-identity establishment and relationship maintenance is included in Kantor and Houston, *ibid.*

[10] Research methods for categorizing worker-group relationships according to intensity and intimacy will be cited in future reports.

as the basis of involvement in organized activities; (2) Serving as intermediary between group members and adult institutions; (3) Utilizing techniques of direct influence.

The workers devoted considerable effort to changing group relational systems from the informal type of the street gang to the formal type of the club or athletic team, and involving the groups so reorganized in a range of activities such as club meetings, athletic contests, dances, and fund-raising dinners. In most cases this effort was highly successful. Clubs formed from the corner groups met regularly, adopted constitutions, carried out extensive and effective club activities. Athletic teams moved from cellar positions to championships in city athletic leagues. One group grossed close to a thousand dollars at a fund-raising dance.

Project use of the "organized group and planned activities" method was buttressed by rationale which included at least five premises. (1) The experience of learning to operate in the "rule-governed" atmosphere of the formal club would, it was felt, increase the group members' ability to conduct collective activities in an orderly and law-abiding fashion. (2) The influence of the more lawfully oriented leaders would be increased, since authority-roles in clubs or teams would be allocated on different bases from those in the corner gang. (3) The need for the clubs to rely heavily on the adult worker for advice and facilitation would place him in a strategic position to influence group behavior. (4) The need for clubs to maintain harmonious relations with local adults such as settlement house personnel and dance hall owners in order to carry out their activity program, as well as the increasing visibility of the organized group, would put a premium on maintaining

a public reputation as non-troublesome, and thus inhibit behavior which would jeopardize this objective. (5) Active and extensive involvement in lawful and adult-approved recreational activities would, it was felt, substantially curtail both time and energy potentially available for unlawful activity. This devil-finds-work premise was taken as self-evidently valid, and was reinforced by the idleness-boredom explanation frequently forwarded by group members themselves—"We get in trouble because there's nuthin to do around here." On these grounds as well as others, the use of this method appeared amply justified.[11]

In performing the role of intermediary, workers proceeded on the premise that gang members were essentially isolated within their own adolescent slum world and were either denied, or lacked the ability to seek out, "access" to major adult institutions. This blocked access, it was felt, prevented the youngsters from seeking prestige through "legitimate" channels, forcing them instead to resort to "illegitimate" forms of achievement such as thievery, fighting, and prostitution. On this assumption, the Project aimed deliberately to open up channels of access to adult institutions—particularly in the areas of education and employment.

In the world of work, Project workers arranged appointments with employment agencies, drove group members to job interviews, counseled them as to proper demeanor as job applicants and as employees, urged wavering workers not to quit their jobs.

[11] Further elaboration of the rationale behind the "group-organization-and-activity" method, as well as some additional detail on its operation, is contained in David Austin, "Goals for Gang Workers," *op. cit.*, p. 49, and Walter B. Miller, "*The Place of the Organized Club in Corner-Group Work Method*, Boston: on file Special Youth Program, mimeo, 7 pp. (November 1956).

Workers also contacted business firms and urged them to hire group members. In the area of education, workers attempted to solidify the often tenuous bonds between group members and the schools. They visited teachers, acted to discourage truancy, and worked assiduously—through means ranging from subtle persuasion to vigorous argument—to discourage the practice of dropping out of school at or before the legally permissible age. Workers arranged meetings with school personnel and attempted to acquaint teachers and other school staff with the special problems of corner youngsters. Every effort was made to arrange scholarships (generally athletic) for those group members for whom college seemed a possibility.

Workers also acted as go-between for their youngsters and a variety of other institutions. They arranged for lawyers in the event of court appearances, and interceded with judges, probation officers, correctional officials, and parole personnel. They obtained the use of the recreational facilities and meeting places in settlement houses and gyms which would not have considered admitting the rough and troublesome gang members in the absence of a responsible adult sponsor. They persuaded local storekeepers and businessmen to aid the groups in their money-raising efforts. They arranged for the use or rental of dance halls, and solicited radio stations to provide locally famous disc-jockeys to conduct record hops. They organized meetings between gang members and local policemen during which both sides were given the opportunity to air their mutual grievances.

During later stages of the Project, workers brought together the clubs of the corner gangs and the adult organizations formed by the Project's Community Organization program, and gang members and community adults served together on joint committees working in the area of community improvement. One such committee exerted sufficient pressure on municipal authorities to obtain a $60,000 allocation for the improvement of a local ball field; another committee instituted an annual "Sports Night" during which most of the community's gangs—some of whom were active gang-fighting enemies—attended a large banquet in which city officials and well-known sports figures made speeches and presented awards for meritorious athletic achievement.

Thus, as a consequence of the workers' activities, gang members gained access to a wide variety of legitimate adult institutions and organizations—schools, business establishments, settlement houses, municipal athletic leagues, public recreational facilities, guidance services, health facilities, municipal governmental agencies, citizens groups, and others. It could no longer be said that the groups were isolated, in any practical sense, from the world of legitimate opportunity.[12]

While Project methods placed major

[12] Project research data made it possible to determine the relative amount of worker effort devoted to various types of activity. The frequency of 12 different kinds of activity engaged in by workers toward or in behalf of group members ("worker functions") was tabulated for all seven workers. Of 9958 recorded worker functions, 3878 were executed in connection with 22 organizations or agencies. Of these "institutionally-oriented" functions, workers acted in the capacity of "intermediary" for group members 768 times (19.8%), making "intermediation" the second most frequent type of "institutionally-oriented" worker function. The most frequent function was the exercise of "direct influence" (28.7%), to be discussed in the next section. Thus about one-half of all institutionally-oriented worker activity involved two functions—acting as intermediary and engaging in direct influence efforts. Of the 768 intermediary functions, 466 (60.7%) were exercised in connection with six kinds of organizations or groups—business organizations, schools, social welfare agencies, families, and other gangs.

stress on changing environmental conditions through organization, activity involvement, and opening channels of access, workers were also committed to the use of methods designed to induce personality change. The training of most workers had involved exposure to the principles of, and some practice in the techniques of, psychodynamic psychotherapy, and serious consideration was given to the possibility of attempting some form of direct application of psychotherapeutic principles, or techniques based on "insight" therapy. After much discussion workers decided that the use of techniques appropriate to the controlled therapist-patient situation would not be practicable in the open and multi-cliented arena of the corner gang world, and arrangements were made to utilize this approach through indirect rather than direct means.

Psychodynamic methods and individual treatment approaches were utilized in two ways. First, a contract was made with a well-known child-psychiatry clinic, and workers consulted with psychodynamically trained psychiatrists on a regular basis. During these sessions the psychiatrists analyzed individual cases on the basis of detailed case summaries and recommended procedures for the workers to execute. In this way the actual operating policies of the workers were directly influenced by the diagnostic concepts and therapeutic procedures of psychodynamic psychiatry. Second, in cases where the workers or the psychiatric consultants felt that more direct or intensive therapy for group members or their families was indicated, arrangements were made to refer these cases either to the psychiatric clinic or to local casework or family-service agencies.

Another type of direct influence technique utilized by the workers was "group-dynamics"—a method which combined approaches of both psychodynamic and small-group theory. As adult advisors during club meetings, during informal bull-sessions, and in some instances during specially arranged group-therapy sessions, workers employed the specific techniques of persuasion and influence developed out of the group-dynamics approach (indirect suggestion, non-directive leadership, permissive group guidance, collective reinforcement). Sessions based on the group-therapy model were generally geared to specific emergent situations—such as an episode of sexual misbehavior among the girls or an upsurge of racial sentiment among the boys.[13]

The direct-influence technique which operated most consistently, however, was simply the continued presence with the group of a law-abiding, middle-class-oriented adult who provided active support for a particular value position. This value stance was communicated to the youngsters through two principal devises—advice and exemplification. The worker served as counsellor, advisor, mentor in a wide range of specific issues, problems, and areas of behavioral choice as these emerged in the course of daily life. Should I continue school or drop out? Can we refrain from retaliatory attack and still maintain our honor? How does one approach girls? How does one handle an overly romantic boy? Should I start a pimping operation? In all these issues and many more—sometimes broached by the worker, more frequently by the youngsters—the workers put their support—often subtle but nonetheless consistent—behind the law-abiding versus the law-violating choice, and, to a lesser extent, the middle-class-oriented over the

[13] A description of the use of group-dynamics techniques by Project workers is included in A. Paul Hare, "Group Dynamics as a Technique for Reducing Intergroup Tensions," Cambridge, Mass.: Harvard University, unpublished paper, 1957, pp. 14–22.

lower-class-oriented course of action in regard to long-term issues such as education, occupation, and family life.[14]

But the continued association of worker and group engaged a mechanism of influence which proved in many ways more potent than advice and counsel. The fact of constant association, and the fact that workers became increasingly accepted and admired, meant that they were in a particularly strategic position to serve as a "role-model," or object of emulation. A strong case can be made for the influencive potency of this device. Adolescents, as they move towards adult status, are often pictured as highly sensitive to, and in search of, models of estimable adult behavior, and as particularly susceptible to emulation of an adult who plays an important role in their lives and whom they respect and admire. It appeared, in fact, that gang members were considerably more impressed by what the workers *were* than by what they said or did. The youngsters were particularly aware that the workers were college people, that they were responsible spouses and parents in stable mother-father families, that they were conscientious workers under circumstances which afforded maximum opportunities for goofing-off. The workers' statuses as college people, "good" family people, and responsible workers constituted an implicit endorsement of these statuses, and the course of action they implied.

In some instances the admiration of group members for their worker approached hero-worship. One group set up a kind of shrine to their worker after his departure; on a shelf in the corner store where they hung out they placed his photograph, the athletic trophies they had won under his aegis,

[14] For the frequency of use of "direct influence" techniques, see footnote 12.

and a scrap-book containing accounts of the many activities they had shared together. Visitors who knew the worker were importuned to relay to him a vital message—"Tell him we're keepin' our noses clean. . . ."

Phase III: Termination

Since the Project was set up on a three-year "demonstration" basis, the date of final contact was known well in advance. Due largely to the influence of psychodynamic concepts, workers were very much concerned about the possibly harmful effects of "termination," and formulated careful and extensive plans for effecting disengagement from their groups. During the termination phase the workers' efforts centered around three major areas: scheduling a gradual reduction in the frequency of contact and "services" so as to avoid an abrupt cut-off; preparing the groups emotionally for the idea of termination by probing for and discussing feelings of "desertion" anger and loss; and arranging for community agencies to assume as many as possible of the services workers had provided for the groups (e.g., recreational involvement, counseling, meeting places for the clubs).

Despite some difficult moments for both workers and group members (one worker's car was stolen during the tearful farewell banquet tendered him by his group the night before he was to leave for a new job in another city; group members explained this as a symbolic way of saying "Don't leave Midcity!"), termination was effected quite successfully; workers moved off to other involvements and the groups reassumed their workerless position within the community.

In sum, then, the methods used in the Project's attempt to inhibit delinquent behavior were based on a sophisticated rationale, utilized both sociocultural and psychological concepts and methods, encompassed an unusually wide range of practice techniques, and were executed with care, diligence, and energy by competent and professionally trained workers. It was impossible, of course, to execute all planned programs and methods as fully or as extensively as might have been desired, but in overall perspective the execution of the Project showed an unusually close degree of adherence to its ambitious and comprehensive plan of operation.[15] What, then, was the impact of these efforts on delinquent behavior?

THE IMPACT OF PROJECT EFFORTS

The Midcity Project was originally instituted in response to a community perception that uncontrolled gang violence was rampant in Midcity. Once the furor attending its inception had abated, the Project was reconceptualized as a "demonstration" project in community delinquency control.[16] This meant that in addition to setting up methods for effecting changes in its client population, the Project also assumed responsibility for testing the efficacy of these methods. The task of

evaluating project effectiveness was assigned to a social science research staff which operated in conjunction with the action program.[17] Since the major effort of the Project was its work with gangs, the evaluative aspect of the research design focused on the gang program, and took as a major concern the impact of group-directed methods on the behavior of target gangs. However, since the focal "client" population of the group-work program (gang members) was a subpopulation of the larger client population of the overall project ("trouble"-prone Midcity adolescents), measures of change in the gangs also constituted a test of the totality of control measures utilized by the Project, including its community organization and family-service programs.

The broad question—"Did the Project have any impact on the behavior of the groups it worked with?"—has, in effect, already been answered. The above description of Project methods shows that workers became actively and intensively involved in the lives and activities of the groups. It is hardly conceivable that relatively small groups of adolescents could experience daily association with an adult—especially an adult committed to the task of

[15] A previous report, "Preventive Work with Street-Corner Groups: Boston Delinquency Project," *op. cit.*, p. 106, cited certain factors which made it difficult to execute some project methods as fully as might have been desired. With greater perspective, derived both from the passage of time and increased knowledge of the experience of other projects, it would now appear that the Midcity Project was relatively less impeded in this regard than many similar projects, especially in regard to difficulties with police, courts, and schools, and that from a comparative viewpoint the Project was able to proceed relatively freely to effect most of its major methods.

[16] Events attending the inception of the Midcity Project are cited in "The Impact of a Community Group Work Program on Delinquent Corner Groups," *op. cit.*, and in Walter B. Miller, "Inter-Institutional Conflict as a Major Impediment to Delinquency Prevention," *Human Organization,* 17 (Fall 1958), pp. 20–23.

[17] Research methods were complex, utilizing a wide range of techniques and approaches. A major distinction was made between "evaluative" (measurement of impact) and "informational" (ethnographic description and analysis) research. No detailed account of research methods has been published, but brief descriptions appear in "The Impact of a Community Group Work Program on Delinquent Corner Groups," *op. cit.*, pp. 392–396, and "Preventive Work with Street-Corner Groups: Boston Delinquency Project," *op. cit.*, pp. 99–100, *passim.* A somewhat more detailed description of one kind of content analysis method used in an earlier pilot study, and modified for use in the larger study, appears in Walter B. Miller, Hildred Geertz, and Henry S. G. Cutter, "Aggression in a Boys' Street-Corner Group," *Psychiatry,* 24 (November 1961), pp. 284–285.

changing their behavior—without undergoing some substantial modification. But the fundamental *raison d'etre* of the Project was not that of demonstrating the possibility of establishing close relationships with gangs, or of organizing them into clubs, or of increasing their involvement in recreational activities, or of providing them with access to occupational or educational opportunities, or of forming citizens' organizations, or of increasing inter-agency cooperation. These objectives, estimable as they might be, were pursued not as ends in themselves but as means to a further and more fundamental end —the inhibition and control of criminal behavior. The substantial effects of the Project on nonviolent forms of behavior will be reported elsewhere; this paper addresses itself to a central and critical measure—the impact of the Project on specifically violative behavior.[18]

The principal question of the evaluative research was phrased as follows: *Was there a significant measurable inhibition of law-violating or morally disapproved behavior as a consequence of Project efforts?* For purposes of research procedure this question was broken down into two component questions: (1) To what extent was there a measurable reduction in the actual or expected frequency of violative behavior by Project group members during or after the period of Project contact? and (2) To what extent could

observed changes in violative behavior be attributed to Project activity rather than to other possible "causative" factors such as maturation or police activity?[19] Firm affirmative answers to the first question would necessarily have to precede attempts to answer further questions such as "Which methods were most effective?"; the value of describing what the workers did in order to reduce delinquency would evidently depend on whether it could be shown that delinquency had in fact been reduced.

Following sections will report three separate measures of change in patterns of violative behavior. These are: (1) disapproved forms of customary behavior; (2) illegal behavior; (3) court appearance rates. These three sets of measures represent different methods of analysis, different orders of specificity, and were derived from different sources. The implications of this for achieved results will be discussed later.

Trends in Disapproved Behavior

A central form of "violative" behavior is that which violates specific legal statutes (e.g., theft, armed assault). Also important, however, is behavior which violates "moral" norms or ethical standards. Concern with such behavior is of interest in its own right (Was there a reduction in morally violative behavior?) as well as in relation to illegal behavior (Were developments in the areas of illegal and immoral behavior related or independent?). The relationship between immoral and illegal behavior is highly complex; most behavior which violates legal norms also violates moral

[18] Detailed analyses of changes in "nonviolative" forms of behavior (e.g., frequency of recreational activities, trends in "evaluatively neutral" behaviors) as well as more generalized "change-process" analyses (e.g., "structural" changes in groups—factions, leadership; overall patterning of change and relations between changes in violative and non-violative patterns) will appear in Walter B. Miller, *City Gangs: An Experiment in Changing Gang Behavior,* John Wiley and Sons, in preparation.

[19] The "study population" toward which these questions were directed was the 205 members of the seven corner gangs subjected to "intensive service" by workers. Unless otherwise specified, the term "Project Groups" will be used to refer to this population.

norms (overtime parking is one example of an exception), but much immoral behavior seldom results in legal action (homosexual intimacy between women; failure to attempt to rescue a drowning stranger).

Designating specific forms of behavior as "illegal" presents a relatively simple task, since detailed and fairly explicit criminal codes are available; designating behavior as "immoral" is far more difficult, both because of the multiplicity of moral codes in American society, and because many important moral norms are not explicitly codified.[20] In addressing the question —"Did the Project bring about a decrease in morally violative behavior?", at least four sets of moral codes are of relevance—those of middle-class adults, of middle-class adolescents, of lower-class adults, and of lower-class adolescents.[21] While there are large areas of concordance among these sets, there are also important areas of noncorrespondence. The method employed in this area was as follows:

A major source of data for Project research was a large population of "behavior sequences" engaged in by group members during the study period. These were derived from a variety of sources, the principal source being the detailed descriptive daily field reports of the workers.[22] All recorded behavioral events involving group members were extracted from the records and typed on separate data cards. These cards were coded, and filed in chronological order under 65 separate categories of behavior such as drinking behavior, sexual behavior, and theft. A total of 100,000 behavior sequences was recorded, coded, and filed.

Fourteen of the 65 behavior categories were selected for the purpose of analyzing trends in immoral behavior.[23] These were: theft, assault, drinking, sex, mating, work, education, religion, and involvement with courts, police, corrections, social welfare, family, and other gangs. Seventy-five thousand behavioral sequences were included under these fourteen categories.

A separate set of evaluative standards, based primarily on the workers' own values, was developed for each of the fourteen areas. The workers as individuals were essentially oriented to the value system of middle-class adults, but due largely to their training in social work, they espoused an "easier" or more permissive version of these standards. In addition, as a result of their experiences in the lower-class community, their standards had been further modified to accommodate in some degree those of the adolescent gangs. The workers' standards thus comprised an easier baseline against which to measure change since they were considerably less rigid than those

[20] A brief discussion of the complexities of the "multiple-moral-norm" system of the United States is contained in William C. Kvaraceus, Walter B. Miller, et al., *Delinquent Behavior: Culture and the Individual*, Washington, D.C.: National Education Association of the United States, 1959, pp. 46–49.

[21] This four-type distinction is very gross; a range of subsystems could be delineated within each of the four cited "systems."

[22] 8870 pages of typescript records were subjected to coding. Of these, 6600 pages were self-recorded field reports by workers; 690 pages were worker reports to the Project Director; 640 were field reports and interviews by research staff; 150 were tape-recorded transcriptions of group interaction.

A brief description of the principles of the data-coding system, based on the concept of the "object-oriented-behavior-sequence," is included in Ernest Lilienstein, James Short, et al., "Procedural Notes for the Coding of Detached Worker Interviews," Chicago: University of Chicago Youth Studies Program (February 1962), pp. 2–7.

[23] These fourteen were selected because they included the largest numbers of recorded events, and because they represented a range of behaviors along the dimension "high violative potential" (theft, assault) through "low violative potential" (church, family-oriented behavior).

which would be applied by most middle-class adults.

Listings were drawn up for each of the fourteen areas which designated as "approved" or "disapproved" about 25 specific forms of behavior per area. A distinction was made between "actions" (behavioral events observed to occur) and "sentiments" (attitudes or intentions).[24] Designations were based on three kinds of information: evaluative statements made by the workers concerning particular areas of behavior; attitudes or actions workers had supported or opposed in actual situations; and an attitude questionnaire administered to each worker. Preliminary listings were submitted to the workers to see if the items did in fact reflect the evaluative standards they felt themselves to espouse; there was high agreement with the listings; in a few instances of disagreement modifications were made.

A total of 14,471 actions and sentiments were categorized as "approved," "disapproved," or "evaluatively neutral." While these data made possible detailed and extensive analysis of differential patterns of behavior change in various areas and on different levels, the primary question for the most general purposes of impact measurement was phrased as—"Was there a significant reduction in the relative frequency of *disapproved actions* during the period of worker contact?" With some qualifications, the answer was "No."

Each worker's term of contact was divided into three equal phases, and the relative frequency of disapproved

[24] Examples of approved and disapproved actions and sentiments in the area of drinking are as follows: *Approved action:* "refusal to buy or accept liquor"; *disapproved action:* "getting drunk, going on a drinking spree"; *approved sentiment:* "stated intention to discontinue or reduce frequency of drinking"; *disapproved sentiment:* "bragging of one's drinking prowess."

actions during the first and third phase was compared.[25] During the full study period, the 205 members of the seven intensive analysis groups engaged in 4518 approved or disapproved actions. During the initial phase, 785 of 1604 actions (48.9%) were disapproved; during the final phase, 613 of 1364 (44.9%)—a reduction of only 4%.

Of the fourteen behavior areas, only one ("school-oriented behavior") showed a statistically significant reduction in disapproved actions. Of the remaining thirteen, ten showed decreases in disapproved actions, one no change, and two (church- and social-agency-oriented behavior) showed increases. Of the seven analysis groups, only one (white, male, younger, higher social status) showed a statistically significant reduction. Of the remaining six, five showed decreases in disapproved actions, one no change, and one (white, male, older, lower social status) an increase.[26]

The unexpected degree of stability over time in the ratio of approved to

[25] Selected findings in regard only to disapproved actions are reported here. Future reports will present and analyze trends in both actions and sentiments, and in approved, disapproved and evaluatively neutral forms, and the relations among these.

[26] Chi-square was used to test significance. For all fourteen behavior areas for all seven groups, chi-square was 4.57 (one d.f.), which was significant between the .02 and .05 level. However, almost all the "change" variance was accounted for by the single area which showed a significant reduction (chi-square for "school" was 14.32, significant beyond the .01 level). The other 13 behavior areas, accounting for 91.6% of the evaluated actions, showed a reduction of only 2.3%. Chi-square was 1.52 (one d.f.) which fails of significance. Chi-square for the one significant change group (Junior Outlaws) was 9.21, significant at the .01 level. However, omitting the one "significant change" behavior area (school) from consideration, chi-square for the remaining 90% of Junior Outlaws behavior areas was 3.19—which fails of significance at the .05 level.

disapproved actions is all the more noteworthy in view of the fact that one might have expected the area of moral behavior to have felt the most direct impact of the workers' presence. One clue to the stability of the change figures lies in the fact that there was a good correspondence between the degree of change in disapproved actions and the social status of the group; in general, the lower the group's social status, the smaller the reduction in disapproved actions.[27]

Trends in Illegal Acts

The central question to be asked of a delinquency control program is— "Does it control delinquency?" One direct way of approaching this question is to focus on that "target" population most directly exposed to program action methods and ask "Was there a decrease in the frequency of crimes committed by the target population during the period of the program?" Under most circumstances this is difficult to answer, owing to the necessity of relying on records collected by police, courts, or other "official" agencies. The drawbacks of utilizing official incidence statistics as a measure of the actual occurrence of criminal behavior have frequently been pointed out; among these is the very complex process of selectivity which governs the conversion of committed crimes into official statistics; many crimes are never officially detected; many of those detected do not result in an official arrest; many arrests do not eventuate in court action,

and so on. At each stage of the conversion process, there is a multiplicity of factors relatively independent of the commission of the crime itself which determines whether or not a crime will be officially recorded, and in what form.

The Midcity Project was able to a large extent to overcome this difficulty by the nature of its base data. Because of their intimate daily association with gang members, workers were in a position both to observe crimes directly and to receive reports of crimes shortly after they occurred. The great majority of these never appeared in official records.[28]

The research question in the area of illegal behavior was phrased: "Was there a significant decrease in the frequency of statute violations committed by Project group members during the period of worker contact?" As in the case of disapproved actions, the answer was, with some qualifications, "No." Methods and results were as follows.

Every statute-violating act committed by a Project group member during the course of the contact period was recorded on an individual record form. While the bulk of recorded acts were derived from the workers' field reports, information was obtained from all available sources, including official records. Very few of the crimes recorded by official agencies were not also recorded

---

[27] Rank-difference correlation between "reduction in disapproved actions" and "lower social status" was —.82. The fact that this kind of association (the lower the social status the less change) appeared frequently in analyses of specific forms of behavior attests to the strength of the influence of group social status on patterns of delinquency and vulnerability to change efforts.

[28] The availability to the Project of both official and unofficial statistics on crime frequency made it possible to derive "conversion ratios" showing the proportion of crimes recorded by official agencies to those recorded by the Project. These ratios will be reported in greater detail in *City Gangs, op. cit.;* in brief, ratios of "Project-recorded" to "court-appeared" offenses were as follows. For all categories of offense for both sexes, 15% of known crimes resulted in court action. For males only this ratio was 16%; fewer than 1% of recorded female crimes were court processed. The highest ratio was in the case of theft-type offenses by males; about 25% were court processed. About 10% of male drinking and assaultive offenses resulted in court appearance.

by the Project; many of the crimes recorded by the Project did not appear in official records. During the course of the Project, a total of 1005 legally violative acts was recorded for members of the seven intensive analysis groups. Eighty-three per cent of the 205 Project group members had committed at least one illegal act; 90% of the 150 males had been so involved. These figures alone show that the Project did not prevent crime, and there had been no expectation that it would. But did it "control" or "inhibit" crime?

Offenses were classified under eleven categories: theft, assault, alcohol violations, sex offenses, trespassing, disorderly conduct, truancy, vandalism, gambling violations, and "other" (e.g., strewing tacks on street, killing cats).[29] Each worker's term of contact was divided into three equal phases, and the frequency of offenses during the initial and final phase was compared.

Seven hundred and fifty-two of the 1005 offenses were committed during the initial and final phases. Of these, 394 occurred during the initial phase, and 358 during the final—a reduction of 9.1%. Considering males only, however, 614 male crimes accounting for 81.6% of all offenses showed an *increase* of 1.3% between initial and final phases. In order to localize areas of greater and lesser change, a distinction was made between "major" and "minor" types of offense, in which theft, assault, and alcohol offenses, accounting for 70.5% of all male offenses, were categorized as "major." On these major offenses the male groups showed an increase of 11.2%—the older male groups showing an increase of 4.7%, and the younger an increase of 21.8%.

In sum, then, it could not be said that there was any significant reduction in the frequency of known crimes during the course of the Project. The modest decrease shown by the total sample was accounted for largely by the girls and by minor offenses; major offenses by boys, in contrast, increased in frequency during the course of the Project, and major offenses by younger boys increased most of all.[30]

Trends in Court Appearances

The third major index to Project impact was based on court appearance statistics. The principal research question in this area was phrased: "Did the Project effect any decrease in the frequency with which Project group members appeared in court in connection with crimes?"[31] The use of court-

---

[29] Determination of illegality was based on the offense classifications of the Massachusetts Penal Code. The complexities of definition of the various offense categories cannot be detailed here, but most categories represent higher-level generality definitions than those of the code. For example, the category "theft" is used here to include all forms of unlawful appropriation of property, thus subsuming the more than 30 distinctions of the Penal Code, e.g., robbery, armed, unarmed; larceny, grand, petty; burglary, etc.). Non-theft auto violations are included under "other" since so few were recorded; similarly, narcotics violations, a major form of crime from a "seriousness" point of view, are included under "other" since virtually no instances were recorded.

[30] None of these changes proved significant on the basis of chi-square. Chi-square for the largest change, the increase of 21.8% for the younger males, was 3.32, which is just below the .05 level. More detailed analyses of these trends, broken down according to type of offense, sex, age, etc., will be presented in *City Gangs, op. cit.*

[31] Phrasing the question in this way was one of the devices used to accommodate the difficulties in using statistics compiled by official agencies. This phrasing takes the court appearance itself as an essentially independent index of impact; it does not assume any systematic connection between frequency of court appearance and frequency of criminal behavior. Having separate measures of Project-recorded and court-processed crimes (see footnote 28) makes possible separate computations of these ratios. Further, since court-appeared crime rather than committed crime can be

appearance data made it possible to amplify and strengthen the measurement of impact in three major ways. (1) It permitted a considerable time-extension. Previous sections describe trends which occurred during the actual period of worker contact. Sound determination of impact makes it necessary to know how these "during" trends related to trends both preceding and following the contact period. Post-contact trends become particularly important in light of the "negligible change" findings of the "during-contact" period, which raise the possibility that the real impact of the Project may have occurred following the workers' departure, as a kind of delayed re-action response. (2) The data were compiled by agencies which were essentially independent of the Project. Although the Project made every attempt to recognize, accommodate to, and correct for the possibility of in-project bias,[32] exclusive reliance on data collected primarily by those in the employ of the Project would admit the possibility that the objectives or values of Project staff would in some way prejudice results. Despite some contact between Project and court personnel, the operations of the courts were essentially independent of those of the Project, and the likelihood that the various courts in which group members appeared would be influenced in any consistent way by Project values or objectives was extremely small. (3) It made possible the application of time-trend measures to groups other than those taken by the Project as ob-

jects of change. The inclusion of a control population as part of the basic evaluative design was of vital importance. Despite the detail obtainable through the continued and intimate contact of group and worker, it would have been difficult to know, without a control population, the extent to which the experience of Project group members during the contact period was a response to worker influence rather than a variety of other possible influencing factors.

Court appearance data were processed in three different ways. The first made these data directly comparable with the other "during-contact" measures by asking—"Was there a significant decrease in the frequency with which Project group members appeared in court in connection with crimes during the contact period?" The second exploited the time-extension potentialities of the data by asking—"How did the frequency of court appearance during the contact period compare with frequency preceding and following this period?" The third utilized a control population and asked—"Did the court-appearance experience of gang members worked with by a delinquency control project for various periods between the ages of 14 and 19 differ significantly from the experience of similar gang members not so worked with?"

CONTACT PERIOD TRENDS. Names of the 205 members of the Project's intensive contact groups were submitted to the state's central criminal records division. Court appearance records were returned for all group members with court experience. These records contained full court appearance and correctional commitment data for the sixteen-year period from 1945 to 1961 —at which time older group members averaged 23 years of age, and younger, 21. It was thus possible to process the full sample as an age cohort in regard

---

seen, from one perspective, as the more serious social problem, Project impact on the likelihood of appearance itself can be taken as one relatively independent measure of effectiveness.

[32] The technical and methodological devices for accommodating to or correcting for the possibility of in-project bias will be detailed in future reporting.

to court experience between the ages of 7 and 23, and including the period of Project contact. Each appearance in court on a new count for all male group members was tabulated.[33] "During-contact" appearance trends were analyzed in the same fashion as disapproved and illegal actions. The contact term for each group was divided into three equal phases, and the frequency of appearances during the initial and final phase was compared.

Trends in court-appeared offenses were essentially the same as trends in illegal actions. Group members appeared in court in connection with 144 offenses during the contact period. Fifty-one appearances occurred during the initial period and 48 during the final —a decrease of 5.8%. However, categorizing offenses as "major" and "minor" as was done in the case of illegal actions showed that for major offenses (theft, assault, alcohol), 31 appearances occurred during the initial phase and 35 during the final—an increase of 12.9%.[34] There was, therefore, no significant decrease in the frequency with which group members appeared in court during the term of worker contact. Neither the slight decrease in all-offense trends nor the increase in major offense trends proved statistically significant. The fact that these "during-

contact" court appearance trends, involving 155 offenses, closely paralleled illegal act trends, involving 1005 offenses, served to corroborate both sets of trends, and to reinforce the finding of "negligible change" in legally violative behavior for the period of worker contact.

BEFORE-DURING-AFTER TRENDS: PROJECT GROUPS. In order to place the "during-contact" offense trends in a broader time perspective, it was necessary to compare them to rates preceding and following the contact period. Since group members were of different ages during the contact period, data were processed so as to make it possible to compare the court experience of the several groups at equivalent age periods. The average age of each group was determined, and the number of court appearances per group for each six-month period between the ages of 7 and 23 was tabulated. One set of results is shown in Table 1. The frequency curve of yearly court appearances resembled a normal distribution curve, skewed to the right. Appearance frequency increased gradually between the ages of 7 and 16, maintained a high level between 16 and 20, and dropped off quite rapidly after 20.

The period of maximum frequency of court appearances coincided, in general, with the period of worker contact. Although no single group remained in contact with a worker during the full period between ages 16 and 20, each of the groups experienced contact for periods ranging from one to two and a half years during this period. It could not be said, then, that frequency of court appearance during the contact period was appreciably lower than during the pre-contact period; on the contrary, groups achieved a peak of appearance frequency during the period of Project service efforts.

Another way of describing these

---

[33] Out of 145 "during-contact" court appearances, only one involved a girl. Since 155 illegal acts involved females, this supports the frequently reported finding that females are far less likely to be subjected to official processing for crimes than males. All following figures, therefore, refer to males only.

[34] Neither of these changes was statistically significant, testing with chi-square and Fisher's Exact Test. The three "major" offenses showed differing trends—with "theft" showing some decrease (23 to 19), "assault" remaining about the same (5 to 6) and "alcohol" showing a considerable increase (3 to 10). "Minor" crimes decreased from 20 to 13. These trends will be reported and analyzed more fully in future reports.

Table 1

NUMBER OF COURT APPEARANCES FOR YEAR:* AGES 7-23. PROJECT AND CONTROL
GROUPS

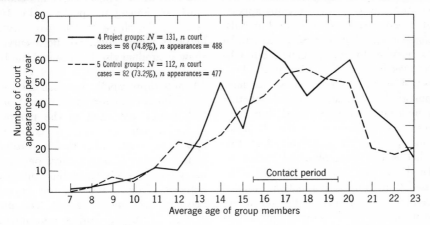

* On new charges, all offenses.

trends is by examining appearance frequency by six-month periods. During the six months preceding contact there were 21 appearances; during the first six months of contact there were 29, and during the last, 27. In the six months following termination appearances rose to 39, dropped to 20 for the next six months, and rose to 39 for the next. Thus, eighteen months after project termination, appearance frequency was at its highest point for the total adolescent period.

The yearly appearance curve (Table 1) does, however, show two rather prominent dips—one at age 15, the other at 18. The dip at 15 could not have been related to the Project, since contact had not yet begun. The dip at 18, however, occurred at a time when each of the three older groups was in contact with workers, and thus admits the possibility of worker influence.[35] It is also possible that the

[35] This "dip" phenomenon—a lowering of the frequency of violative behavior during the "middle" phase of worker contact—was also noted in connection with a

post-20 decline may have represented a delayed action effect. Thus, looking at the period of worker contact as one phase within the overall period of adolescence, it would appear that the presence of the workers did not inhibit the frequency of court appearances, but that a dip in appearance frequency at age 18 and a drop in frequency after age 20 may have been related to the workers' efforts.

COMPARISON OF PROJECT AND CONTROL GROUP TRENDS. Extending the examination of offense trends from the during-contact period to "before" and "after" periods, while furnishing important additional information, also raised additional questions. Was it just coincidental that the 16 to 19 peak in court appearances occurred during the contact period—or could the presence of the workers have been in some way

somewhat different kind of processing of illegal acts reported in "Preventive Work with Street-Corner Groups: Boston Delinquency Project," *op. cit.*, p. 100. Currently available data make it possible to amplify and modify the interpretation presented in the earlier paper.

responsible? Was the sharp decline in frequency of appearances after age 20 a delayed action result of worker effort? To clarify these questions it was necessary to examine the court appearance experience of a control population—a set of corner gangs as similar as possible to Project gangs, but who had *not* been worked with by the Project. The indexes reported so far have provided information as to whether significant change occurred, but have been inconclusive as to the all-important question of cause-and-effect (To what extent were observed trends related to the workers' efforts?). The use of a control population entailed certain risks—primarily the possibility that service and control populations might not be adequately matched in some respects—but the unique potency of the control method as a device for furnishing evidence in the vital area of "cause" outweighed these risks.

Each of the Project's seven intensive service groups was matched with a somewhat smaller number of members of similarly organized corner gangs of similar age, sex, ethnic status, and social status. Most of these groups hung out in the same district as did Project groups, and their existence and membership had been ascertained during the course of the Project. Since the total membership of the Control groups was not known as fully as that of Project groups, it was necessary in some instances to match one Project group with two Control groups of similar status characteristics. By this process, a population comprising 172 members of 11 corner gangs was selected to serve as a control population for the 205 members of the seven Project gangs. Court appearance data on Control groups were obtained, and the groups were processed as an age cohort in the same manner as Project groups.

The court appearance frequency curves for Project and Control groups are very similar (see Table 1). If the two dips in the Project curve are eliminated by joining the peaks at 14, 16, and 20, the shape of the two curves becomes almost identical. Both curves show a gradual rise from ages 7 to 16 or 17, maintain a high level to age 20, and drop rapidly between 20 and 23. Table 2 compares Project and Control groups according to the number of *individuals* per year per group to appear in court, rather than according to the number of *appearances* per year per group. On this basis, the similarity between Project and Control curves becomes even more marked. The dip at age 14 in the Project appearance curve (Table 1) flattens out, and both Project and Control groups show a dip at age 18, making the Project and Control curves virtually identical.[36]

The unusual degree of similarity between the court appearance curves of Project and Control groups constitutes the single most powerful piece of evidence on Project impact obtained by the research. The fact that a group of similar gangs not worked with by the Project showed an almost identical decrease in court appearance frequency between ages 20 and 23 removes any reasonable basis for attributing the post-20 decline of Project groups to worker efforts. Indeed, the high degree of overall similarity in court appearance experience between "served" and

[36] The implications of these court-appearance frequency trends transcend their utility as a technique for "controlling" for worker influence. One implication will be cited in footnote 43; more detailed interpretation and analysis, with special attention to the relative influence of worker activity and subcultural forces on the shape of the curves, will be included in *City Gangs, op. cit.* Also included will be greater detail on the process of locating, selecting, matching, and processing the control population.

Table 2

NUMBER OF INDIVIDUALS APPEARING IN COURT PER YEAR:* AGES 7-23. PROJECT AND
CONTROL GROUPS

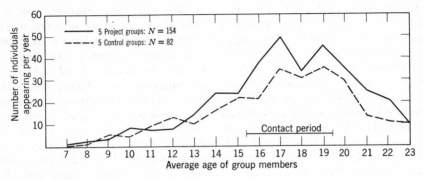

* At least once, on new charges, all offenses.

"unserved" groups makes it most difficult to claim that anything done by the
Project had any significant influence
on the likelihood of court appearance.

Project and Control groups show
equally striking similarities in regard
to three additional measures—the proportion of individuals who had appeared in court by age 23, the proportion who had re-appeared, and the
number of appearances per individual.
Of 131 members of four male Project
groups, 98, or 74.8%, had appeared
in court at least once by age 23. The
fact that 75% of the members of gangs
worked with by social workers had
nevertheless appeared in court by age
23 would in itself appear to indicate
very limited Project impact. This finding, however, still admits the possibility that appearance frequency might
have been even higher in the absence
of the workers, or conversely, that the
high figure was in some way a consequence of the workers' efforts. Both
of these possibilities are weakened by
the Control cohort figures. Of 112 members of five male groups *not* worked
with by the Project, 82, or 73.2%, had

appeared in court by age 23—almost
exactly the same percentage shown by
Project groups.[37]

The possibility still remains that
Project group members, once having
appeared in court, would be less likely
than Control members to *reappear*. This
was not the case. Of 98 members of
Project groups who appeared in court
at least once, 72, or 73.5%, appeared
at least once again; of 82 Control group
members who appeared at least once,
61, or 74.3%, appeared at least once

[37] The finding of negligible difference
in court appearance frequency between
Project and Control groups parallels the
findings of the Cambridge-Somerville
Youth Study—one of the few delinquency
control projects to report findings of careful
evaluative research (Edwin Powers and
Helen Witmer, *An Experiment in the Prevention of Delinquency*, New York: Columbia University Press, 1951). It was found
that 29.5% of a 325-boy treatment group
had appeared in court by the time the
oldest boys were 21, as compared with
28.3% of a 325-boy control group (p. 326).
Despite differences in methods (Cambridge-Somerville used primarily individually focused counseling) and client
populations (Cambridge-Somerville boys
were less delinquent), the degree of similarity between the two projects in treatment and control outcomes is striking.

more. A further possibility exists that while similar proportions of *individuals* might have appeared in court, Project group members might have made fewer *appearances* per individual. However, Project and Control groups were also similar in this respect. Ninety-eight Project members who appeared in court between the ages of 7 and 23 appeared 488 times, or 5.0 appearances per individual. Eighty-two Control males appeared 447 times, or 5.4 appearances per individual. These figures, while not as close to identity as the outcome figures, fail to show a statistically significant difference. The unusual degree of closeness in all these court appearance measures for male Project and Control groups provides a firm basis for concluding that Project impact on the likelihood of court appearance was negligible.

Summary of "Impact" Findings

It is now possible to provide a definite answer to the principal evaluative research question—"Was there a significant measurable inhibition of law-violating or morally disapproved behavior as a consequence of Project efforts?" The answer, with little necessary qualification, is "No." All major measures of violative behavior—disapproved actions, illegal actions, during-contact court appearances, before-during-after appearances, and Project-Control group appearances—provide consistent support for a finding of "negligible impact."

There was a modest decrease, during the period of worker contact, in the frequency of disapproved actions in 14 areas of behavior—but much of this reduction was due to a decrease in a single area—school-oriented behavior. The overall change in the other 13 areas was only −2.3%.[38] The total

number of illegal actions engaged in by group members also decreased slightly, though not significantly, during the course of the Project. Most of this reduction, however, was accounted for by minor offenses; major offenses showed a slight increase. Similarly, while there was a small decrease in the frequency of all categories of court-appeared offenses, major offenses showed an increase. Examining the group members' court appearance trends between the ages 7 and 23 showed that court appearances were most frequent during the age-period when Project workers were with the groups. The possibility that a pronounced decrease in court appearance frequency after age 20 represented a delayed response to the Project was weakened by the fact that a similar decline occurred in the case of a set of similar gangs not worked with by the Project, and which, in fact, showed extremely similar court appearance trends both before, during, and after the age period during which Project groups were in contact with workers.

The fact that the various measures of impact are mutually consistent increases confidence in the overall "negligible impact" finding. Not only do the several indexes delineate similar trends in regard to the direction and magnitude of change (e.g., "during-period" change in disapproved actions, −4.0%; in illegal actions, −9.1%; in court appearance frequency, −5.8%), but also show a high degree of internal consistency in other respects. For example, the rank position of the five male groups in the degree of reduction in violative

---

[38] It is possible that the decrease in disapproved school-oriented actions was due largely to a decrease in the frequency of

truancy brought about by the fact that many of the earlier period truants had, by Project termination, passed the age at which school attendance was compulsory, thus ending their truancy. This possibility will be tested as part of a detailed analysis of change trends in each behavior area.

behavior shown by the three major indexes was very similar.[39]

Two previous papers reporting impact findings of the Midcity Project conveyed the impression of a limited but definite reduction in delinquency.[40] Why does the present report support a different conclusion? In the first place, present findings are based on new data not available in 1957 and 1959, as well as on more extensive analysis of data then available. Both previous papers stated that reported results were preliminary, and cited the possibility of modification by future analysis.[41] Second, present data focus more directly on the specific experience of a specific target population; some of the previous impact findings were based on less focused indexes of general community trends, in which the behavior of the Project's target groups was not as directly distinguishable. Third, the "before" and "after" time extension made possible by the use of court data shows some previously reported trends to have been relatively temporary fluctuations. Fourth, the use of a control population made it possible to anchor results more firmly by showing that important observed trends were common to both Project and non-Project groups, thus making possible a better determination of the extent to which "during" Project variation was in fact related to the workers' efforts.

THE EFFICACY OF PROJECT CONTROL METHODS

Which of the Project's methods were "tested" by the "negligible impact" findings? This complex question can be addressed only briefly here. It is evident that it was those methods which were most extensively employed or successfully executed which were shown most directly to have been least effective in inhibiting delinquency. Fifteen separate methods or techniques were cited earlier in connection with the three major programs (Community Organization, Family Service, Gang Work) of the Midcity Project. Of these, seven could be designated as extensively employed or successfully executed: establishment of district citizens' council; locating and contacting adolescent corner gangs; establishing relationships with gang members; effecting formal organization and involvement in organized recreational activity; provision of access to adult institutions; provision of adult role-model. It is to these seven methods that the "negligible impact" finding applies most directly. Of these, "recreation" is already recognized quite widely to be of limited effectiveness as an exclusive method; "relationship" is still seen in many quarters as quite effective; "adult role-model" was also found, by the Cambridge-Somerville Project, to have had little effect. Of two aspects of "access-provision"—enabling youngsters to avail themselves of existing opportunities, and altering larger societal institutions so as to create new opportunities—the Project achieved the former but exerted limited systematic effort in regard to the latter, so that this aspect of access-provision was only minimally tested.

[39] Rank-difference correlation coefficients were as follows: disapproved acts and illegal acts +.80; disapproved acts and court appearances +.87; illegal acts and court appearances +.97. Even with the small N of 5, the good correspondence between disapproved acts and court appearances is impressive, since the data for the two rank series were derived from completely independent sources.

[40] "The Impact of a Community Group Work Program on Delinquent Corner Groups," *op. cit.*, pp. 390–406, and "Preventive Work with Street-Corner Groups: Boston Delinquency Project," *op. cit.*, pp. 97–106.

[41] It is similarly possible that some of the results cited here will be modified in the final Project report, especially in areas where more extensive internal analysis will enable fuller interpretations of reported trends.

Six methods could be characterized as less extensively employed or implemented with only moderate success: formation of citizens' groups; coordination of efforts of youth groups and adult citizens' groups; coordination of family-service agencies; treatment of "chronic problem" families; psychodynamic counseling and therapy; group dynamics. Some of these programs continued beyond the Project's three year demonstration period, but there is as yet no evidence available that any of these have had an impact on delinquency substantially different from that of the "best-tested" methods.

Two final methods—effecting concerted effort between citizens' groups and professional agencies, and coordinating the varied efforts of professional agencies themselves—were implemented only minimally. It is to these methods, then, that the "negligible impact" finding has least applicability. However, this failure of effectuation, especially in the area of inter-agency cooperation, was achieved only after extensive expenditure of effort, which might suggest that the cost of implementing this type of method, whose potential impact on delinquency is as yet undetermined, might not be commensurate with the degree of delinquency reduction it could perhaps produce.

In addition, granting that some of the Project's methods were tested less fully than others, the fact that all 15 (and others) were applied concurrently and in concert also constituted a test of the "synergism" concept—that the simultaneous and concerted application of multiple and diverse programs on different levels will produce an impact greater than the summed impact of the component programs. Thus the total-community–multiple-programs approach, as executed by the Midcity Project, also fell within the category of methods best tested by the finding of "negligible impact."

In evaluating the significance of these "negligible impact" findings three considerations should be borne in mind. The first concerns the scope and nature of the question to which "negligible impact" is an answer, the second the level on which the answer is presented, and the third the value of the Project to delinquency control as a larger enterprise.

The phrasing of the principal evaluative research question tests the effectiveness of the Project against a single and central criterion—the measurable inhibition of explicitly violative behavior of a designated target population. The Project had considerable impact in other areas. To cite only two of these: the establishment of the control project and the spread of knowledge as to its existence had a calming effect on the adult community. Pre-Project gang activities in Midcity had activated a sense of fear among many adults, and a feeling of helplessness in the face of actual and potential violence. Simple knowledge of the existence of the Project served to alleviate the community's sense of threat, in that there was now an established locus of responsibility for gang crime. The fact that *something* was being done was in itself important quite independent of the possible effectiveness of what was being done.

The Project was also instrumental in establishing new delinquency-control organizations, and left the community a legacy of organizations and programs which it had either brought into being or taken primary responsibility for. Among these were the District Community Council organized by Project staff, the project for providing direct service to "chronic problem" families, an annual sports award dinner for the youth of the community, and a permanent program of area work administered by the municipal government.

The organizational plan of this latter enterprise was drawn up before Project termination, so that the municipal delinquency control bureau, once established, was able to extend the general approach of the Project to the entire municipal area.[42] While the value of these organized enterprises must also be measured against the same "impact on delinquency" criterion which was applied to the Project, it is clear that their existence was one tangible product of the Project.

A second consideration concerns the "level" of the reported findings. Data presented in connection with each of the major indexes to impact are at the most gross analytical level—that is, they neither specify nor analyze systematically the internal variation of the reported trends in three important respects—variations among the several groups, variations among the several behavior areas, and finer fluctuations over time. The finding of "negligible impact" encompasses, most accurately, *all* analyzed forms of behavior of *all* analyzed groups for extended periods. Internal analyses not reported here show that some groups showed considerable change in some areas, and that some areas showed considerable change for some groups. Further, while initial and final levels of violative behavior in many instances showed little difference, a good deal of turbulence or fluctuation characterized intervening periods. The flat "negligible impact" statement, then, by concealing a considerable degree of internal variability, obscures the fact that there was differential vulnerability to change in different areas and for different groups. Fuller analyses of these variations, along with the methods associated with

greater and lesser vulnerability, will furnish specific policy guides to more and less strategic points of intervention.

A final consideration concerns the "value" of the Project in the face of its "negligible inhibition of delinquent behavior" outcome. There can be an important distinction, obscured by the term "evaluation" between the "effect" of an enterprise and its "value." The Midcity Project was established to test the possible effectiveness of its several approaches. These were in fact tested, and the Project was thus successful in the achievement of its "demonstration" objective. The evaluation model used here, based on multiple indexes to change, and using the "behavioral event" as a primary unit of analysis, can be applied in other instances where the impact of a specific change enterprise is at issue. Even more important, perhaps, is the fact that the process of gathering and analyzing the great bulk of data necessary to furnish a sound answer to the question of impact also produced a large volume of information of direct relevance to basic theoretical questions as to the origins of gangs and of gang delinquency. These findings also bear directly on a further question of considerable importance— "Why did the Project have so little impact on delinquency?"—a question to be addressed in some detail in future reports.[43]

[42] See D. Austin, "Recommendations for a Municipal Program of Delinquency Prevention," mimeo, 7 pp., United Community Services of Boston, 1957.

[43] Factors accounting for the limited impact of Project efforts will be treated in detail in *City Gangs, op. cit.* The explanatory analysis will forward the thesis that culturally derived incentives for engaging in violative behavior were far stronger than any counterpressures the Project could bring to bear. This explanation will derive from a general theory of gang delinquency whose central proposition, to be expanded at length, will be that patterned involvement in violative behavior by gangs of the Midcity type occurs where four cultural "conditions" exist concurrently—*maleness, adolescence, urban residence,* and *low-skill laboring class status.* Each of these condi-

tions is conceptualized as a particular type of subcultural system—each of whose "demanded" sets of behavior, taken separately, contribute some element of the motivation for engagement in gang delinquency, and whose concerted operation produces a subcultural milieu which furnishes strong and consistent support for customary involvement in criminal behavior. Data on "impact" presented here document the influence of two of these conditions—age status and social status. Court appearance frequency trends (Tables I and II) would appear to indicate that the single most important determinant of the frequency of that order of criminal behavior which eventuated in court appearance for Midcity male gangs was *age*, or more specifically, movement through a series of age-based subcultural stages. Commission of criminal acts of given types and frequency appeared as a required concomitant of passing through the successive age-stages of adolescence and a prerequisite to the assumption of adult status. The influence of these age-class demands, on the basis of this and other evidence, would appear to exceed that of other factors—including conditions

of the family, school, neighborhood or job world; police arrest policies, sentencing, confinement, probation and parole policies, and others. Data on *social status* (e.g., footnote 27, *passim*) along with much additional data not reported here, indicate a systematic relationship between social status *within* the lower class, and delinquency. 1. Within the 21-gang sample of the Midcity study, crime was both more prevalent and more serious among those whose social status, measured by occupational and educational indexes, was lowest. 2. Relatively small differences in status were associated with relatively large differences in patterned behavior; as lower status levels were approached, delinquency incidence increased exponentially rather than linearly; this indicates the necessity of making refined intra-class distinctions when analyzing the social "location" of criminal behavior. 3. Groups of lower social status showed the least reduction in violative forms of behavior; this lower vulnerability to change efforts would indicate that violative behavior was more entrenched, and thus more central to the subcultural system.

41.   The Highfields Project

H. ASHLEY WEEKS

The Highfields Project for the Short-Term Treatment of Youthful Offenders inaugurated in New Jersey has been in operation since July 5, 1950. This report is an attempt to measure and evaluate various aspects of the Highfields Project for the first several years of its life.

The Short-Term Treatment of Youthful Offenders Program evolved from the need felt by many New Jersey judges for a new law to permit them to make definite sentences of not more than three months to the existing New Jersey facilities such as the reformatories and training schools. These judges believed that such a law would act as a deterrent to many boys—it would demonstrate to delinquent boys that commitment and incarceration for a much longer period would be their lot if they did not mend their ways. The judges felt that many delinquent boys were not yet serious enough offenders to warrant their being sent to the New Jersey State Home for Boys at Jamesburg or to one of the state's reformatories for an indeterminate period of confinement. Such boys had demonstrated that their misbehavior was serious enough to raise doubts in the minds of the judges as to whether they could be placed or continued on probation with safety to the community and protection to themselves. Juvenile court judges are frequently loath to commit a boy to an institution which he is not likely to leave short of a year. They feel, with justification, that a boy often becomes worse when he is kept too long in an institution.[1] . . .

THE PROPOSED PROGRAM

The New Jersey program for the short-term treatment of youthful offenders[2] originally included these points:

Boys, while still officially on probation, would live, work, and play together in a unit which would house only a few boys at any one time.

Small groups of boys—not more than ten in any one group—would meet each day with the director, a trained guided group interactionist, in sessions

---

[1] There is much evidence to show that the longer the stay in a correctional institution the more likely a person is to fail on parole when he is released.

[2] Cf. F. Lovell Bixby, "Short Term Treatment of Youthful Offenders," *Focus*, 30 (March 1951), pp. 33–36.

SOURCE. H. Ashley Weeks, "The Highfields Project," from *Youthful Offenders at Highfields*, Ann Arbor: The University of Michigan Press, 1958, pp. 1–5, 7–10, 20–24, 118–128. Copyright © 1958, The University of Michigan Press. Reprinted with permission.

designed to uncover their problems and help them begin to solve them.

The boys would live as nearly normal lives as possible. There would be no outward symbols of incarceration, force, or even control. There would be no officers or guards. The personnel would consist only of the director, who would be responsible for establishing and maintaining a therapeutic climate, a man and his wife to supervise housekeeping and to assume the role of houseparents, and a handyman or jack-of-all-trades to assist the boys in developing their hobbies and in making themselves useful around the place.

There would be no formal educational program, but boys would listen to the radio and read newspapers and magazines and other material. This material would be thoroughly discussed and would give the residents a chance to evaluate and interpret together the information and opinions with which these mass media continually bombard us all.

The boys would work on some constructive project, not for vocational training but to gain work experience, and they would be paid a small wage for this work.

There would be hobby and craft projects in which all would participate. Each boy would be expected to select and finish one such project during his residency, whether it be "writing a short story, building a radio cabinet, overhauling a gasoline engine, or almost anything else that the individual feels he would like to do."

The boys would be allowed to go to local villages, accompanied by an adult, to shop, attend the movies, have a soda, or indulge in other approved activities of interest to them. On Sundays, religious activities and experiences would be available in the nearby community churches. There would be many opportunities to maintain community contacts. Periodically, during their short stay, they would be granted furloughs home. These would be in the nature of test situations and would also furnish experiences that could be discussed in the group sessions.[3]

As actually established, the project embodies some changes in the original plan as proposed by Dr. Bixby. The guided group interaction sessions are not held every night, but only five nights during each week. Usually, there are no sessions Thursday and Saturday nights. So far as is known, there is no specific discussion session in which the boys evaluate and interpret the information they have received from the mass media. Of course, certain attitudes and expressions received from their reading or listening are often brought forward in the sessions and aired and analyzed there, but this as observed by the writer is more by happenstance than design. Nor is there any hobby or craft program in which all participate. Boys can and do carry on projects, but again it is because of an individual interest and not by design. With these exceptions the program is very similar to the one Dr. Bixby originally conceived.

Certain criteria for the kind of residents were set up. In the first place, it was decided to limit the project to delinquent boys sixteen and seventeen years of age. Boys under this age would have to have school facilities provided for them in accordance with the state law, and those over seventeen are beyond the age when they may be handled as juveniles by the courts of the state. It was also decided to limit the project to first-commitment boys, that is, boys who had not formerly been committed to a state industrial school or other place of confinement. It was reasoned that boys who had had former

[3] Cf. *Focus*, pp. 35–36.

institutional experience might be so conditioned in their behavioral reactions that it would be difficult for them to participate wholeheartedly and freely in the guided group interaction sessions.[4] The kind of resident to be sent to Highfields was further limited by the exclusion of known sexual perverts and feebleminded and/or psychotic boys.

Before Highfields began to accept boys, discussions were held with the judges of the four large northeastern counties which have separate juvenile courts. It was explained to them that Highfields was not necessarily a substitute for either probation or incarceration, but a third choice. Whenever a judge had a boy before him who was sixteen or seventeen years of age and met the other criteria, the judge could consider whether the short-term treatment afforded at Highfields might be preferable to commitment or regular probation. A specialized facility such as Highfields would be helpful when he was in doubt. He could still place a boy on probation provided the boy would agree to spend a relatively short term (up to four months) under the treatment program.[5] If he decided a boy was suitable for Highfields, he could ascertain whether a bed was available there, and if it was he could see whether a boy would volunteer to go to Highfields. If a bed was not available, the former choice was still possible—incarceration or probation. . . .

[4] From time to time these criteria have been disregarded in the interest of a particular boy.

[5] Judges are loath to institutionalize a delinquent if they can possibly avoid it. This can be seen from the fact that boys often have long histories of delinquency and court appearances without commitment. They frequently are placed on probation again and again, or continued on probation. The ordinary delinquent has three or more official prior delinquencies before he is committed to a state institution. This is true not only in New Jersey but elsewhere.

ORIGINAL RESEARCH DESIGN

In order to secure the information needed to evaluate the program proposed by Dr. Bixby, it appeared that there were three basic questions which should be answered:

1. Do delinquents participating in the short-term treatment program show a higher, the same, or a lower recidivist rate than boys participating in other kinds of treatment programs?

2. Do delinquents participating in the short-term treatment program change their expressed attitudes, values, and opinions toward their families, law and order, and their own outlook on life?

3. Do delinquents participating in the short-term treatment program change their basic personality structures or at least the overt manifestations of their personalities?

These questions were based on certain theoretical considerations. It is generally assumed that correctional training, whether punitive or therapeutically oriented, changes and improves the overt behavior of the person undergoing the training. The lay public as well as the professionals at work in the field hope that the experiences persons have in correctional facilities will be reflected in an improvement in the behavior they exhibit after they are released. As Dr. Bixby has written: "The objective of all correctional procedures is the permanent protection of society through the rehabilitation of the greatest possible number of convicted offenders."[6] Recidivist rates, then, should be a general measure of the effectiveness of a correctional program.

But recidivism is not the sole measure of effectiveness. Persons who have

[6] "A Plan for the Short-Term Treatment of Youthful Offenders" (mimeographed), p. 1.

experienced correctional training may be favorably affected by the treatment only to have the good effects discounted by the fact that they are returned to the same family, the same neighborhood, and the same detrimental social groupings and influences which contributed to their antisocial behavior in the first place. But whether or not they subsequently get into further trouble with the law, the treatment they receive, if effective, should alter their attitudes, values, and opinions, and this alteration should be observable at the time they leave the treatment facility. We felt that the short-term treatment program should especially bring about changes in values, attitudes, and opinions. Guided group interaction sessions, we believed, should encourage the participants to recognize their problems in terms of their behavior, attitudes, and values and allow them to explore alternative solutions to their problems.

Fundamentally, attitudes and values serve to motivate certain kinds of behavior and inhibit other kinds. A person who despises the police, feels that laws are totally unfair or apply only to the other fellow, and is antagonistic toward or has no respect for his family or other authority, must be motivated differently from one who has opposite attitudes and values. Of course, some specific values may be held which are similar for the lawbreaker and the law-abider; but when this is the case, the object toward which the values are directed is probably narrower and more restricted for the lawbreaker than it is for the law-abider. In other words, the lawbreaker may have a feeling of loyalty, may uphold the norms of the group, but the object of this loyalty is restricted, for example, to his gang or individual members of it and not to society as a whole. The true gang delinquent growing up in high-delinquency areas is motivated certainly by many of the same values as are prevalent in the larger society, but these values are restricted and operate only in reference to his own in-group and fail to operate in reference to what he considers the out-group—the group, as he sees it, which is against him and repressive in its actions toward him.

In the third place, there are persons who, because of adverse conditions in their life histories, become psychologically maladjusted. These persons frequently engage in delinquent behavior because of their deep-seated anxieties and perplexities. Many delinquents have distorted conceptions of reality. For example, although this is not always verbalized, boys—and girls too—often feel that all adults are against them, that they are alone in a hostile world, and that they must battle to retain their personal significance. Treatment, to be effective, must change these basic personality manifestations in order to give a more realistic picture of society.[7]

In order to insure meaningful answers to the questions we were asking, an experimental design was called for. Therefore, we advocated securing pre- and post-information on each boy sent to the short-term treatment project and like information on boys who were handled in other ways. These other ways might include release with no further action by the court, probation, committal to a training school or reformatory, or even to a jail or other local place of incarceration. Theoretically, at least, samples of boys similar in every way to those sent to the short-

---

[7] We think of these two types as (1) the social deviant or gang delinquent and (2) the psychologically maladjusted. They are essentially the same types that Dr. Richard L. Jenkins calls the adaptive and the maladaptive delinquent. See his "Adaptive and Maladaptive Delinquency," *The Nervous Child*, Vol. 6.

term treatment facility could be drawn from those handled in each of these other ways, and comparisons made between them and the boys experiencing the short-term treatment program.

New Jersey has an excellent Diagnostic Center at Menlo Park, and it was suggested that all boys be screened at the Center and complete diagnostic workups on each boy be obtained when he first came to the attention of the court and again when he was discharged from whatever treatment he had been undergoing. Comparisons could then be made in terms of the changes revealed between the two workups and the particular treatment accorded the various groups of boys.

As the research plan was discussed with the judges of the four separate juvenile courts, it appeared that the great majority of boys would probably be committed to Annandale Farms, the New Jersey State Reformatory for Males, if there were no room for them at Highfields. It could be assumed that if Highfields did not exist almost all of the more serious delinquents as old as sixteen or seventeen would be sent to the reformatory at Annandale. Thus, it was decided for research purposes to use as a control group boys of the same ages as those eligible for Highfields who were committed to this reformatory. The control group would, of course, be selected according to the other criteria established for Highfields eligibility: it would be composed of boys who had not previously been in a state correctional institution, who did not appear to be feebleminded or psychotic, and who were not known sexual perverts. . . .

THE RESEARCH

During the spring of 1951 the following policy, initiated with the co-operation of the juvenile courts and parole offices, became the standard operating procedure carried on for the remainder of the study. Each time a judge decided to send a boy to either Highfields or Annandale, his office notified the research division at New York University and one of the staff traveled to the probation office or parental school of the respective court, where the tests were administered. Each time a boy was released from Highfields the director notified the research office and a member of the staff went to the respective probation office and administered the same tests as were given before. When a boy in the control group was released from Annandale the institution parole officer notified the district parole officer that the boy was in the control sample. This officer in turn notified the research office and arrangements were made to meet with the parolee and administer the tests. In this way almost all of the boys were tested just before they went to their respective facilities and just after they were released.[8] A few boys from counties which do not have a full-time juvenile court, such as Burlington, Monmouth, and Mercer, were first tested after they arrived at Highfields and shortly before they were released from there.[9] No procedure was established whereby the research office was notified when boys were sent to one or the

---

[8] Without the co-operation, interest, and awareness on the part of the judges of the juvenile court or the probation and parole officers and the superintendent of the reformatory of the necessity for this procedure, the research staff would have had much more difficulty than it encountered. We recognize that the procedure added to their already heavy burdens and we are exceedingly grateful.

[9] By far the greatest number of boys were sent to Highfields from the four counties with full-time juvenile courts; only relatively few were sent from all other counties of the state. Boys at Annandale from other than the juvenile court counties were selected for the control sample in about the same proportion as they were found in the Highfields population.

other facility from these counties. Occasionally, through some unusual contingency, the research office was not notified when boys were sent to Highfields or to Annandale by the four larger counties. With Highfields boys this did not appreciably delay the testing because we were informed that the boy had arrived and the tests had not been given, but in the case of Annandale the information was not so readily forthcoming. For this reason, about every two or three months during the course of the study we checked the records at Annandale and tested any boy who had not hitherto been tested. In this way, we secured as complete a sample as possible of all boys who met our criteria.

Because it was believed there might be a fictitious inflationary "halo" reflected in the results of the tests taken so soon after release from either facility, each boy who was still available (that is, still on probation or parole or had not joined the armed services) was called in to his probation or parole office and was given all the tests a third time, after he had been back in his community six months or more.[10]

The administration of these tests and the filling in of the interview schedule took, on the average, somewhat over two hours on the first contact. The post-test could be administered in much less time because it was not

necessary to interview again; and then, too, the boys knew the staff and there was no problem of establishing rapport. However, it should be mentioned that often the boys were somewhat more resistant to filling in the post-test, especially when, as originally was the case, we asked them to do so before they had had a chance to get home and see their families and friends. When this was discovered, we arranged the post-test a day or so after the boy had been home.

In addition to the testing, we have, through co-operation of the probation and parole offices, kept in touch with each boy over the length of the study. Periodically, we received reports from the respective offices on each boy's adjustment. If he got into further trouble and was returned to the court and recommitted to any correctional facility we were immediately notified.

For the purposes of this study the following definition of a recidivist, or failure, was adopted. A recidivist is one who, for any reason, was returned to court and/or violated probation or parole and as a result was committed to an institution. When we speak of failures or recidivists, we mean only boys who, subsequent to their first stay in either Highfields or Annandale, have been committed a second time. This commitment may be in Annandale, as is the case with most of the boys in our sample who have failed, or in a jail for a period of thirty days or longer, or penal institution in another state. Boys who have been called in to the probation or parole office or even brought before the court and admonished or warned but were not recommitted but continued on probation or parole are not failures by this definition.

Beginning November 1, 1951, and continuing until January 1953, another phase of the research was designed and

[10] This was not carried on after the first year or so, for several reasons. First, almost all of the boys tested were those making favorable adjustments, as many of those who failed on probation or parole had done so before the end of a six-month period and were recommitted. Second, by examining the various test scores it could not be seen that the boys changed much from the first post-test to the second. And finally, it added another burden to the probation and parole staffs to call these boys in. Often it was difficult to find a time when they could be tested. No boy was post-post-tested after November 1952.

carried out.[11] This was an attempt to ascertain whether persons who know a boy intimately see any changes in him after he has been out of his respective facility for six weeks or more.

The procedure for this phase of the research was as follows:

1. At the time the boy was first interviewed—before he entered Highfields or Annandale—he was asked if he had any objections to our talking about him with (1) one of his parents or his guardian or another relative, (2) a boy or girl friend, (3) the proprietor of the place where he "hung out," (4) a policeman or other representative of the law, and (5) his probation officer. If he had no objections (very few objected) we asked for names and addresses.

2. Each of the persons suggested was interviewed in order to find out about the boy's behavior and the interviewee's attitudes toward it at the time he got into his present trouble.

3. After the boy had been out of either facility for two months, each of these persons was interviewed again and was asked the same type of questions concerning the boy's behavior as at the first interview. A comparison of the pre- and post-interview shows whether they think the boy's behavior has changed or whether opinions and attitudes toward the boy have altered. It was felt that these interviews would also indicate whether there were any unusual community situations which would make it especially difficult for the boy to adjust.

No boys committed to Annandale were pre-tested after February 1954, and no boys sent to Highfields after

[11] This addition to the study was made possible by a grant-in-aid from the Rockefeller Foundation, to whom we are exceedingly grateful.

April of this same year. It was necessary to cut off the Annandale cases earlier than the Highfields ones because of the longer commitment period of the reformatory boys. Few boys, unless recalled by the committing judge, are released from Annandale earlier than twelve months. Therefore, boys committed through February 1954 would not leave Annandale before the end of January 1955; and because we wished to allow at least a six-month period after release to ascertain whether or not a boy made good, none could be included who would not be out of the institution for at least six months by the end of August 1955. The same reasoning was applied to the Highfields cases. Boys at Highfields stay as long as four months. All of the boys admitted to Highfields through April 1954, therefore, would normally be released by the last of August and would have been on probation in their communities for at least six months by the end of February 1955. The main reason for the earlier six-month cut-off date for the Highfields boys was that many more Highfields than Annandale boys had to be processed. It was also felt that numerically enough boys were in the Highfields sample and nothing would be gained by extending the time. Both groups of boys were finally followed up until October 1955.

From February 1951, when the first boys were tested, to the last of April 1954, two hundred and thirty-three boys were sent to Highfields by the courts, an average of about sixty-one boys a year.

From this beginning date to the end of January 1954, the same courts committed one hundred and twenty-two boys to Annandale. Nearly three-quarters of the boys sent to Highfields came almost equally from two of the most populous counties. One of these counties committed very few boys to Annandale—only three—whereas the second county committed almost two-thirds of the Annandale sample. This discrepancy in commitment rates was an indication that the Highfields and Annandale samples might not be exactly comparable.[12]

CONCLUSION

What answers can be given to the three questions which were proposed to guide this research?

1. Do delinquents participating in the short-term treatment program show a higher, the same, or a lower recidivist rate than boys participating in other kinds of treatment programs?

2. Do delinquents participating in the short-term treatment program change their expressed attitudes, values, and opinions toward their families, law and order, and their own outlook on life?

3. Do delinquents participating in the short-term treatment program change their basic personality structures or at least the overt manifestation of their personalities?

Answer to the First Question

There is no doubt that the Highfields Program for the Short-Term Treatment of Youthful Offenders is effective with a large proportion of the boys who are sent to the project. The data show that over the length of this study, when all the boys sent to the project by the counties of New Jersey are included, sixty-three in every hundred

[12] When we began the Highfields research, fifteen boys had already been there and were released at the end of their treatment or sent back to the court as unsuitable for residence at Highfields. These boys are not, of course, included in our analysis. It should be pointed out, however, that the results would not be altered in any significant way if they were.

Highfields boys, in contrast to only forty-seven in every hundred Annandale boys, complete their treatment and do not get into further difficulty serious enough to require that they be reinstitutionalized.

This better over-all record of the total two hundred and twenty-nine boys sent to Highfields appears to be due in the main to the large difference between the relative number of Negro boys from the two facilities with successful outcomes. There is very little difference in the relative number of white boys from the two facilities with successful outcomes, but fifty-nine in every hundred Highfields Negroes as compared with only thirty-three in every hundred Annandale Negroes complete their stay and do not get into further difficulty.

There is no reason to believe from the data available that this large discrepancy is accounted for by differences in the backgrounds of Negro boys sent to the two facilities. When the number of background variables related to outcome are held constant, Highfields still has relatively more Negro boys with low and high scores who are successful than does Annandale. Nor is the difference accounted for by the disproportionate number of white and Negro boys sent to either facility by each county. A comparison of the counties has shown that the county which sends the most Negroes to Annandale also sends the most Negroes to Highfields. In this county the proportion of boys with successful outcomes is basically the same as it is for all the counties which send boys to Highfields: about three in every five white and Negro boys complete their treatment period at Highfields and get into no further difficulty after release, whereas about the same ratio of Annandale white boys but only three in every ten Annandale Negro boys complete their stay and get into no further difficulty after release.

It must be remembered that boys are sent to Highfields while they are officially on probation to the court from which they are sent.[13] Because this is the case, boys can be sent back to the court if, in the opinion of the director, they are failing to adjust. About one-fifth of the boys, during the length of this study, have been declared unsuitable for residence. These include boys who ran away from Highfields (some within a few days or even a few hours after they first arrived), boys who found that the group and the program offered too great a threat to them, and boys who were so disruptive that they threatened the stability of other boys and the group as a whole. The majority of these boys were returned to the court within the first few weeks they were at the project. They cannot be

[13] The fact that boys sent to Highfields are officially on probation should not be construed to mean that they are less serious delinquents than boys sent to Annandale. Probation is an integral part of the Highfields program. There is little doubt that almost all of the boys in the Highfields sample would have been sent to Annandale or a similar facility, rather than placed on probation, if Highfields were not in existence.
The original research design included the drawing of a second control group from boys placed on probation. This plan was abandoned because of the impossibility of securing a sample of boys on probation which would be reasonably similar to the Highfields sample. It was not possible to find enough boys sixteen to seventeen years of age on probation with the same frequency of prior delinquencies and serious kinds of delinquencies as those of the Highfields boys, to say nothing of the similarity of many other background variables. There is every reason to believe that boys sent to Highfields are more like boys of the same age sent to Annandale than they are to boys placed on probation. All available information points to the fact that the great majority of Highfields boys are serious delinquents and have long histories of delinquency.

considered to have really experienced the Highfields program.

The elimination of the boys who have been returned to the court results in an even more striking contrast between the success rates for Highfields and Annandale boys. More than three-quarters (seventy-seven per cent) of the Highfields boys who completed treatment have been successful. In other words, for every hundred boys who complete residence in the respective facility, the Highfields program rehabilitates twenty-eight more than does the traditional program of caring for such boys.

Furthermore, a separate comparison of the success rates for white and Negro boys from the two facilities shows that Highfields has a higher success rate than Annandale for each group. Eight in every ten Highfields white boys are successful, whereas only six in every ten Annandale white boys are successful. Highfields Negroes succeed at more than double the rate of Annandale Negroes: seven out of ten Negroes are successful after their Highfields treatment, but only slightly over three in ten Negroes are successful after their Annandale stay.

When the differential in length of time after release is held constant the rates for Highfields boys are even more favorable than they are when time is not considered. Eight Highfields boys in every ten are successful a year after being released (there is no difference between whites and Negroes), whereas only five Annandale boys in every ten are likewise successful at the end of the same period of time. Seventeen more Highfields white boys in every hundred and almost fifty more Negro boys in every hundred are rehabilitated twelve months after release than Annandale white and Negro boys.

There is no reason to believe that

these differences in success rates are due to the fact that Highfields may get a "better type" of boy. The expectancy tables constructed on the basis of background variables found to be related to outcome for white and Negro boys have shown that the differences in the relative number of adverse background variables for Highfields and Annandale boys do not account for the differences in outcome.

The simple fact is that all boys who complete their stay at Highfields have a better chance of being successful than do boys who complete their stay at Annandale, and this is especially the case for Highfields Negro boys.

A word of caution is in order here. The fact that Negroes at Highfields appear to profit so much more than they do at Annandale does not necessarily indicate that Highfields-type facilities should be established solely for Negroes or that a higher proportion of Negroes should be sent to the present Highfields project. From the data collected, it cannot be concluded that Negroes would profit to the same extent if a facility were established for them alone or if a higher proportion of them were sent to the present facility. It appears that the success of the Negroes sent to Highfields may be related to the ratio of Negroes to whites there. At present, it is rare that there are, at any one time, more than four or five Negroes at the project in a total of eighteen to twenty boys. If the number were increased to eight or nine the whole acceptance and integration of the Negroes into the group might be different. This integration and acceptance is a fundamental aspect of the program at Highfields. A facility solely for Negroes would not allow the give-and-take between the white and Negro boys both in the guided group interaction sessions and in all their daily living experiences. In our opinion, the fact that white and Negro boys can discuss their common problems together is an important factor in the relatively low failure rate of the Negro boys who have been at Highfields.

Not only are higher proportions of Highfields than Annandale boys successful, but as time has passed since Highfields first opened in 1950 the proportion of boys who are successful has tended to increase. Also as time has gone by, relatively fewer boys have been returned to the court as unsuitable for residence. Of the eighty-five boys who entered Highfields during the last year of the study—from April 1953 to April 1954—only eight were sent back to the court as unsuitable for residence; and of those who completed their treatment nine out of ten had not got into further difficulty requiring institutional care, although every boy had been released and back in his community for more than a year. Sixteen of the seventy-seven boys who completed treatment during this period were Negroes, and every one of them had a successful outcome. In fact, all but two Negro boys have had successful outcomes after Highfields treatment since April 1952. Of course, a few more failures can be expected as the boys are out longer, but the data indicate that the great majority, over three-quarters, of the boys who fail do so within the first year after release. It appears certain that as the Highfields program has become stabilized and traditions have crystallized, it has become even more effective than it was at first.

Answer to the Second Question

There is very little evidence that Highfields boys, over the length of their treatment, change their attitudes toward family and toward law and order, and their outlook toward life, so far as the eight scales used to measure these attitudes show.

Highfields white boys showed no appreciable change on six of the eight scales. They became more favorable on the scale measuring attitude toward obeying the law, and less favorable on the scale measuring attitude toward law enforcement.

Annandale white boys also did not show many changes from pre- to post-test. On five of the eight scales there were no appreciable changes. They became more favorable on the scale measuring attitude toward general authority and less favorable on the scale measuring attitude toward law enforcement. Annandale white boys were more inclined to mark the neutral category on the post-test than they were on the pre-test on the scale measuring attitude toward the family.

On five of the eight scales Highfields Negro boys showed no appreciable difference from pre- to post-test. On three of the scales—attitude toward parental authority, attitude toward law enforcement, and attitude toward behavior norms—Highfields Negro boys became more unfavorable on the post-test than they were on the pre-test.

The Annandale Negro boys showed the greatest tendency to change. On only three of the eight scales did these boys show relatively no difference between pre- and post-test responses. These scales were: attitude toward law enforcement, attitude toward general authority, and attitude indicating acceptance of others. On five of the scales the Annandale Negro boys moved in a favorable direction and on one, attitude toward parental authority, they moved unfavorably.

Although there does not appear to be much evidence that Highfields or Annandale white or Negro boys change their responses on the eight scales, there is evidence that the attitude responses of the boys are related to outcome.

Actually, the pre-test responses of all white boys sent to either Highfields or Annandale on five of the scales significantly differentiate the boys who are likely to be successful from those who are likely to be unsuccessful. These scales are: attitude toward family, attitude toward parental authority, attitude toward obeying the law, attitude toward acceptance of others, and attitude toward behavior norms. On each of these scales boys with more favorable attitudes are more likely to have successful outcomes than boys with less favorable attitudes. An expectancy table constructed on the basis of the cumulative effect of these attitude variables, makes clear that white boys in both Highfields and Annandale who have low scores (zero or one) are much more likely than those with high scores to have successful outcomes; but *there is no appreciable difference between the success rates of Highfields and Annandale white boys who fall in the same score group, whether low or high.*

Only two of these scales show a relationship with outcome for Highfields and Annandale white boys who have completed their stay at either of the facilities: attitude toward obeying the law and attitude toward behavior norms. An expectancy table constructed on the basis of these two scales shows that Highfields white boys with no adverse attitude variables are more likely to be successful than those with one or more variables. This table does not discriminate for Annandale white boys who have completed treatment.

The attitude responses of all Negroes sent to either Highfields or Annandale show a significant relationship with outcome on three of the scales. These same scales also discriminate for only the Negro boys who complete their stay in either of two facilities. The scales which differentiate are: attitude toward family, attitude toward acceptance of others, and attitude toward behavior norms.

On the attitude toward family scale, Negro boys with less favorable attitudes are more likely than those with more favorable attitudes to have successful outcomes; this is especially pronounced for the Highfields Negroes. On the other two scales Negroes with more favorable attitudes are more likely than those with less favorable attitudes to have successful outcomes, as is the case with the white boys. The expectancy table constructed on the cumulative effect of these three scales shows very little discrimination for all Negroes sent to Highfields, but discriminates significantly for all Negroes sent to Annandale. The expectancy table based on these same scales discriminates for both Highfields and Annandale Negroes who have completed treatment. Negro boys with low scores who have completed treatment in either facility are more likely to be successful than those with high scores, but *Annandale Negroes with either low or high scores have lower success rates than do Highfields Negroes.*

Actually, there is much more discrimination on these scales than the above discussion of the expectancy tables would indicate. We have discussed only the pre-test responses on the attitude scales which discriminate in the same direction for boys in both facilities. In addition, some of the other scales show a relationship between the pre-test and/or post-test responses of the boys and outcome. A given scale may discriminate for Highfields boys but not for Annandale boys, or vice versa, or discriminate in opposite ways for boys in the two facilities.

It is interesting that on six of the eight scales the highest success rate is found for the Annandale Negro boys whose post-test responses fall in the most favorable categories. An expectancy table based on Annandale Negroes' post-test responses shows that boys with low scores have much higher success rates than boys with high scores. Only for Annandale Negroes is there this consistency. In all other groups the highest success rate is likely to be found in any of the three categories. This may indicate that few Annandale Negroes can succeed unless they have favorable attitudes, but that Highfields Negroes can hold favorable or unfavorable attitudes and still succeed because they have learned to live with their attitudes without undue disturbance.

Answer to the Third Question

There is no evidence that Highfields white or Negro boys change much from pre- to post-test, judging from the overall responses they made to the ten scales adapted from the Army's Psychoneurotic Screening Adjunct to measure the boys' personality structure.

Highfields white boys show an overall difference in response of as much as ten percentage points between pre- and post-tests on only one scale; and Highfields Negro boys show this much difference on but two. The white boys shift in the direction of better adjustment, whereas the Negroes shift toward poorer adjustment on one of the scales and toward better adjustment on the other.

Annandale white and Negro boys shift at least ten percentage points between pre- and post-tests on more scales than do Highfields white and Negro boys. Annandale white boys show an over-all difference in response of as much as ten percentage points between pre- and post-tests on five of the ten scales; Annandale Negro boys show this much over-all difference in response on three scales. Two of these scales are the same as those on which the Annandale white boys shift, but none is the same as those on which the Highfields

Negroes shift. On one of the scales the Annandale Negroes shift in the direction of poorer adjustment, but on the other two scales the shift is toward better adjustment. On all five scales the Annandale white boys shift in the direction of better adjustment.

There is no consistent relationship between the boys' responses to either the pre- or post-test and outcome. The scales on which there is the most change from pre- to post-test are not necessarily the scales which show the greatest relationship between the boys' responses and outcome. A number of the scales which showed a relationship between boys' pre-test responses and outcome do not show the same relationship between the boys' post-test responses and outcome.

According to the analysis of the Miale-Holsopple Sentence Completions given to a sample of Highfields and Annandale boys, Highfields boys tend to change from pre- to post-test more than Annandale boys, and in a different way. But, as Dr. Holsopple writes: "There is no reason to suppose that the primary goals or basic drives of either group were substantially changed. With the Annandale group on the one hand, the goals remained distorted to unclear, the drives unrecognized or unaccepted. In contrast, among the Highfields group, there was movement toward a clearer view of primary goals and substantially increased acceptance of primary drives."

These changes, however, do not appear to be related to outcome. Just about as many Highfields as Annandale boys whose tests were analyzed have unsuccessful outcomes. It would be worth knowing whether the boys who change the most and in a favorable direction on these tests are the ones who are most likely to be successful. This cannot be ascertained from this analysis because it was done for the group of boys in each sample rather than for the individual boys making up the respective samples.

This research points out the fact that a higher proportion of Highfields than Annandale boys succeed and that this is true even when the background variables which are related to their success or failure are held constant. It has shown that it is possible, by using background and attitudinal variables, to differentiate boys who are likely to have high and low success rates even before they enter the respective facility. It has not shown that the boys' attitudes as measured by the tests change appreciably during their residence and treatment. It may well be that the instruments used in this research do not get at the kinds of changes which the Highfields white and Negro boys undergo during their period of treatment. When almost three more Highfields than Annandale white boys in every ten and five more Highfields than Annandale Negroes in every ten who complete their treatment succeed, there must be some explanation for it.

Highfields rehabilitates this high proportion of boys in a four-month period, whereas most other facilities keep boys at least three times as long. Not only is this fact important in itself, but it is important because Highfields is relatively much less expensive per boy treated than is the conventional facility. The "yearly per capita cost" of the residential aspects of the Highfields and Annandale programs, as figured by the state, is about the same, but this is misleading because it does not take into consideration the total number of boys who have experienced the Highfields program during the course of a year.[14] On a strict per capita basis the

[14] The yearly per capita cost on current maintenance while in the institutions was $1,413.95 for Highfields and $1,479.75 for Annandale during 1953 (see: *Mental Defi-*

Highfields program costs one-third as much as the traditional program for each boy treated. Because of the differential in the outcome rates, this cost differential would be much greater if it

ciency in New Jersey, 1953). These per capita costs are figures on the basis of the number in the facility at the end of the fiscal year and not the total number treated during a year.

took into consideration the number of boys each facility rehabilitated.

It is hoped that research will continue at Highfields so that the many facets of the program can be explored and better understood. It would be very worthwhile to know which boys at Highfields change, how this change takes place, and what form it takes.

42. The Provo Experiment in Delinquency Rehabilitation

LAMAR T. EMPEY AND JEROME RABOW

Despite the importance of sociological contributions to the understanding of delinquent behavior, relatively few of these contributions have been systematically utilized for purposes of rehabilitation.[1] The reason is at least partially inherent in the sociological tradition which views sociology primarily as a research discipline. As a consequence, the rehabilitation of delinquents has been left, by default, to people who have been relatively unaware of sociological theory and its implications for treatment.

This situation has produced or perpetuated problems along two dimensions. On one dimension are the problems engendered in reformatories where

authorities find themselves bound, not only by the norms of their own official system, but by the inmate system as well. They are unable to work out an effective program: (1) because the goals of the two systems are incompatible; and (2) because no one knows much about the structure and function of the inmate system and how it might be dealt with for purposes of rehabilitation.[2] Furthermore, the crux of any treatment program has ultimately to do with the decision-making process utilized by delinquents in the community, *not* in the reformatory. Yet, the deci-

* The inception and continuation of this experiment were made possible through the co-operation of the Judge (Monroe Paxman) and staff of the Third District Juvenile Court, a voluntary group known as the Citizens' Advisory Council, and Utah County Officials. Evaluation is supported by the Ford Foundation. Grateful acknowledgment is made to all involved.

[1] Donald R. Cressey, "Changing Criminals: The Application of the Theory of Differential Association," *American Journal of Sociology*, 61 (July, 1955), p. 116.

[2] Daniel Glaser maintains that the prison social system has not received the study it merits. Most writing about prisons, he says, is "impressionistic," "moralistic," "superficial," and "biased," rather than "systematic" and "objective." "The Sociological Approach to Crime and Correction," *Law and Contemporary Problems*, 23 (Autumn, 1958), p. 697; see also Gresham M. Sykes and Sheldon Messinger, "The Inmate Social System," in *Theoretical Studies in Social Organization of the Prison*, Social Science Research Council, March, 1960, pp. 5–19; and Lloyd W. McCorkle and Richard Korn, "Resocialization Within Walls," *The Annals of The American Academy of Political and Social Science*, 293 (May, 1954), pp. 88–98.

SOURCE. Lamar T. Empey and Jerome Rabow, "The Provo Experiment in Delinquency Rehabilitation," from *American Sociological Review*, Volume 26, October 1961, pp. 679–695. Reprinted with the permission of the American Sociological Association and the authors.

sions which lead to success in "doing time" in the reformatory are not of the same type needed for successful community adjustment. Existing conditions may actually be more effective in cementing ties to the delinquent system than in destroying them.[3]

The second dimension of the problem has to do with the traditional emphasis upon "individualized treatment."[4] This emphasis stems from two sources: (1) a humanistic concern for the importance of human dignity and the need for sympathetic understanding;[5] and (2) a widespread belief that delinquency is a psychological disease and the offender a *"sick"* person.[6] If, however, sociologists are even partially correct regarding the causes for delinquency, these two points of view overlook the possibility that most persistent delinquents do have the support of a meaningful reference group and are

not, therefore, without the emotional support and normative orientation which such a group can provide. In fact, a complete dedication to an individualistic approach poses an impasse: How can an individual who acquired delinquency from a group with which he identifies strongly be treated individually without regard to the persons or norms of the system from whom he acquired it?[7]

A successful treatment program for such a person would require techniques not normally included in the individualized approach. It should no more be expected that dedicated delinquents can be converted to conventionality by such means than that devout Pentecostals can be converted to Catholicism by the same means. Instead, different techniques are required for dealing with the normative orientation of the delinquent's system, replacing it with new values, beliefs, and rationalizations and developing means by which he can realize conventional satisfactions, especially with respect to successful employment.

This does not suggest, of course, that such traditional means as probation for dealing with the first offender or psychotherapy for dealing with the disturbed offender can be discarded. But it does suggest the need for experimental programs more consistent with sociological theory, and more consistent with the sociological premise that most *persistent* and *habitual* offenders are active members of a delinquent social system.[8]

---

[3] Sykes and Messinger, *op. cit.*, pp. 12–13; Richard McCleery, "Policy Change in Prison Management," *Michigan State University Political Research Studies*, No. 5, 1957; Richard A. Cloward, "Social Control in the Prison," in *Theoretical Studies in Social Organization of the Prison, op. cit.*, pp. 20–48; Stanton Wheeler, "Socialization in Correctional Communities," *American Sociological Review*, 26 (October, 1961).

[4] Cressey, *op. cit.*, p. 116.

[5] For example, see John G. Milner, "Report on an Evaluated Study of the Citizenship Training Program, Island of Hawaii," Los Angeles: University of Southern California School of Social Work, 1959, p. 4. Irving E. Cohen implies that anything which interferes with the establishment of "confidence, sympathy and understanding" between adult and offender interferes with the effectiveness of the individualized approach. See "Twilight Zones in Probation," *Journal of Criminal Law and Criminology*, 37, No. 4, p. 291.

[6] Michael Hakeem, "A Critique of the Psychiatric Approach to Juvenile Delinquency," in *Juvenile Delinquency*, edited by Joseph S. Roucek, New York: Philosophical Library, 1958. Hakeem provides a large bibliography to which attention can be directed if further information is desired. See also Daniel Glaser, "Criminality Theories and Behavioral Images," *American Journal of Sociology*, 61 (March, 1956), pp. 433–444.

[7] Cressey, *op. cit.*, p. 117. LaMay Adamson and H. Warren Dunham even imply that the clinical approach cannot work successfully with habitual offenders. See "Clinical Treatment of Male Delinquents: A Case Study in Effort and Result," *American Sociological Review*, 21 (June, 1956), p. 320.

[8] One program consistent with this premise is the Highfields Residential Group Center in New Jersey. Modern penology is indebted to it for the development of many

This paper presents the outlines of a program—the Provo Experiment in Delinquency Rehabilitation—which is derived from sociological theory and which seeks to apply sociological principles to rehabilitation. Because of its theoretical ties, the concern of the Experiment is as much with a systematic evaluation and reformulation of treatment consistent with findings as with the administration of treatment itself. For that reason, research and evaluation are an integral part of the program. Its theoretical orientation, major assumptions, treatment system, and research design are outlined below.

THEORETICAL ORIENTATION

With regards to causation, the Provo Experiment turned to a growing body of evidence which suggests two important conclusions: (1) that the greater part of delinquent behavior is not that of individuals engaging in highly secretive deviations, but is a group phenomenon—a shared deviation which is the product of differential group experience in a particular subculture,[9] and (2)

that because most delinquents tend to be concentrated in slums or to be the children of lower-class parents, their lives are characterized by learning situations which limit their access to success goals.[10]

Attention to these two conclusions does not mean that emotional problems[11] or "bad" homes[12] can be ignored. But only occasionally do these variables lead by themselves to delinquency. In most cases where older delinquents are involved other intervening variables must operate, the most important of which is the presence of a delinquent system—one which supplies status and recognition not normally obtainable elsewhere. Whether they are members

---

unique and important aspects. See Lloyd W. McCorkle, Albert Elias, and F. Lovell Bixby, *The Highfields Story: A Unique Experiment in the Treatment of Juvenile Delinquency*, New York: Henry Holt and Co., 1958; H. Ashley Weeks, *Youthful Offenders at Highfields*, Ann Arbor: University of Michigan Press, 1958; and Albert Elias and Jerome Rabow, "Post-Release Adjustment of Highfields Boys, 1955–1957," *The Welfare Reporter*, January, 1960, pp. 7–11.

[9] Richard A. Cloward and Lloyd E. Ohlin, *Delinquency and Opportunity: A Theory of Delinquent Gangs*, Glencoe, Ill.: The Free Press, 1960; Albert K. Cohen, *Delinquent Boys—The Culture of the Gang*, Glencoe, Ill.: The Free Press, 1955; Albert K. Cohen and James F. Short, Jr., "Research in Delinquent Subcultures," *The Journal of Social Issues*, 14 (1958), pp. 20–37; Solomon Kobrin, "The Conflict of Values in Delinquency Areas," *American Sociological Review*, 16 (October, 1951), pp. 653–661; Robert K. Merton, *Social Theory and Social Structure*, Glencoe, Ill.: The Free Press, 1957, Chapters 4–5; Walter B. Miller, "Lower Class Culture as a

Generating Milieu of Gang Delinquency," *The Journal of Social Issues*, 14 (1958), pp. 5–19; Clifford R. Shaw, *Delinquency Areas*, Chicago: University of Chicago Press, 1929; Clifford R. Shaw, Henry D. McKay, et al., *Juvenile Delinquency and Urban Areas*, Chicago: University of Chicago Press, 1931; Edwin H. Sutherland, *Principles of Criminology*, 4th ed., Philadelphia: Lippincott, 1947; Frank Tannenbaum, *Crime and the Community*, Boston: Ginn and Co., 1938; F. M. Thrasher, *The Gang*, Chicago: University of Chicago Press, 1936; William F. Whyte, *Street Corner Society*, Chicago: University of Chicago Press, 1943.

[10] Richard A. Cloward, "Illegitimate Means, Anomie, and Deviant Behavior," *American Sociological Review*, 24 (April, 1959), pp. 164–176; Cloward and Ohlin, *op. cit.*; Robert K. Merton, "Social Conformity, Deviation, and Opportunity-Structures: A Comment on the Contributions of Dubin and Cloward," *American Sociological Review*, 24 (April, 1959), pp. 177–189; Robert K. Merton, "The Social-Cultural Environment and Anomie," *New Perspectives for Research on Juvenile Delinquency*, edited by Helen Kotinsky, U. S. Department of Health, Education and Welfare, 1955, pp. 24–50; Merton, *Social Theory and Social Structure*, *op. cit.*

[11] Erik H. Erikson, "Ego Identity and the Psycho-Social Moratorium," *New Perspectives for Research on Juvenile Delinquency*, *op. cit.*, pp. 1–23.

[12] Jackson Toby, "The Differential Impact of Family Disorganization," *American Sociological Review*, 22 (October, 1957), pp. 505–511; and F. Ivan Nye, *Family Relationships and Delinquent Behavior*, New York: John Wiley and Sons, 1958.

of a tight-knit gang or of the amorphous structure of the "parent" delinquent subculture,[13] habitual delinquents tend to look affectively both to their peers and to the norms of their system for meaning and orientation. Thus, although a "bad" home may have been instrumental at some early phase in the genesis of a boy's delinquency, it must be recognized that it is now other delinquent boys, not his parents, who are current sources of support and identification. Any attempts to change him, therefore, would have to view him as more than an unstable isolate without a meaningful reference group. And, instead of concentrating on changing his parental relationships, they would have to recognize the intrinsic nature of his membership in the delinquent system and direct treatment to him as a part of that system.

There is another theoretical problem. An emphasis on the importance of the delinquent system raises some question regarding the extent to which delinquents are without any positive feeling for conventional standards. Vold says that one approach to explaining delinquency ". . . operates from the basic, implicit assumption that in a delinquency area, delinquency is the normal response of the normal individual— that the non-delinquent is really the 'problem case,' the nonconformist whose behavior needs to be accounted for."[14] This is a deterministic point of view suggesting the possibility that delinquents view conventional people as "foreigners" and conventional norms and beliefs as anathema. It implies that delinquents have been socialized entirely in a criminal system and have never internalized or encountered the

blandishments of conventional society.[15]

Actually, sociological literature suggests otherwise. It emphasizes, in general, that the subparts of complex society are intimately tied up with the whole,[16] and, specifically, that delinquents are very much aware of conventional standards; that they have been socialized in an environment dominated by middle-class morality;[17] that they have internalized the American success ideal to such a degree that they turn to illegitimate means in an effort to be successful[18] (or, failing in that, engage in malicious or retreatist activities);[19] that they are profoundly

---

[13] Cohen and Short, Jr., *op. cit.*, p. 24.

[14] George B. Vold, "Discussion of Guided Group Interaction in Correctional Work by F. Lovell Bixby and Lloyd W. McCorkle," *American Sociological Review*, 16 (August, 1951), p. 460.

[15] As Glaser points out, sociologists have tended to be deterministic and to ally themselves with psychiatrists in the struggle against classical legalists and religious leaders over the free will versus determinism issue. He labels this struggle as a "phony war," involving polemics more than reality. However, he says the war is losing its intensity because of a declining interest in metaphysical issues and a recognition of the importance of voluntaristic rather than reflexive conceptions of human behavior. Contrary to their protestations, the determinists, for example, recognize that humans are aware of alternative possible courses of behavior and make deliberate choices between them. See "The Sociological Approach to Crime and Correction," *op. cit.*, pp. 686–687.

[16] Sutherland, it will be recalled, maintained that "While criminal behavior is an expression of general needs and values, it is not explained by those general needs and values since non-criminal behavior is an expression of the *same needs and values.*" *Op. cit.*, pp. 6–7, italics ours. The accuracy of the statement would hinge on the definition of "needs" and "values." See also David J. Bordua, *Sociological Theories and Their Implications for Juvenile Delinquency*, U. S. Department of Health, Education and Welfare, 1960, p. 8, and Robin M. Williams, Jr., *American Society*, New York: Alfred A. Knopf, 1955, Chapter 11.

[17] Cohen, *op. cit.*, p. 133.

[18] Merton, *Social Theory and Social Structure*, *op. cit.*

[19] Cloward, *op. cit.*, and Cloward and Ohlin, *op. cit.* See also Robert Dubin, "Deviant Behavior and Social Structure: Continuities in Social Theory," *American Sociological Review*, 24 (April, 1959), pp. 147–164.

ambivalent about their delinquent behavior;[20] and that in order to cope with the claims of respectable norms upon them, they maintain a whole series of intricate rationalizations by which to "neutralize" their delinquent behavior.[21]

This suggests that delinquents are aware of conventional structure and its expectations. In many conventional settings they can, and usually do, behave conventionally. But it also suggests that, like other people, they are motivated by the normative expectations of their own subsystem. Consequently, when in the company of other delinquent boys, they may not only feel that they have to live up to minimal delinquent expectations but to appear more delinquent than they actually are, just as people in church often feel that they have to appear more holy than they actually are.

If this is the case, the problem of rehabilitation is probably not akin to converting delinquents to ways of behavior and points of view about which they are unaware and which they have never seriously considered as realistic alternatives. Instead, the feeling of ambivalence on their parts might be an element which could be used in rehabilitation.

An important sociological hypothesis based on this assumption would be that the ambivalence of most habitual delinquents is not primarily the result of personality conflicts developed in such social *microcosms* as the family but is inherent in the structure of the societal

macrocosm. A delinquent subsystem simply represents an alternative means for acquiring, or attempting to acquire, social and economic goals idealized by the societal system which are acquired by other people through conventional means.

If this hypothesis is accurate, delinquent ambivalence might actually be used in effecting change. A rehabilitation program might seek: (1) to make conventional and delinquent alternatives clear; (2) to lead delinquents to question the ultimate utility of delinquent alternatives; and (3) to help conventional alternatives assume some positive valence for them. It might then reduce the affective identification which they feel for the delinquent subsystem and tip the scales in the opposite direction.

MAJOR ASSUMPTIONS FOR TREATMENT

In order to relate such theoretical premises to the specific needs of treatment, the Provo Experiment adopted a series of major assumptions. They are as follows:

1. Delinquent behavior is primarily a group product and demands an approach to treatment far different from that which sees it as characteristic of a "sick," or "well-meaning" but "misguided," person.

2. An effective program must recognize the intrinsic nature of a delinquent's membership in a delinquent system and, therefore, must direct treatment to him as a part of that system.

3. Most habitual delinquents are affectively and ideologically dedicated to the delinquent system. Before they can be made amenable to change, they must be made anxious about the ultimate utility of that system for them.

4. Delinquents must be forced to deal with the conflicts which the demands

---

20 Cohen, *Delinquent Boys, op. cit.*, p. 133; Cohen and Short, *op. cit.*, p. 21. See also John I. Kitsuse and David C. Dietrick, "Delinquent Boys: A Critique," *American Sociological Review*, 24 (April, 1959), p. 211.

21 Gresham M. Sykes and David Matza, "Techniques of Neutralization: A Theory of Delinquency," *American Sociological Review*, 22 (December, 1957), pp. 664–670.

of conventional and delinquent systems place upon them. The resolution of such conflicts, either for or against further law violations, must ultimately involve a community decision. For that reason, a treatment program, in order to force realistic decision-making, can be most effective if it permits continued participation in the community as well as in the treatment process.

5. Delinquent ambivalence for purposes of rehabilitation can only be utilized in a setting conducive to the free expression of feelings—both delinquent and conventional. This means that the protection and rewards provided by the treatment system for *candor* must exceed those provided either by delinquents for adherence to delinquent roles or by officials for adherence to custodial demands for "good behavior." Only in this way can delinquent individuals become aware of the extent to which other delinquents share conventional as well as delinquent aspirations and, only in this way, can they be encouraged to examine the ultimate utility of each.

6. An effective program must develop a unified and cohesive social system in which delinquents and authorities alike are devoted to one task—overcoming lawbreaking. In order to accomplish this the program must avoid two pitfalls: (*a*) it must avoid establishing authorities as "rejectors" and making inevitable the creation of two social systems within the program; and (*b*) it must avoid the institutionalization of means by which skilled offenders can evade norms and escape sanctions.[22] The occasional imposition of negative sanctions is as necessary in this system as in any other system.

7. A treatment system will be most effective if the delinquent peer group is used as the means of perpetuating

[22] McCorkle and Korn, *op. cit.*, pp. 88–91.

the norms and imposing the sanctions of the system. The peer group should be seen by delinquents as the primary source of help and support. The traditional psychotherapeutic emphasis upon transference relationships is not viewed as the most vital factor in effecting change.

8. A program based on sociological theory may tend to exclude lectures, sermons, films, individual counseling, analytic psychotherapy, organized athletics, academic education, and vocational training as primary treatment techniques. It will have to concentrate, instead, on matters of another variety: changing reference group and normative orientations, utilizing ambivalent feelings resulting from the conflict of conventional and delinquent standards, and providing opportunities for recognition and achievement in conventional pursuits.

9. An effective treatment system must include rewards which are realistically meaningful to delinquents. They would include such things as peer acceptance for law-abiding behavior or the opportunity for gainful employment rather than badges, movies, or furlough privileges which are designed primarily to facilitate institutional control. Rewards, therefore, must only be given for realistic and lasting changes, not for conformance to norms which concentrate upon effective custody as an end in itself.

10. Finally, in summary, a successful program must be viewed by delinquents as possessing four important characteristics: (*a*) a social climate in which delinquents are given the opportunity to examine and experience alternatives related to a realistic choice between delinquent or non-delinquent behavior; (*b*) the opportunity to declare publicly to peers and authorities a belief or disbelief that they can benefit from a change in values; (*c*) a type of social

structure which will permit them to examine the role and legitimacy (for their purposes) of authorities in the treatment system; and (*d*) a type of treatment interaction which, because it places major responsibilities upon peer-group decision-making, grants status and recognition to individuals, not only for their own successful participation in the treatment interaction, but for their willingness to involve others.

THE TREATMENT SYSTEM[23]

The Provo Program, consistent with these basic assumptions, resides in the community and does not involve permanent incarceration. Boys live at home and spend only a part of each day at Pinehills (the program center). Otherwise they are free in the community.[24]

HISTORY AND LOCALE. The Provo Program was begun in 1956 as an "in-between" program designed specifically to help those habitual delinquents whose persistence made them candidates, in most cases, for a reformatory. It was instigated by a volunteer group of professional and lay people known as the *Citizens' Advisory Council to the Juvenile Court.* It has never had formal ties to government except through the Juvenile Court. This lack of ties has permitted considerable experimenta-

tion. Techniques have been modified to such a degree that the present program bears little resemblance to the original one. Legally, program officials are deputy probation officers appointed by the Juvenile Judge.

The cost of treatment is financed by county funds budgeted through the Juvenile Court. So near as we can estimate the cost per boy is approximately one-tenth of what it would cost if he were incarcerated in a reformatory. Research operations are financed by the Ford Foundation. Concentrated evaluation of the program is now in its second year of a six-year operation. Because both the theoretical orientation and treatment techniques of the program were in developmental process until its outlines were given final form for research purposes, it is difficult to make an objective evaluation of the over-all program based on recidivism rates for previous years, especially in the absence of adequate control groups. Such an evaluation, however, is an integral part of the present research and is described below.

Relations with welfare agencies and the community, per se, are informal but extremely co-operative. This is due to three things: the extreme good will and guiding influence of the Juvenile Court Judge, Monroe J. Paxman,[25] the unceasing efforts of the Citizens' Advisory Council to involve the entire county as a community, and the willingness of city and county officials, not only to overcome traditional fears regarding habitual offenders in the community, but to lend strong support to an experimental program of this type.

Community co-operation is probably enhanced by strong Mormon traditions.

[23] Except for the community aspects, the above assumptions and the treatment system are similar to those pioneered at Highfields. See McCorkle, Elias, and Bixby, *op. cit.* The Provo Program is especially indebted to Albert Elias, the present director of Highfields, not only for his knowledge about treatment techniques, but for his criticisms of the Provo Experiment.

[24] The idea of a community program is not new. The Boston Citizenship Training Group, Inc., a non-residential program, was begun in 1934–1936. However, it is for younger boys and utilizes a different approach. A similar program, initiated by Professor Ray R. Canning in Provo, was a forerunner to this experiment. See "A New Treatment Program for Juvenile Delinquents," *Journal of Criminal Law and Criminology,* 31 (March–April, 1941), pp. 712–719.

[25] Judge Paxman is a member of the Advisory Council of Judges to the National Council on Crime and Delinquency and is a member of the symposium preparing a work entitled, *Justice for the Child,* Chicago: University of Chicago, 1962.

However, Utah County is in a period of rapid transition which began in the early days of World War II with the introduction of a large steel plant, allied industries, and an influx of non-Mormons. This trend, both in industry and population, has continued to the present time. The treatment program is located in the city of Provo but draws boys from all major communities in the county—from a string of small cities, many of which border on each other, ranging in size from four to 40,000. The total population from which it draws its assignees is about 110,000.

Despite the fact that Utah County is not a highly urbanized area, when compared to large metropolitan centers, the concept of a "parent" delinquent subculture has real meaning for it. While there are no clear-cut gangs, per se, it is surprising to observe the extent to which delinquent boys from the entire county, who have never met, know each other by reputation, go with the same girls, use the same language, or can seek each other out when they change high schools. About half of them are permanently out of school, do not participate in any regular institutional activities, and are reliant almost entirely upon the delinquent system for social acceptance and participation.

ASSIGNEES. Only habitual offenders, 15–17 years, are assigned to the program. In the absence of public facilities, they are transported to and from home each day in automobiles driven by university students. Their offenses run the usual gamut: vandalism, trouble in school, shoplifting, car theft, burglary, forgery, and so forth. Highly disturbed and psychotic boys are not assigned. The pre-sentence investigation is used to exclude these people. They constitute an extremely small minority.

NUMBER IN ATTENDANCE. No more than twenty boys are assigned to the program at any one time. A large number would make difficult any attempts to establish and maintain a unified, cohesive system. This group of twenty is broken into two smaller groups, each of which operates as a separate discussion unit. When an older boy is released from one of these units, a new boy is added. This is an important feature because it serves as the means by which the culture of the system is perpetuated.

LENGTH OF ATTENDANCE. No length of stay is specified. It is intimately tied to the group and its processes because a boy's release depends not only upon his own behavior, but upon the maturation processes through which his group goes. Release usually comes somewhere between four and seven months.

NATURE OF PROGRAM. The program does not utilize any testing, gathering of case histories, or clinical diagnosis. One of its key tools, peer group interaction, is believed to provide a considerably richer source of information about boys and delinquency than do clinical methods.

The program, per se, is divided into two phases. Phase I is an intensive group program, utilizing work and the delinquent peer group as the principal instruments for change. During the winter, boys attend this phase three hours a day, five days a week, and all day on Saturdays. Activities include daily group discussions, hard work, and some unstructured activities in which boys are left entirely on their own. During the summer they attend an all-day program which involves work and group discussions. However, there are no practices without exceptions. For example, if a boy has a full-time job, he may be allowed to continue the job in lieu of working in the program. Other innovations occur repeatedly.

Phase II is designed to aid a boy after release from intensive treatment in Phase I. It involves two things: (1) an attempt to maintain some reference group support for a boy; and (2) community action to help him find employment. Both phases are described below.

PHASE I: INTENSIVE TREATMENT

Every attempt is made in Phase I to create a social system in which social structure, peer members, and authorities are oriented to the one task of instituting change. The more relevant to this task the system is, the greater will be its influence.

SOCIAL STRUCTURE. There is little formal structure in the Provo Program. Patterns are abhorred which might make boys think that their release depends upon *refraining* from swearing, engaging in open quarrels or doing such *"positive"* things as saying, "yes sir," or "no sir." Such criteria as these play into their hands. They learn to manipulate them in developing techniques for beating a system. Consequently, other than requiring boys to appear each day and work hard on the job, there are no formal demands. The only other daily activities are the group discussions at which attendance is optional.

The absence of formal structure helps to do more than avoid artificial criteria for release. It has the positive effect of making boys more amenable to treatment. In the absence of formal structure they are uneasy and they are not quite sure of themselves. Thus, the lack of clear-cut definitions for behavior helps to accomplish three important things: (1) It produces anxiety and turns boys towards the group as a method of resolving their anxiety. (2) It leaves boys free to define situations for themselves: leaders begin to lead, followers begin to follow, and manipulators begin to manipulate. It is these types of behavior which must be seen and analyzed if change is to take place. (3) It binds neither authorities nor the peer group to prescribed courses of action. Each is free to do whatever is needed to suit the needs of particular boys, groups, or situations.

On the other hand, the absence of formal structure obviously does not mean that there is no structure. But, that which does exist is informal and emphasizes ways of thinking and behaving which are not traditional. Perhaps the greatest difference lies in the fact that a considerable amount of power is vested in the delinquent peer group. It is the instrument by which norms are perpetuated and through which many important decisions are made. It is the primary source of pressure for change.

THE PEER GROUP. Attempts to involve a boy with the peer group begin the moment he arrives. Instead of meeting with and receiving an orientation lecture from authorities, he receives no formal instructions. He is always full of such questions as, "What do I have to do to get out of this place?" or "How long do I have to stay?", but such questions as these are never answered. They are turned aside with, "I don't know," or "Why don't you find out?" Adults will not orient him in the ways that he has grown to expect, nor will they answer any of his questions. He is forced to turn to his peers. Usually, he knows someone in the program, either personally or by reputation. As he begins to associate with other boys he discovers that important informal norms do exist, the most important of which makes *inconsistency* rather than *consistency* the rule. That which is appropriate for one situation, boy, or group may not be appropriate for another. Each merits a decision as it arises.

Other norms center most heavily about the daily group discussion sessions. These sessions are patterned after the technique of "Guided Group Interaction" which was developed at Fort Knox during World War II and at Highfields.[26] Guided Group Interaction emphasizes the idea that only through a group and its processes can a boy work out his problems. From a peer point of view it has three main goals: (1) to question the utility of a life devoted to delinquency; (2) to suggest alternative ways for behavior; and (3) to provide recognition for a boy's personal reformation and his willingness to reform others.[27]

Guided Group Interaction grants to the peer group a great deal of power, including that of helping to decide when each boy is ready to be released. This involves "retroflexive reformation."[28] If a delinquent is serious in his attempts to reform others he must automatically accept the common purpose of the reformation process, identify himself closely with others engaged in it, and grant prestige to those who succeed in it. In so doing, he becomes a genuine member of the reformation group and in the process may be alienated from his previous pro-delinquent groups.[29] Such is an ideal and long-term goal. Before it can be realized for any individual he must become heavily involved with the treatment system. Such involvement does not come easy and the system must include techniques which will impel him to involvement. Efforts to avoid the development of formal structure have already been described as one technique. Group processes constitute a second technique.

Before a group will help a boy "solve his problems" it demands that he review his total delinquent history. This produces anxiety because, while he is still relatively free, it is almost inevitable that he has much more to reveal than is already known by the police or the court. In an effort to avoid such involvement he may try subterfuge. But any reluctance on his part to be honest will not be taken lightly. Norms dictate that no one in the group can be released until everyone is honest and until every boy helps to solve problems. A refusal to come clean shows a lack of trust in the group and slows down the problem-solving process. Therefore, any recalcitrant boy is faced with a real dilemma. He can either choose involvement or relentless attack by his peers. Once a boy does involve himself, however, he learns that some of his fears were unwarranted. What goes on in the group meeting is sacred and is not revealed elsewhere.

A second process for involvement lies in the use of the peer group to perpetuate the norms of the treatment system. One of the most important norms suggests that most boys in the program are candidates for a reformatory. This is shocking because even habitual delinquents do not ordinarily stay out. Vold, in our opinion, is incorrect if his remarks are taken to mean that the group does not discuss groups and group processes, what peers mean to a boy or how the orientations of delinquent groups differ from those of conventional society. *Op. cit.*, p. 360.

---

[26] See F. Lovell Bixby and Lloyd W. McCorkle, "Guided Group Interaction and Correctional Work," *American Sociological Review*, 16 (August, 1951), pp. 455–459; McCorkle, Elias, and Bixby, *The Highfields Story, op. cit.*; and Joseph Abrahams and Lloyd W. McCorkle, "Group Psychotherapy on Military Offenders," *American Journal of Sociology*, 51 (March, 1946), pp. 455–464. These sources present a very limited account of techniques employed. An intimate knowledge would require attendance at group sessions.

[27] Other goals relating to the emphasis upon group development, the role of the group therapist, and the nature of the therapeutic situations have been described briefly elsewhere. See *The Highfields Story, op. cit.*, pp. 72–80.

[28] Cressey, *op. cit.*, p. 119.

[29] Vold maintains that guided group interaction assumes that there is something wrong inside the individual and attempts to correct that. He is right in the sense that it emphasizes that an individual must accept responsibility for his own delinquencies and that no one can keep him out of prison unless he himself is ready to

see themselves as serious offenders.[30] Yet, the tradition is clear; most failures at Pinehills are sent to the Utah State Industrial School. Therefore, each boy has a major decision to make: either he makes serious attempts to change or he gets sent away.

The third process of involvement could only occur in a community program. Each boy has the tremendous problem of choosing between the demands of his delinquent peers outside the program and the demands of those within it. The usual reaction is to test the situation by continuing to identify with the former. Efforts to do this, however, and to keep out of serious trouble are usually unsuccessful. The group is a collective board on delinquency; it usually includes a member who knows the individual personally or by reputation; and it can rely on the meeting to discover many things. Thus, the group is able to use actual behavior in the community to judge the extent to which a boy is involved with the program and to judge his readiness for release. The crucial criterion for any treatment program is not what an individual does while in it, but what he does while he is *not* in it.

The fourth process involves a number of important sanctions which the group can impose if a boy refuses to become involved. It can employ familiar techniques such as ostracism or derision or it can deny him the status and recognition which come with change. Furthermore, it can use sanctions arising out of the treatment system. For example, while authorities may impose restrictions on boys in the form of extra work or incarceration in jail, the group is often permitted, and encour-

aged, to explore reasons for the action and to help decide what future actions should be taken. For example, a boy may be placed in jail over the week-end and told that he will be returned there each week-end thereafter until his group decides to release him. It is not uncommon for the group, after thorough discussion, to return him one or more week-ends despite his protestations. Such an occurrence would be less likely in an ordinary reformatory because of the need for inmates to maintain solidarity against the official system. However, in this setting it is possible because boys are granted the power to make important decisions affecting their entire lives. Rather than having other people do things to them, they are doing things to themselves.

The ultimate sanction possessed by the group is refusal to release a boy from the program. Such a sanction has great power because it is normative to expect that no individual will be tolerated in the program indefinitely. Pinehills is not a place where boys "do time."

AUTHORITIES. The third source of pressure towards change rests in the hands of authorities. The role of an authority in a treatment system of this type is a difficult one. On one hand, he cannot be seen as a person whom skillful delinquents or groups can manipulate. But, on the other hand, he cannot be perceived permanently as a "rejector." Everything possible, therefore, must be done by him to create an adult image which is new and different.

Initially, authorities are probably seen as "rejectors." It will be recalled that they do not go out of their way to engage in regular social amenities, to put boys at ease, or to establish one-to-one relationships with boys. Adult behavior of this type is consistent with the treatment philosophy. It attempts to

---

[30] Delinquents are like other people: The worst can never happen to them. See also Mark R. Moran, "Inmate Concept of Self in a Reformatory Society," unpublished Ph.D. dissertation, Ohio State University, 1953.

have boys focus upon the peer group, not adults, as the vehicle by which questions and problems are resolved.

Second, boys learn that authorities will strongly uphold the norm which says that Pinehills is not a place for boys to "do time." If, therefore, a boy does not become involved and the group is unwilling or unable to take action, authorities will. Such action varies. It might involve requiring him to work all day without pay, placing him in jail, or putting him in a situation in which he has no role whatsoever. In the latter case he is free to wander around the Center all day but he is neither allowed to work nor given the satisfaction of answers to his questions regarding his future status.

Boys are seldom told why they are in trouble or, if they are told, solutions are not suggested. To do so would be to provide them structure by which to rationalize their behavior, hide other things they have been doing, and escape the need to change. Consequently, they are left on their own to figure out why authorities are doing what they are doing and what they must do to get out of trouble.

Situations of this type precipitate crises. Sometimes boys run away. But, whatever happens, the boy's status remains amorphous until he can come up with a solution to his dilemma. This dilemma, however, is not easily resolved.

There is no individual counseling since this would reflect heavily upon the integrity of the peer group. Consequently, he cannot resolve his problems by counseling with or pleasing adults. His only recourse is to the group. But since the group waits for him to bring up his troubles, he must involve himself with it or he cannot resolve them. Once he does, he must reveal why he is in trouble, what he has been doing

to get into trouble or how he has been abusing the program. If he refuses to become involved he may be returned to court by authorities. This latter alternative occurs rarely, since adults have more time than boys. While they can afford to wait, boys find it very difficult to "sweat out" a situation. They feel the need to resolve it.

As a result of such experiences, boys are often confused and hostile. But where such feelings might be cause for alarm elsewhere, they are welcomed at Pinehills. They are taken as a sign that a boy is not in command of the situation and is therefore amenable to change. Nevertheless, the treatment system does not leave him without an outlet for his feelings. The meeting is a place where his anger and hostility can be vented—not only against the program but against the adults who run it. But, in venting his confusion and hostility, it becomes possible for the group to analyze, not only his own behavior, but that of adults, and to determine to what end the behavior of all is leading. Initial perceptions of adults which were confusing and provoking can now be seen in a new way. The treatment system places responsibility upon a boy and his peers for changing delinquent behavior, not upon adults. Thus, adult behavior which was initially seen as rejecting can now be seen as consistent with this expectation. Boys have to look to their own resources for solutions of problems. In this way they are denied social-psychological support for "rejecting the rejectors," or for rejecting decisions demanded by the group. Furthermore, as a result of the new adult image which is pressed upon them, boys are led to examine their perceptions regarding other authorities. Boys may learn to see authorities with whom they had difficulties previously in a new, non-stereotyped fashion.

WORK AND OTHER ACTIVITIES

Any use of athletics, handicrafts, or remedial schooling involves a definition of rehabilitation goals. Are these activities actually important in changing delinquents? In the Provo Experiment they are not viewed as having an inherent value in developing non-delinquent behavior. In fact, they are viewed as detrimental because participation in them often becomes criteria for release. On the other hand, work habits are viewed as vitally important. Previous research suggests that employment is one of the most important means of changing reference from delinquent to law-abiding groups.[31] But, such findings simply pose the important question: How can boys be best prepared to find and hold employment?

Sociologists have noted the lack of opportunity structure for delinquents, but attention to a modification of the structure (assuming that it can be modified) as the sole approach to rehabilitation overlooks the need to prepare delinquents to utilize employment possibilities. One alternative for doing this is an education program with all its complications. The other is an immediate attack on delinquent values and work habits. The Provo Experiment chose the latter alternative. It hypothesized that an immediate attack on delinquent values, previous careers, and nocturnal habits would be more effective than an educational program. Sophisticated delinquents, who are otherwise very skillful in convincing peers and authorities of their good intentions, are often unable to work consistently. They have too long believed that only suckers work. Thus concentration is upon work habits. Boys are employed by the city and county in parks, streets,

and recreation areas. Their work habits are one focus of group discussion and an important criterion for change. After release, they are encouraged to attend academic and vocational schools should they desire.

THE STARTER MECHANISM:
PUTTING THE SYSTEM IN MOTION

There are both theoretical and practical considerations relative to the purposeful creation of the social structure at Pinehills and the process by which it was developed. The foregoing discussion described some of the structural elements involved and, by inference, suggested the means by which they were introduced. However, the following is presented as a means of further clarification.

The first consideration involved the necessity of establishing structure which could pose realistically and clearly the alternatives open to habitually delinquent boys. What are these alternatives? Since in most cases delinquents are lower-class individuals who not only lack many of the social skills but who have been school failures as well, the alternatives are not great. Some may become professional criminals, but this is a small minority. Therefore, most of them have two principal choices: (1) they can continue to be delinquent and expect, in most cases, to end up in prison; or (2) they can learn to live a rather marginal life in which they will be able to operate sufficiently within the law to avoid being locked up. Acceptance of the second alternative by delinquents would not mean that they would have to change their entire style of living, but it does mean that most would have to find employment and be willing to disregard delinquent behavior in favor of the drudgery of everyday living.

Until these alternatives are posed

[31] Glaser, "A Sociological Approach to Crime and Correction," *op. cit.,* pp. 690–691.

for them, and posed in a meaningful way, delinquents will not be able to make the necessary decisions regarding them. The need, therefore, was for the type of structure at Pinehills which could pose these alternatives initially without equivocation and thus force boys to consider involvement in the rehabilitative process as a realistic alternative for them.

By the time delinquents reach Pinehills they have been cajoled, threatened, lectured, and exhorted—all by a variety of people in a variety of settings: by parents, teachers, police, religious leaders, and court officials. As a consequence, most have developed a set of manipulative techniques which enable them to "neutralize" verbal admonitions by appearing to comply with them, yet refraining all the while from any real adherence. For that reason, it was concluded that *deeds*, not *words*, would be required as the chief means for posing clearly the structural alternatives open to them.

Upon arrival the first delinquents assigned to Pinehills had every reason to believe that this was another community agency for which they possessed the necessary "techniques of neutralization." It was housed in an ordinary two-story home, and authorities spent little time giving instructions or posing threats. It must have seemed, therefore, that Pinehills would not constitute a serious obstacle for which they could not find some means to avoid involvement.

The following are examples of happenings which helped to establish norms contrary to this view. After attending only one day, a rather sophisticated boy was not at home to be picked up for his second day. Instead, he left a note on his front door saying he was at the hospital visiting a sick sister. Official reaction was immediate and almost entirely opposite to what he expected.

No one made any efforts to contact him. Instead, a detention order was issued by the court to the police who arrested the boy later that evening and placed him in jail. He was left there for several days without the benefit of visits from anyone and then returned to Pinehills. Even then, no one said anything to him about his absence. No one had to; he did not miss again. Furthermore, he had been instrumental in initiating the norm which says that the principal alternative to Pinehills is incarceration.

A second occurrence established this norm even more clearly. After having been at Pinehills for two months and refusing to yield to the pressures of his group, a boy asked for a rehearing in court, apparently feeling that he could manipulate the judge more successfully than he could the people at Pinehills. His request was acted upon immediately. He was taken to jail that afternoon and a hearing arranged for the following morning. The judge committed him to the State Reformatory.[32] Since that time there has never been another request for a rehearing. In a similar way, especially during the first year, boys who continued to get in serious trouble while at Pinehills were recalled by the court for another hearing and assigned to the reformatory. These cases became legendary examples to later boys. However, adults have never had to call attention to them; they are passed on in the peer socialization process.

Once such traditions were established, they could be used in yet another

[32] Co-operation of this type between the Juvenile Courts and rehabilitative agencies is not always forthcoming. Yet, it also reflects two things: (1) the fact that Judge Paxman sentences only those boys to Pinehills who are habitual offenders; and (2) the fact that it is his conviction that rehabilitation must inevitably involve the Court's participation, both in posing alternatives for boys and in determining the effectiveness of various approaches.

way. They became devices by which to produce the type of uncertainty characteristic of social settings in which negative sanctions should be forthcoming but do not appear. The individual is left wondering why. For example, not all boys who miss a day or two at Pinehills now are sent to jail. In some cases, nothing is said to the individual in question. He is left, instead, to wonder when, and if, he will be sent. Likewise, other boys who have been in serious trouble in the community are not always sent to the State Reformatory but may be subjected to the same kind of waiting and uncertainty. Efforts are made, however, to make it impossible for boys to predict in advance what will happen in any particular case. Even adults cannot predict this, relying on the circumstances inherent in each case. Thus, both rigidity and inconsistency are present in the system at the same time.

The same sort of structural alternatives were posed regarding work. Boys who did not work consistently on their city jobs, where they were being paid, were returned to Pinehills to work for nothing. At Pinehills, they were usually alone and had to perform such onerous tasks as scrubbing the floor, washing windows, mowing the lawn, or cutting weeds. They might be left on this job for hours or weeks. The problem of being returned to work with the other boys for pay was left to them for their own resolution, usually in the group. So long as they said nothing, nothing was said to them except to assign them more work.

This type of structure posed stark but, in our opinion, realistic alternatives. It was stark and realistic because boys were still living in the community, but for the first time could sense the omnipresence of permanent incarceration. However, another type of structure less stringent was needed by which

boys could realistically resolve problems and make choices. Since, as has been mentioned, peer-group decision-making was chosen as the means for problem-resolution, attention was focused upon the daily group meetings as the primary source of information. It became the focal point of the whole treatment system.

The first group, not having any standards to guide it (except those which suggested resistance to official pressures), spent great portions of entire meetings without speaking. However, consistent with the idea that deeds, not words, count, and that a group has to resolve its own problems, the group leader refused to break the silence except at the very end of each meeting. At that time, he began standardizing one common meeting practice: he summarized what had been accomplished. Of silent meetings he simply said that nothing had been accomplished. He did point out, however, that he would be back the next day—that, in fact, he would be there a year from that day. Where would they be, still there? The problem was theirs.

When some boys could stand the silence no longer, they asked the group leader what they might talk about. Rather than making it easy for them he suggested something that could only involve them further: he suggested that someone might recite all the things he had done to get in trouble. Not completely without resources, however, boys responded by reciting only those things they had been caught for. In his summary, the leader noted this fact and suggested that whoever spoke the next time might desire to be more honest by telling all. Boys were reluctant to do this but, partly because it was an opportunity to enhance reputations and partly because they did not know what else to do, some gave honest recitations. When no official action was taken against them, two new and important norms were introduced: (1) the idea that what is said in the meeting is sacred to the meeting; and (2) that boys can afford to be candid—that, in fact, candor pays.

The subsequent recitals of delinquent activities ultimately led to a growing awareness of the ambivalence which many delinquents feel regarding their activities. In the social climate provided by the meeting some boys began to express feelings and receive support for behavior which the delinquent system with its emphasis on ideal-typical role behavior could not permit.

Eventually, the meeting reached a stage where it began to discuss the plethora of happenings which occurred daily, both at Pinehills and elsewhere in the community. These happenings, rather than impersonal, easily speculated-about material, were urged as the most productive subject matter. For example, many boys had reached the stage of trying devious rather than direct methods of missing sessions at Pinehills. They came with requests to be excused for normally laudatory activities: school functions, family outings, and even religious services. But, again adults refused to take the traditional course of assuming responsibility and making decisions for boys. Boys were directed to the meeting instead. This not only shifted the responsibility to them, but provided the opportunity to develop five important norms: (1) those having to do with absences; (2) the idea that the place for problem-solving is in the meeting; (3) that everyone, not just adults, should be involved in the process; (4) that if a boy wants the meeting to talk about his problems, he has to justify them as being more important than someone else's; and (5) that any request or point of view has to be substantiated both by evidence and some relevance to the solution of delinquent problems.

It became obvious that even simple requests could be complicated. Boys found themselves using their own rationalizations on each other, often providing both humorous and eye-opening experiences. The climate became increasingly resistant to superficial requests and more conducive to the examination of pressing problems. Boys who chose to fight the system found themselves fighting peers. A stubborn boy could be a thorn in the side of the whole group.

The daily meeting summaries took on increased importance as the leader helped the group: (1) to examine what had happened each day; (2) to examine to what ends various efforts were leading—that is, to examine what various boys were doing, or not doing, and what relevance this had for themselves and the group; (3) to suggest areas of discussion which had been neglected, ignored, or purposely hidden by group members; and (4) to describe the goals of the treatment system in such a way that boys could come to recognize the meaning of group discussions as a realistic source of problem-resolution.

The structural lines associated with the meeting eventually began to define not only the type of subject matter most relevant to change, but the general means for dealing with this subject matter. However, such structure was extremely flexible, permitting a wide latitude of behavior. Great care was taken to avoid the institutionalization of clear-cut steps by which boys could escape Pinehills. Problem-solving was, and still is, viewed as a process—a process not easily understood in advance, but something which develops uniquely for each new boy and each new group.

Finally, in summary, the Pinehills system, like many social systems, has some rigid prerequisites for continued membership. The broad structural outlines carefully define the limits beyond which members should not go. However, unlike most extreme authoritarian systems, there is an inner structure, associated with the meeting, which does not demand rigid conformity and which instead permits those deviations which are an honest expression of feelings.

The admission of deviations within the structural confines of the meeting helps to lower the barriers which prevent a realistic examination of their implications for the broader authoritarian structure, either at Pinehills or in society at large. Boys are able to make more realistic decisions as to which roles, conventional or delinquent, would seem to have the most utility for them.

This brief attempt to describe a complex system may have been misleading. The complexities involved are multivariate and profound. However, one important aspect of the experiment has to do with the theoretical development of, and research on, the nature of the treatment system. Each discussion session is recorded, and efforts are made to determine means by which treatment techniques might be improved and ways in which group processes can be articulated. All would be very useful in testing theory which suggests that experience in a cohesive group is an important variable in directing or changing behavior.

PHASE II: COMMUNITY ADJUSTMENT

Phase II involves an effort to maintain reference group support and employment for a boy after intensive treatment in Phase I. After his release from Phase I he continues to meet periodically for discussions with his old group. The goal is to utilize this group in accomplishing three things: (1) acting as a check on a boy's current behavior; (2) serving as a law-abiding reference group; and (3) aiding in the solution of new problems. It seeks to continue treatment in a different and

perhaps more intensive way than such traditional practices as probation or parole.

Efforts to find employment for boys are made by the Citizens' Advisory Council. If employment is found, a boy is simply informed that an employer needs someone. No efforts are taken by some well-meaning but pretentious adult to manipulate the boy's life.

These steps, along with the idea that delinquents should be permitted to make important decisions during the rehabilitative process, are consistent with structural-functional analysis which suggests that in order to eliminate existing structure, or identification with it, one must provide the necessary functional alternatives.[33]

APPROPRIATENESS OF TECHNIQUES

Many persons express disfavor with what they consider a harsh and punitive system at Pinehills. If, however, alternatives are not great for habitual delinquents, a program which suggests otherwise is not being honest with them. Delinquents are aware that society seldom provides honors for *not* being delinquent; that, in fact, conventional alternatives for them have not always promised significantly more than delinquent alternatives.[34] Therefore, expectations associated with the adoption of conventional alternatives should not be unrealistic.

On the other hand it should be remembered that, in terms familiar to delinquents, every effort is made at Pinehills to include as many positive

[33] Edwin M. Schur, "Sociological Analysis in Confidence Swindling," *Journal of Criminal Law, Criminology and Police Science,* 48 (September-October, 1957), p. 304.

[34] Gwynn Nettler has raised a question as to who perceives reality most accurately, deviants or "good" people. See "Good Men, Bad Men and the Perception of Realty," paper delivered at the meetings of the American Sociological Association, Chicago, September, 1959.

experiences as possible. The following are some which seem to function:

1. Peers examine problems which are common to all.

2. There is a recurring opportunity for each individual to be the focal point of attention among peers in which his behavior and problems become the most important concern of the moment.

3. Delinquent peers articulate in front of conventional adults without constraint with regard to topic, language, or feeling.

4. Delinquents have the opportunity, for the first time in an institutional setting, to make crucial decisions about their own lives. This in itself is a change in the opportunity structure and is a means of obligating them to the treatment system. In a reformatory a boy cannot help but see the official system as doing things to him in which he has no say: locking him up, testing him, feeding him, making his decisions. Why should he feel obligated? But when some important decision-making is turned over to him, he no longer has so many grounds for rejecting the system. Rejection in a reformatory might be functional in relating him to his peers, but in this system it is not so functional.

5. Delinquents participate in a treatment system that grants status in three ways: (*a*) for age and experience in the treatment process—old boys have the responsibility of teaching new boys the norms of the system; (*b*) for the exhibition of law-abiding behavior, not only in a minimal sense, but for actual qualitative changes in specific role behavior at Pinehills, home or with friends; and (*c*) for the willingness to confront other boys, in a group setting, with their delinquent behavior. (In a reformatory where he has to contend with the inmate system a boy can gain little and lose much for his willingness

to be candid in front of adults about peers, but at Pinehills it is a primary source of prestige.) The ability to confront others often reflects more about the *confronter* than it does about the *confronted*. It is an indication of the extent to which he has accepted the reformation process and identified himself with it.[35]

6. Boys can find encouragement in a program which poses the possibility of relatively short restriction and the avoidance of incarceration.

7. The peer group is a potential source of reference group support for law-abiding behavior. Boys commonly refer to the fact that their group knows more about them than any other persons: parents or friends.

RESEARCH DESIGN

An integral part of the Provo Experiment is an evaluation of treatment extending over a five-year period. It includes means by which offenders who receive treatment are compared to two control groups: (1) a similar group of offenders who at time of sentence are placed on probation and left in the community; and (2) a similar group who at time of sentence are incarcerated in the Utah State Industrial School. Since it is virtually impossible to match all three groups, random selection is used to minimize the effect of sample bias. All three groups are drawn from a population of habitual delinquents who reside in Utah County, Utah, and who come before the Juvenile Court. Actual selection is as follows:

The Judge of the Court has in his possession two series of numbered en-

[35] Support for this idea can be found in a recently developed matrix designed to measure the impact of group interaction. See William and Ida Hill, *Interaction Matrix for Group Psychotherapy*, mimeographed manuscript, Utah State Mental Hospital, Provo, Utah, 1960. This matrix has been many years in development.

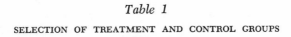

Table 1

SELECTION OF TREATMENT AND CONTROL GROUPS

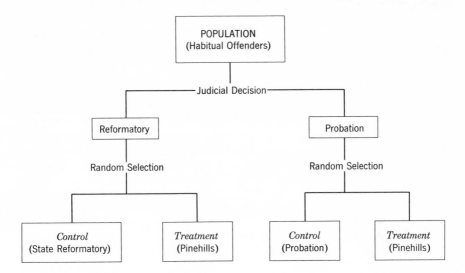

velopes—one series for selecting individuals to be placed in the *probation*
treatment and control groups and one
series for selecting the *reformatory* treatment and control groups. These series
of envelopes are supplied by the research team and contain randomly selected slips of paper on which are
written either *Control Group* or *Treatment Group*.

In making an assignment to one of
these groups the Judge takes the following steps: (1) After hearing a case
he decides whether he would ordinarily
place the offender on probation or in
the reformatory. He makes this decision as though Pinehills did not exist.
Then (2) he brings the practice of
random placement into play. He does so
by opening an envelope from one of the
two series supplied him (see Table 1).
For example, if he decides initially that
he would ordinarily send the boy to the
reformatory, he would select an envelope from the *reformatory* series and
depend upon the designation therein as

to whether the boy would actually go
to the reformatory, and become a member of the *control* group, or be sent to
Pinehills as a member of the *treatment*
group.

This technique does not interfere
with the judicial decision regarding the
alternatives previously available to the
Judge, but it does intercede, after the
decision, by posing another alternative.
The Judge is willing to permit the use
of this alternative on the premise that,
in the long run, his contributions to research will enable judicial decisions to
be based ultimately on a more realistic
evaluation of treatment programs available.

In order to make the comparison of
treatment and control groups more
meaningful, additional research is being
conducted on the treatment process.
Efforts are made to examine the problems involved in relating causation
theory to intervention strategy, the role
of the therapist in Guided Group Interaction, and the types of group inter-

action that seem most beneficial. Finally, a detailed examination is being made of the ways in which boys handle "critical incidents"[36] after release from treatment as compared to the way they handled them prior to treatment.

SUMMARY AND IMPLICATIONS

This paper describes an attempt to apply sociological theory to the treatment of delinquents. It concentrates not only upon treatment techniques, *per se,* but the type of social system in which these techniques must operate. The over-all treatment system it describes is like all other social systems in the sense that it specifies generalized requirements for continued membership in the system. At the same time, however, it also legitimizes the existence of a subsystem within it—the meeting—which permits the discussion and evaluation of happenings and feelings which *may* or *may not* support the over-all normative structure of the larger system.

The purposeful creation of this subsystem simply recognized what seemed to be two obvious facts: (1) that the existence of contrary normative expectations among delinquent and official members of the over-all system would ultimately result in the creation of such a subsystem anyway; and (2) that such a system, not officially recognized, would pose a greater threat, and would inhibit to a greater degree, the realization of the over-all rehabilitative goals of the major system than would its use as a rehabilitative tool.

This subsystem receives not only official sanction but grants considerable power and freedom to delinquent members. By permitting open expressions of

36 John C. Flanagan, "The Critical Incident Technique," *Psychological Bulletin,* 51 (July, 1954), pp. 327–358.

anger, frustration, and opposition, it removes social-psychological support for complete resistance to a realistic examination of the ultimate utility of delinquent versus conventional norms. At the same time, however, the freedom it grants is relative. So long as opposition to the demands of the larger system is contained in the meeting subsystem, such opposition is respected. But continued deviancy outside the meeting cannot be tolerated indefinitely. It must be seen as dysfunctional because the requirements of the over-all treatment system are identified with those of the total society and these requirements will ultimately predominate.

At the same time, the over-all treatment system includes elements designed to encourage and support the adoption of conventional roles. The roles it encourages and the rewards it grants, however, are peer-group-oriented and concentrate mainly upon the normative expectations of the social strata from which most delinquents come: working- rather than middle-class strata. This is done on the premise that a rehabilitation program is more realistic if it attempts to change normative orientations towards lawbreaking rather than attempting (or hoping) to change an individual's entire way of life. It suggests, for example, that a change in attitudes and values toward work *per se* is more important than attempting to create an interest in the educational, occupational, and recreational goals of the middle class.

The differences posed by this treatment system, as contrasted to many existing approaches to rehabilitation, are great. Means should be sought, therefore, in addition to this project by which its techniques and orientation can be treated as hypotheses and verified, modified, or rejected.

43. Custody and Treatment in Juvenile Institutions

MAYER N. ZALD AND DAVID STREET

Correctional organizations, no matter how much they vary in emphasis, must ultimately have the dual purpose of custody and rehabilitation. If one of them attempts to do away with containment and control, the community and relevant officials will build pressure to reinstate controls. On the other hand, given the values of our society and the original definition of the juvenile institution as rehabilitative, even the most custodial institution has to make some effort to reclaim its youth and use *humanitarian* controls. Yet, differences in goals, ranged along a continuum from custody to treatment, have a number of effects on the operation of these organizations.

Organizational analysis, a developing subdiscipline within sociology, directs attention to the broad problems of organizational goals, relations between the organization and its environment, the internal structure of the organization, and relations with and among the clientele. In this article we shall examine the organizational patterns and problems of juvenile correctional institutions, particularly those which have at-

tempted to convert from a custodial to a treatment-oriented type of approach.

Some time ago, we had the opportunity to explore this problem in a comparative study of several institutions for male juvenile offenders.[1] Questionnaires filled in by inmates and staff, historical documents, observations of meetings and organizational practices, extended interviews with executives and others, and consultation with people outside the organization were some of the methods used.

The institutions we studied differed in their goals. Among the four major organizations, one was strongly, even repressively, custodial, emphasizing discipline and hard work; a second was a "moderated custody" institution, beginning to tone down repressive control but not yet committed to a full treat-

[1] Detailed findings of the study, which was directed by Robert Vinter and Morris Janowitz, may be found in *The Comparative Study of Juvenile Correctional Institutions: A Research Report* (Ann Arbor: University of Michigan School of Social Work, 1961). The research was supported by grant M-2104 from the National Institute of Mental Health.

SOURCE. Mayer N. Zald and David Street, "Custody and Treatment in Juvenile Institutions," from *Crime and Delinquency*, Volume 10, July 1964, pp. 249–256. Reprinted with the permission of the National Council on Crime and Delinquency.

ment program; a third emphasized individual treatment; and the last was developing a program of milieu treatment. These institutions, which were located in several states, varied in size —from 400 boys and 180 staff to 75 boys and 40 staff—and were both public and private. In addition, we studied two smaller private institutions which had custodial goals but which were "open" in that they sent their inmates out to ordinary public and parochial schools each day.

Such aspects of organization as departmental structure, balance of power, level and patterns of conflict, staff-inmate relations, and inmate responses to the institutions will be considered both generally and with special reference to those institutions.

DEPARTMENTAL STRUCTURE

One striking difference between institutions with more custodial goals and those with more treatment-oriented goals is the ease of routinization and coordination of the former. The first reason for this is that inmates in the custodial institutions are rendered more passive by the use of dominating and coercive sanctions, whereas in the treatment institutions staff must be continually adapting to the inmates. Secondly, custodial philosophy provides rules for most situations that will arise, while treatment philosophy requires that each situation be handled in terms of the particular inmate involved. Thirdly, custodial institutions establish programs which hold for large groups of boys, while treatment institutions try to set up programs to meet the needs of each boy. Finally, treatment institutions have continually changing programs which require a great deal of individual coordination of staff and boys. This is in marked contrast to the repetitive programing of the custodial institutions.

These differences in the degree of routinization sharply affect other aspects of the institutions. While in custodial institutions little departmentalization occurs and most personnel report directly to the superintendent or assistant superintendent, in treatment institutions the superintendent's span of control becomes extremely attenuated because he must make so many different kinds of decisions. Thus, the clearly custodial institutions are organized simply, while institutions toward the center of the continuum and institutions utilizing mainly individual treatment have what can be called a "multiple department" structure in which each area of the institution—the school, the cottage, the social service, maintenance, business—operates relatively autonomously. Each has a department head who makes decisions for his own area. Both the moderate custodial and the individual treatment institutions are likely to have this type of structure because the activity in one department seems to have no relevance for another. In contrast, in the correctional institution with a program of milieu treatment, all activity with inmates must correspond to that philosophy; thus, action in the school and cottage, for example, must be as treatment-oriented as action elsewhere in the institution. As a result, milieu institutions are likely to have a dual divisional structure: all activity with inmates is placed under a single division head and is guided and supervised by professional treatment personnel, and all business and maintenance staffs are placed in a separate division.

To illustrate these ideas about departmental structure, let us turn specifically to the institutions in our study. The most custodial was only slightly departmentalized. Its farm had a departmental structure, but only so as to achieve better production rather than to supervise staff-inmate relations. The superintendent did not feel hard-pressed to make decisions and spent an hour or two each morning reading the political news. The largest institution in our sample, presently a moderated custodial institution with a multiple department structure, was, at an earlier time, more custodial and had fewer departments, though the size was the same. Indeed, it once resembled our most custodial institution, even though it had over 100 employees. Departmentalization came to this institution when outside pressure groups complained about the autonomy and power of cottage parents in disciplining and treating boys as they wished. In this circumstance, departmentalization helped the executive establish a reasonable span of control so that he could guarantee appropriate behavior from his staff.

Of course, as institutions get larger they require some greater departmentalization, but size alone does not account for departmentalization, as the case of the moderated custodial organization indicates. Similarly, the individual treatment institution had only 40 staff and 75 boys; yet it was fully departmentalized and the assistant superintendent, who was the key person in running the institution, was under a great deal of pressure. However, departmentalization did not solve all the problems of executive control. The lack of routinization and the fact that the assistant superintendent was chief disciplinarian put him in the position of having to make decisions about many things every day.

BALANCE OF POWER

How is power distributed among executives and staff groups in the institutions? What are the orientations and values of the people who hold power?

Looking first at the distribution of power among the executives, we note that as the institution becomes more departmentalized, the superintendent finds it more difficult to control and supervise all personnel; consequently, power must be shared. This sharing of power is especially true, therefore, for the treatment institutions, which are not only departmentalized but also in the public eye, in contrast to custodial institutions, which tend to be relatively isolated and removed from the public. Treatment institutions generally are involved with a wide range of external agencies and because of their open policies, superintendents must be prepared to defend their institutions against attack and share their power as a means of building support for their relatively expensive programs.

We found that in the most custodial institution only the superintendent was perceived by the staff as having a great deal of influence among the executives. In three of the institutions studied, an "inside-outside" split in the executive role occurred. The assistant superintendent in each of the two treatment institutions was seen as having a great deal of power; in fact, the number of staff who thought *he* had a great deal of influence was larger than the number who felt the superintendent had. In the moderate, or intermediate, custodial institution, where the superintendent was ideologically more committed to a treatment goal but was unable to implement this commitment, the second in command—unofficially—was the head of the cottage parents, who had two mottoes: "We're not in the beating business," and "The community has a right to be protected." Thus, in this institution, a person with primarily nonrepressive custodial attitudes was in command. What is important here is that by giving him power, the superintendent could insure containment and control.

In most of the institutions the values of the chief executive and the assistant superintendent tended to parallel the difference in goals. Only in the moderate custodial institution do we see any marked feeling that program and goals were not up to the standards of the figures in power there. The superintendent, for example, felt he had to compromise his aims in order to meet the restricted budget and lack of public support for a more rehabilitative program.

Among staff groups, power distribution took a fairly predictable course. First, in all institutions the teachers and the principal had very little power, reflecting the fact that the schools were relatively isolated from the major operating problems of the organization. Secondly, as we move from the most custodial to the individual treatment institution we see a decreasing amount of power given to cottage parents. Cottage parents have less and less say over discipline, over when the boy goes home, and over what the boy's program should be like. On the other hand, in the milieu institution, where cottage parents participated in the basic decisions, their power was higher than in any of the other institutions. Thirdly, as we move from custodial to treatment institutions, the social service workers move from a position relatively isolated from internal operations, a position in which they deal mainly with the courts and families, to an increasingly central position, in which they make decisions about the boys. He who controls decisions about the boys controls the organization.

LEVEL AND PATTERN OF CONFLICT

The power balance in an organization is also related to its pattern of conflict. The extent to which the institution is committed to both custodial and treatment goals should be related to the amount or level of conflict there. Many objective observers have noted the apparently irreconcilable conflict among treatment personnel—who tend to be professionals, white-collar workers, and younger people—and the custodial cottage parents over such well-known issues as: Should or shouldn't we lock the doors? Must the boys march? Should boys be allowed to go off grounds? How much should we believe the boys? We made it our job to go beyond mere recognition that institutions are conflict-prone organizations and, instead, attempted to account for differences in their level and pattern of conflict.

Our first notion was that institutions near the middle of the goal continuum, with social service workers in one department and cottage parents in another, should have the highest tension level. Our second was that institutions with custodial goals would have fewer social service workers and, since these few would be isolated from the organization, there would be little conflict. In treatment institutions, we thought that careful selection of cottage parents and the clear dominance of treatment goals and social service workers would lead to a decline in conflict. In other words, we hypothesized that the further away from the end points of the continuum, the more the conflict. We were wrong in this hypothesis because we seriously underestimated the problems of the treatment institution.

First, it is hard to know when one is effective in treating a delinquent—one can only know after his means have proved successful ten years later. In other words, good criteria for what means to use are absent in treatment institutions. In the absence of hard criteria, one can debate endlessly about what constitutes appropriate staff behavior even though there may be a basic agreement on goals. This is not the case in custodial institutions, where there is a clear relationship between the means and the end. Furthermore, because communication and coordination are more important in treatment institutions, the personnel have more of an opportunity to express their differences so that the amount of conflict perceived is higher. Although the conflict may be less virulent and less basic, it nevertheless is likely to exist and to be fairly strong. What we found, then, is that conflict was lowest in our two most custodial institutions and highest in the milieu treatment institution. Of course, idiosyncrasies of the institution may help to account for this, but we would not discount this basic pattern.

What about the *pattern* of conflict— that is, who conflicts with whom— within the institution? In any organization, conflict is most likely to occur between those who control the basic definitions of policy and decisions and those who disagree with those policies. Briefly and oversimply, we expected that in the more custodial institutions social service workers and teachers would conflict with cottage parents but not with each other, and that in treatment institutions cottage parents and teachers would conflict with the powerful social service staff but not with each other. In a milieu institution, however, where cottage parents and social service workers are highly integrated, we expected that both would be likely to conflict with teachers but not with each other. These are oversimplified explanations, however, because they make assumptions which are not necessarily met. They assume, for example, that the values of social service workers in a custodial institution will conflict with those of the cottage parents, while in reality institutions may select and train people who can accommodate to the institution. In other words, our predictions would hold true only if these groups did, in fact, have divergent values. Secondly, we had assumed that groups interact and recognize the con-

flict, but if groups are relatively isolated, the partners to the conflict would not be aware of it.

In general, our model worked. In those cases where it did not, we could see that the institution's selection policies had solved the problem. For instance, in the individual treatment institution, we had expected a great deal of conflict between the cottage parents and the social service workers, but since the cottage parents were all college-educated persons who identified with the professional staff and accepted their professional ideals, this institution effectively by-passed such conflict. This does not mean that the cottage parents failed to experience a large degree of role strain; they did feel pressured, were not sure what they were supposed to be doing, and so on. Since they accepted the values of the social service staff, however, they could not come out in open conflict with them. The one case in which we clearly were wrong was the milieu institution: there, cottage parents and social service workers continued to be in conflict even though we had expected them not to be and even though they identified with each other and considered themselves part of the same team. So although they continued to fight, they felt they were fighting on the same side and for the same goals and they attempted to reconcile their differences.

STAFF-INMATE RELATIONSHIPS

In testing out some of our commonsense assumptions about what relationships of staff to inmates would obtain in different organizations, we found that in custodial institutions staff had a relatively dominating relationship with the inmates, while in treatment institutions staff were less domineering and relied more on manipulation and persuasion to control the inmates. To illustrate, in custodial institutions all staff are called "sir" or "ma'am" by the boys, reflecting the emphasis upon social distance; in treatment institutions friendly —and sometimes not so friendly —nicknames are permitted. In the most custodial institution one of the staff members, who was well-liked by both staff and boys, was ordered to paddle any boy who called him by his nickname—a nickname which all the staff used in front of the boys.

These differences in basic relationships were reflected in the staff attitude toward the inmates. Thus, the staff in the more custodial institutions felt that boys should keep to themselves, should conform, should not make too many friends within the institution, and should not have close relationships with many people. Staff in the more treatment-oriented institutions wanted boys to make friends with both the staff and the other boys and to express themselves, articulate their needs, and so on. They also stressed the importance of understanding the boys more than did those in the custodial institutions.

Another difference is subtle. In all the institutions studied, staff were preoccupied with two kinds of inmates— the boy who is quiet and the boy who makes himself known. The quiet, withdrawn boy generally does not get too much attention, although the staff in treatment institutions try to encourage this type of child to come out of himself, to start acting up a little, if you will. Custodial institutions tend to ignore this type of boy. The reasoning used by the treatment personnel is that if a boy is just quietly getting by, the institution is not actually reaching him. He is just "doing time."

In all institutions, however, when staff are among themselves, it is not the quiet one they talk about, but the troublemakers and the heroes who, in all the institutions, tended to be the good athletes. But personnel in the treatment and custodial institutions have fundamentally different attitudes toward the troublemakers. Although staff in custodial institutions tend to talk about them with awe, the only problem they worry about is how to stop them. For the staff in the treatment institution, troublemaking reflects underlying disturbance and is not something to be clamped down on immediately. To know what is bothering the inmate, one must almost encourage disturbance.

INMATE RESPONSE

How do differences in goal emphasis affect the behavior of the inmates? Instead of stretching our resources to gather data on inmate recidivism, we chose to focus on the attitudes and social relations of the inmates while they were in the institution. Findings in this area, we believe, have implications for the inmates' future adjustment.

We asked the inmates a variety of questions as to whether the institution was a better or worse place than they expected, whether they thought the institution had been of some help to them, whether staff members were fair, and other subjects. From the replies, we found that the attitudes of inmates in custodial institutions were less favorable than the attitudes of the inmates in treatment organizations. Further, we found that among the inmates of custodial institutions, those who were more involved in or who were informal leaders of the inmate group were even more antipathetic toward that type of institution than were the other inmates. By contrast, the more involved inmates and leaders in the treatment institutions had more favorable attitudes than the other boys. Overall, then, the results of our inmate questionnaire showed a consistent pattern of differences in inmate attitudes toward themselves, the institution, and the staff, depending on the type of institution they were in. In the custodial institutions emphasizing containment and conformity, the inmate group, by stressing covert opposition and "playing it cool," moved toward behavior more consistent with the institutional policy than did inmates in the treatment institutions. The custodial inmates thus made little move to alter their behavior, while the inmate group in the treatment facility seemed to influence its members toward achieving change, at least insofar as change in behavior requires some cooperation with the staff.

Of special interest were our findings on the ways in which the formal organizational structure influences the informal patterns of inmate social relations. The results clearly challenge the frequently held view that the inmate group is inevitably opposed to the goals of the organization. First, the degree of inmate solidarity against the administration in juvenile institutions was nowhere as high as that reported generally for adult prisons. Second, solidarity —the inmates' belief that they should and do stick together—was not necessarily linked to attitudes opposed to the institution and staff. Third, solidarity was higher in the treatment institutions, where, as we have suggested, inmate attitude was relatively more favorable than it was in the custodial institutions. Finally, in the custodial organizations the staff's repression of inmate social relations effectively reduced the level of inmate solidarity but at the same time tended to assure that whatever inmate group activity did take place

would be oriented against the institution and staff. By contrast, in the treatment institutions, where the inmates were allowed to organize and express hostility overtly, the boys apparently were more day-to-day "trouble" to the staff, but their groupings were less often oriented against the institution and staff and had fewer undesirable effects upon the inmates' attitudes.

Differences between the inmates in the two custodial and two treatment institutions were clear-cut, and our findings for inmates in the two small open institutions paralleled those for the inmates in the treatment institutions. Inmates in these open organizations were almost as favorably disposed to their environment as those in the treatment institutions—a finding which raises the question of whether the great resources used for treatment are really necessary if the same results are produced in an open institution.

This paper is not a prescription for running a correctional institution. Rather, it points to dilemmas which arise from the various goals which institutions set for themselves. Today, professionalization of correctional personnel is leading toward a greater emphasis upon rehabilitation and treatment so that few institutions will be able to cling to predominantly custodial goals in the years ahead. Yet, any executive who wants to move his institution toward treatment goals must be prepared to face conflict among staff members, higher operating costs, and the need for, and risks in, delegating authority. But the effort, as our study indicated, will be worth it.

44. Inter-Institutional Conflict as a Major Impediment to Delinquency Prevention

WALTER B. MILLER

Juvenile delinquency is a major area of concern in the United States today. Although there is evidence of some increase in the actual incidence of juvenile crime, it is equally evident that the intensity of public concern over this issue has increased far more rapidly than the demonstrated statistical increase. This paper will focus, not on juvenile crime as such, but on the larger adult community, and, in particular, on that segment of the community which maintains explicit responsibility in this area.

It is the thesis of this paper that the nature of current concern over juvenile delinquency serves important latent functions for substantial segments of the adult community. If this thesis is true, we would expect to find, as in all areas where a significant discrepancy exists between the overt or recognized aspects of a phenomenon and its covert aspects or latent functions: (1) Discrepancies and contradictions between officially stated policy and actual operating procedure; (2) recurrent failure to follow through on plans whose objectives conform to officially stated posi-

tions but whose execution would in fact run counter to the latent function; (3) much conflict over goals and methods both between concerned institutional systems and between sub-units within these systems. The net result of these forces would be to produce action stalemates both through failure to take action and through mutual blocking of efforts to the end that the latently functional status quo is preserved.

That public concern over juvenile delinquency serves *psychological* functions for adults as individuals has been maintained by several investigators. This paper will attempt to show that the nature of current institutional practice regarding delinquency serves important *structural* functions as well; that is, for the great majority of organized institutions which maintain programs directed at juvenile delinquency, the adoption of operating procedures and philosophies which would be effective in reducing juvenile crime would, in fact, pose severe threats to the viability of the institution. The focus here will be on the area of delinquency *prevention* rather than on methods of

SOURCE. Walter B. Miller, "Inter-Institutional Conflict as a Major Impediment to Delinquency Prevention," from *Human Organization*, Volume 17, No. 3, Fall 1958, pp. 20–23. Reprinted with the permission of the Society for Applied Anthropology.

dealing with the adjudicated delinquent. Since the area of prevention is far less structured and has developed fewer established operating procedures than the area of treatment or disposition, the dynamics of institutional functioning in this area are revealed in much sharper relief.

It has been established that there is far more law-violating behavior by adolescents than is officially acted on; according to one study, the actual number of potentially arrestable delinquents is three times that of those actually arrested. Once an individual is officially apprehended for the commission of a delinquent act or acts, a whole series of established procedures are set into motion; the individual may be released with a warning, put on probation, or sentenced to undergo a variety of corrective measures ranging from a citizenship course through psychiatric treatment to straight confinement. But in the area of "prevention" things are much less well established. There is growing sentiment to the effect that "prevention" of juvenile crime would be a much sounder procedure than attempting to deal with the individual once he has already committed a crime, and would be much more economical in the long run. But then the question becomes—how does one "prevent"? Once something has happened you can take steps as a consequence of that occurrence, but what steps should you take for something that has not happened yet, but which might? Thus, while there are many well-established institutions—courts, police, correctional institutions, psychiatric agencies— whose operating procedures and philosophies are geared to handling individuals who have committed delinquent acts and been apprehended, there are, with a few exceptions, no established institutional structures whose major responsibility is delin-

quency prevention, and whose institutional values and operating philosophies are geared to that objective. Existing organizations undertake prevention, if at all, as a relatively minor adjunct to major institutional responsibilites which lie elsewhere—a fact which has important bearing on the potential effectiveness of prevention programs.

Following sections will describe very briefly the experience of one large eastern city in attempting to institute and maintain a "preventive" program on the community level. In 1950, rising public apprehension over juvenile delinquency in general, and gang violence in particular, produced demands for action from many quarters. Since gang activity was a focus of concern, and much gang delinquency is undetectable or undetected, traditional approaches based on restriction or treatment were seen as unfeasible, and pressures to institute some sort of community-based preventive program were exerted on the major institutional structures with assumed or assigned responsibility in the area of juvenile crime.

I

The city contained scores of intricately interrelated organizations, both public and private, varying widely in size, scope, and method of operations, and in assigned or claimed area of jurisdiction or concern with juvenile crime. Of these, about a dozen public and private organizational groupings maintained major responsibility in the area of juvenile crime. The principal public agencies were the municipal government, the recreation department, the police department, the courts, the public schools, and the state youth corrections division. Major private groupings were medical and psychiatric clinics, social work agencies, churches, universities, and various special cause groups, such as ethnic associations and crime prevention societies.

Initial pressures produced a variety of statements as to the desirability of a preventive program, but no action. A complex set of maneuvers was carried on for about three years, usually involving the appointment of special committees which then appointed a study group which turned in a set of recommendations strongly affirming the desirability of a preventive program, and at the same time explaining why such a program was not the responsibility of that particular organization. This continuing stalemate was finally broken early in 1953, primarily through combined pressures from two ethnic groups, the Jews and the Negroes, after a prominent Jewish clergyman had been murdered, allegedly by a Negro teenage gang. The Jews, acting through their organized representative groupings, inferentially charged the Negroes with anti-semitism; the Negroes, through their organized groupings, intimated that this charge indicated anti-Negro sentiment on the part of the Jews. Two other groups whose interests were being threatened by gang activity —the public schools and the settlement houses—added their pressures to those of the Jews and Negroes, and, in the spring of 1953, a central delinquency committee was created, comprising representatives of over one hundred youth-concerned groupings in the metropolitan area, including the major groups cited above. At the time this committee was formed, many statements were made by all groupings—police, courts, the municipal administration, churches, private agencies—pledging their fullest mutual cooperation in this enterprise aimed at coping with the city gang problem.

Despite the sense of urgency and crisis which attended the organization of the central committee, no concrete action was taken for more than a year. This year was filled with indecision, groping for direction, and constant mutual blocking and conflict, sometimes veiled, sometimes overt, among the agencies represented on the central committee. A great variety of proposals was forwarded and debated, reflecting many divergent conceptions of the causes and proper treatment of juvenile crime, and the group seemed unable to reach any agreement on a positive course of action. After six months, a sociology professor at a local university was persuaded to accept responsibility for formulating a plan of action, and in June of 1954—four and a half years after the initial moves, and a year and a half after the murder which had broken the stalemate—a special demonstration project in delinquency prevention was set up in one district of the city. By this time, several of the major organizations originally represented on the central committee had terminated active affiliation—principally, the police and the Jewish clergy. The Jews lost interest rapidly when it developed that anti-semitism had played a relatively small role in gang attacks on Jews.

The prevention project, which was to operate for three years, was staffed primarily by social workers, and included three service programs—a program of direct service to selected "delinquogenic" families, a community organization program, and, as a major effort, a program of direct work with delinquent corner gangs. Although it was the creation of the central committee, once project operations actually started, the committee became progressively disenchanted with its offspring. As the project took action in more definite and visible ways, it became clear that many of its methods and the operating philosophies behind them were in radical conflict with the institutional ideals of the various groups represented on the central committee. This was evidenced in responses ranging from passive non-participation, through withdrawal, to active opposition.

During the three years of the project's existence, the executive board of the central committee became a battleground for its component organizations, with the project and its methods serving as a pawn in these conflicts. After the first meeting, at which a project worker presented a report on his activities, the representative of the Catholic Archdiocese resigned in indignation from the executive board. Following this incident, a watchdog committee was set up to oversee the project; the chairman of this committee was a Protestant clergyman who was strongly opposed to major methods of the project. About a year later the project became involved in direct conflict with the state division of corrections, with enmity reaching sufficient intensity that the corrections division issued an order forbidding its parolees to participate in project activities, and, in fact, jailed one parolee who defied this order. The social agencies initially regarded the program with great suspicion, as did the schools. During the latter part of the program the city recreation department representative on the central committee, incensed by a report issued by the project, demanded that no further reports be issued unless approved by the central committee. During the second year, funds to support the project, which were raised by the central committee, became increasingly difficult to obtain, and about this time the committee's original chairman, who had been active in initiating and supporting the project, was replaced, without his prior knowledge, by another man who was far less assertive.

Shortly after the start of the project's third year, its director resigned, partly because of increasing difficulties in obtaining financing, and no attempt was made to replace him with a person of equivalent status. Before the director left, he formulated a detailed proposal for the establishment of a permanent delinquency prevention agency under state and municipal auspices, using the project's experience as the basis of recommendations. The three-man committee chosen to present this program to the mayor and governor consisted of an amiable but aged chairman and the two most outspoken opponents of the project on the central committee. The recommendations for a state-municipal program presented under these auspices were rejected both by the mayor and governor. Once the program was officially terminated, the central committee appeared eager to forget that it had ever existed. Although federal support for post-project research had been obtained, members of the central committee were most reluctant to permit such continuation and questioned the right of the project to have sought these funds, despite the fact that authorization had been officially voted.

During the period when the project was subject to increasing opposition by its parent organizations on the central committee, these agencies were also engaged in attacking one another both in the arena of central committee meetings and through other media. A judge accused the police of inefficiency in dealing with delinquents and in keeping adequate crime statistics; a police chief accused the social welfare agencies of coddling delinquents; the director of a medical group accused the corrections division of increasing the delinquency of those in their care; a Catholic prelate accused the social work agencies of neglecting religion in their dealings with delinquents; a psychiatric agency head accused the police of harmful advocacy of punitive measures; the Archbishop accused enforcement agencies of politically motivated laxness in prosecuting delinquents; a group of legislators attempted to oust major officials of the youth corrections department over the issue of personnel qualifications. In addition, sub-units within these larger organizations feuded with one another; a judge accused other judges of excessive leniency in dealing with juvenile offenders; a committee of the school department claimed that some teachers were fostering delinquency by being unable or unwilling to cope with school behavior problems; the Police Commissioner castigated and demoted a sizable group of patrolmen, charging them with inefficiency in dealing with juveniles in their area of jurisdiction; a Protestant clergyman claimed that some Protestant sects were failing in the fight against delinquency by remaining too aloof from community involvement.

II

We have, then, a situation which involves these elements: first, a social phenomenon—gang violence—which is universally condemned; a crisis incident which arouses deep feelings and provides a spur to direct action; the mobilization and pledged cooperation of all the major concerned institutional groupings of a major American city; and then—much delay and misdirected energy by these institutions in setting up a project to which they become progressively more hostile; constant inter-institutional conflict over a variety of issues; and finally a virtual stalemate in launching any sort of effective action to cope with the problem. This situation is by no means unique; it is found in many cities faced with similar problems; in particular, conflicts between the police, churches, courts, social agencies, and schools in the New York City gang situation have been widely publicized. This prevalent phenomenon —apparently universal agreement on a basic objective, gang control, coupled with mutual conflict leading to almost complete blocking of action, may be explained by focusing on the *means* proposed to secure the end—means which derive from the operating philosophies of the various concerned organizations. This paper suggests that operating philosophies may be *non*functional for the purpose of reducing juvenile crime, and that a consequence of differences in institutional philosophies is that a significant proportion of energy potentially directable to delinquency reduction is instead expended in conflict between institutions.

The nature of these differences may be illuminated by specifying six dimensions along which conflict takes place: these relate to differences in conceptions of the *etiology* of delinquency; of the *disposition* of the delinquent; of the *approach priority;* of the appropriate *organizational method,* and of the proper *status of personnel.*

MORALITY-PATHOLOGY. A major difference in assumptions as to the etiology of juvenile crime, as well as other forms of behavior, involves fundamental concepts of human nature. According to one school of thought, deviant or criminal behavior must be viewed in terms of morality and immorality; an individual is morally responsible for his own behavior, and failure to conform to norms and standards represents a triumph of evil forces over good in an inner struggle for which the individual is held personally responsible. The opposing school maintains that deviant or criminal behavior should be viewed in terms of sickness and health; that an individual who violates social and legal norms is, in fact, driven by inner forces over which he has relatively little control, and which have their origins in pathological conditions of the organism.

INDIVIDUAL LOCUS-SOCIAL LOCUS. A second important difference involving etiological concepts relates to the locus of deviant behavior. One school attributes criminal behavior to forces within the *individual*—moral or physical-psychological—which may be dealt with by corrective measures directed at the individual; the other school finds the significant factors in the nature of the *social milieu*, and sees basic alterations in social conditions as the necessary course of action.

RESTRICTION-REHABILITATION. This dimension relates to the proper method of dealing with offenders. The restrictive school of thought advocates the separation or isolation of the individual from normal social intercourse on the assumption, first, that the *protection of society* is the paramount necessity, and second, that punishment both serves as a deterrent to future violation and is merited in consequence of transgression. This dispositional prescription is generally forwarded by those espousing the morality concept of etiology. The treatment or rehabilitative school, basing procedure on the "pathology" conception of etiology, postulates "cure" or directed efforts to modify behavior patterns of the offending individual as of prime importance, with his restoration to normal social interaction a desired objective.

ACTION-RESEARCH. This dimension relates to consideration of priority in approaching the problem. One school maintains that the urgency of the situation, or the intensity of need, demands immediate action, based on the best knowledge currently available; the other maintains that far too little reliable information exists as to the nature of the involved phenomena and methods of treatment, and that the most productive expenditure of energy can be made by undertaking systematic research to gain essential knowledge.

LOCALIZATION-CENTRALIZATION. This dimension concerns the issue of the most desirable method for organizing preventive programs; one school believes that programs should be undertaken within and by the local community, on the grounds that only local people are sufficiently familiar with the special conditions of the local situation for adequate understanding, and that local autonomy must be maintained; the centralization school maintains that the nature and magnitude of the problem demand mobilization of resources which local groups, operating indipendently, could not afford, and that, to be effective, resources must be pooled and efforts coordinated to avoid duplication and overlap.

LAY-PROFESSIONAL. This dimension relates to the qualifications and status of personnel who are to implement preventive programs. One school holds that only those who manifest characteristics similar to those of the subject population—either through similarities in class or locality status—can be effective, and that attributes essential to effectiveness, such as warmth and sympathy, are independent of training; the other school maintains that work in so difficult an area demands that practitioners be exposed to a course of professional training which both imparts knowledge as to specialized procedures and eliminates those whose personality characteristics would be detrimental to this kind of work.

The various institutional structures related to delinquency tend to maintain characteristic syndromes of these etiological and procedural positions. The described positions are seldom maintained in the "pure" form, since they are presented here as polar extremes which define variable dimensions—and "middle positions," such as equal stress on action and research, may be taken, but most institutions involved do maintain definitely identifiable positions of varying intensity along these dimensions. Conflicts along the varying dimensions take place, both *between* and within, concerned institutions, but intra-institutional differences are generally concealed from public notice. The most severe conflict occurs between institutions which take extreme opposing positions on all or most of these dimensions; conflict is less severe when there is disagreement on only one or two. For example, the major juvenile court of the city described above strongly supported the "morality" and "individual locus" concepts of etiology: the restrictive dispositional method, action priority, and localized organization. The major child psychiatry clinic supported the "pathology" etiological concept: rehabilitative treatment method, centralized organization, and use of professional implementary personnel. These positions put the two organizations in direct conflict in four of the six dimensions; in agreement over one—individual etiological locus —and in minor opposition over the action-research issue. Similar comparisons could be made between each set of involved institutions.

SUMMARY

The argument of this paper may be summarized as follows: There is much conflict over the issue of proper procedure among the different groups which maintain varying orders of responsibility for delinquency prevention. This conflict results in a lack of coordination and mutual blocking of efforts leading to a stalemate in reference to a community-supported objective. But these conflicts over method derive from the basic institutional philosophies of the several institutions; although these philosophies may be effective in facilitating achievement of the stated objectives of the institution, their maintenance is vital to the institution's continued existence and this latent objective has greater priority than the achievement of the institution's explicit objectives, and much greater priority than achieving objectives only peripherally related to the institution's primary explicit aims.

This situation would appear to have important implications for delinquency prevention. It would imply that the major impediment to effectiveness in this field relates more to the nature of relations among the various concerned institutions than to a lack of knowledge as to effective procedure. Much is now known about the causes of delinquency and promising ameliorative techniques have been developed. The principal difficulty lies in the *application* of these techniques, and any realistic possibility of such application depends almost entirely on existing institutional structures. This would suggest a shift in emphasis in current research and action efforts, from a primary focus on the relations between implementing institutions and the subject population, to the relationships among the institutions themselves. Both research and action efforts involve severe difficulties since they will touch on areas intimately related to the visibility of the institution —areas all the more charged and sensitive, since they are frequently unconscious or implicit.

Date Due